INDEX

BOOK 1 GRAMMAR (9246 questions))

PART A: **2-50**
14 Elementary tests, 14 Pre-Intermediate tests, 8 Intermediate tests.
Each test is specified on different grammar topics. (1976 questions-) 1-2

PART B: **51-102**
14 tests including Elementary, Pre-intermediate, Intermediate and Upper intermediate level grammar tests.
Every test is focused on a different grammar topic. (2452 questions) 1-2-3

PART C: **103-150**
16 Multi-level grammar tests.
Each test is specified on a different grammar topic. (1418 questions) 4

PART D: **151-190**
20 perfect multi-level grammar tests for assessment.
(2000 questions) 4

PART E: **191-218**
6 Elementary, 5 Intermediate, 3 Advanced grammar tests.
The formats of the tests are similar and the level gradually increases. (1400 questions) 1-2-3

ANSWER KEY

BOOK 1 - PART A ....

BOOK 1 - PART B ....

BOOK 1 - PART C ....

BOOK 1 - PART D ....

BOOK 1 - PART E ....

ELEMENTARY TEST - 1

- Verb to be: am/is/are
- Possessive adjectives: my, your, his, her
- Subject Pronouns - Plural nouns & Numbers

1. A- Hello, what _____ your name?
   A) is   B) are   C) am   D) be

2. _____ name is John. And my _____ is Johnson.
   A) Your / surname   B) My / surname
   C) I / surname   D) I / name

3. My name is Lisa. _____ Lisa Peterson.
   A) My am   B) I is   C) I am   D) I

4. _____ name is Apple. _____ Ann Apple.
   A) His / She   B) His / He's   C) Her / She's   D) His / His

5. "Where _____ John from?" "_____ from the US."
   A) is / He's   B) is / His   C) am / He's   D) is / She's

6. _____ are you from? Japan.
   A) What   B) Who   C) Where   D) When

7. Where _____ you _____ ?
   A) is / from   B) are / in   C) are / is   D) are / from

8. _____ from Spain. I'm Rodriguez.
   A) I'm   B) He's   C) You're   D) She's

9. Pierre is a French boy. _____ from _____ .
   A) He's / France   B) His's / French
   C) His / France   D) He / France

10. Lisa and Max are Americans. _____ from U.S.A.
    A) There   B) Their   C) They're   D) Their're

11. "What ____ their _____?"
    "Alexander and Philip."
    A) are/name   B) is / name   C) is / names   D) are / names

12. I _____ 22 years old, but Andrew _____ 20.
    A) am / am   B) are / am   C) am / is   D) are / are

13. Mark_____ 19, but Brian and Denis _____ 26 and 28.
    A) is / are   B) are / is   C) are / are   D) am / are

14. "What _____ this?"
    "It's _____ umbrella."
    A) are / a   B) is / a   C) is / an   D) its / an

15. Oxford is _____ English university.
    A) an   B) the   C) a   D) *

16. Toyotas _____ Japanese _____ .
    A) is a / car   B) is / car   C) are / cars   D) is / cars

17. "What is _____ ?"
    "She is a bank manager."
    A) his job   B) she job   C) he job   D) her job

18. 0/2/11/18/20 Find the correct alternative.
    A) oh / twelve / eighteen / twenty
    B) zero / two / one-one / eighteen / twenty
    C) zero / two / eleven / eighteen / twenty
    D) zero / two / eleven / eighty / twenty

19. "How old is your aunt?"
    "_____ is 29."
    A) She   B) He   C) She's   D) He's

20. "Where _____ she from?"
    "She _____ from Japan."
    A) are / is   B) is / is   C) is / am   D) are / are

21. This _____ my friend. _____ name's Richard.
    A) are / His   B) is / My   C) is / His   D) his / His

22. They _____ Lisa and Max. They _____ from the USA.
    A) is / is   B) are / is   C) are / are   D) is / is

23. "What is _____ name?" "My name's Carlos."
    A) his   B) her   C) your   D) my

24. This is my sister. _____ name is Laura.
    A) His   B) My   C) Her   D) Its

25. I have _____ brother. _____ name is David
    A) an / His   B) a / Her   C) a / His   D) * / His

26. Hello! My ___ ___ Maria. I ___ ___ Mexico.
    A) name is / from am   B) is name / from am
    C) name is / am from   D) name am / is from

27. Is Catherine _____ sister?
    A) he   B) you   C) your   D) yours

28. We _____ students.
    A) are a   B) is   C) are   D) am

29. I _____ student.
    A) is / an   B) am / *   C) am / a   D) am / the

30. She _____ Italy.
    A) are from   B) is at   C) is from   D) am from

31. He is _____ teacher.
    A) a   B) an   C) *   D) the

32. I live _____ a house _____ Los Angeles.
    A) * / in   B) in / in   C) in / *   D) at / in

33. "_____ is your phone number?"
    "It's 2229"
    A) Where   B) How   C) What   D) Who

34. "_____ are you?"
    "I'm Alex."
    A) Which   B) How   C) What   D) Who

35. What's this _____ English?
    A) *   B) in   C) at   D) on

36. Champaigne is _____ French drink.
    A) a   B) the   C) an   D) *

37. Oxford is _____ English university.
    A) a   B) an   C) the   D) *

38. A Mercedes is _____ German car.
    A) a   B) an   C) the   D) *

39. English is _____ international language.
    A) a   B) an   C) the   D) *

40. Milan is _____ Italian city.
    A) a   B) an   C) the   D) *

41. A JVC is _____ Japanese camera.
    A) a   B) an   C) the   D) *

42. I have two _____ .
    A) sister   B) sisters   C) a sister   D) sister's

43. It's _____ Spanish orange.
    A) a   B) an   C) the   D) *

44. It's _____ green apple.
    A) a   B) an   C) the   D) *

ELEMENTARY TEST - 2

- Verb to be: questions and negatives
- Short answers
- Possessive's
- The family
- Prepositions
- Opposite adjectives
- Food and drink

1. "_____ her name Eliza?"
   "No, _____ ."
   A) What / it isn't
   B) Is / she isn't
   C) Is / it is not
   D) Is / it isn't

2. Is your surname Anderson?
   A) Yes, you are.
   B) Yes, it is.
   C) Yes, I am.
   D) Yes, my is.

3. "Is she American?"
   "No, _____ ."
   A) hers isn't   B) she isn't   C) she is not   D) she her isn't

4. "_____ their names Jack & Benny?"
   "Yes, _____ ."
   A) Are / they are
   B) Aren't / there are
   C) Am / their
   D) Is / they're

5. "Is your dog 2 years old?"
   "Yes, _____ ."
   A) it's   B) dog is   C) it is   D) its

6. "Is your elder brother married?"
   "No, _____ ."
   A) brother isn't
   B) he isn't
   C) he is not
   D) she isn't

7. "Are you from Senegal?"
   "No, _____ ."
   A) I'm not   B) I amn't   C) I are not   D) I not

8. "_____ Martha English?"
   "Yes, she _____ ."
   A) Is / isn't   B) Are / is   C) Is / is   D) Are / is

9. "_____ her surname Smith?"
   "No, it _____ ."
   A) What / isn't   B) Is / is   C) Is / isn't   D) Are / isn't

10. "Are you a student?"
    "Yes, I _____ ."
    A) am   B) have   C) is   D) 'm not

11. "_____ you from Barcelona?"
    "No, I'm not."
    A) Is   B) Are   C) Do   D) Where

12. "_____ you married?"
    "No, I _____ ."
    A) Aren't / am
    B) Are / am
    C) Is / am not
    D) Are / 'm not

13. "_____ is Brenda?"
    "She's Patrick's wife."
    A) What   B) Who   C) Which   D) Where

14. My teacher's name _____ John.
    A) are   B) is   C) am   D) not

15. Marcus and Carlos _____ my brothers.
    A) is   B) am   C) are   D) be

16. My mother and father _____ at work.
    A) is   B) am   C) are   D) *

17. It _____ Monday today.
    A) is   B) am   C) are   D) *

18. This is the photo _____ my family.
    A) in   B) at   C) of   D) on

19. It's good practice _____ you.
    A) for   B) at   C) of   D) in

20. I'm _____ home.
    A) in   B) on   C) at   D) from

21. I'm _____ La Guardia Community College.
    A) in   B) on   C) at   D) of

22. I'm _____ New York.
    A) in   B) for   C) at   D) of

23. I'm _____ a class _____ eight other students.
    A) in / for   B) at / of   C) in / with   D) at / off

24. I live _____ an apartment _____ two American boys.
    A) in / of   B) at / with   C) in / with   D) of / with

25. Central Park is lovely _____ the snow.
    A) at   B) in   C) of   D) with

26. "_____ is his job?"
    "He _____ a policeman."
    A) Which / is   B) What / are   C) What / is   D) Where / is

27. He _____ from Argentina. He is _____ Mexico.
    A) is / from   B) isn't / from   C) isn't / in   D) aren't / in

28. "_____ _____ is a hamburger and chips?"
    "Three pounds fifty."
    A) How many   B) How often   C) How much   D) How long

Find the opposite word.

29. easy - _____
    A) cold   B) cheap   C) difference   D) difficult

30. lovely - _____
    A) old   B) expensive   C) horrible   D) quick

31. fast - _____
    A) slow   B) small   C) quick   D) warm

32. expensive - _____
    A) big   B) cheap   C) cold   D) hot

33. hot - _____
    A) cold   B) new   C) warm   D) small

34. big - _____
    A) high   B) small   C) tall   D) slow

35. young - _____
    A) old   B) big   C) small   D) quick

36. "Are you married?"
    "No, _____ ."
    A) I am not   B) I'm not   C) I amn't   D) I m not

37. Brazil _____ in Asia. _____ in South America.
    A) is / It isn't   B) is / It's   C) is / Is   D) isn't / It's

38. Snow is _____ .
    A) cold   B) hot   C) small   D) cheap

39. A: _____ Greek?
    B: Yes, I am.
    A) You   B) Are you   C) Am I   D) I

40. We _____ in a Russian class.
    We _____ in an English class.
    A) are / are   B) are / not   C) aren't / are   D) are / am

41. Rolls-Royce cars are _____ .
    A) cheap   B) blue   C) expensive   D) tall

42. "_____ your teachers married?"
    "Yes, _____."
    A) Is / he is   B) Is / he's   C) Is / she is   D) Are / they are

43. "Is it hot today?"
    "No, _____."
    A) it isn't   B) it is not   C) it's not   D) it not

44. "Are _____ your parents?"
    "Yes, _____."
    A) they-their are   B) their-they are
    C) they-they are   D) they-they

45. Eliza _____ from Greece. _____ from Poland.
    A) is / Is   B) isn't / She's   C) is / Isn't   D) is / Is not

46. Ann is _____ wife.
    A) John's   B) John is   C) John's is   D) John

47. This is not just my computer. It is 4 _____ computer.
    A) students'   B) students's   C) student's   D) student

48. A: What is _____ ?
    B: She is a bank manager.
    A) his job   B) she job   C) he job   D) her job

49. "How old is your brother?"
    "_____ 29."
    A) They are   B) I am   C) It is   D) He is

50. "How old _____ Mr. & Mrs. White?"
    "_____ 50 and 48."
    A) is / They   B) are / They're
    C) are / They   D) */ They are

51. "How old ___, Andrew?"
    "_____ 21 years old."
    A) are you / I'm   B) is he / He's
    C) is / He is   D) are / I

52. "_____ you now?"
    "I'm at the school."
    A) Where's   B) Where're are
    C) Where're   D) Where

53. "Where _____ now?"
    "In her office."
    A) is he   B) is she   C) is it   D) is

54. "_____ is his father's job?"
    "He's a teacher."
    A) Who   B) When   C) Why   D) What

55. This is those _____ toy.
    A) kid's   B) kid   C) kids's   D) kids'

56. They are not my _____ books.
    A) children's   B) childs   C) children'   D) children of

57. They're not his _____ mistakes.
    A) friend's   B) friend   C) friends   D) friends's

ELEMENTARY TEST - 3

- Present Simple: Positive, Negative, Question
- Verbs - Jobs
- Personal pronouns and possessive adjectives

1. She _____ a uniform.
   A) wear   B) to wear   C) wearing   D) wears

2. He _____ his car every weekend.
   A) wash   B) washes   C) washing   D) washed

3. Rosemary _____ three languages.
   A) speaks   B) talks   C) tells   D) know

4. My dad _____ at 7 o'clock everyday.
   A) stands up   B) looks up   C) gets up   D) jumps up

5. Isabel is a flight attendant. She _____ passengers.
   A) serve   B) to serve   C) serves   D) serving

6. Their son _____ in this hospital.
   A) works   B) begins   C) starts   D) likes

7. Jim's a postman. He _____ letters to people.
   A) answers   B) works   C) delivers   D) serves

8. Jane's a doctor. She _____ ill people.
   A) looks at   B) speaks to   C) helps   D) serves drinks

9. Bern _____ in a flat in Birmingham.
   A) lives   B) stands   C) has   D) wants

10. Nancy's uncle is a pilot. He _____ all over the world.
    A) goes   B) sees   C) travels   D) delivers

11. In winter Sheila _____ skiing and in summer _____ tennis.
    A) makes / plays   B) goes / plays
    C) does / plays   D) starts / *

12. My friend's son _____ Turkish and English at university.
    A) has   B) plays   C) studies   D) goes

13. Most of the people _____ work at 8 o'clock every morning.
    A) finishes   B) goes   C) does   D) starts

14. A: _____ does Tony Blair live?
    B: In Great Britain.
    A) When   B) Where   C) What time   D) How

15. _____ does your father do in his free time?
    A) Why   B) What kind   C) How many   D) What

16. _____ does Andy's little brother play with?
    A) Who   B) Why   C) How old   D) Where

17. A: _____ does Natalie's nephew do?
    B: He's an architect.
    A) How   B) Whom   C) When   D) What

18. A: _____ does it rain here?
    B: Mostly in summer and winter.
    A: _____ snow?
    B: In winter.
    A) When / Why   B) Why / How
    C) What time / Whom   D) When / What about

19. A: _____ does Anthony go to work?
    B: _____ bus.
    A) How / By   B) How well / On
    C) What kind / In   D) How / In

20. She _____ from England.
    A) come   B) comes   C) don't come   D) goes

21. _____ she _____ French?
    A) Do / speaks   B) Does / speaks
    C) Does / speak   D) Is / speak

22. She _____ _____ from America.
    A) don't comes   B) doesn't come
    C) doesn't comes   D) does comes

23. Every time he _____ a glass of lemonade before breakfast.
    A) is   B) have   C) has   D) does

24. _____ he _____ three children?
    A) Does / have   B) Does / has   C) Do / have   D) Has / have

25. _____ a shower.
    A) Come   B) Go   C) Have   D) Has

26. _____ the phone.
    A) Go   B) Read   C) Look   D) Answer

27. She _____ a white coat.
    A) wear   B) wears   C) does wear   D) have

28. _____ a magazine.
    A) Go   B) Read   C) Live   D) Has

29. Our teacher gives _____ a lot of homework.
    A) our   B) us   C) her   D) his

30. He _____ television every evening.
    A) watch   B) watches   C) see   D) buy

31. At ten we go _____ bed.
    A) in   B) on   C) to   D) sleep

32. He picks up the apples _____ the tree.
    A) for   B) from   C) on   D) at

33. Get _____ the bus.
    A) on   B) in   C) to   D) out

34. She lives _____ Switzerland.
    A) at   B) on   C) in   D) city

35. A nurse looks _____ people in hospital.
    A) at   B) for   C) after   D) helps

36. There's a letter _____ you.
    A) for   B) to   C) about   D) on

37. Tourists come _____ boat.
    A) by   B) to   C) of   D) with

38. He drives the children _____ school.
    A) of   B) at   C) to   D) go

39. He speaks to people _____ his radio.
    A) at   B) on   C) of   D) in

40. She likes going _____ walks _____ summer.
    A) for / at   B) to / at   C) for / in   D) on / at

41. She goes skiing _____ her free time.
    A) in   B) on   C) at   D) of

42. He works _____ an undertaker.
    A) as   B) for   C) of   D) in

43. "Does she live in Australia?"
    "No, she _____."
    A) do   B) does   C) don't   D) doesn't

44. We _____ _____ watching television.
    A) doesn't like   B) do like   C) doesn't like   D) don't like

45. He _____ to help people.
    A) flies   B) likes   C) runs   D) swims

46. _____ _____ languages does she speak?
    A) How much   B) How many   C) Why   D) Where

47. _____ sells things.
    A) A postman   B) A nurse   C) A doctor   D) A shopkeeper

48. A barman _____.
    A) sells things   B) serves drinks
    C) delivers letters   D) drinks a lot

49. _____ _____ looks after money.
    A) A nurse   B) A postman
    C) An accountant   D) A dentist

50. _____ designs buildings.
    A) A pilot   B) An architect
    C) An interpreter D) An engineer

51. He lives _____ an island _____ the west of Scotland.
    A) on / in   B) in / in   C) on / on   D) in / at

52. She's married _____ an American man.
    A) with   B) for   C) to   D) on

53. He _____ listening _____ music.
    A) like / to   B) likes / to   C) likes / of   D) likes / with

54. "How _____ he _____ to work?"
    "By car."
    A) do / go   B) does / goes   C) does / go   D) does / play

55. Anna likes Joanna, but Maria doesn't like _____.
    A) her   B) them   C) your   D) their

56. That's my dictionary. Can I have ___ back please?
    A) it   B) you   C) them   D) my

57. Philippe _____ in London.
    A) work   B) starts   C) comes   D) lives

58. "_____ he married?"
    "No, he _____."
    A) Is / doesn't   B) Does / isn't   C) Is / isn't   D) Does / is

59. "What _____ she do?"
    "She is an interpreter."
    A) is   B) do   C) does   D) are

60. _____ he sleep well?
    A) Has   B) Have   C) Do   D) Does

ELEMENTARY TEST - 4

- Present Simple - Verbs
- Leisure activities - Prepositions
- Telling the time - Wh Questions

1. What _____ you _____ at the weekend?
   A) does / does   B) do / does
   C) does / do   D) do / do

2. What _____ Dick and Tom like _____?
   A) do / doing   B) doing / *   C) do / do   D) does / doing

3. Do boys like _____ jeans?
   A) wear   B) wearing   C) to wear   D) worn

4. My classmates _____ on picnic every month.
   A) went   B) goes   C) going   D) go

5. Mary _____ face every morning.
   A) washes his   B) wash my   C) washes her   D) washes their

6. I _____ a cigarette, but my teacher _____ smoke.
   A) don't / smokes   B) smoke / doesn't
   C) smokes / smokes   D) smoke / don't

7. They _____ wash _____ car every day.
   A) don't / my   B) don't / his
   C) don't / their   D) don't / our

8. My parents _____ eat meat.
   A) don't   B) aren't   C) doesn't   D) are

9. Summer holidays _____ in June.
   A) begins   B) begin   C) beginning   D) began

10. We _____ tennis on Monday evenings, but my little sister _____ on Sundays.
    A) play / play   B) plays / plays
    C) play / plays   D) plays / play

11. You _____ a lot of things in _____ free time.
    A) do / our   B) does / your   C) do / my   D) do / your

12. My cat licks _____ tail every evening. But my dogs never lick _____ tails.
    A) its / their   B) its / its   C) their / its   D) * / *

13. I like _____ football, but my brother doesn't.
    A) play   B) played   C) playing   D) plays

14. She likes _____ TV, but her husband doesn't.
    A) watching   B) to watch   C) watches   D) watched

15. Her sister doesn't _____ eating a hamburger.
    A) like   B) likes   C) liking   D) liked

16. Do you like _____ in your free time?
    A) read   B) reads   C) to read   D) reading

17. I like _____ but I _____ like swimming.
    A) sailing / don't   B) sail / doesn't
    C) sail / don't   D) sail / do

18. Tom _____ her but she doesn't like _____.
    A) like / her   B) likes / him   C) likes / he   D) like / him

19. Andrew buys a newspaper everyday. _____ reads _____ at home.
    A) It / he   B) Him / it   C) He / it   D) His / it

20. Mike eats cheeseburgers because _____ likes _____.
    A) he / their   B) him / they   C) he / them   D) him / them

21. "What time is it?" "3:45"
    A) It is quarter past three.
    B) It is fifteen past four.
    C) It is quarter to four.
    D) It is fifteen to four.

22. It is half past eight.
    A) 8:30   B) 7:30   C) 18:30   D) 17:30

23. It is quarter past eight.
    A) 8:30   B) 7:30   C) 8:15   D) 17:15

24. It is five to nine.
    A) 9:55   B) 9:35   C) 8:55   D) 9:05

25. It is five past nine.
    A) 9:55   B) 9:35   C) 8:55   D) 9:05

26. A friend of mine likes _____ on picnic at weekends.
    A) to go   B) going   C) goes   D) go

27. I _____ my teeth every morning.
    A) brushing   B) brush   C) brushes   D) to brush

28. _____ Kate live near Jane?
    A) Is   B) Are   C) Do   D) Does

29. His father _____, but Bill's father _____ smoke.
    A) smokes / don't   B) smokes / doesn't
    C) smoke / don't   D) smokes / isn't

30. My father _____ driving.
    A) doesn't likes   B) don't likes
    C) doesn't like   D) don't like

31. She _____ a bus to university.
    A) always takes   B) always take
    C) takes always   D) take always

32. I _____ to a football match every Sunday but my father _____.
    A) go / don't   B) goes / doesn't
    C) go / doesn't   D) goes / don't

33. Every year millions of people _____ The London Museum.
    A) visit   B) go   C) come   D) want

34. The Buckingham Palace _____ lots of rooms.
    A) have   B) has   C) to have   D) having

35. Visitors _____ to India's Independence Day from all over the world.
    A) visit   B) come   C) leave   D) goes

36. I _____ English, Russian, and Romanian, but I _____ Chinese.
    A) speak / don't speak B) speaks / speak
    C) speaks / speaks   D) speaks / don't speak

37. Many foreigners in our country _____ to the Golden Bazaar.
    A) buy   B) go shopping   C) want   D) come

38. A: What _____ you _____ ?
    B: An architect.
    A) do / do   B) does / do   C) are / do   D) do / are

39. A: What _____ your niece _____ ?
    B: A nurse.
    A) do / do   B) does / is   C) does / do   D) is / do

40. A: Where _____ your parents _____ ?
    B: In the Ministry of Education.
    A) do / do   B) do / work   C) are / work   D) work / *

41. A: _____ languages do they speak?
    B: Just one.
    A) What   B) How many   C) How   D) Which

42. A: Do you _____ Afghani?
    B: No, _____ .
    A) speak / you don't   B) speak / I don't
    C) speak / don't I   D) speaks / don't speak

43. A: _____ does Margaret start work?
    B: At 7 in the morning.
    A) What time   B) What kind   C) What sort   D) What about

44. A: _____ do your brothers like working in this factory?
    B: Because they earn much money.
    A) What   B) When   C) Why   D) Whom

45. _____ he like his job?
    A) Does   B) Do   C) Is   D) Are

46. I _____ an accountant.
    A) do   B) does   C) am   D) is

47. _____ New York exciting?
    A) Are   B) Do   C) Does   D) Is

48. Where _____ they live?
    A) are   B) do   C) does   D) is

49. Why _____ you want to learn English?
    A) do   B) are   C) *   D) is

50. We _____ Algerians.
    A) does   B) are   C) do   D) am

51. What _____ he do at weekends?
    A) do   B) is   C) does   D) are

52. He plays football _____ Friday mornings.
    A) in   B) on   C) at   D) of

53. Do you relax _____ weekends?
    A) at   B) on   C) in   D) by

54. Where do you go _____ holiday?
    A) at   B) in   C) of   D) on

55. I like _____ .
    A) cooks   B) cooking   C) cook   D) cooked

56. She gets up early _____ the morning.
    A) on   B) in   C) at   D) by

57. She gets up early _____ the weekdays.
    A) at   B) of   C) on   D) in

58. He takes photos only _____ spring.
    A) in   B) at   C) on   D) by

59. He hates _____ football _____ television.
    A) watching / on   B) to watch / in
    C) watch / on   D) watching / in

60. They like _____ very much.
    A) sail   B) sailed   C) sailing   D) sail

61. My brother's birthday is _____ March.
    A) in   B) on   C) at   D) to

62. The train leaves Paris _____ 4 p.m.
    A) in   B) at   C) on   D) by

63. Vancouver is very cold _____ winter.
    A) at   B) in   C) on   D) to

64. Sometimes we _____ cards.
    A) plays   B) playing   C) play   D) to play

65. She never _____ meat.
    A) eats   B) eating   C) eat   D) to eat

66. We always _____ lemonade in the evenings.
    A) to drink   B) has   C) drinking   D) have

67. A: I'm sorry. I'm late.
    B: _____ Come and sit down.
    A) Excuse me!   B) Don't worry!
    C) What's the matter?   D) Why are you late?

68. A- _____ your wife _____ English?
    B- Yes, she does.
    A) Do / speak   B) Does / speaking
    C) Does / speak   D) Do / speaking

69. "How many languages _____ you _____ ?"
    "Three: English, German and Spanish."
    A) does / speak   B) do / speak
    C) do / speaking   D) does / speaking

70. Why _____ you like _____ in the hotel?
    A) do / working   B) do / work
    C) does / working   D) does / work

71. They never go out _____ Friday evenings.
    A) on   B) in   C) at   D) by

72. She loves _____ to music.
    A) listening   B) to listen   C) listens   D) listen

73. They often eat in a restaurant ___ Tuesdays.
    A) on   B) in   C) of   D) at

74. _____ summer I play tennis _____ Sundays.
    A) In / in   B) At / on   C) In / on   D) At / in

75. "Do Mr. Adams and his daughter like going _____ ?"
    "No, they _____ ."
    A) ski / don't   B) skiing / don't
    C) skiing / do   D) ski / does

76. "_____ they _____ a winter holiday?"
    "Yes, they do."
    A) Do / wanting   B) Does / want
    C) Do / want   D) Does / wanting

77. What time _____ you go to bed?
    A) do   B) does   C) is   D) have

78. "_____ do you do your homework?"
    "After dinner."
    A) Where   B) What   C) How   D) When

79. "_____ you go out on Friday evenings?"
    "Yes, I do sometimes."
    A) Do   B) Where   C) Are   D) Does

80. "_____ do you like your job?"
    "Because it's interesting."
    A) Why   B) What   C) How   D) Where

81. "_____ do you travel to school?"
    "By bus."
    A) How   B) What   C) Why   D) Where

82. "_____ _____ you live with?"
    "With my mother and sisters."
    A) What / do   B) Who / do
    C) Where / does   D) Who / does

83. "_____ do you _____ on Sundays?"
    "I always relax."
    A) How / doing   B) What / do
    C) Where / does   D) What / relax

84. "_____ do you _____ on holiday?"
    "To Rome or Paris."
    A) Where / like   B) How / relax
    C) Where / go   D) Why / go

ELEMENTARY TEST - 5

- There is/are
- Prepositions of place
- This, that, these, those
- How many ?
- Some and any
- So, but, because

1. A- _____ there _____ desk?
   B- Yes, _____ is.
   A) Is / * / there   B) Are / the / they
   C) Is / a / there   D) Is / one / they

2. A- _____ there three stereos in the living room?
   B- No, there _____ .
   A) Are / aren't   B) Are / are   C) Are / not   D) Are / *

3. Is there _____ apple in the bag?
   A) a   B) an   C) the   D) *

4. There _____ 4 _____ on the sofa?
   A) are / woman   B) is / women
   C) * / woman   D) are / women

5. There _____ one bag. There _____ 3 bags.
   A) isn't / are   B) is / is   C) not / are   D) aren't / are

6. There _____ 3 telephones, but _____ isn't a cooker.
   A) are / they   B) is / there   C) are / there   D) are / their

7. _____ any men in the hall?
   A) Are there   B) Are their   C) Are they   D) Is there

8. A: _____ there many mice in the house?
   B: No, there _____ .
   A) Are / are   B) Are / not   C) Are / aren't   D) Are / *

9. _____ there _____ chairs in the class?
   A) Are / a   B) Are / some   C) Are / there   D) Are / any

10. Yes, there are _____ chairs, but there are not _____ desks.
    A) some / any   B) any / some   C) any / any   D) some / some

11. A: _____ is there in the bedroom?
    B: There _____ 2 beds, 3 televisions, and 2 cupboards.
    A) How many / are   B) What / is
    C) What / are   D) How many / is

12. A- _____ books _____ there under your desk?
    B- There _____ one.
    A) How much / are / is   B) How many / is / is
    C) What / are / is   D) How many / are / is

13. There are _____ sandwiches, but there _____ any chips.
    A) some / aren't   B) any / aren't
    C) some / are   D) any / are

14. A: Do you have any _____ ?
    B: No, I don't. But I have _____ grammar books.
    A) dictionary / any   B) a dictionary / some
    C) dictionaries / some   D) dictionaries / any

15. There is _____ photo of _____ teachers.
    A) some / some   B) a / some
    C) some / any   D) any / some

16. How many _____ are there in the cupboard.
    A) glass   B) of glasses   C) a glass   D) glasses

17. In our garden there is _____ huge pine tree, and there are _____ bushes.
    A) a / a lot of   B) an / many   C) a / lot of   D) * / many

18. Is there _____ garden?
    A) any   B) *   C) a   D) some

19. There's _____ open-fire in the living room?
    A) a   B) some   C) an   D) any

20. There are _____ big cupboards in the kitchen.
    A) a   B) some   C) any   D) *

21. Are there _____ trees and flowers in the garden?
    A) a   B) some   C) any   D) *

22. There's _____ electric cooker.
    A) an   B) some   C) any   D) a

23. There are _____ good restaurants nearby.
    A) a   B) any   C) some   D) *

24. Upstairs there's _____ big bathroom.
    A) some   B) a   C) an   D) any

25. Does the cottage have _____ dining room?
    A) any   B) an   C) a   D) some

26. The village of the Kingmore has _____ post office and _____ shop.
    A) some / a   B) some / any   C) a / a   D) an / a

27. Are there _____ good beaches near the cottage?
    A) any   B) some   C) a   D) the

28. "_____ there any cups?"
    "Yes, _____ are."
    A) Are / there   B) There / is   C) This / is   D) Is / this

29. "Is _____ a television?"
    "Yes, there _____."
    A) this / are   B) there / is   C) this / is   D) that / is

30. There _____ any flowers.
    A) are   B) is   C) aren't   D) isn't

31. It's the best home _____ the world.
    A) on   B) in   C) all   D) at

32. The front door is _____ the top of the steps.
    A) on   B) at   C) in   D) by

33. There _____ a photo _____ the television.
    A) are / on   B) is / in   C) is / on   D) are / in

34. There are two pictures _____ the wall.
    A) at   B) on   C) of   D) in

35. The cinema is _____ the left.
    A) in   B) at   C) off   D) on

36. _____ there a table? Yes, there _____.
    A) Are / are   B) Is / is   C) Are / is   D) Is / are

37. There _____ an armchair.
    A) any   B) is   C) are   D) some

38. "_____ there any photos?"
    "No, there _____."
    A) Are / aren't   B) Is / isn't   C) Is / aren't   D) Are/isn't

39. There _____ magazines under the table.
    A) is   B) are   C) some   D) any

40. There _____ a post box in front of the chemist's.
    A) are   B) is   C) some   D) any

41. How much are _____ glasses?
    A) this   B) they   C) these   D) that

42. "Is _____ book john's?"
    "Yes, _____ is."
    A) these / it   B) this / it   C) it / it's   D) that / its

43. Take _____ bags into the kitchen.
    A) these   B) this   C) that   D) it

44. I don't like _____ music.
    A) they   B) these   C) this   D) it

45. Bob, _____ is my mother.
    A) these   B) it   C) this   D) that

46. "Is _____ exercise very easy?"
    "No, _____ isn't."
    A) these / it   B) this / its   C) these / this   D) that / it

47. I like Tom, _____ I don't like his wife.
    A) and   B) but   C) because   D) so

48. I like living here _____ it's near the shops.
    A) because   B) so   C) and   D) but

49. We both like sailing, _____ we live near the sea.
    A) and as   B) because   C) so   D) but

50. Our flat is small, _____ it's comfortable.
    A) but   B) so   C) because   D) and

51. New York is expensive, _____ I like it.
    A) because   B) but   C) and   D) so

52. I like New York, _____ it's very exciting.
    A) because   B) but   C) and   D) so

53. I like Judy, _____ I often visit her.
    A) so   B) because   C) but   D) for

54. I like Chinese food, _____ my husband doesn't like it at all.
    A) so   B) but   C) because   D) and

55. We live in a flat on the top floor, _____ we don't have a garden.
    A) so   B) but   C) because   D) and

56. I like my job _____ it's interesting.
    A) because   B) and   C) so   D) but

57. In my bedroom there's a bed _____ a wardrobe.
    A) but   B) so   C) and   D) also

ELEMENTARY TEST - 6

- Can / can't
- Could
- Prepositions
- Was / were
- Was born

1. Our homework _____ very difficult yesterday, but today it _____ easy.
   A) is / is   B) was / is   C) was / was   D) is / was

2. I know that I _____ late 2 days ago, but this time I _____ late.
   A) am / were   B) am not / am not
   C) was / was   D) wasn't / am

3. A: _____ was she born?
   B: She _____ born in New Zealand.
   A) Where / was   B) Where / were
   C) When / were   D) When / was

4. A: _____ were they late for the meeting?
   B: Because they _____ asleep.
   A) What / were   B) Why / was
   C) Why / were   D) Why / are

5. The weather _____ nice today, but it _____ nasty yesterday.
   A) is / was   B) was / is   C) is / is   D) is / were

6. A: _____ was Mr. Black born?
   B: He was born _____ 1963.
   A) When / at   B) Where / in   C) What / in   D) When / in

7. The students _____ very tired today.
   Because they _____ at a party last night.
   A) were / are   B) are / was   C) are / were   D) were / were

8. A: _____ was Jennifer's job 2 years ago?
   B: She _____ a flight attendant.
   A) Why / were   B) What / was   C) Who / was   D) Who / were

9. A: _____ is the briefcase?
   B: It _____ 200 dollars, but it _____ 100 dollars before.
   A) How much / is / was   B) How many / is / was
   C) How much / was / is   D) How much / is / is

10. A: How old _____ you in 1990?
    B: I _____ 10, but I _____ 25 now.
    A) are / are / was   B) were / was / am
    C) was / are / were   D) were / was / are

11. A: How _____ they after the accident?
    B: They _____ shocked, but now they _____ better.
    A) were / are / were   B) were / were / were
    C) was / were / are   D) were / were / are

12. A: How much _____ the tea cups before?
    B: They _____ 10 euros each, they _____ 8 euros now!
    A) were / were / are   B) were / are / were
    C) are / were / were   D) are / were / are

13. A: Where _____ they born?
    B: They _____ born _____ .
    A) were / were / in 1995   B) was / were / in Italy
    C) were / were / in Denmark   D) was / were / in 1995

14. I _____ play chess _____ I was five.
    A) can / when   B) could / when
    C) could / what   D) can / where

15. _____ could you do when you _____ seven.
    A) Were / was   B) What / was
    C) What / are   D) What / were

16. A: _____ languages _____ Nicola speak when he _____ a child?
    B: 2 languages.
    A) How many / could / was   B) How much / could / was
    C) What / was / could   D) What / could / was

17. A: _____ languages could they speak when they _____ teenagers?
    B: Italian and Russian.
    A) Which / was   B) What / were
    C) What / was   D) How / were

18. My little sister _____ paint pictures alone when she _____ nine, but she _____ now.
    A) could / can / can   B) can / was / could
    C) couldn't / was / can   D) was / can / could

19. Kim _____ ski 4 years ago, but he _____ ski very well now.
    A) could / can   B) can / could
    C) could / can't   D) couldn't / can

20. _____ Ben and Jane married ten years ago?
    A) Was   B) Were   C) Are   D) Is

21. Tim _____ run very well, but I _____ run like him, because I was bad at running.
    A) could / couldn't   B) could / could
    C) can / could   D) can / can

22. I _____ play football well, but I _____ play ice-hockey very well.
    A) can't / can   B) could / can't
    C) could / can   D) can / could

23. Last year they _____ in Europe, and visited Germany, _____ they traveled only in Berlin.
    A) was / but   B) were / but   C) were / so   D) was / and

24. I _____ born in Amsterdam _____ I live in New York now.
    A) was / and   B) was / but   C) were / and   D) were / but

25. She _____ understand English, _____ she can't speak it.
    A) could / and   B) can / and   C) can / but   D) can't / but

26. I love Netherlands, _____ I came to Amsterdam.
    A) and   B) however   C) for   D) so

27. A: _____ you _____ the piano?
    B: Yes, _____ .
    A) Can / use / I can   B) Can / play / I can
    C) Can / play / I   D) Can / use / *

28. A: _____ of food _____ our cook cook?
    B: Italian & French food.
    A) What of / can   B) Which / can
    C) What kind / can   D) What / can

29. A: _____ can she _____ the guitar?
    B: Very well.
    A) How / play   B) Why / play   C) What / play   D) When / play

30. A: _____ can they _____ a computer?
    B: In the office.
    A) What time / use   B) Where / use
    C) When / use   D) Where / using

31. A: _____ languages can her aunt _____ ?
    B: 2 languages.
    A) How many / speak   B) How much / speak
    C) What / use   D) What / speak

32. A: _____ languages can Mrs. Brown speak?
    B: English & Irish.
    A) How   B) What   C) Why   D) Where

33. A: _____ can you cook Italian food for us?
    B: On Friday evening.
    A) What   B) When   C) What time   D) Why

34. A: _____ can my students come?
    B: At 3 in the afternoon.
    A) What   B) Where   C) How   D) What time

35. A: _____ can Alison go skiing?
    B: On her winter holiday.
    A) Where   B) Why   C) When   D) What

36. A: _____ Paul play rugby?
    B: No, he can't. But he can _____ baseball.
    A) Can / play   B) Can / plays   C) Does / play   D) Does / play

37. A: _____ can't you come to the party?
    B: Because I have an exam tomorrow.
    A) When   B) *   C) Why   D) What

38. Adam _____ ride a motorbike and he _____ drive a car.
    A) can't / can   B) can / can   C) can / is   D) can / can't

39. Adam _____ use a computer, but he _____ program a computer.
    A) is / isn't   B) can / can   C) can / can't   D) can't / can't

40. Flora _____ drive a car but she _____ ride a motorbike.
    A) can / can't   B) is / can't   C) can't / can't   D) is / can

41. The homework _____ very difficult yesterday.
    A) were   B) was   C) is   D) could

42. The children _____ very tired today. They _____ at a party yesterday evening.
    A) were / was   B) are / were   C) was / was   D) am / was

43. Hello, everybody! I _____ sorry, I _____ late!
    A) am / is   B) am / am   C) was / was   D) am / was

44. Was it hot yesterday? Yes, it _____ .
    A) is   B) was   C) were   D) wasn't

45. She paints _____ two hours _____ bedtime.
    A) at / to   B) for / at   C) for / until   D) until / for

46. Yesterday there was a party _____ my house.
    A) at   B) in   C) for   D) on

47. I was _____ a party last night.
    A) at   B) in   C) on   D) for

48. I could play chess when I _____ five.
    A) am   B) were   C) was   D) is

49. Can I speak _____ you?
    A) to   B) with   C) for   D) of

50. The weather _____ beautiful today. But it _____ terrible yesterday.
    A) is / were   B) is / is   C) was / was   D) is / was

51. They were _____ England _____ 1998.
    A) at / in   B) in / in   C) at / of   D) for / in

52. "Where _____ you born?"
    "I _____ born in India.
    A) are / am   B) were / was   C) were / were   D) was / were

53. We _____ married when I _____ eighteen and Roger _____ twenty.
    A) are / was / was   B) are / is / was
    C) were / was / was   D) are / am / was

54. "Where _____ your sister born?"
    "She _____ born in India, too."
    A) were / was   B) are / is   C) was / was   D) was / were

55. "_____ you drive?"
    "No, I can't."
    A) Could   B) Are   C) Can   D) Is

56. Only Sam _____ play the piano.
    A) can   B) was   C) is   D) were

57. Nobody _____ play the guitar.
    A) can't   B) can   C) couldn't   D) isn't

58. I was _____ Adam's party _____ Saturday.
    A) in / at   B) at / on   C) in / on   D) on / at

59. Tom is _____ the garden _____ his friend Sam.
    A) in / with   B) in / of   C) at / of   D) on / with

60. She was _____ the cinema _____ her brother.
    A) in / in   B) on / of   C) at / with   D) of / with

61. John lives _____ home _____ his parents.
    A) in / with   B) at / with   C) at / of   D) on / with

62. I go _____ work _____ bus.
    A) to / by   B) at / on   C) to / with   D) by / to

63. I work _____ 6 a.m. _____ 6 p.m.
    A) from / to   B) to / at   C) at / at   D) at / until

64. Look _____ this photo _____ my brother. Isn't he tall?
    A) at / of   B) of / on   C) in / in   D) in / at

65. Queen Elizabeth was born _____ London _____ 1926.
    A) at / in   B) of / on   C) in / in   D) on / in

66. "Can you help me with my homework?"
    "_____ course I can; give it _____ me."
    A) Of / for   B) Of / to   C) It / at   D) For / of

67. "Could she cook?"
    "Yes, she _____"
    A) can   B) is   C) could   D) was

68. "_____ you cook Italian food?"
    "No, I _____ but I love eating it."
    A) Are / am not   B) Can / can't
    C) Could / can't   D) Can't / can

69. Everybody _____ drive a car in my family.
    A) was   B) can   C) is   D) are

70. _____ you _____ any other languages?
    A) Could / know   B) Could / use
    C) Can / speak   D) Can / speaking

71. "_____ your friend speak English?"
    "No, she _____."
    A) Is / isn't   B) Can / can't
    C) Could / could   D) Can/can

72. He _____ paint pictures when he was just three.
    A) can   B) could   C) is   D) are

73. "_____ you in England in 1999?"
    "Yes, I _____."
    A) Could / could   B) Are / am
    C) Were / was   D) Was / were

74. _____ you swim when you were five?
    A) Could   B) Can   C) Do   D) Are

75. Where _____ you now?
    A) were   B) do   C) are   D) is

76. What month _____ it last month?
    A) was   B) is   C) were   D) did

77. _____ your teacher speak English when he was seven?
    A) Can   B) Could   C) Does   D) Are

ELEMENTARY   TEST - 7

- Past Simple
- Regular verbs, irregular verbs
- Time expressions

1. He _____ some new shoes last month.
   A) bought   B) buying   C) buy   D) buys

2. Where _____ you _____ on holiday last year?
   A) did / went   B) go / did   C) did / go   D) do / go

3. A: _____ you _____ Jane last month?
   B: No, I _____.
   A) * / saw / didn't   B) Did / see / didn't
   C) Did / saw / didn't   D) Did / see / did

4. A: _____ did she _____ a job?
   B: In the car factory.
   A) When / get   B) Where / got
   C) Who / get   D) Where / get

5. Max didn't _____ yesterday afternoon; he _____ at home.
   A) go out / stayed   B) go out / stay
   C) went out / stayed   D) went out / stay

6. Geoffrey _____ French before, but he _____ at university now.
   A) study didn't / studies   B) didn't study / study
   C) did not study / studies   D) didn't studied / studies

7. A: _____ did they have _____ lunch?
   B: Soup & fish.
   A) What / on   B) What / for   C) Where / in   D) Who / for

8. A: Where _____ you last week?
   B: I _____ in Alabama.
   A) were / were   B) was / is   C) were / was   D) was / were

9. I usually _____ for 6 hours a day, but I _____ for 8 hours yesterday.
   A) work / worked   B) works / worked
   C) worked / worked   D) work / work

10. Rosemary often _____ to work by bus, but she _____ to work by taxi yesterday.
    A) got / get   B) gets / got   C) get / got   D) got / got

11. Bonny and Nick _____ tennis last weekend, but they rarely _____ tennis.
    A) played / play   B) play / play
    C) play / plays   D) play / played

12. It _____ a lot in winter here, but it _____ last year.
    A) snows / rains   B) snowed / rained
    C) snow / rain   D) snows / rained

13. Last year it _____ for three months, but it _____ just for two weeks.
    A) snows / rains   B) snowed / rained
    C) snowing / raining   D) snow / raining

14. A: _____ it snow a little in winter in Holland?
    B: Yes, it _____. But last winter it _____ snow at all.
    A) Do / do / didn't   B) Does / do / doesn't
    C) Does / does / didn't   D) Do / does / don't

15. A: _____ you usually work for 8 hours a day?
    B: Yes, I _____. But last week I _____ for 8 hours a day.
    A) Do / do / didn't work   B) Do / did / didn't worked
    C) Did / did / don't work   D) Do / did / don't work

16. A: _____ Alex _____ you yesterday evening?
    B: No, he _____.
    A) Did / helped / didn't   B) Did / helped / did
    C) Did / help / did   D) Did / help / didn't

17. It _____ Jack's birthday two days ago.
    A) was   B) were   C) is   D) are

18. A: Who _____ you eat with?
    B: Well, I _____ dinner with friends.
    A) did / eat   B) did / eats   C) did / ate   D) did / eaten

19. Ann usually _____ to work, but yesterday she_____ .
    A) drive / walks   B) drives / walked
    C) drove / walked   D) drive / walk

20. It usually _____ a lot in winter but last year it _____ .
    A) rains / snowed   B) rains / snows
    C) rain / snowed   D) rain / snow

21. Ann and Max usually _____ sailing at weekends, but last weekend they _____ tennis.
    A) goes / played   B) go / played
    C) went / play   D) went / played

22. My family left London and moved _____ a small village.
    A) to   B) in   C) at   D) for

23. People all _____ the world speak English.
    A) of   B) for   C) over   D) from

24. What do you know _____ George Washington?
    A) with   B) about   C) for   D) off

25. Now she _____ alone, but when she was a child she _____ with her mother and sisters.
    A) live / lived   B) lives / lived   C) lived / lives   D) live / lived

26. Where _____ she live now ?
    A) did   B) do   C) does   D) is

27. She _____ learn to read until she was 86.
    A) didn't   B) doesn't   C) isn't   D) don't

28. Where _____ she live in 1950?
    A) does   B) is   C) did   D) do

29. She _____ work when she was 8.
    A) started   B) starts   C) start   D) starting

30. "_____ you like the film?"
    "No, I _____ ."
    A) Are / am not   B) Did / didn't
    C) Do / didn't   D) Are / didn't

31. She thinks _____ her past life.
    A) off   B) for   C) about   D) with

32. He was tired _____ politics.
    A) of   B) at   C) from   D) with

33. She died _____ a car crash.
    A) at   B) for   C) in   D) on

34. People were afraid _____ her.
    A) from   B) of   C) at   D) on

35. I _____ in Paris when I was six.
    A) lived   B) live   C) living   D) lives

36. We _____ move to London.
    A) did   B) didn't   C) aren't   D) isn't

37. "When _____ you have your last holiday?"
    "Last August."
    A) do   B) are   C) did   D) is

38. He _____ the school in 1994.
    A) left   B) leaved   C) leave   D) leaves

39. He _____ his wife, Maria, in 1998.
    A) met   B) meted   C) meet   D) meets

40. In my bedroom there's a bed _____ a wardrobe.
    A) but   B) so   C) and   D) also

41. Millions of people _____ to London for her Funeral when he died.
    A) come   B) coming   C) came   D) comes

42. Peter stayed _____ his grandmother _____ Christmas.
    A) at / in   B) to / in   C) on / at   D) with/at

43. We arrived _____ the airport _____ New York _____ 5:45 am.
    A) at / in / at   B) to / in / at   C) on / at / at   D) at / at / in

44. Speak _____ me in English. It's good practice _____ us.
    A) to / with   B) of / of   C) to / for   D) with / on

45. There's a postman _____ a letter _____ you.
    A) with / for   B) with / to   C) at / to   D) at / at

46. I often think _____ the day we met.
    A) off   B) on   C) about   D) for

47. Tuncay Atakan is an English teacher. He _____ English.
    A) teaching   B) like   C) teaches   D) study

48. 'Was there anyone at the office yesterday?'
    ' No, _____.'
    A) they weren't   B) there isn't
    C) there wasn't   D) they didn't

49. 'Did she go to the cinema last night?'
    'No, she _____.'
    A) did   B) wasn't   C) can't   D) didn't

50. '_____ they come by train?'
    'No, they came by plane.'
    A) Do   B) Does   C) Were   D) Did

51. I came to live here three years _____ .
    A) ago   B) before   C) last   D) always

52. _____ month I went to Paris.
    A) This   B) That   C) Last   D) Next

53. In my family we _____ dinner at seven o'clock.
    A) take   B) do   C) go   D) have

54. There's a bank _____ the bookshop.
    A) between   B) on   C) opposite   D) straight ahead

55. I usually take the car because I don't like _____ .
    A) working   B) running   C) going   D) walking

56. We _____ in a hotel in Frankfurt.
    A) stayed   B) was   C) spent   D) had

57. 'Where can I buy some medicine?'
    'At the _____ in Cook Street.'
    A) chemist's   B) bank   C) market   D) baker's

58. '_____ ?'
    'He's very nice.'
    A) What does he look like?
    B) What's he like?
    C) How is he?
    D) How does he look?

ELEMENTARY TEST - 8

- Past Simple
- Negatives and ago
- Time expressions
- What is the date?
- Linking words (because, when, until)
- Prepositions

1. Prince Charles _____ Canadian. He _____ English.
   A) is not / is   B) is not / was
   C) was not / is   D) was not / were

2. I _____ to be _____ artist when I _____ a child.
   A) wanted / an / was   B) want / a / was
   C) wants / an / was   D) to want / an / is

3. He _____ blind _____ the car accident _____ the beach.
   A) came / in / on   B) went / in / on
   C) went / on / in   D) came / in / in

4. My friend _____ a present _____ me _____ the Ramadan Holiday last year.
   A) give / to / in   B) give / at / to
   C) gives / to / at   D) gave / to / on

5. It _____ a lot _____ our holiday.
   A) didn't rain / during   B) didn't / during
   C) didn't rained / on   D) not rain / in

6. What a man he is! He _____ his passport and _____ keys _____ his car yesterday.
   A) forgot / lose / of   B) forget / lost / of
   C) forgot / lost / of   D) forgot / lost / from

7. A: Did you watch a football match _____ TV?
   B: No, I didn't. But it was broadcast _____ radio.
   A) on / in   B) on / on   C) in / in   D) in / to

8. Can I talk _____ Mr. Adams _____ your mobile phone?
   A) with / on   B) on / in   C) on / on   D) to / on

9. It _____ a really bad joke; no one laughed _____ his joke.
   A) was / with   B) was / at   C) were / at   D) is / at

10. I learned _____ the Internet that a pop concert is _____ the third _____ November.
    A) in / on / of   B) on / in / of   C) in / in / of   D) on / on / of

11. Who's the blonde girl _____ the first row?
    A) in   B) on   C) at   D) over

12. You'll find the poem _____ page 16.
    A) at   B) on   C) in   D) *

13. They lived in this city _____ 1980.
    A) since   B) for   C) about   D) before

14. The Greens lived in London _____ six years.
    A) since   B) for   C) in   D) at

15. A: _____ is Amanda's birthday?
    B: It is _____ the 25th _____ December.
    A) What / on / in   B) When / on / of
    C) When / in / on   D) What / on / of

16. A: What is _____ today?
    B: Today is _____ 1st of _____ .
    A) the day / the / May   B) the / the / Monday
    C) the month / the / July   D) the date / the / October

17. A: When _____ Turkmenistan become Independent?
    B: It _____ Independent on _____ .
    A) did / became / the 27th of October, 1991
    B) became / did / 27 the 1991, October
    C) did / became / the 27th of 1991, October
    D) did / did / 1991, the 27th, October

18. A: _____ century is it now?
    B: It is _____ .
    A: What _____ the last century?
    B: It was _____ .
    A) What / the 21st century / was / the 20 century
    B) What / the 21st century / was / the 20th century
    C) What / the 21 century / is / the 20 century
    D) When / the 21st century / was / the 20th century

19. A: _____ is the _____ month?
    B: It is May.
    A: Which is _____ 2 _____ month?
    B: It is February.
    A: Which is _____ 12th month?
    B: It is December.
    A) What / 5th / * / st / the
    B) Which / 5 / the / th / the
    C) Which / 5th / the / nd / the
    D) Which / 5th / the / rd / the

20. We _____ see Tom last night.
    A) don't   B) didn't   C) doesn't   D) isn't

21. I _____ to the U.S.A. ten years ago.
    A) went   B) go   C) visit   D) gone

22. What's _____ television this evening?
    A) at   B) on   C) in   D) of

23. Today's the third _____ April.
    A) in   B) on   C) of   D) at

24. I left the party early _____ I didn't feel well.
    A) because   B) but   C) until   D) so

25. They didn't go to bed _____ midnight.
    A) when   B) until   C) so   D) because

26. We met Ken's brother last Saturday _____ they came for dinner.
    A) but   B) until   C) when   D) so

27. I am _____ the mobile phone.
    A) on   B) in   C) of   D) at

28. Some people try to find friends _____ the Internet.
    A) at   B) on   C) in   D) of

29. We didn't laugh _____ his joke.
    A) at   B) with   C) for   D) on

30. There was a knock _____ the door.
    A) of   B) in   C) at   D) for

31. We met fifty years _____ .
    A) until   B) ago   C) of   D) after

32. I didn't feel well _____ I left the party early.
    A) so   B) because   C) but   D) until

33. Peter couldn't speak _____ he was 6.
    A) until   B) because   C) so   D) where

34. I didn't enjoy math lessons _____ I was at school.
    A) until   B) when   C) because   D) and

35. Sally didn't buy the red shoes _____ she couldn't afford them.
    A) until   B) so   C) because   D) when

36. We met Ken's wife _____ her parents last Saturday.
    A) until   B) when   C) because   D) and

37. She _____ see me.
    A) don't   B) aren't   C) isn't   D) didn't

38. Our teacher _____ come to school.
    A) aren't   B) isn't   C) wasn't   D) didn't

39. Paul _____ read until he was eight.
    A) can't   B) can   C) couldn't   D) could

40. I often _____ have a lot of time, so I _____ do the shopping myself.
    A) don't / don't   B) doesn't / does
    C) didn't / did   D) didn't / didn't

41. I _____ him three months ago.
    A) see   B) sees   C) saw   D) seen

42. We _____ in 1965.
    A) met   B) meets   C) meet   D) meeting

43. Princess Diana _____ in 1997.
    A) die   B) died   C) dies   D) dye

44. Alice _____ back from America last month.
    A) come   B) came   C) comes   D) coming

45. Their son _____ born at 2 o'clock this morning.
    A) were   B) is   C) was   D) are

46. I _____ have a shower yesterday evening.
    A) don't   B) didn't   C) doesn't   D) haven't

Book 1 Part A   13   Elementary Test 8

47. I _____ the answer now.
    A) know   B) known   C) knows   D) knew
48. I _____ bread this morning.
    A) buy   B) bought   C) sell   D) buying
49. He was born _____ 1955.
    A) on   B) at   C) of   D) in
50. 130 _____
    A) one hundred and thirty   B) one hundred and fifteen
    C) one hundred and fifty   D) one hundred and thirteen
51. 862 _____
    A) eight hundred and forty-two
    B) eight hundred and sixty-two
    C) eight hundred and sixty
    D) eight hundred and sixteen
52. 999 _____
    A) nine hundred and nineteen—nine
    B) nine hundred and ninety-six
    C) one thousand and ninety-nine
    D) nine hundred and ninety-nine
53. 603 _____
    A) six hundred and thirteen   B) six hundred and thirty
    C) six hundred and three   D) six hundred and nine
54. 387 _____
    A) three hundred and eighty-seven
    B) three hundred and eighteen
    C) three hundred and eighty
    D) three hundred and eighty-eight
55. I liked the movie _____ I didn't like the book.
    A) until   b) but   C) so   D) when
56. I went to university, _____ Sandy didn't.
    A) until   B) so   C) but   D) and
57. She married _____ she was just eighteen.
    A) when   B) until   C) but   D) and
58. We were together nearly every day _____ we left school twelve years later.
    A) when   B) until   C) so   D) and
59. I didn't see Sandy very often _____ we talked on the telephone.
    A) and   B) but   C) until   D) when
60. We stopped for three-quarters of an hour _____ New York Airport.
    A) at   B) in   C) over   D) on
61. Where is your mother? Is she _____ the hairdresser's again?
    A) in   B) on   C) at   D) *
62. I'll finish the work _____ two weeks.
    A) by   B) for   C) since   D) in
63. I'll be home _____ 7 o'clock.
    A) by   B) in   C) on   D) since
64. He lived with Nomads _____ the Sahara desert for two years.
    A) over   B) on   C) in   D) of
65. I won't stay _____ bed; I'll just lie down _____ the bed for an hour.
    A) in / in   B) at / in   C) at / on   D) in / on
66. I last saw her _____ the car park.
    A) in   B) under   C) on   D) *
67. He grows corn _____ his farm.
    A) over   B) with   C) at   D) on
68. They lived in Spain _____ the Second World War.
    A) during   B) for   C) since   D) at
69. She opened her mouth so the doctor could look _____ her throat.
    A) to   B) on   C) at   D) for
70. I cut myself _____ a knife.
    A) by   B) with   C) in   D) over
71. You'd better go _____ the next plane to London.
    A) at   B) in   C) by   D) on
72. She said hello _____ everyone except me.
    A) to   B) *   C) at   D) of

73. She is worried _____ her exams.
    A) of   B) about   C) with   D) *
74. Tell us _____ your holiday.
    A) *   B) of   C) about   D) with
75. Mr. Collins always talks _____ himself.
    A) to   B) with   C) at   D) in
76. Is it possible for me to keep it _____ Tuesday?
    A) by   B) at   C) since   D) until
77. Who's the man _____ the funny hat?
    A) in   B) from   C) at   D) to
78. Will you come _____ bus or _____ a late train?
    A) by-by   B) on-in   C) by-on   D) in-by
79. I saw an accident _____ my way home.
    A) on   B) at   C) in   D) to
80. The doctor gave me a prescription _____ my cough.
    A) with   B) to   C) at   D) for
81. I usually stay at home _____ night.
    A) at   B) with   C) in   D) over
82. I called you _____ seven o'clock yesterday.
    A) in   B) on   C) at   D) of
83. Can't you come _____ your bicycle?
    A) in   B) with   C) on   D) by
84. She arrived _____ Friday.
    A) in   B) on   C) at   D) over
85. We'll go _____ Rio _____ June.
    A) * - in   B) at - on   C) to - on   D) to - in
86. I was born _____ September 9th.
    A) in   B) on   C) at   D) of
87. John and Mary are talking _____ the telephone.
    A) *   B) to   C) on   D) with
88. Classes began _____ last week.
    A) in   B) *   C) at   D) on
89. They took my temperature _____ the operation.
    A) before   B) by   C) *   D) of
90. Do you want sugar _____ your tea?
    A) with   B) on   C) by   D) *
91. I'm afraid _____ falling trees.
    A) from   B) of   C) with   D) at
92. She didn't get a passing grade _____ her test.
    A) from   B) with   C) at   D) of
93. I sometimes listen _____ the radio or watch _____ TV.
    A) of - on   B) to - on   C) * - to   D) to - *
94. I always lie down _____ a swim.
    A) by   B) with   C) on   D) after
95. Did you stay _____ a tent on your last holiday?
    A) in   B) over   C) on   D) of
96. She put a bandage _____ the boy's cut finger.
    A) at   B) to   C) on   D) in
97. He has a pain _____ his leg.
    A) on   B) over   C) in   D) at
98. The Prime Minister arrived _____ Tokyo last night.
    A) *   B) in   C) at   D) to
99. I couldn't get _____ school in time.
    A) to   B) at   C) *   D) in
100. Ann stirred her coffee _____ a spoon.
    A) with   B) by   C) in   D) to

ELEMENTARY TEST - 9

- Countable and uncountable nouns
- Do you like ..?   - Would you like..?
- A/an and some   - Much and many
- Polite requests (Could you ..?, Can I ..?)
- Prepositions

1. Would you like _____ rice?
   A) a   B) some   C) an   D) any

2. Can I have _____ stamps, please?
   A) a   B) an   C) some   D) any

3. Can you give me _____ money?
   A) some   B) a   C) any   D) an

4. I usually have _____ biscuit and _____ cup of coffee at 11 a.m.
   A) a/some   B) some/some   C) a/a   D) a/any

5. He always has _____ egg for breakfast.
   A) an   B) a   C) any   D) the

6. Do you like _____ ?
   A) cook   B) cooking   C) to cook   D) cooked

7. "_____ you like some tea?"
   "No, thanks."
   A) Does   B) Do   C) Would   D) Are

8. "_____ you _____ your teacher?"
   "Yes, he is a good man."
   A) Would / like   B) Do / like
   C) Did / liked   D) Are / like

9. Would you like _____ apple or _____ strawberries?
   A) a / any   B) an / some   C) any / any   D) a / some

10. Would you like _____ milk?
    A) a   B) some   C) any   D) an

11. Do you like _____ homework ?
    A) making   B) do   C) doing   D) does

12. I have got a book _____ Stephen King.
    A) by   B) for   C) from   D) in

13. Help me _____ my homework.
    A) to   B) with   C) of   D) about

14. There is _____ cheese on the table.
    A) any   B) some   C) a   D) the

15. There are _____ oranges on the table.
    A) any   B) an   C) a   D) some

16. _____ rice is there?
    A) How many   B) How much   C) How long   D) How

17. Are there _____ chips?
    A) any   B) some   C) a   D) the

18. Can I have _____ tea?
    A) a   B) the   C) any   D) some

19. I'd like _____ bananas.
    A) any   B) a   C) an   D) some

20. Is there _____ tea?
    A) a   B) the   C) some   D) any

21. _____ coffee is there?
    A) How many   B) How   C) How much   D) How long

22. There isn't _____ coffee.
    A) many   B) a   C) the   D) much

23. Can I have _____ bread?
    A) a   B) some   C) any   D) an

24. Do you like _____ ?
    A) shop   B) shopping   C) to shop   D) shopped

25. Do you like _____ English?
    A) learn   B) learned   C) learning   D) learnt

26. She _____ the Rolling Stones records.
    A) like   B) liking   C) likes   D) to like

27. Would you like to listen to _____ music?
    A) any   B) some   C) many   D) a

28. I need to put _____ petrol in the car.
    A) some   B) a   C) any   D) an

29. _____ English books do you have?
    A) How many   B) How some   C) How much   D) How any

30. I want _____ book from the library.
    A) the   B) a   C) some   D) any

31. Are there _____ letters for me this morning?
    A) some   B) a   C) the   D) any

32. You have _____ lovely pictures in your house.
    A) some   B) a   C) an   D) any

33. There was _____ rain during the night.
    A) an   B) some   C) any   D) a

34. "Are you Canadian?"
    "No, but I have _____ good friends in Canada."
    A) any   B) a   C) an   D) some

35. Do you have _____ sisters or brothers?
    A) some   B) a   C) the   D) any

36. _____ I have a cheese sandwich, please?
    A) Do   B) Does   C) Can   D) Am

37. I don't have _____ milk left.
    A) much   B) some   C) many   D) a

38. We have _____ of homework today.
    A) many   B) a lot   C) much   D) a few

39. How _____ milk is there in the fridge?
    A) much   B) a lot   C) many   D) a few

40. I'd like _____ mineral water.
    A) any   B) a   C) the   D) some

41. Where do you come _____ ?
    A) from   B) *   C) of   D) in

42. We stayed _____ the Heathrow Hotel.
    A) on   B) into   C) at   D) to

43. I waited _____ the bus-stop for ten minutes.
    A) at   B) in   C) on   D) for

44. I'm not very good _____ mathematics.
    A) of   B) on   C) in   D) at

45. What are you interested _____ ?
    A) in   B) of   C) on   D) over

46. Please, put your homework _____ my desk.
    A) at   B) to   C) on   D) with

47. It takes about five minutes to walk _____ the bridge.
    A) *   B) to   C) at   D) till

48. I took the train _____ Dover to Ostend.
    A) by   B) on   C) *   D) from

49. David was very busy _____ the afternoon.
    A) *   B) on   C) at   D) in

50. Toshio is _____ Japan. He isn't American.
    A) of   B) in   C) at   D) from

51. Bob ran 100 meters _____ 11 seconds.
    A) in   B) at   C) on   D) with

52. They arrived _____ plane.
    A) by   B) on   C) with   D) at

53. "Did they come _____ bus ?"
    No, they came _____ foot.
    A) on / on   B) by / on   C) with / by   D) by / with

54. Switch _____ the light. It's getting dark.
    A) of   B) off   C) out   D) on

55. Is there a fridge _____ your kitchen?
    A) at   B) on   C) with   D) in

ELEMENTARY TEST - 10

- Comparatives and superlatives
- Have got, has got
- Prepositions   - Linking words (which, where)

1. You are _____ me.
   A) older   B) oldest   C) older than   D) older then

2. New York is _____ Paris.
   A) dirty   B) dirtier than   C) the dirtiest   D) dirtier

3. Prague is one of the _____ cities in Europe.
   A) most beautiful   B) more beautiful
   C) beautiful   D) the most beautiful

4. How many children _____ they _____?
   A) have / got   B) have / get
   C) does / got   D) has / got

5. A country is quieter _____ a city.
   A) with   B) to   C) than   D) ago

6. The house is 50 meters _____ the sea.
   A) to   B) by   C) for   D) from

7. He spends his time _____ the banks of the river.
   A) in   B) to   C) about   D) on

8. She came _____ the garage.
   A) out   B) of   C) out of   D) up

9. He jumped _____ the lake.
   A) into   B) to   C) in   D) at

10. He walked _____ the hill.
    A) to   B) at   C) out   D) up

11. A country is _____ than a city.
    A) cheap   B) cheaper   C) cheapest   D) more cheaper

12. A city is _____ than the country.
    A) the most exciting   B) exciting
    C) more exciting   D) excited

13. Your class is _____ than my class.
    A) noisy   B) noisiest   C) noisier   D) more noisy

14. Life in a country is _____ in a city.
    A) slow   B) slower than   C) slower   D) slowly

15. Brain's car is _____ in our district.
    A) fast   B) faster   C) the fastest   D) more fast

16. Paris is _____ Madrid.
    A) big than   B) bigger   C) bigger than   D) biggest

17. Madrid is much _____.
    A) cheap   B) cheaper   C) cheapest   D) the cheapest

18. Why did you leave London? You had a _____ job.
    A) better   B) best   C) gooder   D) the best

19. London _____ got a lot of parks.
    A) has   B) have   C) does   D) do

20. Our school _____ a library, but it doesn't _____ any computers.
    A) has / have   B) have / has   C) has / has   D) have / have

21. My parents _____ a new stereo.
    A) has   B) have   C) have get   D) have got

22. Does your sister _____ a fiancé?
    A) has   B) has got   C) have   D) has get

---

56. I'm still waiting _____ the Blue Train.
    A) to   B) *   C) for   D) of

57. What was the temperature _____ Ankara yesterday?
    A) at   B) of   C) in   D) off

58. I look forward _____ meeting you next month.
    A) at   B) for   C) with   D) to

59. "You can't come in _____ a ticket," the man told us.
    A) without   B) through   C) by   D) with

60. I get up _____ six o'clock _____ Tuesdays.
    A) at / on   B) at / in   C) about / at   D) around / in

61. My father takes a nap _____ dinner.
    A) with   B) after   C) on   D) at

62. When people go _____ picnic they always eat a lot.
    A) *   B) on   C) to   D) at

63. Boys and girls go _____ dancing.
    A) to   B) at   C) *   D) with

64. When do you take _____ your wrist watch?
    A) off   B) on   C) out   D) of

65. I'll phone _____ you tomorrow.
    A) to   B) at   C) on   D) *

66. Our village lies _____ two high mountains.
    A) among   B) over   C) in   D) between

67. You may write _____ a pen or _____ a pencil.
    A) with / by   B) with / with   C) in / in   D) by / by

68. A lot of planes fly _____ the city every day.
    A) on   B) through   C) over   D) between

69. They went _____ a museum.
    A) to   B) at   C) of   D) *

70. There were no planes _____ the past.
    A) in   B) on   C) at   D) over

71. We waited _____ you _____ 11.00.
    A) at / to   B) for / until   C) for / to   D) with / since

72. Marie Curie was born _____ Warsaw.
    A) on   B) at   C) in   D) from

73. Chocolate _____ harmful for your teeth, but strawberries _____ useful for your health.
    A) is / is   B) are / is   C) are / are   D) is / are

74. There _____ apple juice in the fridge. And apples _____ so delicious.
    A) are / are   B) is / are   C) is / was   D) is /is

75. Would you like _____ chips?
    A) some   B) any   C) a   D) the

76. Would you like _____ tea _____ mineral water?
    A) some / and   B) any / or   C) some / or   D) any / and

77. A: Is there _____ juice in the fridge?
    B: No, there isn't _____ juice, but there is _____ lemonade.
    A) some / some / any   B) any / any / some
    C) some / any / any   D) any / any / any

78. A: Would you like _____ oranges? Oh, sorry! There aren't _____ oranges. But we have apples.
    B: That's all right. Can I have _____ tea?
    A: OK.
    A) any / any / some   B) some / any / some
    C) any / some / any   D) some / some / any

79. A: _____ you like _____ cold water?
    B: No, thanks. _____ _____ green tea.
    A) Do / some / I love / some
    B) Would / any / I'd love / any
    C) Would / some / I'd love / some
    D) Did / some / I liked / some

80. A: _____ you like _____ biscuit?
    B: Yes, please. And I _____ some milk, too.
    A) Would / a / 'd like
    B) Do / a / would like
    C) Would / some / 'd love
    D) Would / * / would love

23. I don't _____ a problem with this exercise.
    A) has B) to have C) have D) has got

24. Do you have _____ homework?
    A) some B) a C) any D) the

25. I've got _____ pencils than you.
    A) many B) more C) much D) most

26. The Plaza is the _____ hotel.
    A) cheap B) cheapest C) the cheapest D) cheaper

27. Claridge's is the _____ hotel.
    A) old B) oldest C) older D) the oldest

28. The Plaza _____ a swimming pool.
    A) have got B) has got C) does have D) do has

29. I _____ for a walk in the country and ___ a farm.
    A) went / see B) go / saw C) went / saw D) look / saw

30. Yesterday was _____ than today.
    A) most hottest B) more hot
    C) hot D) much hotter

31. She's _____ than her brother.
    A) tall B) tallest C) taller D) the tallest

32. She is smaller _____ her sister.
    A) that B) this C) than D) this

33. I'm the _____ in the class.
    A) youngest B) most youngest
    C) young D) younger

34. Last week was _____ than this week
    A) busier B) busiest C) more busy D) busy

35. He _____ got any sisters.
    A) haven't B) doesn't C) hasn't D) don't

36. Do you _____ any bread?
    A) got B) have C) has D) had

37. My homework is the _____ in class.
    A) worst B) worse C) worthy D) bad

38. This exercise is _____ difficult in the book.
    A) most B) more C) the most D) the more

39. I'm the most _____.
    A) intelligent B) clever C) cleverer D) the intelligent

40. Its university, founded ___ 1965, is one of the oldest in Europe
    A) on B) in C) at D) of

41. I've got a book _____ Mark Twain.
    A) by B) from C) off D) in

42. Help me _____ my homework.
    A) in B) by C) with D) on

43. These exercises are _____ in the exam.
    A) the difficulties B) the most difficult
    C) the difficult D) most difficult

44. His exam marks were _____ for several months.
    A) the baddest B) the bad C) badder D) the worst

45. Have you _____ any rice?
    A) have B) got C) have got D) had

46. Bill _____ got any friends.
    A) has no B) hasn't C) doesn't D) not

47. Last week was _____ than this week.
    A) busy B) more busy C) busier D) the busiest

48. Hey! You are _____ employee in our firm.
    A) youngest B) younger C) young D) the youngest

49. She is taller _____ her elder sister.
    A) than B) then C) that D) the

50. Yesterday it was ____ the day before yesterday.
    A) colder the B) colder than C) colder them D) colder

51. Nancy's car is ____than mine, but Ben's car is ____ car.
    A) the most expensive / more expensive
    B) more expensive / the most expensive
    C) expensiver / expensivest
    D) most expensive / the more expensive

52. Your essay was _____ than Jim's, but it was _____ than Mary's.
    A) better / worse B) gooder / badder
    C) better / worst D) best / worse

53. New houses are _____ than old ones.
    A) more modern and clean
    B) modern and cleaner
    C) more modern and cleaner
    D) moderner/cleaner

54. A: _____ she _____ a new job?
    B: Yes, she does.
    A) Has / got B) Does / got C) Does / * D) Does / have

55. A: _____ they got any problems?
    B: No, they _____ .
    A) Have / haven't B) Do / have
    C) Do / does D) Does / has

56. Maya _____ got a camera. And she _____ have a car either.
    A) haven't / doesn't B) hasn't / doesn't
    C) doesn't / hasn't D) haven't / don't

57. She dived _____ the lake and went _____ the water quickly.
    A) into / out of B) in / out of
    C) into / out D) in / out

58. Who can run first _____ and _____ the hill?
    A) up / on B) upper / down
    C) down / under D) up / down

59. The chemist is 2 kilometers _____ the port.
    A) off B) from C) along D) via

60. Cairo is located _____ the banks _____ the Nile River.
    A) of / on B) on / off C) on / of D) in / of

61. Walk _____ this path and ____ the stream.
    A) along / in B) along / over C) over / in D) in / on

62. Go _____ the bus stop _____ is at the corner.
    A) close / what B) past / where
    C) past / which D) near / went

63. Drive me to the _____ , or I'll be late _____ my plane.
    A) port / of B) airport / on C) airport / for D) port / of

64. Izmir is the sea _____ _____ hundreds of ships come to.
    A) port / where B) port / that
    C) stop / which D) port / when

65. Is there a car ____ _____ I can park my Porche?
    A) center / where B) park / where
    C) station / where D) bank / which

66. We went on picnic to the _____ of the Nile River _____ is very beautiful in spring.
    A) banks / where B) where / banks
    C) banks / which D) which / banks

ELEMENTARY   TEST - 11

- Present Continuous
- Possessive pronouns (mine, yours, hers)
- Linking words (although, but)
- Prepositions

1. We _____ watching a good documentary _____ BBC World now.
   A) are / in   B) am / on   C) are / on   D) is / in

2. I always _____ _____ credit card.
   A) pay / by   B) am paying / with
   C) 'm paying / by   D) pay / with

3. _____ you _____ a girl _____ fair hair?
   A) Do / knowing / of   B) Does / know / of
   C) Do / know / with   D) Are / knowing / with

4. _____ she got a dress _____ white?
   A) Does / in   B) Has / on   C) Have / in   D) Has / in

5. _____ is reading a letter _____ bed now.
   A) She / in   B) I / in   C) You / on   D) He / at

6. A: What _____ you _____?
   B: I'm a lecturer.
   A) do / do   B) are / do   C) is / do   D) do / doing

7. A: What _____ she _____ now?
   B: I don't know.
   A) does / do   B) do / do   C) is / doing   D) is / do

8. A: _____ are we _____?
   B: To the class.
   A) When / going   B) Where / go
   C) When / go   D) Where / going

9. A: Oh no! It _____. We can't go out.
   B: It always _____ here in March.
   A) is snowing / snows   B) snows / 's snowing
   C) 's snow / snows   D) snows / snows

10. I _____. Because it's my happiest day today.
    A) jumping   B) jump   C) 'm jumping   D) jumped

11. Benedit and Nina are _____ only salads. Because vegetarians don't _____ meat.
    A) eat / eat   B) eating / eating
    C) eat / eating   D) eating / eat

12. Sorry, I _____ understand you. I _____ speak Russian.
    A) do / don't   B) do / do
    C) don't / don't   D) am / am

13. A: Why _____ we _____ to a park?
    B: A good idea!
    A) do / go   B) don't / go
    C) aren't / going   D) are / going

14. What _____ you _____ to know?
    A) do / want   B) are / wanting
    C) do / wanting   D) are / want

15. A: _____ she _____ a problem now?
    B: No. She _____ _____ how to solve.
    A) Is / solve / doesn't / know
    B) Does / solve / isn't / knowing
    C) Is / solving / doesn't / know
    D) Does / solving / doesn't / know

16. Can you translate this letter _____ English _____ Chinese _____ me?
    A) from / into / for   B) into / from / for
    C) from / in / her   D) for / from / in

17. We watched the program called Hard Talk _____ CNN. Because we are interested _____ politics.
    A) in / to   B) on / from   C) on / in   D) off / of

18. _____ child _____ playing in _____ yard.
    A) Who's / is / our   B) Whose / is / our
    C) Whose / is / ours   D) Whose / are / our

19. A: _____ are you doing under the trees?
    B: I'm _____ my keys.
    A) What / looking off   B) Whom / looking in
    C) When / looking up   D) What / looking for

20. _____ hair is blonder than _____.
    A) Her / yours   B) Hers / yours
    C) Her / your   D) Hers / your

21. _____ is hiding behind _____ car?
    A) Whose / my   B) Who's / mine
    C) Who / my   D) Whose / mine

22. I am _____ English.
    A) study   B) to study   C) studying   D) studied

23. She's _____ jeans.
    A) wearing   B) wear   C) to wear   D) wore

24. I am _____ tennis this afternoon.
    A) play   B) playing   C) to play   D) played

25. We are not _____ outside.
    A) go   B) went   C) going   D) to go

26. Where are you _____?
    A) go   B) going   C) to go   D) went

27. "Are you _____ a good time?" "Yes, we _____."
    A) having / are   B) have / is
    C) having / do   D) have / aren't

28. I _____ from Switzerland.
    A) come   B) coming   C) to come   D) came

29. Is my English _____ better.
    A) gets   B) get   C) getting   D) to get

30. Jane's _____ her friend tonight.
    A) sees   B) seeing   C) see   D) saw

31. He _____ as a clerk in a bank.
    A) working   B) work   C) works   D) to work

32. "Why are you _____ a suit?" "You usually wear jeans."
    A) wears   B) wore   C) wear   D) wearing

33. I read _____ bed.
    A) at   B) in   C) to   D) under

34. We've got this jumper _____ red
    A) in   B) to   C) with   D) at

35. He's talking _____ Mandy.
    A) with   B) to   C) at   D) for

36. There's a girl _____ fair hair.
    A) with   B) on   C) at   D) out

37. I'm looking _____ jumper.
    A) at   B) for   C) on   D) in

38. I always pay _____ credit card.
    A) in   B) on   C) at   D) by

39. He's _____ down.
    A) sit   B) sitting   C) sits   D) sat

40. It is _____ .
    A) rains   B) to rain   C) raining   D) rained

41. I'm _____ gum.
    A) chew   B) chewing   C) chews   D) chewed

42. I _____ a shower every morning.
    A) am having   B) have   C) having   D) had

43. I like _____ house.
    A) your   B) you   C) yours   D) your

44. _____ house is smaller than _____ .
    A) Ours / theirs   B) Our / their
    C) Ours / their   D) Our / theirs

45. _____ children are older than _____ .
    A) My / her   B) Mine / hers   C) My / hers   D) Mine / her

46. _____ talking to _____ sister?
    A) Whose / yours   B) Who's / your
    C) Whose / your   D) Who's / yours

47. This book isn't _____ . Is it _____ ?
    A) my / yours   B) mine / your
    C) my / your   D) mine / yours

48. "_____ dictionary is this?" "It's _____ ."
    A) Whose / him   B) Who's / his
    C) Whose / his   D) Who's / him

49. "_____ going to the party tonight?" "I am not."
    A) Whose   B) Which   C) Who's   D) Where

50. And _____ garden is bigger than _____ .
    A) their / ours   B) theirs / ours
    C) their / our   D) theirs / ours

51. _____ dog is running round _____ garden.
    A) Whose / ours   B) Who's/our
    C) Whose / our   D) Who's / ours

52. I _____ tennis this afternoon.
    A) 'm playing   B) play   C) playing   D) plays

53. We _____ pizza for dinner tonight.
    A) having   B) have   C) are having   D) had

54. _____ boots are these?
    A) Whose   B) Which   C) What   D) Whose

55. _____ do you do after school today?
    A) Which   B) Why   C) What   D) Where

56. Where _____ you going tonight.
    A) do   B) is   C) does   D) are

57. She _____ tennis every day.
    A) play   B) playing   C) plays   D) to play

58. My daughter _____ French and German.
    A) speaks   B) 's speaking   C) speak   D) to speak

59. Sally _____ a breakfast at the moment.
    A) has   B) having   C) is having   D) had

60. I'm not _____ to buy you lunch, today.
    A) go   B) going   C) goes   D) to go

61. How many languages do you _____ ?
    A) speaking   B) speaks   C) spoke   D) speak

ELEMENTARY TEST - 12

- Going to
- Wh questions
- Infinitive of purpose
- Making suggestions
- Prepositions

1. She _____ to be a ballet dancer when she _____ up.
   A) go / grow   B) going / grows
   C) goes / grows   D) 's going / grows

2. We _____ to stay in a villa in France this summer.
   A) going   B) 're going   C) to go   D) go

3. I _____ Peter tonight.
   A) 'm seeing   B) see   C) seeing   D) to see

4. I'm going _____ Peter tonight.
   A) see   B) seeing   C) to see   D) saw

5. Careful! The glass is _____ fall.
   A) going   B) going to   C) goes to   D) go to

6. We _____ to Paris this weekend.
   A) going   B) go   C) 're going   D) to go

7. Tom and Tim _____ for lunch tomorrow.
   A) to come   B) coming   C) came   D) are coming

8. I'm saving my money _____ a CD player.
   A) buying   B) to buy   C) buy   D) bought

9. We're going to Paris _____ a holiday.
   A) to have   B) have   C) having   D) had

10. I'm going to Florida _____ a year's time.
    A) at   B) on   C) in   D) by

11. He's interested _____ flying.
    A) at   B) in   C) on   D) with

12. She's good _____ singing.
    A) on   B) at   C) in   D) with

13. She was afraid _____ cars.
    A) at   B) with   C) in   D) of

14. What's the weather _____ today?
    A) like   B) with   C) in   D) about

15. What's _____ TV tonight?
    A) in   B) at   C) on   D) by

16. There's a film _____ channel 4.
    A) at   B) in   C) by   D) on

17. What's _____ the cinema?
    A) on   B) at   C) on at   D) at on

18. They _____ both _____ to become TV stars.
    A) are / go   B) are / going to
    C) is / going   D) are / going

19. What's she going _____ ?
    A) do   B) doing   C) to do   D) did

20. She's going _____ home.
    A) to walk   B) walking   C) walk   D) to walking

21. She wants _____ in Paris and Moscow.
    A) dancing   B) dance   C) is dancing   D) to dance

22. They _____ going _____ a car this year.
    A) aren't / get   B) aren't / getting
    C) aren't / to get   D) aren't / got

23. _____ he play tennis last Sunday?
    A) Did   B) Does   C) Do   D) Are

24. _____ he playing tennis now?
    A) Are   B) Does   C) Is   D) Did

25. _____ you wash it yesterday ?
    A) Do   B) Does   C) Did   D) Are

26. I _____ going to wash it tonight.
    A) do   B) am   C) are   D) do

27. We _____ having dinner at the moment.
    A) do   B) is   C) are   D) did

28. _____ you have a dinner at this time every evening?
    A) Did   B) Do   C) Does   D) Are

29. What _____ your parents going to do when they retire?
    A) is   B) do   C) are   D) did

30. When _____ your parents first meet?
    A) did   B) does   C) do   D) are

31. What time _____ Maria usually arrive at school?
    A) does   B) is   C) do   D) did

32. Look _____ that picture. Isn't it beautiful?
    A) on   B) at   C) in   D) by

33. What have we got _____ dinner?
    A) at   B) of   C) for   D) from

34. Our hotel is fifty meters _____ the sea.
    A) of   B) in   C) than   D) from

35. What is the longest river _____ the world?
    A) at   B) on   C) in   D) at

36. France is bigger _____ England.
    A) from   B) on   C) like   D) than

37. I'm looking _____ Jane. Do you know where she is?
    A) about   B) for   C) at   D) in

38. Can you buy me a bottle _____ lemonade _____ the shop?
    A) of / at   B) at / of   C) from / at   D) from / of

39. Maria is _____ her sister in many ways. They're both beautiful and intelligent.
    A) from   B) like   C) of   D) about

40. What did you do _____ the weekend?
    A) of   B) in   C) at   D) for

41. _____ Saturday night we went to a party.
    A) In   B) On   C) At   D) For

42. I _____ going out, because it _____ going to rain.
    A) 'm not / is   B) amn't / is   B) isn't / am   D) aren't / is

43. _____ you going _____ wash your car this afternoon?
    A) Are / too   B) Are / to   C) 're / to   D) Am / to

44. She _____ going to the post office _____ some stamps.
    A) is / to buy   B) is / for buying
    C) 's / for to buy   D) * / buy

45. I'm _____ home early next week.
    A) go   B) going for going
    C) going   D) going to

46. What _____ the weather _____ in Las Vegas the day before yesterday.
    A) were / like   B) was/as
    C) is / like   D) was/like

47. A : _____ is the weather like _____ ?
    B : _____ is sunny & warm. But yesterday _____ cold.
    A) What / today / it / was   B) How / today / it / was
    C) What / it / today / *   D) How / it / today / was

48. A : What _____ we _____ ?
    B : _____ go swimming.
    A) will / do / Let me   B) shall / do / Let's
    C) would / do / Let her   D) shall / do / Let me

49. A: What is the weather _____ like tomorrow?
    B: Sunny. _____ we go on picnic?
    A) going to / Shall   B) going to be / Will
    C) going to be / Are   D) going to be / Shall

50. A : _____ are you going to eat?
    B : Pizza.
    A : _____ 're you going to eat?
    B : In the cafeteria.
    A) Where / What   B) What / Where
    C) What / When   D) Who / Whom

51. A : _____ is Jim going to get married?
    B : Next month.
    A : _____ is he going to marry?
    B : His colleague.
    A) What time / Who   B) Who / Where
    C) When / Whom   D) Where / *

52. A: _____ are you going to the chemist's?
    B: I'm going to the chemist's _____ some medicine.
    A) Why / too buy   B) Why / to buy
    C) When / two buy   D) Where / buy

53. A: _____ is Pittsburg _____ Ohio?
    B: About 500 kilometers.
    A) How long / from   B) How far / from
    C) How big / off   D) How small / since

54. German is _____ English in some ways, but it is more difficult _____ English.
    A) like / then   B) as / that   C) like / than   D) like / like

55. Nicola's _____ to Liverpool _____ his grandparents.
    A) coming / visit   B) to come/visit
    C) going to come / to visit   D) coming / to visit

ELEMENTARY — TEST - 13

- Question forms (Why-how many- how much)
- Why questions
- Adverbs and adjectives

1. "_____ did the first man walk on the moon?"
   "In 1969."
   A) When   B) Where   C) Who   D) What

2. "_____ did she marry?"
   "She married to John."
   A) What   B) Who   C) Which   D) Why

3. A _____ dog.
   A) bigger than   B) big   C) biggest   D) the biggest

4. A _____ driver.
   A) care   B) careful   C) carefully   D) the careful

5. She ran _____.
   A) quick   B) quicker   C) quickly   D) the quickly

6. He drives too _____ .
   A) fastly   B) fast   C) faster   D) fastest

7. What is the story _____?
   A) of   B) on   C) at   D) about

8. What happened _____ the end of the story?
   A) on   B) in   C) at   D) from

9. The train leaves _____ platform 9.
   A) of   B) at   C) from   D) for

10. "_____ did you buy your new jacket?"
    "At supermarket."
    A) What   B) Where   C) When   D) How

11. "_____ did you pay?"
    "$ 1000."
    A) How many   B) How
    C) How much   D) Which one

12. "_____ did you buy?"
    "A new jacket."
    A) Who   B) When   C) How much   D) What

13. _____ did you buy with?
    A) Which one   B) Why   C) When   D) Who

14. "_____ did you go?"
    "This morning."
    A) Why   B) What   C) When   D) How

15. "_____ did you go?"
    "To buy some new clothes."
    A) When   B) Why   C) Where   D) How

16. "_____ did you go?"
    "To the shops."
    A) When   B) Why   C) Where   D) How

17. "_____ did you go?"
    "By car."
    A) When   B) Why   C) How much   D) How

18. "_____ do you want to go?"
    "To Paris."
    A) Why   B) Where   C) How   D) What

19. "_____ is she?"
    "Our cousin."
    A) Who   B) What   C) How   D) Where

20. "_____ old was she?"
    "60 years old."
    A) What   B) How much   C) How many   D) How

21. _____ you like learning English?
    A) Does   B) Are   C) Do   D) Have

22. What _____ you do last night?
    A) does   B) did   C) do   D) done

23. How many languages _____ your mother speak?
    A) do   B) are   C) does   D) is

24. When _____ you go shopping last?
    A) do   B) does   C) are   D) did

25. _____ do you weigh?
    A) How many   B) How   C) How much   D) What

26. Smoking is a _____ habit.
    A) badly   B) worth   C) worst   D) bad

27. The team played _____ and lost the match.
    A) badly   B) worth   C) worst   D) bad

28. Please listen _____ .
    A) careful   B) carefully   C) care   D) carely

29. The homework was the _____ .
    A) easy   B) easier   C) easily   D) easiest

30. Peter's very _____ at tennis. He won the game.
    A) goodly   B) well   C) good   D) best

31. I know the Prime Minister _____ .
    A) good   B) best   C) better   D) well

32. My husband's a _____ cook.
    A) bad   B) worst   C) badly   D) worse

33. Teachers work _____, but they don't earn much money.
    A) hardly   B) harder   C) hard   D) hardest

34. Lunch is a _____ meal for many people.
    A) quick   B) quickly   C) quicker   D) quickest

35. Life in New York is very _____ .
    A) excited   B) exciting   C) exciter   D) excitely

36. The teacher was _____ when nobody did the homework.
    A) annoyed   B) annoying   C) annoy   D) annoys

37. The news is very _____ .
    A) worried   B) worrying   C) worry   D) worringly

38. Everybody was very _____ about you.
    A) worried   B) worrying   C) worry   D) worringly

39. The game of tennis was very _____ .
    A) tired   B) tire   C) tiring   D) tires

40. "_____ did the story take place?"
    "A long time ago."
    A) How many   B) What   C) Where   D) When

41. We use adverbs _____ the beginning and the end of a sentence, but sometimes _____ the middle of a sentence.
    A) at / in   B) in / at   C) on / at   D) at / on

42. A train leaves _____ Berlin and arrives _____ Bonn in time.
    A) from / to   B) from / in   C) from / at   D) in / from

43. A plane arrived _____ the airport _____ .
    A) in / late   B) at / lately   C) at / late   D) in / lately

44. What is the story _____?
    A) in   B) from   C) off   D) about

45. A - _____ is it _____ London _____ New York?
    B - 6000 km.
    A) How long / from / to B) How fast / to / from
    C) How much / from / to D) How wide / from / to

46. My friend never comes school _____. He is always _____.
    A) early / late B) early / lately
    C) earlily / lately D) earlily / late

47. At first we draw _____ then _____.
    A) quickly / slowly B) quick / slowly
    C) quickly / slow D) quick / slow

48. They are _____ readers, they read _____.
    A) slowly / hard B) slow / hard
    C) slow / hardly D) slowly / hardly

49. I turned around _____, because there was a _____ shout.
    A) immediately / sudden B) immediate / suddenly
    C) immediate / sudden B) immediately / suddenly

50. Are you _____? Or is the book _____?
    A) boring / boring B) boring / bored
    C) bored / bored D) bored / boring

51. A- I am really _____ about my exam marks.
    B- Oh, no! You are sometimes so _____.
    A) worried / tired B) worried / tiring
    C) worrying / tired D) worrying / tiring

52. I am _____ in the Mexican Culture, because it is _____ .
    A) interesting / excited B) interested / exciting
    C) interesting / exciting D) interesting / excited

53. Be _____! Walk _____.
    A) careful / quietly B) careful / quiet
    C) carefully / quietly D) carefully / quiet

54. She paints _____; she is a _____ painter.
    A) goodly / well B) goodly / good
    C) well / good D) good / good

ELEMENTARY TEST - 14

- Present Perfect
- Ever and never
- Yet and just
- Present Perfect and Past Simple

1. She _____ traveled to most parts of the world.
   A) have B) is C) has D) will

2. _____ you ever _____ in a car accident?
   A) Has / been B) Have / been
   C) Have / be D) Have / was

3. She _____ to Russia two years ago.
   A) go B) went C) gone D) goes

4. I _____ in a crash when I _____ 10.
   A) were / was B) am / was C) was / am D) was / was

5. I _____ last night.
   A) leave B) leaves C) leaving D) left

6. "_____ you _____ to Russia."
   "Yes, I _____ ."
   A) Had / be / haven't B) Has / been / have
   C) Have / be / have D) Have / been / have

7. Have you _____ your homework?
   A) do B) to do C) done D) did

8. I haven't done it _____ .
   A) yet B) already C) just D) since

9. I have _____ done it.
   A) yet B) ago C) just D) since

10. She has _____ to Portugal.
    A) going B) went C) gone D) went

11. She has _____ to Portugal.
    A) be B) been C) being D) were

12. She works _____ a big company.
    A) to B) with C) for D) of

13. 'Hamlet' is a play _____ Shakespeare.
    A) of B) by C) at D) on

14. Brad and Marilyn are _____ honeymoon.
    A) on B) for C) at D) of

15. Wait _____ me.
    A) to B) for C) at D) on

16. Monica _____ many tournaments?
    A) have / won B) has / win
    C) have / win D) has / won

17. _____ she go to America 10 years ago?
    A) Has B) Does C) Had D) Did

18. Have they _____ been to Australia?
    A) never B) just C) yet D) ever

19. _____ they go to Australia last month?
    A) Have B) Do C) Has D) Did

20. Has she won the Wimbledon Tennis Tournament _____ ?
    A) just B) yet C) already D) since

21. I've _____ the latest Star Wars film. I _____ it last week.
    A) seen / saw B) see / saw C) seen / seen D) saw / saw

22. She's _____ the letter. She _____ it yesterday.
    A) wrote / wrote B) written / written
    C) wrote / written D) written / wrote

23. They've _____ lunch. They _____ it at 12 o'clock.
    A) have / had   B) had / have   C) had / having   D) had / had

24. I've _____ my homework. I _____ it after supper.
    A) done / done   B) did / done
    C) done / did   D) did / did

25. A: Have you tidied your room _____ ?
    B: Yes, I've _____ tidied it.
    A) yet / just   B) just / yet
    C) already / just   D) already / just

26. I've never _____ anyone who_____ more than you.
    A) saw / eats   B) seen / eat   C) saw / eaten   D) seen / eats

27. Bob's not here. He's _____ to work.
    A) been   B) went   C) gone   D) being

28. My brother's _____ to America 4 times.
    A) been   B) gone   C) went   D) being

29. It's good to see you again. Where have you _____ ?
    A) gone   B) being   C) been   D) went

30. Mary's hair looks nice. She's just _____ to the hairdresser's.
    A) gone   B) been   C) was   D) went

31. It's terribly difficult to give _____ smoking.
    A) on   B) off   C) of   D) up

32. Why don't we turn _____ the T.V. to watch the news.
    A) of   B) on   C) off   D) out

33. When I grow _____, I'm going to be a T.V. Star.
    A) up   B) on   C) of   D) out

34. Angela _____ Thai food but Frank _____ .
    A) have eaten / hasn't   B) has ate / hasn't
    C) have ate / hasn't   D) has eaten / hasn't

35. I _____ John yesterday.
    A) see   B) seen   C) 'm seeing   D) saw

36. _____ she already bought a new car?
    A) Did   B) Has   C) Does   D) Have

37. They've _____ on a double-decker bus.
    A) travel   B) traveled   C) traveling   D) travels

38. He _____ cooking when he _____ 15 years old.
    A) started / was   B) has started / has been
    C) 's started / was   D) started / has been

39. In 1992 I _____ for the Italian President
    When he _____ to France.
    A) cooked / has come   B) have cooked / came
    C) cook / came   D) cooked / came

40. She is only 14 years old, but she _____ many tournaments in her life.
    A) already won   B) 's already won
    C) already win   D) 've already won

41. I _____ been _____ Ireland.
    A) have / too   B) have / to   C) has / to   D) has / too

42. _____ Sandra _____ ridden a horse?
    A) Has / never   B) Have / never
    C) Have / never   D) Has / ever

43. _____'ve _____ played golf.
    A) They / yet   B) She / never
    C) We / ever   D) I / just

44. When _____ the watchman _____ work?
    A) has / started   B) did / start
    C) started / *   D) * / start

45. _____ she _____ a new carpet yet?
    A) Does / buy   B) Did / buy
    C) Has / bought   D) Is / buying

46. A- Have your parents come _____?
    B- Yes, they _____ just come.
    A) yet / 're   B) just / do   C) already / 've   D) yet / 've

47. Mason _____ his homework 10 minutes ago, but I've not finished mine _____ .
    A) finished / yet   B) finish / just
    C) finished / just   D) finish / just

48. A- Have you ever _____ a holiday in India?
    B- Yes, we have. We _____ there in 2000.
    A) had / 've gone   B) * / went
    C) had / went   D) have / went

49. A- Welcome back. _____ have you been?
    B- I've _____ to Afghanistan.
    A) Where / gone   B) Where / been
    C) When / been   D) When / gone

50. There's nobody in the class. All the students have _____ home.
    A) been   B) went   C) gone   D) be

51. _____ the TV and _____ the lights. Let's watch news.
    A) Turn out / turn off   B) Turn off / turn out
    C) Turn back / on   D) Turn on / turn off

52. First he _____ his jumper, then _____ his best shirt.
    A) took off / put on   B) took after / put on
    C) turned up / tried on   D) tried on / turned up

53. The new couples watched a play _____ Shakespeare _____ their honeymoon.
    A) of / in   B) by / on   C) off / at   D) by / in

54. When I _____ , I'm going to work _____ my dad's company.
    A) go out / in   B) give up / at
    C) grow up / for   D) look up / on

55. Nurses _____ ill people, and gardeners _____ flowers & plants.
    A) look after / grow up   B) look up / get up
    C) look around / grow up   D) look before / get up

PRE-INTERMEDIATE TEST - 1

- Present, Past, Future Tenses
- Questions with Who, Why, How much
- Phrases with more than one meaning

1. _____ three languages: French, Spanish, and English.
   A) I'm speak B) I'm speaking
   C) I speaking D) I speak

2. Where _____ from?
   A) Hans come B) does Hans come
   C) does Hans coming D) Hans came

3. What _____ tonight?
   A) do you do B) you do
   C) are you doing D) did you do

4. "Where is George"
   "He _____ a shower."
   A) has B) will have C) is having D) have

5. "What _____ ?"
   "I don't know. Look it up."
   A) does this word mean B) means this word
   C) does mean this word D) is meaning this word

6. "Do you want a cigarette?"
   "No, thanks. I _____ ."
   A) no smoke B) smoke not
   C) am not smoking D) don't smoke

7. Last year I _____ to America.
   A) was go B) go C) was going D) went

8. How long _____ in America?
   A) you stay B) did you stay
   C) stayed you D) you staying

9. The weekend was boring. I _____ anything.
   A) don't do B) no do
   C) didn't do D) wasn't doing

10. "I'm going to university next year"
    "What _____ study?"
    A) you going to B) do you
    C) did you D) are you going to

Enrique __(11)__ in Puebla, a town in Mexico. He __(12)__ medicine because he __(13)__ to be a doctor. He's married, but he __(14)__ any children. His wife, Silvia, __(15)__ in a primary school. Enrique __(16)__ cooking. He can make an excellent enchilada!

11. A) lived B) lives
    C) was living D) live

12. A) studied B) was studying
    C) is studying D) doesn't study

13. A) is wanting B) was wanting
    C) will want D) wants

14. A) has B) have
    C) doesn't have D) is going to have

15. A) was teaching B) teaches
    C) teach D) thought

16. A) loved B) used to love
    C) loves D) love

17. At the weekend, I usually _____ go swimming.
    A) am B) *
    C) was D) want

18. Are you _____ the party?
    A) enjoy B) enjoyed C) enjoying D) enjoys

19. How many sisters _____ ?
    A) do you have B) you have
    C) are you have D) do you has

20. I _____ understand what you are saying.
    A) no B) don't C) am not D) didn't

21. What time _____ home last night?
    A) did you get B) you get
    C) do you get D) did you got

22. Last weekend I _____ some friends and we _____ a meal.
    A) see / having B) saw / have
    C) seeing / had D) saw / had

23. I _____ English food. It's wonderful!
    A) am loving B) loved C) love D) loves

24. Pierre is French. He _____ from Toulouse.
    A) is coming B) came C) come D) comes

25. _____ the computer at the moment?
    A) Does Mr. Taylor use B) Is Mr. Taylor using
    C) Did Mr. Taylor use D) Will Mr. Taylor use

26. Dave _____ a student with her work now.
    A) helped D) help C) is helping D) helping

27. "It's very noisy"
    "Suzy _____ to rock music."
    A) listen B) listens C) listened D) is listening

28. Carol _____ hard for her exam last week.
    A) didn't study B) isn't studying
    C) don't study D) aren't study

29. Most of the students _____ these days.
    A) didn't smoke B) aren't smoking
    C) isn't smoking D) don't smoke

30. You look nice, Anne. _____ a new dress?
    A) Do you wear B) Does she wear
    C) Are you wearing D) Did you wear

31. Many birds _____ south every winter.
    A) fly B) flew C) are flying D) will fly

32. Usually Jim _____ to work on Saturdays.
    A) is going B) went C) go D) goes

33. Japan _____ many high mountains.
    A) have B) is having C) has D) are having

34. Cats _____ very well in darkness.
    A) are seeing B) see C) will D) sees

35. "What _____ ?"
    "I'm studying computer science."
    A) are you studying B) were you studying
    C) was you studying D) is she studying

36. "_____ born?"
    "I was born in London."
    A) When did you B) Where were you
    C) Where are you D) Where do you

37. "Are _____ ?"
    "No, I'm single."
    A) he marries B) you married
    C) you marry D) she married

38. "_____ a job ?"
    "No, I don't. I'm a student."
    A) Did you have B) Do you have
    C) Have you had D) Are you having

39. "_____ Liverpool?"
    "It's in the north west of England."
    A) Where were   B) Where are
    C) Where is   D) When was

40. "What _____?"
    "My name's Ben."
    A) was your name   B) were your name
    C) is your name   D) is his name

41. "Are _____ your course?"
    "Yes, I'm enjoying it very much."
    A) you enjoying   B) they enjoying
    C) they enjoyed   D) enjoying

42. "Do _____ clubs?"
    "I go sometimes."
    A) you do   B) you go to
    C) you usually go   D) you do go to

43. "What _____ doing in you free time?"
    "I like watching sport on TV."
    A) are you   B) sport are you
    C) do you like   D) would you like to

44. "_____"
    "Yes, can I help you?"
    A) Thank you!   B) Cheers!
    C) Excuse me!   D) Nothing much.

45. "What are you doing this weekend?"
    "_____."
    A) Nothing much   B) Not at all. Don't mention it
    C) Cheers   D) Bye for now

46. "Make your self at home."
    "_____."
    A) Sleep well   B) Thank you
    C) Thanks. Same to you D) Excuse me

47. "Thank you so much for helping."
    "_____."
    A) Nothing much   B) Cheers
    C) Not at all. Don't mention it   D) Sleep well

48. "Good morning!"
    "_____"
    A) Good morning!   B) Thank you!
    C) Cheers!   D) Sleep well!

49. "See you next week."
    "_____."
    A) Cheers   B) Thank you
    C) Good morning   D) Bye for now

50. "Have a nice day!"
    "_____."
    A) Thanks. Same to you B) Not at all. Don't mention it.
    C) Nothing much   D) Sleep well

51. A- Where _____ from?
    B- _____ am from Milano.
    A) are you / I   B) are / you
    C) are they / they   D) you / I

52. A- _____ Leo eat Chinese food?
    B- Yes, he _____ it _____ he was 10.
    A) Did / eaten / when B) Does / ate / what
    C) Did / ate / when   D) Do / eat / what

53. What _____ they going _____ do?
    A) are / too   B) are / to   C) is / to   D) is / too

54. A- How _____ languages can your son speak?
    B- Three _____.
    A) much / languages   B) many / language
    C) many / languages   D) much / language

55. A- When _____ it _____ raining?
    B- Yesterday.
    A) Did / started   B) Does / start
    C) Does / starts   D) Did / start

56. _____ kind _____ music do you like?
    A) What / *   B) How / of   C) What / of   D) What / *

57. A- Good night!
    B - _____!
    A) Sleep well   B) Cheers   C) Fine, thanks   D) Bye

58. Oh! Welcome, Jack! _____.
    A) Pleased to meet you B) That's very kind
    C) Make yourself at home   D) Same to you

59. Customer: _____!
    Shop assistant: _____?
    A) Good morning / Good morning
    B) Excuse me / Yes, can I help you
    C) Bless you / Thank you
    D) How do you do / How do you do

60. A- Thank you very much!
    B- _____.
    A) Same to you   B) Thanks
    C) Bye   D) Not at all

61. Mobile phones, televisions, and radios are a means of _____.
    A) communication   B) transport
    C) media   D) civilization

62. Romans _____ a unique system of the Roman alphabet.
    A) improved   B) developed
    C) persuaded   D) exchanged

63. Nowadays media has a huge influence on the _____.
    A) neighbors   B) society
    C) printing pressing   D) Greeks

64. We send _____ through the internet.
    A) a letter   B) a fax   C) mail   D) an e-mail

65. Romans, Greek and Egyptians are all _____ nations.
    A) ancient   B) old   C) dated   D) modern

PRE-INTERMEDIATE TEST - 2

- Present Simple, Present Continuous
- Have/has got
- But, and, however

1. Where _____ on holidays?
   A) you go   B) do you go
   C) do you going   D) are you go

2. I _____ to work now. Good-bye!
   A) go   B) went   C) am going   D) goes

3. I _____ a book about astrology these days.
   A) am reading   B) read   C) am reads   D) reading

4. I _____ lots of books every year.
   A) will read   B) am reading
   C) read   D) am going to read

5. Nurses _____ after people in hospital.
   A) looks   B) is looking   C) will look   D) look

6. Annie _____ from Ireland.
   A) come   B) is coming   C) comes   D) coming

7. We _____ to a party next Saturday.
   A) go   B) goes   C) are going   D) went

8. She _____ for dinner this evening.
   A) come   B) came   C) comes   D) is coming

9. _____ to go out tonight?
   A) Do you want   B) Are you wanting
   C) Is you want   D) Would you want

10. I _____ four languages.
    A) am speaking   B) speak
    C) speaks   D) am speak

11. Every morning Tessa _____ at 7.30.
    A) is getting up   B) got up
    C) get up   D) gets up

12. Oh, someone _____ in my seat!
    A) is sitting   B) sits   C) will sit   D) sit

13. I'm sorry. I can't help you at the moment. I _____ dinner.
    A) will cook   B) am cooking   C) cook   D) cooked

14. I _____ a pain in my leg.
    A) has   B) having   C) have   D) am having

15. Mrs. Steele _____ to her boss. I'll tell her you phoned.
    A) talked   B) talks   C) talk   D) is talking

16. Turn the T.V off. No one _____ it!
    A) watches   B) watch   C) is watching   D) watched

17. She is not ready. She _____ her hair.
    A) is washing   B) washes   C) washed   D) wash

18. Derek's good at golf but he _____ very often.
    A) aren't play   B) isn't playing   C) doesn't play   D) didn't play

19. The sun _____ in the day time.
    A) shine   B) shone   C) is shining   D) shines

20. In Britain people _____ on the right.
    A) are driving   B) drives   C) drive   D) drove

21. This is a great party! Everyone _____.
    A) dance   B) is dancing   C) dances   D) are dancing

22. Jack's a policeman but he _____ a uniform.
    A) doesn't wear   B) isn't wearing
    C) no wear   D) wears

23. What _____ in your free time?
    A) are you doing   B) do you do
    C) you do   D) are you do

24. How many children _____?
    A) are you having   B) do you have
    C) do you have got   D) are you have

25. I _____ a shower every morning.
    A) have got   B) am having   C) have   D) has

My sister and I are very different, __(26)__ we get on well together. She likes staying at home in the evening __(27)__ watching television with parents. __(28)__ I prefer going out with my friends. We like to go to clubs or the cinema. Sometimes we just go to a café. I have exams soon, __(29)__ I'm not going out very much these days. My sister is six years older than me, __(30)__ she works in a bank. She's trying to save some money __(31)__ she's going to get married this year. Her fiancé's name is Ferdinand. __(32)__, we all call him Freddy. People say I look like my sister __(33)__ we both have brown eyes __(34)__ dark hair. __(35)__, we are very different in character. She's very quiet, __(36)__ I'm a lot more sociable.

26. A) and   B) but   C) so   D) because
27. A) however   B) so   C) and   D) because
28. A) Because   B) And   C) So   D) But
29. A) so   B) however   C) but   D) and
30. A) however   B) so   C) because   D) and
31. A) and   B) so   C) because   D) but
32. A) However   B) So   C) But   D) And
33. A) so   B) because   C) and   D) however
34. A) but   B) so   C) however   D) and
35. A) But   B) So   C) However   D) And
36. A) however   B) but   C) and   D) so

37. I _____ a bicycle when I was young.
    A) have   B) am having   C) had   D) have got

38. He _____ a shower in the morning.
    A) have got   B) has   C) am having   D) have

39. He _____ milk in his coffee.
    A) never has   B) has never got
    C) has never   D) have never

40. What time _____ lunch in general?
    A) does you have   B) have you got
    C) do you have   D) are you having

41. The Pope _____ in Vatican.
    A) live   B) lived   C) lives   D) will live

PRE-INTERMEDIATE TEST - 3

- Past Simple   - Past Continuous
- Irregular verbs - Linking words
- Prepositions

1. I was born in Africa _____ 1970.
   A) on   B) at   C) in   C) last

2. My parents moved back to England _____ I was five.
   A) when   B) ago   C) *   D) for

3. We lived in Bristol _____ three years.
   A) last   B) for   C) at   D) *

4. I left college three years _____.
   A) nothing   B) ago   C) for   D) in

5. I found a flat on my own _____ last year.
   A) at   B) for   C) *   D) on

6. I usually go home _____ the weekend.
   A) in   B) when   C) at   B) of

7. I didn't go home _____ weekend because some friends came to stay.
   A) for   B) last   C) *   D) at

8. They arrived _____ three o'clock _____ the afternoon.
   A) at / in   B) in / for C) when / ago   D) last / *

9. _____ Saturday evening we went out to a concert.
   A) Last   B) In   C) For   D) On

10. _____ we got home we listened to some music.
    A) For   B) Last   C) Last   D) When

11. We got up late _____ Sunday morning.
    A) *   B) at   C) on   D) in

12. _____ the afternoon we went for a walk.
    A) At   B) For   C) On   D) In

13. I bought a car a few weeks _____.
    A) last   B) when   C) ago   D) for

14. I had an accident _____ last night.
    A) in   B) *   C) on   D) at

15. It happened _____ seven o'clock _____ the evening.
    A) when / * B) in / at   C) at / last D) at / in

16. I took my car to the garage _____ this morning.
    A) in   B) when   C) *   D) at

17. It will be ready _____ two weeks.
    A) *   B) in   C) on   D) for

18. I _____ a friend while I _____ the shopping
    A) was meeting / did   B) met / was doing
    C) meet / do   D) met / did

19. I _____ for my things when I _____ someone call my name.
    A) paid / was hearing   B) pay / heard
    C) was paying / hear   D) was paying / heard

20. I _____ round and _____ Paula.
    A) turned / saw   B) was turning / was seeing
    C) turn / was seeing   D) was turning / saw

21. She _____ a bright red coat yesterday.
    A) wore   B) was wearing
    C) wear   D) was wear

22. We _____ to have a cup of coffee.
    A) decided   B) were deciding
    C) decides   D) will deciding

23. While we _____ a drink, a waiter _____ a pile of plates.
    A) had / was dropping   B) have / dropped
    C) have / drop   D) were having / dropped

24. We all _____ a terrible shock.
    A) were getting   B) gets
    C) getting   D) got

25. While the waiter _____ up the broken plates, he _____ his finger.
    A) picked / was cutting B) was picking / cut
    C) pick / cut   D) picks / cut

This morning I __(26)__ to work. I __(27)__ to go by bus because the sun __(28)__. While I __(29)__ past the supermarket, I __(30)__ something strange. A man __(31)__ near me and he __(32)__ a song very loudly on his own! He __(33)__ for a few minutes. Then he __(34)__ a friend and he __(35)__ singing.

26. A) was walking B) walked   C) walk   D) walking
27. A) didn't want   B) wasn't wanting
    C) don't want   D) am not wanting
28. A) shone   B) is shining C) was shining D) shines
29. A) walked   B) am walking C) was walked   D) was walking
30. A) was seeing   B) saw   C) am seeing   D) see
31. A) passed   B) was passing C) pass   D) passes
32. A) sang   B) sing   C) was singing D) song
33. A) was continuing   B) continues
    C) is continuing   D) continued
34. A) will met   B) met   C) was meeting D) meet
35. A) was stopping   B) stop
    C) stopped   D) is stopping

36. I _____ a very good program on TV last night.
    A) was seeing   B) see   C) am seeing   D) saw

37. While I _____ this morning, I _____ my money. I don't know how.
    A) shopped / lose   B) was shopping / lost
    C) shopped / was losing   D) shop / lose

38. Last week the police _____ Alan in his car because he _____ over eighty miles an hour.
    A) were stopping / was driving
    B) stop / drived
    C) stopped / was driving
    D) was stopping / drove

39. How _____ your finger?
    A) are you cutting   B) were you cutting
    C) did you cut   D) you cut

40. I _____ and I _____ the knife.
    A) cooked / was dropping   B) cook / drop
    C) was cooking / dropped   D) cooked / dropped

41. When I _____ at the party, everyone _____ a good time.
    A) was arriving / had   B) arrived / was having
    C) arrived / had   D) arrived / were having

42. _____ a good time last night?
    A) Did you have   B) Were you having
    C) Will you have   D) Are you having

43. While I _____ to work this morning I _____ an old friend.
    A) went / meet   B) am going / met
    C) go / was meeting   D) was going / met

44. I _____ to get up this morning. It _____ and it was cold, and my bed was so warm.
    A) don't want / is raining   B) am not wanting / rains
    C) wasn't wanting / rained   D) didn't want / was raining

45. I _____ to the news on the radio when the phone _____.
    A) listened / was ringing   B) am listening / was ringing
    C) was listening / rang   D) listen / is ringing

46. But when I _____ up the phone, there was no one there.
    A) pick   B) am picking C) picked   D) was picking

47. I _____ hello to the children, but they didn't say anything because they _____ television.
    A) say / watched   B) said / were watching
    C) was / saying   D) said / watched

48. What _____ at 8.00 last night?
    A) did you do   B) you did
    C) were you doing   D) are you doing

49. We played tennis _____ two hours.
    A) during   B) while   C) nothing   D) for

50. I worked on a farm _____ the holidays.
    A) for   B) since   C) while   D) on

PRE-INTERMEDIATE TEST - 4

- Much, many
- Some, any
- How much, how many
- Something, anyone, nobody, everywhere
- A few, a little, a lot of
- Articles

1. A: Did you meet _____ at the party?
   B: Yes, I met _____ who knows you!
   A) someone / anyone   B) anything / nobody
   C) anybody / somebody   D) everybody / nothing

2. A: Ouch! There's _____ in my eye!
   B: Let me look. No, I can't see _____.
   A) something / anything   B) anything / anywhere
   C) somebody / everywhere D) something / nothing

3. A: Let's go _____ hot for our holidays.
   B: But we can't go _____; that's too expensive.
   A) everywhere / nowhere   B) somewhere / anywhere
   C) anywhere / everywhere D) anybody / someone

4. A: I don't want to talk to _____.
   B: And I want to talk to _____ either.
   A) anyone / no one   B) somebody / everyone
   C) nobody / somebody   D) everybody / anybody

5. I lost my glasses. I looked _____, but I couldn't find them.
   A) anywhere   B) everywhere
   C) somewhere   D) everything

6. A: Did you buy _____ at the shops?
   B: No, _____. I didn't have any money."
   A) something / anything   B) everything / something
   C) anything / nothing   D) no one / anybody

7. It was a great party. _____ loved it.
   A) Everything B) Anyone
   C) Somebody   D) Everybody

8. I'm bored. I want _____ interesting to read, or _____ to talk to, or _____ interesting to go.
   A) anything / everyone / something
   B) somebody / anyone / anywhere
   C) something / somebody / somewhere
   D) everything / nobody / somewhere

9. Have you got _____ homework?
   A) many   B) much   C) a few   D) some

10. We don't need _____ eggs. Just half a dozen.
    A) a little B) many   C) much   D) a few

11. Is there _____ traffic in your town?
    A) a few   B) many   C) some   D) much

12. I have _____ close fiends. Two or three.
    A) a lot of B) a little C) a few D) much

13. I don't know _____ students in this class. Because I am a newcomer.
    A) many   B) a few   C) some   D) much

14. How _____ people live in your house?
    A) any   B) much   C) many   D) a lot of

15. He has _____ money. He's a millionaire.
    A) many   B) a lot of   C) a little   D) a lot

16. A: Do you take sugar in coffee?"
    B: Just _____. Half a spoonful."
    A) a few   B) many   C) a little   D) a lot of

17. A: Have you got _____ CD's?
    B: Yes, hundreds.
    A) much   B) a little   C) a few   D) lots of

18. I'll be ready in _____ minutes.
    A) a lot   B) a little   C) much   D) a few

19. She speaks good Spanish, but only _____ Russian.
    A) a few   B) a lot of   C) much   D) a little

20. I come to _____ school by _____ bus.
    A) * / the   B) the / a   C) * / *   D) the / the

21. This morning _____ bus was late.
    A) a   B) *   C) an   D) the

22. My favorite subject is _____ history, but I'm not very good at _____ math.
    A) * / the   B) a / a   C) the / the   D) * / *

23. Ankara is _____ capital of Turkey.
    A) the   B) a   C) *   D) an

24. I work in _____ company that makes _____ carpets.
    A) a / *   B) the / the   C) the / *   D) a / a

25. My friend lives in _____ same street as me.
    A) a   B) *   C) an   D) the

26. A: How much are the driving lessons?
    B: Fifteen pounds _____ hour.
    A) *   B) the   C) an   D) a

27. I was at _____ home all day yesterday.
    A) the   B) *   C) an   D) a

28. There are _____ apples.
    A) most   B) a lot of   C) a little   D) much

29. The shop hasn't got _____ washing powder.
    A) a few   B) few   C) much   D) many

30. Why aren't there _____ magazines?
    A) little   B) much   C) a little   D) many

31. The shop hasn't got _____ birthday cards.
    A) many   B) much   C) some   D) a little

32. I saw _____ change on the table a minute ago.
    A) much   B) some   C) many   D) any

33. I can see _____ newspapers.
    A) lots of   B) most   C) a little   D) much

34. The shopkeeper has got _____ cheese.
    A) a lot of   B) many   C) few   D) a few

35. I need _____ help with my homework. Are you free?
    A) a few   B) much   C) any   D) some

36. Let's have _____ ice-cream.
    A) a   B) *   C) an   D) the

37. I eat _____ apple every day.
    A) the   B) a   C) an   D) *

38. Would you like _____ coffee or tea?
    A) *   B) the   C) an   D) a

39. They don't like _____ chocolate.
    A) a   B) the   C) *   D) an

40. I'd like _____ glass of milk, please.
    A) the   B) a   C) an   D) *

41. Please have _____ cake.
    A) a   B) *   C) the   D) an

42. How often do you eat _____ chocolate?
    A) the   B) an   C) *   D) a

43. This table is made of _____ glass.
    A) *   B) the   C) an   D) a

44. I never drink _____ coffee.
    A) an   B) *   C) a   D) the

45. Does he like _____ cake?
    A) the   B) a   C) an   D) *

46. She needs _____ to help her choose a birthday present.
    A) something   B) anybody   C) someone   D) somewhere

47. Is _____ listening to me!
    A) somebody   B) anyone   C) something   D) anywhere

48. Would _____ please explain what happened?
    A) anything   B) somewhere   C) anybody   D) someone

49. He doesn't care. He will watch _____ on television!
    A) somewhere   B) something   C) anything   D) anybody

50. If _____ asks, tell them I've got a cold.
    A) anyone   B) anything   C) somewhere   D) somebody

PRE-INTERMEDIATE / TEST - 5

- Infinitive, gerund
- Going to, will
- Prepositions

1. "_____ a drink?"
   "Yes, please. I'll have an orange juice."
   A) Do you like   B) Are you liking
   C) Would you like   D) Did you like

2. "What _____ at the weekend?"
   "I like putting my feet up and relaxing. Sometimes I play tennis."
   A) will you like to do   B) do you like doing
   C) would you like to do   D) are you like to do

3. "_____ your teacher?"
   "Yes, she's very nice."
   A) Did you like   B) Would you like
   C) Will you like   D) Do you like

4. "What _____ to do in the evening?"
   "Why don't we pop round and see Pat and Peter?"
   A) do you like   B) are you
   C) would you like   D) did you like

5. "_____ for walks?"
   "What a good idea! It's so hot today!"
   A) Are you going to go   B) Did you like going
   C) Do you like going   D) Would you like to go

6. "My bag is so heavy."
   "Give it to me. _____ it for you."
   A) I'm going to carry   B) I carry
   C) I'll carry   D) I carried

7. I bought some warm boots today because _____ skiing.
   A) I went   B) I'm going   C) I'll go   D) I go

8. "Tony's back from holiday."
   "_____ him a ring."
   A) I'll give   B) I gave
   C) I'm going give   D) I give

9. "What are you doing tonight?"
   "We _____ a play at the theatre."
   A) saw   B) will see
   C) are going to see   D) seeing

10. You can tell me your secret. I _____ anyone.
    A) am not going tell   B) won't tell
    C) don't tell   D) didn't tell

11. "I need to post these letters."
    "I _____ shopping soon. I _____ them for you."
    A) will go / will post   B) am going / will post
    C) am going / am going post D) go / am going to post

12. "Now, holidays. Where _____ this year?"
    "We don't know yet."
    A) did you go   B) you going
    C) will you go   D) do you going

13. We've decided _____ married in the spring.
    A) get   B) to get   C) getting   D) got

14. I hope _____ some money soon.
    A) earning   B) earn   C) to earn   D) to earning

15. I want _____ a film on TV this evening.
    A) seeing   B) see   C) see to   D) to see

16. Some people like _____ breakfast in bed, but I don't.
    A) having   B) too have   C) have   D) had

17. I'm looking forward _____ you again soon.
    A) to see   B) seeing   C) to seeing   D) see

18. I _____ my job soon.
    A) think changing   B) am thinking of changing
    C) am thinking to change   D) think change

19. This book is full _____ pictures.
    A) with   B) in   C) to   D) of

20. Julie is married _____ Sam.
    A) in   B) with   C) to   D) at

21. I don't agree _____ him.
    A) for   B) at   C) with   D) to

22. He isn't good _____ French.
    A) at   B) in   C) to   D) of

23. My brother is interested _____ math.
    A) to   B) in   C) of   D) at

24. Look _____ those birds!
    A) at   B) to   C) for   D) in

25. Are you afraid _____ flying?
    A) with   B) at   C) in   D) of

26. Wait _____ me in the street.
    A) to   B) for   C) at   D) in

27. Bill is looking _____ his keys but he can't find them.
    A) for   B) at   C) to   D) in

28. Please ask _____ help if you want.
    A) to   B) for   C) of   D) in

29. Do you work _____ someone special?
    A) at   B) for   C) of   D) in

30. Can I speak _____ you for a minute?
    A) with   B) of   C) at   D) for

31. Barbara hopes _____ a lawyer.
    A) become   B) to become   C) of becoming   D) becoming

32. I'd love _____ with you.
    A) to going   B) go   C) to go   D) going

33. She enjoys _____ the news on television.
    A) watching   B) to watch   C) to watching   D) watch

34. I'm looking forward _____ more free time.
    A) to having   B) to have   C) of having   D) having

35. Do you want _____ it again?
    A) try   B) trying   C) to trying   D) to try

36. We're _____ a party next Saturday. Would you like _____?
    A) have / to go   B) having / to come
    C) had / to have   D) having to / had

37. You must see my new flat. _____ round and _____ a drink some time.
    A) Go / come   B) Have / come
    C) Go / have   D) Come / have

38. "I _____ out now, Mum. Bye!"
    "OK. Have a good time. What time _____ home?"
    A) went / did you come   B) am going / are you coming
    C) go / will you come   D) am going / do you come

39. Hi, Dave. Pete _____ a shower at the moment. I'll just _____ and tell him.
    A) is having / go   B) had / went
    C) is having / come   D) will have / will go

40. "I feel nervous. I've got an exam today."
    "_____"
    A) Cheer up! Things can't be that bad!
    B) That's great. Have a good time.
    C) Poor you! That happens to me sometimes.
    D) Good luck! Do your best.

41. "I feel really depressed at the moment. Nothing's going right in my life."
    "_____"
    A) I know. We really need some sunshine, don't we?
    B) Cheer up! Things can't be that bad!
    C) I'm sorry to hear that, but I'm sure he'll be all right.
    D) That's good. I'm pleased to hear it.

42. "I'm really excited. I'm going on holiday to Australia tomorrow."
    "_____"
    A) Good luck! Do your best.
    B) Why don't you go home to bed?
    C) That's great. Have a good time.
    D) Cheer up! Things can't be that bad!

43. I don't feel very well. I think I'm getting the flu.
    "_____"
    A) Poor you! That happens to me sometimes.
    B) Why don't you go home to bed?
    C) I'm sorry to hear that but I'm sure he'll be all right.
    D) Cheer up! Things can't be that bad!

44. "I'm cold."
    "I _____ the heating on."
    A) am going to put
    B) will put
    C) put
    D) will be putting

45. "Can I speak to Marco?"
    "Hold on. I _____ him."
    A) got
    B) am going to get
    C) get
    D) will get

46. "Coffee or tea?"
    "I ____ tea, please."
    A) will have
    B) have
    C) am going to have
    D) had

47. "Has Amy got any plans for the weekend?"
    "Yes, she _____ her grandparents.
    A) will visit
    B) visits
    C) is going to visit
    D) visited

48. "Alison's on the phone for you."
    "Can she call back? I ____ a bath."
    A) will have
    B) am going to have
    C) have
    D) having of

49. "I _____ to the supermarket."
    "Oh, ____? I think I _____ with you."
    A) go / are you / am going to come
    B) will go / will you / will come
    C) am going to go / are you / will come
    D) am going / do you / come

50. A: Did you get my fax?
    B: No, I didn't.
    A: OK, I _____ it again.
    A) send
    B) will send
    C) am going to send
    D) am sending

PRE-INTERMEDIATE TEST - 6

- What's it like?
- Comparative and superlative adjectives
- Relative pronouns (who, which, what, where)
- Vocabulary

1. He's _____ older than he looks.
   A) much   B) more   C) *   D) the

2. Jessica's as tall _____ her mother.
   A) than   B) like   C) more   D) as

3. "What _____ New York like?"
   "It's really exciting!"
   A) does   B) is   C) was   D) did

4. Trains in London are more crowded _____ in Paris.
   A) that   B) as   C) than   D) like

5. Oxford is one of ___ oldest universities in Europe.
   A) the   B) *   C) much   D) more

6. He isn't as intelligent _____ his sister.
   A) like   B) as   C) than   D) nothing

7. This is _____ than I expected.
   A) more hard   B) hard   C) the hardest   D) harder

8. Who is the _____ man in the world?
   A) rich   B) most richest   C) richest   D) most rich

9. Everything is _____ in my country.
   A) more cheaper   B) cheaper   C) cheap   D) cheapest

10. Rome was hotter _____ I expected.
    A) than   B) that   C) nothing   D) as

11. My dad's really ____. He always buys presents for everyone.
    A) romantic   B) fortunate   C) generous   D) depressed

12. Before you can get a credit card, you have to provide a lot of _____ details.
    A) wealth   B) person   C) happiness   D) personal

13. I try to lead a _____ lifestyle - lots of exercises, fruit, and no junk food.
    A) depressed   B) dirty   C) healthy   D) mess

14. The disco was so _____ that you couldn't hear yourself speak.
    A) noisy   B) finance   C) windy   D) difference

15. After the earthquake, the country needed a lot of _____ equipment to look after the sick and wounded.
    A) depressed   B) medical   C) personal   D) financial

16. She had a car crash, but she was _____ to escape with no injuries at all.
    A) depressed   B) romantic   C) lucky   D) healthy

17. Venice is a very _____ city. A lot of people go there on honeymoon.
    A) dirty   B) polluted   C) wealthy   D) romantic

18. Here is the ____ news. Share prices on the Dow Jones Index have fallen dramatically.
    A) cheap   B) financial   C) depressed   D) wealthy

19. After a heart attack, he needed a major surgery, but fortunately the operation was _____.
    A) happy   B) different   C) successful   D) personal

Book 1 Part A   30   Pre-Intermediate Test 6

20. I didn't like that city at all. The streets were so _____ and the air was so _____.
    A) dirty / messy		B) dirty / polluted
    C) personal / noisy		D) messy / polluting

21. There's the boy _____ broke the window.
    A) which	B) where	C) *	D) who

22. That's the palace _____ the King lives.
    A) who	B) which	C) where	D) when

23. They are the policemen _____ caught the thief.
    A) where	B) who	C) which	D) *

24. He gave him a watch _____ stopped after two days.
    A) that	B) *	C) when	D) where

25. The Red Lion is the pub _____ we met for a drink.
    A) which	B) that	C) where	D) when

26. Here are the letters _____ arrived this morning.
    A) who	B) which	C) *	D) where

27. That's the house _____ I was born.
    A) when	B) that	C) where	D) which

28. Where is the woman _____ ordered the fish.
    A) who	B) which	C) when	D) where

29. The hotel _____ we stayed was very comfortable.
    A) which	B) that	C) where	D) when

30. I bought the coat _____ was in the shop window.
    A) who	B) where	C) that	D) *

31. Are you as tall _____ your brother?
    A) like	B) as	C) than	D) more

32. Was Joan's party better _____ Maria's?
    A) than	B) much	C) like	D) as

33. "Wasn't that film wonderful!"
    "Yes, it was _____."
    A) modern	B) wealthy	C) brilliant	D) depressed

34. "I'm bored with this lesson!"
    "I know, I'm really _____ with it, too!"
    A) generous	B) fed up	C) healthy	D) happy

35. "Mary's family is very rich."
    "Well, I knew her uncle was very _____."
    A) finance	B) polluted	C) wealthy	D) windy

36. "Ann's bedroom's really untidy again!"
    "Is it? I told her it was _____ yesterday, and she promised to clean it."
    A) clean	B) shining	C) modern	D) messy

37. She's _____ than her sister.
    A) much nicer		B) more nicer
    C) much more nicer		D) more nicer

38. He's _____ boy in the class.
    A) the funnier		B) funniest
    C) funnier		D) the funniest

39. Barbara's _____ than Sarah.
    A) intelligenter		B) much intelligent
    C) more intelligent		D) intelligent

PRE-INTERMEDIATE TEST - 7

- Present Perfect & Past Simple
- For & since
- Adverbs (slowly, carefully, just, still, too)
- Relative Clause (who, which, that)

1. _____ to a rock concert?
    A) Were you ever go		B) Have you ever been
    C) Do you ever go		D) Have you ever go

2. I _____ the champion last week.
    A) saw	B) have seen	C) see	D) seen

3. I love rock and roll. I _____ it all my life.
    A) am liking	B) like	C) liking	D) have liked

4. The Flash's concert _____ fantastic 3 years ago.
    A) was	B) has been	C) have been	D) are

5. I _____ all their records since then.
    A) bought	B) buy	C) buyed	D) have bought

6. The Flash _____ together for over fifteen years.
    A) are	B) have been	C) are being	D) *

7. He's my sister's son. He's my _____.
    A) uncle	B) nephew	C) niece	D) bride

8. I run in races. I'm a(n) _____.
    A) pilot	B) teenager	C) athlete	D) chef

9. In my job I wear the latest fashions. I'm a(n) _____.
    A) actor	B) professor	C) nurse	D) model

10. I serve you drinks on a plane flight. I'm a _____.
    A) cousin		B) flight attendant
    C) niece		D) child

11. I cook food for a restaurant. I'm a(n) _____.
    A) chef	B) musician	C) uncle	D) professor

12. The wedding was wonderful. The _____ looked beautiful, and the _____ was very handsome.
    A) bridegroom / bride		B) niece / nephew
    C) bride / bridegroom		D) sir / madam

13. He's the man _____ Anna loves.
    A) which	B) *	C) this	D) when

14. The film star gave a party _____ cost $10.000.
    A) *	B) who	C) which	D) where

15. The man _____ you met at the party was a famous film star.
    A) who	B) when	C) where	D) which

16. What's the name of the woman _____ was wearing the gold dress?
    A) *	B) which	C) where	D) who

17. You're reading the book _____ I wanted to read.
    A) when	B) who	C) which	D) where

18. There's someone at the door _____ wants to speak to George.
    A) who	B) that	C) which	D) *

19. I don't like food _____ is very spicy.
    A) which	B) *	C) who	D) when

20. That's the dictionary _____ Bill gave me for my birthday.
    A) *	B) who	C) when	D) where

21. Those are old cars _____ only take leaded petrol.
    A) who	B) when	C) *	D) which

22. Do you like the people _____ Sarah invited to her party?
    A) which	B) who	C) where	D) when

23. I called Tom at 10.00 in the morning, but he was _____ in bed.
    A) of course	B) still	C) only	D) especially

24. It's our anniversary today. We've been _____ for fifteen years.
    A) at last	B) exactly	C) together	D) nearly

25. Kate is very fussy about food. She _____ eats pasta and crisps.
    A) only	B) hard	C) exactly	D) too

26. She was very ill and _____ died, but fortunately, she got better.
    A) carefully   B) nearly   C) too   D) usually

27. "I hate ironing."
    "Me, _____. It's so boring."
    A) just   B) at last   C) slowly   D) too

28. I like all Russian novelists, _____ Tolstoy.
    A) usually   B) especially   C) together   D) only

29. I met her on December 23, _____ before Christmas.
    A) too   B) slowly   C) just   D) still

30. _____ I have finished this exercise. Thank goodness! It was so boring.
    A) Together   B) At last   C) Exactly   D) Just

31. Sarah's English is getting better. She _____ a lot of English since she _____ here.
    A) learnt / has come   B) has learnt / has come
    C) has learnt / came   D) learnt / came

32. Mike and Jack _____ here five months ago. They _____ in this city for five months.
    A) came / have been   B) have come / have been
    C) come / were   D) has come / has been

33. David can go to bed now. He _____ his homework.
    A) finish   B) has finished
    C) finishes   D) finished

34. Alison _____ in Chicago, but she would like to go there one day.
    A) was   B) has been
    C) wasn't   D) has never been

35. Peter _____ his work 3 hours ago.
    A) has finished   B) will finish
    C) finished   D) finish

Dennis Heal __(36)__ a politician. He __(37)__ to Oxford University in 1975, and in 1982 he __(38)__ a Member of Parliament. He __(39)__ an MP since then. He __(40)__ Defense Minister from 1989-95. He __(41)__ three books, including his autobiography "The Time of my Life", and a spy story called "The Time to Run". He is married to the artist Edna Heal, and they have two children. They __(42)__ in Oxford for 10 years, then they __(43)__ to London in 1995. They now __(44)__ in a house in Queen Square in central London.

36. A) was   B) is   C) is being   D) has been
37. A) go   B) has gone   C) went   D) goes
38. A) became   B) become   C) becomes   D) has become
39. A) was   B) is being   C) is   D) has been
40. A) was   B) is   C) has been   D) were
41. A) has written   B) wrote   C) write   D) writes
42. A) lives   B) has lived   C) have lived   D) live
43. A) move   B) moved   C) is moving   D) has moved
44. A) lives   B) have lived   C) lived   D) live

45. I haven't seen Keith _____ a while.
    A) since   B) *   C) for   D) in

46. He and his wife have lived next to me _____ their son, Tom, was born.
    A) for   B) when   C) since   D) *

47. I have known them _____ many years.
    A) *   B) for   C) on   D) since

48. Anna has had a bad cold _____ the last few days.
    A) for   B) after   C) since   D) in

49. I have written a letter _____ breakfast.
    A) *   B) before   C) for   D) since

50. I'm looking after Tom today. He's been at my house _____ 8.00 this morning.
    A) at   B) for   C) since   D) from

PRE-INTERMEDIATE TEST - 8

- Have to, must, should   - Gerunds, infinitives
- Future tense   - Ever, since, for

1. "Why have you got so much food?"
   "Because I _____ a meal for two people."
   A) cook   B) am going to cook
   C) will cook   D) had cook

2. "Jane told me you have a place at university."
   "That's right. I _____ math at St. Andrews in Scotland."
   A) studied   B) will study
   C) study   D) am going to study

3. "My car isn't working."
   "Ask Joe to look at it. He _____ you."
   A) will help   B) helps
   C) is going to help   D) helped

4. "I passed my driving test!"
   "That's great! I _____ some champagne to celebrate!"
   A) am going to buy   B) will buy
   C) bought   D) am buying

5. "Why have you got your old clothes on?"
   "Because I _____ the grass.'
   A) had cut   B) cutted
   C) am going to cut   D) cut

6. He's worked there _____ many years, _____ 1988, I believe.
   A) since / ever   B) for / ever
   C) for / since   D) ever / never

7. I have _____ loved anyone as much as I love you.
   A) never   B) since   C) for   D) ever

8. We've known Paul _____ two years. Have you _____ met him?
   A) since / for   B) since / ever   C) for / ever   D) never / ever

9. I've known him _____ we went to school together, but I've _____ met his parents.
   A) ever / ever   B) for / never   C) since / for   D) since / never

10. Your hair's too long. I think you _____ get it cut.
    A) have to   B) should   C) *   D) will

11. Your clothes smell, and you've got a cough. You _____ smoke.
    A) don't have to   B) should
    C) shouldn't   D) have to

12. I'm going to bed. I _____ be up early tomorrow.
    A) should   B) shouldn't
    C) don't have to   D) have to

13. I'd like to meet your boyfriend. You _____ invite him round.
    A) must   B) have to   C) would   D) don't have to

14. I _____ tell my parents where I am, then they don't worry.
    A) should   B) don't have to
    C) have to   D) shouldn't

15. You _____ come with me if you don't want to. I'll go on my own.
    A) don't have to   B) must
    C) should   D) shouldn't

16. Our train leaves in two minutes! We _____ hurry.
    A) would   B) have to
    C) must   D) don't have to

17. If you need some help with your homework, you _____ go to the library.
    A) should   B) mustn't   C) have to   D) shouldn't

18. If you've got a ticket, you _____ queue. You can go straight in."
    A) shouldn't   B) don't have to
    C) have to   D) should

19. You _____ tell lies. It's wrong.
    A) don't have to   B) should
    C) have to   D) shouldn't

20. Geoff works too much. I think he _____ take it easy.
    A) must   B) have to
    C) should   D) don't have to

21. My bedroom is a real mess. I _____ clean it.
    A) have to   B) must
    C) don't have to   D) should

22. There's a wonderful new restaurant opened in town. You _____ go there.
    A) shouldn't   B) must
    C) don't have to   D) should

23. You can borrow my tennis racquet, but you _____ keep it very well. It was very expensive.
    A) don't have to   B) should
    C) must   D) have to

24. It's my mother's birthday tomorrow. I _____ buy her a present.
    A) must   B) have to
    C) shouldn't D) don't have to

25. Joanna Trollope _____ a lot of books. She _____ her first in 1980.
    A) wrote / wrote   B) has written / wrote
    C) had written / wrote   D) wrote / had written

26. I _____ in London for eight years, and I don't want to move.
    A) live   B) lived   C) had lived   D) have lived

27. What is the weather _____ in January?
    A) likes   B) like   C) liked   D) don't like

John Frantz is American. He has a wonderful lifestyle and he wants __(28)__ it with an English girl. He enjoys __(29)__ on exotic holidays, but he wouldn't like __(30)__ outside the United States. He hopes __(31)__ an English wife through the English Rose dating agency. He'd like __(32)__ someone who likes __(33)__.

28. A) sharing   B) share   C) shared   D) to share

29. A) to go   B) went   C) going   D) to going

30. A) living   B) to live C) live   D) lives

31. A) to find   B) found   C) finding   D) to be founded

32. A) meets   B) to met   C) meeting   D) to meet

33. A) traveling B) traveled C) travel   D) to traveling

34. You _____ have a driving license if you want to drive a car.
    A) should   B) have to   C) have   D) had to

35. I don't think people _____ get married until they're 21.
    A) have to   B) would   C) should D) are

36. They liked the hotel because they _____ do any cooking.
    A) have to   B) had to   C) should D) didn't have to

37. I _____ swim when I was three.
    A) could   B) can   C) have to D) must

38. She _____ work on Monday. It's her day off.
    A) must   B) doesn't have to
    C) have to   D) shouldn't

39. You _____ sit so close to the TV. It's bad for your eyes.
    A) don't have to   B) have to
    C) shouldn't   D) can

40. You _____ do the washing-up. I've got a washing machine.
    A) should   B) have to   C) mustn't   D) don't have to

41. "I'm working 16 hours a day."
    "I think you _____ talk to your boss."
    A) have to   B) can   C) mustn't   D) should

42. "I can't sleep."
    "You _____ drink coffee at night."
    A) must   B) shouldn't   C) don't have to   D) have

43. "My friend is getting married."
    "I _____ go to the wedding."
    A) think you should   B) think you have to
    C) think you can   D) think you may

44. "I've had a terrible toothache for weeks."
    "You _____ go to the dentist."
    A) have to   B) would   C) shouldn't   D) should

45. Anne was upset because she didn't _____ in the race. She really wanted to win.
    A) come last   B) go up   C) come first   D) turn out

46. We always _____ for our holidays.
    A) go abroad   B) go off   C) go on   D) go away

47. I'm _____. There's nothing to do.
    A) annoyed   B) interested   C) kind   D) fed up

48. If you want to do well in life you _____ believe in yourself.
    A) can   B) don't have to
    C) have to   D) should

49. If you want to keep fit, you _____ do some sport.
    A) shouldn't   B) have to   C) should   D) don't have to

50. If you want to learn English, you _____ speak your language in English lessons.
    A) should   B) don't have to
    C) must   D) shouldn't

PRE-INTERMEDIATE TEST - 9

- Before, after, until, when, as soon as
- Prepositions

1. I will have a bath _____ I go to bed.
   A) when   B) if   C) before   D) until

2. I'm coming to London tomorrow. I'll ring you _____ I arrive.
   A) before   B) when   C) until   D) if

3. _____ it is a nice day tomorrow, we can go swimming.
   A) If   B) Until   C) When   D) Before

4. Wait here _____ I get back.
   A) until   B) before   C) as soon as   D) when

5. _____ you have any problem, just ask for help.
   A) When   B) After   C) Before   D) Until

6. I want to get home _____ Jim comes back.
   A) if   B) before   C) until   D) when

7. I'm going to have driving lessons _____ I pass my test.
   A) before   B) when   C) if   D) until

8. Give me your address _____ you go home.
   A) if   B) before   C) as soon as   D) until

9. Bye! I _____ you when I _____ home.
   A) phoned / get   B) will phone / will get
   C) phone / get   D) will phone / get

10. I'm going to bed when this TV program _____.
    A) ended   B) will end
    C) is going to end   D) ends

11. I'm sorry you are leaving. I _____ when you _____.
    A) am glad / you are back   B) glad / will be back
    C) will be glad / are back   D) am glad / will be back

12. "Give me your phone number."
    "Sure. I _____ it to you before I _____."
    A) will give / go   B) give / will go
    C) will give / will go   D) am going to give / go

13. What's _____ TV tonight?
    A) at   B) in   C) on   D) with

14. I often go abroad _____ business.
    A) to   B) by   C) for   D) on

15. Do you come to school _____ bus?
    A) on   B) by   C) at   D) in

16. I'm very busy _____ the moment.
    A) in   B) on   C) by   D) at

17. I can't understand the instructions. They're _____ Chinese.
    A) by   B) at   C) in   D) for

18. "Romeo and Juliet" is a play _____ William Shakespeare.
    A) for   B) by   C) with   D) on

19. "Is Mr. James _____ work this week?"
    "No. He's _____ holiday."
    A) on / in   B) at / in   C) in / for   D) at / on

20. I hate being late. I like to arrive _____ time.
    A) by   B) on   C) at   D) for

21. I spoke to her _____ the phone last week.
    A) at   B) like   C) on   D) by

22. I read an interesting article _____ the paper this morning.
    A) in   B) on   C) at   D) for

23. "Can I ask you something?"
    "Not now. _____ a moment."
    A) At   B) For   C) On   D) In

24. "Here's a birthday present _____ you."
    "Oh, thank you!"
    A) by   B) in   C) for   D) at

25. "Why did you open my letter?"
    "I'm sorry. I did it _____ mistake."
    A) with   B) at   C) by   D) on

26. I arrived _____ England last month.
    A) at   B) to   C) in   D) for

27. I live _____ the third floor.
    A) at   B) on   C) by   D) in

28. I met my classmates _____ the party.
    A) in   B) for   C) on   D) at

29. "Why does Jane look so happy?"
    "Because she's _____ love."
    A) at   B) on   C) in   D) by

30. Let's go _____ a walk.
    A) on   B) to   C) in   D) for

31. We arrived _____ the station five minutes late.
    A) to   B) at   C) for   D) on

32. The doctor will be ready in ten minutes. Take a seat while you _____.
    A) are wait   B) will wait   C) are waiting   D) wait

33. I'm going out before the shops _____.
    A) will shut   B) shuts   C) are shutting   D) shut

34. I _____ by the phone until _____.
    A) wait / you ring   B) will wait / you will ring
    C) wait / you will ring   D) will wait / you ring

35. You must phone me as soon as _____ your exam results.
    A) you get   B) you will get
    C) you got   D) you are going to get

36. I hope to see you while I _____ in London.
    A) am   B) will be
    C) am going to be   D) was

37. _____ I win a lot of money, I'll buy you a Ferrari.
    A) When   B) If   C) Until   D) As long as

38. Please turn out the lights _____ you go to bed.
    A) after   B) as soon as   C) while   D) before

39. I like to relax _____ I'm on holiday.
    A) while   B) before   C) if   D) as soon as

40. _____ you are the first person up in the morning, make me a cup of coffee.
    A) When   B) If   C) As soon as   D) While

41. I'm going to keep asking you to marry me _____ you say "Yes".
    A) while   B) when   C) until   D) before

42. We can go _____ you're ready.
    A) if   B) after   C) before   D) while

43. _____ I'm having my hair cut, you can do the shopping.
    A) When   B) While   C) As soon as   D) If

44. Stop at a petrol station _____ we run out of the petrol.
    A) before   B) until   C) after   D) when

45. _____ you've read the newspaper, can I have it?
    A) Until   B) After   C) Before   D) *

46. I am so worried about James, _____ you hear any news, phone me.
    A) while   B) until   C) as soon as   D) before

47. _____ we discover life on another planet, will it be intelligent?
    A) As soon as   B) When   C) Until   D) If

48. I'll have a bath _____ I go to work.
    A) after   B) as soon as   C) before   D) while

49. _____ the lesson ends, I'll go home.
    A) Before   B) Until   C) If   D) As soon as

50. I'll study English _____ I speak it perfectly.
    A) if   B) after   C) until   D) when

PRE-INTERMEDIATE / TEST - 10

- Infinitive, gerund
- Describing feelings and situations

1. He agreed _____ the job as soon as possible.
   A) start   B) starting   C) to start   D) starts

2. I stopped _____ my book and went to bed.
   A) to read   B) read   C) will read   D) reading

3. My teachers always expected me _____ well in exams.
   A) did   B) doing   C) do   D) to do

4. Let me _____ for the meal. You paid last time.
   A) pay   B) to pay   C) paid   D) paying

5. The dentist told me _____ more careful when I brush my teeth.
   A) will be   B) being   C) to be   D) be

6. I asked Monica _____ some stamps.
   A) buys   B) buying   C) to buy   D) buy

7. I never liked _____ to church when I was a child.
   A) going   B) to do   C) went   D) go

8. Have you finished _____ that letter yet?
   A) to write   B) writing   C) writes   D) write

9. You can't _____ your car outside the hospital.
   A) parks   B) to park   C) park   D) parking

10. David always enjoyed _____ football at school.
    A) to be played   B) playing   C) to play   D) play

11. The TV program was so _____ that I felt asleep.
    A) tired   B) surprising   C) annoyed   D) boring

12. Children can't get to sleep on Christmas Eve. They're too _____.
    A) bored   B) excited   C) frightened   D) worrying

13. "Hi, Mum!"
    "Carol! Thank goodness you rang! Where have you been? We've been so _____ about you."
    A) interested   B) annoying   C) worried   D) frightening

14. A: Hello, darling. I've got a present for you.
    B: For me?
    A: Don't look so _____. I often buy you presents.
    B: But it isn't my birthday!
    A) bored   B) exciting   C) tiring   D) surprised

15. The art exhibition was very _____. I loved it.
    A) surprised   B) boring   C) interesting   D) excited

16. My feet are killing me! I find going round art galleries and museums very _____.
    A) tiring   B) worrying   C) boring   D) frightening

17. Some people don't go out at night because they're _____ that someone will rob them.
    A) worried   B) annoying   C) surprised   D) frightened

18. Our financial situation is very _____. We spend more and more, but we're earning less and less.
    A) worrying   B) exciting   C) frightened   D) interesting

19. A: You are yawning. Are you listening to what I am saying?"
    B: I am! I'm really _____. I want to know what happened. It's just that I feel very _____. I went to bed very late last night.
    A) surprised / tiring   B) excited / worrying
    C) interested / tired   D) frightened / bored

20. "I'm going on a three-month holiday to the Far East."
    "How _____! Lucky you!"
    A) frightening   B) interested   C) boring   D) exciting

21. "Was your father _____ when you told him your exam results?"
    "He was furious."
    A) annoyed   B) worrying   C) frightened   D) tired

22. "What _____ to do?"
    "I'm looking for my contact lens. Can you see it?"
    A) do you try   B) will you try
    C) are you trying   D) did you try

23. "I'll help you. What _____ me to do?"
    "Could you do the washing-up while I am doing the cooking?"
    A) you want   B) are you wanting
    C) did you want   D) do you want

24. "What _____ you to do?"
    "She (the doctor) told me to stay in bed for a few days."
    A) will she tell   B) did she tell
    C) is she going to tell   D) does she tell

25. "My mother was so helpful while she was staying with us"
    "What _____ to do?"
    A) did she help you   B) does she help you
    C) will she help you   D) was she helping you

26. "What _____ to do tonight?"
    "What about going out for a meal?"
    A) do you like   B) would you like
    C) are liking   D) will you like

27. "What _____ to do after university?"
    "I'd like to get a job in publishing."
    A) do you hope   B) will you hope
    C) are you going to hope   D) are you hope

28. My family is trying _____ where to go on holiday.
    A) decided   B) decide   C) to decide   D) deciding

29. I'd like _____ somewhere different for a change.
    A) went   B) to go   C) go   D) going

30. I enjoy _____ places I've never been to before.
    A) visiting   B) to visit   C) visits   D) visit

31. But my children hate _____.
    A) sightsee   B) to sightsee   C) sightseeing   D) will sightsee

32. They prefer _____ in a swimming pool all day.
    A) playing   B) plays   C) to play   D) to playing

33. They refuse _____ out on trips if it's too hot.
    A) to going   B) to go   C) going   D) go

34. Last year we managed _____ a holiday that suited everyone.
    A) found   B) to find   C) find   D) finding

35. We decided _____ a house with a swimming pool.
    A) renting   B) rent   C) to renting   D) to rent

36. A woman from a travel agency helped us _____ a nice house.
    A) to choose   B) choosing   C) chooses   D) too choose

37. When we arrived, the people next door invited us _____ a drink with them.
    A) have   B) to have   C) to had   D) having

38. We began _____ about next year's holiday two months ago.
    A) talked   B) talking   C) talks   D) talk

39. Everyone hopes _____ themselves on holiday but it isn't always easy.
    A) enjoy   B) to enjoy   C) be enjoyed   D) enjoying

40. My wife and I are starting _____ we should stay at home.
    A) thinking   B) think   C) to think   D) thought

41. I went to the shops _____ some shoes.
    A) buy   B) for to buy   C) to buy   D) for buy

42. Do you enjoy _____?
    A) dance   B) dancing   C) danced   D) to dance

43. When I was young, I _____ ice-skating.
    A) went to   B) go   C) used to go   D) going

44. He told me he loved me. I didn't know what _____.
    A) to say   B) say   C) will I say   D) saying

45. Their house is _____ mess! I don't know how they live in it.
    A) so   B) such an   C) so many   D) such a

46. There were _____ people at the party! There was nowhere to dance.
    A) such a   B) so many   C) so much   D) such

47. I'm _____ hungry. I could eat a horse.
    A) so   B) such a   C) such   D) so much

48. Jane and Pete are _____ nice people! But I can't stand their kids.
    A) so many   B) so   C) such a   D) such

49. I've spent _____ money this week! I don't know where it's all gone.
    A) such   B) so many   C) so much   D) so

50. A present! For me? You're _____ kind!
    A) such   B) so many   C) so   D) such a

PRE-INTERMEDIATE TEST - 11

- Passives   - Tenses

Concorde, the world's fastest passenger plane, __(1)__ by France and Britain together. In the 1950s, both countries dreamed of having a supersonic plane, and the project __(2)__ in 1962. £1.5 billion __(3)__ on developing the Concorde, and it __(4)__ for over 5.000 hours, which makes it the most tested plane in history. The first passenger plane __(5)__ by British Airways and Air France in 1976. The Concorde holds many world records, including the fastest crossing of the Atlantic Ocean from New York to London, which __(6)__ in 2 hours 45 seconds! Flying at twice the speed of sound means that flying time __(7)__ by half, which is why the Concorde flight between London and New York __(8)__ a lot by business people and film stars - you can leave Britain at 10.30 and arrive in New York an hour earlier! Twenty planes __(9)__ up to the present day. But there are no plans to build any more. Each plane __(10)__ at a cost of £55 million, which makes them very expensive!

1. A) developed   B) have been developed
   C) was developed D) develops

2. A) was started   B) starts
   C) have been started D) started

3. A) spend   B) was spent
   C) have been spent D) spent

4. A) has tested   B) tested
   C) have been tested D) was tested

5. A) introduce   B) has been introduced
   C) introduces   D) was introduced

6. A) have been achieved B) was achieved
   C) will achieve D) achieved

7. A) was reduced   B) has reduced
   C) is reduced   D) will be reduced

8. A) had been used B) uses
   C) used   D) is used

9. A) were built   B) are built
   C) have been built D) build

10. A) is being produced B) is produced
    C) was produced D) has been produced

11. Where _____ these shoes made?
    A) was   B) were   C) did   D) is

12. I was given this watch _____ my aunt.
    A) to   B) from   C) *   D) by

13. Someone _____ my bag!
    A) was stolen   B) has been stolen
    C) has stolen   D) is stolen

14. A newsagent _____ stamps.
    A) sells B) is sold C) was sold D) sell

15. A British policeman _____ guns.
    A) aren't carried   B) don't carry
    C) hasn't been carried D) doesn't carry

16. All the apple juice _____ by nine o'clock.
    A) drunk B) was drunk C) was drank D) drink

17. Have all the sandwiches _____?
    A) been eaten B) eaten C) was ate D) ate

18. _____ hello to your parents from me when you see them.
    A) Tell   B) Say   C) Give   D) Keep

19. I was late for work because I _____ the bus.
    A) carried B) lost C) waited for D) missed

20. This is my grandfather's watch. He _____ it every day until he died.
    A) gave   B) carried   C) wore   D) kept

21. I _____ just _____ a good idea. Let's eat out tonight.
    A) have / kept B) have / had C) am / told D) had / carried

22. My uncle _____ £500 on the stock exchange.
    A) keeps B) grows C) carries D) earns

23. We _____ a complaint to the manager because our meal was so bad.
    A) made B) said C) gave D) told

24. Rolls Royce cars _____ in England.
    A) were made B) is made C) makes D) are made

25. They _____ rice in China.
    A) are grown   B) grow
    C) have been grown D) grows

26. The telephone _____ by Bell in 1876.
    A) has invented   B) is invented
    C) was invented   D) invented

27. Thieves _____ two pictures from the museum last night.
    A) have stolen B) stole C) was stolen D) had stolen

28. They _____ the picture for £3.000.
    A) has sold B) are sold C) sold D) sell

29. Three new factories _____ this year.
    A) built   B) were built
    C) have been built D) has built

30. 10.000 cars _____ next year.
    A) will produce   B) produced
    C) are produced   D) will be produced

31. The television _____ by Bell.
    A) was invented   B) is invented
    C) wasn't invented D) invented

32. _____ they _____ many cars last year?
    A) Have / made   B) Did / make
    C) Will / make   D) Been / made

Nylon __(33)__ in the early 1930s by an American chemist, Julian Hill. Other scientists __(34)__ with his invention, and finally on 27 October, 1938 nylon __(35)__ to the world. It was cheap and strong and immediately __(36)__ successful, especially in the making of women's stockings.

During the Second World War, the best present for many women was a pair of nylon stockings, but more importantly, nylon __(37)__ to make parachutes and tires.

Today, nylon __(38)__ in many things: carpets, ropes, seat belts, furniture, computers, and even spare parts for the human body. It __(39)__ an important part in our lives for over 50 years. Next year about 36 million tons of it __(40)__.

33. A) invented B) has been invented
    C) is invented D) was invented

34. A) has worked B) worked
    C) were working D) have been working

35. A) was introduced B) introduces
    C) has introduced D) introduced

36. A) have become B) became
    C) is became D) becomes

37. A) has been used B) used
    C) was used D) was been used

38. A) found B) founded
    C) has founded D) is found

39. A) played B) has played C) is playing D) plays

40. A) is manufactured B) will be manufactured
    C) manufactured D) is going to manufacture

41. English _____ all over the world.
    A) speaks B) is spoken
    C) was spoken D) has been spoken

42. The animals _____ by a loud noise.
    A) frightened B) were frightening
    C) has been frightened D) were frightened

43. My children _____ with their homework.
    A) helped B) help C) are helping D) aren't helped

44. How many times _____ playing football?
    A) have you been hurt B) did you hurt
    C) were you hurted D) are you hurt

45. The thieves _____ by anyone.
    A) saw B) have been seen
    C) weren't seen D) didn't seen

46. Coffee _____ in England.
    A) grows B) isn't grown
    C) grew D) have been grown

47. _____ last night?
    A) Have the plants been watered
    B) Did the plants water
    C) Were the plants watered
    D) Are they watered

48. Driving should _____ in city centers.
    A) ban B) be banned C) banned D) being ban

49. America _____ by Christopher Columbus.
    A) has discovered B) have discovered
    C) had been discovered D) was discovered

50. The house is going _____.
    A) to knock down B) to be knocked down
    C) to been knocked down D) knocking down

PRE-INTERMEDIATE TEST - 12

- Second conditional
- Might, will, going to
- Phrasal verbs

1. Don't wait for me. I _____ late. It depends on the traffic.
   A) will be B) am
   C) might be D) am going to be

2. "What are you doing tonight?"
   "I don't know. I _____ out, or I _____ at home."
   A) will go / am staying B) might go / might stay
   C) am going / am staying D) go / stay

3. We have guests coming for Saturday lunch. I _____ cook roast beef and Yorkshire pudding. I have bought all the ingredients.
   A) might B) will C) am going to cook D) can

4. A- I'm going to buy George a green shirt.
   B- I wouldn't if I were you.
   A- Why not?
   B- I'm sure he _____ the green color.
   A) might not like B) will like
   C) isn't going to like D) won't like

5. "Goodbye, darling. I _____ phone as soon as I arrive."
   "Thanks. Bye!"
   A) can B) will C) am going to D) might

6. Catherine wants to be a politician. Who knows? One day she _____ Prime Minister!
   A) is going to be B) will be
   C) might be D) is

7. _____ on your warm coat. It's cold today.
   A) Try B) Fill C) Dress D) Put

8. Could I _____ on these shoes, please? Size nine.
   A) look B) put C) try D) turn

9. Don't forget to _____ off the lights when you come to bed.
   A) down B) turn C) fall D) fill

10. You look tired. Sit _____ and have a cup of tea.
    A) away B) on C) down D) put

11. I'm looking for yesterday's newspaper. Did you throw it _____?
    A) out B) down C) back D) away

12. Turn _____ the music! It's too loud!
    A) on B) round C) down D) after

Laura __(13)__ in a big city. If she lived in the country, she __(14)__ a dog. Laura __(15)__ a flat with three other girls. But if it __(16)__ possible, she __(17)__ on her own. If she __(18)__ in the country, she __(19)__ a small cottage, and she __(20)__ her own flowers and vegetables. She __(21)__ by underground and __(22)__ shopping in big department stores, but she __(23)__ this at all. If she __(24)__ in the country she __(25)__ her bike, and she __(26)__ things in a small village shop.

13. A) was living B) lived
    C) would like to live D) lives

14. A) has B) would have C) had D) will have

15. A) share B) is sharing C) shares D) shared

16. A) will be B) was C) is D) were

17. A) lives B) is living C) will be living D) would live

18. A) was living B) were living C) is living D) lived

19. A) will buy B) is going to buy
    C) would buy D) buys

20. A) grows B) wants to grow
    C) will grow D) would grow

21. A) is traveling B) would travel
    C) travels D) will travel

22. A) go B) goes C) is going D) would go

23. A) likes B) would like C) doesn't like D) is liking

24. A) were B) is C) will be D) would being

25. A) rides B) rode C) would ride D) is riding

26. A) bought B) would buy C) buys D) will buy

27. "What's for supper?"
    "We _____ lamb. It's in the oven."
    A) might have B) would have C) had D) are having

28. "What time are we eating?"
    "Don't worry. It _____ ready before your TV program."
    A) is B) will be C) might be D) *

29. I'm going to the town tomorrow. I _____ lunch with Joe at 1.00."
    A) will have B) am having C) might have D) have

30. "Are you going to have a winter holiday this year?"
    "I _____. I haven't decided yet."
    A) am B) might C) am not D) can't

31. How do you _____ your parents?
    A) look forward to B) look up a word
    C) get on with D) look out

32. You shouldn't smoke in here. Put _____.
    A) it off B) it down C) it out D) it away

33. I haven't get time to fill in this form. I'll fill _____ later.
    A) it B) in it C) on it D) *

34. I _____ tennis tomorrow. But I'm not sure.
    A) play B) am playing C) will play D) might play

35. If I _____ younger, I _____ to play the piano, but I'm too old now.
    A) am / will learn B) will be / are learning
    C) were / would D) were / would learn

36. I'm _____ forward to meeting her very much.
    A) fallen B) looking C) trying D) giving

37. She _____ off her horse and hurt her wrist.
    A) put B) turned C) ran D) fell

38. What a pretty dress! Turn _____ ! Let me look at it from the back.
    A) up B) round C) away D) on

39. Don't worry about the baby. I'll look _____ her while you're out.
    A) for B) with C) to D) after

40. Pick _____ your litter! Don't drop it on the street!
    A) on B) up C) out D) back

41. If I _____ Prime Minister, I _____ increase tax for rich people.
    A) would be / shall B) will be / will
    C) am / would D) were / would

42. If I _____ in a big house, I _____ a party.
    A) lived / would have B) am / am having
    C) will live / have D) would live / will have

43. Thank you for the invitation. _____ I can't come.
    A) Suddenly B) Upstairs
    C) Unfortunately D) Hardly

44. If she _____ a lot of clothes, she _____ money.
    A) bought / would have B) would buy / has
    C) wouldn't bought / had D) didn't buy / would have

45. If he _____ a watch, he _____ always late.
    A) will have / won't be B) had / isn't
    C) has / is D) had / wouldn't be

46. They _____ their baby Lily, but they aren't sure yet.
    A) will call B) are calling C) call D) might call

47. I'd visit you more often if you _____ so far away.
    A) will be living B) didn't live
    C) don't live D) wouldn't live

48. If I _____ perfect English, I _____ in this class.
    A) could spoke / won't be B) can speak / would be
    C) could speak / wouldn't be D) can't speak / will not be

49. I _____ to work if I _____ better, but I feel terrible.
    A) went / felt B) would go / feel
    C) will go / feel D) would go / felt

50. What _____ if a stranger _____ you £1 million?
    A) will you do / gave B) would you do / gave
    C) do you do / will give D) would you do / will give

PRE-INTERMEDIATE TEST - 13

- Present Perfect
- Present Perfect Continuous
- Past Simple
- Vocabulary

1. How long _____ in Paris?
   A) do you live   B) are you living
   C) have you been living D) you live

2. Anna _____ a good job.
   A) finds   B) has found
   C) founded   D) has been finding

3. Pete and I _____ for over six month.
   A) are gone   B) have gone out
   C) went out   D) have been going out

4. I _____ a new flat a few months ago.
   A) bought   B) have been buying
   C) have bought   D) buy

5. How long _____ your car?
   A) have you had   B) you have
   C) are you have   D) have you been having

6. Tom _____ as a postman for the past month.
   A) has worked   B) worked
   C) works   D) has been working

7. I _____ an essay all day.
   A) write   B) have been written
   C) am writing   D) have been writing

8. I _____ six pages.
   A) am written   B) have been writing
   C) have written   D) write

9. "Are you going out?"
   "_____. I don't know yet."
   A) Carefully   B) Possibly   C) Mainly   D) Nearly

10. The exam was _____ difficult. I couldn't do any of it.
    A) fluently   B) seriously   C) exactly   D) real

11. "How old are you?"
    "I'm _____ eight. It's my birthday next week."
    A) possibly   B) fluently   C) nearly   D) exactly

12. I travel a lot in my job, _____ to Europe.
    A) exactly   B) nearly   C) really   D) mainly

13. Sorry I'm late. _____ for a long time?
    A) Did you wait   B) Have you waited
    C) Have you been waiting D) Did you wait

14. The streets are wet. _____?
    A) Was it raining   B) Has it been raining
    C) Has it rained   D) Did it rain

15. I'm hot because I _____!
    A) have run   B) run
    C) have been running D) am run

16. I _____ my finger! It really hurts.
    A) cut   B) cutted
    C) have cut   D) have been cutting

17. _____ Paul Simon's latest record?
    A) Have you heard   B) Have you been hearing
    C) Did you hear   D) Are you heard

18. She's tired because she _____ all day.
    A) shopped   B) shops
    C) has been shopping D) has shopped

19. Sorry. I _____ one of your glasses.
    A) have broken   B) broke
    C) break   D) have been breaking

20. How long _____ this book?
    A) do you read   B) are you reading
    C) have you been reading   D) have you read

21. They _____ here for three years.
    A) lives   B) are living
    C) live   D) have been living

22. I _____ the living room, but I haven't finished yet.
    A) have painted   B) paint
    C) painted   D) have been painting

23. I _____ my wallet. Where did I last put it?
    A) lost   B) have lost
    C) have been losing D) lose

24. Look what Pat _____ me for my birthday! A bike!
    A) gave   B) have been giving
    C) gives   D) has given

25. There's my wallet! I _____ for it for ages.
    A) have been looking B) looked
    C) have looked   D) look

We __(26)__ in our new house for several months. Since we __(27)__ in, we __(28)__ very busy. Everyone __(29)__ to get the house ready. So far we __(30)__ the living room and the kitchen. Soon after we arrived the central heating __(31)__ down, so we __(32)__ to spend a lot of money to repair it.
We __(33)__ gardening very much, but we __(34)__ time to do anything in the garden yet. And it __(35)__ very heavily recently, so we'll just wait till the weather gets better.

26. A) lives   B) lived
    C) have lived   D) have been living

27. A) have moved   B) moved
    C) have been moving   D) are moving

28. A) are   B) have been being
    C) were   D) have been

29. A) has been helping   B) has helped
    C) helps   D) helped

30. A) decorated   B) decorate
    C) have decorated   D) have decorating

31. A) have broken   B) broke
    C) breaks   D) are breaking

32. A) have been having   B) have
    C) had   D) have had

33. A) are liking   B) liked   C) have liked   D) like

34. A) don't have   B) haven't had   C) had not   D) aren't having

35. A) is raining   B) rained
    C) have been raining D) has rained

36. "Can I speak to Mr. Thompson, please?"
    "I'm afraid he's just _____ out of the office."
    A) been   B) has   C) gone   D) *

37. I _____ to most countries in Europe, but I've never _____ to Russia.
    A) was / gone   B) have gone / been
    C) have been / been   D) went / gone

38. _____ me that you'll always tell the truth.
    A) Advise   B) Waste   C) Promise   D) Invent

39. He was taken to hospital by ambulance, but he was _____ on arrival.
    A) mad   B) dead   C) alive   D) various

40. I love the _____ and quite of the countryside.
    A) peace   B) feeling   C) comfort   D) wealth

41. I saw a(n) _____ for a job as a waiter.
    A) invention   B) mystery   C) waste   D) advertisement

42. The sofa was so _____ that I felt asleep.
    A) successful   B) comfortable   C) honest   D) comforting

43. I gave the police a(n) _____ of the man who attacked me.
    A) beauty   B) describing   C) advice   D) description

44. I had a few problems, but Bob gave me some good _____.
    A) advice   B) promises   C) inventions   D) *

45. I was sitting at home when suddenly I had a funny _____ that I wasn't alone.
    A) belief   B) government   C) mystery   D) feeling

46. I used to speak French _____, but I've forgotten it now.
    A) successfully   B) fluently   C) honestly   D) carefully

47. Please drive _____. The roads are so dangerous.
    A) carefully   B) seriously   C) comfortably   D) wealthy

48. I have _____ £5.17 until the end of the week.
    A) exactly   B) suddenly   C) peacefully   D) really

49. There was an accident, but fortunately no one was _____ injured.
    A) mainly   B) seriously   B) possibly   D) exactly

50. "Where does their money come from?"
    "They have a very _____ business."
    A) wealthy   B) comfortable   C) successful   D) various

PRE-INTERMEDIATE TEST - 14

- Past Perfect
- Reported statements

1. Lisa _____ me a lift because I _____ the bus.
   A) gave / missed   B) have given / have missed
   C) gave / had missed   D) had gave / missed

2. I _____ her for everything she _____.
   A) thanking / did   B) thanked / had done
   C) have thanked / has done   D) had thanked / had done

3. When I got to the office, I _____ that I _____ to lock the front door.
   A) had realized / forget   B) realized / had forgotten
   C) realized / forget   D) had realized / had forgotten

4. After they _____ their work, they ___ home.
   A) had finished / went   B) finished / went
   C) had finished / had gone   D) finished / had gone

5. I _____ you at 8.00, but you _____ just _____ out.
   A) call / have / gone   B) called / have / gone
   C) called / had / gone   D) have called / have / gone

6. I took my family to Paris last year. I _____ there as a student, so I _____ my way around.
   A) was / know   B) were / knew
   C) had been / have known   D) had been / knew

7. After I _____ to the news, I _____ to bed.
   A) listened / went   B) had listened / went
   C) have listened / had gone   D) listen / go

8. He _____ he was at school the day before.
   A) says   B) told   C) said   D) is telling

9. Sandra _____ Bob that she didn't see the Taj Mahal.
   A) told   B) tells   C) said   D) talked

10. Why did you _____ that?
    A) talk   B) said   C) tell   D) say

11. Could I _____ your pen?
    A) give   B) lend   C) borrow   D) make

12. I'm English. I come from Brighton. In Paris I am a _____.
    A) cooker   B) stranger   C) travel   D) foreigner

I went to a school reunion last week. I __(13)__ very surprised. So many things __(14)__. They __(15)__ the old gymnasium, and the library __(16)__. I __(17)__ slowly round the school. Everything __(18)__ much smaller, although they __(19)__ some impressive new buildings. I __(20)__ lots of my old schools friends, too, and they __(21)__ the same either. Some of them __(22)__ to London, and the most of them __(23)__ married. I __(24)__ to the headmaster for a while. He __(25)__. He __(26)__ that he __(27)__ every boy who __(28)__ the school since he __(29)__ working there in 1978. But when I asked him what my name was, he __(30)__ confess that he __(31)__ which __(32)__ me realize that I __(33)__ too!

13. A) am B) have been C) was D) had been

14. A) changed B) had changed
    C) has changed D) has change

15. A) had knocked down B) knocked down
    C) knock down D) have knocked down

16. A) disappeared B) was disappeared
    C) had disappeared D) have been disappeared

17. A) have walked B) walked
    C) was walking D) had walked

18. A) seems B) have seemed
    C) had seemed D) seemed

19. A) were building B) built
    C) have built D) had built

20. A) met B) meet C) had met D) have meet

21. A) hadn't stayed B) weren't stayed
    C) didn't stay D) not stayed

22. A) have moved B) moved
    C) had moved D) was moving

23. A) are get B) had got C) were got D) have got

24. A) talked B) had talked C) was talking D) have talked

25. A) haven't left B) had not left
    C) didn't leave D) hadn't leave

26. A) said B) was saying C) had said D) have said

27. A) remembers B) have remembered
    C) remembered D) had remembered

28. A) attended B) had attended
    C) have attended D) attending

29. A) had started B) starts C) started D) have started

30. A) had to B) have had to C) had had to D) was having to

31. A) forget B) forgot
    C) have forgotten D) had forgotten

32. A) have made B) made C) had made D) was made

33. A) was changed B) had changed
    C) have changed D) changed

34. _____ I had had a bath I went to bed.
    A) Before B) Soon as C) After D) Until

35. I had read the book _____ I saw the film.
    A) when B) before C) until D) after

36. I _____ to sleep until I _____ my homework.
    A) don't go / did B) had not gone / had done
    C) didn't go / did D) didn't go / had done

37. As soon as he _____ his driving test, he _____ a car.
    A) passed / bought B) had passed / bought
    C) passes / had bought D) passed / had bought

38. When I _____ the letter, I _____ it away.
    A) read / had thrown B) had read / had thrown
    C) had read / threw D) read / threw

39. "You can move in immediately."
    She told me I _____ immediately.
    A) will move in B) would move in
    C) can move in D) could move in

40. "The people who I looked after are very well."
    She said that the people who she _____ after _____ very well.
    A) were looking / are B) have looked / are
    C) would looked / were D) had looked / were

41. "You'll have to make up your mind soon."
    She told me I _____ make up my mind soon.
    A) had to B) will have had to
    C) would have to D) could have to

42. I didn't recognize him because he _____ a haircut.
    A) had had B) has C) had D) have had

43. He always makes me _____.
    A) to laugh B) laughing C) laugh D) be laughed

44. She refused _____ for the meal.
    A) paying B) to pay C) pays D) the pay

45. I'll never forget _____ him for the first time.
    A) meet B) meeting C) to meet D) to met

46. "It's a quite flat, and the neighbors are nice."
    "Mrs. Deon said it __a quite flat, and the neighbors __ nice."
    A) has been / are B) is / were
    C) was / were D) had been / have been

47. "You look brown. Have you _____ on holiday?"
    "Yes, we've _____ got back."
    A) been / now B) gone / just
    C) been / just D) did / already

48. I live in a house now, but before I _____ in a flat.
    A) am using to live B) used to live
    C) had used to live D) have used to live

49. "I need £100 deposit."
    Then she said she _____ £100 deposit.
    A) needs B) had needed
    C) needed D) have needed

50. I _____ the book back to the library after I _____ reading it.
    A) take / finished B) have taken / have finished
    C) took / had finished D) had taken / finished

INTERMEDIATE TEST - 1

- Auxiliary verbs (do, be have)
- Prepositions

1. _____ you ever stayed at the Ritz?
   A) Did B) Have C) Was D) Were

2. We _____ breakfast in bed.
   A) were have B) has C) was having D) had

3. _____ John give you those flowers?
   A) Did B) Have C) Was D) Is

4. I _____ my homework very quickly last night.
   A) do B) have C) did D) am

5. She _____ a shower every morning before school.
   A) does B) has C) did D) is

6. We _____ talking to James about his exam.
   A) don't B) haven't C) wasn't D) aren't

7. Lots of trees _____ blown down by the wind.
   A) were B) has C) did D) is

8. Where _____ you yesterday?
   A) was B) have C) did D) were

9. Mary never _____ the washing up.
   A) does B) has C) did D) is

10. Thank goodness we _____ a dishwasher!
    A) was B) have C) did D) were

11. How many people _____ you invited to the party?
    A) was B) have C) did D) were

12. Why _____ you leaving so early?
    A) was B) have C) is D) are

13. We _____ got a beautiful puppy called Molly.
    A) was B) have C) did D) were

14. We _____ a beautiful puppy called Molly.
    A) was B) having C) did D) had

15. I have been to Australia but Anna _____ .
    A) haven't B) hasn't C) isn't D) doesn't

16. Anna likes ice-cream but John _____ .
    A) haven't B) hasn't C) isn't D) doesn't

17. I don't like ice-cream but Jill _____ .
    A) have B) has C) is D) does

18. Maria isn't studying hard but I _____ .
    A) have B) has C) am D) are

19. John loves flying but we _____ .
    A) haven't B) don't C) isn't D) doesn't

20. I watched TV last night but my sister _____ .
    A) hasn't B) didn't C) isn't D) doesn't

21. Bill hasn't finished his work but we _____ .
    A) have B) do C) don't D) doesn't

22. We don't want to leave early but they _____ .
    A) have B) do C) is D) does

23. They didn't remember my birthday but you _____ .
    A) have B) don't C) did D) does

24. Your English is really improving but mine _____ .
    A) haven't B) don't C) isn't D) doesn't

25. _____ you speak three languages?
    A) Do B) Does C) Did D) Are

26. _____ you having a holiday soon?
    A) Do B) Does C) Did D) Are

27. _____ you have a good holiday last year?
    A) Do B) Does C) Did D) Are

28. _____ you ever been to Amsterdam?
    A) Do B) Does C) Have D) Did

29. _____ you often travel abroad?
    A) Do B) Does C) Have D) Did

30. _____ your best friend sometimes go on holiday with you?
    A) Do B) Does C) Have D) Did

31. I think you're wrong. I don't agree _____ you at all.
    A) to B) on C) with D) about

32. I'm not interested _____ what you think or what you want.
    A) to B) on C) with D) in

33. We might have a picnic. It depends _____ the weather.
    A) to B) on C) with D) about

34. What are you listening _____ ?
    A) to B) on C) with D) about

35. If you have a problem, talk _____ the teacher.
    A) to B) on C) at D) in

36. "What did you talk _____ ?"
    "Oh, this and that."
    A) to B) on C) with D) about

37. You aren't concentrating on your work. What are you thinking _____ ?
    A) to B) on C) with D) about

38. "What do you think _____ Pete?"
    "I really like him."
    A) to B) at C) with D) of

39. Where's the cash desk? I'd like to pay _____ this book.
    A) to B) for C) with D) about

40. "I've lost your pen. Sorry ..."
    "It's all right. Don't worry _____ it."
    A) to B) on C) with D) about

INTERMEDIATE TEST - 2

- Present Simple and Continuous
- Present Passive
- Prepositions

1. Sue and Geoff _____ a shop.
   A) work   B) study   C) run   D) runs

2. This kind of shop _____ a milk bar.
   A) is called   B) called
   C) is calling   D) is being called

3. Most days the shop _____ at 10.00 p.m.
   A) sells   B) opened   C) closes   D) run

4. They _____ camping any more.
   A) go   B) doesn't go   C) don't go   D) have gone

5. Ursula _____ four brothers and sisters.
   A) have   B) has   C) haven't   D) having

6. It _____ her fifteen minutes _____ to school.
   A) took / go   B) has taken / walk
   C) takes / walk   D) takes / to walk

7. She _____ school at 7:45 a.m.
   A) go   B) begin   C) starts   D) goes

8. I _____ lunch in the university canteen.
   A) eats   B) have   C) drink   D) has

9. I _____ extra money teaching computer studies.
   A) earn   B) earns   C) win   D) buy

10. I _____ the traffic in Bangkok.
    A) play   B) have   C) hate   D) has

11. English is _____ here.
    A) speak   B) spoke   C) is speaking   D) spoken

12. Volvos are _____ in Sweden.
    A) produced   B) produce   C) produces   D) producing

13. Is service _____ in the bill?
    A) including   B) include   C) to include   D) included

14. Our kitchen _____ decorated at the moment.
    A) is   B) is being   C) being   D) was being

15. Our factory is being _____ over by an American company.
    A) taken   B) bought   C) sold   D) run

16. About one thousand people are _____ in the factory.
    A) taken   B) cleaned   C) employed   D) worked

17. Lots of tulips are _____ in Holland.
    A) grown   B) growing   C) grow   D) grew

18. That block of flats is being _____ because it is unsafe.
    A) pulled down   B) pulled
    C) pulled up   D) pulling down

19. In Britain milk is _____ to your doorstep.
    A) shown   B) sold   C) bought   D) delivered

When you __(20)__ at an airport, you should go straight to the check-in desk where your ticket and luggage __(21)__. You __(22)__ your hand luggage with you but your suitcases __(23)__ to the plane on a conveyor belt. You can now go to the departure lounge.
If you are on an international flight, your passport __(24)__, and then you and your bags __(25)__ by security cameras; sometimes you __(26)__ a body search and your luggage __(27)__ by a security officer. You __(28)__ in the departure lounge until your flight __(29)__ and you __(30)__ which gate number to go.
Finally you __(31)__ your plane and you __(32)__ your seat by a flight attendant.

20. A) start   B) started   C) arrive   D) are arrived
21. A) are checked   B) control   C) check   D) is changed
22. A) kept   B) keeping   C) wait   D) keep
23. A) take   B) took   C) are taken   D) taking
24. A) check   B) checked   C) is checking   D) is checked
25. A) are x-rayed   B) x-rayed   C) control   D) check
26. A) give   B) are given   C) gave   D) giving
27. A) is searched   B) searching   C) searched   D) search
28. A) waiting   B) waits   C) wait   D) waited
29. A) calling   B) call   C) is called   D) called
30. A) are told   B) telling   C) told   D) tell
31. A) boarded   B) boarding   C) sit   D) board
32. A) show   B) are shown   C) showing   D) come

33. "Hello. Can I speak to Mr. James, please?"
    "I'm sorry. He isn't _____ at the moment. Can I take a message?"
    A) in   B) on   C) at   D) off

34. "Hello. Can I speak to Mr. James, please?"
    "I'm sorry. He is _____ on holiday at the moment. Can I help you?"
    A) in   B) on   C) away   D) off

35. "I feel like going to the cinema tonight."
    "Good idea! What's _____ at the moment?"
    A) in   B) on   C) at   D) off

36. I think this milk's _____ . It smells horrid.
    A) in   B) on   C) at   D) off

37. "Where shall we go for a meal?"
    "It's _____ you. It's your birthday. You choose."
    A) in   B) on   C) at   D) up to

38. Come on, kids! Aren't you _____ yet? Breakfast's on the table.
    A) in   B) on   C) up   D) off

39. I wonder why they aren't answering the door. There must be someone _____ .
    A) in   B) on   C) at   D) off

40. All the lights are _____ . I can see nothing.
    A) in   B) on   C) at   D) off

41. I must be _____ soon. I want to get to the shops before they close.
    A) in   B) on   C) at   D) off

42. "Why isn't there any hot water?"
    "The central heating is _____ . That's why."
    A) in   B) on   C) at   D) off

43. "You're crying. What's _____ ?"
    "I'm just a bit sad. That's all."
    A) in   B) on   C) up   D) off

INTERMEDIATE TEST - 3

- While, during, for
- Past Simple - Continuous - Perfect
- Past Passive
- Prepositions

1. My uncle died _____ the war.
   A) via   B) during   C) for   D) in

2. The phone rang _____ I was having supper.
   A) while   B) during   C) for   D) in

3. I lived in Paris _____ several years.
   A) while   B) during   C) for   D) in

4. _____ I was in Paris, I made a lot of friends.
   A) While   B) During   C) For   D) In

5. I was in hospital _____ three weeks.
   A) while   B) during   C) for   D) in

6. _____ my stay in hospital, the nurses looked after me very well.
   A) While   B) During   C) For   D) In

7. A football match lasts _____ ninety minutes.
   A) while   B) during   C) for   D) in

8. I hurt my leg _____ I was playing football yesterday.
   A) while   B) during   C) for   D) in

9. I hurt my leg _____ the second half of the match.
   A) via   B) until   C) for   D) in

10. Traffic is always bad _____ the rush hour.
    A) while   B) during   C) for   D) in

11. Last week I was held up _____ three hours.
    A) while   B) during   C) for   D) in

12. Peter came round _____ we were eating.
    A) while   B) during   C) for   D) in

13. Peter came round _____ the meal.
    A) while   B) during   C) on   D) in

14. It's my birthday _____ next week.
    A) at   B) in   C) on   D) *

15. "When?"
    "_____ Monday."
    A) At   B) In   C) On   D) *

16. _____ when were you born?
    A) At   B) In   C) On   D) *

17. _____ 8.00 _____ the morning.
    A) At / in   B) In / in   C) On / in   D) * / in

18. I'm meeting Alan _____ this evening.
    A) at   B) in   C) on   D) *

19. "What time?"
    "_____ six."
    A) At   B) In   C) On   D) *

20. What did you do _____ the weekend?
    A) at   B) in   C) with   D) *

21. _____ Friday evening we went to a party.
    A) At   B) In   C) On   D) *

22. We slept late _____ Saturday morning.
    A) at   B) in   C) on   D) *

23. _____ the afternoon we went shopping.
    A) At   B) In   C) On   D) *

24. _____ 7:00 some friends came round for a drink.
    A) At   B) In   C) On   D) *

25. We didn't do anything _____ Sunday.
    A) at   B) in   C) on   D) *

26. The weather in England is unreliable. _____ summer it can be hot, but it often rains _____ April and June.
    A) At / in   B) In / in   C) On / in   D) * / in

27. _____ last year the summer was awful.
    A) At   B) In   C) On   D) *

28. The best English weather is _____ spring and autumn.
    A) at   B) in   C) on   D) *

29. I learned to drive _____ 1980 _____ the age of 17.
    A) at / at   B) in / at   C) on / at   D) * / at

30. My brother learned _____ the same time as me, but I passed first.
    A) at   B) in   C) on   D) *

31. I'll phone you _____ next week. _____ Thursday.
    A) at / On   B) in / On   C) on / On   D) * / On

32. I'll phone you _____ about 3.00.
    A) at   B) in   C) on   D) *

Helen Keller's deafness and blindness __(33)__ by a severe illness when she was a baby. Her parents __(34)__ what to do, and they __(35)__ it difficult to control their growing daughter. One day they __(36)__ about a brilliant young teacher called Anne Sullivan. She __(37)__ to work with Helen. Very firmly and patiently, she __(38)__ her that every object __(39)__ a name. Eventually Helen __(40)__ a place at university. After this she __(41)__ the world helping people like herself. In 1962 the story of her life __(42)__ into a film, The Miracle Worker.

33. A) cause   B) caused   C) were caused   D) has caused

34. A) didn't know   B) doesn't know
    C) knew   D) knows

35. A) find   B) finds   C) were found   D) found

36. A) tell   B) were told   C) telling   D) told

37. A) came   B) begin   C) start   D) helping

38. A) studied   B) helped   C) thought   D) taught

39. A) has   B) had   C) have   D) having

40. A) offer   B) offered   C) was offered   D) offering

41. A) tour   B) toured   C) touring   D) tours

42. A) was made   B) make   C) is making   D) was making

INTERMEDIATE TEST - 4

-Modal verbs (can, could, have to)

1. I _____ work very hard because I have an exam next week.
   A) am having   B) has to   C) had to   D) have to

2. You _____ work hard after your exam. You can have a holiday.
   A) had to   B) won't have to
   C) have too   D) won't have

My father is a customs official so he always __(3)__ wear a uniform at work, but my mother is a teacher so she __(4)__ wear one.

3. A) doesn't have to   B) have to
   C) has to   D) don't have to

4. A) doesn't have to   B) have to
   C) has to   D) don't have to

When we were teenagers, we __(5)__ be home by nine o'clock. But we __(6)__ take as many exams as teenagers nowadays.

5. A) had to   B) won't have to
   C) have to   D) don't have to

6. A) had to   B) didn't have to
   C) have to   D) don't have to

7. I can't see the small print very well. I think I ____ wear glasses soon.
   A) will have to   B) won't have to
   C) have to   D) don't have to

8. Nobody enjoys _____ get up at five o'clock in the morning.
   A) have to   B) has to   C) having to   D) will have to

9. _____ we _____ have any vaccinations before we go to Barbados?
   A) Will / have to   B) Did / have to
   C) Won't / have   D) Are / having

10. _____ your grandmother _____ leave school when she was only fourteen?
    A) Will / have to   B) Did / have to
    C) Won't / have   D) Are / having to

11. You _____ be a millionaire to shop in Harrods. Everything is expensive there.
    A) will have to   B) won't have to
    C) have to   D) don't have to

12. If I fail my exam, ____ I ___ take it again?
    A) will / have to   B) did / have to
    C) does / have to   D) do / won't have

13. I phoned the plumber because I _____ smell gas in the kitchen.
    A) can   B) could   C) managed to   D) couldn't

14. Jane and John saved and saved, and finally they _____ buy the house of their dreams.
    A) can   B) could   C) managed to   D) couldn't

15. I phoned yesterday, but I ____ get an answer. Where were you?
    A) can   B) could   C) managed to   D) couldn't

16. The neighbors were having a row, and I _____ hear every word they said.
    A) can   B) could   C) managed to   D) couldn't

17. ____ you speak French before you moved to Paris?
    A) Can   B) Could   C) Managed to   D) Couldn't

18. I went for a ten-mile run last Saturday. It nearly killed me! I _____ move on Sunday.
    A) can   B) could   C) managed to   D) couldn't

19. _____ you _____ find all the things you wanted at the shops?
    A) Did / have to   B) Did / can
    C) Did / manage to   D) Did / could

20. The police _____ find the man who had stolen my car. He was sent to prison.
    A) can   B) could   C) managed to   D) couldn't

21. My grandfather _____ speak four languages when he was alive.
    A) can   B) could   C) managed to   D) couldn't

22. When we got to the top of the mountain we _____ see for miles.
    A) can   B) could   C) managed   D) couldn't

23. In my country you _____ get married when you're sixteen.
    A) can   B) could   C) managed to   D) couldn't

24. Speak up! I _____ hear you!
    A) can   B) could   C) can't   D) couldn't

25. _____ I borrow your dictionary?
    A) Can't   B) Could   C) Manage to   D) Couldn't

26. I'd love _____ help you, but I can't. I'm sorry.
    A) can   B) could
    C) managed to   D) to be able to

27. I _____ get into my house last night because I'd lost my key.
    A) can   B) could   C) managed to   D) couldn't

28. Women _____ vote in England until 1922.
    A) can   B) are able to   C) managed to   D) couldn't

29. I'm learning Spanish because I want _____ speak when I'm in Mexico.
    A) can   B) could
    C) will be able to D) to be able to

30. The doctor says I _____ walk again in two weeks' time.
    A) can   B) could
    C) will be able to D) to be able to

I asked the teacher if I __(31)__ open the window, but she said I __(32)__ because it would be too noisy.

31. A) can   B) could   C) managed to   D) couldn't

32. A) can   B) could   C) managed to   D) couldn't

33. I'm sorry, but I _____ come to your party next week.
    A) can't   B) couldn't   C) can   D) 'll be able to

34. I love driving! _____ drive has changed my whole life.
    A) Can   B) Could
    C) Will be able to D) Being able to

35. Children in my country _____ go to school when they're 7.
    A) doesn't have to   B) has to
    C) have to   D) don't have to

36. Adults _____ go to school.
    A) doesn't have to   B) has to
    C) have to   D) don't have to

37. Every adult _____ go to work.
    A) doesn't have to   B) has to
    C) have to   D) don't have to

38. A retired person _____ go to work.
    A) doesn't have to   B) has to
    C) have to   D) don't have to

39. Teenagers _____ study for exams.
    A) doesn't have to   B) has to
    C) have to   D) don't have to

40. You _____ drive on the right in Britain.
    A) mustn't   B) has to   C) have to   D) don't have to

INTERMEDIATE TEST - 5

- Make, do
- Present Continuous
- Somebody, anywhere, nothing...
- Prepositions

1. Is there a public call box near here? I have to _____ a phone call.
   A) do   B) make   C) get   D) hear

2. First she said "Yes", then she said "No", but in the end she _____ up her mind to marry him.
   A) did   B) made   C) got   D) said

3. When you're not sure what to do, the best thing is to _____ nothing.
   A) do   B) make   C) get   D) hear

4. Ssh! You mustn't _____ a noise. The baby's asleep.
   A) do   B) make   C) get   D) hear

5. My teacher says I must work harder, but I can't work any harder. I'm _____ my best.
   A) doing   B) trying   C) making   D) showing

6. We asked to see the manager and we _____ a complaint about the terrible service in the restaurant.
   A) did   B) made   C) had   D) heard

7. At first I found learning English very easy, but now I don't think I'm _____ any progress at all.
   A) doing   B) making   C) showing   D) getting

8. Could you _____ me a favor please? Could you give me a lift to the airport?
   A) make   B) do   C) give   D) want

9. My uncle died without _____ a will, and it was very difficult for our family to sort out his money and possessions.
   A) doing   B) make   C) get   D) making

10. We have some lovely new neighbors; we've already _____ friends with them.
    A) did   B) made   C) done   D) make

11. I like to keep fit, so I _____ exercises every day.
    A) do   B) make   C) get   D) hear

12. Before you go on holiday, you should _____ sure that the doors and windows are shut and locked.
    A) do   B) make   C) get   D) hear

13. _____ money, not war!
    A) Do   B) Make   C) Study   D) Get

14. I was _____ a queue waiting to buy some bread.
    A) in   B) on   C) at   D) by

15. I looked _____ all the shelves and _____ all the cupboards.
    A) in / on   B) on / in   C) at / in   D) at / on

16. They certainly weren't _____ the table or _____ the floor.
    A) in / on   B) on / in   C) at / in   D) on / on

17. Had I left them _____ work?
    A) in   B) on   C) at   D) near

18. Were they _____ the car?
    A) in   B) on   C) at   D) of

19. Then I realized where they were. They were _____ my favorite armchair.
    A) on   B) into   C) at   D) off

20. "Where were you at 2:00?" "_____ the beach."
    A) In   B) On   C) At   D) To

21. "Where were you at 2:00?" "_____ Sally's house doing my homework."
    A) Of   B) On   C) At   D) From

22. "Where were you at 2:00?" "_____ a cave."
    A) In   B) On   C) At   D) By

23. Would you like _____ to eat?
    A) something   B) anything   C) nothing   D) everything

24. Can I have _____ to drink?
    A) something   B) anything   C) nothing   D) everything

25. Can we go _____ quiet?
    A) somewhere   B) anywhere   C) nowhere   D) everywhere

26. If you need _____, just ask.
    A) something   B) anything   C) nothing   D) everything

27. Come and see me _____ you want. I don't mind.
    A) some time   B) any time   C) no time   D) every time

28. Help yourself to food. You can have _____ you want.
    A) something   B) anything   C) nothing   D) everything

29. _____ will tell you that two and two is four.
    A) Someone   B) Anyone   C) No one   D) Nothing

30. 'Does _____ want a game of tennis?' 'Yes.'
    A) someone   B) anyone   C) no one   D) everyone

31. Did _____ phone me while I was out?
    A) someone   B) anyone   C) no one   D) everyone

32. What's that smell? Can you smell _____ burning?
    A) something   B) anything   C) nothing   D) everything

33. I asked if _____ wanted an ice-cream, but _____ did, so I just bought one for myself.
    A) anyone / no one   B) no one / somebody
    C) anybody / somebody   D) no body / no one

34. Your face looks terribly familiar. Haven't I seen you _____ before?
    A) somewhere   B) anywhere   C) nowhere   D) everywhere

35. She left the room without saying _____.
    A) something   B) anything   C) nothing   D) everything

36. This doesn't look a very nice restaurant. Can we go _____ else?
    A) somewhere   B) anywhere   C) nowhere   D) everywhere

37. I have _____ more to say to you. Goodbye!
    A) something   B) anything   C) nothing   D) everything

38. I have never been _____ more beautiful than Scotland.
    A) somewhere   B) anywhere   C) nowhere   D) everywhere

39. I felt so embarrassed. _____ was laughing at me.
    A) Everyone   B) Anyone   C) No one   D) Something

40. "What do you want for supper?" "_____, I don't mind."
    A) Something   B) Anything   C) Nothing   D) Everything

41. It was Sunday, and the town was deserted. _____ was in the streets, and _____ was open.
    A) Somebody / somewhere   B) Anybody / anywhere
    C) Nobody / nowhere   D) Everybody / everywhere

42. "Who was at the party?" "_____: Pete, Ann, James, Kathy, all the Smiths, Sally Beams and Sally Rogers."
    A) Someone   B) Anyone   C) No one   D) Everyone

43. "Where do you want to go on holiday?" "_____ hot. I don't care if it's Greece, Spain, Italy or Sahara, but it has to be hot."
    A) Somebody   B) Anywhere   C) Nowhere   D) Everywhere

INTERMEDIATE TEST - 6

- As, like
- Questions with like
- Phrasal verbs
- Infinitive, gerund

1. I'm really looking forward to _____ my new course.
   A) start   B) starting   C) started   D) to start

2. They can't help us _____ the house.
   A) move   B) moving   C) moved   D) move to

3. She refused _____ the phone.
   A) answer   B) to answer   C) answered   D) answering

4. I don't mind _____ to the restaurant.
   A) driving   B) drive   C) drove   D) to drive

5. We encouraged them _____ a new business.
   A) setting up   B) to set up   C) set up   D)'d setup

6. His parents don't allow him _____ after ten o'clock.
   A) stay up   B) to stay up   C) stay up   D) stayed up

7. I'll be back in touch _____ soon _____ possible.
   A) as   B) like   C) like / as   D) as / as

8. This wine tastes _____ vinegar!
   A) likes   B) as / as   C) like   D) as

9. I've known Andy for years. He went to the same school _____ I did.
   A) liked   B) similar to   C) like   D) as

10. My sister's a teacher _____ me.
    A) likes   B) similar   C) like   D) as

11. 'We had a new teacher today called Mary.'
    'What was she _____?'
    A) liked   B) look like   C) like   D) as

12. Who do I look _____ , my mother or my father?
    A) like   B) more   C) likes   D) as

13. She really annoys me. I can't stand people _____ her.
    A) likes   B) compared to   C) like   D) as

14. I'll see you tomorrow at 11.00 _____ usual.
    A) like   B) as - as   C) like   D) as

15. It's July and the weather's awful! It's _____ in winter!
    A) likes   B) as like   C) like   D) as

16. I need to buy all sorts of things _____ socks, shirts and knickers.
    A) likes   B) such   C) like   D) as

17. My wife has found a job _____ a personal assistant.
    A) likes   B) as - as   C) like   D) as

18. Dave drinks _____ a fish! I've never seen anyone drink as much.
    A) likes   B) as such   C) like   D) as

19. My brother has a car _____ yours.
    A) likes   B) such   C) like   D) as

20. Don't touch anything. Leave everything _____ it is.
    A) likes   B) so   C) like   D) as

21. It's freezing. My feet are _____ blocks of ice.
    A) likes   B) such   C) like   D) as

22. I want _____ more careful with your homework in future.
    A) you be   B) you to be   C) that you are   D) you being

23. I stopped _____ when I was thirty.
    A) to smoke   B) smoke   C) smoking   D) too smoke

24. Why did I agree _____ with you? I can't stand it.
    A) to work   B) work   C) working   D) to working

25. I tried _____ you that you were making a mistake, but you didn't listen.
    A) tell   B) to tell   C) telling   D) told

26. I'm looking forward _____ you again soon.
    A) to see   B) to seeing   C) seeing   D) too seeing

27. My parents let me _____ what I wanted when I was young.
    A) do   B) to do   C) doing   D) does

28. I wasn't allowed _____ out unless they knew where I was going.
    A) going   B) go   C) to go   D) going to

29. I finished _____ the television, and then I went to bed.
    A) watching   B) to watch   C) watch   D) watch to

30. I don't like people _____ arrive late.
    A) which   B) whose   C) who   D) where

31. The company _____ he works for is based in Germany.
    A) which   B) whose   C) who   D) where

32. Where are the scissors _____ I bought yesterday?
    A) which   B) whose   C) who   D) where

33. I want you to meet the woman _____ taught me how to drive.
    A) which   B) whose   C) who   D) where

34. The meal _____ you cooked was delicious.
    A) which   B) whose   C) who   D) where

35. I like animals _____ don't make a mess.
    A) which   B) whose   C) who   D) where

36. The film _____ I've always wanted to see is on TV tonight.
    A) whose   B) which   C) who   D) where

37. The flat _____ they bought was very expensive.
    A) which   B) whose   C) who   D) where

38. The room in our house _____ is most used is the kitchen.
    A) which   B) whose   C) who   D) where

39. I didn't like the meal _____ we had yesterday.
    A) which   B) whose   C) who   D) where

40. The people _____ work here are very interesting.
    A) which   B) whose   C) who   D) where

41. The man _____ you were talking about has just come in the room.
    A) which   B) whose   C) who   D) where

42. I received a letter this morning _____ really upset me.
    A) who   B) which   C) where   D) whose

43. Toby, a boy _____ I went to school with, is ill in hospital.
    A) who   B) which   C) where   D) whose

44. He's going to have an operation _____ could save his life.
    A) who   B) which   C) where   D) whose

45. Toby, _____ parents both died a few years ago, is the same age as me.
    A) who   B) which   C) where   D) whose

46. I recently went back to the town _____ I was born.
    A) who   B) which   C) where   D) whose

47. The people _____ used to live next door moved a long time ago.
    A) who   B) which   C) where   D) whose

48. I met a girl _____ I used to play tennis with.
    A) who   B) which   C) where   D) whose

49. She told me a story _____ I found hard to believe.
    A) who   B) which   C) where   D) whose

50. She said she'd married a man _____ had been married ten times before.
    A) who   B) which   C) where   D) whose

51. I'll dry the dishes if you _____ them _____.
    A) put / away   B) find / out   C) put / out   D) wash / up

52. 'Can you _____ the time of the next train to London?' 'O.K. I'll phone the station.'
    A) put away   B) find out   C) put out   D) clear up

53. "Look at these shoes! They're brand new, and the heel's fallen off already."
"_____ them _____ and change them, then."
A) Put / away   B) Find / out   C) Put / out   D) Take / back

54. "Oh, dear! The washing machine isn't working. I haven't got any clean clothes, and I've got to go to work. What am I going to do?'
'Don't worry. I'll ___ them all ___. Just go to work.'
A) put / away   B) find / out   C) sort / out   D) clear / up

55. The fire was so intense that it took the firemen three hours to _____ it _____.
A) put / away   B) find / out   C) put / out   D) clear / up

56. The government wants to _____ a new scheme to encourage people to start their own businesses.
A) put away   B) find out   C) try out   D) clear up

57. 'Can I _____ these jeans _____ please?'
'Sure. The changing rooms are over there.'
A) put / away   B) try / out   C) put / out   D) try / on

58. I won't be able to go shopping with you today, I'm afraid. I've got a lot to do at the moment. Can we _____ it _____ till next week?
A) put / off   B) find / out   C) put / out   D) take / back

59. I don't mind your baking a cake, but just make sure you ___ everything __ when you've finished.
A) put /away   B) clear / up   C) put / out   D) take / back

60. 'What should I do with this form?'
'_____ it _____.'
A) Find / out   B) Fill / in   C) Put / out   D) Clear / up

61. I wanted to _____ to you yesterday.
A) to speak   B) speaking   C) speak   D) to speaking

62. They enjoyed _____ on holiday by the sea.
A) be   B) being   C) to be   D) too be

63. We hope _____ by half past seven.
A) arriving   B) to arrive   C) arrive   D) arrived

64. The weather was awful. It didn't stop _____ all week.
A) raining   B) to rain   C) rain   D) rain too

65. My sister has agreed _____ with the decorating.
A) help   B) helping   C) to help   D) helps

66. She loves _____ for herself.
A) to work   B) work   C) working   D) works

67. Please let me _____ for the drinks.
A) to pay   B) pay   C) paying   D) paid

68. My health wasn't very good so I stopped _____.
A) smoking   B) to smoke   C) smoke   D) smoked

69. We chose _____ by boat rather than by plane.
A) traveling   B) travel   C) to travel   D) traveled

70. We've finished _____ the house.
A) decorate   B) decorating   C) decorated   D) to decorate

71. I can't stand _____ in an office.
A) working   B) work   C) worked   D) to work

72. We expect you _____ on time.
A) arrive   B) arriving   C) arrived   D) to arrive

73. It was a wonderful holiday. I will always remember _____ the Niagara Falls.
A) seeing   B) to see   C) saw   D) see

74. I would hate _____ your party.
A) miss   B) miss to   C) missed   D) to miss

75. They can't promise _____ the work today.
A) finish   B) finishing   C) finished   D) to finish

76. He hates _____ calculators.
A) use   B) using   C) used   D) to use

INTERMEDIATE TEST - 7

- Present Perfect
- Past Simple
- Present Perfect Passive
- Phrasal Verbs

1. I was born _____ 1974.
A) for   B) since   C) in   D) ago

2. I've been a journalist _____ two years.
A) for   B) since   C) in   D) ago

3. I waited for you _____ hours.
A) for   B) since   C) in   D) ago

4. She left university three years _____.
A) for   B) since   C) in   D) ago

5. He's lived abroad _____ 1990.
A) for   B) since   C) in   D) ago

6. They got acquainted with each other _____ last year.
A) for   B) since   C) in   D) *

7. Have you _____ been to China?
A) never   B) ever   C) since   D) yet

8. Don't worry about phoning him because I've _____ done it.
A) ever   B) already   C) yet   D) never

9. I haven't finished my lunch _____.
A) never   B) ever   C) already   D) yet

10. I've not _____ been skiing, but I'd like to try it.
A) never   B) ever   C) already   D) just

11. I can't come out because I've _____ washed my hair.
A) never   B) ever   C) just   D) yet

12. Have you met our new teacher _____?
A) just   B) ever   C) already   D) yet

13. I'm delighted because I've been _____ a pay rise.
A) gave   B) have given   C) given   D) was given

14. The director's children _____.
A) have been kidnapped   B) have kidnapped
C) kidnapped   D) was kidnapped

15. They're really angry because someone _____ their car.
A) has been damaged   B) has damaged
C) damage   D) was damaged

16. She's going to be late because her plane _____.
A) has been delayed   B) has delayed
C) delayed   D) was delayed

17. He _____ to a senior designer.
A) has been promoted   B) has promoted
C) promoted   D) are promoted

18. Hundreds of people _____ for the jobs.
A) have been applied   B) have applied
C) have applying   D) was applied

19. Four people _____ in a train crash.
A) have been killed   B) have killed
C) are killed   D) was killed

20. Local police _____ the bank robber.
A) have been arrested   B) have arrested
C) has arrested   D) was arrested

21. Floods _____ serious damage.
A) have been caused   B) have caused
C) has caused   D) was caused

22. My job application _____.
A) haven't been accepted   B) haven't accepted
C) hasn't been accepted   D) hasn't accepted

23. The workers _____ a new representative.
A) have been elected   B) have elected
C) has elected   D) was elected

24. An occupation which gives opportunities for promotion is a/an _____ .
    A) applicant   B) CV   C) career   D) retirement

25. A document which lists your personal and professional details is a(n) _____ .
    A) applicant   B) CV   C) application   D) retirement

26. A person who has reached an age where they no longer work is _____ .
    A) an applicant   B) a CV
    C) an application   D) retired

27. When you want to leave a job, you have to give your _____ .
    A) resignation   B) Resume   C) career   D) retirement

28. If you have the right talents and experience for a job, then you are _____ for it.
    A) resignation   B) resume   C) career   D) qualified

29. When you try and get a job, you usually have to complete a/an _____ form.
    A) resignation   B) resume   C) application   D) retirement

30. If an employee is no longer needed, he or she can be made _____ .
    A) resigned   B) redundant   C) employer   D) retiring

31. You can often find about a new job by a/an _____ in a newspaper.
    A) news   B) completion
    C) sensation   D) advertisement

32. If an employer is interested in meeting you, you will be asked to come to a/an _____ .
    A) sensation   B) add   C) completion   D) interview

33. Tom's just _____ to the area manager of Eastern Europe.
    A) promoted   B) been promoted
    C) promoted   D) to promote

34. I _____ for a new job.
    A) have applied   B) have been applied
    C) apply   D) been applied

35. How many times _____ redundant?
    A) were you   B) have you been made
    C) you   D) have you made

36. Bob's wife _____ her job.
    A) has lost   B) were lost
    C) was losing   D) has been lost

37. My father _____ early retirement.
    A) was taken   B) has taken
    C) has been taken   D) take

38. My brother _____ the sack. His boss said he was lazy.
    A) has been given   B) gave
    C) given   D) has given

39. The number of people out of work _____ to nearly 3 million.
    A) has risen   B) have risen
    C) have been risen   D) has been risen

40. A strike _____ by the air traffic controllers.
    A) called   B) has called
    C) has been called   D) is given

41. They _____ more money by the management.
    A) haven't offered   B) haven't been offered
    C) offer   D) offered

42. How much money _____ for your retirement?
    A) saved   B) have you been saved
    C) have you saved   D) you saved

43. The factory workers are _____ strike because they want more money.
    A) in   B) on   C) out of   D) of

44. Thousands of people are _____ work in this town. It's really difficult to get a job.
    A) in   B) on   C) out of   D) of

45. I got a cheque _____ a hundred pounds this morning.
    A) in   B) on   C) out of   D) of

46. You're really annoying me. You're doing it _____ purpose, aren't you?
    A) in   B) on   C) out of   D) of

47. Can you tell the difference _____ butter and margarine.
    A) between   B) on   C) out of   D) of

48. There have been a lot of complaints _____ your behavior.
    A) in   B) on   C) out of   D) about

49. You are always _____ trouble because you don't listen to anybody.
    A) in   B) on   C) with   D) of

50. I'm fed up _____ cooking. Let's eat _____ for a change.
    A) in / out   B) on / now   C) with / out   D) at / out

51. How much do you spend a week _____ average?
    A) in   B) on   C) out of   D) of

52. Watch your step with Dad. He's _____ a terrible mood.
    A) in   B) on   C) out of   D) of

53. Could you take a photo _____ me, please?
    A) in   B) on   C) with   D) of

54. I had a crash this morning. Fortunately, I didn't do much damage _____ my car.
    A) in   B) on   C) out of   D) to

55. 'Where's Peter?'
    'He's _____ on holiday.'
    A) in   B) gone   C) been   D) being

56. Where have you _____ ? You're so brown!
    A) been   B) in   gone   C) D) being

57. 'Are you going to the shops this afternoon?'
    'No, I've already _____ . I went this morning.'
    A) going   B) gone   C) been   D) being

58. 'Can I speak to Jenny, please?'
    'I'm afraid she's _____ to lunch. Can I take a message?'
    A) going   B) gone   C) been   D) being

59. I've never _____ to Australia, but I'd like to go.
    A) went   B) gone   C) been   D) being

60. 'When's your holiday?'
    'We've already _____ . We went to France.'
    A) gone   B) were   C) been   D) being

61. 'Where's Harry these days?'
    'Didn't you know? He's _____ to another company.'
    A) went   B) gone   C) been   D) being

62. The Prime Minister of Italy _____ .
    A) has been resigned   B) have resigned
    C) resigned   D) has resigned

63. A new prime minister _____ .
    A) has elected   B) has been elected
    C) have elected   D) elected

64. The Italian people _____ of his resignation on television yesterday evening.
    A) was told   B) have been told
    C) told   D) were told

65. I _____ my glasses. _____ them anywhere?
    A) have been lost / Have you seen
    B) lost / Have you seen
    C) have lost / Did you see
    D) lost / Did you see

66. "Where _____ Liz _____ on holiday?"
    "She's in Paris."
    A) did / went   B) has / been   C) did / go   D) has / gone

67. "Where _____ Liz _____ on holiday?"
    "She went to Paris."
    A) did / went   B) has / been   C) did / go   D) has / gone

68. "____ John ever ____ to Paris?"
    "Oh, yes. Five times."
    A) Did / go   B) Has / gone   C) Has / been   D) Does / go

69. The police _____ the public that the man is dangerous.
    A) have warned   B) have been warned
    C) has warned   D) warned

INTERMEDIATE TEST - 8

- Pronunciation
- Conditionals
- Time clauses (when, as soon as)

1. Suppose! If it _____ last weekend, we _____ to play tennis.
   A) rained - wouldn't be able   B) rains - won't be able
   C) rain - would be able   D) had rained - could

2. Give me Peter's letter. If I _____ him, I _____ it to him.
   A) see-will give   B) saw-would give
   C) meet-would visit   D) had seen- would give

3. I have to work about 80 hours a week, so I'm very busy. But if I _____ any spare time, I _____ a sport like golf.
   A) will have / will take up   B) had / will take up
   C) will have / had   D) had / would take up

4. If I _____ taller, I _____ be a policeman, but I'm too short.
   A) was / can   B) had / could
   C) were / could   D) am / will

5. Please, start your meal. If you _____ your soup now, it _____ cold.
   A) didn't have / would go   B) had / got
   C) can eat / doesn't go   D) don't have / will go

6. What noisy neighbors you've got! If my neighbors _____ as bad as yours, I _____ crazy.
   A) were / would go   B) are / will go
   C) are / would go   D) had been / would have gone

7. If you _____ any problems, let me know and I _____ and help you straight away
   A) had / would come   B) have / will come
   C) had had / would come D) have / would go

8. You're a brilliant cook! If I _____ cook as well as you, I _____ a restaurant.
   A) could / would open   B) can / will open
   C) could / will open   D) can / would open

9. If there _____ some nice fish in the supermarket, _____ you _____ some for supper tonight?
   A) had been / would / buy   B) were / would / buy
   C) is / will / buy   D) are /will / buy

10. I'm small. I wish I _____ small.
    A) am not   B) was   C) were   D) weren't

11. I'm small. If only I _____ taller.
    A) were   B) wasn't   C) am   D) have

12. "We have mice in the kitchen."
    "If you _____ a cat, the mice _____ soon _____ ."
    A) had / would / disappear   B) have / will / disappear
    C) are / will / disappear   D) had / will / disappear

13. We live in the city. We wish we _____ in the country.
    A) have lived   B) living   C) lived   D) live

14. We live in the city. If only we _____ in the city!
    A) lived   B) didn't live   C) haven't lived   D) living

15. I'm not having a holiday this year. I wish I _____ a holiday.
    A) was having   B) is having   C) will have   D) have

16. I'm going to the dentist tomorrow. I wish I _____ to the dentist.
    A) am not going   B) will go
    C) wasn't going   D) went

17. I can't ski. I wish I _____ ski.
    A) can   B) could   C) will   D) couldn't

18. I wasn't happy at school. I wish I _____ happy.
    A) has been   B) had had   C) will have   D) had been

19. He didn't pass his driving test. He wishes he _____ it.
    A) have passed   B) had passed
    C) will pass   D) pass

20. I haven't been to Beijing. I wish I _____ to Beijing.
    A) had been   B) have been   C) has been   D) will be

PART B — ELEMENTARY PRE-INTERMEDIATE 1
pronouns – adverbs – adjectives – determiners

Choose the best alternative.

1. I can see Amanda. _____ is waiting for the New York plane.
   A) I   B) She   C) His   D) He
2. The clerk is speaking to the women. He is talking to _____.
   A) them   B) they   C) him   D) he
3. I haven't got the keys. Father has got _____.
   A) him   B) her   C) it   D) them
4. Can you see those boys and _____ father?
   A) they   B) them   C) their   D) him
5. Today _____ weather is very hot.
   A) a   B) an   C) the   D) _
6. He is Mrs. Taylor's _____ husband.
   A) a   B) _   C) the   D) an
7. Butterflies are _____ insects.
   A) a   B) an   C) the   D) them
8. Is a bee _____ insect?
   A) a   B) an   C) _   D) the
9. I'll wait for you half _____ hour.
   A) _   B) an   C) a   D) the
10. I haven't got _____ paint.
    A) any   B) some   C) _   D) many
11. We are late. The teacher will get angry with _____.
    A) we   B) they   C) us   D) I
12. My father is _____ engineer.
    A) a   B) the   C) _   D) an
13. This is not my bicycle. It is my _____ bicycle.
    A) _   B) father   C) father'   D) father's
14. Cats can wash _____ paws and fur.
    A) they   B) his   C) its   D) their
15. There is some milk. I'd like to drink _____.
    A) they   B) it   C) them   D) its
16. Terry is talking to two _____.
    A) women   B) woman   C) woman's   D) women's
17. All the _____ are following the man.
    A) policeman   B) woman   C) dog   D) children
18. There are many _____ on the shelf.
    A) paper   B) magazines   C) book   D) dust
19. I can see a lot of _____ outside the building.
    A) person   B) man   C) people   D) child
20. There is a lot of ice in _____ refrigerator.
    A) a   B) _   C) an   D) the
21. Give me two _____ cake, please.
    A) piece   B) pieces   C) slice   D) pieces of
22. _____ students are looking for their ball.
    A) That   B) Those   C) This   D) They
23. Please hand me _____ dictionary.
    A) that   B) these   C) it   D) them
24. A: Is this your suitcase?
    B: No, _____ is my suitcase.
    A) that   B) these   C) it   D) they
25. Bill and Jack are going to _____ house.
    A) they   B) their   C) them   D) his
26. My brother and I are hungry. _____ are thirsty too.
    A) They   B) He   C) We   D) Us
27. Take Janet and Anna to _____ rooms.
    A) her   B) them   C) they   D) their
28. Father is calling Ali and me. He wants _____.
    A) we   B) us   C) them   D) him
29. Serpil dropped some books, so I picked _____ up for her.
    A) them   B) it   C) its   D) they
30. The boys are holding up _____ hands.
    A) their   B) there   C) they   D) them

31. Seda and I washed _____ hands.
    A) us   B) our   C) ours   D) we
32. Look at that house. All _____ windows are broken.
    A) their   B) his   C) it   D) its
33. The sea is dirty. There is oil on _____.
    A) them   B) they   C) it   D) her
34. The girls can go home. They have finished _____ work.
    A) its   B) ours   C) hers   D) their
35. Do you want those shoes? I don't want _____.
    A) them   B) they   C) him   D) its
36. We called Allan. He came to _____.
    A) our   B) us   C) we   D) ours
37. Look at these books. Are _____ yours?
    A) they   B) them   C) this   D) that
38. We went to _____ seaside and played on the beach.
    A) a   B) the   C) an   D) _
39. Many tourists visit _____ Turkey.
    A) a   B) the   C) an   D) _
40. There is only _____ water in the glass. Please give me some more.
    A) many   B) much   C) a few   D) a little
41. There were not _____ people at the market yesterday.
    A) many   B) much   C) a few   D) a little
42. I put _____ sugar on the fruit. I do not like sugar very much.
    A) many   B) much   C) a few   D) a little
43. We can all get on the bus. There are only _____ passengers on it now.
    A) many   B) much   C) a few   D) a little
44. The policeman is holding the _____ right arm.
    A) robber   B) robber's   C) robbers   D) robbers'
45. It was my _____ watch.
    A) grandfathers   B) of grandfather
    C) grandfather's   D) grandfather
46. I can see the _____ bicycles.
    A) boys'   B) boys   C) boy   D) of the boys
47. I checked the answers. Two of _____ were wrong.
    A) it   B) its   C) them   D) they
48. The postman gave me two letters, so I gave _____ to my mother.
    A) them   B) its   C) they   D) it
49. The army lost the battle because _____ was not strong.
    A) they   B) them   C) it   D) its
50. My parents are coming. I'll open the door for _____.
    A) they   B) them   C) him   D) her
51. Is this radio _____?
    A) to you   B) of you   C) you   D) yours
52. Give that ball to Tom and me. It _____.
    A) is mine   B) is ours   C) is theirs   D) is our
53. We washed _____ and then had our dinner.
    A) myself   B) himself   C) herself   D) ourselves
54. You must learn to defend _____, Tom.
    A) yourself   B) yourselves   C) himself   D) ourselves
55. I cut _____ on that piece of wire.
    A) himself   B) myself   C) oneself   D) herself
56. I saw the girls, so I spoke to _____.
    A) she   B) her   C) they   D) them
57. You can have these books. _____ are too hard for me.
    A) It   B) They   C) Its   D) There
58. The rope was not very strong, so we did not use _____.
    A) them   B) its   C) they   D) it
59. The policeman spoke to my sister and me. He told _____ about the bridge.
    A) us   B) he   C) I   D) we

60. The bananas were not ripe, so we did not buy _____ .
    A) it	B) its	C) them	D) they
61. Please open the window. I can't reach _____ .
    A) him	B) her	C) them	D) it
62. My father listened to the news. He was very pleased with _____ .
    A) they	B) them	C) it	D) its
63. Can you tell me _____ best way to the station?
    A) a	B) an	C) the	D) _
64. She works as _____ clerk in a very large bank.
    A) a	B) an	C) the	D) _
65. Cyprus is _____ island in the Mediterranean.
    A) a	B) _	C) the	D) an
66. There is _____ excellent film on television this evening.
    A) a	B) _	C) the	D) an
67. In England there is a saying. "_____ apple a day keeps the doctor away". This means that apples keep you healthy.
    A) An	B) A	C) The	D) _
68. It is going to rain. I must buy _____ umbrella quickly.
    A) an	B) a	C) the	D) _
69. _____ other day I had a letter from my friend.
    A) A	B) An	C) _	D) The
70. They enjoyed _____ at the party.
    A) himself	B) themselves	C) them	D) _
71. My friend cut _____ when she was cooking.
    A) myself	B) himself	C) herself	D) her
72. Help _____ to some more coffee.
    A) yourself	B) myself	C) you	D) yours
73. I taught _____ to play the guitar. I've never had lessons.
    A) me	B) myself	C) himself	D) herself
74. The cow hurt _____ when it tried to get through the fence.
    A) himself	B) herself	C) itself	D) themselves
75. That machine is automatic. It runs by _____ .
    A) itself	B) it	C) themselves	D) herself
76. She is wearing _____ unusual dress .
    A) a	B) _	C) the	D) an
77. The car was traveling at more than 90 miles _____ hour when the accident happened.
    A) an	B) a	C) _	D) the
78. It's _____ time for us to go home.
    A) _	B) a	C) the	D) an
79. This cake was made with _____ butter so it should be good.
    A) a	B) _	C) the	D) an
80. His parents and _____ went to a concert last weekend.
    A) me	B) our	C) mine	D) us
81. I enjoyed _____ vacation. Did you enjoy _____ too ?
    A) me / yours	B) my / yourself	C) mine / yours	D) my / yours
82. _____ of the children is sick today.
    A) One	B) Fewer	C) Many	D) Some
83. Everyone is responsible for _____ own composition.
    A) his	B) their	C) nobody's	D) all their
84. I asked her _____ was on the phone.
    A) which	B) who	C) whom	D) whomever
85. I don't have _____ petrol in my car.
    A) some	B) no	C) any	D) lots of
86. He knows _____ about sports.
    A) nothing	B) anything	C) at all	D) something
87. The children ran screaming into _____ own rooms.
    A) his	B) they're	C) their	D) its
88. _____ of us are staying home.
    A) Some	B) A little	C) Couples	D) Much
89. There is _____ food in the house.
    A) none	B) some	C) no	D) any
90. Misfortunes like that aren't _____ fault.
    A) each	B) anybody	C) no one's	D) anybody's

91. This test is for students _____ native language is not English.
    A) that	B) whose	C) of whom	D) which
92. Please lend me _____ dollar.
    A) a	B) an	C) any	D) a few
93. Her mother wants _____ to wash the dishes.
    A) she	B) her	C) hers	D) she herself
94. Each of the children _____ given a box of chocolate.
    A) was	B) were	C) are	D) aren't
95. Everyone _____ in the room now.
    A) are	B) is	C) were	D) weren't
96. Everybody in the classroom _____ sleepy.
    A) is	B) has	C) are	D) weren't
97. They were here, but they have gone back to _____ apartment.
    A) they're	B) theirs	C) hers	D) their
98. A couple of the players _____ leaving now.
    A) is	B) are	C) was	D) were
99. All the businessmen _____ staying at the hotel.
    A) isn't	B) was	C) is	D) are
100. A: Whose coat it that?
     B : It's _____ .
     A) my daughter's	B) of my daughter
     C) to my daughter	D) of my daughter's
101. A: Do you have five dollars?
     B: No, I don't, but Oswald has _____ money with him.
     A) a lot of	B) much of	C) many	D) lots
102. Someone forgot an umbrella. I'll try to find out _____ it is.
     A) whom	B) of whom	C) whose	D) who
103. Most of the students _____ in the classroom now.
     A) were	B) was	C) are	D) is
104. A: May I help you?
     B: Yes, I want three _____ .
     A) cans beans	B) cans of beans	C) can of beans	D) can beans
105. Half of the salad _____ yours.
     A) is	B) were	C) are	D) aren't
106. "That coat is expensive, isn't it?" "Yes, it costs _____ ."
     A) very many	B) a lot of
     C) too much money	D) too many
107. A: Let's have lunch at the Sultan Restaurant.
     B: I can't. I didn't bring _____ money today.
     A) some	B) any	C) none	D) no
108. A: Would you like some coffee?
     B: Yes please, but just _____ .
     A) few	B) a few	C) little	D) a little
109. A: Whose house is that?
     B: It's _____ .
     A) the Taylor	B) the Taylors	C) the Taylor's	D) the Taylors'
110. Would you like _____ of this cake?
     A) some	B) a few	C) few	D) little
111. The boy has a knife. Don't let him cut _____ .
     A) himself	B) itself	C) herself	D) yourself
112. A: Do you read a lot?
     B: Yes, I read _____ books every year.
     A) a lot	B) a lot of	C) too much	D) very few
113. A: What is the matter with the baby?
     B: She is _____ hungry.
     A) a few	B) a little	C) little	D) few
114. My niece can't find her umbrella. Is this blue one _____ ?
     A) of her	B) his	C) mine	D) hers
115. He paid for an ice-cream for _____ .
     A) I	B) mine	C) my	D) me
116. A: Have you read this new book by Robert O'Neill?
     B: No, I haven't. _____ like to read it.
     A) He'd	B) She'd	C) We'd	D) I'd
117. A: Is Ashley's new dress blue?
     B: No, _____ is green. Helen's is blue.
     A) hers	B) her	C) mine	D) ours

118. If the police _____ arrive soon, they'll be too late.
    A) isn't   B) doesn't   C) don't   D) wasn't
119. He has two friends. That's not very _____ .
    A) few   B) many   C) much   D) a lot
120. There _____ some fish very near the coast.
    A) weren't   B) was   C) wasn't   D) were
121. The police _____ looking for a man who escaped from prison.
    A) is   B) was   C) are   D) has been
122. Plastic surgery doesn't cost _____ .
    A) a lot of   B) much   C) many   D) very few
123. He knows _____ about classical music.
    A) a lot   B) a lot of   C) many   D) a few
124. He is very honest. He is _____ than David.
    A) honest   B) more honestly   C) more honest   D) honestly
125. Some people think that life was _____ a hundred years ago.
    A) badly   B) worst   C) well   D) better
126. A bee is _____ than a bird.
    A) smaller   B) smallest   C) the smallest   D) small
127. A bicycle moves _____ than a car.
    A) slowly   B) fast   C) very slow   D) more slowly
128. Concorde is _____ other planes.
    A) the safest   B) safest   C) as safe as   D) safer
129. The news _____ bad.
    A) was   B) are   C) were   D) aren't
130. _____ everybody here?
    A) Are   B) Is   C) Were   D) Does
131. He has a lot of friends. He is _____ than Tony.
    A) much less friendly   B) less friendly
    C) the most friendly   D) more friendly
132. Other planes are not so _____ Concorde.
    A) more expensive   B) expensive
    C) expensive as   D) as expensive
133. The Boeing 747 makes _____ noise than Concorde.
    A) much   B) less   C) most   D) least
134. It was a very _____ journey.
    A) interesting   B) more interested
    C) interested   D) interestingly
135. Venus is the _____ planet to the earth.
    A) far   B) nearest   C) farther   D) near
136. What are the _____ sports in Turkey?
    A) interested   B) as interesting   C) better than   D) most popular
137. This team is bad. It plays _____ .
    A) badly   B) bad   C) not good   D) well
138. He runs _____ than David.
    A) better   B) slowly   C) well   D) very fast
139. Jim is 19 years old. Tony is 15. Jim is _____ than Tony.
    A) younger   B) oldest   C) older   D) youngest
140. He came late because he can't run _____ the others.
    A) as fast as   B) faster   C) the fastest of   D) quickly as
141. Bill swims _____ than Robert.
    A) faster   B) very badly   C) good   D) worst
142. How _____ butter do you need?
    A) much   B) many   C) few   D) a lot
143. Colombia is the _____ country in the world.
    A) as wet as   B) wetter than   C) wetter   D) wettest
144. He thinks that their team is the _____ one in Italy.
    A) better than   B) better   C) best   D) good
145. Who sings the _____ in your class?
    A) happy   B) more happily   C) happily   D) most happily
146. My father is sick. I'm worried about _____ .
    A) his   B) him   C) her   D) me
147. I saw Ann at the party but I didn't talk to _____ .
    A) hers   B) him   C) she   D) her

148. A: Why doesn't Pete have any teeth?
    B: Because he _____ brushed them.
    A) usually   B) often   C) frequently   D) never
149. Almost all of my father's teeth are good because he _____ brushes them.
    A) usually   B) ever   C) never   D) sometimes
150. Paul doesn't feel very good now. In six weeks he's going to feel _____ .
    A) bad   B) better   C) best   D) badly
151. Kate is _____ than any other actress on TV.
    A) as pretty   B) not pretty   C) prettier   D) the prettiest
152. It's very _____ . It's going to rain.
    A) cloudy   B) cloudless   C) clouds   D) more cloudy
153. They're good players, but we can beat _____ .
    A) their   B) they   C) theirs   D) them
154. Lisa likes to read _____ horoscope.
    A) hers   B) her   C) mine   D) yours
155. The kitchen looks beautiful. Have you cleaned _____ , Mary?
    A) its   B) it's   C) it   D) them
156. Sam and Bob went swimming with _____ sister, Lisa.
    A) their   B) theirs   C) hers   D) them
157. I think he was driving _____ .
    A) dangerous   B) less careful   C) hardly   D) carelessly
158. I don't know why she behaves so _____ sometimes.
    A) careless   B) badly   C) worse   D) strange
159. This bag isn't _____ it looks.
    A) as lightly as   B) lighter   C) as light as   D) the lightest
160. I haven't _____ been as fat as I'm now.
    A) ever   B) never   C) usually   D) sometimes
161. She is a _____ driver. She drives her car _____ .
    A) carelessly / careless   B) slowly / slow
    C) well / good   D) careful / carefully
162. He is _____ at painting. He paints _____ .
    A) bad / worse   B) bad / badly
    C) worse / bad   D) badly / the worst
163. She behaves _____ every day.
    A) good   B) strange   C) bad   D) worse
164. Not every American _____ English.
    A) doesn't speak   B) don't speak
    C) speak   D) speaks
165. Terry hasn't come to school _____ .
    A) almost   B) yet   C) just   D) never
166. Janet has _____ left home.
    A) just   B) yet   C) almost   D) ever
167. I can't find my homework _____ .
    A) nowhere   B) everywhere   C) anywhere   D) somewhere
168. I've looked for my book _____ but I can't find it.
    A) anywhere   B) somewhere   C) nowhere   D) everywhere
169. I'm sure it's here _____ .
    A) somewhere   B) everywhere   C) anywhere   D) nowhere
170. The bus is very _____ .
    A) quickly   B) slow   C) well   D) noisily
171. She listens to the teacher very _____ .
    A) good   B) carefully   C) better   D) careless
172. The author writes _____ .
    A) bad   B) good   C) well   D) careful
173. He plays the piano _____ than his father.
    A) very good   B) better   C) the best   D) very well
174. A: _____ did you go yesterday? B: I went to a restaurant.
    A) Where   B) Why   C) When   D) What
175. A: _____ didn't you phone him?
    B: I haven't got his telephone number.
    A) What   B) Why   C) When   D) How
176. A: _____ did you come to school?
    B: On the school bus.
    A) When   B) What   C) Why   D) How

177. Horses _____ drive automobiles.
    A) often   B) usually   C) never   D) sometimes
178. Students _____ shout in the library.
    A) always   B) often   C) frequently   D) seldom
179. Tourists _____ visit museums.
    A) often   B) seldom   C) never   D) rarely
180. The sun is _____ hot.
    A) always   B) often   C) usually   D) never
181. A: Do you ever fail tests?
    B: No. I _____ fail tests.
    A) sometimes   B) usually   C) never   D) ever
182. Susan fails all of her history exams. She _____ passes them.
    A) ever   B) never   C) often   D) seldom
183. Bob saw only one film last year. He _____ goes to the cinema.
    A) often   B) seldom   C) sometimes   D) never
184. David eats a lot of pears and apples. He _____ eats fruit.
    A) sometimes   B) rarely   C) ever   D) frequently
185. We can't do our homework. Can you help _____ ?
    A) we   B) me   C) them   D) us
186. I'm a strong player, he can't beat _____ .
    A) I   B) mine   C) me   D) him
187. Swimming is _____ excellent sport.
    A) __   B) a   C) an   D) the
188. Mike wants to watch TV _____ tonight.
    A) __   B) a   C) an   D) the
189. I'd like _____ bowl of soup, please.
    A) an   B) a   C) __   D) the
190. Can you see those two men? They are _____ policemen.
    A) __   B) the   C) a   D) an
191. My father hates _____ hospitals.
    A) __   B) the   C) a   D) an
192. _____ traffic in Turkey is bad.
    A) The   B) __   C) A   D) An
193. I'd like _____ ice-cream, please.
    A) a few   B) few   C) a little   D) a lot
194. A: How _____ apples did you eat?
    B: I ate _____ apples.
    A) many / a few   B) much / some
    C) many / a little   D) a lot of / a few
195. Carol writes well. Andy writes _____ than Carol. Mary writes _____ .
    A) good / the best   B) better / better
    C) good / better   D) better / the best
196. Maria sings _____ Julia.
    A) better than   B) as good as   C) as bad as   D) worse
197. Julia gets up early. Mike gets up _____ than Julia. Anderson gets up _____ .
    A) as early as / earlier   B) earlier / the earliest
    C) early / earlier   D) the earliest / earlier
198. She arrives at work much _____ than anyone else.
    A) earliest   B) the earliest   C) earlier   D) as early as
199. Robert works less _____ than Tom.
    A) carefully   B) careful
    C) careless   D) as carelessly as
200. Which student in the class works _____ ?
    A) more careful   B) less careful
    C) the most carefully   D) the least careful
201. Tom wasn't hungry, so he ate only _____ soup.
    A) a few   B) a little   C) a lot   D) little
202. Which is _____ place you've ever been to?
    A) more beautiful   B) as beautiful as
    C) the most beautiful   D) the most beautifully
203. David's sister is thin but not _____ Mike's.
    A) so thin   B) thinner   C) the thinnest   D) so thin as
204. _____ Amazon is _____ longest river in the World.
    A) The / the   B) __ / the   C) __ / __   D) The / __
205. _____ Lake Oregon is _____ large lake.
    A) The / a   B) __ / a   C) A / a   D) __ / __

206. He always drinks _____ tea with _____ milk.
    A) the / __   B) __ / __   C) a / __   D) a / a
207. A: Where is _____ coffee I bought?
    B: It's in _____ kitchen.
    A) __ / the   B) __ / __   C) the / the   D) the / a
208. They went to France by _____ plane but we're planning to go on _____ bus.
    A) the / the   B) __ / a   C) __ / __   D) a / a
209. My father has gone into _____ hospital for _____ operation.
    A) __ / __   B) __ / an   C) the / __   D) the / an
210. _____ ABC cinema is opposite _____ hospital.
    A) __ / the   B) The / __   C) An / the   D) The / the
211. We visited _____ Birmingham Museum _____ last year.
    A) __ / __   B) the / the   C) the / __   D) __ / the
212. _____ Atlantic Ocean is larger than _____ Mediterranean Sea.
    A) The / the   B) The / __   C) __ / __   D) __ / the
213. He is _____ vegetarian. He doesn't eat _____ meat.
    A) __ / __   B) a / __   C) a / __   D) the / __
214. There is _____ horror film on _____ TV tonight.
    A) a / the   B) an / __   C) __ / __   D) a / __
215. _____ earth moves round _____ sun.
    A) An / the   B) The / __   C) __ / the   D) The / the
216. What is _____ capital of _____ Switzerland?
    A) the / the   B) the / __   C) a / __   D) __ / a
217. _____ milk is good for you. Why don't you drink _____ milk in your glass?
    A) The / the   B) __ / the   C) __ / a   D) A / the
218. Tracey has been in _____ prison for a year. Last Sunday his father went to _____ prison to see him.
    A) __ / __   B) the / the   C) a / the   D) __ / the
219. _____ weather was terrible yesterday, so we spent all day at _____ home.
    A) The / __   B) __ / the   C) The / the   D) A / __
220. Good health is _____ than money.
    A) more important   B) very important
    C) as important as   D) the most important
221. Who is _____ footballer in Turkey?
    A) very good   B) a better   C) the best   D) best
222. The world's population is getting _____ every year.
    A) big   B) bigger   C) very big   D) the biggest
223. Janet is almost _____ her father. She's 176 cm and he is 178 cm.
    A) tall as   B) as tall as   C) taller than   D) a little shorter
224. Today isn't _____ yesterday.
    A) cold as   B) as sunny as   C) a little warmer   D) a lot hotter
225. Where is the _____ place in the world?
    A) hottest   B) as peaceful as
    C) more interesting   D) colder
226. I can't speak English as _____ my elder brother.
    A) good as   B) fluently as   C) better than   D) well
227. The plane arrived _____ than we'd expected.
    A) very late   B) later   C) as late as   D) lately
228. I've got very _____ money.
    A) few   B) a few   C) little   D) some
229. She's got _____ records of classical music.
    A) very much   B) very little   C) a few   D) plenty
230. A: Were there _____ passengers on the plane?
    B: Not _____ .
    A) a few / many   B) a lot of / many
    C) many / a few   D) a lot of / much
231. Only _____ Simon's friends went to the match, not _____ .
    A) a few / much   B) a few of / many
    C) some / much   D) a lot of / many
232. _____ I want is a cup of tea.
    A) All   B) Every   C) Whole   D) Everything
233. Listen to me. I can explain _____ .
    A) all   B) every   C) everything   D) whole

INTERMEDIATE UPPER-INTERMEDIATE 2
pronouns - adverbs - adjectives - determiners

Choose the best alternative.

1. The series of TV programs that has just finished _____ very useful.
   A) are   B) weren't   C) wasn't   D) were

2. A new means of detecting gold in travelers' luggage _____ recently been brought into use.
   A) has   B) have   C) is   D) was

3. Physics _____ a subject that has grown enormously in importance during this century.
   A) are   B) was   C) is   D) have been

4. A pack of cards _____ scattered over the table.
   A) is   B) are   C) were   D) have been

5. The few words he spoke _____ well chosen.
   A) is   B) was   C) were   D) wasn't

6. Some of his advice _____ funny.
   A) are   B) were   C) was   D) aren't

7. Let's get _____ lettuce.
   A) head of   B) a head of   C) head of a   D) a head

8. There were _____ snow on the car.
   A) two feet of   B) two feet   C) a two-feet   D) a foot

9. The poor _____ unable to look after themselves.
   A) are   B) is   C) was   D) has been

10. Two dozens of cows _____ lying peacefully in the shade.
    A) were   B) was   C) has been   D) is

11. The Town Council _____ against raising the rents of its houses.
    A) are   B) were   C) is   D) aren't

12. A _____ of vitamin C results in skin infections and slow healing.
    A) short   B) shortage   C) shorten   D) shortly

13. What is the difference in _____ between the Amazon and the Nile?
    A) long   B) wide   C) length   D) deep

14. How many of _____ are present in class?
    A) the girls   B) girls   C) girls'   D) the girl's

15. This isn't _____ bottle.
    A) a big enough   B) big enough
    C) big enough a   D) enough big a

16. We don't have _____ vacation.
    A) long enough   B) a long enough
    C) long enough a   D) enough a long

17. That's too _____ for swimming.
    A) a shallow lake   B) a lake shallow
    C) shallow a lake   D) lake shallow

18. It isn't _____ job for me to do alone.
    A) easy enough a   B) an easy enough
    C) enough an easy   D) an enough easy

19. That's too _____ for me to carry.
    A) heavy a suitcase   B) heavy suitcase
    C) a heavy suitcase   D) a suitcase heavy

20. It wasn't as clear _____ today.
    A) day as   B) day as is   C) a day as   D) is a day

21. I guess I didn't buy her _____ gift.
    A) expensive enough   B) an expensive enough
    C) expensive enough a   D) an enough expensive

22. You don't need as fast _____ she bought.
    A) a car as   B) car as one   C) car as   D) as a car

23. That isn't as busy _____ this one.
    A) as a corner   B) corner as a   C) a corner as   D) as a corner as

24. Rome isn't _____ as Milan is.
    A) as near to us   B) as near us   C) near us to   D) to us near

25. It cost me _____ than I thought it would.
    A) fewer   B) much   C) more   D) a lot

26. It took us _____ time to get here than usual.
    A) a lot   B) little   C) less   D) long

27. Do you walk _____, now that you live in a village?
    A) a lot of   B) little   C) very many   D) more

28. I have two boys, but _____ of them likes pop music.
    A) either   B) both   C) neither   D) none

29. I think my answer on the test was _____.
    A) the best possible choice   B) best beyond all the choices
    C) the better of all choices   D) the possible best choice

30. Not all English people _____ fish and chips.
    A) likes   B) doesn't like   C) don't like   D) like

31. It is very difficult to drive in _____.
    A) rush houred slow-moving traffic
    B) slow moving traffic of rush hour
    C) rush-hour slow moving traffic
    D) slow moving rush hour traffic

32. Nobody _____ objecting to the decision to closedown the factory.
    A) is   B) are   C) isn't   D) wasn't

33. The audience _____ listening to a Beethoven symphony.
    A) are   B) is   C) were   D) have been

34. Neither of these roads _____ to the airport.
    A) go   B) goes   C) don't go   D) doesn't go

35. Neither of the footballers _____ well.
    A) played   B) play   C) didn't play   D) do play

36. Neither of us _____ hungry.
    A) is   B) aren't   C) wasn't   D) weren't

37. Neither of them _____ interested in history.
    A) was   B) were   C) are   D) have been

38. All that glitters _____ not gold.
    A) are   B) is   C) were   D) aren't

39. Measles _____ an infectious disease.
    A) are   B) were   C) is   D) aren't

40. Neither Colin nor Digby _____ there.
    A) are   B) isn't   C) wasn't   D) was

41. Either your brakes or your eyesight _____ at fault.
    A) is   B) are   C) were   D) aren't

42. Either David or his parents _____ at home.
    A) is   B) are   C) was   D) aren't

43. It was a _____.
    A) thirty-minute show   B) TV show thirty minute
    C) thirty minutes TV show   D) TV show of thirty minute

44. We saw _____ last week.
    A) award winning of French film
    B) A French film award winning
    C) an award winning French film
    D) a film of French winning award

45. A: What is the characteristic of people who live alone?
    B: Some of them have tendency to talk to _____.
    A) himself   B) oneself   C) itself   D) themselves

46. This used to be the home _____.
    A) my old friend Terry   B) of my old friend Terry
    C) my old friend of Terry   D) my old friend Terry's

47. Terry is _____.
    A) an old friend of mine   B) an old friend's
    C) old friend of me   D) my friend's

48. Our family is quite _____ united family.
    A) _   B) a   C) the   D) an

49. The committee decided to award the prize to you and _____.
    A) I   B) we   C) his   D) me

50. They always give the available seats to _____ comes first.
    A) whoever   B) whom   C) whichever   D) whomever

51. She heard a sound _____ brought her heart into her mouth.
    A) what   B) who   C) whenever   D) which

52. A: Why are you sitting there?
    B: Frankly, there is _____ interesting to do.
    A) anything   B) nothing   C) something   D) nothing else

53. A: What do you think of politics?
    B: Oh, I find politics really _____.
    A) depress   B) depressing   C) depressed   D) be depressed

54. I agree. I get terribly _____ when people talk about politics.
    A) depression   B) depressing   C) depressed   D) be depressed

55. I find people who spit in the street _____.
    A) offensive   B) offensively   C) offender   D) offence

56. Since divorce became easier to obtain in Europe, the divorce rate has gone up _____.
    A) dramatic   B) dramatically   C) dramatics   D) to be dramatic

57. They play the guitar _____.
    A) beautiful   B) beautifully   C) very beautiful   D) a lot beautiful

58. I'm going to _____ next term, because the exams are getting closer.
    A) study hard   B) hardly study   C) study hardly   D) studying hard

59. The migration of the ducks was due to the _____ of colder weather.
    A) arriving   B) arrive   C) arrival   D) arrived

60. Since the old lady's husband died, she's been living _____.
    A) herself   B) on her own   C) by itself   D) by her

61. The weather changed _____. There was an _____ change in the weather.
    A) unexpected / unexpectedly   B) unexpectancy / unexpected
    C) unexpectedly / unexpected   D) unexpectedly / unexpectation

62. Her condition improved _____. There was a _____ improvement in her condition.
    A) steady / steadiness   B) steadiness / steady
    C) steady / steadily   D) steadily / steady

63. Fleming discovered penicillin _____.
    A) accidentally   B) accidental   C) accident   D) on accident

64. The _____ discovery of penicillin by Fleming in 1928 made the effective treatment of many bacterial diseases possible.
    A) accidental   B) by chance   C) accident   D) accidentally

65. The _____ of the forest will result in the ____ of many animal species.
    A) destruction / disappear   B) destruction / disappearance
    C) destructing / disappear   D) destruct / disappearance

66. A: Who told you they were moving?
    B: They told me _____.
    A) by themselves   B) on their own
    C) themselves   D) himself

67. The toes of her shoes are open. She always wears open _____ shoes.
    A) toe   B) toehold   C) tiptoe   D) toed

68. I didn't buy the sweater because it wasn't _____.
    A) washing   B) washable   C) washer   D) washed

69. My chest hurts _____ I breathe.
    A) whenever   B) whatever   C) wherever   D) whichever

70. Larry is a friendly person. He meets new people _____ he goes.
    A) whenever   B) whatever   C) wherever   D) whoever

71. You must do _____ he says.
    A) whomever   B) whatever   C) whenever   D) wherever

72. _____ solved that problem must be very smart.
    A) Whomever   B) Whatever   C) Who   D) Whoever

73. We haven't enjoyed _____ so much for years.
    A) myself   B) oneself   C) ourselves   D) us

74. Have you heard about Sally? She killed_____.
    A) itself   B) herself   C) on her own   D) by herself

75. Her children are too young to look after_____.
    A) them   B) by themselves
    C) on their own   D) themselves

76. That is a beautiful dress you're wearing. Did you make it_____?
    A) you   B) yourselves   C) yourself   D) herself

77. Many lakes and rivers are being _____ polluted.
    A) dangers   B) danger   C) dangerous   D) dangerously

78. Vitamins are produced synthetically in large quantities. This has made them _____ and _____ available to most of the population.
    A) cheaply / easily   B) cheap / easy
    C) cheap / easily   D) cheaply / easy

79. Several new dams are being constructed. This will help to control floods and provide water for_____.
    A) irrigate   B) irrigated   C) irrigating   D) irrigation

80. A problem of fundamental _____ for the developing countries is that of slowing down population growth.
    A) importance   B) vital   C) urgent   D) serious

81. "The Alfa River is 100 km long. The Beta River is 200 km long." means: The Beta River is _____ the Alfa River.
    A) shorter than   B) half as long as
    C) twice as long as   D) half as short as

82. "Lake Beta is 20 m deep. Lake Alfa is 80 m deep." means: The depth of Lake Beta is _____ that of Lake Alfa.
    A) one-fourth   B) four times   C) one-third   D) three times

83. The height of Mt Vesuvius is about 1200 m and that of Mt Blanc is 4800 m. Mt Blanc is the _____ of the two mountains. Its height is about _____ of Mt Vesuvius
    A) higher / one fourth that   B) highest / one fourth
    C) highest / four times that   D) higher / four times that

84. A: Will you boil the potatoes?
    B: Yes. I like _____ potatoes.
    A) boiling   B) boiled   C) boil   D) boiler

85. A: Shall I write the recipe?
    B: Yes, please. I need a _____ recipe.
    A) wrote   B) write   C) writing   D) written

86. We didn't have much money, so we stayed at a/an _____ hotel.
    A) luxurious   B) inexpensive   C) comfort   D) quietness

87. The nurse is very _____. She spoke _____.
    A) politely / politely   C) polite / politely
    B) politely / polite   D) polite / polite

88. Annie _____ lives in London. She moved to Bristol.
    A) any more   B) any longer   C) no longer   D) any better

89. I don't want to stay here _____.
    A) any more   B) no longer   C) never   D) no more

90. Are you _____ or do you want me to switch on the heating?
    A) warm enough   B) too warm
    C) pretty cold   D) quite cold

91. I've got _____ a lot to do today. I'm really busy.
    A) such   B) so   C) very   D) too

92. I've made _____ many mistakes in this letter. I think I'll type it again.
    A) such   B) so   C) very   D) too

93. The poor girl looked _____ _____.
    A) miserable / unhappy   B) miserably / unhappy
    C) miserable / unhappily   D) miserably / unhappily

94. This is not_____.
    A) a big enough van   B) big a enough van
    C) an enough big van   D) a van enough big

95. The boss looked at him _____.
    A) astonishing   B) unhappy   C) angrily   D) hardly

96. It was _____ hot in the train.
    A) extreme   B) intolerable   C) worse   D) terribly

97. She ran _____ to the telephone.
    A) very quick   B) hopefully   C) impatient   D) miserable

98. "Shall we go?" David looked _____ at Susan.
    A) happily   B) surprised   C) astonishing   D) glad

99. The child looked _____.
    A) neglected   B) a beggar   C) hunger   D) poverty

100. The world has gone _____.
    A) difficult   B) coldness   C) crazy   D) foregoing

101. The situation resolved itself _____ than I had expected.
    A) much more easily   B) the most easily
    C) a lot easier   D) much easier

102. The young man struck his boss and_____ killed him.
    A) sudden   B) accidentally   C) bloody   D) angry

103. Every child reacts _____ _____.
    A) rather / different   B) quite / differ
    C) a lot / difference   D) somewhat / differently

104. He stood up slowly and _____.
    A) with difficulty   B) too difficult
    C) very difficult   D) too much difficulty

105. A: I'm afraid we can expect _____ temperatures over the holiday.
    B: I'm _____ sorry about it.
    A) extreme / extremely   B) extremely / extremely
    C) extremely / extreme   D) extreme / extreme

106. I thought _____ of the idea.
    A) highly   B) extraordinary   C) clear   D) thorough

107. The supper looked _____.
    A) badly   B) delicious   C) well   D) awfully

108. It's _____ to use and _____ to carry than other computers.
    A) simple / easy   B) simply / easily
    C) simpler / easier   D) more simply / more easily

109. Yesterday the temperature was 20 degrees below zero. It hasn't been so cold this year. Yesterday was _____ day of the year.
    A) very cold   B) too cold   C) such a cold   D) the coldest

110. The Taylors have three sons. They are all clever, but Bill is outstanding. He is _____ of all.
    A) a lot clever   B) the least cleverest
    C) the cleverest   D) far much cleverer

111. There were _____ people in the queue that it was impossible to get on the bus.
    A) so many   B) so much   C) so few   D) such a lot

112. "There was a lot of traffic. The bus took half an hour to get from 5th Avenue to Broadway." means: _____.
    A) The traffic was heavy but we could get to Broadway in half an hour.
    B) The traffic was heavy. That is why we got to Broadway late.
    C) If the traffic hadn't been heavy, we could have got to Broadway earlier.
    D) There was so much traffic that it took us half an hour to get to Broadway.

113. She went _____ a sheet when she heard the news.
    A) as white as   B) as light as   C) as mute as   D) as deaf as

114. The _____ the problem _____ it is to find a solution.
    A) more complicated / hardly
    B) most complicated / the hardest
    C) more complicated / the harder
    D) more complicated / the hardest

115. _____ we leave, _____ we'll arrive.
    A) The sooner / the earlier   B) Sooner / earlier
    C) The soonest / the earliest D) The soonest / earlier

116. The car went _____ and _____ down the hill.
    A) very fast / dangerous   B) silently / safe
    C) faster / faster   D) later / slow

117. Although we hear about terrible air crashes, flying is still the _____ way to travel. It is much _____ than walking down the road!
    A) safer / a lot safe   B) safest / safer
    C) less safer / safer   D) least / a lot safer

118. A Volvo is expensive. A Mercedes is very much more expensive, but a Rolls Royce is _____.
    A) by far the most expensive   B) far more expensive
    C) a lot more expensive   D) too expensive

119. I backed three horses. Night Star ran _____. The Sun ran _____ and Wind ran the _____.
    A) bad / badly / worst   B) badly / worse / worst
    C) good / better / best   D) well / best / better

120. He has _____ Rolls Royce and _____ Audi 7 and _____ MG.
    A) a / a / a   B) an / an / a   C) a / an / an   D) the / _ / an

121. His father is _____ architect; quite _____ expert.
    A) an / a   B) the / __   C) an / an   D) _ / an

122. We'd booked the table for eight, and we got there fifteen minutes _____.
    A) very late   B) lately   C) too late   D) late

123. The food looked perfectly _____ to me.
    A) well   B) nicely   C) deliciously   D) good

124. He works so hard that there are _____ minutes in the day when he's not busy doing something.
    A) some   B) few   C) none   D) a few

125. _____ way is acceptable.
    A) Either   B) Both   C) None   D) All

126. There was _____ anyone could do to help.
    A) a little   B) none   C) few   D) little

127. They were all strangers to me. I'd met _____ of them before.
    A) either   B) neither   C) none   D) all

128. I suppose he wanted to get home as _____ as _____.
    A) quickly / possibly   B) quick / possibly
    C) quick / possible   D) quickly / possible

129. It seemed _____ that we would _____ have a crash.
    A) certain / final   B) certain / finally
    C) certainly / finally   D) certainly / final

130. I think _____ truthfulness is _____ greatest value.
    A) __ / a   B) _ / _   C) a / the   D) __ / the

131. Everything is fair in _____ love and _____ war.
    A) __ / the   B) a / _   C) _ / _   D) the / the

132. What _____ terrible news!
    A) a   B) an   C) the   D) _

133. In _____ past _____ most people lived by _____ agriculture.
    A) the / the / __   B) _ / _ / _
    C) _ / the / _   D) the / _ / _

134. In _____ fog or rain, you should reduce _____ speed.
    A) the / _   B) _ / _   C) __ / a   D) a / _

135. He's studying _____ chemistry at _____ university at _____ present.
    A) __ / the / the   B) a / the / _
    C) _ / _ / _   D) _ / a / the

136. She turned this way and that, admiring _____ in the mirror.
    A) himself   B) herself   C) hers   D) him

137. The couple in the flat upstairs are making _____ unpopular by shouting _____ at the top of their voices every night.
    A) themselves / each other   B) them / one another
    C) herself / one another   D) as / each other

138. She expresses _____ very clearly, though sometimes she doesn't remember _____ the right word.
    A) himself / _   B) herself / her   C) her / _   D) herself / _

139. They were fighting with _____ and making _____ cry, but then their mother told them to behave _____.
    A) each other / themselves / themselves
    B) _ / _ / themselves
    C) each other / each other / themselves
    D) each other / _ / yourselves

140. The story seems to be _____ _____.
    A) true / whole   B) wholly / true
    C) truly / wholly   D) wholly / truly

141. I make _____ mistakes much too _____.
    A) stupid / frequent   B) stupidly / frequently
    C) stupidly / frequent   D) stupid / frequently

142. It's _____ low season now, and _____ most of _____ hotels are half empty.
    A) the / _ / the   B) a / _ / the   C) _ / _ / the   D) a / _ / _

143. _____ great improvement in _____ patient's condition was brought about by _____ use of _____ newly developed antibiotic.
    A) _ / the / _ / a   B) A / the / _ / _
    C) The / the / _ / _   D) A / the / the / a

144. _____ abnormal behavior can be caused by _____ fear, but there are _____ other causes as well.
    A) _ / _ / _   B) An / _ / _   C) An / _ / the   D) The / _ / the

145. Only doctors and nurses can go into the Intensive Care Unit. _____ is allowed inside.
    A) Anybody else   B) No one else
    C) Anyone else   D) Someone else

146. You looked _____ this morning but you look a bit _____ now.
    A) depressing / happy   B) depressed / happier
    C) depressed / happily   D) depressingly / happily

147. The teacher looks _____.
    A) sadly   B) angry   C) angrily   D) nicely

148. The teacher is looking _____.
    A) good   B) angry   C) angrily   D) nice

149. The soup tastes _____.
    A) nicely B) well C) suspiciously D) wonderful

150. I tasted the soup _____.
    A) wonderful B) suspiciously C) happy D) haste

151. Poor people from rural areas are migrating to the cities to find work and _____ the circles of slum housing in many suburbs are growing larger.
    A) consequently B) however C) as D) whereas

152. Heart disease remains the _____ of diseases. It killed about 750,000 Americans last year, almost 40 percent of all _____.
    A) more danger / death B) most killing / die
    C) threateningly / deaths D) most deadly / deaths

153. He's got two very _____ daughters.
    A) alike B) like C) similar-looking D) much like

154. My brother is _____ yours.
    A) the same age B) younger
    C) as old D) the same age as

155. Of the two toys, the child chose _____ .
    A) the less expensive B) the least expensive
    C) the one most expensive D) the most expensive of them

156. The more we looked at the abstract painting, _____.
    A) we liked it less B) better we liked it
    C) the less we liked it D) it looked better

157. A: There is someone at the door.
    B: _____ it is, I don't want to see them.
    A) Whichever B) Whoever C) Wherever D) Whatever

158. _____ you say to her, she still keeps smiling.
    A) Whatever B) Whichever C) Whoever D) Whenever

159. _____ you go, I'll go with you.
    A) Whoever B) Whichever C) Wherever D) Whatever

160. You look very _____. What's the matter?
    A) unhappily B) happily C) unhappy D) angrily

161. It is _____ interesting book. It gives _____ wonderful picture of what _____ life was like in _____ Victorian times.
    A) an / _ / the / _ B) an / a / _ / _
    C) an / a / the / _ D) a / a / the / the

162. I have noticed that _____ English people do not seem to shake _____ hands as much as people do in _____ Turkey.
    A) the / __ / the B) _ / _ / _
    C) the / _ / _ D) _ / _ / the

163. Although _____ brown rice is better for you, _____ most people prefer _____ white rice.
    A) _ / _ / _ B) the / _ / the C) _ / the / _ D) the / the / the

164. Taylor knows a lot about _____ classical music. He seems to like _____ string quartets of Beethoven best.
    A) _ / the B) _ / _ C) the / _ D) a / the

165. I studied ____ modern history at ____ university. In ____ last year I specialized in ____ history of ____ Turkish Independence War.
    A) _ / the / _ / _ / the B) the / the / _ / a / a
    C) a / _ / the / _ / _ D) _ / the / the / the / the

166. Do you think that I could learn _____ Japanese _____ way _____ Japanese speak it?
    A) _ / the / _ B) a / the / _ C) _ / the / the D) the / a / the

167. They say that _____ Turkish language is particularly difficult for _____ Europeans.
    A) _ / the B) _ / _ C) the / _ D) the / the

168. _____ physical fitness can help you live longer, feel healthier and cope with _____ life's problems.
    A) The / _ B) _ / the C) A / _ D) _ / _

169. A coalition government was in _____ power in Britain during _____ Second World War.
    A) _ / _ B) the / the C) _ / the D) the / _

170. _____ Swiss Alps are _____ good place to go if you like ____ skiing. There is usually plenty of _____ snow during _____ winter months.
    A) _ / a / the / _ / _ B) the / _ / _ / the / _
    C) a / _ / a / _ / _ D) the / a / _ / _ / the

171. _____ cafeteria is located to _____ left of _____ Faculty of Engineering.
    A) A / the / _ B) A / _ / _
    C) The / the / the D) The / _ / the

172. _____ solar energy is produced in _____ central core of _____ sun.
    A) _ / the / _ B) _ / the / the
    C) The / the / the D) The / the / _

173. _____ Indian elephant is smaller than _____ African elephant.
    A) The / _ B) _ / _ C) An / the D) _ / a

174. At ___ beginning of _____ Pre-Cambrian era there was no life on ___ earth.
    A) _ / the / _ B) _ / _ / the C) the / _ / the D) the / the / the

175. __ ancient Egypt consisted of __ desert regions surrounding __ Nile.
    A) _ / the / the B) _ / _ / the C) The / the / _ D) The / _ / the

176. It came out many years later that _____ pair had been happily married since _____ beginning of _____ century.
    A) the / _ / _ B) _ / the / the C) the / the / _ D) the / the / the

177. It is not known whether _____ high blood pressure is due to _____ increased sodium intake.
    A) the / the B) _ / the C) _ / _ D) a / an

178. In _____ past, _____ air pollution was generally considered basically _____ urban phenomenon.
    A) the / _ / _ B) the / _ / an C) _ / _ / _ D) the / _ / _

179. Many statues and monuments have been eroded in _____ last fifty years than had been in _____ previous two hundred years.
    A) __ / the B) the / the C) _ / _ D) the / _

180. _____ price of sugar has risen by _____ penny _____ kilo.
    A) The / a / a B) _ / a / a C) The / _ / a D) _ / _ / a

181. _____ Finance Minister increased _____ tax on _____ petrol in his last budget.
    A) _ / the / the B) The / the / the
    C) _ / the / the D) The / the / _

182. Economic growth is not _____ sufficient condition on its own to ensure _____ increase in _____ economic welfare.
    A) _ / the / _ B) a / an / _ C) the / _ / _ D) a / an / the

183. _____ inflation is defined as _____ persistent rise in _____ general level of prices.
    A) The / _ / the B) _ / _ / the C) _ / a / the D) _ / a / _

184. In 1937 ____ explorer Sir Hubert Wilkens set out to search for ____ Soviet airman whose plane had gone down over ____ North Pole.
    A) _ / a / the B) the / the / _ C) _ / the / _ D) the / a / the

185. _____ protein can only be found in _____ meat.
    A) _ / _ B) The / _ C) _ / the D) A / _

186. When we read _____ lives of _____ great, we can catch their courage as if by _____ contagion.
    A) _ / the / _ B) the / the / _ C) the / the / a D) the / the / _

187. Pressure is inversely proportional to volume; _____ greater the volume _____ lower the pressure.
    A) the / the B) _ / _ C) _ / the D) the / _

188. ___ Macy is ___ department store on ___ 34th Street in New York.
    A) _ / a / _ B) The / a / _ C) _ / a / the D) The / a / the

189. ____ Queen of England lives in ____ Buckingham Palace in London.
    A) _ / _ B) _ / the C) The / _ D) The / the

190. _____ life is going to be ____ little easier in ____ economic terms.
    A) _ / a / _ B) The / a / _ C) _ / _ / _ D) _ / a / the

191. _____ problem of fundamental importance for _____ developing countries is that of slowing down _____ population growth.
    A) _ / the / _ B) A / the / _ C) A / _ / _ D) The / the / the

192. We won't get much benefit from _____ removal of _____ import duty from _____ European goods.
    A) the / _ / _ B) the / _ / the C) a / _ / _ D) the / _ / the

193. You won't reach to _____ back of _____ auditorium; so we'll have to use _____ amplifier.
    A) _ / the / an B) _ / the / _ C) the / the / an D) _ / the / the

194. ____ primary task of ____ development is to eliminate ____ poverty.
    A) The / _ / _ B) _ / the / _ C) The / _ / the D) A / the / the

195. In ____ kingdom of Nepal, high up in ____ Himalayas and within sight of ____ Mt. Everest ____ world's highest mountain, ____ way of life in ____ villages has hardly changed in hundreds of years.
    A) the / _ / the / the / _ / the B) the / the / _ / the / the / the
    C) the / the / the / the / the / _ D) _ / the / _ / _ / the / the

ELEMENTARY PRE-INTERMEDIATE 3 — tenses - passives

Choose the best alternative.

1. _____ you students?
   A) Do   B) Are   C) Am   D) Is

2. _____ the man at work?
   A) Am   B) Does   C) Are   D) Is

3. Who _____ an optician?
   A) is   B) are   C) am   D) does

4. Where _____ Mary and Julia going?
   A) is   B) are   C) do   D) does

5. She _____ working at the library.
   A) does   B) can   C) is   D) are

6. Frank and I _____ engineers.
   A) am   B) is   C) was   D) are

7. _____ there a hamburger on the table?
   A) Does   B) Are   C) Isn't   D) Is

8. There _____ any soup on the menu.
   A) aren't   B) are   C) isn't   D) is

9. There _____ any dentists in hospital.
   A) are   B) aren't   C) isn't   D) is

10. There _____ no chalk in the classroom.
    A) is   B) isn't   C) are   D) aren't

11. There _____ no surgeons in that hospital.
    A) isn't   B) are   C) aren't   D) was

12. _____ you have any other questions?
    A) Are   B) Aren't   C) Were   D) Do

13. How much milk _____ there?
    A) are   B) do   C) is   D) were

14. How many vacation days _____ there?
    A) are   B) do   C) is   D) was

15. What _____ those?
    A) is   B) was   C) are   D) have

16. _____ photocopiers.
    A) There's   B) They're   C) We're   D) It's

17. She _____ a sweater.
    A) has   B) have   C) is   D) are

18. We _____ a video.
    A) has   B) are   C) don't   D) have

19. David _____ a stereo.
    A) doesn't have   B) not have   C) don't have   D) don't

20. _____ she got a watch?
    A) Does   B) Have   C) Has   D) Was

21. _____ they have an old car?
    A) Are   B) Aren't   C) Have   D) Do

22. A: What is wrong with Lisa?
    B: She _____ a fever.
    A) is   B) has   C) does   D) got

23. I _____ a fever but I _____ have sore throat.
    A) have / don't   B) am / not   C) have / don't   D) don't / got

24. _____ Tom a test today?
    A) Does   B) Is   C) Is there   D) Has

25. Has he _____ flu?
    A) have   B) does   C) has   D) got

26. _____ Tom and Betty have measles?
    A) Are   B) Has   C) Do   D) Have

27. Sally has a headache but she _____ have a fever.
    A) not got   B) doesn't   C) don't   D) haven't

28. I _____ walk to school. I take a bus.
    A) am not   B) doesn't   C) don't   D) haven't

29. They like slow music. They _____ like fast music.
    A) don't   B) not   C) are   D) doesn't

30. My brother _____ like Indian films.
    A) isn't   B) don't   C) not   D) doesn't

31. She wants to go to the park. She _____ want to go to the zoo.
    A) doesn't   B) don't   C) isn't   D) wasn't

32. How much _____ an egg sandwich?
    A) does   B) is   C) are   D) were

33. How much _____ bananas?
    A) was   B) is   C) are   D) do

34. Peter has a pocket calculator. He _____ it almost every day.
    A) use   B) uses   C) using   D) is using

35. Mr. and Mrs. Taylor _____ to watch horror films.
    A) likes   B) doesn't like   C) like   D) not like

36. Robert reads sports magazines. He wants _____ them now.
    A) reads   B) is reading   C) read   D) to read

37. Tom _____ mathematics. He _____ it at school.
    A) like / study   B) likes / studies
    C) likes / studying   D) to like / studies

38. She _____ her homework at night.
    A) do   B) does   C) is doing   D) doing

39. It is 8.30. Let's _____ on the TV.
    A) to turn   B) turning   C) turn   D) is turning

40. They _____ never late.
    A) are   B) aren't   C) be   D) don't

41. Please _____ a bottle of ketchup, Janet.
    A) buys   B) buying   C) is buying   D) buy

42. Her hands are dirty. She'd _____ a bar of soap.
    A) like   B) likes   C) to like   D) liked

43. Let him _____ two tubes of toothpaste.
    A) to buy   B) buying   C) buy   D) buys

44. Peter _____ his hair now. He _____ it every day.
    A) is washing / washes   B) washes / is washing
    C) wash / is washing   D) is washing / wash

45. She is setting the table. They are _____ lunch.
    A) have   B) will have   C) go to have   D) going to have

46. A: Does his father play tennis?
    B: No. He _____ to learn.
    A) is going   B) plays   C) will   D) playing

47. It's dark in here. Can you _____ the light?
    A) turning on   B) turn on   C) to turn on   D) will turn on

48. We _____ to the theatre tonight.
    A) goes   B) are going   C) didn't go   D) went

49. She usually _____ breakfast at 7:30.
    A) have   B) eat   C) eats   D) having

50. I _____ Turkish folk music.
    A) listens to   B) likes   C) listen   D) like

51. My brother and I _____ football on Sundays.
    A) play   B) am playing   C) going to   D) likes

52. His sister _____ tennis on Wednesday.
    A) play   B) plays   C) go to   D) practice

53. George _____ television before bed.
    A) looks   B) going to watch   C) looking   D) watches

54. _____ you at home yesterday morning?
    A) Did   B) Were   C) Are   D) Will

55. He _____ late yesterday.
    A) be   B) were   C) is   D) was

56. They _____ ready in class yesterday.
    A) didn't   B) aren't   C) weren't   D) don't

57. Yesterday he _____ lunch in a restaurant.
    A) had   B) has   C) eats   D) is having

58. She _____ a sweater last Tuesday.
    A) buys   B) bought   C) is buying   D) will buy

59. He _____ his father yesterday morning.
    A) phones   B) is phoning   C) phone   D) phoned
60. I won't _____ to class tomorrow.
    A) come   B) came   C) comes   D) coming
61. She is going _____ shopping tomorrow.
    A) go   B) will go   C) to go   D) goes
62. I _____ home when it started to rain.
    A) was walking   B) have walked
    C) walk   D) will walk
63. He has _____ English for three years.
    A) learns   B) learn   C) been learning   D) learning
64. They _____ working here for six months.
    A) been   B) have been   C) would   D) will
65. How long _____ her ?
    A) do you know   B) you know
    C) you knew   D) have you known
66. Who _____ first this morning ?
    A) get up   B) gets up   C) got up   D) getting up
67. _____ Peggy happy ?
    A) Is   B) Do   C) Does   D) Can
68. John was singing while he _____ a bath.
    A) is taking   B) was taking   C) takes   D) take
69. When Peter talks, everybody _____.
    A) are listening   B) listened   C) listen   D) listens
70. Policemen often _____ traffic.
    A) directing   B) is directing   C) directs   D) direct
71. Buses _____ every ten minutes.
    A) runs   B) is going   C) run   D) has gone
72. Good children always _____ their parents.
    A) obey   B) obeys   C) obeying   D) has obeyed
73. He usually _____ coffee but today he _____ tea.
    A) drank / is drinking   B) drunk / drinks
    C) drinks / is drinking   D) drinks / was drinking
74. I always buy lottery tickets but I never _____ anything.
    A) don't win   B) had won   C) won   D) win
75. The police _____ the thief yet.
    A) haven't caught   B) didn't catch
    C) hasn't caught   D) don't catch
76. I _____ him for five years. I don't know where he is.
    A) didn't see   B) haven't seen
    C) don't see   D) not to see
77. He _____ his leg in a skiing accident last winter.
    A) has broken   B) broke   C) breaks   D) was broken
78. Have you seen my ball-point pen anywhere? I _____ for it for ten minutes.
    A) looked   B) was looking
    C) am looking   D) have been looking
79. I _____ to the dentist tomorrow.
    A) went   B) have gone   C) am going   D) going
80. She _____ an operation next Tuesday.
    A) had   B) have   C) is having   D) has had
81. The Prime Minister _____ on TV tonight.
    A) is speaking   B) spoken   C) had spoken   D) speak
82. He is _____ the car.
    A) has washed   B) will wash   C) washed   D) going to wash
83. I _____ this day all my life.
    A) am remembering   B) will remember
    C) remembered   D) have remember
84. I hope I _____ it.
    A) found   B) will find   C) am finding   D) finding
85. _____ me with my suitcase, please ?
    A) Did you help   B) Are you going to help
    C) Are you helping   D) Will you help
86. This time tomorrow I _____ on a beach in Antalya.
    A) lie   B) am lying   C) will be lying   D) have been lain

87. We _____ play basketball without a ball.
    A) can't   B) needn't   C) could   D) doesn't
88. Does he _____ go to school at eight ?
    A) must   B) should   C) has to   D) have to
89. Tom gets up early, but Sarah _____.
    A) didn't   B) isn't   C) does   D) doesn't
90. My father _____ an apple now. He _____ an apple every day.
    A) eating / eats   B) eats / is eating
    C) ate / is eating   D) is eating / eats
91. John _____ the guitar, but he _____ it now.
    A) is playing / doesn't play   B) plays / doesn't play
    C) plays / wasn't playing   D) plays / isn't playing
92. Teresa _____ to the theatre, but Jack doesn't.
    A) want to go   B) wants to go   C) can go   D) wanted to go
93. Mike likes to play tennis. So _____.
    A) is Fred   B) does Fred   C) Fred does   D) can Fred
94. Two wrongs _____ make a right.
    A) doesn't   B) haven't   C) isn't   D) don't
95. Please go away, I _____ to finish my I work.
    A) try   B) am trying   C) was trying   D) have tried
96. He always _____ while he _____ a bath.
    A) sang / is having   B) sing / has
    C) sings / is having   D) is singing / has
97. I _____ like the film on TV last night.
    A) didn't   B) don't   C) am not   D) haven't
98. He likes cowboy films, but I _____.
    A) don't   B) didn't   C) am not   D) haven't
99. She likes science fiction films, and so _____.
    A) am I   B) do I   C) I do   D) I have
100. How many brothers _____ you got ?
    A) do   B) has   C) have   D) did
101. I don't think he _____ pass.
    A) won't   B) doesn't   C) would   D) will
102. Does she _____ some ice ?
    A) wanted   B) want   C) wants   D) to want
103. Who _____ play tennis with me ?
    A) wants   B) want to   C) wants to   D) to want
104. I don't _____ study, but I have to.
    A) want to   B) want   C) to want   D) wanted
105. The weather _____ sunny yesterday morning.
    A) is   B) was   C) are   D) did
106. We usually _____ table tennis every Saturday.
    A) to play   B) plays   C) will play   D) play
107. Drive carefully. It _____ heavily this morning.
    A) snows   B) snowing   C) snow   D) is snowing
108. You are hungry. Why _____ you eating ?
    A) aren't   B) don't   C) won't   D) didn't
109. Sally _____ her hair when the doorbell rang.
    A) will be washing   B) washed
    C) has washed   D) was washing
110. The planet Mercury _____ round the sun every eighty-eight days.
    A) traveled   B) is traveling   C) travel   D) travels
111. The traffic _____ very slowly on the motorway today. Workmen _____ the road.
    A) moves / were repairing   B) is moving / repaired
    C) are moving / are repairing   D) was moving / are repairing
112. James Dean _____ a sports car when he died.
    A) drove   B) will drive   C) was driving   D) is driving
113. The plane _____ at 11.45.
    A) leaves   B) leave   C) are leaving   D) to leave
114. Does she _____ to Mozart ?
    A) listening   B) listens   C) listen   D) listened
115. Excuse me. Do you know where I can _____ a color film ?
    A) buy   B) buying   C) to buy   D) bought

116. _____ you free on Saturday evening?
    A) Do B) Did C) Are D) Was

117. _____ I talk to you in a few minutes?
    A) Am B) Can C) Was D) Do

118. I didn't _____ any money yesterday.
    A) spent B) spend C) spending D) was spending

119. What time are you _____ to school tomorrow?
    A) go B) will go C) going D) went

120. Fifty million years ago there _____ no people.
    A) were B) was C) are D) weren't

121. He _____ an aspirin half an hour ago.
    A) takes B) is taking C) took D) taken

122. The Nile _____ into the Mediterranean Sea.
    A) flowing B) flowed C) is flowing D) will flow

123. The weather forecast says it _____ tomorrow.
    A) was snowing B) is going to snow
    C) snows D) snowed

124. _____ he married?
    A) Does B) Is C) Were D) Did

125. A: _____ tennis this afternoon?
    B: Yes, I am.
    A) Will you play B) Are you playing
    C) Did you play D) Were you playing

126. A: We visited the Hitit Museum.
    B: Where else _____?
    A) have you visited B) did you visit
    C) do you visit D) you visited

127. A: Was he waiting for you?
    B: No. He _____ still _____.
    A) is / working B) will / work
    C) was / working D) were / working

128. It's a nice day, _____?
    A) isn't it B) doesn't it C) was it D) wasn't it

129. The war _____ in 1939.
    A) start B) will start C) is starting D) started

130. The Government has _____ the price of petrol.
    A) increasing B) increased C) increases D) is increasing

131. A: _____?
    B: Not yet.
    A) Have you read today's paper?
    B) Did you sleep well last night?
    C) Do you usually get up early?
    D) Are you early?

132. Why _____ the little girl crying?
    A) is B) did C) are D) does

133. It's _____ rain soon.
    A) going to B) goes C) gone D) to go

134. How long will she _____ in London?
    A) staying B) stays C) to stay D) stay

135. You will _____ tired after work.
    A) being B) are C) be D) been

136. I'd like _____ out tonight.
    A) going B) be going C) go D) to go

137. I _____ because I had forgotten my homework.
    A) will apologize B) apologized
    C) am apologizing D) have apologized

138. Is it going _____ sunny tomorrow?
    A) be B) to be C) will be D) being

139. You _____ too fast. Please slow down.
    A) are driving B) drive C) drove D) were driving

140. The train leaves at 4.18, _____ it?
    A) isn't B) does C) doesn't D) didn't

141. I am _____ to some piano music.
    A) listen B) listened C) listening D) will listen

142. I _____ phone you after lunch.
    A) am B) was C) going to D) will

143. A: Where is Anna?
    B: She's just _____.
    A) leaves B) left C) leaving D) to leave

144. Prophet Mohammed _____ born in 570.
    A) did B) is C) to be D) was

145. He _____ in 632.
    A) dies B) dying C) was dying D) died

146. Don't _____ during the exam.
    A) talking B) talk C) to talk D) talked

147. What nationality _____ she?
    A) is B) does C) are D) were

148. He _____ a packet of cigarettes a day.
    A) smoking B) were smoking
    C) smokes D) smoke

149. She _____ shopping every weekend.
    A) goes B) go C) were going D) to go

150. Can I turn off the TV? You _____ it.
    A) don't watch B) aren't watching
    C) didn't watch D) aren't watched

151. _____ you have a good time last summer?
    A) do B) did C) Will D) Were

152. When I saw her, she _____ reading.
    A) was B) is C) will be D) were

153. Who _____ to Janet?
    A) is he speaking B) was speaking
    C) did he speak D) was he speaking

154. Who _____ Janet _____ to?
    A) is / speaking B) does / speaks
    C) did / spoke D) were / speaking

155. _____ you often in a hurry?
    A) Are B) Did C) Do D) Was

156. _____ he usually eat very quickly?
    A) Is B) Was C) Do D) Does

157. Last week _____ terrible for me.
    A) did B) were C) was D) had

158. _____ you got a dishwasher?
    A) Did B) Were C) Had D) Have

159. A: They are not very fond of chips.
    B: Neither _____.
    A) do I B) am I C) I am D) I don't

160. A: She is studying now.
    B: So _____.
    A) is her brother B) has her brother
    C) her brother is D) was her brother

161. I don't like maths. I don't like science, _____.
    A) too B) either C) so D) neither

162. Galatasaray _____ the championship last year.
    A) was winning B) going to win
    C) won D) had won

163. What will you _____ this time tomorrow?
    A) doing B) are doing C) did D) be doing

164. Water _____ at 100 centigrade degrees.
    A) is boiling B) boils C) boil D) was boiling

165. She _____ the prize because she wrote the best composition.
    A) won B) to win C) is winning D) wins

166. Sally _____ because she doesn't want to be late.
    A) hurry B) is hurrying
    C) is going to hurry D) was hurrying

167. We've _____ in Ankara since 1992.
    A) be B) being C) to be D) been

168. He's already _____ his homework.
    A) done B) doing C) does D) did

169. She _____ in Spain for over three years.
A) has been   B) be staying   C) is living   D) travels

170. I went to the gym and _____ volleyball.
A) will play   B) played   C) have played   D) were playing

171. I _____ to learn a lot of new words.
A) am going   B) will   C) will be   D) going

172. They _____ basketball when I saw them.
A) were playing   B) played   C) play   D) are playing

173. A: Where _____ at three?
B: I was at the library.
A) have you gone   B) was he   C) were you   D) you saw him

174. They will be here when _____.
A) he is coming   B) you telephoned   C) your father arrives   D) she will be there

175. I always brush my teeth before I _____ to bed.
A) don't go   B) will go   C) am going   D) go

176. I'll go out after I _____ reading this detective story.
A) am finishing   B) finished   C) finish   D) will finish

177. It is a fine day. The sun _____.
A) was shining   B) is shining   C) shines   D) shining

178. _____ you ever _____ Japanese food?
A) Did / eat   B) have / eaten   C) Have / ate   D) Do / eaten

179. A: Shall we go out?
B: No, it _____.
A) is snowing   B) snows   C) was snowing   D) snowed

180. It _____ snowing for five hours.
A) has been   B) is   C) was   D) will be

181. My brother never _____ football when he was younger.
A) didn't play   B) played   C) doesn't play   D) will play

182. A: Do you mind if I _____ your dictionary?
B: No, that's all right.
A) will use   B) used   C) use   D) to use

183. She always _____ about her weight when she was younger.
A) worries   B) worry   C) will worry   D) worried

184. It _____ cloudy tomorrow.
A) was   B) to be   C) will be   D) has been

185. She is going _____ a dentist.
A) being   B) to be   C) be   D) will be

186. A: Would you like a cigarette?
B: No, thanks _____.
A) I am not smoking   B) I don't smoke   C) I didn't smoke   D) I haven't smoked

187. I'm tired, so I _____ to bed.
A) went   B) have gone   C) am going   D) had gone

188. When Fred _____ happy he sings.
A) will be   B) was   C) is   D) has been

189. Has he ever _____ to Paris ?
A) been   B) were   C) was   D) go

190. A: Where is your mother?
B: She's _____ to the dry-cleaner's.
A) been   B) went   C) gone   D) goes

191. We _____ to a new flat next week.
A) are moving   B) moved   C) to move   D) moving

192. I'll wait until he _____.
A) arrives   B) will arrive   C) is arriving   D) arrived

193. He's been _____ since nine-thirty.
A) studies   B) studied   C) study   D) studying

194. How long _____ you _____ learning English ?
A) do / do   B) did / do   C) have / been   D) have / done

195. What _____ UNICEF mean ?
A) is   B) does   C) do   D) was

196. When they _____ she was vacuuming the house.
A) arrive   B) will arrive   C) were arriving   D) arrived

197. This time tomorrow I _____ visiting my parents.
A) was   B) will be   C) have been   D) been

198. How many people _____ to the meeting yesterday?
A) come   B) did come   C) came   D) are coming

199. When she _____ her room, she broke her reading lamp.
A) was cleaning   B) is cleaning   C) cleaned   D) were cleaning

200. Our friends are going to be late, _____?
A) aren't we   B) do we   C) are they   D) aren't they

201. Let's _____ this crossword puzzle together.
A) do   B) doing   C) did   D) to do

202. It is very cloudy. I am sure it's _____.
A) rained   B) rains   C) going to rain   D) will rain

203. I _____ the doctor next week.
A) am seeing   B) saw   C) have seen   D) had seen

204. John is eating too much. _____.
A) He is going to get fat   B) He spends a lot of money   C) Give him some more   D) He was very thin

205. He _____ never _____ a camel before he came to Turkey.
A) has / seen   B) did / see   C) will / see   D) had / seen

206. A : When are you going to do your homework?
B : I've _____ done it.
A) yet   B) still   C) already   D) soon

207. My young brother _____ three centimeters this month.
A) grew   B) has grown   C) is growing   D) grown

208. I arrived at he bus station late yesterday. When I got there, my bus _____.
A) left   B) has left   C) leaves   D) had left

209. When I _____ home my father wasn't there. He had gone out.
A) arrive   B) had arrived   C) arrived   D) will arrive

210. I'll phone Mike as soon as I _____ any news.
A) will get   B) get   C) got   D) had got

211. A: Where is Ken?
B: I think he _____ a bath.
A) was having   B) has   C) is having   D) took

212. Sarah _____ Simon for a long time.
A) has known   B) knew   C) doesn't know   D) didn't know

213. Robert de Niro began acting in the 1970s. He has been _____ for about 35 years.
A) acted   B) acting   C) acts   D) to act

214. It started raining on Saturday. It hasn't _____ since then.
A) stopping   B) stops   C) had stopped   D) stopped

215. When did Fatih Sultan conquer Istanbul? Istanbul _____ by Fatih Sultan in 1453.
A) was conquered   B) conquered   C) be conquered   D) is conquered

216. Turkish is _____ in Turkey.
A) speaks   B) spoke   C) spoken   D) be spoken

217. A: Who wrote "War and Peace"?
B: It _____ by Leo Tolstoy.
A) is written   B) wrote   C) writes   D) was written

218. That film has _____ on TV.
A) showed   B) been shown   C) shown   D) showing

219. She _____ to hospital yesterday.
A) was taken   B) took   C) is taken   D) can take

220. They grow coffee in Brazil. Coffee is _____ in Brazil.
A) grown   B) grows   C) grew   D) grow

221. A: Where did the gunman shoot President Kennedy?
B: He _____ in Dallas, Texas.
A) is shot   B) shoots   C) was shot   D) been shot

222. I'll do everything. Everything _____ done.
A) is   B) was   C) has   D) will be

223. America _____ in 1492.
    A) discovered   B) was discovered
    C) has been discovered   D) is discovered

224. Many cameras _____ in Japan.
    A) is made   B) was made   C) are made   D) make

225. The English test _____ yesterday.
    A) given   B) gave   C) is given   D) was given

226. A: Did Alexander Graham Bell invent the telephone?
    B: Yes, it _____ invented by him.
    A) was   B) has been   C) is being   D) to be

227. French _____ in our school.
    A) isn't taught   B) doesn't teach
    C) taught   D) teaches

228. The 1990 World cup for football _____ in Italy.
    A) was played   B) was being played
    C) has been played   D) will be played

229. The computer _____ delivered tomorrow.
    A) are   B) was   C) has   D) will be

230. Experiments are often _____ by scientists.
    A) do   B) done   C) doing   D) been

231. A patient _____ by a doctor.
    A) examined   B) is examining
    C) will examine   D) is examined

232. The electric light bulb _____ by Edison.
    A) invented   B) invents   C) is invented   D) was invented

233. The history exam _____ given next Friday.
    A) was   B) will be   C) were   D) are

234. The letter _____ by the secretary now.
    A) is being typed   B) typing
    C) typed   D) types

235. Television _____ by millions of people every day.
    A) watches   B) watched   C) is watched   D) are watched

236. Why _____ you learning English ?
    A) will   B) are   C) have   D) did

237. Julia _____ feeling well this morning.
    A) aren't   B) doesn't   C) didn't   D) wasn't

238. I _____ tired today.
    A) feeling   B) is feeling   C) were feeling   D) felt

239. A: I'd like a salad.
    B: So _____.
    A) I will   B) would I   C) did I   D) am I

240. How long has he _____ that old car?
    A) had   B) buy   C) sold   D) have

241. _____ there a toilet upstairs ?
    A) Is   B) Does   C) Will   D) Did

242. My English is _____ better.
    A) gets   B) will get   C) get   D) getting

243. A: Why are you late?
    B: I _____ on the wrong bus.
    A) get   B) got   C) am getting   D) will get

244. The French Revolution _____ about 200 years ago.
    A) had happened   B) happen
    C) happening   D) happened

245. A: Who discovered penicillin?
    B: _____?
    A) Penicillin was discovered by him.
    B) It was discovered by Alexander Fleming
    C) It has been discovered by Fleming
    D) Alexander Fleming may discover penicillin

246. A: Was Kennedy killed by Lee Harvey Oswald?
    B: Yes, _____.
    A) Lee Harvey Oswald was killed by Kennedy
    B) Lee Harvey Oswald killed Kennedy
    C) He is killed by Lee Harvey Oswald
    D) Kennedy killed Lee Harvey Oswald

247. Who _____ next to you now?
    A) sits   B) is sitting   C) sit   D) sitting

248. A: Can I speak to Mr. Rich?
    B: I'm sorry, he _____.
    A) is sleeping   B) sleeps   C) slept   D) was sleeping

249. Lucy often _____ red.
    A) wear   B) is wearing   C) worn   D) wears

250. A: How was the party?
    B: Very nice but Thomas _____ too much.
    A) drinks   B) drunk   C) drink   D) drank

251. We can't eat rice before it's _____.
    A) cooked   B) cooking   C) cooks   D) to cook

252. You cannot take good photographs when it _____ cloudy.
    A) was   B) been   C) be   D) is

253. It was raining when I _____ the house this morning.
    A) leave   B) leaving   C) left   D) have left

254. Bread _____ from wheat.
    A) is made   B) made   C) are made   D) was made

255. She _____ to the market just now.
    A) goes   B) went   C) is going   D) going

256. I saw you on the bus yesterday. Where _____ you _____?
    A) are / going   B) did / went   C) will / go   D) were / going

257. Our house _____ painted at the moment.
    A) was   B) is   C) is being   D) has been

258. She's going _____ an operation.
    A) having   B) to have   C) will have   D) has

259. _____ the meat smell bad?
    A) Is   B) Was   C) Does   D) Do

260. I _____ them since Tuesday.
    A) I didn't see   B) don't see   C) haven't seen   D) hasn't seen

261. A: How did he die? B: He _____ in the earthquake.
    A) killed   B) had killed   C) was killed   D) is killed

262. A: Do they allow smoking?
    B: No, smoking _____ inside the terminal building.
    A) doesn't allow   B) wasn't allowed
    C) hasn't been allowed D) is not allowed

263. Are girls _____ the same opportunities as boys?
    A) given   B) be given   C) to be given   D) gave

264. The road has _____ to traffic.
    A) been closed   B) been closing
    C) closing   D) be closed

265. Has the country _____ by pollution ?
    A) be spoiled   B) spoiled
    C) been spoiling   D) been spoiled

266. How many languages _____ in Switzerland?
    A) spoken   B) are spoken   C) are speaking   D) spoke

267. The first pyramids of Egypt _____ around 3000 BC.
    A) was built   B) built   C) were built   D) were building

268. Walt Disney _____ the cartoon character Mickey Mouse.
    A) created   B) was created
    C) had been created D) has been created

269. This problem _____ at the last meeting.
    A) was discussed   B) has been discussed
    C) discussed   D) will be discussed

270. A: Who does the ironing in your family?
    B: It _____ by grandmother.
    A) is being done   B) is done
    C) has been done   D) was done

271. A: Are they _____ down that old house?
    B: Yes, it is being pulled down.
    A) pulling   B) pulled   C) have pulled   D) were pulling

272. A: _____ they sell their car ?
    B: Yes, their car will be sold.
    A) Will   B) Do   C) Did   D) Are

273. A: Who is going to clean the office?
B: _____.
A) My mother cleaned it
B) It was cleaned
C) It's already been cleaned
D) It is not clean

274. A: _____?
B: Tomorrow.
A) Where was the old man taken
B) When was he arrested
C) Why is he going to Istanbul
D) When will the hospital be opened

275. A: Water the plants, please.
B: _____.
A) Yes, I did
B) They were watered
C) They've already been watered
D) No, not yet.

276. A man _____ by the police last night.
A) arrested
B) was arrested
C) was arresting
D) were arrested

277. The Mona Lisa _____ by Leonardo da Vinci.
A) painted
B) were painted
C) is painted
D) was painted

278. A new motorway _____.
A) is being built
B) was building
C) have already been built
D) is building

279. Someone has opened this letter. This letter _____.
A) have been opened
B) has been opened
C) was opened
D) has opened

280. When _____ television _____?
A) did / invent
B) was / invent
C) was / invented
D) is / invented

281. I _____ you were in hospital.
A) don't know
B) didn't know
C) am not known
D) wasn't known

282. The doctor says he _____ a few weeks' rest.
A) needs   B) is needed   C) need   D) needed

283. She _____ married next month.
A) has got
B) is going to get
C) has been
D) had got

284. One of my uncles _____ just _____.
A) have / died   B) has / died   C) was / died   D) is / dying

285. I _____ never _____ such a beautiful house.
A) am / seen   B) has / seen   C) had / seen   D) have / seen

286. The dentist _____ my tooth out the other day.
A) will take   B) is taking   C) took   D) was taken

287. We played tennis until _____.
A) school opens
B) the weather gets cold
C) we got tired
D) it starts raining

288. When he _____ angry he always starts shouting at everyone.
A) is getting   B) gets   C) got   D) will get

289. The book, Gone With the Wind, _____ by Margaret Mitchell.
A) wrote   B) was written   C) are written   D) were written

290. How long ago _____?
A) does she study in the library
B) will she stay in Paris
C) did they leave
D) have you known her

291. The restaurant _____ very crowded. They couldn't find anywhere to sit down.
A) was   B) is   C) were   D) has been

292. They missed their plane because they _____ home early.
A) came   B) didn't get   C) called   D) didn't leave

293. Who _____ you they were moving?
A) tell   B) told   C) tells   D) was told

294. A: When ____ the next train ____ for Liverpool? B: In eight minutes.
A) did / leave   B) has / left   C) had / left   D) does / leave

295. It is the best holiday I _____ ever _____.
A) have / had
B) am / having
C) had / had
D) was / having

INTERMEDIATE / UPPER-INTERMEDIATE 4 — tenses - passives

Choose the best answer.

1. When I last talked to him, he _____ English.
   A) studies
   B) study
   C) was studying
   D) studied

2. I met her at yesterday's party, but I _____ her by sight for years before that.
   A) had known
   B) have known
   C) will have known
   D) had been known

3. By 2010, scientists surely _____ a cure for cancer.
   A) are discovering
   B) have been discovered
   C) will have discovered
   D) had discovered

4. Since the day he _____ ill he _____ a lot of reading.
   A) was / had done
   B) is / has done
   C) was / has done
   D) is / has been done

5. A: What's the time?   B: I'm sorry I _____. My watch _____.
   A) can't tell / stopped
   B) didn't know / stopped
   C) don't know / has stopped
   D) don't know / had stopped

6. He _____ in the library every night for the last two months.
   A) would be studying
   B) will have studied
   C) has been studied
   D) has been studying

7. Last Sunday we ____ out of the house where we ____ for five years.
   A) had moved / lived
   B) have moved / had lived
   C) moved / had lived
   D) will move / have lived

8. We spent hours talking about what we _____ since we left school.
   A) have done
   B) had been doing
   C) have been doing
   D) were doing

9. They _____ married but in the end they changed their mind.
   A) are going to get
   B) will have been
   C) were going to get
   D) had been

10. A: Would you like me to give Mike a message for you?
    B: Oh, I don't want to trouble you.
    A: It's no trouble, really. I _____ Mike tomorrow anyway.
    A) am seeing
    B) saw
    C) have seen
    D) would see

11. When I counted my change I realized they _____ me $ 3 too much.
    A) gave
    B) had given
    C) have given
    D) had been given

12. When he'd counted his change he _____ it in his pocket.
    A) was put
    B) put
    C) had put
    D) has put

13. As soon as she _____ out of bed she got dressed.
    A) had got
    B) gets
    C) has got
    D) would get

14. In a fortnight's time they _____ their exams.
    A) have taken
    B) will have taken
    C) will have been taken
    D) had taken

15. They were very rude to us. We _____ there again.
    A) won't go
    B) hadn't gone
    C) didn't go
    D) wouldn't go

16. In about forty years' time we'll probably _____ on pills.
    A) be living
    B) have been living
    C) have been lived
    D) have lived

17. A: Why have you set your alarm clock to go off at 5.30?
    B: Because I _____ then. I have to catch the early train.
    A) get up
    B) was going to get up
    C) am going to get up
    D) have got

18. A: I've planned my future for the next five years.
    B: That is very clever of you. What _____ when you retire?
    A) will you do
    B) are you going to do
    C) have done
    D) do you do

19. You'll feel a lot better after you _____ a rest.
    A) had
    B) have had
    C) will have
    D) had had

20. Next August, while you _____ for your exams, I _____ on a Mediterranean beach.
    A) are preparing / will be
    B) were preparing / would be
    C) prepare / will be
    D) were preparing / was

21. He _____ my name, so I reminded him.
    A) forgets
    B) has forgotten
    C) had forgotten
    D) forgot

22. By 5.30 this afternoon, Tom _____ at work for eight hours.
    A) had been
    B) would have been
    C) will have been
    D) has been

23. She _____ unwell for several days when she was taken to hospital.
    A) had been feeling
    B) has been feeling
    C) was feeling
    D) had felt

24. During this year we _____ many advances in computer science.
    A) had seen
    B) have seen
    C) saw
    D) are seeing

25. Our maths teacher _____ us a lot of homework last week but he _____ us very much so far this week.
    A) would give / didn't give
    B) had given / didn't give
    C) gave / didn't given
    D) gave / hasn't given

26. It is expected that man _____ on several planets by the end of this century.
    A) would have landed
    B) will be landing
    C) will have been landed
    D) will have landed

27. A: I'm going to the pop concert. _____ with me?
    B: Thank you very much. I'd love to.
    A) Are you going to come
    B) Do you come
    C) Will you come
    D) Were you coming

28. It rained! I didn't think it _____.
    A) is going to rain
    B) was going to rain
    C) was raining
    D) had rained

29. I _____ to see you tomorrow, but now I find I can't.
    A) will come
    B) come
    C) was coming
    D) am coming

30. He found everything rather strange as he _____ never _____ abroad before.
    A) has / been
    B) will / be
    C) hasn't / been
    D) had / been

31. I _____ you know as soon as the telegram _____.
    A) will let / arrives
    B) would let / arrives
    C) will let / arrived
    D) let / had arrived

32. Please _____ until after the plane _____.
    A) not smoke / takes off
    B) don't smoke / has taken off
    C) don't smoke / took off
    D) not smoke / has taken off

33. It is the first time I _____ of anything like that.
    A) had heard
    B) have heard
    C) hear
    D) am hearing

34. You're always late. This is the third time you _____ late this week.
    A) had been
    B) were
    C) have been
    D) will be

35. It was the first time she _____ ever _____ a prize.
    A) has / won
    B) had / won
    C) is / won
    D) would / win

36. He _____ about to give up his job when they offered him a rise.
    A) was
    B) is
    C) has been
    D) had been

37. Yesterday while I _____ in class I _____ the hiccups. The boy next to me told me _____ my breath.
    A) was sitting / had got / to hold
    B) sat / got / to hold
    C) was sitting / got / to hold
    D) am sitting / got / hold

38. Hello! I _____ to phone you all week. Where _____?
    A) am trying / were you
    B) have tried / did you go
    C) tried / were you
    D) have been trying / have you been

39. It is time we _____ goodbye to each other. The train is due to leave in a minute.
    A) said
    B) say
    C) will say
    D) had said

40. I think you should apologize when you _____ her.
    A) will see
    B) see
    C) saw
    D) are seen

41. His clothes are in a mess because he _____ the house all morning.
    A) has been painting
    B) will be painting
    C) had been painting
    D) will have painted

42. Since I last met him he _____.
    A) will get married
    B) gets married
    C) had got married
    D) has got married

43. They quarreled last week. They _____ to each other since.
    A) didn't talk
    B) haven't talked
    C) don't talk
    D) hadn't talked

44. I _____ much of the film because I fell asleep half-way through.
    A) had seen
    B) didn't see
    C) wasn't seen
    D) saw

45. There is nothing we can do that ____ people from driving too fast.
    A) is stopping
    B) stop
    C) will stop
    D) stopped

46. I didn't answer the phone when it _____ because I _____ a shower, so I _____ it until it was too late.
    A) rang / was having / didn't hear
    B) rung / was having / wasn't heard
    C) was ringing / had / didn't hear
    D) rang / was having / wasn't heard

47. Last night I _____ you, but the phone was out of order.
    A) would phone
    B) phoned
    C) were going to phone
    D) didn't phone

48. She wants us to meet at the cafeteria, but I'd rather we _____ here.
    A) meet
    B) will meet
    C) met
    D) had met

49. We met at the cafeteria as she wanted. I'd rather we _____ here.
    A) meet
    B) would meet
    C) met
    D) had met

50. It is likely that by the time you _____ to the shop it _____ shut.
    A) will get / will be
    B) got / will be
    C) would get / will
    D) get / will be

51. _____ you ever _____ of him? He is a world-famous violinist.
    A) Won't / hear
    B) Didn't / hear
    C) Haven't / heard
    D) Had / heard

52. A: Did you turn off the photocopier?
    B: The manager _____ already _____ it off.
    A) had / turned
    B) has / turned
    C) was / turned
    D) had been / turned

53. I _____ what the problem is by tomorrow.
    A) will be discovering
    B) have discovered
    C) will have discovered
    D) will be discovered

54. By the time I got to the stadium they _____ already _____ for ten minutes.
    A) have / been playing
    B) were/playing
    C) had / been playing
    D) will / have played

55. Someone _____ my bike last night. _____ you ever _____ your bike stolen?
    A) stole / Did / have
    B) stolen / Have / had
    C) was stolen / Have / had
    D) stole / Have / had

56. The doctor _____ the patient with a smile and told him that he _____ better.
    A) approached / is looking
    B) approached / was looking
    C) approaches / is looking
    D) had approached / looked

57. I used to smoke at one time but now I _____ it up.
    A) have given
    B) gave
    C) had given
    D) am given

58. He _____ silly questions until my patience finally ran out.
    A) has kept asking
    B) kept asking
    C) had been kept asking
    D) was kept asking

59. He _____ at tennis since he came to the USA.
    A) isn't beaten
    B) hasn't beaten
    C) hasn't been beaten
    D) wasn't beaten

60. It is probably about time we _____ the car serviced.
    A) had
    B) would have
    C) will have
    D) have had

61. A: _____ we _____ somewhere before?
    B: Yes, I _____ you at your sister's wedding.
    A) Didn't / meet / saw
    B) Haven't / met / saw
    C) Hadn't / met / had seen
    D) Haven't / meet / have seen

62. The weather _____ worse last year than I _____ it to be.
    A) was / had expected
    B) was / have expected
    C) had been / expected
    D) had been / have expected

63. I _____ hungry at four because I _____ a big lunch at one.
    A) wasn't / had had
    B) am not / had
    C) was / had had
    D) wouldn't be / had

64. I woke up feeling tired this morning because I _____ very well.
    A) haven't slept
    B) wasn't sleeping
    C) hadn't slept
    D) haven't been sleeping

65. Go out and get some fresh air! You _____ here reading all morning.
    A) had been sitting
    B) were sitting
    C) are sitting
    D) have been sitting

66. A: Why are you crying?
    B: Well, I _____ up onions for the last five minutes.
    A) have been cutting
    B) will have cut
    C) am cutting
    D) will be cutting

67. A: Did you spend your holiday in Miami?
    B: No. I was _____. It there, but I changed my mind and went to Antalya instead.
    A) spent
    B) have spent
    C) to have spent
    D) to be spent

68. I don't think your brother _____ rid of his bad cold.
    A) won't get
    B) had got
    C) has got
    D) hasn't got

69. Transport systems _____ likely to change in the future. One probable difference is that there _____ more electric vehicles.
    A) is / will be
    B) are / will be
    C) will / are
    D) will / would be

70. The men were to _____ but the manager decided to give them a second change.
    A) have been dismissed
    B) dismissed
    C) being dismissed
    D) be dismissing

71. Mike _____ in a travel agency for six months in 1990. He already had some experience of the tourist industry because he _____ in a Tourist Information office in Bristol two years before.
    A) had worked / had worked
    B) was working / worked
    C) worked / has worked
    D) worked / had worked

72. The film _____ already _____ when we sat down.
    A) has already / started
    B) was / starting
    C) had / started
    D) have / started

73. It is due _____ in five years' time.
    A) to complete
    B) be completed
    C) be completing
    D) to be completed

74. I _____ her a week ago but she _____ yet.
    A) wrote / hasn't answered
    B) wrote / didn't answer
    C) had written / hasn't answered
    D) was written / doesn't answer

75. A: What happens to traffic in a traffic jam?
    B: It _____ up.
    A) is held
    B) will hold
    C) has been held
    D) was held

76. No one brought up that question at the meeting. That question _____ up at the meeting.
    A) was brought
    B) won't be brought
    C) hasn't been brought
    D) wasn't brought

77. By the end of this century most of the world's oil supplies _____.
    A) have used up
    B) will have used up
    C) have been used up
    D) will have been used up

78. My brother _____ in a restaurant for the summer, but he _____ it very much.
    A) worked / doesn't like
    B) is working / doesn't like
    C) has been working / didn't like
    D) working / doesn't like

79. Someone saw him. He was driving a Renault Manager. He _____ a Renault Manager.
    A) saw driving
    B) was seen driving
    C) is seen driving
    D) has been seen drive

80. There has been a serious accident on the E5, and a section of the motorway _____ to traffic.
    A) was closed
    B) has been closed
    C) had been closed
    D) are closed

81. People say that Istanbul is one of the world's most interesting cities. Istanbul _____ one of the world's most interesting cities.
    A) said to be
    B) is said to be
    C) told to be
    D) was said to be

82. Long ago, people thought that the earth was flat. Long ago, the earth _____ flat.
    A) was thinking to be
    B) was thought to be
    C) is thought to be
    D) thought to be

83. When I arrived, no arrangements _____.
    A) had been made
    B) weren't made
    C) hadn't been made
    D) have been made

84. The pilot _____ thought to _____ in the crash.
    A) was / have died
    B) was / be dying
    C) had / have died
    D) has / would die

85. A: Who's going to meet him at the airport?
    B: He _____ by our ambassador.
    A) is going to be met
    B) will have been met
    C) is going to meet
    D) has gone to meet

86. This week we've had the house _____ into by thieves.
    A) to break
    B) be broken
    C) broken
    D) being broken

87. A: What do they use this building for?
    B: Well, years ago it _____ as a dance hall but now it _____ for offices.
    A) is used / being used
    B) had been used / is using
    C) was used / is used
    D) has been used / is used

88. A: Were you able to cure the patient?
    B: He _____ already _____ by the time I got there.
    A) will / have been cured
    B) had / been cured
    C) had / cured
    D) has / been cured

89. Mars is the first planet _____.
    A) to discover
    B) was discovered
    C) to be discovered
    D) to have been discovered

90. They were unhappy with the way things _____.
    A) are going
    B) were going
    C) have been going on
    D) will be going on

91. Don't touch that electric stove while it _____.
    A) was being repaired
    B) being repaired
    C) is being repaired
    D) will be repairing

92. He was 8 kilos overweight and _____ to go on a diet.
    A) is advised
    B) has been advised
    C) was advised
    D) had advised

93. People like policemen _____ always _____ against flu.
    A) do / vaccinate
    B) are / vaccinated
    C) to be / vaccinated
    D) is / to be vaccinated

94. His novels _____ into eight languages.
    A) to be translated
    B) has been translated
    C) have translated
    D) have been translated

95. We usually _____ the news on TV at eight o'clock, but tonight we _____ that new soap opera.
    A) are watching / watched
    B) watch / are watching
    C) are watching / are watching
    D) watch / watched

96. He noticed that the room _____ recently.
    A) hasn't been cleaned
    B) was not cleaned
    C) hadn't been cleaned
    D) won't be cleaned

97. I hate it when my boiled egg _____ properly.
    A) not done
    B) isn't done
    C) wasn't done
    D) won't be done

98. A speech to the nation was _____ by the Prime Minister, but it had to be cancelled at the last minute because of a cabinet crisis.
    A) would make
    B) has been made
    C) being made
    D) to have been made

99. He _____ empty the contents of his suitcases onto the counter.
    A) was made
    B) was made to
    C) had made
    D) will be made

100. The authorities feared the missing man was dead. The missing man was feared _____.
    A) being dead
    B) dead
    C) to be dead
    D) was dead

101. Someone heard him shout for help. He _____ shout for help.
    A) has been heard
    B) is heard to
    C) was heard
    D) was heard to

102. The authorities will make him pay all his debts. He _____ pay all his debts.
    A) is going to be
    B) will be made
    C) was made to
    D) will be made to

103. She's spring-cleaning the house from bottom to top. The house _____ from top to bottom.
    A) is being spring-cleaned
    B) was to be spring-cleaned
    C) has been spring-cleaned
    D) is to be spring-cleaned

104. The last days of the holiday _____ by rain.
    A) was spoiled
    B) are spoiled
    C) have been spoiled
    D) were spoiled

105. They have used up all the petrol in the tank. All the petrol in the tank _____ up.
    A) has been using
    B) has been used
    C) will have been used
    D) have been used

106. I expect the police will find him. I expect he _____ by the police.
    A) to be found
    B) would be found
    C) be found
    D) will be found

107. People don't bring up children properly these days. Children _____ properly these days.
    A) didn't bring up
    B) aren't bringing up
    C) aren't brought up
    D) weren't brought up

108. They _____ the traffic problem when the plans for the project _____ made last year.
    A) haven't considered / were being
    B) weren't considered / were
    C) didn't consider / was being
    D) didn't consider / were being

109. Because of the patient's health, _____.
    A) the doctor was advised to lose weight
    B) he was advised by the doctor to lose weight
    C) the doctor wants to lose weight
    D) he advised the doctor to lose weight

110. They hadn't done any damage to it. No damage _____ to it.
    A) was done
    B) had been done
    C) hadn't been done
    D) has been done

111. "They say he robbed the bank." means: _____.
    A) they say he's been robbed in the bank.
    B) He is said to rob the bank.
    C) He said he'd robbed the bank.
    D) He is said to have robbed the bank.

112. A: Did Arsenal beat Galatasaray in the final?
    B: _____.
    A) Yes, Arsenal was beaten by Galatasaray in the final.
    B) Yes, Galatasaray beat Arsenal in the final.
    C) No, Galatasaray was beaten by Arsenal
    D) No, Arsenal was beaten by Galatasaray in the final.

113. People think he is guilty. He _____ guilty
    A) thought to be
    B) thinks he is
    C) is thought to be
    D) thought he was

114. Foreign investments _____ reduced by 20 per cent since the election.
    A) have been
    B) were
    C) have had
    D) has been

115. It _____ that the Government would do something to relieve the situation.
    A) is assumed   B) assumed
    C) was assuming   D) was assumed

116. The man who _____ by a snake was given a serum.
    A) is bitten   B) has been bitten
    C) had been bitten   D) had bitten

117. A cease-fire _____ expected to _____ later this month.
    A) was / be declaring   B) is / be declared
    C) is / declare   D) has expected / to be declared

118. A great deal of research _____ into the possible causes of cancer.
    A) are being done   B) have been done
    C) has been done   D) has done

119. She promised that she _____ hospital until she _____ better.
    A) would not leave / was   B) wouldn't leave / would be
    C) doesn't leave / was   D) didn't leave / was

120. New sources of energy _____ developed. This will become increasingly important as oil reserves _____ up.
    A) is being / are used   B) has been / have been used
    C) are being / are used   D) have been / is used

121. The transistor _____ in 1948. As a result of this, both the size and the cost of electronic equipment _____ greatly reduced.
    A) was invented / have been   B) had been invented / has been
    C) was invented / have had   D) had invented / will be

122. Radio waves _____ by the ionosphere. This makes it possible _____ short-wave radio signals over great distances.
    A) is reflected / to send   B) are reflecting / sent
    C) are reflected / sending   D) are reflected / to send

123. Plans to develop cars on methanol are likely _____ in the future.
    A) will be realized   B) will have been realized
    C) to be realized   D) being realized

124. There is no bread left because we _____ it all.
    A) have eaten   B) has been eaten
    C) had eaten   D) have been eaten

125. Little _____ she realize that the evening was _____ out very differently.
    A) did / turning   B) will / to turn
    C) does / to have turned D) did / to turn

126. It is highly probable that more and more solar energy _____ in the future.
    A) will be used   B) be used
    C) to be used   D) will be using

127. There isn't any more chalk, it _____ all _____.
    A) has / used up   B) was / used up
    C) has / been used up   D) had / been used up

128. You can stop looking for his watch. He _____ just _____ it.
    A) has / been found   B) has / found
    C) had / found   D) will / have found

129. Don't ask me what cauliflower tastes like. I _____ eating it.
    A) am not trying   B) didn't try
    C) haven't tried   D) don't try

130. I bought another concert ticket in case you _____ to come with me.
    A) wanted   B) will want
    C) have wanted   D) would want

131. We'll close all the windows in case it _____ while we are out.
    A) rains   B) rained
    C) will rain   D) rain

132. Take an umbrella with you in case it _____.
    A) rained   B) will rain
    C) should rain   D) is raining

133. She ought to pass her exams so long as she _____.
    A) doesn't panic   B) won't panic
    C) shouldn't panic D) didn't panic

134. His hopes of making a fortune _____ when his factory burned down.
    A) were dashed   B) have dashed
    C) was dashed   D) will be dashed

135. When eleven o'clock came and he still _____, I began to wonder if he _____ an accident.
    A) didn't arrive / had   B) hadn't arrived / had had
    C) won't arrive / had had   D) didn't arrive / had had

136. Some patients shout in pain while _____ an injection.
    A) giving   B) being given
    C) given   D) have been given

137. For various reasons, clothing of some type _____ by human beings since the beginning of time.
    A) has worn   B) was worn
    C) is being worn   D) has been worn

138. Considering the weather is so uncertain, the reception _____ indoors.
    A) was held   B) will be held
    C) to be held   D) has held

139. In most non-western countries punishment _____ as a deterrent.
    A) is not seen   B) hasn't seen
    C) weren't seen   D) aren't seen

140. If we compare the mass of hydrogen in a star with the rate at which energy _____, we can estimate its potential life.
    A) is being emitted   B) be emitted
    C) was emitted   D) will be emitted

141. It has been predicted that within the next 50 years, scientists _____ a drug to prolong life up to 150 years or more.
    A) are producing   B) to be produced
    C) will be produced   D) will have produced

142. We _____ at the Italian restaurant last night, but it was full, so we ate somewhere else.
    A) were eating   B) were going to eat
    C) are going to eat   D) had eaten

143. The door _____ unless you _____.
    A) won't open / push   B) doesn't open / will push
    C) won't open / will push   D) isn't open / push

144. His parents _____ married for eight years when he was born.
    A) have been   B) will be
    C) had been   D) were

145. By April 2010, he _____ for this organization for fifteen years.
    A) has been working   B) will be working
    C) will have been working   D) had been working

146. He _____ from the company for several years before they found him out.
    A) has been stealing   B) had been stealing
    C) was stealing   D) will have been stolen

147. He _____ a cold for the last three days.
    A) is fighting off   B) will have fought off
    C) has been fighting off   D) was fighting off

148. The Prime Minister refuses to enter into negotiations with the railway men until they _____ all _____ to work.
    A) are / return   B) have / returned
    C) had / returned   D) will / have l returned

149. In the years ahead, it seems likely that people _____ even greater control over nature.
    A) to acquire   B) will be acquired
    C) will acquire   D) will have been acquired

150. You _____ pleased to hear that your father _____ to the committee.
    A) have been / selected   B) will be / has been selected
    C) are / is selecting   D) have been / was selected

151. Hardly _____ I _____ the phone down when it started ringing again.
    A) did / put   B) will have / put
    C) did / to have put   D) had / put

152. The day she agreed to marry him was the happiest he _____ ever _____ in his life.
    A) has / had   B) had / had
    C) will / have   D) would / have

ELEMENTARY PRE-INTERMEDIATE 5

adjective - adverb - noun clauses

Choose the best answer.

1. I'll stay home if it _____.
   A) rained   B) rains   C) will rain   D) won't rain

2. If I _____ out, I'll buy a newspaper
   A) go   B) will go   C) am going   D) went

3. I'll help him if he _____.
   A) ask   B) asked   C) asks   D) will ask

4. If I fail the exam, I _____ it again.
   A) took   B) wouldn't take   C) will take   D) didn't take

5. If I _____ time, I could go with you.
   A) have   B) will have   C) am having   D) had

6. I'll go to the park if it _____ cold.
   A) weren't   B) wasn't   C) isn't   D) doesn't

7. If I _____ a bird, I could fly home.
   A) were   B) will be   C) would be   D) be

8. If the weather were nice, I _____ to the beach.
   A) will go   B) would go   C) went   D) go

9. If she _____, she usually does well on the tests.
   A) studied   B) had studied   C) studies   D) will study

10. If you needed the money, I _____ it to you.
    A) would lend   B) lent   C) will lend   D) lend

11. I _____ to you if you don't come.
    A) wouldn't talk   B) won't talk   C) didn't talk   D) doesn't talk

12. If I _____ a lot of money, I'd take a long holiday.
    A) won   B) win   C) would win   D) had won

13. You wouldn't _____ your car if you had driven more carefully.
    A) damage   B) damaged   C) has damaged   D) have damaged

14. If I had time, _____ see the new film at the cinema.
    A) I'll   B) I'd   C) I can   D) I am

15. A: I smoke too much.
    B: If I _____ you, I _____ smoke at all.
    A) was / won't   B) were / weren't   C) am / won't   D) were / wouldn't

16. I don't have much money so I can't travel. If I _____ a lot of money, I _____ travel.
    A) have / could   B) had / would   C) had / can   D) had had / would

17. I'm going out. If the phone _____, please answer it.
    A) rang   B) rings   C) would ring   D) will ring

18. I _____ the car if I had the right tools.
    A) can repair   B) repaired   C) could repair   D) will repair

19. If you mix yellow and blue, you _____ green.
    A) get   B) got   C) would get   D) gets

20. I usually take some aspirin if I _____ a headache.
    A) had   B) have   C) will have   D) would have

21. If flowers _____ enough water, they die.
    A) don't get   B) get   C) didn't get   D) doesn't get

22. I _____ write to you if you don't give me your address.
    A) can't   B) couldn't   C) wouldn't   D) didn't

23. Your cough _____ get better if you don't stop smoking.
    A) will   B) would   C) won't   D) didn't

24. If he _____ a promise, he always keeps it.
    A) made   B) would make   C) make   D) makes

25. If you _____ me, I'd have helped you.
    A) asked   B) would ask   C) had asked   D) ask

26. If I _____ ill yesterday, I wouldn't have stayed at home.
    A) weren't   B) had been   C) hadn't been   D) wasn't

27. He is fat because he doesn't take any exercise. If he _____ some exercise, he _____ so fat.
    A) took / won't be   B) will take / won't be   C) takes / wouldn't be   D) took / wouldn't be

28. I'd like to go to the concert, but I haven't got a ticket. If I _____ a ticket, I _____ go to it.
    A) had / will   B) have / will   C) will have / can   D) had / could

29. Would he have passed if he _____ hard?
    A) studied   B) had studied   C) studies   D) would study

30. If you _____ practice, you can't learn English.
    A) aren't   B) didn't   C) won't   D) don't

31. If I could go anywhere in the world, I _____ to Japan.
    A) would go   B) will go   C) went   D) had gone

32. You will kill yourself if you _____ stop smoking.
    A) aren't   B) didn't   C) don't   D) weren't

33. If the teacher _____ a little more slowly, I could understand him.
    A) speak   B) will speak   C) speaks   D) spoke

34. If people _____ ill, they go to see a doctor.
    A) is   B) are   C) were   D) will be

35. If she _____ him, she would marry him.
    A) loved   B) would love   C) loves   D) had loved

36. Perhaps he would excuse you if you _____ to him yourself.
    A) spoke   B) will speak   C) speak   D) had spoken

37. I could tell you the time if I _____ a watch.
    A) had had   B) had   C) would have   D) will have

38. If you don't take your medicine, you _____ get well quickly.
    A) won't   B) wouldn't   C) couldn't   D) aren't

39. I'd have been there on time if I _____.
    A) get up early   B) could get on the first train   C) had caught the earlier bus   D) set my alarm clock

40. If the sun _____ the world _____ dark.
    A) won't rise / will be   B) hadn't risen / would have been   C) doesn't / will be   D) didn't rise / would be

41. If Neil Armstrong had lived in 1453, he _____ on the moon.
    A) couldn't walk   B) wouldn't walk   C) can't walk   D) couldn't have walked

42. If she _____ younger, she could start jogging.
    A) were   B) would be   C) is   D) will be

43. He _____ angry if you argue with him.
    A) got   B) get   C) gets   D) would get

44. Diana would have got up earlier if _____ .
    A) she knew the train left at 6.30
    B) the alarm clock went off on time
    C) you could have woken her up
    D) she could sleep well

45. If I had listened to the weather forecast _____.
    A) I would stay at home
    B) I'd know it was windy
    C) I wouldn't have watered the flowers
    D) we were going to play football

46. _____ they'd take you to hospital.
    A) If you are seriously ill   B) If you have a terrible headache   C) If you got any worse   D) If you'd become worried

47. Everything would be all right if _____.
    A) I could start on the 9th of September
    B) you'd apologize to her
    C) it hadn't rained
    D) she hadn't phoned the police

48. _____, I wouldn't have told you.
    A) If it was a piece of bad news
    B) If I failed the driving test
    C) If you were dismissed
    D) If I'd known you were going to be upset

49. She'd go on a diet if _____.
    A) you ask her to do B) she had had some complaints
    C) she will marry a rich man D) she appeared on TV

50. She wouldn't have married him if _____.
    A) she weren't beautiful B) he didn't have a lot of money
    C) she had a villa D) he hadn't been an engineer

51. Tell me _____.
    A) where is the station B) what is your name
    C) why she is crying D) how did you learn English

52. Ask the driver _____.
    A) how long does it take to the airport
    B) how much we'll pay
    C) if he had any change
    D) the car is his own

53. Does anybody know why _____ ?
    A) does the teacher get angry B) Ray is absent
    C) is he waiting outside D) are they late

54. "Are you ready?" she asked. She asked _____ ready.
    A) if I was B) when I am C) to be D) why I was

55. I don't know_____.
    A) when is it B) what time it is
    C) what time is it D) when was it

56. I wonder why _____.
    A) is the sky blue B) was the sky blue
    C) the sky was blue D) the sky is blue

57. "Why is he smiling?" I want to know_____.
    A) why he was smiling B) why was he smiling
    C) why is he smiling D) why he is smiling

58. I wonder whether _____ on other planets.
    A) is there life B) there was C) there's life D) was there

59. Could you tell me where _____?
    A) the bus station was B) is the bus station
    C) the bus station is D) was the bus station

60. She said, "My brother is a student." She said that _____ a student.
    A) my brother is B) her brother was
    C) my brother was D) your brother was

61. "When will you be here?" she asked. She asked me when _____ there.
    A) I would be B) would I be C) she will be D) she would be

62. He said, "I will watch TV". He said _____.
    A) I would watch TV B) I will watch TV
    C) she would watch TV D) he would watch TV

63. "Do you need a pen?" Anne asked me _____ a pen.
    A) do you need B) did I need
    C) if I needed D) whether she needed

64. "I may be late." Mike told me_____ late.
    A) he might be B) I might be
    C) he may be D) he was

65. "What are you talking about?" Dick asked me what_____.
    A) am I talking about B) I was talking about
    C) he is talking about D) was he talking about

66. "Can you come to the party?" David asked me ____ to the party.
    A) could he come B) can he come
    C) if I could come D) whether I can come

67. "I have to study." Barbara said_____.
    A) she had to study B) if he had to study
    C) she has to study D) if she has to study

68. I don't know if I _____ succeed in passing my exam or not.
    A) will B) could C) would D) will be

69. "Have you seen my grammar book?" Nancy wanted to know _____ grammar book.
    A) whether she'd seen my B) if I'd seen her
    C) did I see her D) I'd seen her

70. He explained why _____.
    A) did he come late B) was he late
    C) late he was D) he was late

71. My friend said, "I can't believe it." He said _____ it.
    A) he can't believe B) I couldn't believe
    C) he couldn't believe D) he didn't believe

72. The nurse doesn't understand why the girl_____.
    A) is coughing B) was coughing
    C) would cough D) cough

73. I didn't know if he _____ there.
    A) were B) is going to be
    C) would be D) will be

74. Peter asked his brother _____.
    A) where are the hammers B) where was the hammer
    C) where is the hammer D) where the hammer was

75. Father said that _____.
    A) I'm at my office B) he was at his office
    C) you are at your office D) "I'm at my office"

76. I heard that you _____ at the basketball match.
    A) are B) were C) been D) gone

77. George said that _____ to Tom.
    A) he'd spoken B) he's spoken
    C) you speak D) I have spoken

78. They promised that they _____ Mike next year.
    A) visit B) would visit C) will visit D) won't visit

79. She was sorry that _____.
    A) she was late B) she is late C) was she late D) to be late

80. "May I use your telephone?" He asked me if _____.
    A) I might use his telephone B) he may use his telephone
    C) he might use my telephone D) he might use his telephone

81. "Can you help me?" She wondered if _____.
    A) I can help her B) she could help me
    C) I could help her D) she can help me

82. I don't know where _____.
    A) the lavatory is B) is the lavatory
    C) was the lavatory D) the lavatory was

83. She asked me if _____ to the meeting.
    A) I was going B) I am going
    C) she is going D) would she go

84. The surgeon says, "You may have some pain for a few days." He says that _____ some pain for a few days.
    A) I might have B) he may have
    C) he might D) I may have

85. She asked me, "Can you help us?" She wanted to know if _____.
    A) could we help her B) I could help them
    C) we could help her D) I can help them

86. "Don't walk on the bridge." He warned us _____ on that bridge.
    A) didn't walk B) to walk C) don't walk D) not to walk

87. "Please be quiet." I asked them _____ quiet.
    A) be B) not to be C) to be D) are

88. "Shall I call a taxi?" He asked me if _____ a taxi.
    A) he should call B) I should call
    C) should he call D) he will call

89. The teacher told me _____ the board.
    A) he is cleaning B) I clean
    C) cleaning D) to clean

90. "Open your mouth." The dentist told me _____.
    A) to open his mouth B) opened my mouth
    C) open your mouth D) to open my mouth

91. "Don't be late." The teacher told us _____.
    A) not to be late B) not being late
    C) to be late D) we don't be late

92. "Are you free now?" He asked her if _____ then.
    A) I was free B) is she free C) she was free D) was she free

93. The teacher said, "Pick up your book, Mike."
    The teacher told Mike _____.
    A) pick up his book B) to pick up her book
    C) to pick up my book D) to pick up his book

94. A: Who is that woman?
    B: I don't know _____.
    A) who's that woman
    B) who was that woman
    C) who that woman is
    D) who that woman was

95. A: What started the fire?
    B: Nobody knows _____.
    A) who started the fire
    B) what started the fire
    C) what starts the fire
    D) who'd started the fire

96. A: What did Julia buy?
    B: I don't know _____.
    A) what she bought
    B) what she's bought
    C) what did she buy
    D) what she had bought

97. Don't look at your friend's paper. The teacher warned me _____ my friend's paper.
    A) to look at
    B) I don't look at
    C) you don't look at
    D) not to look at

98. He said that _____.
    A) it is raining
    B) she is unable to come
    C) it was somebody else's bike
    D) I didn't come

99. I don't know _____.
    A) will he come
    B) what time the next train is
    C) he is there
    D) why did he fail

100. I can't imagine how _____ the children.
     A) they are going to rescue
     B) did they rescue
     C) do they rescue
     D) are they going to rescue

101. Janet said that she was hungry. Janet said, "_____"
     A) I was hungry
     B) I am hungry
     C) She was hungry
     D) She is hungry

102. Mike says his father is ill. Mike says, "_____"
     A) My father is ill
     B) His father is ill
     C) My father was ill
     D) Your father is ill

103. We said that we were leaving on Saturday. We said, "_____"
     A) You are leaving on Saturday
     B) We leave on Saturday
     C) We are leaving on Saturday
     D) You were leaving on Saturday

104. The secretary told me that Mr. Rich had gone out. The secretary told me, "_____"
     A) Mr. Rich was going out
     B) Mr. Rich goes out
     C) Mr. Rich has gone out
     D) Mr. Rich is going out

105. Bill said he didn't like to study. Bill said, "_____"
     A) I don't like to study
     B) You don't like to study
     C) He doesn't like to study
     D) We don't like to study

106. The old lady said she wasn't feeling well. The old lady said, "_____"
     A) I'm not feeling well
     B) She isn't feeling well
     C) I don't feel well
     D) She hasn't been feeling well

107. Carol said that she would see me the next day. Carol said, "_____"
     A) You will see me tomorrow
     B) I will see you tomorrow
     C) She will see you tomorrow
     D) She will see me tomorrow

108. You told me that you would be careful. You said to me, "_____"
     A) You will be careful
     B) You would be careful
     C) I will be careful
     D) Be careful

109. He asked me what I was reading. "_____?" he asked me.
     A) What do you read
     B) What you are reading
     C) What are you reading
     D) What you were reading

110. I asked the clerk if they had a double room. "_____?" I asked the clerk.
     A) Have you got a double room
     B) Did you have a double room
     C) Is there a double room
     D) They have got a double room

111. I asked her what her name was. "_____?" I asked her.
     A) What is your name
     B) What my name was
     C) What is her name
     D) What her name is

112. They asked me if I was Turkish. "_____?" they asked me.
     A) You are Turkish
     B) Am I Turkish
     C) Are they Turkish
     D) Are you Turkish

113. My father told me to do my homework. My father said, "_____"
     A) You do your homework
     B) You don't do your homework
     C) I don't do my homework
     D) Do your homework

114. He warned me not to touch the wire. "_____" he warned me.
     A) I don't touch the wire
     B) Touch the wire
     C) Don't touch the wire
     D) I didn't touch the wire

115. The doctor told him not to eat much. "___" the doctor said to him.
     A) You eat very little
     B) Don't eat much
     C) I don't eat much
     D) Eat very little

116. He says he is cold. He says, "_____"
     A) You are cold
     B) I am cold
     C) He is cold
     D) I was cold

117. The book _____ is on the table is mine.
     A) who B) which C) whose D) where

118. The man _____ car was stolen phoned the police.
     A) who B) which C) whose D) that

119. Bryan Adams is the singer _____ songs I like best.
     A) whom B) whose C) that D) who

120. A river _____ is polluted is not safe for swimming.
     A) whose B) where C) when D) which

121. People _____ study the weather are called meteorologists.
     A) that B) when C) whom D) whose

122. I like photographs _____ are in black and white.
     A) when B) which C) whom D) whose

123. Is there a time _____ we can discus this problem?
     A) when B) which C) that D) where

124. A library is a place _____ we can borrow books.
     A) where B) which C) when D) that

125. The factory _____ he works is closing down.
     A) that B) which C) where D) whom

126. I've got a friend _____ father is a pilot.
     A) whom B) of which C) who D) whose

127. His wife, _____ lives in Paris, is a fashion model.
     A) who B) that C) whom D) whose

128. Elvis Presley, _____ name was probably one of the best known in the world, died in 1977.
     A) who B) whose C) whom D) of which

129. A thermostat is something _____ controls temperatures.
     A) who B) where C) when D) which

130. Miss Snow, _____ you met at the theatre, is my classmate.
     A) who B) whom C) where D) that

131. Mustafa Kemal, _____ was born in 1881, became the first President of Turkey on October 29th, 1923.
     A) that B) who C) whom D) when

132. It was the blue car _____.
     A) it caused the accident
     B) caused the accident
     C) it is expensive
     D) which caused the accident

133. The man _____ is an electrical engineer.
     A) who lives next door
     B) makes cars
     C) works in a factory
     D) whose job

134. That is the film _____.
     A) it is about Turkish people
     B) we are liked
     C) I watched last week
     D) it is a western

135. A teacher is a man _____.
     A) works at a school
     B) makes us study
     C) who teaches
     D) which is liked by everybody

136. Your heart is the part of your body _____.
     A) which pumps blood
     B) can't live without it
     C) it causes heart attacks
     D) makes us sad or happy

137. I like films _____.
     A) they are interesting
     B) which hasn't got a sad story
     C) are not sad ones
     D) that are funny

138. _____ I was watching TV, the telephone rang.
     A) While B) Before C) After D) Until

139. He broke his leg _____ he was skiing.
     A) as soon as B) after C) when D) before

140. I always brush my teeth _____ I go to bed.
    A) before   B) as soon as   C) while   D) until

141. We waited _____ the plane took off.
    A) as soon as   B) when   C) as   D) until

142. We went out _____ it stopped raining.
    A) until   B) as soon as   C) as   D) while

143. I hope he gets here _____ the train leaves. There isn't another train today.
    A) before   B) while   C) until   D) after

144. You must wait _____ the light changes to green.
    A) after   B) before   C) until   D) as soon as

145. He hasn't written to us _____ he left.
    A) since   B) until   C) while   D) when

146. _____ she doesn't enjoy her job, she works hard.
    A) Since   B) Although   C) Because   D) As

147. They went out for a walk, _____ the weather was bad.
    A) even though   B) so
    C) therefore   D) for

148. He was late _____ he took a taxi to go to work.
    A) as   B) because   C) so   D) in order to

149. I use my umbrella _____ it rains.
    A) until   B) after   C) whenever   D) although

150. _____ the film is over, I'll go to bed.
    A) While   B) As soon as   C) By the time   D) Until

151. I'll never speak to her _____ I live.
    A) as long as   B) until   C) whenever   D) whereas

152. She is sneezing _____ she has a cold.
    A) so   B) before   C) whereas   D) because

153. It was hot; _____ we went swimming.
    A) because   B) therefore   C) as long as   D) even though

154. He didn't know the answers to the exercises, _____ he guessed.
    A) as   B) even though   C) because   D) so

155. I had toothache _____.
    A) because I am going to the dentist
    B) so I went to the dentist
    C) why I went to the dentist
    D) I seldom brush my teeth

156. We went out _____ the bell rang.
    A) so   B) although   C) after   D) until

157. By the time he _____ here, it will be too late for the theatre.
    A) will get   B) got   C) gets   D) get

158. I have known him _____ he was a baby.
    A) for   B) since   C) because   D) when

159. We can leave as soon as _____.
    A) the train arrived   B) the plane will take off
    C) you are ready   D) they are going to phone

160. I'll be at the airport when _____.
    A) the plane landed   B) the plane will take off
    C) you arrive   D) you will get there

161. She left the clothes out although _____.
    A) the sun is shining   B) it was raining
    C) it isn't hot   D) the weather was good

162. _____ as soon as I get home.
    A) I will phone you   B) I have taken a shower
    C) I went to bed   D) I would have a cup of coffee

163. Always turn your television off _____.
    A) when you went to bed   B) as soon as you got bored
    C) after you have fallen asleep   D) before you leave home

164. She was not listening while _____.
    A) I was talking   B) we are complaining
    C) she is very angry with you   D) you tell him something to do

165. He went out as _____.
    A) she came in   B) the sun is shining
    C) I am leaving home   D) he is worried about something

166. The lights went out _____.
    A) when the eight o'clock news started
    B) after I have finished my homework
    C) as soon as you arrive home
    D) before the Prime Minister enters the conference hall

167. They studied hard although _____.
    A) they were tired   B) they were good friends
    C) they were happy   D) they had a lot to eat

168. When I got home, _____.
    A) my sister opens the door for me
    B) I will have a good rest
    C) my mother was setting the table
    D) my father hasn't come back home

169. I swim every day when _____.
    A) the weather was very hot   B) I will be in Marmaris
    C) I am on holiday   D) the sea will get hot

170. I usually listen to some classical music _____ I am reading.
    A) as   B) because   C) for   D) since

171. No buses were running _____.
    A) because I had no ticket   B) however I was late
    C) as I was at the bus-stop   D) so I had to walk to school

172. It is raining now. We'd better wait until it _____.
    A) will stop   B) stop   C) stops   D) stopped

173. I have a mark on my coat but _____.
    A) it is not noticeable   B) I've cleaned it
    C) you can see it   D) it was very small

174. I couldn't solve the problem so _____.
    A) I telephoned the police   B) I called an ambulance
    C) I asked my father to help me   D) I answered the advertisement

175. You'd better take care of yourself, otherwise, _____.
    A) it is very cold outside   B) you will catch cold
    C) put on a sweater   D) you should take a hot shower

176. She is very healthy, but _____.
    A) she can play tennis   B) she is also rich
    C) she might get sick   D) she reads a lot

177. Although he eats a lot, _____.
    A) he is losing weight   B) he is gaining weight
    C) he is getting fatter   D) he is putting on weight

178. The doctor examined me; however, _____.
    A) he found nothing wrong with me
    B) he prescribed some medicine
    C) I wasn't feeling very well
    D) I was given an injection

179. There is 'no smoking' sign in our library but _____.
    A) I never smoke there   B) a lot of people ignore it
    C) nobody smokes   D) everybody must obey this

180. We can't do anything before _____.
    A) the doctor comes   B) the doctor didn't come
    C) the doctor will come   D) the doctor doesn't come

INTERMEDIATE / UPPER-INTERMEDIATE 6

adjective - adverb - noun clauses

Choose the best answer.

1. I don't know _____ to telephone.
   A) whom did Tom want B) why was Tom going
   C) when is Tom D) who Tom was going

2. No one seemed to know _____.
   A) why was he angry
   B) which party has won
   C) when the festival was due to start
   D) what is his latest decision

3. "Why don't we go out for dinner?" His wife suggested that _____.
   A) they would go out for dinner
   B) they should go out for dinner
   C) we will go out for dinner
   D) we'd like to go out for dinner

4. "Oh dear! It looks as if it is going to rain again." Mother was afraid that _____.
   A) it was raining again B) it was going to rain
   C) it is going to rain again D) it looked like rain again

5. "Fantastic! I've actually passed my exam!" exclaimed Janet. Janet was delighted to find that _____.
   A) I'd passed my exam B) I've passed my exam
   C) she's passed her exam D) she'd passed her exam

6. I doubt _____ anybody knows how to solve the housing problem in Turkey.
   A) whether B) which C) why D) what

7. It is important that you _____ late.
   A) don't be B) won't be C) not to be D) not be

8. The doctor recommended that she _____ in bed for a few days.
   A) will stay B) stay C) would stay D) to stay

9. The bank manager suggested that I _____ again the following year.
   A) should apply B) applied C) to apply D) would apply

10. _____ is still uncertain.
    A) Why did they lose the match B) He is really guilty
    C) When will they come D) Who first reported the fire

11. The accused pretended that he _____ the lawyer's question.
    A) didn't understand B) hasn't understood
    C) doesn't understand D) wouldn't understand

12. His doctor recommended that he _____ taking sleeping pills for a while.
    A) would try B) should try C) tries D) tried

13. _____ next was lost in the general uproar.
    A) What the speaker said B) That the speaker said
    C) What did the speaker say D) The speaker said that

14. _____ is where you get all your energy from.
    A) It amazes me B) That amazes me
    C) What amazes me D) That amazed me

15. _____ me to do is out of question.
    A) What you are asking B) How you are asking
    C) That you ask D) That you asked

16. No one doubted _____ sincere in his beliefs.
    A) what he was B) that he was
    C) why was he D) that he is

17. He didn't even apologize. This made her really angry. _____ he didn't even apologize made her really angry.
    A) Why B) What C) The fact that D) The reason

18. _____ made her angry was the fact that her husband had forgotten her birthday.
    A) Why B) The fact that C) What D) The thing

19. On entering the restaurant, I immediately realized _____ so popular.
    A) why was it B) how is it
    C) the fact that was D) why it was

20. Where the pilot finally managed to land _____.
    A) is not known B) nobody knows;
    C) we don't know D) nobody knew

21. Teachers have found the overhead projector to be invaluable as a teaching aid.
    Teachers have found that the overhead projector _____.
    A) to be invaluable as a teaching aid
    B) is invaluable as a teaching aid
    C) was invaluable as a teaching aid
    D) invaluable as a teaching aid

22. The law requires that all cars _____ regularly tested for safety and efficiency.
    A) should be B) to be C) were to be D) have to be

23. I assured him that he _____ pneumonia.
    A) should get B) would get C) get D) gets

24. He began to realize that he _____ mistake.
    A) is making B) has made C) had made D) will make

25. The Prime minister warned that higher wages _____ higher prices.
    A) would mean B) will mean C) mean D) to mean

26. Many people considered it to be cruel to send animals in rockets into outer space.
    Many people consider that _____ cruel to send animals in rockets into further space.
    A) to be B) it to be C) it is D) it was

27. The Prime Minister clearly suspects his party to have little chance of winning the next election.
    The Prime Minister clearly suspects that his party _____ little chance of winning the next election.
    A) to have B) has C) would have D) had

28. The witness later disclosed the evidence to have been destroyed.
    The witness later disclosed that the evidence _____.
    A) to be destroyed B) had been destroyed
    C) has been destroyed D) would be destroyed

29. Researches have now proved that earlier theories _____ incorrect.
    A) were B) had been C) to have been D) to be

30. "May I have my letters addressed in care of your office?" asked Mr. Taylor.
    Mr. Taylor asked if _____ letters addressed in care of _____ office.
    A) he may have his / my B) I might have my / your
    C) he may have his / his D) he might have his / my

31. The doctor says, "The moisture in the air might affect your breathing." He thinks that the moisture in the air _____.
    A) might affect my breathing B) might affect your breathing
    C) would affect my breathing D) may affect your breathing

32. "I'd love to come." she said. She said _____ to come.
    A) she'd liked B) I'd like C) she'd like D) I'd liked

33. "Which of these films have you seen?" My friend asked me which of the films _____.
    A) have I seen B) I had seen C) you had seen D) have you seen

34. "Whom did you see at the concert last night?" She asked us whom _____ the other night.
    A) I'd seen B) we'd seen C) we saw D) I saw

35. They asked, "Is the work going to be easy?" They wondered if _____.
    A) was work going to be easy B) the work is going to be easy
    C) the work was easy D) the work was going to be easy

36. He asked "Have you read *The old Man and the Sea*, Ted?" He wanted to know if _____ *The old Man and the Sea*.
    A) I'd read B) he'd read C) I have read D) he has read

37. "Please give me a pain killer." the patient said.
    The patient begged the nurse _____ a pain killer.
    A) to give her B) she would give her
    C) she would give me D) to give me

38. "Don't eat those cherries, they are poisonous," said David. David _____ not to eat those cherries because they were poisonous.
    A) didn't want me B) said to me that
    C) warned me D) suggested that

39. "Did she agree with me?" He wondered if _____.
    A) she'd agreed with he B) she agreed with him
    C) she'd agreed with him D) she'd agree with him

40. I wanted to know why no one _____.
    A) had come   B) hadn't come   C) has come   D) hasn't come

41. Everybody said, "We're glad the danger is over."
    Everybody said that _____.
    A) he was glad the danger was over
    B) they are glad the danger is over
    C) they were glad the danger was over
    D) he is glad the danger is over

42. _____ was to have dinner after the meeting.
    A) What we are to do   B) Which we needed
    C) What I wanted to do   D) Why he comes

43. I recommended that the patient _____ on as soon as possible.
    A) is operated   B) operated
    C) would be operated   D) be operated

44. George told me that _____ with his roommate next semester.
    A) he'd rather not live   B) he wouldn't have lived
    C) he won't live   D) he hadn't lived

45. "I'll hit you!" _____ to hit me.
    A) He suggested   B) He threatened
    C) He promised   D) He offered

46. "Would you like to come to my party?" He invited her _____.
    A) she'd like to come to his party
    B) she'd like to come to my party
    C) if she'd come to his party
    D) to come to his party

47. I didn't hear _____ because there was so much noise where I was sitting.
    A) what was he saying   B) what he has said
    C) what did he say   D) what he said

48. I had hoped _____ my letter.
    A) that she answer   B) she answers
    C) that she would answer   D) she will answer

49. I have no idea _____.
    A) what does this word mean   B) why he has left
    C) when will he arrive   D) how was he killed

50. "Let's go to the cinema this evening," she said.
    She suggested that they _____ to the cinema that evening.
    A) should go   B) would go   C) will go   D) had gone

51. A: Are you going to complain to the police?
    B: Yes, that is _____.
    A) what I have done   B) what I'm going to do
    C) what I was going to do   D) what I would do

52. He _____ to me that he had written a new book.
    A) told   B) tells   C) has said   D) said

53. She said _____ to walk back home.
    A) she'd rather   B) she'd prefer
    C) she'd better   D) she has got

54. I knew that _____ would be difficult.
    A) their coming   B) they would come
    C) they came   D) they were coming

55. It is important that _____ the bilateral talks.
    A) he attend   B) he attends
    C) he attended   D) he'll attend

56. We urge that the plans _____.
    A) not approved   B) not be approved
    C) not to be approved   D) won't be approved

57. We now insist that all cars _____ seat belts to reduce the death toll.
    A) to have   B) will have   C) have had   D) have

58. _____ makes visiting him very difficult.
    A) The fact that he is very busy
    B) The reason why he is very busy
    C) What I know is that he is very busy
    D) It is a fact that he is very busy

59. _____ was clear from his letter.
    A) He was angry
    B) He resented being treated rudely
    C) That he was not interested
    D) What I knew

60. The fact that the experts say stagnation will continue for some time _____.
    A) industry will suffer a lot
    B) we should be prepared for higher inflation
    C) is annoying
    D) we cannot avoid it

61. If grades are going to be given to students for their reports, it is suggested that these _____ for expression and use of language.
    A) given   B) to be given   C) are given   D) be given

62. _____ best is riding horses.
    A) She likes   B) That she likes
    C) What she liked   D) What she likes

63. We had hoped _____ the game, but other team played very well.
    A) the National Team to win
    B) that the National Team win
    C) that the National Team would win
    D) the National Team's winning

64. It is important that he _____ his reservations by Saturday.
    A) will confirm   B) confirm   C) confirms   D) must confirm

65. He asked me if I had ever played the piano. He asked me, "____?"
    A) Do you ever play the piano
    B) Did you ever play the piano
    C) Have I ever played the piano
    D) Have you ever played the piano

66. The doctor asked the patient if she had had a heart attack before. The doctor asked the patient," _____ a heart attack before ?"
    A) Has she had   B) Have you had
    C) Did she have   D) Did you have

67. It is urgent that he _____ on time.
    A) arrived   B) will arrive   C) would arrive   D) arrive

68. It is important that you _____ honest.
    A) will be   B) be   C) were   D) to be

69. The doctor recommended that I _____ weight.
    A) should lose   B) would lose   C) must lose   D) will lose

70. Julia must understand the question. It is necessary.
    It is necessary that Julia _____ the question.
    A) understood   B) understands
    C) must understand   D) should understand

71. Bill must talk to the teacher. It is urgent. It is urgent that Bill _____ to the teacher.
    A) must talk   B) talk   C) talks   D) has talked

72. _____ because he got bored so easily.
    A) Why he left early   B) Why he was embarrassed
    C) Why did he get angry   D) Why he acted as he did was

73. I can't imagine _____.
    A) why did he recommend him
    B) who recommended him for training
    C) when will he recommend me
    D) how will he recommend him

74. What would have suited him better _____.
    A) would be to be a politician
    B) to give up smoking
    C) he shouldn't have married her
    D) than his father's job

75. I suggested that she _____ a doctor.
    A) will see   B) would see   C) must see   D) see

76. I don't know _____.
    A) they were thinking about
    B) that they were thinking about
    C) what do they think about
    D) what they were thinking about

77. I insisted that he _____ me the money.
    A) was paid   B) be paid   C) pay   D) will pay

78. It is not probable that _____ in the next ten years.
    A) the world's population stopped
    B) man must discover a cure for cancer
    C) computers must become more important
    D) air pollution will decrease

79. _____ still puzzles me.
    A) He got selected president
    B) Where they got the idea from
    C) He has got a lot of money
    D) How can they beat us

80. I don't know much about art but I know _____.
    A) what I like
    B) who is a good artist
    C) what is it like
    D) why are people paying that much

81. Do you think _____ man will travel to Mars in this century?
    A) is it possible that   B) it is possible that
    C) will it be possible   D) it became possible

82. Mike must explain his idea. It is important. It is important that Mike _____ his ideas.
    A) explain   B) will explain   C) explains   D) would explain

83. Why is it necessary that _____?
    A) for him to study   B) he will have an operation
    C) he consult an expert   D) he applied for a job

84. He advised that she _____ the bad news.
    A) not be told   B) not to be told
    C) isn't told   D) wouldn't tell

85. He asked us whom we would visit. He asked us, "Whom _____?"
    A) will you visit   B) would you visit
    C) you will visit   D) we would visit

86. The teacher insisted on the students' arriving punctually for their lessons.
    The teacher insisted that the students _____ punctually for their lessons.
    A) had arrived   B) should arrive
    C) would arrive   D) have to arrive

87. Most people don't even know _____.
    A) why has he resigned   B) where was he buried
    C) what good music is   D) where did they take him

88. I refuse to believe her having told me the truth. I refuse to believe that she _____ me the truth.
    A) tell   B) tells   C) had told   D) would tell

89. They proposed that a new highway _____.
    A) should build   B) must build   C) to be built   D) be built

90. It is desirable that no one else _____ about the problem.
    A) doesn't know   B) know   C) to know   D) will know

91. That she was chosen Miss Turkey _____.
    A) made me happy
    B) nobody was glad about it
    C) everybody approved it
    D) everyone present voted in her favor

92. Whether they do it or not _____.
    A) don't make any difference   B) depends on various factors
    C) created a big problem   D) will cause a lot of disturbance

93. I am satisfied _____.
    A) that she came third in the competition.
    B) it was our victory against enemies
    C) what you promised to do
    D) will make her happy, I believe

94. The fact that they blamed us for the accident _____.
    A) which was not our fault   B) was surprising
    C) at which a person was killed D) I wasn't involved

95. _____ is a fact.
    A) That the poor have a hard life B) The world is round
    C) He came first   D) What is he saying

96. Did _____ help him in his career?
    A) the fact that his father was a professor
    B) he was rich and friendly
    C) that he won a scholarship
    D) his teacher recommended him

97. It is incredible that _____.
    A) she study very hard   B) will be the result
    C) he undergo an operation   D) he has passed his exams

98. It is necessary that everyone _____ here on time.
    A) will be   B) be   C) are   D) to be

99. "If I were you, I'd open a bank account because interest is high now" I told her.
    I suggested that she _____ a saving account.
    A) would open   B) will open   C) open   D) had opened

100. Our teacher wishes he _____ another profession.
    A) chose   B) had chosen
    C) would choose   D) has chosen

101. I wish the teacher _____ us more about the exam before it takes place.
    A) would tell   B) has told   C) had told   D) tells

102. I wish you _____ here now. I miss you a lot.
    A) are   B) were   C) had been   D) will be

103. I wish you _____. I'm sure you would enjoy joining us.
    A) could come   B) had come   C) may come   D) would come

104. She won't help me. I wish she _____ me.
    A) will help   B) would help   C) helps   D) had helped

105. I wish I _____ the last bus. Now I'll have to walk.
    A) didn't miss   B) hadn't missed
    C) wouldn't miss   D) wouldn't have missed

106. Don't you wish we _____ tonight?
    A) weren't going   B) aren't going
    C) don't go   D) hadn't gone

107. It is raining. I wish it _____.
    A) hadn't rain   B) didn't rain
    C) weren't raining   D) isn't raining

108. When it was too late, he wished he _____ a better husband.
    A) has been   B) had been   C) were   D) would be

109. You can't change things simply by wishing they _____ different.
    A) are   B) will be   C) would be   D) were

110. I wish he _____ to Tokyo with me last weekend.
    A) came   B) would come   C) had come   D) could come

111. I wish that you _____ such a bad headache because I'm sure that you'd have enjoyed the party.
    A) didn't have   B) hadn't had
    C) wouldn't have   D) won't have

112. I wish that I _____ with you last summer.
    A) went   B) could go   C) have gone   D) could've gone

113. You might have cleaned the bath after you'd used it.
    I wish you _____ the bath after using it.
    A) had cleaned   B) cleaned   C) would clean   D) clean

114. You might come to work a bit earlier on Mondays. I wish you _____ a bit earlier on Mondays.
    A) had come   B) would've come
    C) were coming   D) would come

115. You might have remembered my birthday. I wish you _____ my birthday.
    A) had remembered   B) remembered
    C) would remember   D) could remember

116. You might make less noise. If only you _____ less noise.
    A) had made   B) made   C) would make   D) might make

117. If only I _____ busy yesterday. I could have helped you with the problem.
    A) weren't   B) hadn't been   C) wasn't   D) haven't been

118. He wishes his father _____ him some shoes before the new term starts.
    A) was buying   B) was going to buy
    C) would buy   D) had bought

119. I wish our school _____ a bigger library than it has.
    A) had had   B) would have   C) had   D) will have

120. I wish we _____ late for this film. I can't follow the story.
    A) didn't arrive   B) hadn't arrived
    C) wouldn't arrive   D) wouldn't have arrived

121. She wishes she _____ younger than she is.
    A) were   B) would be   C) had been   D) is

122. A: Janet couldn't come to the concert last night.
    B: I wish she _____ .
    A) is able to come   B) was able to come
    C) could have come   D) had come

123. I couldn't get through the traffic in time.
    I wish I _____ through the traffic in time.
    A) am able to get   B) had been able to get
    C) was able to get   D) would have got

124. My father wasn't able to pay the money back.
    I wish my father _____ the money back.
    A) could have paid   B) were able to pay
    C) could pay   D) would be able to pay

125. It is a pity you drink too much. If only you _____ so much.
    A) don't drink   B) won't drink   C) didn't drink   D) hadn't drunk

126. It is a pity that we rejected their proposal. If only we _____ their proposal.
    A) won't reject   B) hadn't rejected
    C) wouldn't reject   D) didn't reject

127. A: I must go home now. B: I wish you _____ home now.
    A) don't have to go   B) mustn't have gone
    C) didn't have to go   D) needn't have gone

128. A: Don't you have enough time to learn English?
    B: No, I don't. I wish I _____ time to learn English.
    A) did have   B) had had   C) do have   D) will have

129. The bus always stops at every bus-stop. I wish it _____ at every bus-stop.
    A) didn't stop   B) would stop   C) hadn't stopped   D) won't stop

130. The party was so bad that they left early. They wish _____.
    A) they didn't go   B) they wouldn't have gone
    C) they didn't have to go D) they hadn't gone

131. A: Sandy had an accident because she wasn't careful.
    B: If only she _____.
    A) had been careful   B) were careful
    C) would be careful   D) would have been careful

132. A: Robert is unhappy because he can't find his passport.
    B: If only he _____.
    A) could have found it   B) had been able to find
    C) could find it   D) had found it

133. A: We have to cancel the match because it is raining.
    B: If only it _____.
    A) won't be raining   B) isn't raining
    C) didn't rain   D) weren't raining

134. A: Mary is sorry that she bought such an expensive dress.
    B: If only she _____ such an expensive dress.
    A) didn't buy   B) wouldn't have bought
    C) hadn't bought   D) could have bought

135. Don't you think it is significant _____?
    A) in case he fails   B) that he has been re-elected
    C) how comfortable is it D) if we had been offered the job

136. Water is a compound _____ molecule consists of two atoms of hydrogen and one atom of oxygen.
    A) which   B) whom   C) whose   D) of which

137. A dynamo is a machine _____ is used for producing electricity.
    A) who   B) which   C) whom   D) of which

138. The student couldn't remember the year _____ Hitler was born.
    A) when   B) which   C) at which   D) where

139. That is the hotel _____ I stayed at.
    A) where   B) which   C) that   D) whose

140. Hydrogen is an element _____ atomic number is 1 and _____ atomic weight is 1.008.
    A) whose / whose   B) of which / whose
    C) which / of which   D) which / which

141. Neron, _____ was Emperor of Rome, from 45 to 68 A.D, is believed to have murdered both his mother and his wife.
    A) whom   B) whose   C) who   D) that

142. Marlon Brando, _____, is a friend of my fathers.
    A) whose son is in jail now
    B) which is famous worldwide
    C) that you met at the seminar
    D) has just arrived in Spain

143. The problem was with the battery _____ a dead cell.
    A) that has   B) which had   C) who had   D) in which has

144. There were fifty questions on the test, _____.
    A) either was easy
    B) all of which were difficult
    C) all of them were very hard
    D) all of whom were very interested

145. I'm looking for something with _____ I can clean the board.
    A) whom   B) which   C) that   D) whose

146. Gentlemen, from _____ we expect politeness, ought not to lose their tempers.
    A) which   B) who   C) whom   D) where

147. Your information, for _____ I'm grateful, is very helpful.
    A) that   B) which   C) whom   D) whose

148. Men _____ work is good receive high wages.
    A) who   B) that   C) whom   D) whose

149. He did his medical training at a hospital _____.
    A) who is very famous as a surgeon
    B) of which is located just beside a river
    C) which specializes in heart surgery
    D) whose patients are treated very carefully

150. That evening we went to the opera, _____.
    A) where we met the newly appointed general director
    B) that was opened last week by the Minister of Culture
    C) which were fully booked
    D) when all the lights went out

151. His father, _____, said he didn't like to work.
    A) that had retired a few weeks ago
    B) he gave a series of interviews
    C) is an electrical engineer
    D) who was already over sixty - five

152. Mr. Benson, _____, shot himself.
    A) that was known to be very rich
    B) whose firm closed because of complaints
    C) we haven't ever met him
    D) he owns several factories

153. Crops can now be grown in deserts _____.
    A) most of them are in Africa
    B) it was impossible to cultivate the land
    C) where farming would be impossible without irrigation
    D) these are known as dry areas

154. The boys _____ are having special lessons.
    A) which need more care
    B) they are behind the other boys
    C) who have been offered a scholarship
    D) their fathers own factories

155. It was they _____.
    A) who told us the news   B) are against the proposal
    C) when they came to see us   D) which is very late

156. They refused to be reasonable about the delay, _____.
    A) the rain was late   B) that caused a lot of trouble
    C) which made me angry   D) whose passengers were tourists

157. George ordered an enormous steak, _____.
    A) it wasn't well — done   B) which cost him a lot
    C) was very delicious   D) he ate all by himself

158. The students in the early class, _____, did very well on yesterday's maths test.
    A) they study very hard all semester
    B) very few of them had studied very hard
    C) most of whom had studied the night before
    D) they studied hard last week

159. He forgot to get the tickets, _____.
    A) whose wife got very angry with him
    B) his wife had booked yesterday
    C) where his wife wanted to see
    D) which annoyed his wife very much

160. It is nuclear war, which could exterminate mankind, _____.
    A) which is a great danger
    B) its power is unquestionable
    C) that we must avoid
    D) everybody knows it is dangerous

161. The book was _____ boring _____ I only could read two chapters.
    A) such / that   B) so / that   C) very / that   D) too / that

162. It was _____ a boring book _____ I only could read two chapters.
    A) such / that   B) so / that   C) too / as   D) very / as

163. _____ you talk to him, _____ you like him.
    A) Much / the more
    B) The more / the less
    C) More / more
    D) The most / the most

164. _____ I didn't know anybody at the reception, I had a good time.
    A) In spite of that   B) Even so
    C) Even if   D) Even though

165. _____ I've finished "A Tale of Two Cities, I'll read "Oliver Twist".
    A) Therefore   B) Even if   C) Though   D) Now that

166. No sooner had I opened the door _____ the telephone rang.
    A) when   B) before   C) than   D) as soon as

167. _____ you're happy about it, I have no objection.
    A) As long as   B) Whatever   C) Therefore   D) Even so

168. He didn't have any money, _____ he couldn't buy a ticket.
    A) moreover   B) however   C) because   D) consequently

169. He had enough money to buy a ticket, _____, he decided not to go.
    A) consequently   B) nevertheless
    C) moreover   D) because

170. He wanted to go with us; _____ he packed his suitcase.
    A) so   B) nevertheless   C) moreover   D) but

171. It is late; _____, it is raining cats and dogs.
    A) therefore   B) nevertheless   C) because   D) moreover

172. I didn't have enough time; _____, I couldn't go.
    A) nevertheless   B) moreover   C) therefore   D) however

173. She's been working for eight hours; _____, she is tired.
    A) consequently   B) however
    C) nevertheless   D) because

174. I'll finish this. Then I'll join you. When I _____ this, I'll join you.
    A) was finished   B) will finish
    C) finished   D) have finished

175. She dressed the child in a heavy overcoat, _____ he should catch cold.
    A) because   B) therefore   C) however   D) lest

176. I've written it down for her, _____ she forgets it.
    A) so as to   B) therefore   C) in case   D) in order to

177. I will go home for vacation as soon as I _____ my exams.
    A) will finish   B) finish   C) am finishing   D) finished

178. When she arrived, I was pretty fed up, because I _____ since eight o'clock.
    A) had been waiting   B) have waited
    C) have been waiting   D) had waited

179. We left early _____ avoid the traffic.
    A) because   B) so as not to   C) so as to   D) not to

180. They tiptoed up the stairs _____ wake the children.
    A) in order to   B) so as not to   C) so as to   D) because of

181. We won't go unless the weather _____ fine.
    A) will be   B) is   C) won't be   D) isn't

182. I was on vacation; _____, I didn't get your letter.
    A) therefore   B) however   C) even if   D) although

183. Dr. King gives interesting lectures; _____, he is very popular with his students.
    A) however   B) consequently
    C) but also   D) not only

184. Robert didn't study for the test; _____ he did very veil.
    A) consequently   B) therefore
    C) moreover   D) nevertheless

185. James wants to buy a new car, _____ he doesn't have enough money.
    A) however   B) therefore   C) moreover   D) consequently

186. He found everything rather strange, as he _____ abroad before.
    A) would never   B) had never been
    C) has never been   D) will never be

187. _____ coal reserves are abundant, taking advantage of them requires an active program of development.
    A) Even though   B) Therefore
    C) So that   D) Nevertheless

188. _____ the price of petrol is so high, I can't afford to run a car any more.
    A) However   B) Now that   C) So that   D) Even though

189. _____ the bans remained in force, Turkey could not claim to be fully democratic.
    A) Unless   B) Provided   C) As long as   D) Because of

190. Doctors often use X-rays _____ they can pass through skin and flesh.
    A) so that   B) as long as   C) provided   D) nevertheless

191. Within another hundred years we will have to find alternative sources of energy, _____ the world's reserves of oil will not last that long.
    A) so that   B) since   C) unless   D) while

192. An airline pilot and a racing driver are similar _____ they must possess good judgment and the ability to react quickly in a crisis.
    A) however   B) so that   C) in that   D) even if

193. They built a high fence around the building _____ no one could get out.
    A) as   B) so that   C) since   D) because

194. The old woman had to stand all the way _____ no one let her sit down on the bus.
    A) so   B) so that   C) since   D) although

195. He stole the money _____ I warned him not to.
    A) due to   B) in case   C) because   D) although

196. We were _____ late _____ we missed the plane to Istanbul.
    A) so / that   B) such / than   C) very / then   D) too / to

197. I had to work until midnight _____ I was very tired.
    A) although   B) so that   C) in case   D) provided that

198. _____ I took an aspirin, I still have a headache.
    A) Even though   B) Nevertheless   C) Because   D) As

199. A: You studied hard. Did you pass the test?
    B: No, _____ I studied hard, I didn't pass the test.
    A) because   B) as   C) even though   D) unless

200. It was cold; _____ we went on a picnic.
    A) even though   B) nevertheless
    C) so   D) while

201. _____ he had a broken leg, he continued to go to class.
    A) Nevertheless   B) In spite of the fact that
    C) In spite of   D) Because of

202. Some people are fat, _____ others are thin.
    A) because   B) in spite of   C) despite of   D) whereas

203. _____ some students think physics is easy, others find it difficult.
    A) As   B) even   C) Nevertheless   D) While

204. Do you want to walk? The rain has stopped.
    _____ the rain's stopped, do you want to walk?
    A) In spite of   B) As long as   C) Now that   D) Due to

205. _____ it's raining, I think I'll stay at home.
    A) As long as   B) Because of
    C) Despite of   D) On the other hand

206. _____ Monday is a national holiday, all government offices will be closed.
    A) Whereas   B) Since   C) While   D) Because of

207. I'll eat lunch with you _____ there is enough for both of us.
    A) provided   B) so as   C) therefore   D) whereas
208. We'll get along just fine _____ he minds his own business.
    A) as   B) therefore   C) as long as   D) so that
209. Apparently Betty is jealous _____ I get better grades than she does.
    A) in spite of   B) in case   C) moreover   D) because
210. _____ I apologized, he looked as if he wanted to strangle me.
    A) In spite of   B) Even though   C) Because   D) Therefore
211. The government puts up taxes _____ get more money from us.
    A) in order to   B) as   C) because   D) so that
212. I wrote down the address _____ I wouldn't forget it.
    A) because   B) so as to   C) so that   D) as
213. Roy talks _____ nonsense that no one listens to him any more.
    A) although   B) as if   C) like   D) such
214. She doesn't mind working overtime _____ she's paid for it.
    A) provided that   B) so that
    C) as a result   D) in case
215. We have to do the job _____ we like it or not.
    A) if   B) whether   C) unless   D) provided that
216. I did my homework _____ our teacher had instructed.
    A) as   B) in order that   C) for fear that   D) so that
217. I'll give you my telephone number _____ you want to get in touch with me again.
    A) although   B) in case   C) so that   D) as if
218. I obeyed her _____ she should be angry.
    A) provided that   B) but   C) unless   D) lest
219. Please turn down the TV. I want to be able to get to sleep. Please turn down the TV so that _____.
    A) I am getting to sleep   B) I'll be able to sleep
    C) I could get to sleep   D) I can get to sleep
220. Please be quiet so that _____.
    A) the teacher will get angry
    B) I can hear what the teacher is saying
    C) I heard what the teacher said
    D) to hear what the teacher is saying
221. Mike decided to become an anthropologist _____.
    A) so he can study the life of a primitive tribe
    B) that's why he will watch the documentary film on a primitive tribe
    C) after he saw a documentary film on a primitive tribe
    D) due to the fact that the film is- on a primitive tribe
222. "Having seen that film before, she wants to see a different one." means: _____
    A) As she has seen a different film before, she can see this film.
    B) Because she's seen that film before, she wants to go to different one.
    C) As she'd seen that film before, she wanted to see a different one.
    D) Because she wants to see that film, she can watch it.
223. "Having worked all day, I was tired last night." means: _____.
    A) As I had worked all day, I was feeling tired last night.
    B) I worked tiringly hard all day yesterday.
    C) Since I've worked all day, I am tired now.
    D) Because I was tired last night, I worked all day.
224. "I got to the airport at 9.15. My plane left ten minutes later." means: _____.
    A) My plane had left ten minutes ago.
    B) Before I got to the airport, my plane had taken off.
    C) I got to the airport just before my plane left.
    D) I couldn't catch my plane.
225. Since he's not interested in classical music, he _____.
    A) hasn't gone to the concert
    B) would have gone to the concert
    C) had decided not to go to the concert
    D) was supposed to go to the concert
226. _____ the semester is finished, I'm going to rest a few days and then take a trip.
    A) Whenever   B) Now that   C) In spite of   D) In order to

227. This is _____ book that I don't think I'll finish it.
    A) such a boring   B) very boring   C) such boring   D) so boring
228. I can't repair the dishwasher myself _____.
    A) that it has broken down
    B) because I had it repaired
    C) so I will get someone to do it for me
    D) unless the repairman had helped me
229. I've gained _____ weight that I can't wear any of my old clothes.
    A) so many   B) too many   C) so much   D) too much
230. I've met _____ people in the last few days that I can't possibly remember all of their names.
    A) so many   B) too many   C) so much   D) too much
231. Ever since I was a child, I _____ afraid of dogs.
    A) am   B) was   C) have been   D) will be
232. Janet's contact lens popped out while she _____.
    A) was playing   B) is playing
    C) has been playing   D) played
233. Be sure to reread your composition for errors before you _____ it in to the teacher tomorrow.
    A) are handed   B) hand
    C) having handed   D) handed
234. By the time I leave this city, I _____ here for ten years.
    A) have lived   B) would have lived
    C) will live   D) will have lived
235. "We can't leave now. We have to wait Peggy." means: _____.
    A) We can't leave because Peggy isn't here.
    B) We must leave now, because Peggy is waiting for us.
    C) Peggy is waiting; we can't leave.
    D) We must stay here until Peggy arrives.
236. "_____ the terrible weather, we enjoyed ourselves.
    A) In spite of   B) Because   C) Although   D) However
237. "My roommate walked into the room. Immediately, I knew that something was wrong." means: _____ I knew that something was wrong.
    A) As soon as my roommate entered the room,
    B) Before my roommate walked into the room,
    C) By the time my roommate came into the room,
    D) After my roommate came into the room,
238. _____ the harm she's done him, he still loves her.
    A) In spite of   B) Although
    C) Because   D) Even though
239. _____ hard I try, I still can't do it.
    A) In spite of   B) Although
    C) Therefore   D) However
240. _____ quickly you work, you'll never catch up.
    A) Although   B) even though
    C) Moreover   D) However
241. You'd better leave now. _____, you'll have to get a taxi home.
    A) otherwise   B) in case   C) yet   D) still
242. He left school at sixteen, _____ he has had no real education.
    A) because   B) for   C) so   D) even though
243. She didn't seem to recognize me _____ we had never met.
    A) like   B) as if   C) although   D) yet
244. The food may be good at the Harvard but it's _____ expensive.
    A) very much   B) far too   C) even so   D) quite a lot
245. People normally treat you just _____ you treat them.
    A) the same   B) as if   C) as though   D) as
246. He acted strangely, _____ he was frightened,
    A) otherwise   B) like   C) as though   D) the way
247. The weather was _____ bad _____ we didn't go to the seaside.
    A) such / then   B) very / that   C) so / that   D) too / that
248. It was hot, _____ I didn't need my coat.
    A) because   B) so   C) however   D) although
249. She doesn't like phones in living rooms, and _____ does her sister.
    A) so   B) but   C) neither   D) too

250. ____ everybody seemed to be out of cigarettes, I passed mine round.
   A) As   B) So   C) So that   D) In order that

251. ____ she had sung, the whole audience stood and applauded loudly.
   A) Although   B) After   C) Now that   D) So long as

252. _____ he is very rich, he lives very simply.
   A) After   B) While   C) As   D) Although

253. _____ you say to her, she still keeps smiling.
   A) However   B) Moreover   C) Whatever   D) Whenever

254. You shouldn't be rude, _____ you're very angry.
   A) even if   B) however   C) as if   D) therefore

255. You can phone me _____ you like.
   A) whichever   B) in case   C) whatever   D) whenever

256. He speaks English much _____ he writes it.
   A) better than   B) worse   C) clearer than   D) a lot worse

257. Mr. Taylor, I'm here just in case _____.
   A) they will come earlier
   B) anything out of the ordinary happens
   C) they telephoned to meet them at the airport
   D) you might need my help

258. I'm in a difficult situation in that _____.
   A) I've been offered two jobs and they both sound interesting
   B) I had better study, harder
   C) I don't want to get disillusioned
   D) there was some misunderstanding

259. He feels himself to be dependent in that_____.
   A) he is not free to question decisions affecting his daily life
   B) he isn't in good health and spirits
   C) the company collapsed within six months
   D) early retirement is a means of reducing the workforce

260. Be clear and factual in order that _____.
   A) to protect the employee's rights
   B) there will be many exciting opportunities in the future
   C) agriculture and rural industry are flourishing
   D) there may be no misunderstanding

261. I'd have married her even _____.
   A) her parents had given their consent
   B) she'd rather I had married her
   C) she had been penniless
   D) she was in love with another man

262. He grabbed me and shook me till _____.
   A) my teeth rattled
   B) the police have arrived
   C) I'd apologized to him
   D) he would have noticed I had a gun

263. Long before you return _____.
   A) everybody has already left
   B) we'd sold out of your size
   C) she will have forgotten you
   D) I'd finished all the work

264. I had no sooner checked in to the hotel_____.
   A) when two gunmen ordered me to open my briefcase
   B) than he arrived with the appropriate documents
   C) a young lady approached me with a smile
   D) before all rooms have been reserved

265. Hardly had he uttered the words _____.
   A) than we left the room
   B) when he began laughing
   C) as soon as everybody sat down
   D) the manager came in

266. Nobody gets anything unless _____.
   A) they ask for it
   B) he has enough money
   C) they don't work harder
   D) he isn't very determined

267. I get an electrician to check all my electrical appliances every autumn   whether or not _____.
   A) they are giving trouble
   B) they don't need checking
   C) he is very good at it
   D) he charges me a lot

268. "They built a statue of him lest people should forget what he had done." means: _____.
   A) They built a statue of him so that people would not forget what he had done.
   B) They built a statue of him because people wouldn't forget what he had done
   C) As people would forget what he had done one day, they built a statue of him
   D) Believing that it was necessary for people not to forget what he had done, they had a statue of him built

269. Tourism is a good thing inasmuch as _____.
   A) if we are to pay our debts
   B) foreign exchange is concerned
   C) foreign trade is essential
   D) it brings people into contact with other nations

270. I used to love listening to her, even though _____.
   A) she has nothing interesting to mention
   B) we didn't have a radio to listen to
   C) she was a good friend of mine
   D) I could only understand about half of what she said

271. Nobody said a thing except that _____.
   A) one or two asked me if I was better
   B) I would tell them everything in detail
   C) they had already told everything in their mind
   D) a man who has been involved in the accident

272. In Turkey, _____ you come across ceremonies.
   A) which is rich in history   B) I'm sure you'll enjoy it
   C) wherever you go   D) its people are very hospitable

273. I was never allowed to do the things_____.
   A) the way I wanted to do them
   B) I've always thought of realizing
   C) I'm very keen on carrying out
   D) nevertheless I am very determined to solve

274. She felt as if _____.
   A) she is a stranger   B) the fur coat was very nice
   C) she had a fever   D) she is in a crowded stadium

275. His hair looked as if _____.
   A) it has just been dyed
   B) it had been combed with his fingers
   C) it hasn't been cut for ages
   D) it needs cutting

276. I felt as if _____.
   A) I'm going to get selected
   B) I've done my best for the realization of the project
   C) I were the center of the universe
   D) I would have fainted

277. He behaved as though _____.
   A) it was nothing to be ashamed of
   B) he is a millionaire
   C) he has come to a garden party
   D) he lost all his money

278. Our aim is to recruit the most qualified person, _____.
   A) unless there are some really good ones
   B) whether or not we liked them
   C) no matter where he is from
   D) whichever way you looked at it

279. I'd do anything to get that contract, but it is highly unlikely _____.
   A) my firm would get it
   B) that my firm will get it
   C) for my firm getting it
   D) if my firm can get it

280. They decided to postpone the match, _____ the weather conditions were better than they had expected.
   A) yet   B) nevertheless
   C) even though   D) because

ELEMENTARY PRE-INTERMEDIATE 7

modals

Choose the best alternative.

1. _____ you speak Spanish?
   A) May B) Are C) Can D) Is

2. A: _____ I go? B: Yes, you can.
   A) Could B) Am C) Need D) Did

3. _____ you help me with my homework?
   A) Are B) May C) Can D) Need

4. You _____ enter without a tie.
   A) aren't B) can't C) ought not D) weren't

5. Cigarettes _____ seriously damage your health.
   A) are B) do C) can D) were

6. _____ you post this letter for me?
   A) Will B) Shall C) May D) Are

7. _____ I open the window?
   A) Will B) Shall C) Am D) Do

8. We _____ leave now or we'll be late.
   A) has to B) must C) can D) will

9. If you had video, you _____ record it yourself tonight.
   A) could B) can C) must D) may

10. Please _____ make noise.
    A) didn't B) don't C) can't D) may not

11. _____ open the windows. I'm cold.
    A) Don't B) Can't C) Mustn't D) Needn't

12. Shoes _____ be either black or brown.
    A) don't B) are C) may D) need

13. A: My car has been stolen.
    B: _____.
    A) You should ring the police. B) Will you phone the police?
    C) Could you ring the police? D) You are phoning the police.

14. A: I bought this pen today and it doesn't work.
    B: _____.
    A) Could you fill it with ink? B) Shall I give you another one?
    C) You should take it back. D) It cannot be expensive.

15. He _____ read faster a few years ago.
    A) can B) could C) might D) must

16. _____ you pass the salt, please?
    A) Do B) Are C) Should D) Could

17. _____ you remember which shoe you put on first this morning?
    A) May B) Can C) Should D) Were

18. You _____ be hungry. You've just had dinner.
    A) aren't B) can't C) may D) must

19. You _____ be hungry. You had no lunch.
    A) can't B) shouldn't C) must D) couldn't

20. Sorry, this _____ be my bag. Mine is brown.
    A) can't B) must C) can D) could

21. I _____ not have time to phone you this evening.
    A) may B) must C) would D) didn't

22. He probably _____ be back in time for dinner.
    A) isn't B) wasn't C) won't D) doesn't

23. Take a sweater with you. It _____ get cold later.
    A) won't B) might C) would D) need

24. A: She can't sing.
    B: Neither _____.
    A) do I B) could I C) am I D) can I

25. It's very cold. You _____ to put a sweater on.
    A) should B) ought C) has D) must

26. A: Will the director be back in the office today?
    B: He said he _____ be, but he wasn't sure.
    A) can B) might C) may D) has to

27. A: Is this a 24 bus coming?
    B: It__ be. I can't see the number yet.
    A) might B) can't C) may not D) must

28. A: _____.
    B: I'm sorry, but I haven't got my car.
    A) Will you give me a lift? B) Shall I drive you to school?
    C) Could you drive a bit faster? D) When shall we meet?

29. A: _____.
    B: Yes, please. Can I give you the money now?
    A) Will you lend me some money?
    B) Will you buy some fruit on the way back home
    C) Shall we go to the opera tonight?
    D) Shall I get you a ticket for the Madonna Concert?

30. If you don't feel better you _____ go to bed.
    A) ought B) should C) don't have to D) needn't

31. I'll _____ go now.
    A) should B) must C) have to D) ought to

32. You _____ get the 8.45 train. It doesn't stop at Yorkshire.
    A) had better B) mustn't C) should D) don't have to

33. You _____ go near that dog! It's very dangerous.
    A) may not B) don't have to
    C) mustn't D) needn't

34. We _____ play football today because it is raining.
    A) couldn't B) can't C) aren't D) didn't

35. When I was a child I _____ drink a lot of milk.
    A) should B) may C) used to D) need

36. A: I've got toothache. B: You'd _____ go to the dentist.
    A) better B) should C) used to D) must

37. Betty has a temperature. She _____ be ill.
    A) had better B) used to C) can not D) must

38. Good morning sir, what _____ I do for you?
    A) would B) can C) shall D) must

39. We _____ to stop pollution.
    A) must B) should C) had better D) ought

40. _____ careful! You are making mistakes.
    A) Be B) Must C) Do D) Did

41. _____ you answer the phone?
    A) Were B) Will C) Are D) Shall

42. A: I _____ play the guitar.
    B: But you said yesterday you _____ play it.
    A) can't / could B) can / could
    C) couldn't / can D) could / could

43. I missed the bus this morning so I _____ walk to school.
    A) have to B) must C) had to D) ought

44. Vegetables _____ be washed carefully.
    A) has to B) have to C) ought D) might

45. He _____ drive a car when he was eighteen.
    A) is able B) could C) can D) is used to

46. You _____ watch TV when you are studying.
    A) didn't B) shouldn't C) couldn't D) aren't

47. I _____ like to listen to guitar music.
    A) will B) can C) would D) could

48. We _____ see him tomorrow.
    A) might B) would C) had to D) ought

49. _____ you able to understand the lesson this morning?
    A) Were B) Could C) Would D) Should

50. I don't think we _____ be able to get to the airport in time?
    A) can B) are C) will D) could

51. I _____ see the President. There were too many people.
    A) weren't able to B) don't have to
    C) couldn't D) am not able

52. _____ you mind if I used your dictionary?
    A) Do B) Will C) Shall D) Need

53. _____ run if you feel tired.
    A) Mustn't B) Don't
    C) Don't have to D) Shouldn't

54. A horse _____ go twice as fast as an elephant.
    A) used to B) can C) is used to D) is able

55. A: I don't like this medicine.
    B: Don't worry. I'm sure you'll soon _____ it.
    A) used to B) get used to C) is used to D) use to

56. A: Do you like Florida?
    B: Not really. I'm not _____ the heat.
    A) used to B) be able to C) get used to D) got used to

57. A: Does your father smoke?
    B: He _____ but not any more.
    A) used to B) was able to C) got used to D) was used to

58. It is funny. I really enjoy jogging now but I_____.
    A) used to B) was used to
    C) didn't used to D) got used to

59. A: Did your mother tell you stories when you were small?
    B: Yes, she _____ tell me Nasrettin Hodja's stories.
    A) would B) used C) was used to D) is used to

60. A: I'm getting a bit fat. B: _____.
    A) You might eat a bit more. B) You shouldn't eat so much.
    C) You cannot be hungry. D) You used to eat a lot.

61. A: We must go soon, mustn't we? B: Yes, we_____ go.
    A) had better B) would C) had to D) will have to

62. I_____ get up than stay in bed.
    A) had better B) should C) would rather D) have to

63. When I was a child I _____ bite my nails.
    A) was used to B) used to C) got used to D) had better not

64. Nobody _____ come yesterday.
    A) wasn't able to B) should C) could D) were able to

65. If I were you I_____ see a doctor.
    A) would B) had better C) would rather D) should

66. A: _____.
    B: No, thank you. I've had enough.
    A) Would you like a coffee? B) Do you like strawberries?
    C) Could you set the table? D) Would you like some more?

67. This _____ be the right road. There is no other way.
    A) had better B) must C) have to D) would rather

68. You _____ get the 9.45 train. You could get the 9.55 and still arrive in time.
    A) don't have to B) mustn't
    C) should D) had better

69. Hurry up! It is a quarter past! We really_____ be late.
    A) don't have to B) wouldn't rather
    C) mustn't D) needn't

70. You _____ play an instrument to enjoy classical music.
    A) don't have to B) didn't used to
    C) didn't have to D) mustn't

71. A: I thought there was a cinema here.
    B: There _____ be. It's now a supermarket.
    A) should B) would C) used to D) had to

72. A: Isn't there a toilet?
    B: _____.
    A) There must be one somewhere.
    B) There can be after the interval.
    C) I'm afraid I need more details.
    D) It isn't in the program.

73. You _____ hurry if you want to catch that bus.
    A) would rather B) has got to C) had better D) had to

74. Last year Janet_____ run 800 meters in 2 minutes 45; now she _____ do it in 2 minutes 20.
    A) was able to / is able B) couldn't / could
    C) could / can D) can't / is able to

75. I've got toothache. I _____ go to the dentist.
    A) have got B) must C) couldn't D) needed to

76. I _____ to study for tomorrow's exam.
    A) don't need B) may not C) couldn't D) will not

77. A: Why didn't you come to the concert last night?
    B: Because I _____ visit a friend in hospital.
    A) had to B) might C) have to D) must

78. A: I'm putting on weight.
    B: You _____ go on a diet.
    A) ought B) had to C) needed to D) should

79. You _____ to write and thank him.
    A) has B) must C) ought D) needed

80. Jack is preparing for his exams. We _____.
    A) should go and visit him B) ought not to disturb him
    C) ought to phone him D) had better watch TV

81. A: _____?
    B: I'm going to study in the library.
    A) What do you usually do at the weekend
    B) What are you doing now
    C) When are you going to study
    D) Are you coming with us to the cinema

82. A: I've got a cold.
    B: Then you'd _____ stay in bed.
    A) need to B) better C) have to D) should

83. A: I've got a headache.
    B: You _____ take an aspirin.
    A) has to B) should C) would D) used to

84. I _____ like jazz when I was a teenager.
    A) should B) could C) were D) used to

85. A: _____?
    B: Yes, they do.
    A) Do your friends write to you
    B) Do you and your brother like tea
    C) Do we have to leave now
    D) Do they live in Vancouver or Edinburgh

86. A: Were they playing tennis?
    B: No, they _____.
    A) aren't B) weren't C) didn't D) don't

87. Mother is still in bed, and _____ my sister.
    A) so is B) neither is C) nor is D) too

88. My brother was very hungry, I _____too.
    A) am B) were C) do D) was

89. We live in a small flat, and they do, _____.
    A) either B) neither C) too D) so

90. A: Colin didn't like the film.
    B: _____.
    A) So did I B) Neither did I
    C) So do I D) Nor do I

91. A: Nick isn't good at maths.
    B: _____.
    A) Nor is his sister B) So is his brother
    C) Neither does his father D) His elder brother is, too.

92. A: I haven't said anything.
    B: _____.
    A) Nor did I B) Neither did I
    C) Nor have I D) I didn't, either

93. A: My father plays chess very well.
    B: _____.
    A) So does my father B) Nor does my father
    C) Neither my father D) My father is, too

94. He said, "It may rain later in the day." He said that it_____ rain later in the day.
    A) would B) may C) might D) must

95. He _____ take his medicine three times a day. The doctor told him to.
    A) has to B) need C) had better D) have to

96. I feel tired. I _____ go to bed.
    A) had to B) has to C) had better D) used to

97. You _____ do your homework. If you don't, you'll fail the examination.
    A) must B) had to C) had better D) might

98. We haven't got much time. We _____ hurry.
    A) needn't B) must C) don't have to D) has to

99. We have got plenty of time. We _____ hurry.
    A) needn't B) didn't use to C) mustn't D) didn't need to

100. You _____ do it now. You can do it this afternoon.
    A) mustn't B) had better C) needn't D) should

INTERMEDIATE / UPPER-INTERMEDIATE 8

modals

Choose the best alternative.

1. His illness got worse and worse. In the end he _____ go into hospital for an operation.
   A) will have to   B) must   C) had to   D) ought to have

2. You _____ any more aspirins; you've had four already.
   A) mustn't take   B) needn't have taken
   C) shouldn't have taken   D) had better not take

3. I've searched everywhere for Bob but I _____ to find him.
   A) wasn't able   B) am not able
   C) haven't been able   D) couldn't

4. A: Mrs. Taylor was found dead with a wire around her neck.
   B: She _____ strangled.
   A) had to be   B) ought to have been
   C) should have   D) must have been

5. You _____ spanked her. She didn't deserve it.
   A) shouldn't have   B) needn't have
   C) mustn't have   D) couldn't have

6. A: I wonder who took my alarm clock.
   B: It _____ Julia. She _____ supposed to get up early.
   A) might be / is   B) could be / is
   C) had to be / was   D) must have been / was

7. In a hundred years' time we _____ out of water to drink.
   A) must have run   B) might have been/run
   C) should have run   D) may have run

8. If you'd explained your problem to me, I _____ to help you.
   A) was able   B) will have been able
   C) would have been able   D) could have

9. Joe ran all the way. It wasn't necessary. Joe _____ run all the way.
   A) needn't have   B) need have
   C) didn't need to   D) doesn't need to

10. Tom was serious when he said he wanted to be an actor when he grew up. We _____ at him. We hurt his feelings.
    A) shouldn't have laughed   B) needn't have laughed
    C) mustn't have laughed   D) shouldn't have been laughed

11. He _____ hungry. He isn't eating his food.
    A) should be   B) needn't have been
    C) might not have been   D) must not be

12. All the lights in Terry's room are turned off. He _____ sleeping.
    A) must have been   B) had to be
    C) must be   D) must not be

13. Let's go to the seminar. It _____ interesting.
    A) used to be   B) is supposed to be
    C) must have been   D) needs to be

14. Children _____ taught to respect their elders.
    A) should be   B) had better   C) has to be   D) must have

15. This application _____ last week.
    A) should be sent   B) must have been
    C) ought to have been sent   D) should have sent

16. We can't wait any longer! Something _____ immediately.
    A) should have been done   B) had to be done
    C) ought to do   D) must be done

17. A: I overslept this morning.
    B: You _____ your alarm clock.
    A) had better set   B) had to set
    C) should have set   D) ought to have been

18. Rice _____ have water in order to grow.
    A) must   B) should   C) had better   D) ought to

19. I _____ to go now. I have a class in ten minutes.
    A) had better   B) have got   C) must   D) should

20. "Doctors are supposed to help sick people" means: _____.
    A) They help sick people.
    B) They should help sick people.
    C) They must be helping sick people.
    D) They might have helped sick people.

21. I _____ to the doctor. I'm feeling much better.
    A) don't have to go   B) needn't have gone
    C) should have gone   D) mustn't go

22. This is an opportunity that comes once in a lifetime. We _____ let it pass.
    A) don't have to   B) shouldn't have
    C) needn't have   D) mustn't

23. I _____ go to the cinema than study English.
    A) would rather   B) had better   C) need to   D) should

24. When I was a child my father _____ read me a story every night before bed.
    A) was going to   B) was used to
    C) would   D) got used to

25. A: Did you enjoy the concert?
    B: It was OK, but I ___ to the theatre.
    A) needn't have gone   B) must have gone
    C) had better go   D) would rather have gone

26. A: How much do you weigh?
    B: _____.
    A) I needn't have told you   B) I'd rather not tell you
    C) I couldn't have told you   D) I'd better not be told

27. When I was a child, I _____ a flashlight to bed with me so that I _____ read comic books without my parents' knowing them.
    A) used to take / could   B) was used to taking / could
    C) would take / can   D) would have taken / was able to

28. After looking at his notes again, he _____ to complete the exercise.
    A) could   B) was able   C) can   D) has been able

29. If we don't book seats soon, we _____ to get into the concert.
    A) are able   B) won't be able
    C) will be able   D) can't

30. If we went to live in the tropics. I _____ buy some thin clothes.
    A) will have to   B) have to
    C) would have to   D) have had to

31. If there is fuel shortage, solar energy _____.
    A) has to develop   B) will have to be developed
    C) will have to develop   D) had to be developed

32. When she got thinner she _____ take her dress in.
    A) will have to   B) should   C) has to   D) had to

33. Mary _____ any chocolates but she did.
    A) shouldn't eat   B) ought not to have eaten
    C) ought not to eat   D) must not have eaten

34. Your umbrella is wet. It _____ raining.
    A) must be   B) was   C) can't be   D) might

35. _____ the pains come again, don't hesitate to phone me.
    A) Would   B) Should   C) Will   D) Had

36. _____ it been raining, I'd have needed my umbrella.
    A) Should   B) Would   C) Might   D) Had

37. A: I took Janet to the cinema last night.
    B: You _____ me too. I was at home.
    A) might take   B) may have been taken
    C) might have taken   D) must have taken

38. I don't think she _____. Call her again.
    A) can have heard   B) might have heard
    C) must hear   D) can be heard

39. Lucy is very late. She _____ her train.
    A) may miss   B) may have missed
    C) had to miss   D) should have missed

40. I walked to school this morning, but I _____ a bus.
    A) didn't need to take   B) had better take
    C) might take   D) could have taken

41. The flower is dead. Maybe I _____ it more water.
    A) might give   B) needed to give
    C) should have given   D) ought to have been given

42. These flowers _____ twice a week, but I always forget to water them.
    A) ought to water   B) ought to have been watered
    C) should be watered   D) needn't have been watered

43. Why don't you buy a lottery ticket. You _____ a large prize.
    A) might win   B) might have won
    C) could have won   D) must have won

44. Why did you take such a risk? You _____ died!
    A) could   B) must be   C) might have   D) may be

45. We _____ our towels because we knew the hotel would provide some.
    A) didn't need to pack   B) needn't pack
    C) don't have to pack   D) needn't have been packed

46. It was very cold in the morning. You _____ your sweater.
    A) could wear   B) need to wear
    C) should have worn   D) might wear

47. "I was supposed to call her at seven." means: _____.
    A) I called her at seven.   B) I was called by her at seven
    C) I could call her at seven. D) I should have called her at seven

48. You _____ for me; I could have found the way all right.
    A) needn't have waited   B) could have waited
    C) don't have to wait   D) didn't need to wait

49. Janet _____ some problem. She keeps crying.
    A) must have had   B) must have
    C) needs to have   D) may have had

50. The lights have gone out. _____.
    A) A fuse might blow   B) A fuse could blow
    C) A fuse must have blown   D) A fuse will have blown

51. I _____ to the butcher's on the way home, but I forgot.
    A) need to go   B) ought to have gone
    C) must have gone   D) should go

52. She _____ about the time. Her friends were also late.
    A) needn't worry   B) won't need to worry
    C) doesn't need to worry   D) needn't have worried

53. The plane _____ already-it's not due to go until 9.55.
    A) must not leave   B) needn't have left
    C) can't leave   D) can't have left

54. A: Is it Sunday? All the shops are closed.
    B: Well, if all the shops are closed, it _____ Sunday.
    A) can't be   B) might have been
    C) must be   D) must have been

55. A: You bought the tickets, didn't you?
    B: No. I _____, but I didn't have enough money.
    A) couldn't   B) ought to have been
    C) was supposed to   D) must have

56. The boy _____ walk again soon after he had had an operation.
    A) can   B) is able to   C) might   D) was able to

57. He was crying just a moment ago. He _____ singing already.
    A) is not able to   B) must be
    C) must not   D) can't be

58. George is reading a Spanish newspaper. He _____ Spanish.
    A) is to know   B) must know
    C) had to know   D) need to know

59. No wonder you always look pale. You _____ get more fresh air.
    A) will need   B) ought to   C) had to   D) must have

60. To keep fit and stay healthy, you _____ enough of the right kinds of exercise.
    A) have to take   B) used to take
    C) might have taken   D) ought to have taken

61. Transport systems _____ likely to change in the future. One probable difference is that there _____ more electric vehicles.
    A) is / will be   B) will / are
    C) are / will be   D) will / would be

62. If you want antibiotics, you _____ to ask the doctor for a prescription.
    A) must   B) had better   C) will have   D) should

63. "You weren't supposed to do that." means: _____.
    A) You should do that, but you don't.
    B) You should have done it, but you didn't.
    C) You shouldn't have done it.
    D) You shouldn't do that, but you do.

64. The wound has healed now. You _____ that bandage any longer.
    A) needn't have worn   B) didn't need to wear
    C) don't have to wear   D) didn't have to wear

65. You _____ this to Kate, or she'll get upset.
    A) needn't tell   B) shouldn't have told
    C) mustn't have told   D) mustn't tell

66. A: His office is empty. He must have gone home.
    B: But his briefcase is here. He _____ home.
    A) might not go   B) can't have gone
    C) ought not to go   D) could have gone

67. He _____ with us if he doesn't want to.
    A) needs to come   B) needn't have come
    C) didn't need to come   D) needn't come

68. The package _____ to the wrong address.
    A) must have been sent   B) ought to be sent
    C) could have sent   D) might have sent

69. Since you have been working for hours, you _____ tired.
    A) could be   B) can't be
    C) must have been   D) might have been

70. We _____ or we'll be late.
    A) had better hurry   B) didn't need to hurry
    C) had to hurry   D) needn't have hurried

71. The car broke down, and we _____ have it towed to a service station.
    A) have to   B) had to   C) should   D) ought to

72. No one likes _____ work at the weekend.
    A) has to   B) had to   C) will have to   D) having to

73. It is very difficult choice to _____ make.
    A) have to   B) having to   C) had to   D) must

74. You _____ to see a doctor. You're perfectly healthy.
    A) mustn't   B) don't need C) may not   D) shouldn't

75. Alcohol _____ be bad for his health, but it is for me.
    A) must not   B) didn't need to
    C) doesn't have to   D) may not

76. Children under twelve _____ travel free of charge.
    A) can   B) is able to C) can not be   D) must be

77. Father is mending the car. After that we _____ to go for a drive.
    A) can   B) might   C) may   D) will be able

78. It is very important to me, and I really_____ be late.
    A) might not B) ought not   C) don't have to D) mustn't

79. We _____ write an essay on the book after we'd read it.
    A) had to   B) have to   C) will have to   D) must

80. The sky _____ seen because of the pollution.
    A) can not   B) can't be   C) might be D) must be

81. I_____ sorry if she had left.
    A) will be   B) would've been
    C) would be   D) had been

82. Robert is a millionaire's son. He _____ never_____ worry about anything in life.
    A) is / has to   B) had / had to
    C) has / had to   D) doesn't / have to

83. You'd better not try to bribe him. He _____ you to the police.
    A) could report   B) might have reported
    C) needs to report   D) could have reported

84. I wish you'd told me they were on the phone. I _____ all the way to their house.
    A) didn't have to go   B) didn't need to go
    C) needn't go   D) needn't have gone

85. If only you'd mentioned that your friend played tennis. We _____ a game of doubles.
    A) can have   B) could have had
    C) might have   D) could have

86. If my car _____ stuck in a traffic jam, I'd be very angry, but I _____ my horn.
    A) is / won't bang   B) was / don't bang
    C) were / won't bang   D) were / wouldn't bang

87. I wouldn't buy it unless I _____ it.
    A) can't afford   B) could have afforded
    C) could afford   D) couldn't afford

88. A: Williams. Jack Williams.
    B: Sorry. I _____ the wrong number.
    A) must dial   B) must have dialed
    C) might dial   D) might have been dialed

89. A: He was driving on the right in Cyprus when he crashed.
    B: He _____ on the left.
    A) had to be driving   B) could be driving
    C) ought to have been driving   D) shouldn't have been driving

90. A: The attendant was smoking near the petrol pump.
    B: He _____ smoking there.
    A) shouldn't be   B) ought not to be
    C) wouldn't be   D) shouldn't have been

91. You say you saw him sitting in the canteen today. He _____ sitting there. He has been in hospital for two days.
    A) couldn't have been   B) must not be
    C) can not be   D) might have been

92. A: Look at the magician. He is sawing that woman in half!
    B: He _____ sawing her in half. It _____ a trick.
    A) mustn't be / might be   B) can not be / must be
    C) ought not to be / can be   D) must be / might be

93. A: His brother won the marathon last year.
    B: He _____ very fast.
    A) might have been   B) must be
    C) may have been   D) might be

94. A: How on earth did the thief get in?
    B: He _____ a window.
    A) is able to break   B) might have been broken
    C) could have broken   D) had to break

95. I wish he _____ a little more tactful!
    A) must be   B) would be   C) will be   D) might be

96. The Government recommended that the housing problem _____ speeded up.
    A) would be   B) must be   C) is to be   D) should be

97. A: Surely he has woken up.
    B: Well, I can hear snoring coming from his room.
    A: He _____ then.
    A) can't wake up   B) might not wake up
    C) must have woken up   D) can not have woken up

98. You cannot wash these curtains. They _____.
    A) to be dry-cleaned   B) must have been dry-cleaned
    C) have been dry-cleaned   D) have to be dry-cleaned

99. The reports _____ by four o'clock because the manager is going to sign them.
    A) must be finished   B) must finish
    C) should have been finished   D) had to be finished

100. I _____ very hard but I do now.
    A) don't need to work   B) don't have to work
    C) didn't have to work   D) should have worked

101. George King ___ filter-tipped cigarettes, but now he smokes cigars.
    A) is used to smoking   B) was used to smoke
    C) is accustomed to smoking   D) was accustomed to smoking

102. "It isn't necessary for us to leave soon." means: _____.
    A) We needn't have left soon.
    B) We didn't need to leave soon.
    C) We don't need to leave soon
    D) We have to leave soon

103. A: I went out last night, and my cold got worse.
    B: You _____ at home.
    A) must stay   B) had better stay
    C) ought to stay   D) should have stayed

104. A: The Chinese described flying machines.
    B: They _____ tremendous imaginations.
    A) could have   B) must have
    C) must have had   D) need to have

105. A: Do you think they'll have my size?
    B: They _____ have your size.
    A) are used to   B) should   C) has to   D) will have to

106. If you worked in industry, you _____ the value of money.
    A) had to know   B) would know
    C) should have known   D) might have known

107. His life _____ if he had worn his seat belt.
    A) would be saved   B) might have saved
    C) could have been saved   D) may be saved

108. I _____ go out than be stuck in bed.
    A) had better   B) should   C) have to   D) would rather

109. I _____ to learn English fluently.
    A) must   B) have got   C) should   D) would rather

110. A: Is he going to have his operation this month?
    B: Well, he _____ have had it this month, but now he is going to have it next month.
    A) was to   B) will   C) used to   D) needs to

111. A: _____ Barcelona _____ Real Madrid last night?
    B: Yes, it could. It has got more skillful players.
    A) could / beat   B) could / have been beaten
    C) could / have beaten   D) could / be beaten by

112. I can't find my keys. I have a feeling I _____ them in the library.
    A) might leave   B) must have left
    C) could leave   D) should have left

113. My car has been making a strange noise lately. I _____ it to the garage and get it seen to.
    A) had to take   B) shall have to take
    C) should have taken   D) was to have taken

114. Joan suggested that they _____ all go for a walk in the afternoon - provided it didn't keep on raining.
    A) would   B) could   C) should   D) might

115. You say I _____ a screwdriver. What _____ I _____?
    A) could have used / should / have used
    B) shouldn't have used / should / have used
    C) might not use / should / be used
    D) mustn't use / could / have used

116. He was so unsure of himself that he _____ even buy a box of chocolates without consulting his mother.
    A) wouldn't   B) won't
    C) can't   D) might not have

117. Before his illness he _____ anything but now he _____ very careful with his diet.
    A) could eat / can be   B) must have eaten / had to be
    C) could eat / has to be   D) couldn't eat / has to be

118. Powerful though they were, they never _____ to challenge the authority of the King.
    A) will have   B) dared   C) would have   D) could've been

119. If those two people _____ leave, the Whole firm would probably collapse.
    A) must   B) are to   C) were to   D) had to

120. We _____ be late for work. Our boss is very particular about time-keeping.
    A) wouldn't   B) weren't to   C) daren't   D) didn't use to

ELEMENTARY PRE-INTERMEDIATE 9 — prepositions

Choose the best answer.

1. Are you afraid _____ exams?
   A) at   B) from   C) on   D) of

2. My friend and I always go to school _____ the bus.
   A) by   B) on   C) in   D) at

3. He tried to open the tin _____ a knife.
   A) with   B) by   C) from   D) out of

4. His office is _____ the second floor of the building.
   A) at   B) in   C) of   D) on

5. Mike is sitting _____ the desk _____ front of the door.
   A) at / in   B) in / on   C) on / on   D) at / at

6. Listen! I think there is someone _____ the front door.
   A) on   B) at   C) in   D) with

7. There's a paper _____ the floor. Please put it _____ the wastebasket.
   A) at / into   B) on / at   C) on / in   D) over / at

8. There was a storm _____ the night, it rained _____ three or four hours.
   A) at / in   B) during / for   C) in / since   D) during / at

9. See you _____ Monday morning.
   A) under   B) at   C) in   D) on

10. We are giving him a surprise party _____ his birthday.
    A) in   B) at   C) with   D) on

11. What's the price _____ this tie?
    A) of   B) at   C) in   D) to

12. We are meeting _____ next Thursday.
    A) on   B) _   C) at   D) in

13. They have lived in Spain _____ the second World War.
    A) during   B) for   C) since   D) at

14. How do the children get _____ school in the morning?
    A) to   B) at   C) off   D) _

15. A dictionary has information _____ words.
    A) to   B) about   C) in   D) at

16. The children wore boots to play _____ the snow.
    A) at   B) by   C) of   D) in

17. There's a good restaurant _____ the Bolu road.
    A) between   B) in   C) on   D) at

18. We stopped for three-quarters of an hour _____ Heathrow Airport.
    A) at   B) in   C) over   D) on

19. Where is your mother? Is she _____ the hairdresser's again?
    A) in   B) on   C) at   D) _

20. Who's the blonde girl _____ the first raw?
    A) in   B) on   C) at   D) over

21. You'll find the poem _____ page 16.
    A) at   B) on   C) in   D) _

22. He lived with Nomads _____ the Sahara desert for two days.
    A) over   B) on   C) in   D) of

23. I won't stay _____ bed; I'll just lie down _____ the bed for an hour.
    A) in / in   B) at / in   C) at / on   D) in / on

24. I last saw her _____ the car park.
    A) in   B) at   C) on   D) —

25. He grows corn _____ his farm.
    A) over   B) with   C) at   D) on

26. She opened her mouth so the doctor could look _____ her throat.
    A) to   B) on   C) at   D) for

27. He will stay here _____ Monday.
    A) by   B) till   C) at   D) to

28. You'd better go to London _____ the next plane.
    A) at   B) in   C) by   D) on

29. She said hello _____ everyone except me.
    A) to   B) _   C) at   D) of

30. She is worried _____ her exams.
    A) of   B) about   C) with   D) _

31. Tell us _____ your holiday.
    A) _   B) of   C) about   D) with

32. Mr. Collins always talks _____ himself.
    A) to   B) with   C) at   D) in

33. Is it possible for me to keep it _____ Tuesday?
    A) by   B) at   C) since   D) until

34. Who's the man _____ the funny hat?
    A) in   B) from   C) at   D) to

35. Will you come _____ bus or _____ a late train?
    A) by / by   B) on / in   C) by / on   D) in / by

36. I saw an accident _____ my way home.
    A) on   B) at   C) in   D) to

37. The doctor gave me a prescription _____ my cough.
    A) with   B) to   C) at   D) for

38. I usually stay at home _____ night.
    A) on   B) at   C) in   D) over

39. Have you seen the new bridge they've built _____ the river?
    A) over   B) under   C) between   D) at

40. I'll call you _____ seven o'clock.
    A) in   B) on   C) at   D) of

41. Can't you come _____ your bicycle?
    A) in   B) with   C) on   D) by

42. She arrived _____ Friday.
    A) in   B) on   C) at   D) over

43. We'll go _____ Marmaris _____ June.
    A) _ / in   B) at / on   C) to / on   D) to / in

44. I was born _____ September 9th.
    A) in   B) on   C) at   D) of

45. John and Mary are talking _____ the telephone.
    A) _   B) to   C) on   D) with

46. Classes began _____ last week.
    A) in   B) _   C) at   D) on

47. They took my temperature _____ the operation.
    A) before   B) by   C) _   D) of

48. Do you take sugar _____ your tea?
    A) in   B) on   C) by   D) _

49. I'm afraid _____ falling trees.
    A) from   B) of   C) with   D) at

50. She didn't get a passing grade _____ her test.
    A) on   B) with   C) at   D) of

51. I sometimes listen _____ the radio or watch _____ TV.
    A) of / on   B) to / on   C) _ / to   D) to / _

52. I always lie down _____ a swim.
    A) by   B) with   C) on   D) after

53. Are they going to stay _____ a tent?
    A) in   B) over   C) on   D) of

54. She put a bandage _____ the boy's cut finger.
    A) at   B) to   C) on   D) in

55. He has a pain _____ his leg.
    A) on   B) over   C) in   D) at

56. The Prime Minister arrived _____ Tokyo last night.
    A) _   B) in   C) at   D) to

57. I couldn't get _____ school in time.
    A) to   B) at   C) _   D) in

58. The student apologized _____ being late.
    A) to   B) at   C) of   D) for

59. Ann stirred her coffee _____ a spoon.
    A) with   B) by   C) in   D) to

60. Petrol is sold _____ the liter.
    A) by   B) from   C) at   D) on

61. What time does this train get _____ Liverpool?
    A) _   B) to   C) at   D) for

62. Sorry, I didn't phone you last night. I was _____ the theatre.
    A) on   B) in   C) at   D) over

63. Where do you come _____ ?
    A) from   B) -   C) of   D) in

64. We stayed _____ the Heathrow Hotel.
    A) on   B) into   C) at   D) to

65. I waited _____ the bus-stop for ten minutes.
    A) at   B) in   C) on   D) for

66. I'm not very good _____ mathematics.
    A) of   B) on   C) in   D) at

67. What are you interested _____ ?
    A) in   B) of   C) on   D) over

68. Please put your homework _____ my desk.
    A) at   B) to   C) on   D) with

69. He's lived _____ that street for many years.
    A) of   B) on   C) at   D) to

70. It takes about five minutes to walk _____ the bridge.
    A) over   B) to   C) at   D) till

71. I took the train _____ Dover to Ostend.
    A) by   B) on   C) of   D) from

72. David was very busy _____ the afternoon.
    A) with   B) on   C) at   D) in

73. Toshio is _____ Japan. He isn't American.
    A) of   B) in   C) at   D) from

74. Bob ran 100 meters _____ 11 seconds.
    A) in   B) at   C) on   D) with

75. They arrived _____ plane.
    A) by   B) on   C) with   D) on

76. A: Did they come _____ bus?
    B: No, they came _____ foot.
    A) on / on   B) by / on   C) with / by   D) by / with

77. Switch _____ a light. It's getting dark.
    A) of   B) off   C) out   D) on

78. What was the temperature _____ Ankara yesterday?
    A) at   B) of   C) in   D) off

79. I look forward _____ meeting you next month.
    A) at   B) for   C) with   D) to

80. "You can't come in _____ a ticket," the man told us.
    A) without   B) through   C) by   D) with

81. I get up _____ six o'clock _____ Tuesdays.
    A) at / on   B) at / in   C) about / at   D) around / in

82. My father takes a nap _____ dinner.
    A) with   B) after   C) on   D) at

83. When people go _____ a picnic they always eat a lot.
    A) _   B) on   C) to   D) eat

84. Boys and girls go _____ dancing.
    A) to   B) at   C) __   D) with

85. When do you take _____ your wrist watch?
    A) off   B) on   C) out   D) of

86. I'll phone _____ you tomorrow.
    A) to   B) at   C) on   D) __

87. Our village lies _____ two high mountains.
    A) among   B) over   C) in   D) between

88. You may write _____ a pen or _____ a pencil.
    A) with / by   B) with / with   C) in / in   D) by / by

89. I woke up _____ five o'clock _____ the morning.
    A) in / in   B) at / on   C) at / in   D) at / at

90. The weather is pleasant here _____ the spring.
    A) at   B) in   C) on   D) as

91. His birthday is _____ August 20.
    A) in   B) on   C) at   D) from

92. They met _____ Istanbul _____ 1989.
    A) at / at   B) to / in   C) at / in   D) in / in

93. We are leaving for Paris _____ Sunday.
    A) on   B) in   C) at   D) from

94. The plane will stay on the runway _____ five minutes.
    A) at   B) on   C) in   D) for

95. Get _____ the bus. It is about to go.
    A) over   B) for   C) on   D) at

96. Are you going to study _____ the afternoon or _____ night?
    A) on / on   B) in / in   C) in / at   D) at / in

97. We had a wonderful time at the party _____ Saturday night.
    A) on   B) in   C) at   D) by

98. Fuel is a source _____ energy.
    A) of   B) for   C) over   D) in

99. George fell _____ a wall and broke his leg.
    A) of   B) by   C) off   D) up

100. _____ the future, people will be living on pills.
    A) In   B) On   C) By   D) At

101. They lived in Ankara _____ 1990 _____ 1993.
    A) in / to   B) from / till   C) until / to   D) from / by

102. We have been living in Ankara _____ ten years.
    A) for   B) since   C) in   D) until

103. The bridge will be finished _____ two months' time.
    A) by   B) for   C) since   D) in

104. I'll be home _____ 7 o'clock.
    A) by   B) in   C) on   D) since

105. Don't hurry. The train won't leave _____ 5.50.
    A) by   B) in   C) until   D) for

106. I've been in this class _____ the beginning of the semester.
    A) for   B) since   C) until   D) at

107. They live _____ West End Avenue.
    A) at   B) in   C) on   D) along

108. Mr. Lee works _____ 66 Moon Fleet Street.
    A) at   B) in   C) to   D) on

109. He sat _____ the back of the car.
    A) behind   B) at   C) in   D) on

110. How did you enjoy your vacation _____ Europe last summer?
    A) at   B) in   C) on   D) by

111. There are national parks _____ some parts of the country.
    A) in   B) on   C) at   D) over

112. Tokyo is the most crowded city _____ the world.
    A) on   B) at   C) in   D) upon

113. Turn left _____ the corner. The shop is _____ the left side.
    A) on / at   B) in / to   C) at / on   D) in / at

114. Don't walk _____ the street! Walk here _____ the sidewalk.
    A) in / on   B) on / at   C) at / on   D) in / to

115. I'm going to meet my friends _____ Taksim square tonight.
    A) in   B) at   C) on   D) over

116. We arrived _____ Leeds at midnight.
    A) at   B) to   C) in   D) on

117. We couldn't arrive _____ the airport in time.
    A) at   B) to   C) in   D) on

118. A lot of planes go _____ the city.
    A) on   B) through   C) over   D) along

119. There were no planes _____ the past.
    A) in   B) on   C) at   D) over

120. We waited _____ you _____ 11 p.m.
    A) at / to   B) for / until   C) for / to   D) with / since

121. Is there a fridge _____ your kitchen?
    A) at   B) on   C) over   D) in

122. I'm still waiting _____ the Blue Train.
    A) to   B) of   C) for   D) at

123. Marie Curie was born _____ Warsaw.
    A) on   B) at   C) in   D) from

124. He died in 1990 _____ a car accident.
    A) on   B) of   C) after   D) before

125. Who is that pretty young girl _____ the short blue skirt?
    A) _   B) with   C) in   D) on

126. She writes _____ her parents every week.
    A) at   B) to   C) _   D) for

127. She has been _____ the USA _____ three years.
    A) in / since   B) at / for   C) on / for   D) in / for

128. What kind _____ music do you like?
    A) _   B) in   C) of   D) on

129. How do you get _____ home to your school?
    A) at   B) to   C) into   D) from

130. The earth goes _____ the sun.
    A) round   B) over   C) on   D) to

131. Who was the first man _____ the moon?
    A) in   B) at   C) on   D) of

132. Galileo was also interested _____ astronomy.
    A) at   B) _   C) on   D) in

133. That is very nice _____ you.
    A) of   B) in   C) at   D) off

134. Let me help you _____ your cleaning.
    A) with   B) at   C) on   D) in

135. Shevchenko was born _____ Ukraine.
    A) at   B) in   C) on   D) from

136. There is a bus station directly _____ the entrance.
    A) beside   B) opposite   C) on   D) of

137. He lives _____ number five.
    A) at   B) on   C) of   D) in

138. Can you get the eggs _____ the fridge, please?
    A) out   B) out of   C) over   D) off

139. The glass fell _____ the table and broke.
    A) out   B) out of   C) off   D) over

140. Someone is waiting _____ the library.
    A) through   B) on   C) out of   D) outside

141. I'm waiting _____ the Paris plane.
    A) at   B) after   C) for   D) before

142. Would you like to come _____ us?
    A) with   B) from   C) by   D) at

143. Are you _____ or against Nuclear Power?
    A) on   B) for   C) in   D) near

144. Can I come in with my dirty shoes _____?
    A) with   B) on   C) in   D) off

145. I like sitting _____ the sun.
    A) on   B) at   C) in   D) of

146. Have you ever flown _____ the Alps?
    A) over   B) out of   C) on   D) up

147. The teacher is standing _____ the board.
    A) on   B) in   C) of   D) at

148. Are you short _____ breath?
    A) from   B) at   C) off   D) of

149. Do you suffer _____ heartburn?
    A) of   B) on   C) from   D) at

150. In which part _____ the head do you get the pain?
    A) on   B) of   C) in   D) over

INTERMEDIATE / UPPER-INTERMEDIATE 10 — prepositions

Choose the best answer.

1. Wreckage from the plane was scattered _____ a wide area.
   A) over   B) from   C) on   D) at

2. The toilet is straight____ that door, then___ the stairs on the left.
   A) through / up   B) opposite / from
   C) next to / over   D) across / down

3. He makes reading-lamps _____ old wine bottles.
   A) with   B) by   C) out of   D) of

4. He began his career twenty years ago_____ a doctor.
   A) like   B) as   C) of   D) such as

5. She sighed _____ relief.
   A) with   B) on   C) of   D) at

6. The chairman is opposed _____ giving the affair any publicity.
   A) to   B) at   C) by   D) with

7. He shared his property _____ his daughter and his sister.
   A) among   B) between   C) amongst   D) within

8. She was standing laughing _____ a crowd of fans.
   A) among   B) between   C) within   D) next to

9. She got married _____ her childhood sweetheart.
   A) _   B) with   C) at   D) to

10. Will you marry _____ me?
    A) _   B) with   C) to   D) at

11. I dreamt _____ you last night.
    A) with   B) of   C) about   D) for

12. Sometimes I dream _____ running away to a farm.
    A) _   B) about   C) of   D) on

13. She always dresses _____ green.
    A) on   B) in   C) of   D) _

14. I was in hospital _____ two weeks _____ the semester.
    A) for / during   B) for / for   C) since / in   D) since / during

15. Turkey has entered _____ a new trade agreement with Germany.
    A) to   B) with   C) _   D) into

16. When I entered _____ the room everybody was speaking loudly.
    A) _   B) into   C) to   D) in

17. Let's go _____ skiing next weekend.
    A) for   B) to   C) _   D) into

18. This is the solution _____ all problems.
    A) of   B) by   C) with   D) to

19. The country is rich _____ natural resources.
    A) for   B) by   C) with   D) in

20. You can borrow my dictionary, but I must have it back _____ Monday.
    A) by   B) until   C) till   D) to

21. If you are _____ the North Pole, every direction is south.
    A) against   B) in   C) on   D) at

22. It would have been nice to live _____ the eighteenth century.
    A) in   B) at   C) under   D) on

23. My suit is a little too long _____ the arms.
    A) of   B) at   C) over   D) in

24. I last saw her _____ the car park.
    A) in   B) at   C) on   D) over

25. I kissed her_____ both cheeks.
    A) by   B) in   C) at   D) on

26. He hit me _____ the eye.
    A) by   B) in   C) on   D) at

27. He was wounded _____ the shoulder.
    A) by   B) in   C) on   D) at

28. They moved the chair because it was _____ their way.
    A) at   B) on   C) off   D) in

29. We drove about _____ taxis all day.
    A) by   B) in   C) on   D) with

30. _____ a nine-month follow-up, not a single case of chicken pox occurred in the vaccinated group.
    A) By   B) Until   C) During   D) As

31. They may have come _____ an earlier train.
    A) on   B) by   C) with   D) in

32. This wardrobe was made _____ my father. He made it _____ some old packing cases _____ a few simple tools.
    A) by / from / by   B) by / with / with
    C) by / of / by   D) by / out of / with

33. The safe had been blown open _____ dynamite.
    A) with   B) by   C) at   D) on

34. The situation had occurred _____ a misunderstanding.
    A) for   B) of   C) with   D) because of

35. The police accused him _____ going through a red light.
    A) of   B) for   C) in   D) through

36. They are very similar. I often mistake one _____ the other.
    A) through   B) of   C) with   D) for

37. He suffers rather badly _____ migraines.
    A) of   B) from   C) for   D) as

38. Our TV isn't working. A repairer is coming to see _____ it today.
    A) for   B) through   C) like   D) -

39. Animals are not completely devoid _____ intelligence.
    A) on   B) in   C) of   D) without

40. The teacher was disappointed _____ the work of the class.
    A) at   B) on   C) for   D) with

41. Divide 16 _____ 4. 4 is the square root _____ 16.
    A) by / of   B) with / for   C) with / by   D) by / for

42. Write these exercises either _____ ink _____ pencil.
    A) with / with   B) in / in   C) by / by   D) of / of

43. Bill was too ill to travel _____ a doctor or a nurse.
    A) with   B) without   C) by   D) against

44. _____ Denmark, teachers are _____ the best-paid workers.
    A) At / between   B) In / among
    C) In / between   D) In / in

45. Many countries today are suffering _____ lack of food, and unfortunately some people have to do _____ food several days.
    A) from / without   B) of / on   C) of / with
    D) with / without

46. If _____ smoking cigarettes, more people smoked a pipe, they would be more likely to go through the day _____ eating.
    A) without / for   B) for / without
    C) on / without   D) instead of / without

47. There is an interesting article ____ pensions _____ today's newspaper.
    A) of / in   B) on / in   C) on / at   D) with / on

48. He became addicted _____ drugs and went from worse _____ worse.
    A) on / to   B) with / by   C) to / to   D) at / by

49. Flu and measles are both caused _____ a virus.
    A) by   B) with   C) for   D) on

50. I reminded her _____ her promise.
    A) by   B) with   C) from   D) of

51. He recovered _____ his illness only last week.
    A) on   B) up   C) over   D) from

52. He is longing _____ the day when he will be able to earn his own living.
    A) with   B) for   C) at   D) against

53. The boy who got full marks was suspected _____ cheating.
    A) by   B) from   C) of   D) for

54. She complained _____ pains in her back.
    A) by   B) with   C) over   D) about

55. _____ her fine clothes, everyone knows how poor she is.
    A) For all   B) Due to   C) Because of   D) In spite of

56. _____ the day he read the article on lung cancer _____ the day he died, he didn't touch another cigarette.
    A) On / to   B) From / till   C) From / on   D) In / until

57. I'm very obliged _____ her helping me to get that job.
    A) of   B) to   C) for   D) by

58. This year there has been an increase _____ the number of books sold.
    A) on B) for C) in D) at
59. The government imposed a new tax _____ luxuries.
    A) of B) in C) over D) on
60. His efforts resulted _____ success.
    A) in B) for C) from D) with
61. His illness resulted _____ bad food.
    A) in B) from C) with D) for
62. The cost of living has been high _____ June.
    A) from B) for C) since D) on
63. Wrap your scarf _____ your neck to keep warm.
    A) of B) with C) at D) around
64. Each coat in the store has a tag _____ its price on it.
    A) with B) of C) at D) by
65. His illness was _____ bad food.
    A) due to B) by C) against D) as
66. Clouds formed _____ a rapid fall in the temperature.
    A) due to B) as C) because of D) for
67. The formation of clouds was _____ a rapid fall in the temperature.
    A) because B) due to C) like D) from
68. Almost everyone _____ the city was vaccinated _____ cholera.
    A) on / for B) at / against C) in / against D) in / from
69. We show other people that we are happy _____ smiling.
    A) with B) by C) at D) in
70. _____ the company's high profits this year, the employees did not receive a bonus.
    A) Because of B) Due to C) As D) In spite of
71. She remarried _____ the sake of her children.
    A) for B) at C) with D) from
72. He could swim _____ the age of five.
    A) on B) at C) in D) _
73. She was _____ the point of leaving when I arrived.
    A) with B) in C) at D) on
74. The car had been left _____ the side of the road.
    A) on B) with C) at D) in
75. He's sitting _____ the front of the car.
    A) at B) on C) over D) in
76. They found it _____ the bottom of the sea.
    A) at B) in C) on D) upon
77. She's genius _____ telling the wrong thing _____ the wrong time.
    A) in / at B) for / on C) at / at D) at / on
78. What's more important _____ you, independence or security?
    A) of B) to C) with D) for
79. The importance _____ washing one's hands is that it prevents infection.
    A) of B) to C) for D) off
80. He's rather tall _____ his age, and looks older than he is.
    A) as B) to C) for D) in
81. He spends hours _____ a time _____ the countryside looking _____ rare birds and flowers.
    A) at / at / at B) at / in / for C) at / in / after D) on / in / for
82. I'm very keen ___ bread usually, but I'm very fond ___ home bread.
    A) at / of B) in / at C) on / at D) on / of
83. It's supposed to be good _____ the nerves and sleeplessness.
    A) to B) at C) for D) in
84. He got used _____ funny customs, living _____ the country.
    A) to / in B) of / in C) in / at D) for / in
85. I object _____ being treated as a fool.
    A) of B) to C) at D) in
86. She's not used _____ being alone.
    A) at B) to C) of D) by
87. Consumed _____ excess, alcohol is a leading contributor _____ premature death, fatal accidents and suicide.
    A) for / to B) of / for C) in / of D) in / to
88. I can't think _____ the name, but it's _____ the tip of my tongue.
    A) on / on B) about / at C) of / on D) of / at

89. What can you buy _____ a half dollar?
    A) for B) at C) with D) by
90. What do you do when you run _____ petrol?
    A) off B) with C) out of D) without
91. We are not yet _____ danger.
    A) out of B) with C) over D) up
92. We must write our letters _____ ink.
    A) at B) by C) in D) with
93. How can you send a message faster than _____ letter?
    A) at B) with C) on D) by
94. We always review _____ taking an exam.
    A) before B) since C) with D) to
95. She depended _____ their meeting her _____ the airport.
    A) for / at B) on / at C) at / at D) in / on
96. The museum will be open _____ half past eight _____ five o'clock.
    A) at / to B) from / till C) till / at D) of / until
97. Our ideas differ _____ those _____ grandparents.
    A) from / of B) of / from C) as / with D) with / as
98. He kept on working _____ his illness.
    A) according to B) due to
    C) in spite of D) on account of
99. _____ his poor grades, their son had trouble getting into university.
    A) On account of B) In spite of
    C) Despite D) According to
100. As the boxer realized he was getting _____ the end of the round he started to relax.
    A) ahead of B) at C) away from D) towards
101. Did you hear about the architect who designed a three-story house _____ any stairs?
    A) off B) without C) instead of D) in spite of
102. Break this chocolate _____ pieces and share it _____ all the children.
    A) to / among B) into / among
    C) into / between D) off / to
103. If you're _____ trouble, you ought to confide _____ someone and ask _____ advice.
    A) at / to / for B) in / in / for C) in / with / of D) on / in / for
104. She's struggling _____ difficulties.
    A) on B) of C) at D) under
105. He lives _____ a village _____ the hills.
    A) in / beneath B) at / under C) on / in D) below / with
106. He has difficulties _____ paying his taxes.
    A) at B) by C) over D) for
107. I can't get my needle _____ this thick cloth.
    A) to B) at C) on D) through
108. I was walking _____ the hospital with a friend when it happened.
    A) for B) among C) past D) beneath
109. Will you please send _____ Jack? I want to talk to him.
    A) for B) to C) with D) after
110. I'm afraid we can't agree _____ each other _____ anything.
    A) to / on B) with / on C) in / with D) with / for
111. Common politeness is all I ask _____ you _____ return _____ mine.
    A) of / in / for B) from / for / of
    C) from / in / to D) of / to / for
112. He was charged _____ murder and brought _____ trial _____ jury.
    A) for / to / in front of B) at / into / by
    C) with / up to / by D) with / to / through
113. The teacher gave me ninety marks _____ a hundred for literature.
    A) from B) of C) out of D) off
114. Who's the girl _____ blue _____ yellow hair?
    A) in / with B) with / with C) of / in D) on / of
115. Don't play the fool. You should be _____ such childish games _____ your age.
    A) on / at B) above / in C) above / at D) below / of
116. The rider fell _____ his horse as it was jumping _____ a stream.
    A) from / through B) off / over
    C) out of / on D) of / from

117. If you're sure he'll be back _____ then, I'll wait, thank you.
  A) until   B) till   C) to   D) by
118. The human body is made _____ a number of different systems.
  A) off   B) up of   C) from   D) out of
119. Children _____ sixteen years _____ age are not admitted _____ their parents.
  A) over / with / without   B) at / of / with
  C) under / of / without   D) of / at / with
120. Wait _____ eleven o'clock. If your teacher doesn't come _____ then you can leave the class.
  A) at / by   B) till / at   C) until / by   D) to / till
121. The heart pumps blood _____ the body.
  A) by   B) throughout   C) at   D) on
122. Mary thinks that David is _____ love _____ her.
  A) in / with   B) on / with   C) in / at   D) at / in
123. Who takes care _____ the office when the manager is away _____ business?
  A) in / for   B) of / on   C) at / for   D) of / in
124. I was _____ work when thieves broke _____ our house.
  A) in / in   B) at / in   C) on / to   D) at / into
125. _____ his age, he still enjoys jogging.
  A) Concerning   B) According to
  C) Instead of   D) Despite
126. _____ the weather report, it's going to be sunny tomorrow.
  A) About   B) For   C) Although   D) According to
127. I want to ask your advice _____ one or two questions.
  A) considering   B) concerning   C) close to   D) depending on
128. _____ the circumstances, this was an important win for them.
  A) Considering   B) Concerning   C) On top of   D) Over
129. _____ inflation, the general cost of living in Turkey rose by 70% last year.
  A) Except for   B) In spite of   C) Due to   D) Excluding
130. _____ Greenland and Antarctica, the world has 13.15 billion hectares of land.
  A) On   B) Excluding   C) Throughout   D) As of
131. The mines had been closed _____ a geological survey.
  A) except for   B) excluding   C) following   D) due to
132. A: Which way do you have to go if you travel _____ air?
  B: You go _____ Bahrain
  A) on / through   B) by / via
  C) by / to   D) by means of / through
133. _____ popular belief, the desert can produce crops.
  A) By means of   B) As   C) Contrary to   D) Through
134. Different methods are used _____ what results are required.
  A) depending on   B) in favor of
  C) contrary to   D) following
135. Many incompatible couples stay together _____ their children.
  A) in support of   B) for the sake of
  C) in favor of   D) contrary to
136. We just can't agree. Her opinions on this subject are totally _____ mine.
  A) opposite to   B) for the sake of
  C) in support of   D) in favor of
137. _____ the inclusion of the unacceptable clause, the contract was signed.
  A) Despite   B) Under   C) Due to   D) For all
138. I can't get the top _____ this bottle.
  A) off   B) of   C) out of   D) onto
139. _____ receiving bad reviews, the film was a success.
  A) Despite   B) Under   C) By   D) For
140. Severe steps will be taken against those responsible _____ their rank.
  A) in spite of   B) including
  C) irrespective of   D) in favor of
141. We walked along _____ silence.
  A) in   B) in spite of   C) without   D) for the sake of
142. They are taught to respect everyone _____ race.
  A) regardless of   B) regarding   C) pending   D) owing to

143. Mike's completely cured _____ smoking now.
  A) from   B) of   C) with   D) without
144. _____ the first sign of illness, see your doctor.
  A) With   B) On   C) In   D) At
145. We are looking forward _____ your visit _____ pleasure.
  A) for / with   B) to / in   C) at / by   D) to / with
146. Darwin said that people were related _____ monkeys.
  A) to   B) with   C) in   D) of
147. Vitamin D is essential _____ the growth of bones and teeth and is found _____ fish, liver, oil and milk.
  A) to / at   B) of / in   C) on / with   D) for / in
148. They stood _____ silence for a while.
  A) on   B) off   C) with   D) in
149. Exposure _____ radiation may result _____ sickness and even death.
  A) to / in   B) with / in   C) of / with   D) to / from
150. Robert was _____ a brother to me.
  A) as   B) of   C) to   D) like
151. It is always difficult to stand up _____ the opinion of the majority.
  A) for   B) to   C) at   D) against
152. _____ a boy, he had been very fond _____ swimming.
  A) Like / of   B) As / of   C) At / in   D) In / on
153. They were just _____ the range of the big guns.
  A) by   B) beyond   C) below   D) beside
154. We're on your side. We are all _____ you.
  A) for   B) against   C) on   D) by
155. We won _____ two goals _____ nil.
  A) by / to   B) with / by   C) with / to   D) by / in
156. Mexico is situated _____ North America.
  A) to   B) in   C) at   D) throughout
157. Europe is situated _____ the west of Asia.
  A) to   B) in   C) at   D) on
158. The earth is not _____ right angles _____ its path round the sun.
  A) in / on   B) at / on   C) at / to   D) in / to
159. Thermostats make use _____ the principle of expansion.
  A) up   B) from   C) over   D) of
160. The pressure of a gas varies _____ temperature.
  A) from   B) in   C) over   D) of
161. Pressure is _____ inverse proportion _____ volume.
  A) in / to   B) at / of   C) in / in   D) on / in
162. We react _____ stress _____ two ways.
  A) - / in   B) to / in   C) at / on   D) - / for
163. Heavy drinkers are more prone _____ cirrhosis of the liver.
  A) of   B) at   C) with   D) to
164. _____ objections, he came to the meeting.
  A) Instead of   B) Despite   C) According to   D) Between
165. _____ a 1982 survey, one third of Americans regard alcohol as the single greatest threat to family life.
  A) Because of   B) Instead of   C) Despite   D) According to
166. He was found guilty _____ murder in the second degree.
  A) off   B) from   C) by   D) of
167. He was sentenced _____ four years' imprisonment.
  A) -   B) to   C) in   D) at
168. _____ days she remained _____ a deep coma.
  A) On / at   B) Since / in   C) For / in   D) For / -
169. There is a growing awareness _____ the link _____ emotions and backaches.
  A) in / among   B) for / in   C) of / between   D) of / from
170. Many studies have shown less heart disease _____ groups _____ low blood cholesterol.
  A) between / of   B) among / with
  C) in / of   D) within / at
171. As long as the bans remained _____ force, Turkey could not claim to be fully democratic.
  A) with   B) at   C) on   D) in
172. The cost of living index rose _____ 70 percent last year.
  A) in   B) by   C) to   D) up

INTERMEDIATE / UPPER-INTERMEDIATE 11 — prepositions after adjectives

Choose the best answer.

1. The runner is anxious _____ his success in the competition.
   A) of   B) about   C) at   D) on

2. Your criticisms are not applicable _____ the subject.
   A) with   B) on   C) about   D) to

3. He looked ashamed _____ his foolishness.
   A) at   B) of   C) about   D) with

4. He was accused _____ theft by the police.
   A) on   B) over   C) from   D) of

5. They felt quite certain _____ their failure.
   A) of   B) at   C) about   D) with

6. His opinions are directly contrary _____ yours.
   A) to   B) with   C) about   D) on

7. She was absorbed _____ an exciting story.
   A) with   B) in   C) on   D) of

8. I was quite astonished _____ his quick reaction.
   A) with   B) of   C) at   D) on

9. Is this proposal acceptable _____ you?
   A) by   B) in   C) to   D) from

10. The house was built according _____ the owner's plan.
    A) with   B) to   C) by   D) of

11. We are not well acquainted _____ our neighbors yet.
    A) by   B) to   C) of   D) with

12. She is very fond _____ Turkish films.
    A) of   B) on   C) in   D) about

13. Bursa is famous _____ silk and peaches.
    A) by   B) on   C) with   D) for

14. I am not good _____ languages.
    A) on   B) with   C) of   D) at

15. I'm glad _____ the opportunity to repay you for your help.
    A) with   B) on   C) of   D) at

16. Never become addicted _____ drugs.
    A) to   B) in   C) with   D) by

17. The question was not relevant _____ the subject of the lecture.
    A) for   B) to   C) in   D) on

18. I was disgusted _____ the sight of the butcher's shop.
    A) at   B) with   C) on   D) of

19. A child born _____ poverty will always be disadvantaged.
    A) with   B) by   C) in   D) about

20. She was born _____ a beautiful mother.
    A) of   B) in   C) from   D) by

21. The poor old man has gone blind _____ his left eye.
    A) from   B) in   C) on   D) by

22. You are always blind _____ your own faults.
    A) in   B) from   C) at   D) to

23. Most men are anxious _____ the advancement of their children.
    A) for   B) from   C) on   D) with

24. She is cautious _____ telling secrets.
    A) in   B) on   C) of   D) about

25. Are you content _____ the quality of the teaching?
    A) with   B) on   C) at   D) by

26. The teacher was angry _____ the student's conduct.
    A) at   B) about   C) with   D) by

27. Are you angry _____ me?
    A) at   B) about   C) with   D) by

28. Mary is envious _____ Janet's beauty.
    A) by   B) from   C) of   D) with

29. What do you think inflation is due _____?
    A) to   B) from   C) about   D) on

30. I'm familiar _____ your work.
    A) on   B) about   C) with   D) to

31. I'm familiar _____ his family.
    A) on   B) about   C) to   D) with

32. She was disappointed _____ her exam results.
    A) with   B) over   C) on   D) by

33. Your composition is full _____ mistakes.
    A) with   B) by   C) about   D) of

34. The film was based _____ a novel by Hemingway.
    A) on   B) in   C) over   D) at

35. He stole the car belonging _____ his friend.
    A) by   B) to   C) with   D) from

36. His speech was not appropriate _____ the occasion.
    A) for   B) on   C) to   D) about

37. I was not aware _____ your intention.
    A) of   B) about   C) on   D) in

38. You should always be faithful _____ your promise.
    A) on   B) to   C) with   D) over

39. He is a man devoid _____ all fine feelings.
    A) from   B) without   C) on   D) of

40. The supply of material is not adequate _____ the needs of the industry.
    A) for   B) to   C) about   D) in

41. I'm very concerned _____ my mother's illness.
    A) in   B) over   C) of   D) for

42. I was startled _____ the loud knock on the door.
    A) at   B) on   C) by   D) with

43. Our plans may change subject _____ the weather.
    A) over   B) with   C) to   D) at

44. Her ability makes her successful _____ everything she does.
    A) on   B) in   C) about   D) at

45. He thinks he is superior _____ us because his father is very rich.
    A) to   B) over   C) on   D) from

46. I was very surprised _____ the news of your marriage.
    A) by   B) with   C) on   D) at

47. Terry was jealous _____ Tom's success.
    A) of   B) on   C) by   D) at

48. They are innocent _____ the crime.
    A) in   B) on   C) of   D) at

49. I'm short _____ money this week. Can you lend me some?
    A) without   B) of   C) at   D) on

50. Please don't be proud _____ your homework. I know you haven't done it.
    A) of   B) on   C) at   D) about

51. We are quite satisfied _____ the result of the survey so far.
    A) at   B) in   C) on   D) with

52. She is married _____ a rich man.
    A) with   B) to   C) by   D) of

53. He soon got involved _____ serious difficulties.
    A) in   B) with   C) at   D) by

54. She was impatient _____ the arrival of her boyfriend.
    A) with   B) at   C) for   D) on

55. The teacher is always impatient _____ slow learners.
    A) with   B) at   C) for   D) on

56. I was completely ignorant _____ her intentions.
    A) at   B) from   C) by   D) of

57. What are you interested _____?
    A) at   B) on   C) by   D) in

58. He is deeply involved _____ her and feels he must marry her because everyone expects it.
    A) in   B) with   C) about   D) at

59. I'm so tired _____ your complaints.
    A) from   B) about   C) of   D) in

60. His courage is worthy _____ the highest praise.
    A) of   B) with   C) about   D) at

61. The sum covers the cost inclusive _____ postage.
    A) of   B) at   C) with   D) on

62. He was occupied _____ doing his homework.
    A) with   B) in   C) at   D) by

63. I was most grateful _____ you for your kindness.
    A) with   B) by   C) in   D) to

64. Do you plead guilty _____ stealing the car?
    A) to   B) from   C) with   D) of

65. He is occupied _____ the latest report at the moment.
    A) with   B) in   C) at   D) by

66. My mother was pregnant _____ me at the time.
    A) with   B) by   C) of   D) on

67. You should be thankful _____ her for telling you the truth.
    A) for   B) with   C) at   D) to

68. I'm glad to get rid _____ the responsibility.
    A) from   B) of   C) with   D) without

69. This chair is made _____ good solid oak.
    A) from   B) in   C) with   D) of

70. You are responsible ____ your mother ____ keeping the house tidy.
    A) for / to   B) in / for   C) to / for   D) to / from

71. Most people realize that toilet soap is made _____ coal and its by-products.
    A) from   B) by   C) at   D) of

72. George has been cured _____ his cold.
    A) with   B) of   C) from   D) against

73. I was annoyed _____ my failure.
    A) at   B) with   C) by   D) in

74. She was annoyed _____ you for being impertinent.
    A) at   B) with   C) by   D) in

75. Regular exercise is beneficial _____ health.
    A) to   B) on   C) with   D) by

76. He is a man apart _____ others.
    A) at   B) by   C) from   D) with

77. I'm becoming more and more displeased _____ your laziness.
    A) to   B) at   C) with   D) from

78. Mike is quite equal _____ his sister in brain.
    A) to   B) at   C) with   D) by

79. It's wise to be careful _____ one's health.
    A) to   B) by   C) of   D) at

80. She was conscious _____ being admired.
    A) to   B) by   C) with   D) of

81. Her exam results are not corresponding _____ her true abilities.
    A) with   B) at   C) on   D) to

82. They are confident _____ his parents for money.
    A) of   B) from   C) at   D) with

83. He is not dependent _____ his parents for money.
    A) of   B) from   C) on   D) with

84. Your conduct was not consistent _____ your usual politeness.
    A) with   B) by   C) at   D) on

85. I'm ever so grateful _____ you for help.
    A) at   B) to   C) with   D) from

86. He was always attentive _____ my ideas.
    A) with   B) to   C) of   D) for

87. He is very generous _____ his money.
    A) with   B) of   C) for   D) to

88. The manager was quite agreeable _____ my suggestion.
    A) of   B) for   C) with   D) to

89. Sue became very excited _____ receiving a promotion.
    A) at   B) to   C) for   D) in

90. This material is inferior _____ the kind we had last year.
    A) in   B) to   C) for   D) of

91. Dr. Baker is very good _____ children.
    A) by   B) of   C) with   D) from

92. He is capable _____ being an excellent student.
    A) of   B) for   C) to   D) with

93. I'm not accustomed _____ being interrupted.
    A) of   B) for   C) to   D) with

94. I don't see why he is so unkind _____ his brother.
    A) of   B) at   C) with   D) to

95. He was sick _____ hunger. He hadn't eaten anything for two days.
    A) by   B) at   C) with   D) from

96. China is rich _____ minerals.
    A) from   B) in   C) by   D) of

97. I'm not absolutely certain _____ it.
    A) with   B) of   C) by   D) in

98. It's nice _____ you to be concerned _____ me.
    A) of / on   B) from / of   C) of / about   D) with / of

99. I hope you don't think it is rude _____ me to refuse.
    A) of   B) with   C) in   D) from

100. I'm not very keen _____ modern music.
    A) at   B) in   C) with   D) on

101. I feel confident _____ the future of our country.
    A) in   B) at   C) off   D) about

102. They are incapable _____ expressing themselves _____ decent English.
    A) in / in   B) of / in   C) at / on   D) of / at

103. These days everybody is aware _____ the dangers of smoking.
    A) about   B) of   C) at   D) with

104. My problems are very similar _____ yours.
    A) to   B) with   C) for   D) at

105. I can't stop to talk to you now. I'm a bit short _____ time.
    A) with   B) at   C) about   D) of

106. The police are responsible _____ maintaining law and order.
    A) of   B) about   C) for   D) in

107. I was very impressed _____ the lesson he taught.
    A) at   B) about   C) by   D) over

108. I was delighted _____ the present you gave me.
    A) at   B) with   C) by   D) about

109. She is quite nice but I wouldn't like to be married _____ her.
    A) with   B) to   C) by   D) of

110. Nancy is engaged _____ a friend of mine.
    A) with   B) to   C) by   D) on

111. We are virtually immune _____ certain diseases which cause death elsewhere.
    A) with   B) to   C) by   D) on

112. Breathing asbestos-laden air may be hazardous _____ health.
    A) to   B) for   C) with   D) against

113. Strong winds are expected to make roads hazardous _____ drivers today.
    A) to   B) for   C) due to   D) against

114. I'm interested _____ chess but I'm not very good _____ it.
    A) in / at   B) on / at   C) with / on   D) at / at

INTERMEDIATE UPPER-INTERMEDIATE 12 — prepositions after verbs

Choose the best answer.

1. Why did you quarrel _____ your friends _____ such a small matter?
   A) at / about   B) with / on   C) with / over   D) against/over

2. I disagree _____ you.
   A) with   B) at   C) to   D) from

3. He disapproves _____ mothers going out to work.
   A) on   B) with   C) by   D) of

4. I definitely prefer traveling by air _____ traveling by train.
   A) by   B) at   C) to   D) in

5. There is no way we can prevent people _____ talking _____ this matter.
   A) by / over   B) without / on   C) from / with   D) from / about

6. Did you finally succeed _____ convincing them they were wrong?
   A) for   B) at   C) in   D) on

7. The teacher suspected the student _____ cheating on the test.
   A) of   B) in   C) about   D) on

8. You really shouldn't boast _____ your success _____ other people.
   A) with / to   B) of / to   C) about / at   D) over / to

9. I don't know why you insist _____ blaming me _____ all my troubles.
   A) on / for   B) in / for   C) at / on   D) over / for

10. You shouldn't rely _____ getting assistance from Frank.
    A) at   B) in   C) on   D) about

11. Mr. Green always worries _____ losing his position.
    A) in   B) at   C) on   D) about

12. Our boss objects _____ using any different method.
    A) of   B) to   C) with   D) over

13. My father doesn't approve _____ studying late at night.
    A) of   B) with   C) on   D) about

14. Forgive me _____ using these pompous words.
    A) of   B) for   C) with   D) on

15. Why are you laughing _____ me?
    A) of   B) over   C) to   D) at

16. I don't want to argue _____ you _____ that matter at this time.
    A) at / over   B) with / at   C) with / about   D) on / about

17. Terry always depends _____ his brother for assistance.
    A) on   B) in   C) at   D) of

18. Mary reminded her boss _____ his appointment the next day.
    A) at   B) of   C) on   D) with

19. I am translating this book _____ English _____ Turkish.
    A) on / over   B) from / over   C) to / into   D) from / into

20. All of the members objected _____ the chairman's suggestion.
    A) to   B) in   C) about   D) for

21. Aren't you going to introduce me _____ your friend?
    A) with   B) by   C) to   D) at

22. We suspected him _____ stealing the tape recorder.
    A) at   B) with   C) of   D) on

23. A : What are you looking _____?   B : My pen.
    A) about   B) after   C) around   D) for

24. I thought the nurse was looking _____ you.
    A) to   B) after   C) into   D) of

25. Police are looking _____ the disappearance of a quantity of uncut gems.
    A) into   B) after   C) on   D) about

26. I look _____ him as a friend.
    A) about   B) at   C) over   D) on

27. She had been looking forward _____ leaving the hospital wards for a holiday in Turkey.
    A) to   B) at   C) on   D) over

28. Look _____ this word in the dictionary.
    A) at   B) for   C) up   D) into

29. A man in prison longs _____ freedom.
    A) at   B) for   C) on   D) about

30. The canteen provides the workers _____ meals.
    A) for   B) _   C) on   D) with

31. The canteen provides meals _____ the workers.
    A) for   B) to   C) _   D) with

32. A queue of people were waiting _____ the last bus.
    A) on   B) at   C) of   D) for

33. They wait _____ you very well in this restaurant.
    A) for   B) on   C) at   D) in

34. He is thinking _____ retiring _____ his post several years before the normal age.
    A) of / from   B) about / of   C) of / of   D) of / for

35. The child spends almost all his money _____ chocolate.
    A) at   B) over   C) on   D) about

36. People are always mistaking him _____ his twin brother.
    A) with   B) for   C) about   D) on

37. Mr. Taylor was operated _____ for a constriction of the intestine.
    A) with   B) in   C) at   D) on

38. He had the keys of the city presented _____ him.
    A) to   B) in   C) on   D) for

39. In Britain milk is supplied _____ each house in bottles.
    A) at   B) to   C) with   D) in

40. The government supplies them _____ the basic necessities.
    A) at   B) to   C) with   D) on

41. I entirely agree _____ you; that road is very dangerous.
    A) in   B) on   C) at   D) with

42. Will you just run _____ the facts again?
    A) to   B) with   C) over   D) off

43. Drug abuse brought _____ his death.
    A) over   B) up   C) at   D) about

44. He gets _____ 40 cigarettes a day.
    A) through   B) off   C) over   D) with

45. He agreed _____ all the proposal we made.
    A) with   B) on   C) to   D) at

46. He aimed his gun _____ a policeman, and fired.
    A) by   B) to   C) at   D) of

47. People are always accusing me _____ being forgetful.
    A) for   B) at   C) of   D) with

48. The condemned man appealed _____ the court for mercy.
    A) at   B) by   C) with   D) to

49. Could you run _____ 10 copies of this hand-out, please?
    A) at   B) off   C) on   D) out of

50. He has applied _____ the banker _____ a loan.
    A) at / for   B) to / for   C) for / for   D) to / on

51. They went _____ sleep for several days.
    A) without   B) out of   C) for   D) off

52. I must apologize _____ you _____ not answering your letter at once.
    A) from / for   B) at / for   C) from / in   D) to / for

53. I met Mike this morning, he was asking _____ you.
    A) about   B) of   C) after   D) to

54. Do not argue _____ a newspaper editor, he can always have the last word.
    A) with   B) at   C) for   D) about

55. He never asked me _____ anything.
    A) of   B) after   C) from   D) for

56. I know he is always ready to back _____ his friends.
    A) of   B) up   C) from   D) by

57. Don't expect him to approve _____ your design at once.
    A) of   B) at   C) on   D) with

58. Beware _____ the dog!
    A) from B) about C) at D) of
59. The dictionary belongs _____ me.
    A) at B) to C) from D) with
60. The two scientists arrived _____ the same conclusion quite independently.
    A) to B) at C) on D) in
61. Moslems believe _____ God.
    A) in B) to C) at D) with
62. They blamed Peter _____ the failure.
    A) on B) about C) with D) for
63. The police are going to charge him _____ having murdered.
    A) by B) about C) with D) on
64. Our next-door neighbor said he'd complain _____ us _____ the police if we made any more noise.
    A) about / to B) at / by C) of / with D) to / of
65. Paralysis has deprived him _____ the use of his right hand.
    A) from B) of C) out D) to
66. He did not die _____ hunger or cholera. He died _____ an accident.
    A) from / at B) on / in C) in / at D) of / in
67. Some members of parliament voted _____ the proposal.
    A) against B) to C) in D) with
68. We all perform, and we all hope _____ approval.
    A) about B) of C) in D) for
69. Please excuse me _____ being late.
    A) by B) from C) for D) on
70. He feeds his horse _____ corn and beans.
    A) on B) with C) by D) from
71. We can call _____ Mary at her office at 10 tomorrow.
    A) in B) off C) on D) over
72. He boasted _____ the big fish he had caught.
    A) of B) on C) with D) from
73. The teacher explained the principles of nuclear fission _____ the class.
    A) at B) about C) for D) to
74. He insisted _____ being paid the full sum.
    A) at B) on C) with D) by
75. I introduced Terry _____ Janet, 2 years before they were married.
    A) with B) by C) to D) at
76. She would sit for hours listening _____ the songs of the birds.
    A) to B) from C) at D) with
77. They all praised her _____ being brave.
    A) on B) upon C) with D) for
78. He stood looking _____ the picture for a long time.
    A) through B) for C) after D) at
79. If you don't know what this means, refer _____ the dictionary.
    A) at B) for C) to D) with
80. The chance which he had looked _____ was now freely offered to him.
    A) for B) at C) up D) about
81. Have you replied _____ her letter?
    A) at B) to C) for D) with
82. I am intending to resign _____ the committee.
    A) to B) from C) at D) with
83. They knocked him down and robbed him _____ his watch.
    A) of B) from C) at D) with
84. I sent _____ the doctor without any delay because my father had started vomiting blood.
    A) from B) for C) on D) to
85. Water pollution, of course, is not new. We've worried _____ it for years.
    A) from B) about C) with D) of
86. The book speaks _____ the writer's childhood.
    A) of B) by C) with D) to
87. At our next meeting Mr. Mill will be speaking _____ the early development of surgery.
    A) about B) to C) with D) on

88. In the Roman numerals, C stands _____ one hundred.
    A) for B) up C) at D) on
89. He really succeeds _____ anything he really puts his mind to.
    A) at B) in C) on D) about
90. The ice-cream tasted _____ soap.
    A) in B) of C) with D) from
91. The old lady thanked me _____ helping her across the street.
    A) with B) on C) about D) for
92. I'll have to think _____ this before I give you an answer.
    A) about B) on C) in D) of
93. We're thinking _____ going to Spain for our holidays but we've not decided for certain yet.
    A) over B) about C) on D) of
94. Whether you vote _____ or against the proposal doesn't seem to matter very much.
    A) to B) for C) on D) before
95. Worrying _____ your health can make you ill.
    A) to B) of C) about D) on
96. He operates _____ the patient in an operating-theatre.
    A) at B) on C) in D) of
97. His accident prevented him _____ riding a bike for a year.
    A) at B) on C) with D) from
98. Everybody admired him _____ saving the child's life.
    A) at B) in C) for D) upon
99. Nothing can make up _____ his rudeness.
    A) for B) with C) against D) by
100. The teacher congratulated all the students _____ passing the exam.
    A) on B) for C) with D) by
101. The danger from any radioactive substances depends _____ where they are located.
    A) in B) at C) on D) to
102. He decided to give up sport in order to concentrate _____ his studies.
    A) in B) at C) on D) to
103. The policeman charged him _____ driving a car while under the influence of alcohol.
    A) with B) for C) of D) against
104. Government notice on each packet warns the public _____ the dangers of cigarette smoking.
    A) of B) for C) about D) off
105. I always run _____ money at the end of the month.
    A) out of B) off C) on D) without
106. Pneumonia may lead _____ death.
    A) towards B) to C) up to D) for
107. A shortage of vitamin C result _____ skin infections and stow healing.
    A) in B) from C) to D) for
108. The sun appeals _____ both Labor and Conservative supporters.
    A) from B) of C) to D) within
109. Don't turn _____ alcohol to handle pressure.
    A) at B) into C) to D) for
110. I rely _____ my wife, my two children and a small but solid group of friends.
    A) at B) in C) of D) on
111. If you do not comply _____ the traffic regulations you will get _____ trouble with the police.
    A) with / into B) at / into C) at / with D) on / in
112. I pride myself _____ the fact that I read two or three books a week.
    A) in B) at C) on D) for
113. This town reminds me _____ the place where I was born.
    A) about B) of C) for D) from
114. Don't blame me _____ what happened. It wasn't my fault.
    A) for B) of C) about D) at
115. When I was driving home I almost crashed _____ a bus.
    A) at B) in C) into D) on to

ELEMENTARY PRE-INTERMEDIATE 13 — gerund - infinitive

Choose the best alternative.

1. He wants _____ a cold drink.
   A) drink   B) to drink   C) drinking   D) drinks

2. He never _____ by plane.
   A) travels   B) to travel   C) traveling   D) travel

3. Will you _____ off the photocopier?
   A) to turn   B) turning   C) turned   D) turn

4. Would she like _____ to the moon?
   A) going   B) go   C) to go   D) goes

5. Do you like _____ football on TV?
   A) watch   B) watched   C) watches   D) watching

6. We must _____ back the mixer back to the shop. It doesn't work.
   A) taking   B) take   C) took   D) to take

7. She can _____ German and Italian.
   A) speak   B) speaking   C) to speak   D) speaks

8. Could you _____ more slowly?
   A) speaking   B) spoke   C) speak   D) speaks

9. I hope _____ you soon.
   A) to see   B) seeing   C) see   D) saw

10. We'd better _____ to the manager.
    A) to talk   B) talking   C) talked   D) talk

11. It takes him an hour _____ to the bank.
    A) getting   B) get   C) gets   D) to get

12. I am sorry _____ you.
    A) disturbing   B) to disturb   C) disturb   D) disturbed

13. He spoke too quickly for us _____.
    A) to understand   B) understand
    C) understanding   D) understood

14. He's not strong enough _____ me.
    A) beating   B) beats   C) to beat   D) beaten

15. She is able _____ 100 meters in 9 seconds.
    A) running   B) run   C) to run   D) ran

16. It is important _____.
    A) to win   B) winning   C) win   D) won

17. A: This problem is too difficult. I can't solve it.
    B: Is it really too difficult for you _____?
    A) solving   B) solve   C) to solve   D) solved

18. A: He is a doctor. He looks very young.
    B: Yes. He doesn't look old enough _____ a doctor.
    A) being   B) be   C) been   D) to be

19. A: Shall I buy meat or fish?
    B: I've already told you what _____.
    A) to buy   B) buying   C) buy   D) bought

20. A: What are you _____?
    B: I'm resting.
    A) done   B) do   C) doing   D) to do

21. Thank you for _____ me.
    A) helping   B) help   C) to help   D) helped

22. Let's _____ in the sun.
    A) sitting   B) to sit   C) sat   D) sit

23. A: Why do we go to school?
    B: _____.
    A) To learn   B) Learning   C) Learned   D) Learn

24. Could you _____ me the time?
    A) telling   B) to tell   C) tell   D) told

25. There is nothing _____.
    A) to do   B) doing   C) did   D) do

26. Have you got anything _____?
    A) reading   B) to read   C) read   D) reads

27. She is good at _____.
    A) to swim   B) swimming   C) swims   D) swum

28. It takes a long time _____ a foreign language.
    A) learning   B) learned   C) learns   D) to learn

29. A: I've got a headache. B: Well, why don't you _____ an aspirin?
    A) to take   B) take   C) taken   D) taking

30. Why are you _____ my tea?
    A) drinking   B) to drink   C) drunk   D) drink

31. She typed the letters carefully without _____ any mistakes.
    A) made   B) to make   C) makes   D) making

32. I haven't _____ Anna more than five years.
    A) seeing   B) seen   C) to see   D) see

33. Why don't we go and _____ the film at the Moonstar?
    A) see   B) seen   C) to see   D) seeing

34. My son wants _____ a manager.
    A) been   B) to be   C) be   D) being

35. I'd rather not _____ late for my interview.
    A) be   B) to be   C) been   D) being

36. A farmer uses tractors _____ fields with.
    A) ploughing   B) to plough   C) ploughed   D) ploughs

37. She wants _____ a complaint about the waiter.
    A) to make   B) making   C) makes   D) made

38. My father does the _____ himself.
    A) ironing   B) irons   C) to iron   D) iron

39. My mother does all the _____.
    A) cleaning   B) to clean   C) cleans   D) clean

40. Shall I _____ you a glass of lemonade?
    A) making   B) made   C) make   D) to make

41. Do you lie in bed after _____?
    A) to wake up   B) waking up   C) woken up   D) wake up

42. Let him _____ that for you.
    A) to do   B) do   C) doing   D) does

43. How long has he _____ the manager?
    A) been   B) to be   C) being   D) be

44. She is _____ to school by her mother every morning.
    A) takes   B) taken   C) to take   D) taking

45. A new factory is _____ here.
    A) being built   B) to build   C) build   D) building

46. I'm afraid of _____ mistakes.
    A) to make   B) made   C) make   D) making

47. I'm looking forward to _____ you next summer.
    A) visit   B) visited   C) visiting   D) visits

48. It is not necessary for him _____ every page.
    A) reading   B) read   C) to read   D) reads

49. I don't _____ sugar, thank you.
    A) take   B) to take   C) taking   D) taken

50. He prefers walking to _____.
    A) driving   B) drive   C) drives   D) drove

51. I expect she will _____.
    A) comes   B) coming   C) come   D) to come

52. I expect her _____.
    A) to come   B) comes   C) coming   D) come

53. Hadn't we better _____ soon?
    A) leaving   B) leave   C) leaves   D) left

54. He usually goes _____ tennis at the weekend.
    A) to play   B) playing   C) plays   D) play

55. She can't stand _____ to rock music.
    A) listening   B) to listen   C) listen   D) listens

56. Will you _____ to what I'm saying?
    A) listening   B) to listen   C) listen   D) listened

57. Haven't you _____ your calculator?
    A) finding   B) find   C) found   D) to find

58. It is difficult _____ a good hotel, in this town.
    A) find   B) to find   C) found   D) finding

59. May I _____ you tomorrow?
    A) seeing   B) to see   C) seen   D) see

60. I can see a man _____ towards us.
    A) come   B) coming   C) comes   D) to come

61. Terry wants to read, but he hasn't got a _____ lamp.
    A) read   B) to read   C) reading   D) read

62. They don't have _____ water in their house.
    A) running   B) to run   C) run   D) ran

63. Everyone is expected _____ to school.
    A) going   B) goes   C) to go   D) gone

64. Turkey is not an oil _____ country.
    A) producing   B) to produce   C) produces   D) produced

65. I've just eaten a _____ potato.
    A) boiling   B) to boil   C) boils   D) boiled

66. She didn't get a _____ grade on the test.
    A) to pass   B) passing   C) passed   D) passes

67. Let her _____ the potatoes.
    A) fry   B) fries   C) frying   D) fried

68. We'll eat the _____ potatoes with salt and pepper.
    A) fried   B) frying   C) to fry   D) fry

69. Did somebody _____ the dishes?
    A) wash   B) washing   C) to wash   D) washed

70. Yes, I saw the _____ soldiers.
    A) wounding   B) wound   C) wounded   D) to wound

71. The boy _____ in the dentist's chair has got toothache.
    A) sitting   B) sat   C) sit   D) sits

72. Everything is _____.
    A) changes   B) to change   C) changing   D) change

73. Will you _____ here tomorrow?
    A) to be   B) been   C) being   D) be

74. He should give up _____.
    A) to smoke   B) smoking   C) smoke   D) smoked

75. He would like _____ after dinner.
    A) to rest   B) resting   C) rests   D) rested

76. We are peace _____ people.
    A) love   B) loved   C) loving   D) to love

77. He agreed _____ us with our assignment.
    A) to help   B) helping   C) helped   D) helps

78. The doctor advised him _____ a little exercise every day.
    A) takes   B) taking   C) to take   D) taken

79. She told him not _____ too much noise.
    A) making   B) make   C) to make   D) made

80. Do you mind if I _____ you question?
    A) asked   B) ask   C) to ask   D) asking

81. The plane has _____ off.
    A) taken   B) took   C) taking   D) takes

82. Our house was _____ in 1984.
    A) building   B) builds   C) built   D) been built

83. He is too ill _____.
    A) moving   B) moves   C) moved   D) to move

84. Does she have _____ up early?
    A) gets   B) getting   C) got   D) to get

85. _____ in Ankara is expensive.
    A) Don't live   B) Living   C) Live   D) Lived

86. You must _____ at once.
    A) apologize   B) to apologize   C) apologizing   D) apologized

87. You ought _____ exercise regularly.
    A) take   B) to take   C) taking   D) takes

88. The man _____ in that car is my father.
    A) sits   B) sit   C) sitting   D) sat

89. She punished the child for _____ lies.
    A) telling   B) to tell   C) told   D) tells

90. You can't live without _____.
    A) eat   B) to eat   C) eating   D) eaten

91. They can _____ in now.
    A) to come   B) coming   C) came   D) come

92. I saw the bus _____ towards me.
    A) to come   B) comes   C) coming   D) come

93. His father was _____ in a car accident.
    A) killing   B) kills   C) be killed   D) killed

94. English is an easy language _____.
    A) be learned   B) to learn   C) learning   D) learned

95. Could you tell me where _____ off the bus?
    A) to get   B) get   C) getting   D) got

96. When I was young I used _____ to school on my bicycle.
    A) going   B) to going   C) to go   D) gone

97. This problem is hard _____ because it is very complicated.
    A) solving   B) to solve   C) solved   D) be solved

98. I expected Mary _____ me last night but she didn't.
    A) to phone   B) phoning   C) phones   D) phone

99. I'll never again ask you _____ me.
    A) helping   B) help   C) to help   D) helped

INTERMEDIATE / UPPER-INTERMEDIATE 14
gerund - infinitive - participles - causative

Choose the best answer.

1. I felt someone _____ me on the shoulder but when I turned round, there was no-one there.
   A) tapping   B) to tap   C) tapped   D) tap

2. Look at that old man _____ to cross the road.
   A) trying   B) tries   C) to try   D) tried

3. I can feel something _____ up my leg.
   A) crawling   B) crawl   C) to crawl   D) crawls

4. I won't waste time _____ to his letter.
   A) reply   B) to reply   C) replying   D) to have replied

5. It's high time we _____.
   A) go   B) to go   C) went   D) going

6. I'd rather _____ in tonight.
   A) stayed   B) stay   C) to stay   D) staying

7. There is no point in _____ with her.
   A) to argue   B) arguing   C) argued   D) to have argued

8. I think we'd better _____.
   A) going   B) to go   C) gone   D) go

9. Would you care _____ a look at my latest report?
   A) having   B) to have   C) have   D) had

10. She seems _____ better today.
    A) to be feeling   B) feeling   C) feel   D) felt

11. I daren't _____ out after dark.
    A) to go   B) go   C) went   D) going

12. Passengers are forbidden _____ to the driver.
    A) to talk   B) talking   C) talk   D) talked

13. A: Won't you stay? There is a good Japanese film on TV.
    B: No thanks, I hate _____ Japanese films.
    A) to watching   B) watch   C) watching   D) having watched

14. She is afraid of the dentist, so she always puts off _____ till the last possible moment.
    A) to go   B) going   C) go   D) gone

15. I simply couldn't resist _____ you to tell you the good news!
    A) phoning   B) to phone   C) phone   D) phoned

16. They were expected _____ back by eleven.
    A) being   B) been   C) have been   D) to be

17. We'll get Robert _____ it.
    A) delivers   B) delivering   C) to deliver   D) deliver

18. Let's not waste time _____ about this.
    A) argue   B) arguing   C) having argued   D) to have argued

19. I went to the airport _____ to meet her, but she didn't arrive.
    A) to have expected   B) expecting   C) to expect   D) to be expected

20. _____ that I would be late for school, I took a taxi instead of a bus.
    A) Thinking   B) Thought   C) To think   D) To be thinking

21. A: Why does your sister bite her nails?
    B: She doesn't enjoy _____ them; she just can't help _____ it.
    A) bite / do   B) biting / to do   C) biting / doing   D) to bite / doing

22. You seem to be _____ problems with your washing machine.
    A) have   B) to have   C) have had   D) having

23. Susan _____ the mechanic _____ her car yesterday.
    A) had / repair   B) has / to repair   C) had / to repair   D) having / repair

24. Richard is _____ the doctor _____ his chest.
    A) to be having / examine   B) to have / to examine   C) having / examine   D) being had / to examine

25. The police are looking for a man with dark hair. A _____ man is being sought by the police.
    A) dark hair   B) dark-haired   C) to have dark hair   D) having dark hair

26. Living in London is expensive. It is expensive _____ in London.
    A) to live   B) living   C) to have lived   D) lived

27. She left without _____ goodbye.
    A) to say   B) said   C) having said   D) saying

28. I can't forgive Tim's _____ his promise.
    A) to break   B) breaking   C) break   D) broken

29. Will you come _____ with me?
    A) to shopping   B) to shop   C) shopping   D) shop

30. You must see their newly _____ supermarket.
    A) decorating   B) be decorated   C) decorated   D) to be decorated

31. The boy _____ a blue jacket is an excellent tennis player.
    A) worn   B) wearing   C) to be worn   D) wears

32. The freshly _____ store is clean.
    A) has been painted   B) painted   C) painting   D) to paint

33. She is the person whom you should see. She's the person _____.
    A) seeing   B) should be seen   C) ought to see   D) to see

34. The person who was driving the blue truck almost had an accident. The person _____ the blue truck almost had an accident.
    A) to drive   B) to have driven   C) had been driving   D) driving

35. Mr. Hopkins plans on ___ his students ___ the English test tomorrow.
    A) to have / take   B) having / take   C) having / to take   D) to have / to take

36. Galileo is supposed _____ the telescope.
    A) having invented   B) have invented   C) to have invented   D) to invent

37. She went into the kitchen _____ dinner ready.
    A) getting   B) to get   C) get   D) to have got

38. Can you tell me how _____ to the library?
    A) getting   B) to get   C) got   D) to have got

39. Do you want _____ something _____ now?
    A) having / drinking   B) to have / drinking   C) have / for drink   D) to have / to drink

40. They were waiting _____ what the Premier had to say.
    A) to hear   B) heard   C) to have heard   D) hear

41. A: Did someone really write those words on the wall?
    B: Yes, I actually saw them _____ on the wall.
    A) written   B) to write   C) to be written   D) writing

42. A: Did they play that song on the radio?
    B: Well, I heard it _____ on the radio this morning.
    A) play   B) playing   C) played   D) to be played

43. I regret _____ you that you are to be dismissed next month.
    A) inform   B) to inform   C) informing   D) having informed

44. I don't regret _____ her what I thought, even if it upsets her.
    A) tell   B) to tell   C) to have told   D) telling

45. I tried _____ her flowers but it didn't have any effect.
    A) to send   B) sending   C) sent   D) to be sent

46. I once tried _____ Spanish.
    A) to learn   B) learning   C) have learned   D) learnt

47. It was a tragedy that she was killed on her wedding-day.
    To _____ was a tragedy.
    A) killed on her wedding-day
    B) have been killed on her wedding-day
    C) being killed on her wedding-day
    D) have killed on her wedding day

48. They should have shown me more consideration.
    I ought _____.
    A) been shown more consideration
    B) be shown more consideration
    C) to have been shown more consideration
    D) to have shown more consideration

49. I remember _____ for the job, but t forgot the exact amount.
    A) to be paid   B) be paid   C) being paid   D) paid

50. I have to do a lot of work today. There is a lot of work _____.
    A) done today   B) to be done today
    C) be done today   D) being done today

51. You should give your baby Vitamin C. Vitamin C ought _____ to all babies.
    A) to give   B) given   C) be given   D) to be given

52. Dust the furniture thoroughly. The furniture is _____ thoroughly.
    A) dusted   B) to be dusted
    C) be dusted   D) being dusted

53. I insist on _____ this small present as a token of my appreciation.
    A) your accepting   B) you to accept
    C) yours accepting   D) you accept

54. I wonder if Mary posted that letter.
    A) Yes, I remembered her post it.
    B) Yes, I remember her posting it.
    C) Yes, I remember her to post it.
    D) Yes, I remembered her to post it.

55. Did you notice the little boy _____ away?
    A) take the candy and run
    B) took the candy and ran
    C) taking the candy and run
    D) who is taking the candy and running

56. I bought a camera last year but I never use it. I _____ a record player instead.
    A) ought to buy   B) should buy
    C) must buy   D) ought to have bought

57. _____ about his problem, Susan wrote Tom a letter.
    A) Hearing   B) Heard   C) To hear   D) To be heard

58. _____, Mrs. Young returned to the house.
    A) Waiting tiredly   B) For waiting
    C) After tiring   D) Tired of waiting

59. It must have been an interesting performance. I would like _____.
    A) to go   B) to be there   C) to have gone   D) having gone

60. Before taking a test, it is important _____.
    A) to have studied   B) studying
    C) that you will study   D) you would study

61. The roof _____ before winter comes.
    A) requires to be repaired   B) must be repairing
    C) has to repairing   D) needs repairing

62. _____ she washed the cup and put it away.
    A) Having the coffee   B) Drinking the coffee
    C) Having drunk the coffee   D) Has drunk the coffee

63. _____ he ran out of the classroom.
    A) Turning suddenly, with tears in his eyes
    B) Having tears in his eyes and turned suddenly
    C) With a sudden turn, tearful eyes
    D) With tears in his eyes and a sudden turn

64. When the teacher fell off his chair, the students _____.
    A) weren't able to stop laughter
    B) could not stop but laughing
    C) couldn't help laughing
    D) could not avoid to laugh

65. Have you met the secretary _____ last week?
    A) hired   B) was hired
    C) she was hired   D) when she was hired

66. "War and Peace" is a long novel _____ by Leo Tolstoy.
    A) was written   B) it was written
    C) written   D) when it was written

67. I would appreciate _____ it a secret.
    A) your keeping   B) you to keep
    C) that you would give   D) that you are keeping

68. Before the computer could be repaired, a special part had _____ from Germany.
    A) to import   B) a very long delivery
    C) to have been important   D) to be imported

69. Susan hoped _____ to Terry's party.
    A) for being invited   B) to be invited
    C) she will be invited   D) being invited

70. If you need advice, Mr. Wisdom is the person you should talk to.
    If you need advice, Mr. Wisdom is the person _____.
    A) should talk to   B) being talked to
    C) talking to   D) to talk to

71. The easiest thing you can do is to start again.
    The easiest thing _____ is to start again.
    A) being done   B) to do   C) done   D) to have done

72. The hardest thing to do is to start again.
    The hardest thing you _____ is to start again.
    A) have to do   B) having to do
    C) should have done   D) to do

73. Where is the computer that was sent this morning?
    Where is the computer _____ this morning?
    A) to be sent   B) being sent   C) sent   D) to send

74. I told him _____ so bad-tempered.
    A) not being   B) not to be
    C) not to have been   D) not be

75. His eyes need _____.
    A) to have been tested   B) be tested
    C) to test   D) testing

76. A: Your hair needs _____, doesn't it?
    B: Yes, I'm getting it _____ this weekend.
    A) to be cut / cut   B) cutting / to be cut
    C) be cut / cutting   D) cutting / be cut

77. _____ in every match this season, Borussia Dortmund will go down to the second division.
    A) Having been beaten   B) Beaten
    C) To be beaten   D) Having beaten

78. They say he is terribly stingy. He is supposed _____ terribly stingy.
    A) to be   B) being   C) to have been   D) been

79. They say the universe is expanding all the time.
    The universe is supposed _____ all the time.
    A) to expand   B) expanding
    C) to have expanded   D) to be expanding

80. A: Do you think I should take an umbrella?
    B: Yes, you should. It is almost bound _____.
    A) raining   B) to rain   C) rained   D) to have rained

81. Many people think that the Vikings sailed to Canada.
    The Vikings are thought _____ to Canada.
    A) to be sailing   B) to have been sailed
    C) to have sailed   D) to sail

82. Tensing and Hillary were the first men _____ Everest.
    A) climbed   B) climb   C) climbing   D) to climb

83. The last one who was caught was a bank robber.
    The last one _____ was a bank robber.
    A) to have been caught   B) to catch
    C) to be caught   D) to be catching

84. I saw him _____ to a taxi driver.
    A) speaking   B) spoke   C) speak   D) to speak

85. They don't allow _____ in the hall.
    A) to smoke   B) smoking   C) smoke   D) to smoking

86. I don't allow my students _____ during an exam.
    A) to smoke   B) smoking   C) smoke   D) to smoking

87. The developing countries that are producers of primary products are those that have minerals and foodstuffs _____ by the _____ countries.
    A) needing / industrialized   B) needed / to industrialize
    C) needed / industrialized   D) be needed / industrializing

88. A: I've got a headache. Shall I take an aspirin?
    B: Well, you can try _____ an aspirin, if you like.
    A) to be taken   B) to take   C) taking   D) taken

89. _____ his job, he is now unemployed.
    A) Having lost   B) To lose   C) To be lost   D) Losing

90. _____ some money, he didn't need to work any more.
    A) Having made   B) Making
    C) To make   D) Made

91. You should have your visa _____ before it expires.
    A) extended   B) to extend
    C) be extended   D) to be extended

92. The examiner made us _____ our identification in order to be admitted to the test.
    A) showing   B) show   C) to show   D) showed

93. Robert was absent this morning because he had his tooth _____.
    A) to fill   B) filled   C) filling   D) to be filled

94. It is probably about time we _____ the car serviced.
    A) have   B) having   C) had   D) to have

95. _____ him do some of the work.
    A) Tell   B) Make   C) Allow   D) Ask

96. Jack's parents should _____ study because his grades are poor.
    A) let him   B) make him   C) get him   D) to make him

97. If you don't get out of my house, I'll have you _____.
    A) to arrest   B) arresting   C) arrested   D) be arrested

98. If you ask nicely, Mother will probably _____ a piece of cake.
    A) let you have   B) get you to have
    C) make you have   D) to let you have

99. What made you _____ it?
    A) do   B) to do   C) doing   D) done

100. If the car won't start, try _____ it.
    A) push   B) to push   C) pushing   D) to be pushed

101. I lay in bed warm and comfortable _____ to the rain _____ against the windows.
    A) listening / beating   B) listen / beat
    C) to listen / beaten   D) listen / beaten

102. The drunk was _____ against a lamp-post _____ to himself.
    A) leaning / talking   B) leaning / talked
    C) leaned / talking   D) leaned / talked

103. I didn't expect _____ by him to his marriage ceremony.
    A) be invited   B) being invited
    C) to be invited   D) would be invited

104. Janet is fortunate _____ a scholarship.
    A) to have been given   B) being given
    C) having been given   D) be given

105. I'm angry with her for _____ me the truth.
    A) not to have told   B) not having told
    C) not to have been told   D) not having been told

106. He admitted _____ the money.
    A) to have stolen   B) to steal
    C) having been stolen   D) having stolen

107. I can't help _____ about it.
    A) worry   B) to worry
    C) worrying   D) having worried

108. She deserves _____ the prize.
    A) winning   B) to win   C) having won   D) to have won

109. I urged her _____ for the job.
    A) to apply   B) apply   C) applying   D) applies

110. He is lucky _____ alive after the accident.
    A) having been   B) being   C) to be   D) been

111. The boy did nothing but _____ throughout the lesson.
    A) yawning   B) yawn   C) to yawn   D) yawns

112. She can do everything except _____.
    A) is cooking   B) cooks   C) cook   D) to cook

113. Hadn't you better _____ in with that cold?
    A) stay   B) to stay   C) staying   D) stayed

114. I would rather _____ out last night.
    A) not to have gone   B) not go
    C) not to go   D) not have gone

115. _____ ill, my father could not attend his old friend's funeral.
    A) To be   B) Being   C) For being   D) To have been

116. You should avoid _____ during the rush hour.
    A) traveling   B) to travel   C) traveled   D) to traveling

117. I greatly regret _____ those boots when they were so cheap.
    A) not having bought   B) not to have bought
    C) not to buy   D) didn't buy

118. I am not used _____ a suit and tie every day.
    A) to wear   B) having worn   C) to wearing   D) to have worn

119. Did you remember _____ the letter I gave you yesterday?
    A) to have posted   B) to be posted
    C) to post   D) posting

120. I prefer _____ by bus to _____ by train.
    A) traveling / traveling   B) to travel / traveling
    C) traveling / to travel   D) being traveled / having traveled

121. They say she left home at the age of 15. He's supposed _____ home at the age of 15.
    A) to leave   B) leave   C) to have left   D) leaving

122. My friend specially asked that nothing should be said about what she told me. My friend specially asked me _____ anything about what she told me.
    A) not saying   B) not to be said
    C) not having been said   D) not to say

123. He is very skillful at _____ animal noises.
    A) being made   B) to make   C) made   D) making

124. I expect that I'll be able to pass my class this year.
I expect _____ my class this year.
A) to be able to pass B) to be passed
C) passing D) having passed

125. The child was punished _____ his tongue out his uncle.
A) for putting B) to put C) to be put D) having put

126. A: Why didn't you enjoy your holiday?
B: Well, _____ a long story short, the hotel was dirty and the food _____ gave me incessant indigestion.
A) cutting / being served B) to cut / serving
C) having cut / served D) to cut / served

127. There will be a crisis if nothing is done _____ inflation.
A) for controlling B) to control
C) to be controlled D) control

128. I am against children _____ to school before they are six.
A) being sent B) to send
C) to be sent D) having been sent

129. She is very clever at _____ people _____ her ideas are their own.
A) making / to think B) to make / thinking
C) making / think D) being made / think

130. He hates _____ when he is having his after-lunch nap.
A) to disturb B) being disturbed
C) to have disturbed D) having been disturbed

131. We were made _____ a lot of boring history books at school.
A) read B) reading C) to read D) having read

132. He's the second man _____ in this way.
A) stabbing B) having stabbed
C) to stab D) to be stabbed

133. It's stupid of you _____ so much.
A) smoked B) smoking C) to smoke D) smoke

134. The woman _____ in the _____ house was screaming hysterically.
A) to be trapped / blazing B) trapping / blazed
C) trapped / blazing D) trapped / blazed

135. The drunkard spoke aggressively when _____ by the police to accompany them to the police station.
A) asking B) asked C) having asked D) to be asked

136. Floods _____ away the bridge, the river was impassable,
A) to have carried B) carrying
C) to be carried D) having carried

137. We spent a very enjoyable evening _____ about old times.
A) talking B) talked C) having talked D) to talk

138. _____ their final check, the astronauts boarded their spacecraft.
A) Received B) To be received
C) Having received D) To have received

139. It's no use _____ to him. He's asleep.
A) to talk B) talking C) talk D) having talked

140. Come in now. I'm sorry _____ you waiting so long.
A) keeping B) to have kept
C) kept D) had kept

141. He lost his interest, _____ to obtain promotion.
A) to fail B) have failed C) failing D) having failed

142. The film was so terrifying that I could hardly bear _____ it.
A) watching B) to watch
C) to be watching D) to have watched

143. The police found the money _____ in a disused cottage house.
A) hidden B) hiding C) to have hidden D) hide

144. A job worth _____ is worth _____ well.
A) to do / doing B) doing / to do
C) doing / doing D) to do / to do

145. Don't stand there _____ nothing.
A) to do B) doing C) to have done D) being done

146. If I catch you _____ again, I'll make you _____ in after school _____ some extra work.
A) cheating / to stay / to do B) to cheat / to stay / to do
C) to cheat / stay / to do D) cheating / stay / to do

147. This form is _____ in ink.
A) has been filled B) to be filled
C) to fill D) to have been filled

148. You mentioned _____ in a car accident last month.
A) to have been B) to be
C) having been D) to have

149. I'm annoyed about your _____ to phone me yesterday.
A) forgetting B) forget
C) to forget D) to have forgotten

150. Do you object to _____?
A) have smoked B) be smoked
C) smoke D) smoking

151. I'm not used to _____ up early.
A) got B) have got C) getting D) to get

152. Every half hour he stops work _____ a cigarette.
A) to smoke B) smoking C) smoked D) smoke

153. He advised me _____ a Renault.
A) buy B) buying C) bought D) to buy

154. He advised _____ a Renault.
A) buy B) buying C) to buying D) to buy

155. I got my friend _____ me to the airport.
A) to drive B) driving C) drive D) driven

156. I had my friend _____ me to the airport.
A) to drive B) driving C) drive D) driven

157. I had a hard time _____ his house.
A) find B) to find C) found D) finding

158. Mary spent all day _____ ready to leave on vacation.
A) get B) getting C) to get D) to be

159. When she needed a passport photo, she had her picture _____ by a professional photographer.
A) taken B) to be taken C) take D) taking

160. The main idea behind _____ a lot of buildings is _____ new office blocks.
A) to demolish / to erect B) demolishing / erect
C) demolishing / to erect D) to demolish / erecting

161. Excuse me. Would you mind _____? It makes it impossible for me to enjoy my meal.
A) my smoking B) to have smoked
C) not smoking D) not to smoke

162. _____ a horseshoe on the door is supposed _____ good luck.
A) To have / bringing B) Having / to bring
C) Having had / bringing D) To have / to be brought

163. I'd intended _____ on you, but was prevented from _____ so.
A) to call / doing B) calling / doing
C) call / to do D) to be called / doing

164. He knows enough English and German to make himself _____ and _____ other people.
A) understand / understanding B) understood / understood
C) understood / to understand D) understood / understand

165. I'm not accustomed to _____ in that way.
    A) be treated   B) treat
    C) have been treated D) being treated

166. Don't let yourself _____ by your failure.
    A) to be depressed   B) be depressed
    C) being depressed   D) depress

167. He wanted nothing except _____ in peace.
    A) to be left B) to leave C) be left D) being left

168. Was she very upset at not _____ the job?
    A) offered B) to be offered C) being offered D) to offer

169. What makes me _____ all the time, stuffs up my nose, and makes my eyes _____?
    A) cough / water   B) to cough / to water
    C) coughing / watering D) coughs / water

170. He saw me _____ in the garden and asked me what I _____.
    A) working / was doing B) work / was doing
    C) to work / did   D) working / done

171. It's very expensive _____ by ship.
    A) to go B) is going C) go D) for going

172. Always put medicine after _____ it.
    A) take B) took C) you took D) taking

173. You should always check your tires before _____ your car.
    A) drive B) you drove C) driving D) you're driving

174. Mary's father approved of _____ in England for another year in order to improve her English.
    A) her staying B) her to stay C) she will stay D) she to stay

175. Little boys like _____ trees.
    A) climb   B) climbing
    C) swing from   D) having a swing

176. I couldn't help _____ when you fell down.
    A) laughed B) to laugh C) at laughing D) laughing

177. Don't be nervous. I want you _____.
    A) not nervous B) relax C) to relax D) relaxing

178. Excuse me, officer, I'd like you _____ me.
    A) helping B) help C) to help D) for helping

179. If you're not careful in the crowd, you _____ your money _____.
    A) get / steal   B) got / stolen
    C) will get / stolen D) will get / steal

180. We are both looking forward _____ next Saturday.
    A) to going on vacation   B) to go on vacation
    C) to be going on vacation D) to have gone on vacation

181. George wants me _____.
    A) going along with him   B) go along with him
    C) to go along with him   D) will go along with him

182. People are not allowed _____ in the lecture hall.
    A) smoking B) smoke C) to smoking D) to smoke

183. I'm considering _____ your offer.
    A) to accept B) accept C) accepted D) accepting

184. They were in danger of _____.
    A) injuring   B) to be injured
    C) being injured D) been injured

185. He should _____ care of now that he is old.
    A) to be taken B) to take C) taking D) be taken

186. There was no way of _____ the accident.
    A) avoiding B) avoided
    C) to avoid D) to have avoided

187. I forgot _____ off the lights again.
    A) to switch B) switching
    C) switched   D) to have switched

188. She found her radio _____.
    A) break B) broken C) breaking D) broke

189. He tried _____ us by _____ huge cigars.
    A) impressing / smoking   B) to be impressed / smoking
    C) to impress / smoked   D) to impress / smoking

190. On _____ the news she drove straight home.
    A) heard B) to hear C) hearing D) being heard

191. I'd rather she _____ away next week rather than this week.
    A) stays B) stay C) stayed D) had stayed

192. I'd rather she _____ away last week rather than this week.
    A) stays B) stay C) stayed D) had stayed

193. He imagined the man _____ him.
    A) to want to follow B) to be following
    C) were following   D) follows

194. After _____ questioned, he left.
    A) being B) to be C) having D) asking

195. The doctor advised _____ in bed for a week.
    A) stay B) to staying C) staying D) to stay

196. The doctor advised her _____ in bed for a week.
    A) stay B) to staying C) staying D) to stay

197. I can't help _____ her.
    A) liking B) to liking C) to like D) liked

198. What they need is clean, well-_____, and reasonably-_____ houses.
    A) equipped / priced   B) equipping / pricing.
    C) equipped / pricing D) equipping / priced

199. One way of _____ the wealth or poverty is by _____ out how much it produces in one year.
    A) to determine / finding B) determining / finding
    C) determine / finding   D) determining / to find

200. The term _____ to describe the amount of goods and services _____ in a country for each person in one year is per capita GNP.
    A) using / produced B) used / producing
    C) used / produced   D) used / used

201. Per capita GNP is just a rough way of _____ the ability of different countries _____ goods and services, _____ into account the fact that they have different populations.
    A) compared / producing / taking
    B) comparing / producing / taken
    C) comparing / to produce / taking
    D) comparing / producing / to take

202. Can the rich live for ever, _____ to their affairs?
    A) attending   B) attended
    C) to attend   D) having attended

203. Peace and stability cannot be achieved unless progress is made toward _____ solutions to the world's most _____ problems, including poverty.
    A) finding / pressing   B) to find / pressed
    C) to find / pressing   D) finding / pressed

204. The children made this mess, so see that they get it _____ up right away.
    A) cleaning B) to clean C) cleaned D) clean

205. It is no use _____ over _____ milk.
    A) crying / spilt   B) crying / spilling
    C) to cry / spilt   D) cry / spilt

206. I'm sorry I didn't mean _____ you.
    A) hurting B) to be hurt C) to hurt D) hurt

207. She tried _____ high heels, to make herself _____ taller.
    A) to wear / look   B) wearing / to look
    C) wearing / look   D) to wear / looking

Book 1 Part B   101   Gerund - infinitive (Intermediate / Upper-Intermediate)

208. I think you'd better _____ by the time they return.
A) having gone B) have gone C) to have gone D) gone

209. I prefer my meat well _____.
A) to be done B) be done C) been done D) done

210. _____ ill, she couldn't participate in the contest.
A) Being B) To be C) Been D) Was

211. The teacher made us _____ the whole exercises.
A) to rewrite B) rewrite C) rewritten D) rewriting

212. His wife got him _____ drinking.
A) stops B) stopping C) stop D) to stop

213. _____ that tea will make you feel _____.
A) To drink / relaxing B) Drinking / relaxing
C) Drinking / relaxed D) To drink / relax

214. I'll have the clothes _____ and _____.
A) wash / iron B) washed / ironed
C) to wash / to iron D) to be washed / ironed

215. They were _____ it but they forgot.
A) brought B) have been brought
C) to have brought D) to be brought

216. I was just about _____ you when you phoned me.
A) phoned B) phoning
C) to phone D) having phoned

217. She is certain _____ by plane.
A) to come B) come C) coming D) comes

218. I would _____ him if I had seen him in time.
A) tell B) have told C) told D) had told

219. He seems _____ something.
A) to have lost B) to be lost
C) to have been lost D) lost

220. The new bridge should _____ by now.
A) be finished B) to be finished
C) have been finished D) have finished

221. It's said that he retired last month. He is said _____ last month.
A) to retire B) retired
C) retiring D) to have retired

222. Do you happen _____ when Kennedy was assassinated?
A) knowing B) to know
C) to have known D) knew

223. I happen _____ him in 1983.
A) to meet B) meeting C) met D) to have met

224. It's well worth _____ that book again.
A) to study B) study C) studying D) be studied

225. It's no good _____ that. I've tried it before.
A) doing B) to do C) done D) to be done

226. It's a waste of time _____ his advice.
A) to ask B) asking C) ask D) having asked

227. The children have their teeth _____ every six months.
A) check B) checking C) to check D) checked

228. Mind you don't get your fingers _____ in the door.
A) to catch B) catching C) caught D) catch

229. I had my binoculars _____ when I was at the stadium.
A) stolen B) stole C) to steal D) stealing

230. The Olympic Games were held in Tokyo in 1964. As a result, many new stadiums and hotels were built.
As a result of the Olympic Games _____ in Tokyo in 1964, many new stadiums and hotels were built.
A) had held B) held C) being held D) was held

231. Murat studied until late last night. As a result he did very well on today's English test.
As a result of _____ until late last night, Murat did very well on today's English test.
A) he had studied B) having been studying
C) he studied D) (his) studying

232. The population of Moscow has increased rapidly. As a result there is a housing shortage.
As a result of the population of Moscow _____ rapidly, there is a housing shortage.
A) increasing B) had increased
C) having increased D) has increased

233. Because we didn't hurry, we were late.
Because of _____ we were late.
A) our not hurrying B) hadn't hurried
C) we not hurried D) we didn't hurry

234. I expect her _____ the job by five o'clock.
A) finishing B) to have been finished
C) to have completed D) to be completed

235. Tokyo was destroyed during World War II. As a result of _____ during World War II, there's remaining of old Tokyo.
A) Tokyo destroyed B) Tokyo was destroyed
C) Tokyo's being destroyed D) Tokyo's been destroyed

236. _____ a dancer myself, I have excellent posture.
A) Having been B) Being
C) To be D) Having to be

237. Anyone _____ in seeing the film can leave now.
A) not interesting B) interesting
C) not interested D) not to be interested

238. Planners who want to eliminate heavy traffic have suggested that people _____ to share their cars.
A) asking B) asked
C) have been asked D) be asked

239. Can you swear to his _____ in your house that evening?
A) been B) to have been C) to be D) having been

240. We were made _____ still with our arms folded.
A) sat B) to sit C) sitting D) to sitting

241. When fully _____ the men cut off all the lower branches.
A) growing B) to grow C) had grown D) grown

242. Would you approve if I had this article _____?
A) to be copied B) to copy
C) been copied D) copied

243. _____ them, she didn't answer.
A) Not having heard B) Not having been heard
C) Not to have heard D) Not being heard

244. Mr. Walker, _____ the opportunity, could become a first class mathematician.
A) given B) giving C) to give D) to be given

245. It is essential that he _____ the computer test.
A) will take B) takes C) take D) taken

246. I should _____ the exam in January, but I was ill.
A) be taking B) be taken
C) have taken D) have been taken

247. All relevant documents, duly _____, should _____ in at the secretary's office one week before the start of term.
A) completed / hand B) completing / handed
C) completed / be handed D) to be completed / hand

PART C — TEST 1 — articles

1. On ___ bright January morning ___ telephone kept ringing in my office.
   A) the/the   B) a/the   C) -/-
   D) -/the   E) the/-

2. On ___ first day they stopped at ___ river and decided to make ___ camp.
   A) the/a/a   B) the/-/a   C) the/an/a
   D) -/the/-   E) the/an/an

3. At ___ first they began to look for ___ dry place.
   A) the/a   B) -/a   C) a/the
   D) an/a   E) the/-

4. To climb ___ tree is not to climb ___ mountain.
   A) a/a   B) a/the   C) the/the
   D) -/-   E) the/-

5. Where there's ___ will, there's ___ way.
   A) a/a   B) -/-   C) the/the
   D) a/the   E) the/a

6. ___ man always went to ___ same bar at ___ same time every day and asked for two glasses of ___ soda.
   A) A/the/the/-   B) A/the/the/a   C) A/the/-/-
   D) -/the/the/-   E) A/-/the/a

7. ___ weather was rainy and we made ___ bet whether you would come.
   A) The/a   B) -/the   C) A/a
   D) -/a   E) An/a

8. - Are you afraid of ___ him?
   - Not ___ bit.
   A) the/the   B) -/a   C) -/-
   D) the/-   E) an/a

9. ___ USA is ___ country. It is in North America.
   A) -/a   B) the/a   C) the/
   D) the/the   E) -/-

10. If ___ guest has to leave ___ table during ___ meal he always asks his hostess, "Will you please excuse me for ___ minute".
    A) a/the/a/a   B) -/the/a/-   C) the/the/-/the
    D) an/the/a/a   E) -/-/-/a

11. ___ most favorite game is cricket, which is called by ___ English "___ greatest game in ___ world".
    A) the/the/the/the   B) the/a/the/the   C) -/the/-/the
    D) a/the/-/the   E) the/an/-/the

12. In his childhood he lived with ___ grandfather, ___ poor tailor.
    A) a/the   B) -/the   C) the/a
    D) a/a   E) the/the

13. ___ night being sharp and frosty, we trembled from ___ foot to ___ head.
    A) the/the/the   B) the/-/-   C) a/-/-
    D) -/a/a   E) -/-/-

14. My ___ friend likes to listen to ___ good story.
    A) -/the   B) a/a   C) the/the
    D) -/a   E) a/-

15. ___ idea of helping ___ man was unpleasant in itself.
    A) -/the   B) the/the   C) the/a
    D) -/-   E) a/a

16. When I lived in Paris some years ago I used to buy ___ copy of Le Monde every evening at ___ same local newspaper kiosk.
    A) -/a   B) a/the   C) a/a
    D) the/a   E) the/the

17. ___ death of her husband resulted in ___ loss of her home also.
    A) -/-   B) -/the   C) the/the
    D) a/-   E) a/a

18. Peter is on ___ night duty. When I go to ___ bed, he goes to ___ work.
    A) the/-/a   B) -/-/-   C) a/a/a
    D) the/the/-   E) -/the/a

19. R.Peary was ___ famous American polar traveler. He was ___ first to reach ___ North Pole in 1909.
    A) a/the/the   B) the/the/a   C) a/the/a
    D) -/the/-   E) an/the/-

20. He likes to have ___ rest in ___ country.
    A) -/-   B) -/the   C) the/-
    D) a/-   E) a/the

21. Don't stay outside in ___ cold; come in by ___ fire.
    A) the/the   B) the/a   C) -/a
    D) the/-   E) a/the

22. It's ___ pity that my birthday comes only once ___ year.
    A) a/-   B) the/a   C) a/a
    D) an/the   E) -/a

23. ___ boy was shy and always looked down when ___ grown-ups spoke to him.
    A) a/the   B) the/-   C) an/-
    D) -/a   E) the/a

24. There was ___ good restaurant near ___ cinema and Joan decided to have ___ dinner there.
    A) the/a/-   B) -/the/-   C) an/-/the
    D) a/the   E) a/the/a

25. Kate ate ___ meat with ___ vegetables for ___ second course.
    A) -/-/the   B) a/the/-   C) the/a/the
    D) -/an/-   E) an/-/a

26. I'll never forget ___ first time I saw ___ real American Christmas tree.
    A) a/the   B) an/-   C) -/a
    D) the/a   E) the/-

27. "___ English cannot make ___ good coffee", she thought leaving ___ restaurant.
    A) the/a/an   B) an/-/the   C) -/the/the
    D) a/-/a   E) the/-/the

28. At ___ first it was difficult for her to drive ___ car in ___ London.
    A) -/the/-   B) the/the/-   C) -/-/the
    D) a/-/the   E) a/a/-

29. ___ few days later I entered ___ reading room of ___ public library.
    A) A/the/the   B) The/the/the   C) -/the/-
    D) A/a/-   E) -/a/-

30. ___ book is always ___ acceptable gift.
    A) A/an   B) The/   C) The/the
    D) An/the   E) -/a

31. Sofia is ___ capital of ___ Bulgaria.
    A) -/-   B) the/the   C) the/-
    D) the/a   E) -/a

32. Many years ago ___ Tower Bridge of London was ___ fortress.
    A) -/a   B) the/the   C) a/-
    D) the/-   E) the/a

33. ___ youth of Great Britain wants to have ___ better life for ___ British people.
    A) -/-/the   B) the/a/the   C) the/the/the
    D) the/-/the   E) -/the/-

34. ___ Moon has no ___ light. It is bright because ___ Sun shines on it.
    A) The/-/the   B) The/a/the   C) -/-/the
    D) The/the/the   E) A/an/the

35. ___ shortest man in ___ world and ___ tallest man in ___ world live in ___ Africa.
    A) The/the/the/the/-   B) The/the/-/an/an   C) -/the/-/an/an
    D) The/a/-/-/an   E) The/-/-/-/-

36. Hope is ___ good breakfast, but ___ bad supper.
    A) a/a   B) the/the   C) a/the
    D) a/an   E) a/-

37. I always wear sunglasses when I go ___ beach. ___ sun bothers my eyes.
    A) the/the   B) a/the   C) -/a
    D) an/a   E) the/a

38. She ordered ___ fried chicken with ___ green salad and black coffee for ___ dessert.
    A) -/-/-   B) the/-/-   C) an/the/
    D) -/a/the   E) a/an/the

39. My aunt lived on ___ ground floor of ___ old house on ___ River Thames.
    A) the/an/the   B) -/the/a   C) the/the/-
    D) -/an/the   E) a/an/a

40. On the New Year Eve some of ___ pupils stayed at ___ school later than usual.
    A) the/-   B) the/the   C) -/the
    D) a/a   E) the/a

41. ___ best runner in the race was ___ young girl.
    A) a/an   B) the/an   C) -/the
    D) the/a   E) the/the

42. The first of ___ January is ___ great holiday in many countries.
    A) the/a   B) -/an   C) -/a
    D) the/-   E) the/the

43. On ___ Sundays my father stays in ___ bed till ten o'clock reading ___ Sunday papers.
    A) the/the/-   B) -/-/the   C) an/-/-
    D) the/the/the   E) -/-/-

44. After ___ fourth lesson English pupils have ___ break of ___ hour and ___ half for dinner.
    A) a/a/a/a   B) the/a/-/a   C) a/the/an/a
    D) the/a/an/a   E) -/-/an/a

45. On ___ day of ___ race many people came to the skating.
    A) -/-   B) a/the   C) the/a
    D) the/-   E) the/the

46. ___ Sahara is in the northern part of Africa.
    A) -   B) a   C) an
    D) the   E) any

47. ___ fog was so thick that we couldn't see ___ side of ___ road.
    A) a/the/a   B) the/-/-   C) the/the/the
    D) -/the/a   E) the/the/a

48. I remember an episode in ___ my life when I had to spend ___ month in the country.
    A) a/-   B) the/a   C) -/an
    D) -/a   E) an/the

49. In ___ afternoon ___ wind increased and they soon found themselves in ___ difficulties.
    A) the/the/-   B) an/a/the   C) -/the/-
    D) the/the/the   E) the/a/the

50. They took part in ___ demonstration in ___ Independence Square.
    A) -/the   B) a/a   C) the/-
    D) -/-   E) the/the

51. And what ___ beautiful picture there is over there on ___ wall!
    A) -/a   B) a/the   C) a/-
    D) the/a   E) a/a

52. Roger looked at him and, without ___ word, gave him ___ ten-dollar note.
    A) a/a   B) -/-   C) -/the
    D) the/-   E) a/-

53. ___ longest river in ___ world is ___ Mississippi.
    A) a/the/an   B) the/a/the   C) he/an/the
    D) an/the/the   E) the/the/the

54. It took us ___ hour and ___ half to do shopping and we got ___ home at 4.
    A) an/a/-   B) the/an/the   C) on/the/the
    D) an/the/a   E) a/the/the

55. ___ apple ___ day keeps ___ doctor away.
    A) an/a/a   B) an/-/a   C) the/a/a
    D) a/a/the   E) an/the/the

56. We had ___ good talk with him about ___ weather, ___ literature and other things.
    A) -/the/the   B) a/the/-   C) a/-/the
    D) the/the/a   E) a/a/-

57. ___ girl from ___ farm came once ___ week to help to clean ___ house.
    A) a/a/the/the   B) a/the/the/the   C) the/the/a/the
    D) the/a/a/a   E) the/the/the/a

58. ___ questions Ann asked always seemed to be ___ questions which Paul knew ___ answer.
    A) a/the/the   B) the/a/a   C) the/-/a
    D) the/-/the   E) -/the/the

59. Before the New Year we usually have ___ wonderful party at ___ school.
    A) a / the   B) the / the   C) a / -
    D) an/ -   E) - / the

60. There is ___ hair in my soup and ___ plate is dirty.
    A) -/-   B) the/the   C) a/the
    D) the/a   E) -/the

61. Soon our team scored ___ goal and won ___ game.
    A) the/the   B) a/a   C) a/the
    D) the/a   E) an/the

62. Let's have ___ good breakfast and start the day
    A) the   B) -   C) any
    D) a   E) an

63. ___ youngest boy has just started going to school, ___ eldest boy is at ___ college.
    A) the/the/-   B) the/-/the   C) the/-/the
    D) -/-/-   E) a/-/a

64. -Did you come by ___ air?
    -No, I came by ___ sea. I had a lovely voyage on ___ Queen Elizabeth II.
    A) an/the/the   B) -/-/the   C) an/a/a
    D) the/the/the   E) -/-/a

65. We have a very good train service from here to ___ city centre and many people go to ___ work by train.
    A) a/a   B) the/the   C) -/-
    D) the/-   E) an/a

66. - I didn't recognize you. You look different.
    - I know I lost ___ lot of ___ weight.
    A) a/-   B) an/the   C) a/the
    D) the/a   E) the/the

67. ___ sun came out right after ___ rain and there was ___ beautiful rainbow in ___ sky.
    A) The/the/a/the   B) The/a/the/the   C) A/a/the/a
    D) The/the/the/a   E) A/the/a/the

68. I always have ___ breakfast at 8 a.m. Today I had ___ very nice breakfast.
    A) a/the   B) -/a   C) -/-
    D) the/-   E) a/-

69. He was ___ very tall man with ___ dark hair.
    A) a/the   B) a/-   C) the/the
    D) -/-   E) a/a

70. Would you like to be ___ English teacher at ___ college.
    A) the/-   B) the/the   C) a/-
    D) an/-   E) the/a

71. We had ___ very nice meal. ___ vegetables were especially good.
    A) -/-   B) -/the   C) a/-
    D) a/the   E) the/the

72. All ___ books on ___ top of the shelf belong to me.
    A) -/a   B) the/-   C) the/the
    D) -/the   E) on/with

73. If you live in ___ foreign country you should try and learn ___ language.
    A) a/the   B) -/-   C) -/a
    D) the/the   E) the/a

74. Washington is situated on ___ Potomac River in ___ District of Columbia.
    A) -/-   B) the/-   C) -/the
    D) the/the   E) a/an

75. David picked up ___ nut from ___ hole.
    A) the/the   B) a/a   C) a/the
    D) the/a   E) an/a

76. Once ___ pupils of ___ fifth form read ___ book about Robin Hood.
    A) -/the/a   B) a/an/the   C) the/the/a
    D) an/a/the   E) -/the/an

77. ___ concert began with ___ song about ___ peace and ___ work.
    A) the/a/-/-   B) a/the/the/the C) a/the/-/-
    D) the/the/a/a   E) a/a/-/-

78. ___ Penguins live in the South Pole.
    A) a   B) an   C) -
    D) the   E) some

79. France covers ___ area of 551000 sq kms.
    A) the   B) a   C) -
    D) an   E) one

80. Open ___ books at ___ page 20 and read ___ text.
    A) -/the/the   B) the/-/the   C) -/-/the
    D) the/-/a   E) -/the/a

81. You realize that ___ time to choose one job out of ___ hundreds has come.
    A) the/-   B) a/the   C) the/a
    D) an/a   E) -/the

82. There were ___ three shelters on ___ cliff.
    A) -/the   B) -/a   C) the/the
    D) a/a   E) a/the

83. I saw ___ good deal of him during ___ war.
    A) -/a   B) the/the   C) a/a
    D) the/-   E) a/the

84. He sat down at ___ piano and played ___ piece that he had played in the morning.
    A) a/a   B) a/the   C) the/the
    D) the/a   E) the/-

85. ___ doctor says ___ child must eat ___ apple ___ day.
    A) the/the/a/a   B) a/a/the/a
    C) the/the/an/the D) a/a/an/a
    E) the/the/an/a

86. ___ Browns invited me to ___ dinner.
    A) -/the   B) the/a   C) -/a
    D) the/-   E) the/an

87. They went on ___ expedition to ___ North.
    A) a/the   B) an/the   C) -/the
    D) the/the   E) the/a

88. ___ Rome was not built in ___ day.
    A) the/a   B) -/the   C) -/a
    D) -/-   E) an/a

89. The beautiful child gave Pinocchio ___ some medicine and ___ piece of sugar.
    A) a/the   B) the/a   C) -/a
    D) the/the   E) a/an

90. Italy is in ___ South of ___ Europe, isn't it?
    A) an/a   B) the/-   C) the/the
    D) the/an   E) an/the

91. ___ West End is ___ richest part of ___ capital.
    A) a/an/the   B) the/a/a   C) the/the/the
    D) the/-/the   E) the/the/-

92. -When will ___ next bus be?
    -___ next will be tomorrow morning.
    A) -/-   B) the/the   C) a/a
    D) a/the   E) the/a

93. ___ Latin America is on ___ South of America.
    A) the/a   B) -/the   C) the/the
    D) -/-   E) the/-

94. Spring is ___ best season of ___ year.
    A) the/a   B) I/the   C) a/a
    D) the/the   E) a/-

95. ___ long walk in ___ country is very interesting.
    A) the/a   B) the/a   C) the/the
    D) a/a   E) -/the

96. ___ Smiths enjoyed their rest at the coast of ___ Black Sea last summer.
    A) -/the   B) the/the   C) the/
    D) the/a   E) a/a

97. "___ Queen Mary" is one of ___ biggest ships in the world.
    A) -/a   B) -/the   C) the/the
    D) -/-   E) the/a

98. They stayed only ___ day at the hotel.
    A) a   B) the   C) an
    D) -   E) some

99. It is ___ holiday of all European people. ___ people have ___ two days' holiday.
    A) -/-/-   B) a/-/the   C) the/-/the
    D) the/the/a   E) a/the/a

100. This is ___ lion that I saw in the circus yesterday.
    A) a   B) -   C) the
    D) an   E) any

TEST 2

prepositions

1. Our government pays great attention ___ the education ___ the youth.
   A) -/of   B) of/of   C) to/to
   D) to/of   E) by/of

2. ___ summer holidays many boys and girls like to go ___ the country ___ their teachers.
   A) at/by/to   B) into/at/with   C) -/to/to
   D) during/to/with E) during/to/by

3. The girl saw a beautiful garden ___ the end of the corridor with red flowers ___ it.
   A) at/in   B) at/on   C) to/in
   D) in/in   E) of/on

4. At night when there are no clouds ___ the sky you can see many stars.
   A) on   B) in   C) at
   D) to   E) a/an

5. He is very good ___ maths.
   A) in   B) at   C) -
   D) about   E) with

6. He's got a very good head ___ his shoulders.
   A) over   B) beyond   C) on
   D) since   E) for

7. I asked him ___ help.
   A) in   B) about   C) for
   D) by   E) with

8. Father was very angry ___ his son: "You'll be punished according ___ the seriousness ___ your guilt.
   A) to/-/of   B) for/to/to   C) to/to/to
   D) with/to/of   E) with/-/of

9. An electric lamp hangs from the centre ___ the ceiling ___ the table.
   A) to/in   B) of/above   C) to/on
   D) in/from   E) on/near

10. Everybody wanted to come here ___ time.
    A) by   B) for   C) in
    D) without   E) at

11. It is very warm. I am going to take ___ my scarf.
    A) out   B) in   C) off
    D) for   E) of

12. There is something very attractive ___ him.
    A) in   B) about   C) with
    D) by   E) at

13. What is there ___ the ground floor ___ your school?
    A) in/in   B) on/at   C) on/of
    D) in/at   E) near/in

14. They will be fighting ___ political reforms.
    A) in   B) on   C) at
    D) by   E) for

15. It's better to wait for five minutes before crossing the street than stay ___ a month at the hospital.
    A) at   B) on   C) for
    D) of   E) till

16. The famous explorer left ___ the North ___ the fifth of March.
    A) to/on   B) to/in   C) for/at
    D) from/on   E) for/on

17. They put ___ illuminations ___ front of all buildings.
    A) down/over   B) up/on   C) down/near
    D) up/at   E) -/in

18. In England the cars go ___ the left side.
    A) in   B) near   C) of
    D) to   E) on

19. ___ general everything was all right. They thought they were walking ___ the direction ___ the village when they lost the way.
    A) for/-/to   B) in/to/of   C) in/in/of
    D) by/to/to   E) in/in/to

20. I know that he is a noisy boy, but ___ the same time I can't be angry ___ him.
    A) -/to   B) at/with   C) -/with
    D) in/about   E) by/for

21. What are curtains usually made ___?
    A) in   B) with   C) of
    D) -   E) at

22. Great Britain consists ___ three parts.
    A) of   B) with   C) from
    D) in   E) by

23. The train stopped ___ all the stations and long before we got ___ London every seat was taken and people were standing ___ the corridors.
    A) to/at/in   B) in/to/   C) at/in/on
    D) at/to/in   E) -/in/at

24. I congratulated all my classmates ___ passing the exam.
    A) for   B) with   C) on
    D) in   E) within

25. - ___ what time will you arrive?
    - I don't know. It depends ___ the traffic.
    A) at/-   B) in/from   C) -/on
    D) by/with   E) for/out of

26. My father died three years ago ___ a sudden heart attack.
    A) from   B) on   C) at
    D) by   E) in

27. This house reminds me ___ the one I lived ___ when I was a child.
    A) of/in   B) about/at   C) near/-
    D) -/in   E) on/with

28. We shall be waiting ___ a bus ___ 2 till 3.
    A) -/to   B) -/until   C) for/from
    D) for/to   E) of/for

29. There is a place ___ 6 stamps ___ each page ___ Nick's stamp book.
    A) for/on/of   B) to/in/in   C) for/at/of
    D) at/on/for   E) for/in/of

30. Alice drank ___ the bottle and turned ___ a very small girl.
    A) of/in   B) for/at   C) out/of
    D) from/on   E) from/into

31. When we draw we make pictures ___ a pen, a pencil or chalk.
    A) by   B) with   C) of
    D) at   E) in

32. He suddenly jumped ___ a bus.
    A) by   B) at   C) to
    D) on   E) of

33. Who is the girl ___ the blue dress, sitting ___ the head of the table?
    A) with/in   B) on/upon   C) in/at
    D) without/in   E) in/of

34. Children are very fond ___ swimming.
    A) of   B) about   C) till
    D) at   E) in

35. The old woman could go ___ foot, but she preferred going ___ car.
    A) with/in   B) without/at   C) in/on
    D) on/to   E) on/by

36. ___ the top of the hill the tourists could see hundreds of cars running quickly ___ the road.
    A) from/along   B) at/to   C) on/along
    D) from/in   E) with/for

37. Please go on ___ your work while I am out.
    A) to   B) with   C) in
    D) up   E) at

38. We arrived ___ London ___ 6 p.m. ___ a foggy November day.
    A) in/at/on   B) to/at/in   C) at/in/in
    D) on/of/-   E) -/in/on

39. He started going ___ school ___ the age of five.
    A) to/in   B) at/on   C) to/at
    D) before/of   E) into/on

40. I'm going to wait ___ it stops raining.
    A) till   B) before   C) on
    D) at   E) for

41. He came ___ . I told him about my plan and he ___ once agreed ___ it.
    A) into/at/with B) in/at/to   C) in/-/with
    D) out/for/-   E) -/at/to

42. We have worked ___ the plan ___ the new district ___ six months.
    A) over-off /about B) at/of/for   C) of/in/in
    D) about/of/to E) of/at/for

43. There is a man sitting ___ the TV set ___ the hall.
    A) to/at   B) before/on   C) near/at
    D) towards/or   E) in front of/in

44. Did they enjoy ___ their trip down the river?
    A) -   B) with   C) in
    D) for   E) into

45. I think Dan fell ___ love with Alice.
    A) for   B) with   C) in
    D) to   E) into

46. My friends went ___ a cycling tour last week.
    A) to   B) on   C) in
    D) for   E) before

47. She was ___ duty and had to stay ___ the classroom ___ classes.
    A) after/at/at B) on/in/after   C) on/at/at
    D) in/in/in   E) on/with/at

48. "Be careful ___ the crossing," he said ___ the children.
    A) for/at   B) at/to   C) for/to
    D) to/at   E) on/for

49. It was difficult ___ him to earn money ___ the country, so he went ___ town.
    A) at/in/after B) through/under/to C) for/in/to
    D) on/at/before E) for/to/in

50. They drove ___ London ___ Paris, stopping ___ Vienna.
    A) into/from/at B) from/to/on   C) to/for/near
    D) from/to/in   E) to/from/on

51. We lived ___ the suburb ___ a big city ___ the factory where father worked.
    A) at/in/at   B) in/before/of   C) of/by/to
    D) through/at/on E) in/of/near

52. He thought ___ a plan and stayed there ___ a few weeks.
    A) on / of   B) about / at   C) of / in
    D) of / for   E) on / for

53. He stared ___ her ___ amazement.
    A) at/in   B) -/with   C) to/of
    D) with/besides E) on/at

54. Pete was tired, he lay down ___ the sofa ___ his fur coat and fell asleep.
    A) in/to   B) on/under   C) at/by
    D) near/by   E) near/at

55. We've neither been ___ the theatre, nor ___ the cinema ___ a long time.
    A) to/to/for   B) at/with/on   C) on/to/at
    D) with/at/for E) at/on/to

56. The captain looked ___ his glasses and saw a man ___ the sea not far ___ the ship.
    A) after/on/at B) through/at/in   C) with/by/to
    D) through/in/from E) for/of/about

57. The teacher explained the new rule ___ the pupils and they listened ___ her attentively.
    A) at / -   B) to / of   C) from / to
    D) by / of   E) to / to

58. ___ looking ___ his papers he understood it was time ___ him to type them.
    A) on / by / to B) on / after / in C) in / at / before
    D) after / through / for E) for / through / in

59. Don't tell anybody ___ this. It's only ___ us.
    A) -/besides   B) about/between   C) on/by
    D) on/within   E) about/among

60. The girl wanted to cook the meal herself, but Sophia insisted ___ helping her.
    A) on   B) to   C) from
    D) in   E) for

61. He should take care ___ his health.
    A) for   B) on   C) at
    D) to   E) of

62. You must work hard ___ your English.
    A) on   B) at   C) for
    D) from   E) by

63. We are very busy ___ weekdays.
    A) out of   B) in   C) on
    D) at   E) of

64. Mr. Brown had to hurry up as his friend was waiting ___ him ___ the corner ___ the street.
    A) for/at/of   B) for/in/-   C) -/in/-
    D) with/at/in   E) for/in/for

65. He decided to marry ___ Rose ___ money.
    A) -/for   B) for/to   C) on/with
    D) by/for   E) after/-

66. I remember being met ___ zoo station ___ one of their pupils.
    A) near/from   B) in/with
    C) besides/among   D) of/for
    E) at/by

67. They dined ___ a small restaurant which had been "decorated" ___ rather bad pictures ___ young people.
    A) at/with/on   B) near/by/of   C) in/with/by
    D) to/-/with   E) at/towards/from

68. Go ___ the kitchen and get a bottle ___ milk ___ the refrigerator.
    A) at/of/from   B) to/of/out of   C) in/-/from
    D) to/of/of   E) into/of/in

69. He became interested ___ physics ___ the age ___ 14.
    A) in/in/of   B) in/at/of   C) in/for/in
    D) at/at/of   E) of/in/of

70. I remember that it was ___ my fifteenth birthday that she first put them ___ my hands.
    A) in/on   B) on/into   C) on/at
    D) into/on   E) at/on

71. I think we'll have read the article ___ 5 p.m. today.
    A) at   B) to   C) for
    D) by   E) in

72. It's necessary ___ him to do it ___ this year.
    A) of/in   B) for/-   C) to/during
    D) for/by   E) to/-

73. I wanted a book ___ Oscar Wilde and asked the librarian to show ___ me some ___ his books.
    A) by/-/of   B) of/to/by   C) of/with/at
    D) on/on/with   E) by/to/by

74. Take a piece ___ chalk and write the sentence ___ the blackboard.
    A) of/at   B) of/of   C) on/on
    D) of/in   E) of/on

75. ___ Monday morning I had been waiting ___ you ___ two hours but you didn't come.
    A) in/for/at   B) on/-/for   C) -/with/during
    D) on/for/for   E) on/for/-

76. What is happening ___ this picture?
    A) at   B) from   C) of
    D) in   E) off

77. Do you agree ___ her?
    A) to   B) of   C) for
    D) by   E) with

78. "___ your place I'd ask the boy to apologize ___ you," Ann said ___ her friend.
    A) on/with/in   B) in/to/to   C) at/to/for
    D) with/on/on   E) up/with/to

79. I arrived ___ the station ___ a taxi.
    A) to/by   B) at/in   C) to/on
    D) into/by   E) at/by

80. A traveler who visits New York ___ the first time admires ___ the new architecture.
    A) with/of   B) of/of   C) for/-
    D) in/with   E) at/to

81. The girl was dressed ___ the latest fashion but my clothes were quite ___ fashion.
    A) after / out   B) by / out   C) in / out of
    D) for / off   E) on / to

82. He is waiting ___ us ___ .
    A) to / round   B) over / above   C) out of / from
    D) for / outside   E) until / since

83. I looked ___ the box, but there was nothing ___ .
    A) inside / into   B) into / inside   C) around / of
    D) off / upon   E) out of / inside

84. I have read some articles ___ this subject ___ the books you gave me.
    A) about / for   B) except / during
    C) beyond / between   D) down / by
    E) on / besides

85. We protested ___ delays ___ delivery ___ the goods.
    A) against / in / of   B) across / over / after
    C) about / under / of   D) against / of / in
    E) along / behind / beside

86. I can see all the details; the lazy cat spread out ___ the fireplace, my aunt ___ one chimney corner.
    A) with / without   B) in front of / in   C) in / on
    D) within / beyond   E) above / over

87. My contract has been extended ___ another year.
    A) to   B) during   C) in
    D) for   E) over

88. Think ___ the end ___ every beginning.
    A) for/with   B) to/for   C) of/in
    D) with/with   E) about/at

89. "It is ___ no interest ___ me whether we'll win or lose," said the football player.
    A) - / for   B) of / -   C) of / to
    D) - / -   E) in / for

90. Mike failed ___ the exam, but his sister got ___ .
    A) in / through   B) on / on   C) though / out
    D) - / over   E) - / off

91. Mrs. Smith was very good ___ sewing and knitting and she was always well-dressed.
    A) by   B) on   C) for
    D) of   E) at

92. He was interested ___ planes and rockets.
    A) of   B) by   C) in
    D) on   E) with

93. Christmas is the celebration ___ the birth ___ Christ.
    A) in/of   B) of/of   C) of/-
    D) in/-   E) -/of

94. I don't think she is afraid ___ dogs.
    A) -   B) of   C) on
    D) in   E) with

95. ___ my opinion he is a very clever boy.
    A) in   B) on   C) for
    D) with   E) to

96. It was nice ___ you to come to see me.
    A) about   B) of   C) -
    D) about   E) on

97. She was completely blind ___ her faults.
    A) of   B) about   C) on
    D) to   E) for

98. This news is ___ great importance ___ me.
    A) to/to   B) at/for   C) of/for
    D) of/at   E) -/on

99. You can't answer ___ my question again. Why haven't you learned the words ___ heart?
    A) to/on   B) -/by   C) on/by
    D) on/with   E) -/to

100. -Will Mr. Black be at home ___ Saturday evening?
     -Yes, he'll be at home ___ four.
     A) in/after   B) at/before   C) -/after
     D) on/after   E) on/under

TEST 3

pronouns

1. Have you heard that a friend of ___ went to Vietnam
   A) my   B) mine   C) her
   D) their   E) its

2. That is the girl ___ brother came to see ___
   A) that / we   B) whose / us   C) which / they
   D) whom / its   E) what / us

3. If ___ has ___ questions, I'll be pleased to answer them.
   A) someone/any   B) anyone/any   C) none/any
   D) anyone/none   E) someone/none

4. I haven't read ___ of these books but George has read ___ of them.
   A) none/some   B) no/some   C) any/some
   D) any/any   E) any/no

5. That pen isn't ___ . ___ is a green one.
   A) my/my   B) his/he   C) mine/mine
   D) I/me   E) her/its

6. She always thinks of ___ happiness.
   A) another   B) others   C) other
   D) another's   E) others'

7. ___ was not a marriage that could last.
   A) my   B) her   C) them
   D) theirs   E) our

8. If this hat is ___, where have you put ___?
   A) your/mine   B) his/hers   C) mine/her
   D) ours/their   E) hers/my

9. ___ read the book and ___ took it to the library.
   A) He/me   B) I/he   C) You/her
   D) She/her   E) we/them

10. The work done by ___ is very important.
    A) he   B) she   C) we
    D) they   E) you

11. Why is ___ sitting in the dark?
    A) we   B) she   C) you
    D) I   E) her

12. - What has Ann?
    - ___ has a very nice cat.
    A) we   B) it   C) she
    D) he   E) them

13. Will ___ please give me your pen?
    A) he   B) she   C) you
    D) him   E) them

14. MR. WATSON said that THE MYSTERY was over.
    A) he/it   B) he/she   C) she/she
    D) they/it   E) he/them

15. Bad NEWS has wings.
    A) it   B) he   C) they
    D) she   E) them

16. I have a cat. ___ is very nice.
    A) you   B) they   C) it
    D) its   E) who

17. How many children have THE TAYLORS?
    A) them   B) they   C) it
    D) their   E) its

18. ___ didn't take our children to the park as ___ were at school.
    A) her / our   B) we / they   C) us / they
    D) we / them   E) his / her

19. What makes THE SATELLITE rush round the earth at such a great speed?
    A) she   B) its   C) her
    D) it   E) him

20. ___ house is almost the same as ___ neighbors' house. The only difference in appearance is that ___ is grey and ___ is white.
    A) our/ours/ours/theirs   B) ours/ours/our/their
    C) my/hers/my/her   D) our/our/ours/theirs
    E) my/ours/ours/theirs

21. ___ roommate and ___ have to share a bookshelf: ___ keeps ___ books on the top two shelves, and I keep ___ on the bottom two shelves.
    A) my/me/she/her/mine   B) his/me/her/hers/my
    C) my/I/she/her/mine   D) her/hers/she/her/my
    E) my/her/she/hers/mine

22. Later DICKENS described HIS CHILDHOOD in some of his famous novels.
    A) she/them   B) they/it   C) he/us
    D) him/them   E) he/it

23. Of course I ___ used to be very wealthy.
    A) my   B) mine   C) myself
    D) ourselves   E) himself

24. I enjoyed the music, but I didn't like the play ___ .
    A) yourself   B) herself   C) myself
    D) itself   E) himself

25. I always enjoy ___ when I go to concerts of classical music.
    A) himself   B) myself   C) themselves
    D) herself   E) ourselves

26. You know, Mary bought ___ a new dress yesterday.
    A) myself   B) itself   C) himself
    D) oneself   E) herself

27. Let the boys clean the room ___ .
    A) them   B) himself   C) their
    D) theirs   E) themselves

28. We should help everyone as much as possible because we often need help ___ .
    A) themselves   B) ourselves   C) yourselves
    D) himself   E) myself

29. Did you all do the grammar exercises ___?
    A) yourselves   B) yourself   C) herself
    D) themselves   E) ourselves

30. He will sit in the room to keep ___ warm.
    A) himself   B) herself   C) themselves
    D) yourself   E) myself

31. I looked at ___ in the mirror.
    A) me   B) its   C) myself
    D) my   E) mine

32. Dorothy was happy when she found ___ in a magic country.
    A) her   B) she   C) hers
    D) herself   E) himself

33. They always went to places ___ they saw historical monuments.
    A) which   B) what   C) that
    D) where   E) who

34. "___ else is here?" she asked.
    A) my   B) whom   C) which
    D) why   E) who

35. I wonder ___ her sister's boy looks like.
    A) that   B) what   C) which
    D) who   E) whose

36. I like the book ___ I've read recently.
    A) who   B) what   C) which
    D) whose   E) whatever

37. The man ___ works at this table is my friend.
    A) how   B) what   C) who
    D) which   E) as

38. ___ chapter did you like best?
    A) what   B) whose   C) which
    D) that   E) this

39. Cook was an English explorer ___ made three voyages round the world.
    A) what   B) who   C) which
    D) where   E) when

40. You shouldn't live with a man ___ doesn't love you.
    A) that   B) which   C) who
    D) what   E) whom

41. You must find somebody ___ can help you.
    A) whose   B) whom   C) who
    D) what   E) which

42. Who could tell ___ his son's circumstances really was.
    A) which   B) that   C) why
    D) what   E) whose

43. Here are the books, ___ is yours?
    A) what   B) which   C) whose
    D) wherever   E) whether

44. When they saw a POLICEMAN they stopped in the middle of the STREET.
    A) his/him   B) him/it   C) her/its
    D) he/it   E) him/ours

45. He didn't take many clothes with ___
    A) them   B) him   C) his
    D) your   E) ours

46. -On what days do you have English lessons?
    -We have ___ on Tuesday, Wednesday and Friday.
    A) them   B) it   C) her
    D) him   E) they

47. Nick knows English well. Ask ___ to help you.
    A) her   B) hers   C) me
    D) him   E) us

48. He wanted ___ to ring ___ up.
    A) they/them B) her/your   C) you/him
    D) them/their E) us/his

49. I can't find all the books you asked me for. I put ___ I found on your desk.
    A) the   B) this   C) that
    D) those   E) its

50. Leave THE CHILDREN alone.
    A) they   B) us   C) them
    D) its   E) our

51. I have a father, a mother, a grandfather, three brothers and two sisters. ___ my family.
    A) Its   B) These were C) Those were
    D) That was   E) This is

52. ___ your skis?
    A) Is this   B) Are that   C) Is that
    D) Are these E) Those are

53. She would like ___ to go in for sport.
    A) us   B) we   C) our
    D) ours   E) she

54. Father watched ___ crossing the street.
    A) he   B) we   C) him
    D) yourself   E) himself

55. They all ran out of the hotel except ___ .
    A) mine   B) his   C) hers
    D) one   E) nobody

56. Do you see ___ bushes on the ___ side of the river?
    A) this/other B) that/another C) them/other
    D) those/other E) some/other

57. ___ are pencils and ___ are pens.
    A) this/that B) that/these C) these/those
    D) that/this E) those/those

58. Take it from ___ and give it to ___ .
    A) he/I   B) him/me   C) you/you
    D) his/my   E) they/us

59. He put the map before ___ .
    A) him   B) they   C) he
    D) my   E) she

60. - I need a TV-set.
    - Why don't you buy ___ .
    A) them   B) one   C) ones
    D) him   E) its

61. It was clear they loved ___ .
    A) one another B) each other C) their
    D) who ever   E) what ever

62. But now we are both happy and we love ___ .
    A) us   B) each one   C) everyone
    D) each other E) another

63. Michel can only guess ___ ___ think.
    A) whom/he   B) that/me   C) who/our
    D) what/I   E) what/he

64. - ___ is your daughter?
    - ___ is an English teacher.
    A) that / she B) what / she C) she / who
    D) who / her   E) which / that

65. He was very angry because he couldn't find the report ___ .
    A) everywhere B) something C) anywhere
    D) somewhere   E) nowhere

66. ___ of you can play the piano?
    A) where   B) what   C) whose
    D) which   E) whom

67. There is the man ___ ___ saw in the park the other day.
    A) whom / we   B) which / our C) what / ours
    D) what / we   E) whose / we

68. Come at ___ time ___ is convenient to ___ .
    A) any / what / when   B) some / that / us   C) any / that / you
    D) some / which / her E) some / what / you

69. At last we've found our book, but where is ___?
    A) her   B) your   C) you
    D) yours   E) mine

70. ___ met ___ in the street and ___ told ___ all about it.
    A) they/him/he/me   B) he/him/them/they
    C) they/him/he/them   D) he/them/she/him
    E) she/her/he/them

71. I've brought ___ books for you.
    A) any   B) anyone   C) some
    D) someone   E) which

72. ___ want ___ matches. Have ___ got ___?
    A) She / any / any / they   B) I / some / you / any
    C) They / any / we / some   D) I / some / you / some
    E) He / some / you / any

73. The word "Germans" was ___ to be frightened at.
    A) somebody   B) something C) anything
    D) any   E) someone

74. Why didn't you ask ___ to help ___?
    A) somebody / your   B) anybody / you
    C) anyone / yourself   D) somebody / yourselves
    E) anybody / somebody

75. They broke into little groups. ___ had his own wonderful story to tell.
    A) some   B) all   C) every
    D) each   E) other

76. Those seats are not ___, they are ___ .
    A) theirs/ours B) her/mine   C) your/our
    D) themselves/ours E) his/it

77. Kate is a very nice girl and I like ___ for ___ kindness.
    A) him/her   B) her/she   C) she/her
    D) her/her   E) she/his

78. - Here are ___ shoes.
    - These aren't ___ . They are ___ .
    A) my/mine/my   B) her/her/mine
    C) your/mine/yours   D) their/yours/ours
    E) our/yours/their

79. ___ do you like best - your mother or your father?
    A) what   B) who   C) which one
    D) whose   E) why

80. ___ thought ___ could read the story ___ .
    A) You / she /herself   B) You/herself/her
    C) She/she/herself   D) He/him/his
    E) You/yourself/your

81. ___ are ___ maps and ___ are ___ .
    A) these/yours/those/her B) these/your/those/ours
    C) this/you/that/our   D) these/him/those/me
    E) those/hers/these/you

82. Some of the WOMEN watched THE CHILDREN playing with THEIR TOYS.
    A) she/they/them   B) them/them/them
    C) they/they/them   D) us/you/it
    E) them/they/they

83. Summer in ___ place is much cooler than in ___ .
    A) my/her   B) our/their   C) their/ours
    D) mine/yours   E) his/my

84. Is there ___ interesting in the newspaper today?
    A) anything   B) any   C) something
    D) some   E) no

85. She asked ___ to visit ___ sick child.
    A) our/their   B) us/him   C) them/hers
    D) us/her   E) his/her

86. ___ the results of your work.
    A) this is   B) that was   C) this was
    D) those are   E) that is

87. ___ shoes are black, ___ are brown.
    A) me/his   B) our/him   C) my/hers
    D) he/my   E) their/we

88. - Where is the hen?
    - ___ is sitting on ___ nest.
    A) she/hers   B) he's/his   C) she's/hers
    D) it/its   E) it's/his

89. -" I didn't see ___ puppies, Dad".
    -"___ are with ___ mother", said Alice's father.
    A) yours/it is/its   B) our/they/ours   C) my/they/your
    D) my/them/their   E) their/it's/its

90. -Yesterday I found a watch. I don't know whose watch was ___ .
    -___ was ___ if you found it in the garden.
    A) this/that/our   B) they/this/his   C) that/that/mine
    D) these/those/hers   E) that/this/your

91. Ted and Nick looked for ___ dog for a long time. They found a little one but it wasn't ___ .
    A) his/its   B) our/their   C) his/mine
    D) their/theirs E) their/ours

92. Next year famous Mr. Toscanini came to the town to see Mr. Smith again. But ___ couldn't find ___ .
    A) she/him   B) they/her   C) he/her
    D) she/her   E) he/him

93. I want ___ to answer ___ question.
    A) her/them   B) their/our   C) her/him
    D) you/his   E) you/hers

94. Will ___ give ___ your pen? I've left ___ at home.
    A) you/me/my   B) you/him/your C) they/her/his
    D) they/you/their E) you/me/mine

95. There was ___ in my suitcase so I could carry it without ___ effort.
    A) something/no   B) nothing/any
    C) anything/some   D) nothing/some
    E) some/any

96. You are ___ now, and don't let ___ forget it.
    A) anybody/anyone   B) somebody/anybody
    C) something/anything D) something/something
    E) anything/anyone

97. It's not easy to the old man to do shopping. My parents have to do ___ shopping for ___ to help.
    A) him/him   B) his/his   C) him/his
    D) his/him   E) her/him

98. ___ doesn't like to be reminded ___ ___ mother lives in a farmhouse.
    A) he/what/her B) I/-/my   C) she/that/her
    D) we/what/their E) her/which/her

99. How much time does ___ spend on ___ homework?
    A) we/our   B) he/his   C) me/her
    D) them/their   E) her/she

100. ___ presidents elected in years ending in zero died in ___ office.
    A) his/her   B) everybody/their   C) our/her
    D) all/their   E) their/all

101. ___ of them must take an exam.
    A) some   B) nobody   C) every
    D) everybody   E) any

102. ___ mother never regarded ___ with much favor and there was an antipathy between ___ .
    A) my/her/them B) its/her/us   C) his/they/us
    D) your/it/you E) she/we/you

103. We've got a language lab in our college, and ___ is quite up-to-date. Have you got ___ in yours?
    A) it / one   B) one / some   C) it / some
    D) one / any   E) it / it

104. We always want ___ to do the most difficult part of the work.
    A) someone's   B) someone   C) pupils
    D) they   E) ones

105. He might have concealed from ___ but not from ___ .
    A) other/herself   B) others/himself
    C) each other/him   D) themselves/us
    E) on another/it

106. She put out ___ hand and took ___ .
    A) hers/my   B) her/mine   C) she/he
    D) them/his   E) its/ours

107. If ___ can't talk to Mark ___ don't want to talk to ___ .
    A) she/she/somebody B) he/he/anybody   C) I/I/any one
    D) they/they/it   E) you/you/they

108. ___ told ___ a strange "Good bye" and looked at ___ .
    A) He/my/one another B) Which/them/it   C) We/me/us
    D) They/their/them   E) They/me/each other

109. The teacher asked ___ if he did the work ___ .
    A) her/his   B) its/ours
    C) him/themselves   D) him/himself
    E) us/them

110. If ___ comes home early, tell ___ to wait for ___ .
    A) she/him/hers   B) he/her/him   C) he/him/me
    D) we/us/them   E) it/me/her

111. I don't think this pen is ___, it's ___ .
    A) my/yours   B) mine/your   C) his/my
    D) yours/mine   E) their/hers

112. I felt ___ becoming irritated by ___ .
    A) itself/them   B) myself/her
    C) one another/that D) them/theirs
    E) who/which

113. - Did you meet ___ friends at the party?
     - No, I met ___ .
    A) some of yours / no   B) any of your / none
    C) any of your / no   D) some of your / no
    E) any of you / none

114. -Have ___ finished ___ work?
     -Yes, we have. We've done ___ .
    A) she/her/it   B) they/there/it   C) you/your/it
    D) you/their/this   E) he/your/-

115. We asked ___ to join ___ if ___ liked.
    A) you/their/we   B) me/them/theirs   C) you/her/you
    D) him/she/he   E) them/we/he

116. Have ___ seen ___? Is this book ___ ?
    A) she/her/his   B) they/hers/my   C) you/her/hers
    D) him/me/mine   E) you/me/your

117. ___ invited ___ to stay with ___ in the hotel.
    A) I/me/them   B) she/he/they   C) we/us/me
    D) they/us/them   E) you/us/she

118. There is ___ you must believe in.
    A) his   B) anything   C) anybody
    D) something   E) some

119. I'll go to ___ place, ___ time you wish.
    A) some/some   B) any/any   C) no/any
    D) any/no   E) -/-

120. You've got an excellent secretary in your office. We've got ___ too, but ___ doesn't speak ___ foreign language.
    A) one / he / any   B) him / he / some
    C) some / one / any   D) one / one / any
    E) one / he / no

121. Then she saw ___ father. He had laid ___ fishing rod and was taking something from ___ pocket.
    A) his/her/its   B) her/his/his   C) them/his/his
    D) its/his/its   E) they/his/his

122. - "Please, stay a little while"
    - "Of course, mum, ___ was going to suggest ___ ___ .
    A) he/it/myself   B) we/us/ourselves   C) it/it/itself
    D) I/it/myself   E) she/us/myself

123. I wanted to ask ___ both what you thought of my latest films if ___ saw them.
    A) you/you   B) their/we   C) his/him
    D) me/I   E) hers/you

124. I was late. I found ___ in the house.
    A) each   B) nobody   C) one
    D) some   E) any

125. This book is ___, there is ___ name on ___ .
    A) your/your/it   B) his/me/it   C) mine/my/me
    D) his/it/his   E) mine/my/it

126. John left the house without saying ___ to ___ .
    A) nothing / somebody   B) nothing / nobody
    C) anything / anybody   D) anything / nobody
    E) something / nobody

127. We asked her to tell us ___ interesting, but she refused to tell us ___ .
    A) anything / anything   B) anything / nothing
    C) anything / none   D) something / nothing
    E) something / anything

128. MOTHER will send MARY to buy THE TICKETS.
    A) she/herself/it   B) she/her/them
    C) she/it/their   D) she/them/hers
    E) she/your/theirs

129. - Isn't that ___ friend over there?
    - Oh! No, she isn't ___ friend, she is ___ .
    A) your / my / yours   B) your / his / my
    C) my / yours / mine   D) mine / my / yours
    E) ours / your / mine

130. "I'm going out with my friend", she said.
    She said that ___ was going out with ___ friend.
    A) I/my   B) she/her   C) they/their
    D) you/your   E) we/our

131. He always looks unhappy. ___ in the world can make him smile.
    A) anybody   B) something   C) nothing
    D) anything   E) someone

132. Have you packed ___?
    A) anybody   B) someone   C) everybody
    D) everything   E) nobody

133. I don't like the hat of ___ at all. ___ doesn't suit ___ .
    A) hers/it/you   B) her/it/you   C) mine/it/his
    D) theirs/he/them   E) yours/it/you

134. Dick has lost ___ screwdriver. Leave ___ ___ .
    A) yours/her/my   B) his/her/mine   C) his/him/yours
    D) our/him/its   E) my/me/their

135. This isn't ___ book. It must be ___ .
    A) my/yours   B) your/she   C) his/her
    D) her/me   E) our/its

136. A friend of ___ told ___ about it.
    A) his/my   B) mine/me   C) your/me
    D) mine/she   E) their/them

137. I've never heard ___ speak to ___ .
    A) she / he   B) them / they   C) her / him
    D) they / him   E) you / they

138. -Do you know ___ Cindy gave a present to her boss?
    A) who   B) why   C) that
    D) how much   E) what

139. ___ eyes were as bright as ___ .
    A) mine/you   B) his/hers   C) its/she
    D) hers/his   E) ours/our

140. I can't find my watch ___ . I've looked for it ___ .
    A) nothing/anything   B) something/everywhere
    C) everywhere/nowhere   D) anywhere/everywhere
    E) anybody/nobody

141. We got home late. We were very tired and ___ went to bed at once.
    A) anybody   B) nobody   C) somebody
    D) anything   E) everybody

142. I have found ___ lost pen. I don't need ___ .
    A) his/me   B) we/they   C) her/its
    D) your/it   E) your/them

143. ___ say that he is leaving ___ native town tomorrow.
    A) he/his   B) we/us   C) they/his
    D) she/his   E) I/him

144. Could you give ___ book to ___ please. She has forgotten to take ___ .
    A) her/your/hers   B) your/her/hers   C) my/my/mine
    D) him/his/theirs   E) it/him/its

145. Here is ___ notebook, but I can't find ___ .
    A) my/your   B) you/mine   C) your/their
    D) his/her   E) your/mine

146. -Do you know ___ this word means?
    -Yes, it means "continue".
    A) who   B) when   C) that
    D) why   E) what

147. Which of ___ is ___ brother? ___ are so alike.
    A) him/my/they   B) them/your/they   C) us/his/you
    D) you/her/we   E) them/his/you

148. The CHILD was looking for HIS CAP while HIS FATHER called him.
    A) he/it/he   B) he/it/him   C) he/it/his
    D) she/it/her   E) she/it/it

149. When a child, ISAAC lived with HIS MOTHER, UNCLE, AND GRANDMOTHER.
    A) he/them   B) she/him   C) they/him
    D) it/her   E) they/us

150. On ___ way home Peter decided to buy new skates for ___ .
    A) he/him   B) his/his   C) his/herself
    D) his/himself   E) her/him

151. THE HIGH PRICES affected THE POOR.
    A) they/them   B) they/it   C) you/them
    D) they/her   E) be/him

152. A BLIND MAN was groping for the DOOR-HANDLE.
    A) he/it   B) she/it   C) it/them
    D) they/me   E) she/them

153. He asked her name and ___ told ___ ___ .
    A) she/him/her   B) he/her/her   C) she/her/his
    D) she/him/hers   E) he/he/his

154. "But I can't do ___ for him," the girl told ___ friend.
    A) somebody/their   B) anything/her
    C) something/any   D) theirs/nothing
    E) anybody/no

155. THE EIGHTH OF MARCH is WOMEN'S Day.
    A) It/their   B) It/her   C) It/his
    D) It/our   E) She/her

156. ___ own hand shook as ___ accepted a rose or two from ___ and thanked ___ .
    A) his/he/hers/her   B) my/they/theirs/her
    C) her/we/ours/us   D) their/us/we/they
    E) our/he/his/himself

157. Can you give me ___ to eat? I'm very hungry.
    A) anything   B) nothing   C) what
    D) someone   E) anybody

158. There was ___ snakelike in the boy's black eyes.
    A) something   B) someone   C) some
    D) anything   E) none

159. ___ is devoted to ___ family.
    A) I/my   B) he/him   C) he/his
    D) she/mine   E) it/them

160. ___ was evident that ___ wanted ___ to drop the subject, ___ I did accordingly.
    A) she/she/I/who   B) I/she/me/that
    C) it/she/me/which   D) they/theirs/I/me
    E) that/us/him/-

161. I didn't want to think about ___ else but English.
    A) nothing   B) anything   C) someone
    D) everywhere   E) nobody

162. I never have ___ for breakfast but a cup of hot milk.
    A) someone   B) nothing   C) anything
    D) everything   E) anyone

163. MY FRIEND AND I walked in SCOTLAND last year and climbed the MOUNTAINS there.
    A) they/it/them   B) you/he/they   C) we/it/them
    D) you/she/they   E) he/he/them

164. Here is ___ exercise book. Where's ___?
    A) my/her   B) my/yours   C) his/your
    D) her/their   E) me/its

165. ___ are going to give Kate and Bob a washing-machine for ___ wedding.
    A) they/his   B) I / her   C) we/their
    D) you/your   E) some/any

166. Ann took ___ bicycle. Will you give ___ ___ ?
    A) her/my/theirs   B) our/me/him   C) my/you/ours
    D) my/me/yours   E) he/its/hers

167. Father said: "You may go ___ you like."
    A) anywhere   B) nowhere   C) something
    D) anyone   E) somewhere

168. Where is your niece? ___ is somewhere here. Don't you hear singing ?
    A) he/his   B) it/its   C) he/their
    D) she/its   E) she/her

169. My flat is large. What about ___?
    A) mine   B) her   C) their
    D) your   E) yours

170. Has ___ read the text?
    A) any   B) anybody   C) someone
    D) some   E) we

171. Did ___ want ___ to help ___?
    A) you / he / her   B) you / me / them   C) they / her / he
    D) them / her / he   E) he / his / him

172. That test with a bad mark was ___, those were ___
    A) my/her   B) his/her   C) yours/their
    D) me/ours   E) mine/theirs

173. Our goods are not beautiful.
    -Do you think ___ are better?
    A) your   B) their   C) her
    D) its   E) theirs

174. ___ name is Samuel, but ___ may call ___ Sam.
    A) her/he/him   B) his/you/me   C) my/she/him
    D) your/you/me   E) my/you/me

175. POETESS was not in the HALL.
    A) she/it   B) he/it   C) it/it
    D) they/it   E) you/it

176. In the town there were ___ new hospitals.
    A) anybody   B) some   C) any
    D) something   E) oneselves

177. It was ___ he didn't want to remember.
    A) anything   B) nobody   C) anybody
    D) anyone   E) something

178. ___ put on ___ coats and left the room.
    A) we/his   B) you/her   C) they/their
    D) he/his   E) she/her

179. When Peter told ___ about ___ I didn't believe ___ .
    A) her/her/her   B) they/me/them   C) him/it/her
    D) me/it/him   E) us/you/her

180. Let ___ take ___ book, please.
    A) his/her   B) him/-   C) him/your
    D) me/him   E) I/my

181. ___ is ___ watch and ___ is ___ .
    A) that/her/this/you   B) this/him/that/her
    C) this/my/that/yours   D) this/you/that/your
    E) this/her/that/her

182. As ___ is clear to ___, I'm not going to say ___ else.
    A) everything/somebody/anything
    B) everybody/somebody/anybody
    C) everything/everybody/anything
    D) somebody/nobody/something
    E) nothing/nobody/anything

183. Is there ___ in the room? Please, open the door!
    A) somewhere   B) something   C) anything
    D) some day   E) anybody

184. This is ___ watch and that is ___ .
    A) yours/mine   B) my/yours   C) your / yours
    D) my/you   E) mine / your

185. It's very quiet in the office today. There's ___ here. ___ is on holiday.
    A) anybody / everybody   B) anything / nothing
    C) nobody / all of them   D) somebody / nothing
    E) nobody / everybody

186. I'll be very glad if you invite ___ else to join us.
    A) somebody   B) one more   C) friend
    D) aunt   E) something

187. Don't worry. I'll do ___ best to help ___ .
    A) my/you   B) your/you   C) his/him
    D) her/her   E) -/to you

188. ___ friend is going to make a report today. ___ say ___ will be very interesting.
    A) my/he/it   B) her/we/its   C) his/they/it
    D) our/she/he   E) your/it/it

189. Can I use ___ pen today? I've left ___ at home.
    A) his/her   B) your/mine   C) her/his
    D) me/them   E) my/it

190. Here is ___ text-book. Where is ___?
    A) her / my   B) his / their   C) my / them
    D) my / yours   E) it / it

TEST 4 — Present Tenses

1. I'm taking my sister out as she ___ any sun for a long time.
   A) hasn't had   B) haven't had   C) hadn't been
   D) will have   E) shall have

2. He ___ ill for three months already.
   A) was   B) has been   C) is
   D) have been   E) were

3. Who goes sightseeing?
   A) Nina does.   B) We shall.   C) We did.
   D) I did.   E) She has.

4. I usually ___ a blouse and jeans at home, but today I ___ on a new dress.
   A) wear/have put   B) have worn/have put
   C) wore/has put   D) wears/has put
   E) will wear/put

5. What ___ the president ___?
   -He ___ a contract.
   A) does/do/has signed   B) is/doing/is signing
   C) will/do/was signing D) is/going to do/would sign
   E) shall/do/has been signing

6. Look! The cat ___ your cutlet.
   A) is eating   B) was eating   C) eats
   D) has been eating   E) had eaten

7. You look pale. You ___ too hard these days.
   A) have been working   B) worked   C) are working
   D) work   E) were working

8. What ___ you ___ since I saw you last?
   A) do/do   B) are/doing
   C) have/been doing   D) did/do
   E) will/do

9. It is 8.30. Ben and Ann ___ breakfast.
   A) have   B) are having   C) is having
   D) was having   E) were having

10. She ___ a journalist nowadays.
    A) are   B) was   C) is
    D) were   E) am

11. You ___ always ___ your things. Put them into their bag.
    A) are/losing   B) -/lost
    C) have/lost   D) shall/have been losing
    E) had/lust

12. What place ___ the youth of our country occupy in all branches now?
    A) did   B) shall   C) is
    D) does   E) will

13. I ___ home for lunch on Mondays. I have lunch in the canteen.
    A) didn't go   B) was going   C) don't go
    D) doesn't go   E) will not go

14. Westminster Abbey is the ancient old church in which the coronation ceremonies of almost all English kings and queens ___ place.
    A) will take   B) was taken   C) was taking
    D) is taking   E) have taken

15. This is the most interesting film I ___ ever ___.
    A) didn't/see   B) was/seen   C) have/saw
    D) have/seen   E) had/seen

16. "Nobody ___ in that country," said Pinocchio to his friend.
    A) don't learn   B) are learning   C) learns
    D) doesn't learn   E) learn

17. Paul ___ a student of Cambridge University.
    A) were   B) are   C) am
    D) be   E) is

18. "Little boy", said a man, "why do you carry that umbrella over your head? It ___ and the sun ___."
    A) rains/isn't shining   B) doesn't rain/shines
    C) isn't raining/isn't shining   D) is raining/is shining
    E) isn't raining/don't shine

19. Who often has dinner at the canteen?
    A) I did   B) we do   C) he had
    D) they have   E) she will

20. I ___ never ___ him before.
    A) - /met   B) - /meet   C) have/met
    D) has/met   E) -/meets

21. The weather is awful, it ___ all day.
    A) rains   B) is raining   C) rained
    D) has rained   E) has been raining

22. It is 2 o'clock. I ___ afraid I ___ late.
    A) was/am   B) shall be/am   C) am/am
    D) was/was   E) am/wasn't

23. Who usually answers these letters in your office?
    A) My friend can.   B) That man will.   C) I do, of course.
    D) Mary is.   E) Those engineers did.

24. The milk is hot I ___ on it to make it cold.
    A) am blowing   B) blow   C) is blowing
    D) blew   E) had blown

25. - You don't like horror films, do you?
    - ___ . They are so terrifying.
    A) Yes, I can.   B) No, I can't.   C) No, I don't.
    D) Yes, I do.   E) No, we didn't.

26. ___ this engineer work at the Ministry of Foreign Affairs.
    A) do   B) does   C) has
    D) had   E) shall

27. He ___ never ___ him sing.
    A) had___ heard   B) has___heard   C) have___ heard
    D) was___ hearing   E) is___ hearing

28. I think ___ .
    A) if he is about fifty   B) he is about fifty   C) her about fifty
    D) him about fifty   E) be about fifty

29. I miss her very much, almost every minute of the day I think of her, or I think I ___ her.
    A) am hearing   B) hear   C) heard
    D) have heard   E) will hear

30. Look! There ___ a man sitting at the first table near the door. He ___ at us.
    A) was/looks   B) had been/looked
    C) were/had looked   D) is/is looking
    E) is/was looking

31. These engineers always ___ in the office and ___
    A) stayed/learn   B) stay/learn   C) stays/learns
    D) have stayed/learned   E) stay/learned

32. It's the happiest evening I ever ___ .
    A) had   B) have had   C) has
    D) has had   E) had had

33. Let me show the picture that I ___ this week.
    A) am drawing   B) shall be drawing   C) have drawn
    D) drew   E) will be drawing

34. This is the 7th year Ann and Mary ___ this school.
    A) has attended   B) have been attending
    C) had been attending   D) are attending
    E) were attending

35. He ___ his English in the morning, he ___ it in the evening.
   A) doesn't have/is having   B) don't have/had
   C) doesn't have/has   D) didn't have/have
   E) hadn't/will have

36. The sun ___ in the East and ___ in the West.
   A) sets/rises   B) sets/goes   C) rises/sets
   D) goes/rises   E) set/rise

37. While ___ to school we always ___ a bus.
   A) going/take   B) went/take
   C) shall go/will take   D) had gone/took
   E) goes/takes

38. We don't like him because he always ___ lies.
   A) tell   B) was telling   C) tells
   D) are telling   E) has told

39. I ___ all my work. I am free now.
   A) do   B) am doing   C) shall do
   D) have done E) had done

40. She ___ at school since 1984.
   A) teach   B) has been teaching   C) taught
   D) was teaching E) have taught

41. - ___ your father ___ at the Medical College?
    - Yes, he does.
   A) do/work   B) did/work   C) has/worked
   D) does/work E) shall/work

42. He ___ to school at 7:30 and ___ at 2 o'clock.
   A) goes/comes back   B) went/is coming back
   C) go/come back   D) was going/has come back
   E) is going/came back

43. -You ___ not ___ your soup.
    -I'm sorry. I'm not hungry.
   A) are/eat   B) has/eaten   C) are/eating
   D) did/ate   E) will/eat

44. -Who ___ French in your family?
    -I ___ .
   A) speaks/do   B) speak/does   C) spoke/do
   D) speaking/did E) are speaking/did

45. Although Mary has been cooking for many years, she still ___ how to prepare Chinese food.
   A) did not know   B) know   C) don't know
   D) doesn't know   E) hadn't known

46. The aims of the course ___ me willing to begin.
   A) makes   B) is making   C) were made
   D) make   E) making

47. Listen! Somebody ___ in the next room.
   A) sing   B) sings   C) are singing
   D) is singing E) is sung

48. -___ life ___ on Mars?
    -No, it ___ .
   A) Does/exist/doesn't   B) Did/existed/didn't
   C) Has/existed/had   D) Had/existed/had
   E) Will/exist/will

49. I ___ this man at all.
   A) don't know   B) know   C) knew
   D) have known   E) doesn't know

50. The boys ___ four English books this year.
   A) read   B) had read   C) reads
   D) have read   E) read

51. I know he reads every book I ___ ever ___ of.
   A) -/hear   B) -/heard   C) have/heard
   D) has/heard   E) had/heard

52. Nothing will make him ___ back to her.
   A) to come   B) come   C) came
   D) coming   E) would come

53. Listen! Someone ___ at the door.
   A) knocks   B) to knock   C) has knocked
   D) is knocking E) has been knocking

54. "This thief ___ usually promise to steal again," said Sherlock Holmes.
   A) won't   B) didn't   C) isn't
   D) doesn't   E) don't

55. Samuel says he's 25 years old, but nobody ___ him.
   A) is believing   B) believes   C) had believed
   D) don't believe E) doesn't believe

56. The sea ___ to those who ___ to listen to it.
   A) speaks/likes   B) speak/like   C) speaks/like
   D) speak/likes   E) speak/will like

57. Take your umbrella. It ___ .
   A) was raining   B) rained   C) rains
   D) is raining   E) would be raining

58. We can't disturb him now. He ___ .
   A) operate   B) will operate   C) has operated
   D) is operating E) operates

59. The children of the man who works with me ___ the window this morning.
   A) were broken   B) break   C) broke
   D) have broken   E) had broken

60. "Who ___ this picture?" the teacher asks.
   A) is drawn   B) drawn   C) have drawn
   D) draws   E) has drawn

61. -Where is Comrade A?
    -He ___ tennis.
   A) plays   B) is playing   C) played
   D) has been playing E) will play

62. I ___ never ___ such beautiful flowers before.
   A) shall / see   B) had / seen   C) have / seen
   D) has / seen   E) will / see

63. I've got to get him to the station. His train ___ at the moment.
   A) leave   B) has left   C) had left
   D) is leaving E) are leaving

64. -What ___ you ___?
    -I ___ now.
   A) are/doing/am washing up
   B) have/done/am washing up
   C) have/been done/am washed up
   D) were/done/have washed up
   E) is/doing/did not wash up

65. We can go out now. It ___ .
   A) don't rain   B) rains   C) didn't rain
   D) has rained   E) isn't raining

66. You'll see what I ___ about you recently.
   A) shall write   B) have written   C) had written
   D) is written   E) was written

67. She ___ since last week.
   A) is ill   B) was ill   C) had been ill
   D) has been ill   E) will be ill

68. Listen! Somebody ___ at the door.
   A) knocked   B) has knocked   C) is knocking
   D) was knocking E) knocks

69. This year we ___ a good harvest of cotton.
   A) has grown   B) have grown   C) grown
   D) were growing   E) are grown

70. Look at the little boys! They ___ with stones.
    A) play   B) will play   C) are playing
    D) is playing E) played

71. It ___ him 20 minutes to get to the work usually.
    A) take   B) is taking   C) have taken
    D) is not taking E) takes

72. Usually my working day ___ at 8.30 sharp.
    A) start   B) starts   C) would be
    D) won't start E) has started

73. Stop a minute, think what you ___ .
    A) are saying B) say   C) says
    D) is saying E) has said

74. The population of the world ___ very fast.
    A) rise   B) rises   C) is rising
    D) rose   E) is risen

75. Tourists ___ a lot of different information when they travel.
    A) get   B) gets   C) has got
    D) would get E) were getting

76. The English seaside ___ very popular lately.
    A) becomes   B) has become   C) became
    D) will become E) is becoming

77. ___ he already___ the rules in the race ?
    A) did/break B) does/break   C) is/breaking
    D) has/broken E) had/broken

78. Peter ___ his lessons. When he finishes them he'll watch TV.
    A) does   B) do   C) did
    D) is doing   E) has done

79. I ___ never ___ the book.
    A) didn't/read B) haven't/read   C) have/read
    D) don't/read E) was/reading

80. Look! The girls ___ in the park.
    A) skate   B) skated   C) are skating
    D) will skate E) has skated

81. She is sorry, she ___ so rude.
    A) were   B) will be   C) are
    D) has been   E) had been

82. Why ___ nothing ___?
    A) has / been done still   B) hasn't / been done yet
    C) has / been done yet   D) was / done yet
    E) have / been done yet

83. Shh! The teacher ___ on the blackboard.
    A) wrote   B) was writing   C) writes
    D) will write E) is writing

84. I ___ here since 1972.
    A) was living B) had lived   C) lives
    D) am living E) have lived

85. ___ you ___ to England?
    A) were/being B) are/being   C) have/been
    D) were/being E) had/been

86. Hello! Who ___?
    A) spoke   B) speaks
    C) has been speaking   D) is speaking
    E) was spoken

87. Max ___ to be good at interpreting, ___ he?
    A) doesn't seem/does   B) seems/does
    C) seemed/did   D) seems/does
    E) didn't seem/doesn't

88. ___ you ever ___ Herr Boschen sing his great German comic songs?
    A) had/heard B) did/hear   C) do/hear
    D) are/hearing E) have/heard

89. Who ___ writing the text yet?
    A) haven't finished B) didn't finish   C) doesn't finish
    D) won't finish   E) hasn't finished

90. - What ___ you ___?
    - I ___ a letter.
    A) are doing/am writing   B) have done/am writing
    C) did/write   D) have done/am writing
    E) has done/wrote

91. We ___ already twenty words.
    A) learned   B) have learned   C) learn
    D) will learn E) are learning

92. "I can't marry Mr. Fire. I ___ already ___ my word to another man", said the chief's daughter.
    A) don't/give B) had/given   C) shall/give
    D) didn't/give E) have/given

93. Be quick! A dog ___ after your child.
    A) runs   B) ran   C) was running
    D) will run   E) is running

94. I ___ never ___ to the USA.
    A) is/ been   B) has/been   C) have/been
    D) having/been E) was/being

95. Oh, not really, I ___ a minute since I came in.
    A) haven't had B) haven't   C) were not
    D) will have   E) hadn't

96. Take away the crib; the teacher ___ at you.
    A) look   B) is looking   C) looks
    D) looked   E) had looked

97. I ___ them for 10 months.
    A) know   B) knows   C) have known
    D) will know E) shall know

98. Why ___ you ___ the coat? It's not cold.
    A) do/put on B) has/put on   C) have/put on
    D) would/put on E) had/put on

99. Don't enter the classroom. The students ___ an exam.
    A) write   B) were writing   C) have written
    D) are writing E) had been written

100. Look! They ___ in our direction.
    A) come   B) came   C) will come
    D) was coming E) are coming

101. I ___ Paul since Christmas.
    A) don't see B) haven't seen   C) hadn't seen
    D) wasn't seen E) won't see

102. "Fortune" ___ the magazine of business success for over 50 years.
    A) is   B) was   C) will be
    D) has been   E) were

103. She ___ false impressions on those who ___ you.
    A) will produce / hadn't known
    B) produces / don't know
    C) produces / doesn't know
    D) has produced / will not know
    E) would produce / have not known

104. Food prices ___ rapidly in the past few months.
    A) had risen B) has risen   C) have risen
    D) was rising E) rises

TEST 5

Future Tenses

1. I ___ to start a new life tomorrow.
   A) to be going B) am going C) shall go
   D) is going E) were going

2. Mark ___ into the army next year.
   A) was going B) goes C) will go
   D) would go E) will be go

3. They ___ dinner at this time tomorrow.
   A) have B) are having C) will have
   D) having had E) will be having

4. -What's happened to your hair? Your mother ___
   A) didn't like B) liked C) likes
   D) would like E) won't like

5. I ___ if you come too late tomorrow.
   A) shall be sleeping B) will sleep C) sleep
   D) am sleeping E) was sleeping

6. Be quick or we ___ for school.
   A) are late B) is late C) have been late
   D) shall be late E) will not be late

7. What ___ you ___ next Sunday?
   A) were doing B) have done C) are doing
   D) are done E) were done

8. I think I ___ a cassette recorder and use it in class.
   A) buy B) am buying C) shall buy
   D) would buy E) bought

9. We ___ for Niagara tomorrow.
   A) are leaving B) have left C) left
   D) had to leave E) shall be left

10. I'll ask him what he ___ for lunch.
    A) was having B) are having C) would have
    D) should have E) will have

11. Who ___ for a walk tomorrow?
    A) go B) will go C) didn't go
    D) doesn't go E) went

12. They ___ their English exam at this time tomorrow.
    A) will take B) will be taking C) would take
    D) is taking E) take

13. My boss ___ some V.I.P's tomorrow.
    A) will be received B) is receiving
    C) will have received D) receive
    E) has received

14. Ask him when the engineers ___ finish the talks.
    A) will B) would C) had
    D) have E) do

15. He ___ to learn French next year.
    A) was going B) is going C) are going
    D) will be going E) shall be going

16. All the children ___ on an excursion next week.
    A) go B) went C) have gone
    D) will go E) has gone

17. ___ you ___ at 6 tomorrow?
    A) will/sleep B) were/sleeping
    C) will/be sleeping D) do/sleep
    E) are/sleeping

18. I shall be back by 6 and I hope you ___ a good sleep by that time.
    A) will have had B) will have C) would have
    D) have had E) had had

19. This time tomorrow we ___ probably ___ fishing.
    A) are/will B) -/shall C) shall/be
    D) shall/- E) do/are

20. What ___ you ___ at 6 tomorrow?
    A) will/do B) was/doing C) will/be doing
    D) is/doing E) will/have done

21. By the end of the first term we ___ many English books.
    A) shall be read B) read C) shall have read
    D) have read E) shall read

22. What ___ you ___ at 6 tomorrow?
    A) did/do B) will/be doing C) do/do
    D) do/did E) have/done

23. He ___ for you at 7 in the evening next Sunday.
    A) was waiting B) were waiting C) will be waiting
    D) have waited E) had been waited

TEST 6

Past Tenses

1. She never ___ to eat soup.
   A) didn't like   B) like   C) had liked
   D) would not like   E) liked

2. "I'll drink tea from this tin mug."
   "Where ___ you ___ it?"
   A) did/find   B) do/find   C) did/found
   D) were/found   E) are/found

3. It was dark and cold. At one moment he thought that he ___ his way.
   A) lost   B) will lose   C) had lost
   D) was lost   E) loses

4. I didn't know anyone in the city where I ___ to get.
   A) did try   B) was trying   C) would try
   D) have tried   E) shall try

5. -Why ___ you go to the plant?
   -I ___ no time.
   A) do/had   B) will/have   C) did/hadn't
   D) didn't/hadn't   E) didn't/had

6. A policeman ___ me crossing the street yesterday.
   A) seen   B) saw   C) has seen
   D) will see   E) had seen

7. Arthur ___ all his exams by 5 o'clock yesterday.
   A) passed   B) passes   C) has passed
   D) has been passed   E) had passed

8. He evidently ___ his shoes for a very long time. They were worn-out.
   A) were wearing   B) are wearing
   C) had been wearing   D) was wearing
   E) had been worn

9. So, the invisible man ___ into the shop and ___ down.
   A) comes/walked   B) didn't come/walk   C) came/walked
   D) will come/walked   E) comes/would walk

10. -We were at the theatre 2 days ago. The performance was excellent.
    -Who ___ the leading part?
    A) did play   B) play   C) played
    D) would play   E) has played

11. One day the boys found a man in the forest. He ___
    A) will die   B) had been dying   C) had died
    D) was dying   E) die

12. His father ___ a doctor and he ___ to make his son a doctor, too.
    A) was/wants   B) were/wanted
    C) will be/would want   D) was/wanted
    E) were/wanted

13. During his school years Cronin ___ great interest in literature.
    A) take   B) took   C) has taken
    D) had taken   E) would take

14. He ___ the box yesterday, because he had to do it.
    A) would open   B) had opening   C) have opened
    D) opens   E) opened

15. While the gentlemen ___ the recent events, the ladies ___ about the weather.
    A) discuss/talk
    B) are discussing/was talking
    C) being discussed/being talked
    D) were discussing/were talking
    E) have discussed/have talked

16. She ___ you a letter three weeks ago.
    A) had sent   B) has sent   C) sent
    D) send   E) was sending

17. When he ___ home I ___ him the book.
    A) came/shall show   B) comes/showed
    C) has come/has shown   D) came/showed
    E) was coming/shall show

18. They ___ breakfast at 7 and ___ home at eight.
    A) have/left   B) had/left   C) had/leave
    D) have/leaves   E) had/had left

19. Long ago people ___ little about those minerals.
    A) had known   B) knowed   C) will know
    D) knew   E) have known

20. The dentist ___ two of his teeth. One of them ___ quite good.
    A) pulls out/are   B) pull out/was
    C) pulled out/was   D) pull out/was
    E) pulled out/were

21. I couldn't imagine what ___ to her.
    A) had happened   B) has been happened
    C) will happen   D) has been happening
    E) happens

22. He felt that he ___ it wrong.
    A) has made   B) made   C) will make
    D) was made   E) had made

23. I ___ my homework when my mother came.
    A) already did   B) have already done
    C) had already done   D) has already done
    E) already do

24. Turning I found my father sitting beside me on the sofa. I said "How ___ you ___ here?"
    A) do/get   B) did/get   C) does/get
    D) was/getting   E) has/been getting

25. Last summer we ___ a trip to Houston.
    A) made   B) has made   C) are making
    D) shall make   E) will be making

26. He ___ barely ___ of him until that evening.
    A) had/heard   B) has/heard   C) was/heard
    D) did/hear   E) didn't/hear

27. She ___ in Tashkent five years ago.
    A) had lived   B) lived   C) has lived
    D) live   E) have lived

28. We ___ English, so I know it a little.
    A) were learning   B) learned   C) learns
    D) should learn   E) were learning

29. Yesterday at this time it ___ .
    A) had snowed   B) snows   C) snowed
    D) was snowing   E) had been snowing

30. We ___ he ___ ill.
    A) did not know/was   B) knew/am ill   C) knew/will be
    D) had known/is   E) were known/be

31. The plane ___ at 4 and it ___ us 20 minutes to get there.
    A) was landing/was taking   B) was landing/took
    C) landed/took   D) lands/was taken
    E) has landed/is taking

32. We ___ the station by 5 o'clock yesterday.
    A) shall reach   B) were reaching   C) had reached
    D) reached   E) would reach

33. The Browns ___ out of town last Sunday and ___ a good time there.
    A) were going/had   B) went/are having
    C) went/had   D) are going/were having
    E) goes/has

34. Before answering the telephone he ___ down the table.
    A) laid   B) was lying   C) had laid
    D) lay   E) has laid

35. Who ___ at the meeting yesterday?
    A) speak   B) speaks   C) spoke
    D) had spoken   E) will speak

36. He met me with the bird in his hand. It ___ curiously at me.
    A) looks   B) was looking
    C) has been looking   D) would look
    E) should look

37. Nick ___ yesterday.
    A) will not come   B) hadn't come   C) didn't come
    D) hasn't come   E) came not

38. I knew that he ___ the same paper each morning.
    A) was bought   B) buys   C) is buying
    D) bought   E) had bought

39. He asked the children who ___ the book.
    A) tore   B) tear   C) tears
    D) had torn   E) will tear

40. Who ___ on a hike yesterday?
    A) did go   B) will go   C) has gone
    D) went   E) had went

41. I ___ to do it but I ___ no time. I was very busy.
    A) wanted/has   B) want/had have
    C) wanted/had   D) would want/have
    E) have wanted/shall have

42. - What a luck. I haven't seen you for ages.
    - When ___ we ___ last time?
    A) did / meet   B) have / met   C) had / met
    D) did / met   E) will / meet

43. In the summer of 1868, Melville Bell ___ on a lecture tour in the USA and Canada.
    A) goes   B) had gone   C) went
    D) have gone   E) has gone

44. He ___ his work before you came.
    A) finished   B) finishes   C) has finished
    D) had finished   E) finish

45. Why ___ he go to Great Britain last month?
    A) did   B) was   C) will
    D) had   E) has

46. Did you ___ or ___ the potatoes?
    A) mince/peeled   B) minced/peeled
    C) minced/peeling   D) peels/minced
    E) mince/peel

47. When she ___ they ___ and he left the house.
    A) had come/quarreled   B) came/quarreled
    C) has come/quarreled   D) comes/would quarrel
    E) came/had quarreled

48. - Who had left the room by the time I came yesterday?
    A) Tom did   B) Tom does   C) Tom had
    D) Tom has   E) Tom was

49. Neither your parents nor I ___ very glad of the fact that you failed your Math exam.
    A) has been   B) have been   C) were
    D) was   E) are

50. What ___ you ___ at 5 p.m. yesterday?
    A) did/do   B) have/been doing   C) would/do
    D) were/doing   E) will/do

51. Who ___ to see me last week?
    A) comes   B) will come   C) came
    D) has come   E) have come

52. They didn't believe him and ___ to laugh.
    A) begin   B) begins   C) began
    D) had begun   E) have begun

53. Children didn't ___ to school because it ___ Sunday.
    A) went/was   B) go/were
    C) have gone/was   D) gone/was
    E) go/was

54. The train ___ at 8.30 p.m. today, but as a rule it ___ at 8.00 p.m. sharp.
    A) has left / starts   B) left / started
    C) left / has started   D) has left / has started
    E) have left / starts

55. The moon ___ and it ___ surprisingly light at night yesterday.
    A) is rising / is   B) rose / was   C) had risen / was
    D) was rising / were   E) rose / had been

56. Who ___ him yesterday?
    A) has seen   B) did see   C) saw
    D) have seen   E) sees

57. He ___ nobody about his secret that day.
    A) don't tell   B) tell   C) didn't tell
    D) told   E) doesn't tell

TEST 7 — Mixed Tenses

1. Ann ___ that she ___ the visitor before.
   A) thought / saw
   B) thinks / sees
   C) is thinking / sees
   D) thought / had seen
   E) have thought / had seen

2. As it ___ dark we ___ to go home.
   A) gets / decided
   B) would get / shall decide
   C) had got / have decided
   D) was getting / decided
   E) will be getting / had decided

3. He ___ looking at her, wondering where he ___ her.
   A) keep / see
   B) kept / had seen
   C) keeps / saw
   D) had kept / had seen
   E) being kept / would see

4. They ___ to get married last month although they ___ each other for only six weeks.
   A) decide / know
   B) decided / know
   C) decided / had known
   D) decided / knew
   E) decided / has known

5. ___ the weather good when you ___ tennis?
   A) is / played
   B) was / were playing
   C) will be / played
   D) is / will be playing
   E) has been / will play

6. When he ___ to the station the train already ___ .
   A) comes / left
   B) came / leaves
   C) came / had left
   D) had come / left
   E) has come / leaves

7. Last Monday when I ___ the house it ___ heavily.
   A) leave / rain
   B) left / was raining
   C) left / had rained
   D) was leaving / rained
   E) leave / rains

8. Yesterday when Tom ___ the lesson___ .
   A) comes / already begins
   B) came / had already begun
   C) came / already began
   D) will come / already begins
   E) came / already begins

9. I ___ the call because I ___ a shower.
   A) didn't answer / was taking
   B) don't answer / take
   C) doesn't answer / am taking
   D) will not answer / take
   E) am answering / am taking

10. After Mary ___ the room, she ___ the floor.
    A) tidied up / washes
    B) tidies up / has washed
    C) has tidied up / washed
    D) had tidied up / washed
    E) is tidying up / washes

11. Yesterday at this time when his hat ___ he ___ across the bridge.
    A) blows off / is walking
    B) blew off / had walked
    C) has blown off / is walking
    D) blew off / was walking
    E) had blown off / walks

12. He wanted me to go to the skating-rink together. As he ___ I ___ my skates he ___ me his brother's.
    A) knows / broke / offer
    B) knew / broke / offers
    C) knew / had broken / offered
    D) know / had broken / will offer
    E) knew / has broken / offered

13. Tom looked at his hands. He ___ that those hands ___ young and strong before.
    A) knew / was
    B) know / are
    C) had known / were
    D) knew / be
    E) knew / had been

14. He ___ us the firm ___ wool since 1935.
    A) told / had been exporting
    B) tells / would export
    C) said / is exporting
    D) will be told / exports
    E) told / has been exporting

15. He didn't ___ well though he ___ a hard day before.
    A) slept / spent
    B) sleep / spend
    C) sleeping / had spent
    D) sleep / had spent
    E) slept / had spent

16. He___ at the blackboard and ___ that the English teacher ___ the word "apple" there.
    A) was looking / sees/wrote
    B) looks / sees / had written
    C) looked / saw / was writing
    D) is looking / saw / writes
    E) has looked / has seen / is writing

17. Mr. Brown ___ to me 2 hours ago to return the book which he ___ .
    A) comes / borrows
    B) came / had borrowed
    C) will come / borrowed
    D) came / borrowed
    E) was coming / borrowed

18. No sooner he ___ than he ___ ill.
    A) had arrived / falls
    B) had arrived / fell
    C) arrives / has fallen
    D) arrived / will fall
    E) is arriving / is falling

19. I ___ my homework by 6 o'clock yesterday and when my mother came home I ___ supper.
    A) did / have
    B) have done / had
    C) had done / was having
    D) was doing / had
    E) do / have

20. He said that he ___ school and he ___ to enter the academy.
    A) finished / was going
    B) has finished / is going
    C) had finished / was going
    D) finishes / are going
    E) finish / was going

21. It ___ dark and it ___ .
    A) is / are raining
    B) was / was raining
    C) are / was
    D) were / were
    E) were / was

22. The pupils ___ the sentences yet, the teacher ___ the blackboard.
    A) has not written / will clean
    B) had not written / cleaned
    C) did not write / cleans
    D) are not writing / clean
    E) had not written / had cleaned

23. Henry ___ Puerto Rico before he ___ to St. Thomas.
    A) visited / had gone
    B) had visited / went
    C) was visiting / went
    D) would visit / goes
    E) visited / went

24. The company ___ some new equipments before the strike ___ .
    A) have ordered / begin
    B) had ordered / began
    C) ordered / begins
    D) is ordering / began
    E) will order / had begun

25. I ___ he ___ it interesting.
    A) hoped / find
    B) hoped / finds
    C) hopes / would find
    D) hoped / would find
    E) will find / find

26. Mark Twain ___ that they ___ about him.
    A) understand / speaks
    B) understands / speaks
    C) will understand / spoke
    D) understood / are speaking
    E) understood / were speaking

27. On our way home we ___ the problem if we could ___ the fine celebration of our mother's birthday.
    A) discussed / organized
    B) were discussing / organize
    C) had discussed / organize
    D) have discussed / were organizing
    E) discuss / organizes

28. The greater part of London ___ of wood, but after the great fire wider streets and brick houses ___ .
    A) had been / were built
    B) was / were built
    C) is / have been built
    D) are / are built
    E) has been / is built

29. After my parents ___ home my life ___ better.
    A) had returned / became
    B) will return / become
    C) return / have become
    D) return / have become
    E) return / would become

30. Why ___ you come yesterday? We ___ a good time.
    A) don't / can have
    B) didn't / could have had
    C) will / might have
    D) doesn't / will have
    E) did not / shall have

31. He___ even before I ___ a finger on him.
    A) screams / was laid
    B) screamed / had laid
    C) would scream / am laying
    D) screams / laid
    E) screamed / would lay

32. I ___ never ___ to Cambridge, but I once ___ Oxford.
    A) did / go / visit
    B) have / been / visited
    C) have / been / had visited
    D) was / visiting / had been visiting
    E) will / have gone / don't visit

33. We ___ to wait because the man ___ .
    A) told / was questioned
    B) were told / questioned
    C) were told / is questioned
    D) told / was being questioned
    E) were told / was being questioned

34. They didn't know that he ___ from the University in 1990 and then ___ abroad.
    A) had graduated / is working   B) graduated / works
    C) graduated / was working   D) was graduating / worked
    E) had graduated / worked

35. We learned that he ___ the office 5 minutes before he ___ .
    A) left / returned   B) had left / returned
    C) would leave / returned   D) would have left / came
    E) had left / had returned

36. - ___ you ___ him this week?
    - Yes, I ___ him on Sunday.
    A) did / see / saw   B) did / see / have seen
    C) have / seen / see   D) do / see / saw
    E) have / seen / saw

37. I ___ my interview with the vice-president when my daughter ___ me.
    A) had / were calling   B) was having / had called
    C) have had / called   D) had / called
    E) was having / called

38. Ronald Reagan ___ president for 8 years before he ___ .
    A) had been / has retired   B) had been / had retired
    C) was / had retired   D) had been / retired
    E) was / retired

39. I went out of the house. It ___ . It ___ for two weeks.
    A) rained / was raining
    B) had rained / was raining
    C) was raining / had been raining
    D) had been raining / was raining
    E) was raining / rained

40. After long consideration we ___ to the conclusion our behavior ___ .
    A) came / had been justified
    B) came / will be justified
    C) will come / would be justified
    D) are coming / will justify
    E) has come / are being justified

41. The plan ___ for two hours when he ___ .
    A) had been discussed / came
    B) is discussed / comes
    C) will be discussed / come
    D) has been discussed / comes
    E) was discussed / would come

42. Christopher Columbus didn't know where he ___ . When he landed he didn't know where he ___ when he got back to Spain he didn't know where he ___ .
    A) was sailing / was / had been
    B) had sailed / was / was
    C) is sailing / had been / has been
    D) will be sailing / will be / will have been
    E) would sail / hadn't been / haven't been

43. That day after Mr. Brown ___ the letter he ___ me to clarify some details.
    A) has studied / phoned   B) studied / phoned
    C) had studied / phoned   D) had studied / had phoned
    E) studied / is phoning

44. When Christopher Columbus ___ 14 he ___ a sailor.
    A) is / became   B) was / became
    C) was / becomes   D) are / become
    E) were / became

45. When Mr. Brown ___ to the party all the guests ___ at the table.
    A) come / sat   B) came / are sitting
    C) came / were sitting   D) comes / sit
    E) came / had sat

46. Nick ___ he ___ his homework by 4 o'clock.
    A) say / has done   B) said / had done
    C) says / do   D) said / does
    E) said / has done

47. The American ___ the question slowly so that we ___
    A) repeated / should understand
    B) repeat / understood
    C) repeats / would understand
    D) repeated / understand
    E) repeats / understands

48. My sister ___ in Florida for one year when we ___ to New York.
    A) has lived / came   B) have lived / come
    C) lived / come   D) had lived / came
    E) live / came

49. He came to the writing table and ___ through the letters which ___ for him.
    A) look / was waiting   B) looked / were waiting
    C) looks / has been waiting   D) looked / waiting
    E) looks / are waiting

50. Ann ___ her work by 4 o'clock and ___ shopping.
    A) finished / went   B) finishes / will go
    C) had finished / went   D) has finished / go
    E) will finish / went

51. He ___ he ___ lunch an hour before.
    A) say / had   B) said / would have
    C) says / shall have   D) said / had
    E) said / had had

52. When we ___ the station the train ___ already ___ .
    A) reach / has / left   B) reached / had / left
    C) reach / was / leaving   D) shall reach / - / left
    E) were reaching / were / leaving

53. I knew that she ___ Miss Betsy, because I remembered how my mother ___ her.
    A) was / had described   B) is / described
    C) would be / had described   D) had been / described
    E) has been / describes

54. She said that Bob ___ as he ___ research work.
    A) was busy / was doing   B) was busy / had done
    C) was busy / have done   D) was busy / would be doing
    E) is busy / will be doing

55. He says he ___ his friend whom he ___ for many years.
    A) meets / didn't see   B) met / hadn't seen
    C) met / haven't seen   D) will meet / sees
    E) meet / doesn't see

56. That day when we were in the restaurant each one ___ what he ___ .
    A) receive / orders   B) received / had ordered
    C) is receiving / is ordering   D) will receive / would order
    E) is received / is ordered

57. - What ___ you ___ here?
    - I ___ for my friend.
    - How long ___ you ___ for him?
    - For twenty minutes.
    A) are / doing / am waiting / have / been waiting
    B) do / do / am waiting / do / wait
    C) are / doing / wait / have / been waiting
    D) have / done / am waiting / are / waiting
    E) are / doing / am waiting / are / waiting

58. Julia has overslept again. She is going ___ late to her work. "I had better ___ a taxi" she thinks.
    A) being / take   B) to be / take
    C) be / to take   D) to be / to take
    E) to be / taking

59. They ___ just ___ and ___ supper now.
    A) have / come / are having   B) had / come / are having
    C) have / come / is having   D) had / come / had
    E) have / come / have

60. I usually ___ there by train but this week-end I ___ by bus.
    A) go / am going   B) went / go
    C) go / go   D) go / are going
    E) go / was going

61. You ___ very thoughtful. What ___ you ___ about?
    A) looked / was / thinking
    B) look / are / thinking
    C) look / are / think
    D) looking / are / thinking
    E) have looked / had / thought

62. His situation ___ since spring. Now he ___ much better.
    A) has improved / feel   B) improves / felt
    C) improve / is feeling   D) has improved / feels
    E) improved / has felt

63. It's evening. People ___ to their house and ___ TV
    A) come / are watching   B) have come / are watching
    C) come / watch   D) has come / are watching
    E) are coming / have watched

64. Please, ___ me the newspaper a postman ___ today.
    A) show / bring   B) shows / brings
    C) showed / brought   D) show / brought
    E) show / has brought

65. Do you ___ that woman in the corner? She ___ her dog walk.
    A) see / is having   B) saw / was having
    C) to see / is having   D) see / has
    E) seen / have

66. My dog ___ a lot but it ___ at the moment.
    A) is barking / doesn't bark   B) barked / didn't bark
    C) barks / isn't barking   D) was barking / won't bark
    E) will bark / doesn't bark

67. I ___ about it at the moment and I think that I ___ how to use it now.
    A) read / knew   B) was reading / knew
    C) am reading / know   D) read / know
    E) shall read / have known

68. Tom ___ the book since yesterday morning and he ___ it.
    A) has read / just finished
    B) has been reading / has just finished
    C) had been reading / has just finished
    D) will read / just finishes
    E) read / is just finishing

69. I ___ I ___ you there.
    A) thought / meet   B) thinks / meet
    C) think / have met   D) thinks / met
    E) think / has met

70. He ___ a very experienced teacher. He ___ French for 15 years.
    A) to be / taught   B) am / is teaching
    C) is / has been teaching D) will be / was teaching
    E) was / are teaching

71. I'm ___ to tell you the story I ___ at school today.
    A) go / hear   B) going / heard
    C) to go / hear   D) going / have heard
    E) going / had heard

72. Jimmy, Jane and Billy wanted ___ their grandfather who ___ to visit them.
    A) to impress / had come B) impressed / came
    C) will impress / comes   D) had impressed / has come
    E) to impress / to come

73. On ___ the room he ___ left and ___ his way.
    A) entering / turned / went on
    B) having entered / has turned / goes on
    C) entered / turns / went on
    D) enter / turn / goes on
    E) entering / turns / went on

74. ___ you read the book "The Godfather"? If yes, when ___ you read?
    A) did / have   B) will / do   C) have / did
    D) were / done   E) has / does

75. I ___ Tom since he ___ school.
    A) have seen / leave   B) saw / has left
    C) hadn't seen / left   D) haven't seen / left
    E) see / leave

76. He ___ me his name but I ___ it.
    A) tell / am forgetting   B) will tell / forgot
    C) told / have forgotten D) has told / shall forget
    E) was told / forgot

77. They ___ you the money before they ___ .
    A) send / leave   B) sent / left
    C) will send / leave   D) sent / had left
    E) should sent / had left

78. I ___ already ___ the doctor about it, but she couldn't ___ me.
    A) has / seen / helped   B) have / seen / help
    C) had / seen / had helped D) will / have seen / help
    E) is/having seen / is helping

79. The weather ___ as nice today as it ___ yesterday.
    A) is / was   B) are / were
    C) is / will be   D) was / were
    E) were / shall be

80. You ___ six cakes since we ___ .
    A) had / had come   B) had had / came
    C) have / come   D) have had / came
    E) have had / have come

81. The English ___ of sports and ___ themselves as good sportsmen.
    A) are fond / regard   B) is fond / regards
    C) were fond / regards   D) was fond / regards
    E) am fond / are regarding

82. The children ___ their hands and they ___ lunch now.
    A) are washing / are having B) have washed / are having
    C) wash / have   D) washed / are having
    E) wash / have had

83. Don't go out. It ___ . It ___ since morning.
    A) rains / rains   B) has rained / rains
    C) was raining / was raining D) is raining / has been raining
    E) is raining / had rained

84. I ___ you the book after I ___ it.
    A) give / read   B) shall give / had read
    C) shall give / have read D) have given / shall read
    E) am giving / read

85. She ___ all the work and now she ___ in the next room.
    A) did / rest   B) have done / rests
    C) does / rests   D) has done / is resting
    E) had done / is resting

86. She ___ this book this week and she ___ discuss it.
    A) read / can   B) has read / could
    C) had read / can   D) have read / can
    E) has read / can

87. "I hope you ___ well?" "Yes, I ___ ill for two weeks. Now I ___ well."
    A) felt / was / is   B) feel / is / am
    C) is feeling / are / is D) are feeling / have been / am
    E) was feeling / was / am

88. -___ you ___ the man for many years?
    -Yes, we ___ at Cambridge together.
    A) have / known / were   B) do / know / is
    C) were / known / were   D) have / known / was
    E) did / know / was

89. I ___ an exercise now but I ___ it in some minutes.
    A) write / finished   B) writes / will finish
    C) wrote / is finishing   D) am writing / shall finish
    E) have written / had finished

90. Last year he ___ better than he ___ now.
    A) sings / did   B) sang / is doing
    C) had sung / does   D) would sing / did
    E) had been singing / is doing

91. Students ___ already their tests and now they ___
    A) had written / hand   B) are writing / handed
    C) have written / are handing D) wrote / will hand
    E) write / hands

92. It is going to rain. I ___ glad I ___ my umbrella with me today.
    A) am/takes
    B) am/have taken
    C) is/taken
    D) are/took
    E) is/takes

93. Bill ___ his girl-friend now. That's the third time he ___ her this evening.
    A) phones / phones
    B) has phoned / phones
    C) is phoning / has phoned
    D) will phone / has phoned
    E) is phoning / had phoned

94. Here ___ your keys. The boy ___ you up to your rooms and your luggage ___ up straight away.
    A) is/show/will bring
    B) are/show/will be brought
    C) are/will show/will be brought
    D) were/will show/brings
    E) are/has shown/will bring

95. -How long ___ you ___ to stay?
    -I ___ we ___ here for a week at least.
    A) are/going/expect/shall be
    B) were/going/expected/shall be
    C) is/going/expect/are
    D) do/go/expected/are
    E) does/go/expect/will be

96. -Is this your first visit to London?
    -No, I ___ here several times before and I ___ quite at home in London.
    A) was/have felt
    B) have been/feel
    C) had been/felt
    D) has been/felt
    E) were/have felt

97. I don't know when she ___ but when she ___ I'll give her your book.
    A) will come/will come
    B) will come/come
    C) come/will come
    D) will come/comes
    E) comes/will come

98. You ___ here until your mother ___ ready to leave.
    A) will stay/is
    B) would stay/is
    C) stayed/will be
    D) are staying/had been
    E) have stayed/would be

99. Many changes ___ place since I ___ in my native town 10 years ago.
    A) has taken/was
    B) are taking/had been
    C) took/was
    D) has taken/am
    E) have taken/was

100. I ___ to America five years ago. Since then, I ___ American, and ___ nearly all I ___ there.
    A) had gone/haven't spoken/have
    B) had gone/don't speak/forget/learned
    C) was going/haven't spoken/forgot/had learned
    D) went/haven't spoken/ have forgotten/learned
    E) went/hasn't spoken/forgot/had learned

101. It has been long since I ___ him last. I ___ from him all these years.
    A) saw/haven't heard
    B) had seen/haven't heard
    C) see/don't hear
    D) saw/don't hear
    E) have seen/haven't heard

102. He was sure they ___ the station before night ___ .
    A) will reach / came
    B) would reach / came
    C) would have reached / came
    D) would reach / would come
    E) reached / came

103. - "___ you ___ this film yet?"
     - "Yes."
     - "When ___ you ___ it?"
    A) have / seen / have / seen
    B) have / seen / did / see
    C) are / going to see / did / see
    D) did / see / have / seen
    E) have / seen / are / going to see

104. -When ___ you ___ here?
     -I ___ just ___ .
    A) did/come back/have/come back
    B) have/come back/have/come back
    C) will/come/have/come
    D) do/come back/have/has come
    E) are/coming back/was/coming back

105. Look! There ___ nothing here. Everything ___ away.
    A) are / have been taken
    B) is / has been taken
    C) is / is taken
    D) is / is being taken
    E) is / will be taken

106. Everybody ___ at what ___ .
    A) was surprised/has happened
    B) was surprised/had happened
    C) is surprised/happen
    D) surprise/happen
    E) will be surprised/ happened

107. The famous writer Tolstoy ___ forever in our memories, in the books he ___ to us.
    A) will live / has left
    B) is living / will be leaving
    C) lived / leaves
    D) would be living / had left
    E) have been living / left

108. Ernest Hemingway ___ one of those people who ___ in their beds.
    A) had not been / died
    B) are / died
    C) was not / die
    D) was not / dies
    E) is being / have not died

109. If you ___ so rude to her she ___ to us earlier.
    A) were not / had come
    B) hadn't been / would have come
    C) are / would have come
    D) are / will come
    E) are not being / would come

110. "Hello, Mr. Roberts" ___ the clerk. "What ___ you ___ home your the wife today?"
    A) greet / do / take
    B) greeting / were / taking
    C) greeted / are / taking
    D) will greet / did / taken
    E) will greet / did / take

111. Two years ago she ___ and now she ___ her time visiting friends.
    A) retires / spends
    B) retired / spends
    C) had retired / spends
    D) would retire / is spending
    E) will retire / spent

112. He might ___ the accident if he ___ more careful.
    A) avoid / was
    B) have avoided / had been
    C) avoid / had been
    D) had avoided / were
    E) avoids / is

113. -Hello, Ann! I ___ you for ages. Where have you been all this time?
     -I ___ to Italy. I ___ back yesterday.
    A) didn't see/was/came
    B) haven't seen/have been/came
    C) don't see/have been/have come
    D) saw/was/came back
    E) haven't seen/had been/had come

114. -What ___ you ___ at 6 p.m. yesterday?
     -I ___ my homework. After I ___ it I played chess with my friend.
    A) did/do/did/have done
    B) was/doing/was doing/had done
    C) were/doing/was doing/had done
    D) were/doing/did/have done
    E) had/done/had done/did

115. This book ___ quite different from the one I ___
    A) is/have read
    B) was/am reading
    C) has been/read
    D) have been/reads
    E) is/read

116. -___ I ___ after the luggage or ___ you?
     -If you ___ to the luggage and pay the driver I'll go in and see about rooms.
    A) shall/look/will/see
    B) shall/look/will/will see
    C) will/look/shall/saw
    D) should/look/would/would see
    E) would/looked/will/saw

117. Nobody knows what ___ at this meeting but she ___ to him since.
    A) was said / hasn't spoken
    B) is said / hasn't spoken
    C) has said / hasn't spoken
    D) was said / didn't speak
    E) is being said / doesn't speak

TEST 8

Modals

1. Why didn't you help him? You ___ have done it.
   A) must B) can C) could D) were to E) was able to

2. A: ___ I phone you tonight?
   B: Yes, you ___ .
   A) may / may B) must / might C) could / can't D) shouldn't / shouldn't E) have to / had to

3. But I ___ stay in England for six months, and not for a fortnight as I had planned.
   A) had to B) have to C) am able to D) can E) shall have

4. -I ___ draw a circle with a pencil only, and you?
   -Neither can I.
   A) can't B) can C) may D) shan't E) couldn't

5. Last week I ___ go to town on business trip as the Ministry of Education had asked me to come.
   A) had to B) might C) should D) could E) was able to

6. If one person is careless with a library book, then it ___ be read by others.
   A) can't B) couldn't C) may D) can E) mightn't

7. After a book is written, it passes through the heads of very many different workers. Each worker works carefully, for there ___ not be any mistakes.
   A) must B) couldn't C) could D) might E) has to

8. He tried, but ___ persuade nobody.
   A) could B) couldn't C) can D) might E) won't

9. People who know a foreign language ___ learn a second one easily.
   A) may B) should C) mustn't D) can E) needn't

10. ___ I have a word with you, please?
    A) may B) had to C) have to D) must E) am able to

11. At first I ___ skate well, now I ___ .
    A) couldn't / can B) may / can C) mustn't / can D) should / shouldn't E) must / needn't

12. She said they ___ go to the cinema if they liked.
    A) must B) may C) can D) had to E) could

13. - What is your sister doing?
    - She ___ be watching TV.
    A) may B) can't C) needn't D) has to E) could

14. I didn't want to go there but I ___ .
    A) must B) might C) shall D) can't E) had to

15. - ___ I go there now?
    - No, you ___ .
    A) can / hadn't to B) am / aren't C) must / needn't D) might / could E) should / will

16. - Where is he?
    - He ___ be walking in the park.
    A) can't B) is able to C) has to D) must E) ought to

17. Visitors ___ stay in the hospital after ten pm.
    A) might not B) needn't C) couldn't D) must not E) didn't have to

18. We had an appointment yesterday afternoon but he ___ see me.
    A) might not B) cannot C) have to D) mustn't E) wasn't able to

19. I didn't ___ ring her up for she did it herself.
    A) had to B) could C) be to D) have to E) must

20. The rain was so sudden that everybody ___ take a shelter.
    A) can B) could C) have to D) are to E) had to

21. If you ___ fix a radio, you ___ repair a TV too.
    A) can / will be able to B) must / may C) couldn't / can D) need / has to E) may / needn't to

22. -I've examined you very carefully. I think all you ___ is a good rest.
    -But I'm still feeling sick. Why don't you look at my tongue?
    -It ___ a rest too.
    A) must / may B) might / can C) need / could D) should / have to E) need / needs

23. You ___ do this work yourself, if you try.
    A) can B) had to C) must D) was able to E) were to do

24. Guests of the hotel ___ warn the clerk in advance when they leave.
    A) can B) may C) must D) is to E) had to

25. My mother ___ neither read nor write after the operation and now I ___ help her.
    A) have to / must B) could / have to C) couldn't / had to D) were able / can E) might / need

26. ___ I borrow your text-book? I've left mine at home.
    A) am able to B) must C) have to D) need E) may

27. People ___ exercise regularly, otherwise they will get out of shape.
    A) must not B) should C) can D) might E) has to

28. "Ma," said a little girl, "Willie wants the biggest piece of cake, and I think I ___ have it, because he was eating cakes two years before I was born."
    A) couldn't B) has to C) is to D) should E) had to

29. -I live near my work.
    -So you ___ go to the office by crowded buses.
    A) have to B) are able to C) don't have to D) would have to E) can't

30. -I ___ go to the cinema yesterday.
    -Why?
    -Because I ___ complete my work.
    A) can't / must B) couldn't / had to C) didn't have to / may D) wasn't to / need E) should / have to

31. The skier broke his leg and ___ compete in the recent Olympic Games.
    A) couldn't B) mustn't C) had to D) can't E) might

32. I ___ not translate this text yesterday. ___ you help me to translate it tonight?
    A) could / can   B) can / can   C) may / may
    D) had to / could   E) can / must

33. Does Larry ___ leave home at 7.30?
    A) have to   B) must   C) has to
    D) need   E) should

34. -___ any of you speak Italian?
    -No, but we are learning it and I hope we ___ speak it next year.
    A) must / will have to   B) may / have got to
    C) can / shall be able to   D) could / could
    E) might / had to

35. - ___ I take your pen for a moment?
    - Certainly.
    A) must   B) may   C) might
    D) should   E) will

36. I ___ speak English last year but I ___ do it now.
    A) must / can   B) could / can   C) might / may
    D) couldn't / can   E) might / could

37. Mother, ___ I go for a walk? I've done all my work.
    A) have to   B) am to   C) may
    D) must   E) might

38. I was ill and ___ go to school for some days.
    A) can't   B) must   C) could
    D) couldn't   E) can

39. - ___ we do this work now?
    - ___ . You can do it tomorrow.
    A) Can / Yes, you can   B) Must / No, you needn't
    C) May / Yes, you may   D) Could / Yes, you must
    E) Might / No, you might not

40. "___ I do anything for you?", the secretary asked the stranger.
    A) can   B) had to   C) must
    D) have to   E) am

41. - ___ we finish our work today?
    - No, you ___ .
    A) Can / couldn't   B) May / can   C) Have to / can
    D) Must / needn't   E) Had / needn't

42. I ___ go to the library for books as I often write compositions at school.
    A) can   B) could   C) may
    D) might   E) have to

43. It ___ rain this afternoon.
    A) had to   B) may   C) is able to
    D) could   E) might

44. ___ the director receive me now?
    A) Have to   B) Is able   C) Can
    D) Is to   E) Has to

45. Who ___ help him at 2 yesterday?
    A) have to   B) is to   C) can
    D) need   E) had to

46. I said that after all that had happened I ___ run away to my aunt's.
    A) could   B) might   C) had to
    D) need   E) was able to

47. - ___ I go to the cinema?
    - No, you ___ . The film is for grown ups.
    A) may / mustn't   B) can / needn't   C) could / can't
    D) must / may not   E) shall / haven't

48. Teacher: "You ___ ring me up when you ___ my advice.
    A) could / need   B) may / need   C) can / will need
    D) must / needed   E) have to / need

49. "Never put off till tomorrow what you ___ do today."
    A) have to   B) must   C) might
    D) can   E) should

50. -I ___ understand the rule; ___ I take the examination another time?
    -Yes, of course.
    A) could / can   B) may / may   C) can't / may
    D) mustn't / must   E) may / can

51. Pupils ___ speak only English at their English lessons.
    A) must not   B) must   C) cannot
    D) has to   E) had to

52. The lecturer mentioned the name of the town several times, but unfortunately I ___ remember it.
    A) can   B) could   C) may
    D) could not   E) may not

53. -Must I do this exercise too?
    -No, you ___ . It isn't necessary.
    A) can't   B) may not   C) mustn't
    D) needn't   E) oughtn't to

54. Mother, look, I ___ skate well.
    A) can   B) may   C) must
    D) have to   E) ought to

55. I'm sorry you ___ smoke here.
    A) had to   B) can't   C) could
    D) must   E) have to

56. We ___ protect our nature from pollution.
    A) need   B) had to   C) are to
    D) may   E) must

57. He is very helpless, I ___ help him.
    A) need   B) might   C) have to
    D) can   E) may

58. Excuse me, ___ you tell me the time?
    A) may   B) must   C) might
    D) can   E) are able to

59. My grandfather's ill and I ___ go to see him today, I ___ go with you.
    A) can / can't   B) have to / can't   C) may / have to
    D) need / must   E) be able to / may not

60. The Browns ___ not return on Sunday, as the weather was bad.
    A) may   B) could   C) have to
    D) must   E) can't

61. I looked through this book about 2 hours, but ___ find anything interesting.
    A) can't   B) couldn't   C) had to
    D) can   E) hadn't to

62. You ___ do this for it's necessary.
    A) may   B) can   C) have to
    D) has   E) could

63. You ___ work hard at your English.
    A) must   B) mustn't   C) can't
    D) has to E) may not

64. We ___ read much in the original if we want to learn a foreign language.
    A) had to   B) can   C) must
    D) may   E) could

65. We ___ do it by midday if we had the instruments.
    A) may   B) can   C) must
    D) could   E) might

66. You ___ get a visa before you go abroad next summer.
    A) may   B) can   C) could
    D) have to   E) will have to

67. If you want to improve your English you ___ work very hard.
    A) can   B) may   C) are able to
    D) had to   E) must

68. You've been traveling all day. You ___ be very tired.
    A) must   B) can't   C) might
    D) ought to   E) shouldn't

69. My eyesight isn't very good. I ___ wear glasses for reading.
    A) might   B) have to   C) can
    D) may   E) could

70. He said that I ___ look around.
    A) might   B) may   C) can
    D) has to   E) is able to

71. He ___ agree with your suggestion.
    A) may not   B) need   C) are able to
    D) are to   E) have to

72. My son fell ill yesterday, I ___ stay at home.
    A) must   B) can   C) may
    D) need   E) had to

73. I will not read this book, you ___ do it if you want.
    A) can   B) might   C) have to
    D) can't   E) must

74. ___ you show me those black shoes? How much are they?
    A) may   B) must   C) can
    D) have to   E) will have to

75. I ___ leave the party early last night, because I wasn't very well.
    A) must   B) may   C) could
    D) have to   E) had to

76. She ___ lift me up with one hand.
    A) may   B) need   C) can
    D) to have to   E) to be able to

77. You ___ work if you don 't want to.
    A) must not   B) can't   C) needn't
    D) must   E) has to

78. You ___ come and have dinner with us some day.
    A) was able to B) could   C) has to
    D) is to   E) must

79. It was very difficult to hear. I ___ understand what she was saying.
    A) can't   B) may not   C) wasn't able to
    D) couldn't   E) could

80. The teacher told us that we ___ work harder at our English.
    A) have   B) must   C) could
    D) may   E) had to

81. A little girl comes up to her mother and asks if she ___ go to the park with her friend.
    A) couldn't   B) can't   C) must
    D) may   E) has to

82. If you are ill and ___ go to school you ___ learn everything what you have missed.
    A) can / must   B) can't / must   C) may / can
    D) has to / may   E) can't / might

83. The dog had run away and the children ___ find it though they were looking for it the whole day.
    A) can   B) can't   C) could
    D) may   E) could not

84. As Mr. John hadn't got the dictionary at hand, he ___ guess the meaning of the word.
    A) should   B) can   C) has to
    D) must   E) had to

85. Mark Twain ___ easily ___ across the Mississippi River.
    A) must / swim   B) had to / swam   C) may / swim
    D) would / to swim   E) could / swim

86. It was late but the pupils ___ stay at school for an additional lesson.
    A) could   B) must   C) had to
    D) needed   E) might

87. The children have done their homework. I think they ___ have a rest now.
    A) may   B) might   C) are
    D) could   E) will be able to

88. -Shall I retell the text?
    -___ . You can only translate it.
    A) Yes, you will.   B) Do, please.   C) No, you didn't.
    D) No, you needn't.   E) Yes, you may.

89. Patient: Must I go to the hospital?
    Doctor: No, you ___ . You ___ stay at home.
    A) can't / had to   B) mustn't / had to   C) needn't / may
    D) are able to / can   E) shouldn't / might

90. It ___ rain today. There are so many clouds in the sky.
    A) can   B) has to   C) may
    D) should   E) mustn't

91. I understood that he ___ never ___ back.
    A) will / come   B) doesn't / came   C) won't / home
    D) would / come   E) wouldn't / come

92. My son is ill so I ___ stay at home.
    A) mustn't   B) has to   C) can
    D) may   E) have to

93. Must I do it? No, you ___ . It isn't necessary.
    A) couldn't   B) may not   C) needn't
    D) can't   E) shouldn't

94. I feel sick and tired. So I ___ go to school.
    A) can   B) could   C) haven't to
    D) am not able to   E) am able to

95. He was very poor and ___ marry a woman eight years older than himself.
    A) must   B) could   C) needed
    D) had to   E) might

96. Children ___ go to school at the age of 7.
    A) can   B) must   C) may
    D) has to   E) could

97. - ___ I trouble you for a moment?
    - Yes, certainly. What ___ I do for you?
    A) can / might   B) may / can   C) must / may
    D) could / may   E) can / must

98. He ___ know her address. Ask him.
    A) need   B) must   C) could
    D) might   E) have to

99. You knew he was ill. You ___ have visited him.
    A) can   B) might   C) need
    D) have to   E) may

100. May I take this pen? No, you ___ .
    A) can   B) may   C) mustn't
    D) need   E) haven't to

101. -"What's happened to the dog? It isn't here."
     -"Dan ___ have taken it with him."
    A) had to   B) was to   C) might
    D) may   E) could

102. You ___ give it back to me before you go.
    A) might   B) couldn't   C) must
    D) need   E) had to

103. That's a question nobody ___ answer.
   A) must not   B) were to   C) cannot
   D) might   E) can

104. ___ God be with you.
   A) can   B) must   C) may
   D) had to   E) is to

105. A fool man ___ ask more questions than a wise man ___ answer.
   A) may / can   B) can / must   C) may / might
   D) can / might   E) must / could.

106. "Does Jack shave?"
   "No, he's got a beard so he ___ shave."
   A) hasn't to   B) hasn't got to   C) don't have to
   D) can't   E) will be able to

107. Don't worry. You ___ do it just now. You ___ do it tomorrow.
   A) must / can   B) should / may   C) can / could
   D) had to / must   E) needn't / can

108. I ___ speak English well now but I hope I ___ speak next year.
   A) could / can   B) can't / shall be able to
   C) must / shall have to   D) may / may
   E) am able to / shall have to

109. The driver ___ have taken a side road.
   A) shall   B) need   C) may
   D) have to   E) is to

110. He ___ have replaced the tire, it was still quite good.
   A) could   B) can   C) needn't
   D) had to   E) should

111. How ___ I tell her that her life will be ruined from this day on? I think, I can't.
   A) must   B) need   C) may
   D) shall   E) can

112. It was so warm that we ___ wear our coats. It was very pleasant.
   A) couldn't   B) didn't have to   C) shouldn't
   D) mightn't   E) mustn't

113. They will get hungry on the train; I think, you ___ give them some sandwiches.
   A) should   B) could   C) might
   D) had to   E) needn't

114. You ___ a raincoat. You are wet through.
   A) must have worn   B) may wear
   C) should have worn   D) could wear
   E) needn't have worn

115. "You ___ choose any present you like, take it, please", said mother.
   A) might   B) could   C) may
   D) have to   E) are able to

116. -Have you looked through these newspapers?
   -No, I haven't. I ___ write an article.
   A) has to   B) had to   C) mustn't
   D) can   E) might

117. We didn't go out last night. We ___ to the cinema but we decided to stay at home.
   A) could have gone   B) must have gone   C) should go
   D) are to go   E) needn't go

118. I was at home yesterday. You ___ have called and taken the dictionary.
   A) must   B) may   C) could
   D) can   E) had to

119. - When I was a child I ___ draw well.
   - And now? ___ you do it now?
   A) must / may   B) could / can   C) should / need
   D) may / could   E) ought to / can't

120. That day as I ___ to be there at 5 sharp, I ___ to take a taxi.
   A) am / had to   B) is / may   C) was / had to
   D) were / can   E) were / had to

121. You ___ read this book: you are grown up.
   A) may   B) might   C) has to
   D) can't   E) may not

122. I ___ come to see you tonight as I ___ answer many questions.
   A) can / may   B) can't / have to   C) can't / can not
   D) must / had to   E) may / may not

123. Last night the plane ___ land because of the sudden change of the wind.
   A) must   B) may   C) has to
   D) had to   E) can

124. ___ he speak French as English last year?
   A) can   B) may   C) had to
   D) can't   E) could

125. She said that he ___ take her dictionary.
   A) may   B) can   C) is allowed
   D) is able   E) might

126. As my sister was taking an examination I ___ look after her baby yesterday.
   A) could   B) had to   C) must
   D) was able to   E) should

127. "He ___ in the house now," thinks the girl.
   A) could   B) may be   C) might be
   D) had to be   E) will be

128. Your brother is ill, so he ___ go out for a walk.
   A) can   B) could   C) may
   D) might   E) must not

129. It ___ rain today, we ___ see clouds in the sky.
   A) has to / can   B) must / have to   C) could / can't
   D) may / can   E) might / must

130. Charles Dickens ___ go to school at an early age, as he ___ help his family.
   A) should / would   B) couldn't / had to
   C) must / couldn't   D) might / should
   E) had not to / would

131. They ___ tell the truth, but they ___ .
   A) had to / can't   B) have to / couldn't   C) must / can't
   D) are to / couldn't   E) may /had to

132. I have very little time and I ___ take a taxi.
   A) may   B) could   C) should
   D) have to   E) have

133. You ___ this. Why didn't you use a chance?
   A) can do   B) could have done   C) must do
   D) may do   E) need do

134. I ___ send him a letter yesterday.
   A) am   B) can   C) may
   D) had to   E) should

135. She told him he ___ go home.
   A) may   B) can   C) ought
   D) might   E) have to

136. No matter how she ___ try the door ___ open.
   A) can / should   B) could / must   C) should / will
   D) might / wouldn't   E) must / ought to

137. ___ I take your book ? I ___ write many exercises tomorrow.
   A) must / must   B) should / have to
   C) may / shall have to   D) might / had to
   E) can / would

138. She ___ get up and she ___ stay in bed as she is seriously ill.
    A) must / has to   B) can't / has to   C) should / is to
    D) may / must   E) is able / shall

139. My cousin ___ read and write when he was five.
    A) could   B) may   C) have to
    D) must   E) can

140. We ___ to meet at the theatre entrance at a quarter to eight yesterday.
    A) are   B) must   C) have
    D) were   E) couldn't

141. They ___ do this the day after tomorrow. Now they are very busy.
    A) may   B) can   C) must
    D) will be able to E) were able to

142. I ___ write to Ann. I haven't written to her for ages.
    A) can   B) must   C) had to
    D) could E) may

143. This work ___ be done at once.
    A) can   B) must   C) ought
    D) should   E) may

144. The teacher said they ___ all go home.
    A) may   B) have to   C) might
    D) can   E) be able to

145. -How ___ I get to the nearest bus stop?
    -You ___ go straight and then turn to the left.
    A) must / can   B) can / must   C) should / may
    D) may / have to   E) could / might

146. Oh, you are seriously ill. I think you ___ consult a doctor and if he tells you to keep to bed you ___ do.
    A) may / might   B) must / can't   C) should / must
    D) have to / couldn't E) has to / may

147. Tom ___ pass his exam in Literature and now he is working hard as he ___ take it again.
    A) can't / was able   B) must / had to   C) may / could
    D) couldn't / has to E) can't / had to

148. ___ I come in? No, you ___ I am very busy now. I ___ write a report.
    A) can / can / must   B) must / may not / had to
    C) may / can't / must   D) may / may not / can
    E) must / mustn't / may

149. - ___ I smoke here?
    - No, you ___ .
    A) can / may   B) may / mustn't   C) can / should
    D) can / can't   E) may / need

150. You ___ break the body but you ___ break the spirit.
    A) may / can't   B) could / can't   C) must / must
    D) can / might not   E) may / may

151. He ___ tell you how glad he is.
    A) was able   B) couldn't   C) can't
    D) had to   E) have

152. He said that I ___ telephone him any time I liked.
    A) can   B) will   C) might
    D) have to E) will have to

153. I have a terrible headache. I ___ do anything.
    A) could   B) can   C) should
    D) can't   E) might

154. -___ your son speak English?
    -No, but he ___ when he was a schoolboy.
    A) has to / must   B) could / may   C) might / can
    D) can / could   E) may / must

155. Find the synonym of the modal verb "must".
    A) I might be wrong.
    B) We may go there.
    C) He needs a dictionary.
    D) You can say anything.
    E) He was to go to the south.

156. You ___ easily find the newspaper now where his article was printed.
    A) might   B) need   C) couldn't
    D) had to E) can

157. He said that his father was ill and they ___ go to see the doctor yesterday.
    A) can   B) had to   C) are able
    D) can't   E) may

158. Sorry, I ___ go with you. I ___ finish my work.
    A) may not / must   B) couldn't / have to   C) mustn't / can
    D) can't / must   E) am / could

159. Last year in April I ___ use my umbrella more often than in May.
    A) must   B) can   C) were able
    D) had to E) may

160. "___ I have another cup of tea?"
    A) must   B) might   C) may
    D) would   E) need

161. -I wonder where the chief is.
    -He ___ be in his office. I've seen him this morning.
    A) is able to   B) should   C) have to
    D) must   E) had to

162. "I ___ go, Padre, the students will be waiting for me.
    A) is to   B) can   C) be able
    D) must   E) may

TEST 9 — Conditionals

TYPE 1

1. If I ___ my entrance exams I ___ the happiest man in the world.
   A) shall pass / would be   B) passed / am
   C) passed / would have been   D) will pass / be
   E) pass / shall be

2. We ___ to see you next Sunday, if I ___ well.
   A) shall come / shall get   B) come / get
   C) comes / will get   D) will come / get
   E) will come / will get

3. What ___ you ___ if the train ___ in time?
   A) will be / doing / come   B) did / will not come
   C) do / didn't / come   D) have / done / came
   E) will / do / doesn't come

4. If I ___ time I ___ you.
   A) have / help   B) shall have / shall help
   C) shall have / help   D) have / shall help
   E) has / help

5. If you ___ tickets we ___ Paris.
   A) will buy / shall visit   B) bought / visit
   C) buys / visited   D) were buying / should visit
   E) buy / shall visit

6. Tomorrow if the weather ___ fine we ___ out of the town for hours.
   A) is / shall get   B) will be / shall get
   C) be / will get   D) were / get
   E) was / get

7. If you are free, watch the film they ___ on TV.
   A) shows   B) showed
   C) are showing   D) had showed
   E) have showed

8. If the weather ___ fine we ___ to the park.
   A) is / shall go   B) was / go
   C) are / go   D) was / shall go
   E) would / should go

9. If my friend ___ to our town next year I ___ him the sights of the city.
   A) shall come / show   B) comes / shall show
   C) has come / is showing   D) is coming / will show
   E) come / shows

10. They ___ not object to your plan if you ___ it up perfectly.
    A) do / will make   B) did / won't make
    C) will / make   D) would / don't make
    E) don't / shall make

11. If ___ rings me up, tell him that I'll be in at 5.
    A) anything   B) nobody
    C) everything   D) something
    E) somebody

12. Hark will play tennis if he ___ his work in time.
    A) finish   B) finished
    C) finishing   D) finishes
    E) will finish

13. If you ___ after two hares you ___ none.
    A) run / catch   B) run / will catch
    C) will run / will catch   D) will run / catch
    E) ran / catch

14. If we ___ English four times a week we'll learn it.
    A) are having   B) had
    C) have   D) will have
    E) shall have

15. If you ___ in a hurry, leave that to me.
    A) will be   B) were
    C) are   D) was
    E) are being

16. If you ___ to please an English person, be very polite about his garden.
    A) want   B) wanted
    C) are wanting   D) will want
    E) wants

17. You ___ miss the train if you ___ a taxi.
    A) will / don't take   B) - / don't take
    C) will / won't take   D) don't / take
    E) will / would not take

18. We ___ if they ___ .
    A) shall not know / come   B) don't know / will come
    C) didn't know / will come   D) haven't known / come
    E) knew / will come

19. If you want to be healthy you should ___ .
    A) sleep much   B) attend all your classes
    C) go in for sports   D) give up sport
    E) take up art

20. If you ___ Oxford you ___ some interesting old buildings.
    A) will visit / will see   B) visit / see
    C) visited / will see   D) visits / see
    E) visit / will see

21. He ___ the picture if it ___ him.
    A) will buy / impressed   B) would buy / impresses
    C) will buy / impresses   D) will buy / will impress
    E) has bought / impress

22. If you ___ Ann tomorrow, can you tell her to phone?
    A) saw   B) see
    C) will see   D) had seen
    E) shall see

23. They are expecting us. They will be disappointed if we ___ .
    A) won't come   B) didn't come
    C) haven't come   D) don't come
    E) came

24. I wonder whether he ___ if nothing unexpected ___
    A) comes / detains   B) will come / detain
    C) comes / will detain   D) will come / will detain
    E) will come / detains

25. I ___ my work in time if you ___ me.
    A) shall do / help   B) should do / helps
    C) do / will help   D) have done / help
    E) had done / would help

26. The British people think, if you ___ tea ___ you.
    A) were depressed / cheers
    B) are depressed / will cheer
    C) shall be depressed / will cheer
    D) have been depressed / cheered
    E) had been depressed / was cheered

27. If you ___ wisely you ___ cheerfully.
    A) command / will be obeyed
    B) commanded / would have been obeyed
    C) had commanded / would be obeyed
    D) command / will obey
    E) will command / are obeyed

28. If it ___ this winter, we ___ skiing.
    A) snow / go   B) snows / shall go
    C) snowed / went   D) snowed / had gone
    E) had snowed / had gone

29. I ___ them some money if they ___ me for.
    A) send / ask
    B) sent / asked
    C) will send / will ask
    D) would send / ask
    E) shall send / ask

30. If I ___ shopping I ___ some food tomorrow.
    A) went / shall buy
    B) go / buy
    C) am going / would buy
    D) go / shall buy
    E) had gone / would buy

31. We ___ for a walk if the weather ___ fine.
    A) shall go / will be
    B) go / is
    C) shall go / is
    D) go / will be
    E) goes / will be

32. If the weather ___ fine we ___ for a walk.
    A) was / shall go
    B) is / shall go
    C) will be / shall go
    D) is / go
    E) was / went

33. Mike ___ certainly if he ___ not busy.
    A) comes / is
    B) will come / will be
    C) will come / is
    D) comes / will be
    E) come / will be

34. I ___ next week if I can ___ a train ticket.
    A) go / get
    B) shall go / got
    C) went / got
    D) shall go / get
    E) was going / get

35. I ___ happy if I ___ the university.
    A) shall be / shall enter
    B) am / shall enter
    C) am / enter
    D) shall be / enter
    E) was / enter

36. Our fate is in her hands now. If she ___ tickets we ___ away.
    A) has bought / would fly
    B) buys / shall fly
    C) buy / fly
    D) bought / fly
    E) bought / would have flown

37. If you ___ in their talk they ___ .
    A) don't interfere / will quarrel
    B) didn't interfere / have quarreled
    C) doesn't interfere / will quarrel
    D) interfere / should have quarreled
    E) interfere / are quarrelling

TYPE 2

1. If he ___ in Tokyo he ___ us.
   A) was / will visit
   B) were / would visit
   C) will be / will visit
   D) is / would visit
   E) are / will visit

2. If he ___ ill, he would stay at home.
   A) is
   B) be
   C) were
   D) am
   E) are

3. What would you do if a millionaire ___ you a lot of money.
   A) gave
   B) give
   C) will give
   D) giving
   E) gives

4. If it ___ not so late I should go with you.
   A) was
   B) were
   C) is
   D) be
   E) are

5. If I ___ the car myself I ___ you use it.
   A) needed / would let
   B) don't need / would let
   C) didn't need / wouldn't let
   D) didn't need / would let
   E) doesn't need / would let

6. This house ___ better if they ___ it, ___ the grass and ___ flowers.
   A) will look / painted / cut / plant
   B) would look / paint / cut / planted
   C) looks / painted / cut / planted
   D) looked / painted / cut / planted
   E) would look / painted / cut / planted

7. If I ___ you I ___ never her.
   A) am / shall forgive
   B) was / don't forgive
   C) were / would forgive
   D) had been / forgave
   E) shall be / would have forgiven

8. I am sure Mike will lend you some money. I ___ if he refused.
   A) will be surprised
   B) am surprised
   C) would have been surprised
   D) would be surprised
   E) were surprised

9. Many people would be out of work if that factory ___ down.
   A) had been closed
   B) were closed
   C) was closing
   D) is closed
   E) will be closed

10. I ___ living in England if the weather ___ better.
    A) don't mind / was
    B) didn't mind / is
    C) wouldn't mind / is
    D) wouldn't mind / were
    E) wouldn't mind / will be

11. She promised that nothing ___ till he ___ home.
    A) would be done / came
    B) is done / came
    C) will be done / comes
    D) has been done / came
    E) have been done / comes

12. If he ___ generous, he ___ the poor.
    A) were / would have helped
    B) is / would have helped
    C) was / would help
    D) was / will help
    E) were / would help

13. If I ___ you I ___ French next year.
    A) am / learn
    B) was / shall learn
    C) am / should learn
    D) were / should learn
    E) were / learned

14. I ___ so upset, if I ___ you.
    A) am / am
    B) wouldn't be / were
    C) was / were
    D) won't be / are
    E) shall be / would be

15. If you ___ the Prime Minister what ___ you ___ ?
    A) are / would / have done
    B) were / would / do
    C) will be/will / do
    D) have been / are / doing
    E) will have been / would / be doing

16. If he ___ here he ___ help you.
    A) is / would help
    B) were / would help
    C) would be / helped
    D) was / helps
    E) are / helping

17. I hoped if I ___ by the 10 o'clock train I ___ change for a bus.
    A) went / shan't
    B) should go / hadn't
    C) go / shan't
    D) went / shouldn't
    E) go / shouldn't

18. Mr. Bond said if Mr. Blake ___ at 10 o'clock he ___ to see him later.
    A) is busy / will come
    B) will be busy / will come
    C) was busy / came
    D) was busy / would come
    E) is busy / comes

19. ___ your mother wouldn't be angry with you.
    A) If you didn't get bad marks.
    B) If you got bad marks.
    C) If you haven't got bad marks.
    D) If you get bad marks.
    E) If you don't get bad marks.

20. If I were you ___ .
    A) I shall wait
    B) I wait
    C) I would wait
    D) I waited
    E) I'm waiting

21. If all the seas ___ one sea, what a great sea it ___ .
    A) were/would be
    B) is/will be
    C) would be/were will
    D) be/will be
    E) were / will be

22. ___ you really ___ me if I ___ away?
    A) would / follow / go
    B) will / follow / am going
    C) would / follow / went
    D) will / follow / would have gone
    E) will / follow / goes

23. If I ___ you I ___ him.
    A) am / will help
    B) to be / would help
    C) were / would help
    D) is / would have helped
    E) are / will help

24. If my brothers ___ time now they ___ help me.
    A) has / helps
    B) have had / have helped
    C) have / help
    D) is having / helped
    E) had / would help

25. If I ___ the power I ___ people smoking at school and public places.
    A) had / stop
    B) could have / would stop
    C) had / stopped
    D) had / would stop
    E) have / would stop

26. If Helen ___ anywhere in the world she ___ in India.
    A) lived / live
    B) live / would live
    C) could live / would live
    D) didn't live / would live
    E) lives / would live

27. If I ___ you I ___ harder.
    A) am / will work
    B) will be / work
    C) be / shall work
    D) were / would work
    E) am / would have worked

28. If I ___ you I ___ it.
    A) am / regretted
    B) am / regrets
    C) were / wouldn't regret
    D) is / didn't regret
    E) was / regret

TYPE 3

1. The boy ___ at home an hour before, if he ___ his school at one o'clock last Monday.
   A) would be / had left
   B) was / would leave
   C) had been / had left
   D) has been / left
   E) would have been / had left

2. ___ he would have signed his name in the corner.
   A) If he would have painted the picture
   B) If he paints the picture
   C) If he painted the picture
   D) If he shall paint the picture
   E) If he had painted the picture

3. If you ___ him yesterday he ___ you everything.
   A) asked / told
   B) has asked / will tell
   C) asked / would tell
   D) had asked / would have told
   E) would ask / would have told

4. If you had worked more, you ___ to translate this article yesterday.
   A) are able
   B) was able
   C) were able
   D) would have been able
   E) has been able

5. If you ___ to me yesterday, we ___ this article.
   A) came / shall translate
   B) would come / should translate
   C) had come / should have translated
   D) come / having translated
   E) were coming / should be translating

6. If you ___ in time yesterday we ___ this work.
   A) had come / would have done
   B) came / would have done
   C) come / shall go
   D) will come / shall go
   E) come / would go

7. She ___ if she ___ that she was ill.
   A) won't go out / knows
   B) didn't go out / knew
   C) hasn't gone out / has known
   D) wouldn't have gone out / had known
   E) doesn't go out / knows

8. -He failed his exam and he has to take it again in summer.
   -If he ___ so many lessons he ___ it. But he didn't follow the teacher's advice.
   A) didn't miss / would pass
   B) hadn't missed / would have passed
   C) doesn't miss / won't pass
   D) has missed / will pass
   E) will miss / doesn't pass

9. "I ___ my work if you ___ me then. Thank you."
   A) shan't finish / don't help.
   B) haven't finished / don't help.
   C) shouldn't have finished / hadn't helped.
   D) don't finish / won't help.
   E) didn't finish / helped.

10. - Why didn't you do the task?
    - If he ___ everything from the start we ___ it earlier.
    A) hadn't spoilt / would have done
    B) didn't spoil / would have done
    C) doesn't spoil / will do
    D) wouldn't spoil / did
    E) spoils / shall have done

11. The children ___ in the open air if the weather ___ better last Sunday.
    A) had played / was
    B) played / was
    C) would have played / had been
    D) will play / is
    E) would play / were

12. If we ___ a letter at 8 o'clock yesterday, we ___ on the same day.
    A) got / started
    B) had got / had started
    C) would get / had started
    D) had got / should have started
    E) should have got / had started

13. If you ___ so many lessons you ___ all the exams.
    A) didn't miss / passed
    B) hadn't missed / would have passed
    C) haven't missed / would pass
    D) missed / will pass
    E) had missed / would have passed

14. I would have sent you a postcard while I was on holiday if I ___ your address.
    A) had   B) was having
    C) had had   D) will have
    E) would have

15. If the driver ___ the accident wouldn't have happened.
    A) didn't   B) doesn't stop
    C) won't stop   D) hadn't stopped
    E) hasn't stopped

16. If he ___ all right, he ___ with us yesterday.
    A) was / was
    B) had been / would have been
    C) were / would be
    D) had been / would be
    E) would be / would have been

17. If she ___ a new dress, I ___ her then.
    A) hadn't been wearing / might have recognized
    B) didn't wear / might recognize
    C) wasn't wearing / might recognize
    D) wouldn't wear / would recognize
    E) hadn't been wearing / might recognize

18. They ___ for the examination better if they ___ about it earlier.
    A) would prepare / knew
    B) prepare / know
    C) prepared / knew
    D) would have prepared / had known
    E) will prepare / know

MIXED

1. If you ___ the dictionary yesterday I ___ to translate the article today.
   A) had given / would be able   B) give / am able
   C) gave / will be able   D) will give / am able
   E) have given / was able

2. If the help ___ in time, the experiment ___ tomorrow afternoon.
   A) had offered / would he completed
   B) was offered / will be completed
   C) had been offered / would be completed
   D) is offered / would be completed
   E) are offered / will be completed

3. If you ___ these pills yesterday you ___ well now.
   A) had taken / would be   B) took / would be
   C) had taken / had been   D) took / will be
   E) would take / would be

4. If I had gone to the party last night, I ___ tired now.
   A) will be   B) am
   C) would be   D) would have been
   E) was

5. She didn't know if the letter ___ by the time she ___
   A) would be delivered / will come
   B) would deliver / comes
   C) will be delivered / came
   D) would have been delivered / came
   E) was delivered / came

6. If he ___ English well, he ___ the article without difficulty yesterday.
   A) knew / would have translated
   B) know / had been translated
   C) has known / will have translate
   D) would know / will translate
   E) would have known / would have translated

7. If you ___ harder last year you ___ English well now.
   A) worked / had known
   B) work / will know
   C) had worked / would know
   D) will work / know
   E) would work / would have known

8. If you ___ harder you ___ more money and now you ___ to buy a car.
   A) have worked / would earn / could
   B) had worked / would have earned / would be able
   C) had worked / would earn / will be able
   D) has worked / would have earned / could
   E) worked / would earn / might

9. If you ___ your swimming suit you would be able to go for a swim now.
   A) don't leave   B) weren't leaving
   C) will not leave   D) haven't left
   E) hadn't left

Book 1 Part C 132 Conditionals - Mixed

TEST 10 — Comparatives - Superlatives

1. It was ___ music I have ever heard.
   A) more beautiful
   B) less beautiful
   C) the most beautiful
   D) beautiful
   E) most beautiful

2. It's ___ powder I have ever used.
   A) good   B) -   C) the best
   D) best   E) better

3. John is ___ of all to act.
   A) quickest   B) quick   C) -
   D) quicker   E) the quickest

4. He is ___ strong ___ his brother.
   A) as / like   B) similar / as   C) as / as
   D) strong / than   E) so / as

5. English grammar is ___ than Russian one.
   A) easy   B) easier   C) the easiest
   D) as easy as   E) not so easy

6. I have ___ time than he does.
   A) bigger   B) larger   C) most
   D) less   E) least

7. This girl is ___ intelligent than the rest of the class.
   A) most   B) the most   C) more
   D) the more   E) much

8. Two heads are ___ than one.
   A) good   B) bad   C) worse
   D) worst   E) better

9. Alice came late, Philip came later, and Tony ___
   A) latest   B) last   C) the latest
   D) later   E) the last

10. Mark Twain, one of ___ and ___ American writers, lived in a small town in his childhood.
    A) greater / most popular
    B) great / more popular
    C) the greatest / most popular
    D) more great / the most popular
    E) most great / the popular

11. -Why didn't you discuss this question yesterday?
    -It was ___ important than the others.
    A) little   B) least   C) the least
    D) -   E) less

12. Your English is much ___ now. You've made ___ mistakes this time.
    A) best / least   B) better / less   C) the best / less
    D) good / less   E) best / the least

13. The Thames is ___ river in Great Britain.
    A) the longest   B) long   C) longest
    D) -   E) longer

14. Do you have ___ or ___ rain this autumn than the last one.
    A) many / little   B) more / less   C) more / fewer
    D) much / less   E) more / few

15. Please, tell me something ___ than this old joke.
    A) interesting   B) less interesting
    C) more interesting   D) the most interesting
    E) the least interesting

16. This question is ___ than the first one, let's discuss it tomorrow.
    A) important   B) less important
    C) the most important   D) the least important
    E) -

17. Do you have ___ or ___ sunny days this summer?
    A) more / few   B) many / less   C) much / little
    D) more / less   E) many / few

18. We have ___ money than they have.
    A) little   B) much   C) less
    D) few   E) many

19. -Please, give me this bouquet of flowers. I think it is ___ than the rest ones.
    -But it's ___ .
    -Never mind. I'll buy it.
    A) beautiful / expensive
    B) more beautiful / more expensive
    C) the most beautiful / most expensive
    D) beautiful / most expensive
    E) most beautiful / most expensive

20. Of the four girls Marcia is ___ .
    A) prettiest   B) prettier   C) -
    D) the prettiest   E) prettier

21. It's ___ to go by car than by train.
    A) cheap   B) cheaper   C) -
    D) cheapest   E) the cheapest

22. It is much ___ to speak English than to understand
    A) -   B) the most difficult   C) more difficult
    D) difficult   E) most difficult

23. He's ___ intelligent than my brother.
    A) most   B) good   C) better
    D) more   E) last

24. He is ___ among his classmates.
    A) old   B) taller   C) the youngest
    D) short   E) higher

25. This is ___ place I've ever seen.
    A) dirty   B) the dirtiest   C) more dirty
    D) dirtier   E) -

26. What is ___ crime than loss of time.
    A) greater   B) greatest   C) great
    D) -   E) most great

27. He came home in the ___ mood.
    A) sun   B) sunniest   C) more sunny
    D) much sunny   E) sunnier

28. False friend is ___ than open enemies.
    A) worst   B) worse   C) the worst
    D) -   E) bad

29. "Why do you always buy five loaves, no ___ and ___?"
    A) many / little   B) less / fewer   C) more / much
    D) more / less   E) most / less

30. It's ___ in here than it is in the street.
    A) hot   B) the hottest   C) -
    D) hotter   E) hottest

31. Are the streets of London ___ or ___ than the streets of Belfast?
    A) the narrowest / wider   B) narrow / wide
    C) narrower / wider   D) more narrow / wide
    E) most narrow / most wide

32. I make ___ mistakes now than last year.
    A) few   B) fewer   C) -
    D) the fewest   E) fewest

33. The weather is much ___ pleasant than it usually is at this time.
    A) most   B) more   C) the most
    D) little   E) -

34. To spend summer at the seaside is ___ pleasant than in the town.
    A) -   B) less   C) the most
    D) more   E) the least

35. It is ___ and ___ to live here than there.
    A) warm / most pleasant   B) warmer / pleasant
    C) warmest / pleasanter   D) warmer / more pleasant
    E) warm / more pleasant

36. Are the streets ___ and ___ than they were some years ago?
    A) wide / cleaner   B) wider / cleanest
    C) widest / cleaner   D) widest / cleanest
    E) wider / cleaner

37. Lake Baikal is ___ lake in the world.
    A) deeper   B) the deepest   C) deep
    D) deepest   E) -

38. Many people think Scotland is ___ than England.
    A) most beautiful   B) the least beautiful   C) least beautiful
    D) more beautiful   E) beautiful

39. My luggage was ___ than my friend's.
    A) good   B) the best   C) many
    D) less   E) the worst

40. Her love must be ___ than mine.
    A) the deepest   B) most deep   C) deepest
    D) deeper   E) deep

41. His plan is ___ practical of all.
    A) -   B) more   C) much
    D) the most   E) most

42. I think it is ___ beautiful landscape I've ever seen.
    A) more   B) more   C) the most
    D) the best E) worst

43. Our garden is ___ than that of the neighbor's.
    A) little   B) the least   C) most difficult
    D) the best   E) less

44. Which are ___ comfortable, sandals or tennis shoes?
    A) most   B) little   C) more
    D) much   E) any

45. In the second half, the team played ___ and the game ended in a draw.
    A) earliest   B) the worst
    C) interesting   D) the most interesting
    E) worse

46. Area of Brazil is ___ than that of England.
    A) less   B) most   C) much
    D) larger   E) many

47. He was ___ angry than I had expected.
    A) most   B) more   C) much
    D) better   E) good

48. Which question do you think is ___ difficult one?
    A) -   B) much   C) more
    D) the most   E) most

49. There is ___ milk in this jug than in that one.
    A) most   B) the most   C) the least
    D) little   E) less

50. The weather today is ___ than yesterday.
    A) good   B) bad   C) fine
    D) worse   E) the worst

51. Her version is ___ original than yours.
    A) much   B) the most   C) more
    D) many   E) the least

52. Mr. Smith liked his ___ son than others.
    A) older   B) elder   C) the oldest
    D) all   E) the eldest

53. Yesterday Camilla was ___ girl there.
    A) happy   B) happiest   C) the happiest
    D) -   E) happier

54. Traveling is ___ in summer than in winter.
    A) interesting   B) more interesting
    C) the most interesting D) farther
    E) largest

55. Which bird flies ___, the swallow or the gull?
    A) -   B) fast   C) faster
    D) the fastest   E) fastest

56. My clothes have never been ___ than this.
    A) cleaner   B) cleanest   C) clean
    D) -   E) the cleanest

57. My dress is ___ than yours, isn't it?
    A) long   B) -   C) the longest
    D) longest   E) longer

58. Which is ___ country in the UK?
    A) industrial   B) the most industrial
    C) more industrial   D) most industrial
    E) industrial

59. Do you speak English ___ than Spanish?
    A) most fluently   B) fluent   C) rather fluent
    D) fluently   E) more fluently

60. Margaret types ___ than Mary does.
    A) fast   B) -   C) faster
    D) the fastest   E) fastest

61. This chair is ___ comfortable than that one.
    A) -   B) little   C) less
    D) the least   E) least

62. Both of them are skiing very badly, but she is skiing even ___ than he is.
    A) bad   B) -   C) worse
    D) the worst   E) worst

63. The ___ you start, the ___ you'll finish.
    A) soon / more quickly
    B) sooner / more quickly
    C) sooner / quickly
    D) soon / quickly
    E) more sooner / more quickly

64. The play I saw yesterday was ___ than this one.
    A) bad   B) worse   C) worst
    D) the worst   E) -

65. Mary is much ___ than Ann, though they are both alike.
    A) tall   B) taller   C) the tallest
    D) -   E) tallest

66. My arm felt hot but that ache was ___ than the pain that burned in my breast.
    A) stronger   B) the strongest   C) strongest
    D) strong   E) -

67. Your dictation is ___ of all.
    A) bad   B) worse   C) good
    D) well   E) the worst

68. My room is ___ than yours.
    A) large   B) -   C) larger
    D) the largest   E) largest

69. "Family album" is ___ than "Follow me".
    A) interesting   B) most interesting
    C) more interesting   D) the most interesting
    E) as interesting

70. This exercise is ___ than the last one.
    A) -   B) good   C) best
    D) better   E) the best

71. The longer the way the ___ tired we are.
    A) most   B) more   C) the most
    D) -   E) much

72. Today ___ and ___ people come to understand that learning English is ___ .
    A) many / much / most useful   B) many / more / more useful
    C) little / less / useful   D) most / less / less useful
    E) more / more / useful

73. ___ goods you sell, ___ profit you'll make.
    A) more / more   B) the more / more
    C) more / the more   D) the more / the more
    E) the most / the most

74. Yesterday was ___ day we've had this summer.
    A) hotter   B) hot   C) the hottest
    D) hottest   E) much hotter

75. Girls are much ___ than boys.
    A) quiet   B) the quietest   C) so quiet
    D) quieter   E) too quiet

76. Do you need any ___ help?
    A) much   B) more   C) many
    D) most   E) the most

77. Actions speak ___ than words.
    A) loudest   B) less louder   C) most loudest
    D) louder   E) loudly

78. It is ___ work I've ever done.
    A) bad   B) worse   C) better
    D) the worst   E) best

79. Uncle Nick was the ___ son of the family.
    A) old   B) young   C) big
    D) elder   E) next

80. This room is ___ than that one.
    A) large   B) little   C) the smallest
    D) the least   E) smaller

81. The twenty second of December is ___ day of the year.
    A) short   B) much shorter   C) shorter
    D) the shortest   E) less short

82. Who is ___ important person in the history of your country?
    A) more   B) less   C) high
    D) popular   E) the most

83. I think, today the British television program "The Weakest Link" is ___ popular of all the TV programs.
    A) more   B) much   C) the most
    D) -   E) most

84. John is ___ but ___ boy in the family.
    A) taller / the youngest   B) the tallest / the youngest
    C) taller / younger   D) more tall / the most young
    E) the tallest / more young

85. This is ___ rule in this book.
    A) difficult   B) more difficult   C) most difficult
    D) the most difficult   E) much difficult

86. Antalya in my opinion is ___ place for rest.
    A) good   B) less   C) the least
    D) the best   E) better

87. The story I have read is ___ in this book.
    A) the most interesting   B) more interesting
    C) less interesting   D) much interesting
    E) few interesting

88. They showed me their best suits but, if these are their ___ suits, what are their ___ ones like.
    A) best / worst   B) better / worst   C) best / worse
    D) worse / better   E) good / worst

89. He works the ___ but earns the ___ .
    A) harder / less   B) more / most   C) less / harder
    D) hardest / least   E) least / harder

90. Monte Carlo is one of ___ beautiful cities in the world.
    A) much   B) the most   C) much more
    D) the least   E) less

91. Let me know if you hear any ___ news.
    A) many   B) more   C) most
    D) the most   E) much

92. It's ___ weather anyone can remember.
    A) better   B) the worst   C) bad
    D) worse   E) least

93. I think the cotton of Turkmenistan is one of ___ in the world.
    A) better   B) good   C) the best
    D) longer   E) richer

94. I have done ___ part of my homework.
    A) difficult   B) more difficult   C) most difficult
    D) the most difficult   E) -

95. Can't you type ___ ?
    A) shortly   B) more carefully   C) hardly
    D) nearly   E) completely

96. The teacher said that the results of our tests were not good. She added that ___ of all was mine.
    A) bad   B) better   C) worse
    D) good   E) the worst

97. Which season is ___ in Thailand?
    A) rainy   B) the rainiest   C) most rainy
    D) more rainy   E) raining

98. ___ I can stay is three hours.
    A) long   B) longer   C) more longer
    D) the longest   E) much longer

99. Unfortunately her disease was ___ than we thought at first.
    A) more serious   B) serious
    C) the most serious   D) most serious
    E) the more serious

100. This is ___ clown I've ever seen.
     A) good   B) better   C) the best
     D) well   E) bad

101. Vatican is ___ country in Europe.
     A) less   B) the smallest   C) smaller
     D) greater   E) small

102. It's ___ today ___ it was yesterday.
     A) a little warmer / that   B) little warm / than
     C) more warmer / that   D) a little warmer / than
     E) the warmest / than

103. We discover that we were ___ in early youth than somewhat ___ .
     A) wise / late   B) wiser / later   C) wise / latest
     D) wisest / late   E) wise / later

104. The higher is the fence, ___ is the neighbor.
     A) better   B) the best   C) best
     D) good   E) the better

105. ___ people live in the South than in the North of America.
     A) more   B) most   C) the most
     D) much   E) many

106. You won't find ___ restaurant than this. They'll all be ___ expensive ___ this one.
     A) the cheapest / as / as   B) a cheaper / as / as
     C) a cheaper / as more   D) the cheapest / most / than
     E) a cheaper / most / as

TEST 11 — Infinitive - Gerund

1. He admitted ___ the car but denied ___ it by himself.
   A) stealing / doing B) to steal / doing
   C) stealing / to do D) to steal / to do
   E) stealing / to be done

2. How do you feel if someone laughs at you? I hate people ___ at me.
   A) laughed B) laughing C) being laughed
   D) to be laughed E) to be laughing

3. We often hear her ___ at concerts.
   A) sings B) singing C) sang
   D) to sing E) have sung

4. Mother wants him ___ to the country during the summer.
   A) goes B) go C) to go
   D) will go E) went

5. ___ many books on history helps school children to get knowledge about the past of different nations.
   A) read B) reads C) has read
   D) will read E) reading

6. As well as ___ I like ___ .
   A) running/walking B) run/walk C) run/walked
   D) running/walked E) run/to walk

7. The man ___ the newspaper is my brother.
   A) read B) reads C) has read
   D) reading E) will read

8. It is very pleasant ___ in the river on hot days in the summers.
   A) bathe B) bathing C) bathed
   D) to bathe E) having bathed

9. He warmed himself by ___ hot tea.
   A) drinking B) drank C) drunk
   D) to drink E) is drinking

10. It's very pleasant ___ on the beach in summer.
    A) lie B) to lie C) lay
    D) lain E) lying

11. -I hope my dream will come true this year.
    -And what do you dream of?
    -Oh, I dream of ___ a law school and ___ a lawyer.
    A) to enter / to become B) enter / become
    C) entering / becoming D) entered / become
    E) to enter / becoming

12. He sat in the arm-chair ___ a newspaper.
    A) read B) reads C) reading
    D) had read E) is read

13. ___ English is the best way of ___ it.
    A) speak / learn B) speaking / learning
    C) to speak / to learn D) spoke / learning
    E) speak / learning

14. She dreams of her son's ___ a director of the company.
    A) becoming B) is becoming C) become
    D) became E) was becoming

15. Why didn't you try ___ yourself a job?
    A) found B) have found C) finding
    D) to find E) to be found

16. We watched the coastline ___ slowly.
    A) recede B) to recede C) recedes
    D) have receded E) receded

17. Nobody heard her ___ English.
    A) spoke B) speaks C) speak
    D) was speaking E) had spoken.

18. We stopped at the motorway services ___ something to eat.
    A) to get B) to have got C) was getting
    D) get E) got

19. I'm not really interested in ___ to the University.
    A) go B) went C) going
    D) being gone E) have gone

20. This article is worth ___ .
    A) reading B) read C) to read
    D) has read E) will read

21. They have got enough money ___ to the cinema.
    A) go B) having gone C) to have gone
    D) to go E) going

22. I saw him ___ a newspaper.
    A) to read B) to have read C) reading
    D) to be reading E) having read

23. Watch me ___ the fence.
    A) jumping B) jumped C) to jump
    D) had jumped E) did jump

24. She decided ___ to Spain for her holidays.
    A) to go B) go C) goes
    D) to be going E) to have gone

25. In winter he spends much time in the mountains, he is fond of ___ .
    A) to skate B) skated C) skating
    D) to be skated E) having skated

26. The street was full of people ___ and ___ home.
    A) laughed / gone B) laughing / going
    C) having laughed / go D) to laugh / to go
    E) to be laughed / going

27. ___ a foreign language you can ___ great opportunities in your life.
    A) know / have B) knowing / to have
    C) knowing / have D) knows / having
    E) knowing / having

28. On ___ the classroom the teacher asked to the pupil on duty, "Who is absent?"
    A) entering B) entered C) to enter
    D) be entering E) being entered

29. Working in the garden it is pleasant ___ to music.
    A) listening B) listened C) to listen
    D) after listening E) having listened

30. You are lucky you have not got a child ___ .
    A) to look after B) should look after
    C) looking after D) having looked after
    E) is looking after

31. She saw the girl ___ in the yard.
    A) playing B) on playing C) played
    D) to play E) was playing

32. He usually left us without ___ a word.
    A) to say B) saying C) said
    D) say E) having been said

33. I'm fond of ___ in the river.
    A) have swum B) swam C) swim
    D) swimming E) having swum

34. The aim of the exhibition is ___ experience.
    A) to be exchanged B) exchanged
    C) to have exchanged D) to exchange
    E) being exchanged

35. The horse ___ the race ___ the winner of the same event two years ago.
    A) led / was   B) leading / is   C) leading / was
    D) to lead / was   E) leads / being

36. His mother was against his ___ football.
    A) play   B) was playing   C) played
    D) to play   E) playing

37. Miss Benson was looking forward to ___ the title role in the new play.
    A) play   B) playing   C) to be played
    D) played   E) being played

38. Pete likes ___ . His dream is to visit Japan.
    A) painting   B) reading   C) writing
    D) traveling E) swimming

39. My friends need ___ English
    A) learns   B) to learn
    C) to have learned D) to be learned
    E) having learned

40. When I came into the room she stopped ___ T.V.
    A) watching   B) watch   C) watched
    D) on watching E) watches

41. Which of the boys ___ in the yard is Ted?
    A) play   B) played   C) plays
    D) is playing E) playing

42. We saw them ___ the street.
    A) crossed   B) crossing   C) will cross
    D) had crossed E) will be crossing

43. It's never too late ___ .
    A) being learned   B) not to learn   C) learned
    D) learning   E) to learn

44. The girls ___ in the garden are my sisters.
    A) played   B) to play   C) playing
    D) on playing E) are playing

45. I like ___ the people happy.
    A) to have made B) made   C) making
    D) having made   E) being made

46. Besides ___ I like ___ swimming competitions.
    A) swimming / to watch   B) to swim / to watch
    C) swimming / watched   D) to swim / watching
    E) swimming / watch

47. Tom wants to read a book but Susan makes him ___ something in the paper. It's an advertisement for a better job. She wants him ___ for this job.
    A) to read / to apply   B) to read / apply
    C) read / to apply   D) reading / apply
    E) to read / applying

48. She left the room without ___ good bye.
    A) say   B) saying   C) to say
    D) said   E) on saying

49. The friends spoke of their ___ together.
    A) to go   B) going   C) gone
    D) is going   E) on going

50. If your plane has crashed high in the mountains, it's best ___ close to the plane. Rescuers have got a better chance of ___ the plane than one person alone.
    A) to keep / finding   B) keeping / found
    C) kept / to have found   D) kept / not to find
    E) keeping / being found

51. Robert saw the doctor ___ the patient.
    A) to examine   B) to have examined
    C) having examined D) being examined
    E) examine

52. The girl ___ in the yard asked me the time.
    A) play   B) to play   C) played
    D) playing   E) was playing

53. The emperor thought of ___ his state powerful.
    A) becoming   B) become   C) became
    D) having become   E) had become

54. Mother was anxious ___ her family.
    A) to see   B) seeing   C) to be seen
    D) having seen   E) being seen

55. I can't help ___ you about it.
    A) to tell   B) telling   C) having told
    D) having been told E) being told

56. Many builders and engineers from other republics began ___ to build new houses in Moscow in 1995.
    A) helping   B) would help   C) helped
    D) shall help   E) having helped

57. I have never heard him ___ French.
    A) to speak   B) speaking   C) spoken
    D) being spoken   E) to have spoken

58. Nobody expected him ___ Lola.
    A) marry   B) married   C) to marry
    D) will marry E) would marry

59. This holiday is worth ___ .
    A) celebrates   B) celebrated   C) celebrating
    D) have celebrated E) to celebrate

60. Frank is in hospital. He feels bad. He has to give up ___ and ___ beer. But he can't. He says to his wife, "Would you mind ___ some cigarettes next time?"
    A) smoking / to drink / bringing
    B) to smoke / drinking / bringing
    C) smoking / drank / bringing
    D) smoking / drinking / bringing
    E) to smoke / to drink / to bring

61. Ernest Hemingway was fond of ___ books.
    A) read   B) to read   C) reading
    D) be read   E) to be read

62. Turn on the radio. I want ___ to the news.
    A) listen   B) listening   C) to listen
    D) listened   E) have been listened

63. How do you feel if someone interrupts you? I hate people ___ me.
    A) interrupted   B) to be interrupted
    C) not to interrupt D) having interrupted
    E) interrupting

64. After ___ my work I'll join you.
    A) finish   B) to finish   C) have finished
    D) finishing   E) finished

65. Please, try ___ quiet, everyone is sleeping.
    A) be   B) to be   C) being
    D) having been   E) been

66. He enjoyed ___ .
    A) singing   B) sing   C) was singing
    D) to sing   E) sung

67. The man ___ in the garden is listening to music.
    A) work   B) is working   C) working
    D) to work   E) worked

68. ___ the article we began ___ it.
    A) reading / discuss   B) having read / discussing
    C) to read / to discuss   D) read / discussing
    E) reading / discussed

69. The man ___ a cigarette is Tom's cousin.
    A) smoked   B) to smoke   C) smoking
    D) have smoked   E) had smoked

70. I study English again, because ___ a foreign language is very important.
    A) speak   B) spoken   C) having spoken
    D) speaking   E) spoke

71. I like your ___ English.
    A) speak   B) speaking   C) was spoken
    D) have spoken   E) having spoken

72. Instead of ___ for Olga at home I decided ___ her in the street.
    A) to wait / to meet   B) waiting / to meet
    C) waiting / meeting   D) to wait / to meet
    E) wait / meeting

73. They looked at the ___ plane.
    A) flying   B) flown   C) flew
    D) being flown   E) having been flown

74. ___ the language he couldn't understand the question.
    A) know   B) knows   C) not to know
    D) known   E) not knowing

75. Which of these four young men ___ by the fire is your son?
    A) sitting   B) sit   C) will sit
    D) sits   E) sat

76. We expect him ___ tomorrow.
    A) arrived   B) to arrive   C) to have arrived
    D) to be arrived E) having arrived

77. They sat up all night ___ .
    A) talk   B) talked   C) talking
    D) to be talked E) to have talked

78. The young man didn't stop ___ although I asked him twice.
    A) is smoking   B) smoked   C) smoking
    D) smoked   E) to smoke

79. He introduced me to an acquaintance ___ that I did not know her.
    A) to believe   B) believing
    C) to have believed   D) of believing
    E) not to believe

80. I hope ___ you this evening.
    A) to see   B) to be seen   C) have seen
    D) see   E) seen

81. I am thankful for his ___ in time.
    A) came   B) come   C) to have come
    D) coming   E) to come

82. I remember the day when you took me aboard of your ship to help you in ___ the shark.
    A) hunt   B) to hunt   C) hunting
    D) hunted   E) having hunted

83. But the beaver went on ___ lace.
    A) to make   B) make   C) made
    D) making   E) have made

84. ___ with you is real pleasure.
    A) talked   B) is talking   C) on talking
    D) talking   E) talks

85. What time do you come to the office?
    -Usually at 9, but tomorrow I'll have to be there a bit earlier ___ through some documents.
    A) looking   B) looked   C) to be looking
    D) to look   E) to be looked

86. We knew nothing of his ___ a student.
    A) being   B) be   C) been
    D) to be   E) to have been

87. He remembered he was going to buy a new suit ___ the shop.
    A) pass   B) passes   C) to pass
    D) passing   E) will pass

88. ___ for better future many Asians leave their native countries ___ to Europe.
    A) hope / move   B) hoping / moves
    C) hoped / moving   D) hoping / moving
    E) hope / moving

89. She tried to be serious but she couldn't help ___ .
    A) to laugh   B) laughing   C) laughed
    D) laugh   E) having laughed

90. Would you mind ___ the door, please?
    A) to close   B) being closed   C) closing
    D) close   E) closed

91. She has nobody ___ to.
    A) talked   B) to talk   C) talk
    D) talks   E) is talking

92. I enjoy ___ in the garden at week-ends.
    A) work   B) to work   C) to be working
    D) working   E) worked

93. He is an artistic person - very good at ___ poetry.
    A) to write   B) to be written
    C) having written   D) write
    E) writing

94. ___ in Geneva for many years he knew the city well.
    A) Living   B) Lived   C) Being lived
    D) To live   E) Have lived

95. Captain was the last ___ the ship.
    A) leaving   B) is leaving   C) on leaving
    D) to leave   E) left

96. I don't mind ___ .
    A) to walk   B) be walking
    C) walking   D) having been walked
    E) to have walked

97. If you are lost in a snow storm it's best ___ a hole and sit in it until it stops ___ .
    A) digging / snowing   B) dig / snowed
    C) to dig / snowed   D) digging / snowed
    E) to dig / snowing

TEST 12

Passive voice

1. The Remembrance Day and the Veteran's Day ___ on the 11th of November every year.
   A) celebrated
   B) are celebrated
   C) will be celebrated
   D) was celebrated
   E) is celebrated

2. I hope that the truth ___ very soon.
   A) will find out
   B) will be finding out
   C) is found out
   D) will be found out
   E) shall find out

3. Everything ___ before you came.
   A) is done
   B) was done
   C) has done
   D) had been done
   E) has been done

4. -Did the company test the equipment yesterday?
   -Yes it _____.
   A) has tested
   B) had been tested
   C) had tested
   D) was tested
   E) tested.

5. People go to the tomb of the Unknown Soldier to stand in silence for a minute to honor the memory of those who ___ in wars.
   A) is killed
   B) will be killed
   C) was killed
   D) are killed
   E) were killed

6. The sports competitions which ___ on Sunday ___ by a lot of people.
   A) are held / will be visited
   B) was held / will visit
   C) will held / will visit
   D) have been held / have visited
   E) will be held / will be visited

7. The inspector is not in the town. He ___ to another place some days ago.
   A) was sent
   B) sent
   C) will be sent
   D) will send
   E) sends

8. This story ___ to everybody as the name of the first space pioneer ___ in the heart of people all over the world.
   A) knows / lives
   B) knew / lived
   C) is known / is lived
   D) is known / lives
   E) knows / is lived

9. The business letter ___ just ___ .
   A) is / written
   B) has / been written
   C) was / written
   D) were / written
   E) is / going to write

10. Business letters ___ usually on special forms.
    A) will be written
    B) are written
    C) are being written
    D) is written
    E) write

11. Sometimes a lot of guests ___ to his birthday party.
    A) had invited
    B) was invited
    C) were inviting
    D) are invited
    E) is inviting

12. The business letters ___ tomorrow.
    A) are sent
    B) is sent
    C) will be sent
    D) will send
    E) would be sent

13. All the business letters ___ yesterday. They ___ to the post office immediately.
    A) answered / take
    B) were answered / took
    C) are answered / were taken
    D) answered / took
    E) were answered / were taken

14. The special information ___ in an hour or so, that's why it ___ in the newspapers yesterday.
    A) brings / didn't publish
    B) will bring / don't publish
    C) will be brought / wasn't published
    D) will be brought / didn't publish
    E) brought / wasn't published

15. Houses ___ very quickly now.
    A) builds
    B) are building
    C) built
    D) are built
    E) were built

16. In 1834 the Houses of Parliament with the exception of Westminster Hall ___ by fire, they ___ later.
    A) destroyed / was rebuilt
    B) was being destroyed / rebuilt
    C) were destroyed / were rebuilt
    D) is destroyed / has been rebuilt
    E) destroys / rebuilds

17. You can't use this textbook now. It ___ by your friend.
    A) takes
    B) has been taken
    C) took
    D) were taken
    E) had taken

18. Many modern apartments ___ in Berlin since 1980.
    A) are built
    B) are building
    C) were built
    D) have been built
    E) has been built

19. The new film ___ in all the big theatres of the city.
    A) is demonstrated
    B) was being demonstrated
    C) is being demonstrated
    D) would be demonstrated
    E) had been demonstrated

20. Nobody likes ___ for at night.
    A) be sent
    B) is sent
    C) was sent
    D) to be sent
    E) sent

21. I ___ that I ___ at the station at 5.
    A) was told / should be met
    B) told / is being met
    C) tells / am met
    D) am told / was met
    E) will be told / would be met

22. Heroes ___ by people because they served their people and their country.
    A) is remembered
    B) was remembered
    C) are remembered
    D) had been remembered
    E) would be remembered

23. By the time we came to the bookshop all books ___
    A) are sold
    B) were sold
    C) had been sold
    D) are being sold
    E) is being sold

24. Don't touch the door, it ___ just ___ .
    A) is / being painted
    B) has / been painted
    C) is / painted
    D) will / be painted
    E) would / be painted

25. Scientific articles ___ often ___ in this paper.
    A) to be / published
    B) are / being published
    C) are / published
    D) have / published
    E) are / publish

26. The fugitive ___ from prison to prison in Germany until he ___ in prison in 1944.
    A) transferred / killed
    B) was transferred / was killed
    C) is transferred / was killed
    D) has been transferred / has been killed
    E) will be transferred / was killed

27. I ___ a card to the club and in the afternoon I went there to play bridge.
    A) had been given
    B) were given
    C) was given
    D) have given
    E) was giving

28. I hope this book ___ .
    A) will find
    B) will be found
    C) found
    D) were found
    E) had been found

29. ___ about this film tomorrow.
    A) It is an article
    B) He said
    C) I shall be asked
    D) Bob liked to tell
    E) He couldn't

30. New schools ___ in our city every year.
    A) is built
    B) are to be built
    C) will build
    D) are built
    E) have built

31. A liar ___ when he speaks the truth.
    A) don't believe
    B) isn't believed
    C) believed
    D) believe
    E) didn't believe

32. The doctor ___ just ___ for.
    A) is / sent
    B) was / sent
    C) has / sent
    D) has / been sent
    E) will / be sent

33. This year a very beautiful theatre ___ in our city.
    A) built
    B) was built
    C) has been built
    D) had been built
    E) has built

34. The Great Expectations ___ by Charles Dickens.
    A) were written
    B) is written
    C) wrote
    D) are written
    E) was written

35. In 1969 two manned spaceships ___ into space from the first space station.
    A) launch
    B) launched
    C) launches
    D) were launching
    E) were launched

36. We can't get there in time. By the time we get there the papers ___ .
    A) will be destroyed
    B) would be destroyed
    C) will have been destroyed
    D) are destroyed
    E) have been destroyed

37. This school ___ next year.
    A) will close
    B) is closed
    C) will be closed
    D) was closed
    E) would be closed

38. A woman's work ___ never done.
    A) are
    B) is
    C) will
    D) would
    E) were

39. Last Monday I received a telegram ___ by my sister on the 1st of May.
    A) sending
    B) to send
    C) had sent
    D) sent
    E) was sent

40. "I ___ the test yet today," said Ann.
    A) wasn't given
    B) hadn't been given
    C) am not given
    D) haven't been given
    E) have been given

41. I ___ about my father's death before my mother.
    A) is told
    B) shall be told
    C) had been told
    D) were told
    E) have been told

42. Someone wrote this report last week. This report ___ last week.
    A) is written
    B) was written
    C) has been written
    D) had been written
    E) would be written

43. Finally he decided to come back and live in the house of his parents which ___ by his aunt.
    A) kept
    B) was kept
    C) are kept
    D) were kept
    E) keeps

44. The people next door disappeared 6 months ago. They ___ since then.
    A) aren't seen
    B) haven't been seen
    C) weren't seen
    D) weren't being seen
    E) aren't being seen

45. It is winter. Everything ___ with snow.
    A) is covered
    B) covered
    C) were covered
    D) will cover
    E) are covered

46. The men ___ after the explosion.
    A) are said to be arrested
    B) said to be arrested
    C) are said to being arrested
    D) are said to have been arrested
    E) are said to arrest

47. -"Did someone throw those letters away?"
    -"Yes, but it was a mistake. They ___ away."
    A) mustn't be thrown
    B) shouldn't be thrown
    C) shouldn't have been thrown
    D) can't be thrown
    E) need to be thrown

48. A.: Was there any trouble at the yesterday's demonstration?
    B.: Yes, about twenty people ___ .
    A) had been arrested
    B) arrested
    C) were being arrested
    D) were arrested
    E) are arrested

49. Mike didn't have his car yesterday. It ___ at the station.
    A) was serviced
    B) were serviced
    C) had serviced
    D) had been serviced
    E) is serviced

50. You can't come in. She ___ for the TV.
    A) is interviewed   B) interviews
    C) is being interviewed D) was interviewed
    E) has been interviewed

51. I had an unpleasant feeling that I ___ .
    A) watched   B) was watched
    C) have been watched   D) was being watched
    E) will be watched

52. He'll finish the job tomorrow. The job ___
    A) is finished   B) would be finished
    C) will be finished   D) will finish
    E) was finished

53. After a thorough examination the patient ___ home.
    A) was sent   B) were sent
    C) are sent   D) to send
    E) sends

54. I ___ for shopping yesterday.
    A) is sent   B) was sent
    C) am sent   D) are sent
    E) has been sent

55. How much money ___ yesterday?
    A) is stolen   B) stole
    C) will steal   D) will be stolen
    E) was stolen

56. Ron Glib is a successful journalist. He ___ a big salary and his articles ___ in newspaper. He ___ all over the world to write about world events.
    A) pays/publish/sends
    B) paid/are published/isn't sent
    C) was paid/published/shall be sent
    D) is paid/are published/is sent
    E) will play/weren't published/sent

57. This work ___ tomorrow.
    A) is finished   B) was finished
    C) had finished   D) have been finished
    E) will be finished

58. The delegation ___ at the station by the students yesterday.
    A) meet   B) is met
    C) have been met   D) was met
    E) are met

59. Today acupuncture ___ effectively in our country.
    A) were used   B) are used
    C) is used   D) has been used
    E) had used

60. Some scrap metal ___ and ___ in the school yard by the evening last Sunday.
    A) was gathered/heaped
    B) has been gathered/heaped
    C) will be gathered/heaped
    D) had been gathered/heaped
    E) would be gathered/heaped

61. The first coins in America ___ in 1752. They were not regular in shape.
    A) are made   B) made
    C) were made   D) was made
    E) is made

62. Many magnificent palaces and museums ___ in our city lately.
    A) have built   B) has built
    C) has been built   D) have been built
    E) were built

63. A lot of books by this writer ___ into many languages of the world.
    A) translated   B) is translated
    C) were translated   D) has been translated
    E) had been translated

64. The great English scientist Isaac Newton ___ not far from Cambridge.
    A) born   B) is born
    C) are born   D) were born
    E) was born

65. May Day ___ in Great Britain with singing and dancing round a Maypole.
    A) celebrate   B) celebrated
    C) is celebrated   D) is celebrating
    E) has celebrated

66. He ate everything that ___ on the table.
    A) is leaving   B) was left
    C) were left   D) is left
    E) are left

67. He made a rush at the door without realizing it ___ by me earlier.
    A) locks   B) is locked
    C) was locked   D) am locking
    E) had been locked

TEST 13

Indirect speech

1. The teacher promised ___ .
   A) that we can learn three English songs.
   B) if we learn three English songs.
   C) we would learn three English songs.
   D) whether we would learn three English songs.
   E) who will learn three English songs.

2. Bill: "Have you seen any interesting comedy lately, Nancy?"
   Bill asked Nancy ___ .
   A) if he will see an interesting film
   B) if he saw an interesting comedy lately
   C) what comedy Nancy saw lately
   D) if she had seen any interesting comedy lately
   E) if she would see an interesting comedy

3. Nick: "Did you see a bird in the tree?"
   Nick wonders ___ in the tree.
   A) if I saw a bird.
   B) that I saw a bird.
   C) if I had seen a bird.
   D) whether I see a bird.
   E) if I have seen a bird.

4. Dick to Lucy: Have you received my telegram?
   Dick asked if ___ .
   A) Lucy had received his telegram.
   B) Lucy has received his telegram.
   C) Lucy would receive his telegram
   D) Lucy will receive his telegram
   E) Lucy received his telegram

5. Ann: Write down my address.
   Ann asked me ___ .
   A) he wrote down my address
   B) to write down her address
   C) he had written her address
   D) she writes down her address
   E) she wrote down his address

6. He said, "I'm very busy today."
   He said ___ .
   A) he had been very busy that day
   B) he is very busy today
   C) he was very busy that day
   D) I'm very busy today
   E) I had been very busy that day

7. Lena said, "Where have you been yesterday?"
   Lena asked ___ .
   A) where she had been the day before.
   B) where she had been yesterday.
   C) where she was the day before.
   D) where she could be the day before.
   E) where she hasn't been before.

8. He thought: "What am I going to do?"
   He thought ___ .
   A) what was he going to do
   B) what he was going to do
   C) what he is going to do
   D) it he was going to do
   E) what is he going to do

9. Mother asked me ___ .
   A) why I have spent all the money
   B) that I had spent all the money
   C) if I had spent all the money
   D) when I spend all the money
   E) if I will spend all the money

10. "Don't play in the street!"
    A) My mother told me don't play in the street.
    B) My mother said to play in the street.
    C) She asked me to play in the street.
    D) My mother told me not to play in the street.
    E) My mother said I should play in the street.

11. Ann: "Is your sister good at English?"
    Ann asked me ___ .
    A) that my sister is good at English
    B) if my sister was good at English
    C) whether my sister is good at English
    D) my sister is good at English
    E) her sister was good at English

12. Tom: "Don't forget to bring my book, Ann".
    Tom asked Ann: ___ .
    A) that she didn't forget to bring his book
    B) that she doesn't bring his book
    C) not to forget to bring his book
    D) not to forget to bring her book
    E) if she didn't forget to bring the book

13. Mother: "We are going to have supper".
    Mother says ___ .
    A) they are going to have supper
    B) they were going to have supper
    C) that they would have supper
    D) they won't have supper
    E) they haven't had supper yet

14. Jack said: "I was at home yesterday."
    Jack said ___ .
    A) he was at home.
    B) Jack said he was at home the day before.
    C) he will be at home.
    D) he had been at home a week ago.
    E) he had been at home the day before.

15. "Do you go in for sports?", he asked.
    He asked ___ .
    A) he went in for sports.
    B) if I went in for sports.
    C) if I'll go in for sports.
    D) I should go in for sports.
    E) if I had gone in for sports.

16. "Will Tom help me?" she said.
    She asked ___ .
    A) will Tom help her
    B) if Tom would help her
    C) whether he will help her
    D) whether would he help her
    E) that Tom would be helping her

17. Peter said, "Alice, are you busy now?"
    Peter asked Alice ___ .
    A) she was busy.
    B) if she was busy then.
    C) she would be busy.
    D) if she wasn't busy then.
    E) if she is busy.

18. My sister said: "I hope we shall go on an excursion to the lake".
    My sister said that ___ on an excursion to the lake".
    A) she hopes we will go
    B) she didn't hope that we shall go
    C) she hoped they would go
    D) she hoped we were going
    E) she hoped we can go

19. Jim and Julia have been in the restaurant for an hour and they have not been served yet. Julia is angry. "You said ___ a good place"

    A) it is
    B) it has been
    C) it will be
    D) it was
    E) it can't be

20. "Did you work at a factory 3 years ago?" she asked her friend. She asked her friend if she ___ .

    A) worked at a factory 3 years ago.
    B) had worked at a factory 3 years before.
    C) really worked at a factory 3 years before.
    D) work at a factory.
    E) worked at a factory for 3 years.

21. She said she ___ her friend for ages.

    A) didn't
    B) hadn't seen
    C) hasn't seen
    D) doesn't see
    E) saw

22. He asked her "Did anybody call this morning?" He asked her ___ .

    A) if anybody called this morning
    B) if somebody had called that morning
    C) if somebody called that morning
    D) who called that morning
    E) had called anybody that morning

23. Teacher: "Tom, read the story, please". Teacher asked Tom ___ .

    A) to read the story
    B) read the story
    C) that he reads it
    D) whether he reads the story
    E) it he read the story

24. He said "I met him in 1950". He said ___ .

    A) I met him in 1950
    B) he had been met by him in 1950
    C) he used to meet him in 1950
    D) he had met him in 1950
    E) he was meeting him in 1950

25. Jane asked Bob: "What did you buy yesterday?" Jane asked Bob what ___ .

    A) he would buy the next day
    B) he bought yesterday
    C) he had bought the day before
    D) he has just bought
    E) his friend had already bought

26. He said, "I do not want to see this film". He said that ___ .

    A) he did not want to see that film.
    B) he doesn't want to see a film.
    C) he didn't want to see this film.
    D) he wanted to see that film.
    E) not to see that film.

27. He says "What do the pupils study?" He asks ___ .

    A) what do the pupils study.
    B) what the pupils study.
    C) what the pupils studied.
    D) what the pupils have studied study.
    E) whether the pupils study something.

28. My mother told me ___ .

    A) did not go there.
    B) that I can go there.
    C) not to go there.
    D) not going there.
    E) let not go there.

29. The director wondered ___ .

    A) if I know English.
    B) If I knew English.
    C) he knows English.
    D) how I know English.
    E) who has known English.

30. Mary says "I clean my room every day." Mary says that ___ .

    A) I clean her room every day.
    B) she cleans my room every day.
    C) she cleaned her room every day.
    D) she cleans her room every day.
    E) her room was cleaned every day.

31. - "Have you seen my daughter?" a woman is asking her neighbor. A woman is asking her neighbor ___ her daughter.

    A) has she seen
    B) have I seen
    C) if she has seen
    D) if they have seen
    E) have you seen

32. He ___ me if I ___ a taxi yesterday.

    A) will ask / takes
    B) ask / take
    C) is asking / shall take
    D) asked / had taken
    E) will ask / take

33. She asked in surprise ___ .

    A) if he had really read all the books
    B) if this is what her mother buys her
    C) if the cafe is still open
    D) whether I have already read his article
    E) did she caused much trouble

34. The doctor asked his nurse ___ .

    A) when is she going to give the medicine to the
    B) if she would come in time the following day
    C) if the patient prepared for the operation
    D) if the tests are ready for applicants
    E) when the patient feels asleep tell me

35. They ___ us that they ___ from their families for more than a year.

    A) tell / were not hearing
    B) would be told / hear
    C) had told / don't hear
    D) told / had not heard
    E) told / will be hearing

36. Teachers always tell their pupils ___ .

    A) not to cross street when the traffic light is red
    B) doesn't cross the road on red traffic light
    C) don't ask many questions if they are not
    D) when they come to the lesson
    E) they helped their parents

37. I wondered ___ .

    A) if the train had come on time
    B) had the train come on time
    C) whether the train comes on time
    D) if the train will come on time
    E) when the train is due to come

38. She promised her friends she ___ and ___ them the next day.

    A) had come / had seen
    B) will come / see
    C) would come / see
    D) comes / sees
    E) came / saw

39. "You must do what you are told".
    She said ___ .

    A) that must do what I was told
    B) what have to do what I was told
    C) what had to do what I was told
    D) that she must do what she was told
    E) she had to do what she was told

40. The sergeant said that nothing ___ from the two boys since they ___ at the Victoria Station.

    A) was heard / saw
    B) will be heard / were seen
    C) had been heard / were seen
    D) had heard / saw
    E) would have heard / were seen

41. Nick whispered: "I know that the boys were angry with me".
    Nick whispered that ___ .

    A) he knows that the boys were angry with me
    B) he knew that the boys were angry with him
    C) he knows that the boys were angry with him
    D) I know that the boys were angry with me
    E) he knew that the boys had been angry with him

42. Alice is told: "Clean your teeth twice a day!"
    Alice is told ___

    A) clean her teeth twice a day
    B) if she cleans her teeth twice a day
    C) clean your teeth twice a day
    D) to clean her teeth twice a day
    E) cleaned her teeth twice a day

43. I am always asked ___ .

    A) why am I late   B) are you late
    C) is he absent   D) why was I present
    E) if I am on duty

44. Julia continued, "You said ___ good service."

    A) you knew the owner and always got
    B) you know the owner and have got
    C) you know the owner and get
    D) you know the owner and will get
    E) you know the owner and are going to get

45. Julia continued, "You said ___ ."

    A) you have been here before
    B) you were here yesterday
    C) you will be here tomorrow
    D) you are here now
    E) you had been here before

46. He wanted to know ___ .

    A) whether she knows him
    B) if she knew him
    C) that she knew him
    D) what she knew him
    E) did she know him

47. "When will you be there, Tom?" asked Dan.
    Dan asked Tom ___ .

    A) when you will be there
    B) when he will be there
    C) when he would be there
    D) when his friend would be there
    E) when you would be there

48. He said to me: "I'll come as soon as I can".
    He told me that ___ .

    A) he came as soon as he would be able
    B) he would come as soon as I could
    C) he comes as soon as he can
    D) he would come as soon as he could
    E) I would come as soon as I could

49. He has just said, "I want to speak to you".
    He has just said ___ .

    A) he wants to speak to me
    B) he wanted to speak to me
    C) I want to speak to her
    D) he had wanted to speak to me
    E) he will want to speak to me

50. Mother told me "Don't stay out long".
    Mother told me ___ .

    A) did not stay out long
    B) not to stay out long
    C) that I mustn't stay out long
    D) I shouldn't stay out long
    E) stay out long

51. "Where did they spend the vacation?"
    Tom said ___ .

    A) they came back.
    B) they had spent it at the seaside.
    C) they were young.
    D) they left for an hour.
    E) they have spent it at home.

52. The secretary said to the visitor: " When did you graduate from the University?"
    The secretary asked the visitor ___ .

    A) when he graduates from the University.
    B) when did he graduate from the University.
    C) when he had graduated from the University.
    D) when did she graduate from the University.
    E) he graduated from the University.

53. What will you do if Jack is out when you come?
    She asked me ___ .

    A) what would I do if Jack was out when I came
    B) what I will do if Jack is out when I come
    C) what I would do if Jack was out when I came
    D) what Jack would do if I was out when he came
    E) what I will do if Jack was out when I came

54. Jane said, "I shall help you."
    Jane said ___ .

    A) she helped us   B) she will help him
    C) she helps us   D) she would help us
    E) she had helped us

55. The manager wondered ___ .

    A) if the customers' answer can be positive
    B) if the visitors are coming
    C) whether the letters are being posted
    D) if the paper has been typed
    E) if the secretary had come

56. I ___ I ___ her back.

    A) thought / would get   B) thought / shall get
    C) think / had got   D) thinks / am get ting
    E) doesn't think / get

57. The father wondered ___ .

    A) what mark his daughter gets
    B) where the mother is
    C) how his son does at school
    D) if his daughter had passed her exams
    E) whether everybody is at home

58. The teacher asked her pupils ___ .

    A) where are their textbooks
    B) where their textbooks are
    C) where their textbooks were
    D) be quiet, please, listen to me
    E) why they open the text books

59. I ___ my mother___ want to meet her new son-in-law for the first time in my presence.

    A) knows / will not
    B) had known / will not
    C) knew / would not
    D) know / had not
    E) shall know / did not

60. The man said:" I have brought all my things ".
    The man said ___ .

    A) I have brought all his things.
    B) that he had brought all his things.
    C) he has brought all his things.
    D) they have brought all his things.
    E) that he brought all his things.

61. "Don't make so much noise, Michael," said Ellen.
    Ellen told Michael ___ so much noise.

    A) to make
    B) not to make
    C) do make
    D) don't make
    E) didn't make

62. A foreigner asked: "How do English people spend their Sundays?"
    A foreigner asked how ___ their Sundays.

    A) do English people spend
    B) did English people spend
    C) English people spent
    D) English people spend
    E) had English people spent

63. The film director was asked ___ .

    A) if he likes to play on grass
    B) which airline he works for
    C) if he had ever won an Oscar
    D) that he took part in the concert
    E) why he is nervous before the match

64. The police officer asked us ___ .

    A) are we going that way
    B) where we were going
    C) when did the tram stop
    D) if could we stop at the traffic light
    E) whether we speak English

65. He said that ___ .

    A) his friend is learning English
    B) our classroom will be cleaned tomorrow
    C) they were going to the nearest post-office
    D) his car was stolen a few weeks ago
    E) there is nothing to do

66. He said to her, "Don't enter the room".
    He ordered her ___ the room.

    A) not to enter
    B) to enter
    C) didn't enter
    D) doesn't enter
    E) do not enter

67. "How far do I have to walk?" she asked me.
    She wanted to know how far ___ to walk.

    A) she had
    B) she has
    C) I have
    D) I had
    E) she will have

68. She told him that she ___ to see him the following DAY.

    A) will come
    B) come
    C) came
    D) would come
    E) comes

69. "Did you sleep well?" I asked him.
    I asked him if ___ well.

    A) he sleeps
    B) he slept
    C) he had slept
    D) you slept
    E) you did sleep

70. "Were you at the Zoo last night?" asks Jane.
    Jane asks ___ at the Zoo last night.

    A) that I was
    B) if I was
    C) if I had been
    D) if I am
    E) whether was I

71. "Whose birthday is it?" said Jane.
    Jane asked whose birthday ___ .

    A) it is
    B) it
    C) it was
    D) is it
    E) it had been

72. "Where do you live?" the boy asked.
    The boy wanted to know where ___ .

    A) do I live
    B) did I live
    C) I live
    D) I lived
    E) I had lived

73. "Where did you live?" my boss asked.
    My boss wanted to know where ___ .

    A) do I live
    B) did I live
    C) I live
    D) I had lived
    E) I lived

74. "I spoke to Jane last week," she said.
    She said ___ .

    A) I spoke to Jane last week.
    B) she had spoken to Jane last week.
    C) she had spoken to Jane a week before.
    D) I had spoken to Jane a week before.
    E) she spoke to Jane a week before.

75. "Don't wait for me, Ann," said Tom.
    Tom told Ann ___ .

    A) to wait for him
    B) not to wait for him
    C) didn't wait for him
    D) don't wait for him
    E) if she waited for him

76. The manager asks the secretary ___ .

    A) if Mr. Smith would be busy at little next day
    B) if Mr. Smith will be busy at 11 tomorrow
    C) if Mr. Smith had been busy at 11
    D) has Mr. Smith been busy by 11 today
    E) will Mr. Smith be busy at 11 tomorrow

77. He was sure that he ___ this time.

    A) will fail
    B) wouldn't fail
    C) fails
    D) failed
    E) will not fail

78. "Can you open the door for me, my son?" asked an old woman.
    An old woman asked a young ___ the door for her.

    A) can he open
    B) he opens
    C) does he open
    D) if he can open
    E) to open

79. She said, "I lost the key of my room."
    She said that ___ .
    A) she had lost the key of her room
    B) she lost the key of my room
    C) I had lost the key of my room
    D) I lose the key of my room
    E) she lost the key of the room

80. I asked Nelly, "What are you looking for?"
    I asked Nelly what ___ looking for.

    A) are you
    B) she was
    C) were you
    D) was she
    E) she is

TEST 14

When – while – where – as soon as

1. ___ you tell him about it when you ___ him?
   A) did / see   B) does / saw
   C) will / see   D) would / see
   E) do / will see

2. Tomorrow when you ___ the sun ___ .
   A) woke up / shines   B) have woken up / was shining
   C) wake up / will be shining   D) will wake up / will shine
   E) woke up / shined

3. When my sister ___ at the college 2 years ago she ___ to learn several foreign languages.
   A) was studying / tried   B) studies / tries
   C) studied / was trying   D) was studying / was trying
   E) studies / trying

4. When I ___ that morning the sun ___ high in the sky.
   A) will wake up / had shone   B) have waken up / shines
   C) shall wake up / was shining   D) woke up / was shining
   E) woke up / will be shining

5. When I ___ the letter I wondered what ___ .
   A) got / had happened   B) get / happens
   C) got / happened   D) had got / had happened
   E) got / has happened

6. I ___ to know when you ___ .
   A) don't want / will come   B) shall want / come
   C) want / had come   D) didn't want / come
   E) didn't want / are coming

7. When I ___ home my mother ___ me that my friend ___ me an hour before.
   A) had come / told / had called
   B) came / told / called
   C) came / told / had called
   D) was coming / told / called
   E) came / was telling / had called

8. I ___ still, when you ___ .
   A) am working / will return
   B) shall be working / return
   C) was working / are returning
   D) shall have been working / have returned
   E) was working / are returned

9. When Harris ___ her she ___ Paris.
   A) is meeting / was leaving   B) met / was leaving
   C) had met / left   D) meets / left
   E) met / will leave

10. When he ___ in London, it ___ heavily.
    A) arrive / rains   B) arrives / rained
    C) arrived / was raining   D) will arrive / rains
    E) arrived / is raining

11. It ___ when we ___ home.
    A) rained / came   B) rained / was coming
    C) was raining / came   D) will rain / came
    E) rained / shall come

12. When we ___ the beach the rain ___ already ___ .
    A) leave / has / started   B) will leave / have / started
    C) left / had / started   D) left / have / started
    E) are leaving / was / starting

13. What ___ you ___ when I ___ ?
    A) did / do / returned   B) are / doing / shall return
    C) will / be doing / return   D) do / do / return
    E) have done / am returning

14. When I ___ him up they said that he ___ an hour ago.
    A) call / left   B) called / has left
    C) should call / has left   D) call / leaves
    E) called / had left

15. When you ___ me up yesterday it ___ hard.
    A) rings / will rain   B) rang / was raining
    C) will rang / will rain   D) ring / rains
    E) had rung / had rained

16. When the woman was out a postman ___ a letter.
    A) brings   B) bring
    C) brought   D) had brought
    E) has brought

17. I hope it ___ when you ___ to London.
    A) doesn't rain / will get   B) is raining / get
    C) won't be raining / get   D) will rain / will get
    E) rained / have got

18. When the lesson ___ we ___ home.
    A) are over / go   B) is over / goes
    C) is over / shall go   D) will be over / go
    E) will be over / shall go

19. What ___ you ___ when your father returned?
    A) will / do   B) were / doing
    C) was / do   D) will / be doing
    E) were / do

20. When we ___ in Seville we ___ sightseeing.
    A) are / went   B) were / went
    C) shall be / go   D) are / go
    E) had been / go

21. ___ when he was painting the ceiling.
    A) He found his passport   B) He burnt his hand
    C) He bought a new car   D) He wrote a letter
    E) He fell off the ladder

22. It ___ since morning when we ___ .
    A) has rained / went out   B) had been raining / went out
    C) was raining / go out   D) rained / will go out
    E) rained / went out

23. When I ___ back to the table, six soldiers ___ there.
    A) came / were sitting   B) comes / were sitting
    C) has come / sit   D) came / are sitting
    E) came / will sit

24. When I ___ younger I ___ an idea of a wife who ___ with me in my thoughts as well as aims.
    A) was / had / will be   B) was / had / would be
    C) had been / had / is   D) have been / have / will be
    E) was / had had / had been

25. When I ___ school I ___ the university.
    A) shall finish / shall enter   B) finish / enter
    C) shall finish / enter   D) finish / shall enter
    E) finish / entered

26. I visited my sister when she ___ in Moscow.
    A) lived   B) lives
    C) were lived   D) is living
    E) were living

27. We ___ have our supper when our mother ___ from the market.
    A) shall / comes   B) - / comes
    C) - / will come   D) shan't / come
    E) shall / come

28. The passengers ___ for the train for 20 minutes when it ___ into the station.
    A) waited / pulls   B) had waited / pulled
    C) had been waiting / pulled   D) will wait / had pulled
    E) are waiting / was pulled

29. Yesterday when I ___ her she ___ me about you.
    A) have met / told   B) was meeting / told
    C) have met / would tell   D) have met / tell
    E) met / had told

30. When I came in my mother ___ dinner.
    A) cooked   B) were cooking
    C) will cook   D) have cooked
    E) was cooking

31. When I ___ home, I ___ a friend of mine.
    A) was going / met   B) go / meet
    C) was going / was meeting D) are going / meet
    E) were going / met

32. I ___ terrible when I ___ that morning.
    A) felt / wake up   B) feels / wake up
    C) felt / woke up   D) feel / woke up
    E) felt / had woken up

33. When they ___ about it there ___ much trouble.
    A) finds out / be   B) found out / were
    C) is finding out / is   D) find out / will be
    E) found out / had been

34. Lane ___ through the morning papers when the telephone ___ .
    A) was looking / rang   B) were looking / rang
    C) are looking / rung   D) have looked / ring
    E) looked / is ringing

35. A ship ___ near the Malta Islands when the men on board ___ a dolphin in the water.
    A) was fishing / noticed   B) fished / noticed
    C) was fishing / will notice D) is fishing / noticed
    E) fished / notices

36. How fast ___ you ___ when the accident ___?
    A) were / driving / happened   B) did / drive / was happening
    C) will / drive / had happened D) are / driving / will happen
    E) - / drive / happens

37. I ___ my hand when I ___ the dinner.
    A) was burning / cooked   B) had burnt / am cooking
    C) shall burn / shall cook D) burnt / was cooking
    E) have burnt / cooked

38. We ___ ready when you ___ home.
    A) are / will come   B) shall / come
    C) shall be / will come   D) shall be / come
    E) will be / came

39. Two hours ago when the children ___ in the yard a terrible storm ___ .
    A) were playing / began
    B) played / began
    C) were playing / were beginning
    D) played / were beginning
    E) play / begins

40. It ___ for three hours when we ___ home.
    A) will have been raining / came
    B) is raining / come
    C) rained / came
    D) rains / came
    E) had been raining / came

41. While we ___ an article mother ___ dinner.
    A) were translated / was cooking
    B) were translating / cooked
    C) have been translating / is cooking
    D) translated / had cooked
    E) are translating / was cooking

42. He looked at the carpet while ___ for her answer.
    A) to wait   B) be waiting
    C) waiting   D) waited
    E) having waited

43. While the woman ___ her children quickly passed her and ___ upstairs.
    A) was talking / was going B) was talking / went
    C) talks / went   D) were talking / went
    E) talked / went

44. I understood that while the student ___ I couldn't enter the room.
    A) would be examined   B) is examining
    C) was examined   D) was being examined
    E) is examined

45. While we ___ sightseeing the students ___ the book.
    A) went / were reading   B) to go / were reading
    C) went / are reading   D) go / were read
    E) have gone / have read

46. While you ___ a rest, we ___ the task.
    A) were having / did   B) have / do
    C) shall have / done   D) have had / did
    E) is having / do

47. While he ___ to school his elder brother ___ from the Institute. His brother is a teacher now.
    A) had gone / graduated
    B) has been gone / will graduate
    C) is going / has been graduating
    D) went / graduated
    E) goes / graduated

48. ___ while he was having breakfast.
    A) He climbed the fence   B) His pen stopped writing
    C) He fell off the ladder   D) He bit his tongue
    E) He painted the ceiling

49. Mary ___ Nick where he ___ after graduating from the University.
    A) asked / works   B) ask / would work
    C) ask / worked   D) asked / would work
    E) asked / has worked

50. We ___ into the room where the old man ___ . He was seriously ill.
    A) go / lies   B) goes / lie
    C) went / is lying   D) went / was lying
    E) was going / was lying

51. Mrs. Black ___ into the room where her husband ___ and began to cry.
    A) comes / sits   B) came / was sitting
    C) came / sat   D) came / were sitting
    E) was coming / sat

52. As soon as he ___ to Copenhagen he ___ us a letter.
    A) get / send   B) gets / sends
    C) gets / will send   D) got / should send
    E) got / has sent

53. I ___ you as soon as we ___ the contract.
    A) shall call / sign   B) call / sign
    C) called / sign   D) would call / sign
    E) is calling / are signing

54. As soon as I ___ the result I ___ you know.
    A) hear / shall let   B) will hear / will let
    C) hear / let   D) heard / let
    E) have heard / let

55. As soon as the guests ___ we ___ our party.
    A) will come / began   B) comes / begin
    C) will come / begin   D) come / shall begin
    E) come / begin

56. I was in the supermarket. As soon as I ___ for the goods somebody ___ me.
    A) paid / would push   B) had paid / pushed
    C) have paid / pushed   D) pay / will push
    E) have paid / is pushing

57. As soon as we ___ the house we ___ to it.
    A) shall build / move   B) build / shall move
    C) will build / shall move D) built / shall move
    E) build / move

58. As soon as he ___ to see me, we ___ chess.
    A) will come / shall play
    B) comes / shall play
    C) will come / play
    D) comes / play
    E) came / play

TEST 15 — Questions tags

1. He had no practice in composing music, ___ ?
   A) didn't he   B) had he
   C) does he   D) has he
   E) doesn't he

2. You have read all Pushkin's books, ___?
   A) not you   B) have you
   C) haven't you   D) aren't you
   E) isn't it

3. You have a bad headache, ___?
   A) isn't it   B) don't you
   C) does it   D) haven't you
   E) won't we

4. He never thought what might come out of it, ___?
   A) does he   B) hasn't he
   C) didn't he   D) did he
   E) won't he

5. She comes from the family of Donovan, ___?
   A) hasn't he   B) didn't she
   C) do you   D) doesn't she
   E) won't she

6. You have finished your work, ___?
   A) didn't you   B) haven't you
   C) don't you   D) won't you
   E) have you

7. He isn't a student, ___ he?
   A) is   B) does
   C) do   D) isn't
   E) was

8. There are so many people in the street, ___?
   A) are they   B) are there
   C) aren't they   D) aren't there
   E) isn't there

9. You don't play the piano, ___?
   A) don't you   B) do you
   C) doesn't it   D) does it
   E) isn't it

10. This winter is not very cold, ___?
    A) isn't it   B) is it
    C) does it   D) won't it
    E) hasn't it

11. The manner of addressing people in Britain is quite different from ours, ___?
    A) it is   B) isn't there
    C) is there   D) is it
    E) isn't it

12. There won't be any trouble, ___?
    A) wasn't there B) will not there
    C) will there   D) do there
    E) wouldn't there

13. The boy wasn't able to do it alone, ___?
    A) didn't he   B) wasn't he
    C) was he   D) did he
    E) wasn't it

14. They have to ask somebody else to help them, ___?
    A) haven't they B) have they
    C) do they   D) don't they
    E) hasn't he

15. There were many mistakes in your dictation, ___ ?
    A) weren't they B) were there
    C) aren't they   D) weren't there
    E) aren't there

16. He had lunch at home today, ___ ?
    A) hadn't he?   B) wasn't he?
    C) did he?   D) didn't he?
    E) had he?

17. You lived here 3 months ago, ___?
    A) don't you   B) had you
    C) didn't you   D) have you
    E) do you

18. It isn't very early now, ___?
    A) isn't it   B) it is
    C) doesn't it   D) hasn't it
    E) is it

19. Pete doesn't work hard, ___?
    A) is he   B) he does
    C) does he   D) he works
    E) doesn't he

20. A sick man can't go out, can he?
    A) No, he can't. B) I didn't know.
    C) Yes, she could. D) No, he isn't.
    E) Yes, he could.

21. Nothing can stop us now, ___?
    A) don't it   B) doesn't it
    C) can't it   D) can it
    E) does it

22. There is neither electricity nor gas on the island, ___?
    A) is there   B) isn't there
    C) there is   D) there isn't
    E) isn't it

TEST 16

Additions to remarks

1. -Don't you know I'm a football fan?
   -___ . I shout for Galatasaray.
   A) Not, did I   B) He is too
   C) So am I   D) Either do I
   E) Neither was I

2. Our professor thinks we like his subject. What about yours?
   A) So does he.
   B) No, our professor is very young.
   C) Our students don't know anything.
   D) Yes, the student's life is not sugar and candy.
   E) Ours is the best in the world.

3. "I don't like reptiles."
   A) Neither am I.   B) So do I.
   C) Neither do I.   D) I don't like them too.
   E) Me to.

4. I am fond of reading.
   A) So do I   B) Neither can he
   C) So wasn't he   D) So is my son
   E) I am either

5. "I like skating."
   A) So do I   B) Neither do I
   C) Neither does he   D) So is he
   E) I did too

6. Tom: I won't have any more.
   Ann: ___ .
   A) So shall I   B) So do I
   C) Neither do I   D) Neither shall I
   E) Nor I shall

7. I haven't heard him sing.
   A) Neither had we.   B) Neither has my friend.
   C) I haven't either.   D) So do I.
   E) So have he.

8. -"My friend can't go to the theatre tonight."
   - ___ .
   A) Neither can I   B) So can I
   C) I don't either   D) Neither do I
   E) So can he

9. -I haven't read "David Copperfield" by Charles Dickens.
   A) Neither has my brother.   B) Neither can I.
   C) So, did I   D) Either does he.
   E) Haven't they?

10. She didn't see anyone she knew, and ___ did Nick.
    A) either   B) or
    C) neither   D) still
    E) too

11. - My brother is going to enter the Institute.
    - ___ .
    A) So is my sister.   B) Neither am I
    C) So did my brother. D) Nor can I
    E) Neither do we.

12. - I've never been to England.
    - ___ . But I hope I shall visit it some day.
    - ___ . Now that our country has become independent we've got more chances of visiting other countries.
    A) I was there/So shall I   B) I wasn't there/Neither shall I
    C) Neither have I/So do I   D) Really?/Yes, I shall
    E) So have I/Neither do I

13. I can never find my books.
    A) Neither can I.   B) Her too.
    C) Neither does she.   D) I can't too.
    E) We can either.

14. I wasn't at school when I heard the news.
    A) So did I.   B) Yes, I was.
    C) Did you?   D) Neither were they.
    E) No, she wasn't.

15. -I do not like porridge at all.
    -___ .
    A) So do I   B) Neither did we
    C) Neither does your sister   D) Won't you?
    E) Neither am I

16. -He saw nobody in the room, and you?
    - ___ .
    A) neither did I   B) so did I
    C) neither do I   D) so do I
    E) I either

17. - I am proud of my country, and you?
    - ___ .
    A) so we do   B) so did we
    C) so are we   D) we too
    E) we also.

18. -His uncle is a very clever man.
    -And ___ .
    A) his father too.   B) his father also.
    C) so does his father D) so is his father.
    E) so his father is.

19. - I don't like people who tell lies, and you?
    - ___ . I just hate them.
    A) I too   B) I also
    C) So do I   D) Neither do I
    E) I am also

20. - My little brother is very clever.
    - ___ .
    A) so was mine   B) so is mine
    C) my is too   D) mine is either
    E) neither is mine

21. A: George is a student, and you?
    B: ___ .
    A) He is   B) So am I
    C) A student   D) Yes, I am
    E) Yes, I do

22. - I have never been to England.
    - ___ .
    A) Me so   B) Neither was I
    C) Neither have I   D) Neither did I
    E) So have I

23. - I don't like football.
    - ___ .
    A) So does Ann.   B) Ann does neither.
    C) Ann doesn't too.   D) Neither doesn't Ann.
    E) Neither does Ann.

24. - Douglas can't cope with the task.
    - ___ .
    A) His friends can't too   B) So can his friends
    C) I can't either   D) Neither can I
    E) His friends can't neither

25. - Her hopes were realized.
    - ___ .
    A) Mine did too
    B) My were too
    C) Mine were either
    D) Her were too
    E) So were mine

26. - Albert is seldom in time for his classes.
    - ___ .
    A) John is too
    B) So is John
    C) I do too
    D) His friends aren't either
    E) Neither aren't his friends

27. - Alex had to stay in bed for 5 days.
    - ___ .
    A) I had to
    B) So did I
    C) Pier had too
    D) So had I
    E) I do too

28. - He was hardly upset when he heard the news.
    - ___ .
    A) I wasn't either
    B) So was I
    C) His friend was too
    D) Neither I was
    E) Neither was I

29. - He has no money.
    - ___ .
    A) I don't either.
    B) Either have I.
    C) I haven't neither.
    D) Neither do I.
    E) I do too.

30. - It's raining and I have to stay at home.
    - ___ .
    A) Linda have too.
    B) Linda does too.
    C) So does Linda.
    D) Linda has so.
    E) Linda does either.

31. - Brian had English yesterday.
    - ___ .
    A) So did I.
    B) So had I.
    C) I didn't too.
    D) So does I.
    E) Neither did I.

32. - She has lived in Moscow for 20 years.
    - ___ .
    A) I do too.
    B) So do I.
    C) I have too.
    D) So have I.
    E) Neither have I.

33. My sister has graduated from the University.
    A) So is my sister
    B) Her sister has either
    C) So has his brother
    D) Neither did mine
    E) So do they

34. A: I'll not go back with my car, and you?
    B: ___ .
    A) Neither shall I
    B) Neither do I
    C) So shall I
    D) Neither are we
    E) Me too

35. - I had to help my mother about the house.
    - ___ .
    A) Neither had I
    B) Either hadn't we
    C) So had I
    D) So did I
    E) So do I

36. The thief had to run out of the shop when the policeman began shooting.
    A) the customers had to
    B) so the customers did
    C) so had the customers
    D) so did the customers
    E) neither did the customers

37. The guide would like the tourists to see the centre of the city.
    A) They wouldn't either.
    B) Neither would they.
    C) So should they.
    D) A so they would.
    E) So would they.

38. You mustn't stay on the beach in hot weather.
    A) You can't either.
    B) Neither must you.
    C) Neither you must.
    D) Mustn't you either.
    E) You don't have either.

39. She never liked to wear clothes in bright colors.
    A) Neither I did.
    B) So did her friend.
    C) Her friend did either.
    D) Neither did her mother.
    E) Her mother either didn't.

40. Betsy always goes to the country for weekends.
    A) Neither does her friend.
    B) We don't either.
    C) So do we.
    D) So they do.
    E) He doesn't either.

41. My friend doesn't like detective stories.
    A) Neither do I.
    B) Neither I do.
    C) I do either.
    D) So do I.
    E) I do neither.

42. -Have you got any hobbies?
    -Yes, I have. I like English.
    -___ .
    A) So have I
    B) So has he
    C) Neither have I
    D) So do I
    E) Neither do you

43. -I don't like horror films, and you?
    -___ . I can't sleep after seeing such films. I like fantastic films.
    -___ . I've got some at home.
    A) Yes, do / I don't like them
    B) No, don't / I like it
    C) Neither do I / So do I
    D) So do I / Neither do I
    E) Neither I do / So I do

TEST 1

1. _____ a fluent speaker of English?
   A) Is her   B) He   C) Does she   D) Is she

2. This is a desk, and _____ tables?
   A) those are   B) these   C) that are   D) that is

3. This is _____ boyfriend?
   A) hers   B) of her   C) to him   D) her

4. There are _____ people in the office.
   A) the   B) little   C) some   D) any

5. _____ money on Helens table?
   A) There is some   B) There is any
   C) Is it some   D) Is there any

6. A: Where's Helen?
   B: She _____ in the office
   A) is sitting   B) sit   C) sitting   D) sits

7. She _____ French and English, so she has got a good job.
   A) speak   B) speaks   C) speaking   D) is speaking

8. A: What _____ ?
   B: She is writing a letter.
   A) does she do   B) does she   C) is she doing   D) she is doing

9. She _____ speaks no foreign languages.
   A) is not   B) —   C) doesn't   D) don't

10. A: Are Peter and Mary still sitting in the office?
    B: No, _____
    A) they don't sit   B) they standing
    C) there aren't   D) they aren't

11. What language _____?
    A) do you speak   B) you speak
    C) you are speaking   D) speak you

12. A: Are there any people in the bar?
    B: No, _____
    A) any   B) there aren't   C) there isn't   D) are there

13. Helen has got only _____ money.
    A) any   B) a little   C) no   D) few

14. A: Do you want some tea?
    B: No, I don't want _____ thank you.
    A) nothing   B) none   C) anything   D) something

15. I'm sorry, but I _____ the test yet.
    A) don't finish   B) haven't finished
    C) didn't finish   D) aren't finished

16. _____ English before?
    A) Have you   B) Do you study
    C) Are you studying   D) Have you studied

17. Marry _____ to the bank on Monday.
    A) go   B) going   C) gone   D) went

18. Marry _____ hasn't telephoned Peter.
    A) yet   B) still   C) always   D) never

19. Peter _____ in the living room when the phone rang.
    A) was sitting   B) has been sitting
    C) at   D) has she wanted

20. A: What _____?
    B: She wanted to talk to him.
    A) wanted she   B) did she want
    C) she wanted   D) has she wanted

21. Peter can't speak Italian, _____?
    A) isn't   B) can't he   C) does he   D) can he

22. Jack _____ Turkish soon.
    A) goes to learn   B) learns
    C) is going to learn   D) is learning

23. He asked her friend to speak _____ on the telephone.
    A) clear   B) more clearly
    C) very clear   D) too clearly

24. "What _____ this evening?" Marry asked.
    A) you will do   B) do you
    C) very clear   D) are you doing

25. She enjoys _____ to parties.
    A) to go   B) that they go   C) going   D) go

26. His girlfriend _____ while he was still having a bath.
    A) was arriving   B) has arrived   C) arrived   D) is arriving

27. "If I _____ quickly, we wont be late for the party," said Peter.
    A) drive   B) will drive   C) drove   D) would drive

28. She asked him where _____.
    A) the party is   B) the party was
    C) was the party   D) is the party

29. "If I _____ the way to the house, we wouldn't be so late." He replied
    A) knew   B) know   B) would know   D) had know

30. Peter wanted _____ a policeman.
    A) that Mary would ask   B) Mary asking
    C) Mary should ask   D) Mary to ask

31. Marry said she _____ him driving fast, and asked him to slow down.
    A) isn't liking   B) hasn't liking
    C) didn't like   D) doesn't like

32. When they finally arrived, they _____ the car and went in.
    A) had parked   B) were parking
    C) parked   D) have parked

33. They were _____ that they didn't get anything to eat.
    A) such late   B) so late   C) too late   D) very late

34. Peter made Mary _____ all night.
    A) to dance   B) that she danced
    C) dance   D) dancing

35. When you _____ him tomorrow, you will think he is ten years older.
    A) see   C) will be
    C) would see   D) are going to see

36. He promised his wife they _____ here earlier next time.
    A) will get   B) get   C) shall get   D) would get

37. _____ Peter nor I was able to drive home.
    A) Either   B) Not only   C) Nor   D) Neither

38. Helen found a good job, and _____ Peter.
    A) also   B) too did   C) so did   D) so

39. The milk _____ at 8 o'clock the following morning.
    A) was delivering   B) delivered
    C) was delivered   D) is delivered

40. "If I'd known I'd feel so ill, I _____ to party," Peter moaned.
    A) would go   B) wouldn't have gone
    C) didn't go   D) would have gone

41. He heard on the morning news that a family of 6 _____ in an explosion.
    A) were being injured   B) had injured
    C) have injured   D) had been injured

42. The family had just had a new gas cooker _____ in their kitchen.
    A) fitted   B) fitting   C) to be fitted   D) for fit

43. The man who fixed it must _____ a mistake with the connections.
    A) have made   B) to have made
    C) to made   D) made

44. He _____ his job properly because a lot of gas escaped.
    A) shouldn't do   B) must have done
    C) was able to do   D) can't have done

45. After Peter _____ his breakfast, he went to work.
    A) finishing   B) was finishing
    C) had finished   D) has finished

46. He thought he _____ able to read about the explosion when he got home.
    A) will be   B) is   C) would be   D) was

47. "By the time I get home the story _____ in the evening newspaper," he thought.
    A) appears   B) would be
    C) will have appeared   D) has appeared

48. Peter _____ spending weekends alone.
    A) didn't use to   B) wasn't used to
    C) hadn't used to   D) used not to

49. He wished she _____ have to spend so much time away.
    A) didn't   B) hadn't   C) doesn't   D) couldn't

Book 1 Part D   151   Test 1

50. He suggested _____ him on Tuesday evening.
    A) her to meet   B) she should meet
    C) she meeting   D) that her meeting
51. You _____ have worried because the test wasn't difficult, was it?
    A) could   B) needn't   C) must   D) wouldn't
52. Now it's time _____ a short composition.
    A) you write   C) you are writing
    B) for to write   D) you wrote
53. He _____ ill for a long time.
    A) has had   B) has been   C) is   D) were
54. I had two eggs for breakfast and _____ of them was fresh.
    A) either   B) neither   C) no   D) none
55. A: Have you passed the test?
    B: _____
    A) I don't doubt   B) Yes, I doubt it
    C) I doubt   D) I doubt it
56. I usually watch TV, but at present I _____ to the radio.
    A) am listening B) listened C) listen D) will listen
57. He speaks English well _____ he has never been to England.
    A) however   B) even   C) so   D) although
58. How long _____ Mr. Brown?
    A) do you know   B) did you know
    C) have you known   D) will you known
59. Jane is _____ than Mary.
    A) very tall B) taller   C) the tallest D) tallest
60. While I _____ my car I heard a scream.
    A) was parking B) will park C) park D) have parked
61. Turkish is easy, but English _____.
    A) is   B) does not   C) is not   D) is not, either
62. _____ are broken.
    A) The legs of the table   B) Table's leg
    C) One leg of the table   D) One of the legs of the table
63. There is _____ we can do to help you.
    A) nothing   B) anything   C) somewhere D) any
64. My brother is very _____ musician
    A) the most talented   B) talented
    C) more talented   D) talent
65. He wrote a _____ book last year.
    A) good   B) the worst   C) worst   D) very
66. The detective has not solved the mystery _____.
    A) still   B) yet   C) already D) therefore
67. He _____ in Africa this time tomorrow.
    A) is traveling   B) was traveling
    C) will be traveling   D) has been traveling
68. My brother is _____ young to be a team leader.
    A) enough   B) too   C) yet   D) much
69. _____ of his books do you like best?
    A) Which   B) What   C) Who   D) Whom
70. My friend asked me _____ I wanted to drink anything.
    A) what   B) which   C) if   D) that
71. _____ read any good book recently?
    A) Have you B) Do you   C) Did you D) Are you
72. She doesn't have _____ money.
    A) many   B) much   C) no   D) very
73. George enjoys _____ in the sea.
    A) from swimming   B) swim
    C) to swim   D) swimming
74. Can you tell me _____ ?
    A) where does Jack live   B) where Jack lives
    C) where is Jack living   D) where is Jack
75. Did you see the pencil _____ two days ago?
    A) I bought it   B) which I bought it
    C) that I bought it   D) which I bought
76. He would buy a new car if he _____ more money.
    A) had   B) would had   C) would have D) have had

77. Alice is the same age _____ David.
    A) with   B) like   C) as   D) by
78. Who _____ the dinner?
    A) did cook B) cooked   C) was cook D) is cooked
79. How many times a week did you do English at school?
    A) Four times in a week   B) Twice in a week
    C) Once in a week   D) Twice a week
80. She is staying with her parents _____ the time being because she can't afford to rent an apartment.
    A) during   B) for   C) since   D) in
81. The children want me to _____ them a story now.
    A) say   B) talk   C) tell   D) speak
82. He _____ hard because he answered all the questions in the exam.
    A) must have studied   B) should study
    C) should have studied   D) ought to study
83. His aunt died three months ago. Since then he _____ to Ankara twice.
    A) went   B) has gone   C) is going D) was gone
84. She married _____ an Englishman.
    A) by   B) with   C) to   D) too
85. They met some people _____ sons were all football players.
    A) who   B) who's   C) whom   D) whose
86. They really don't know _____.
    A) when does the football game begin
    B) when the football game begin
    C) when begins the football game
    D) when the football game begins
87. He _____ difficulty on the last test he took.
    A) had   B) has   C) is having D) will have
88. After _____ his coffee, he left the restaurant.
    A) drinking B) drank   C) drink   D) to drink
89. She only takes ____ sugar in her tea.
    A) few   B) a lot   C) a little D) a few
90. The teacher's book, _____ lives of great men and women, has 500 pages.
    A) who contains   B) which contains
    C) which is contain   D) whose contains
91. They _____ earlier than the others, but they arrived later.
    A) are leaving C) had left B) leave D) left
92. You can travel _____.
    A) neither by train or by bus   B) either by train or by bus
    C) either by train nor by bus   D) or by train nor by bus
93. They will leave the house as soon as they _____ lunch.
    A) finish eating   B) will finish to eat
    C) finish to eat   D) will finish eating
94. ____ all her efforts, she could not please her family.
    A) In spite of   B) Nevertheless
    C) Although   D) However
95. We _____ helped you even if we had wanted to because we did not know how to do it.
    A) may not have   B) can't have
    C) might not have   D) couldn't have
96. I should have called him right away if I _____ his telephone number.
    A) have know   B) will know
    C) had known   D) would know
97. _____ coffee after dinner.
    A) I'm used to drinking   B) I used to drinking
    C) I'm used drinking   D) would know
98. They were speaking so loudly that I couldn't help _____ what they said.
    A) to overhear   B) overhearing
    C) overhear   D) but to overhear
99. He seems to be director. I remember _____ in school.
    A) saw him   B) seeing him
    C) him to see   D) to see him
100. To travel in the European Community, Dutch people _____ a passport.
    A) haven't got   B) don't need
    C) mustn't get   D) shouldn't get

TEST 2

1. Tom _____ already left when you arrived.
   A) he   B) just   C) had   D) was

2. I _____ working until you came.
   A) am   B) will be   C) had been   D) won't

3. The landlord _____ just rented the apartment when I got there.
   A) almost   B) have   C) had been   D) had

4. _____ they rented it before you called?
   A) How   B) Who   C) Did   D) Had

5. _____ you like to go the movies tonight?
   A) How   B) Had   C) Would   D) Why

6. I _____ rather study in the library..
   A) would   B) can   C) much   D) will

7. _____ it be possible to go next week?
   A) Can   B) How   C) Rather   D) May

8. No, I _____ like to go then.
   A) can't   B) can   C) wouldn't   D) not

9. If my car _____ start, I will be late.
   A) didn't   B) doesn't   C) don't   D) did

10. If Anita doesn't hurry, she _____ be able to finish.
    A) won't   B) would   C) can   D) can't

11. Leonard won't come _____ it rains tomorrow.
    A) will   B) if   C) because   D) and

12. If I _____ a chef, I'd make a great meal.
    A) was   B) were   C) am   D) cooked

13. If it _____ cold outside, Linda would go to the beach.
    A) weren't   B) isn't   C) wasn't   D) won't be

14. Jim _____ study harder if he had more time.
    A) will   B) won't   C) were   D) would

15. Many cameras _____ in Japan.
    A) made   B) here   C) are making   D) are made

16. Watson _____ needed here tomorrow.
    A) not   B) isn't   C) was   D) aren't

17. The computer _____ guaranteed by the company.
    A) is   B) are   C) it's   D) aren't

18. These packages are _____ special care because they're fragile.
    A) give   B) needing   C) given   D) giving

19. When the door _____, Frank was very surprised.
    A) opens   B) is opened   C) was opened   D) shuts

20. "The letter _____ last week," Helen said.
    A) is sent   B) was sent   C) will be sent   D) sent

21. These houses _____ by settlers many years ago.
    A) are maid   B) were built   C) built   D) made

22. America _____ by Christopher Columbus in 1492.
    A) was here   B) was discovered
    C) found   D) had ships

23. Wilma _____ called if she had forgotten her keys.
    A) had   B) would   C) found   D) would have

24. They would have gone home if we _____ here.
    A) aren't   B) won't be   C) hadn't been   D) are

25. If Bruce had been careful, he _____ had an accident.
    A) has   B) have
    C) wouldn't   D) wouldn't have

26. Would Bruce _____ his car if he had driven slowly?
    A) damage   B) had damaged
    C) have damaged   D) damaged

27. Janet taught _____ to play the piano.
    A) myself   B) herself   C) yourself   D) I

28. The Nelsons enjoyed _____ on their vacation on a lonely island.
    A) themselves   B) yourself   C) yourselves   D) ourselves

29. I'm teaching _____ to speak English.
    A) himself   B) us   C) yourself   D) myself

30. It was very cold today. You _____ your sweater.
    A) could wear   B) should have worn
    C) should wear   D) couldn't worn

31. Tom _____ more for the test yesterday.
    A) can always study   B) will be able to study
    C) could have studied   D) always studied

32. Ronald _____ left last week.
    A) should   B) might not   C) have   D) might have

33. By 5:30 this afternoon, Bob _____ been at work for eight hours.
    A) has   B) will   C) have   D) will have

34. Everyone will _____ lunch by 2:30.
    A) be   B) eat for   C) have had   D) had have

35. The painters _____ finished their work by tomorrow.
    A) have   B) will have   C) won't be   D) were

36. The package should be here _____ ten o'clock tomorrow.
    A) delivered   B) sent   C) by   D) by mail

37. Susan will probably work _____ six.
    A) for   B) under   C) until   D) by

38. _____ the time our boss is sixty, he will have worked for forty years.
    A) When   B) Until   C) Over   D) By

39. Always put medicine away after _____ it.
    A) taking   B) took   C) you took   D) you're

40. You should always check your tires before _____ your car.
    A) drive   B) driving   C) you drove   D) you're driving

41. Are you interested in _____ a watch?
    A) by   B) for   C) buying   D) to buy

42. Joan said that _____ .
    A) I'm at my office   B) she was at her office
    C) she's been at my office   D) you are at your office

43. Jack _____ to Tom.
    A) says that he had spoken   B) say that he speaks
    C) said that he had spoken   D) had spoken that he will say

44. Lucy told him that _____ to you.
    A) she wants talk   B) I want to talk
    C) she wanted to talk   D) you wanted to talk

45. I thought that he _____ something for me.
    A) was supposed to do   B) is supposed to do
    C) was supposed   D) is supposed to

46. Carlos heard that you _____ in town.
    A) are   B) been   C) were   D) gone

47. They promised that they _____ Mike next year.
    A) visit   B) will visit   C) would visit   D) won't visit

48. I don't mind _____ for you.
    A) to wait   B) waiting   C) to waiting   D) wait

49. Betty couldn't help _____ when Oscar fell down.
    A) the laugh   B) at laughing   C) to laugh   D) laughing

50. The old man can't stand _____ the bus to work.
    A) riding   B) ride   C) the ride   D) sitting

51. Don't be nervous. I want you _____ .
    A) not nervous   B) to relax   C) relax   D) relaxing

52. Excuse me, officer. I'd like you _____ me.
    A) helping   B) to help   C) help   D) for helping

53. The instructor wants us _____ for the test.
    A) student   B) study hard   C) to prepare   D) writing

54. "Would you like me _____ ?" he asked.
    A) dancing   B) a dance   C) to dance   D) dance

55. Traffic was bad because the highway _____ repaired.
    A) will be   B) is   C) was being   D) being

56. They didn't consider the traffic problem when the plans for the project _____ made last year.
    A) have been   B) was being   C) were being   D) are carefully

57. The English test _____ yesterday.
    A) being   B) was given   C) being here   D) being hard

58. Jean has _____ paid a good salary.
    A) earned   B) being   C) been   D) been earning

59. Mr. Bond's suitcase _____ examined already by the customs officer.
    A) carefully   B) is   C) has   D) has been

60. Their passports _____ checked by the officer.
    A) already have
    B) have already been
    C) already been
    D) have already to be

61. What did the surgeon tell Elizabeth?
    He recommended _____ an operation.
    A) that she have
    B) her have
    C) she has
    D) that she will have

62. John _____ in Japan before he came here.
    A) learned
    B) been educated
    C) been reading
    D) had gone to school

63. A: Our house needs painting.
    B: You can _____ a company paint it.
    A) get   B) have   C) ask   D) tell

64. Roberts seems _____ ready.
    A) it is   B) being   C) to be   D) of being

65. They imagine London _____ like the picture.
    A) be   B) to be   C) being   D) look

66. The teacher seems _____ small for all the people.
    A) to   B) to be too   C) it's to   D) too much

67. Nancy had imagined it _____ different.
    A) much   B) is   C) will be   D) to be

68. When Adam was a child, he _____ to live on a farm.
    A) likes   B) farmed   C) used   D) wishes

69. Mr. Jasper _____ to be a baseball player.
    A) as   B) used   C) has been   D) never

70. Before the invention of he automobile, people _____ use horses for transportation.
    A) to   B) always   C) to travel   D) used to

Decide which of the sentences means the same as the given sentence.

71. She has finished her friendship with him.
    A) She has done for him.
    B) She has done with him.
    C) She has done to him.
    D) She done at him.

72. He cannot be saved. He is certain to die.
    A) He is done down.
    B) He is done up.
    C) He is done to.
    D) He is done for.

73. He took a lot of money from me by cheating.
    A) He did me out a lot of money.
    B) He did me from a lot of money.
    C) He did me up to a lot of money.
    D) He did me out from a lot of money.

74. The army is not capable of fighting any more battles.
    A) The army is not fit to any more battles.
    B) The army is no fit in with any more battles.
    C) The army is not fit for any more battles.
    D) The army is not fit by any more battles.

75. My friend is difficult. He never manages to adapt his plans to ours.
    A) He never fits in to our plans.
    B) He never fits by our plans.
    C) He never fits in for our plans.
    D) He never fits in with our plans.

76. I am trying to pull all these papers in this drawer.
    A) I am trying to fit these papers to the drawer.
    B) I am trying to fit these papers in with the drawer.
    C) I am trying to fit these papers by the drawer.
    D) I am trying to fit these papers into the drawer.

77. These new orders have nothing to do with us.
    A) These new orders do not apply to us.
    B) These new orders do not apply for us.
    C) These new orders do not apply with us.
    D) These new orders do not apply by us.

78. I would like that job. I want to get it.
    A) I am going to apply by that job.
    B) I am going to apply with that job.
    C) I am going to apply for that job.
    D) I am going to apply to that job.

79. He was just to see that mountain through the fog.
    A) He was able to make off with the mountain's shape.
    B) He was able to make out the mountain's shape.
    C) He was able to make over the mountain's shape.
    D) He was able to make up the mountain's shape.

80. Before he died he decided to leave all his money to a stranger.
    A) He made up his money to a stranger.
    B) He made out his money to a stranger.
    C) He made off with his money to a stranger.
    D) He made his money over to a stranger.

81. He loves creating stories for his child.
    A) He loves making out stories for his child.
    B) He loves making over stories for his child.
    C) He loves making up stories for his child.
    D) He loves making of with stories for his child.

82. The robber escaped with all the jewels.
    A) The robber made off with all the jewels
    B) The robber made up with al the jewels
    C) The robber made out with all the jewels
    D) The robber made over with all the jewels

83. This book is very difficult. I don't understand it.
    A) I can't make it up.
    B) I can't make it out.
    C) I can't make it off.
    D) I can't make it over.

84. You must concentrate on your work.
    A) You must settle up to your work.
    B) You must settle down to your work.
    C) You must settle down for your work.
    D) You must settle down your work.

85. He is well off.
    A) He is healthy
    B) He is away
    C) He is wealthy
    D) He is good-hearted

86. He's very calculating.
    A) He is good at managing a business.
    B) He is a good at planning things secretly.
    C) He is good at running games.
    D) He is good at mathematics.

87. He is a hot-head.
    A) He has a fever.
    B) He is fierce.
    C) He is very intelligent.
    D) He is curious.

88. Peter Brown was the sole survivor of the air crash.
    A) He was the only person who wasn't killed in the crash.
    B) He was the only person who was killed in the crash.
    C) He was the first person to reach the scene of the crash.
    D) He was the only one to blame for the crash.

89. He is a man of spirit.
    A) He is strong
    B) He is energetic
    C) He is funny
    D) He is drunk

90. I won't go unless Mary goes.
    A) I will go if Mary doesn't go.
    B) I won't go if Mary goes.
    C) I won't go if Mary doesn't go.
    D) I won't go when Mary goes.

Choose the word closest in meaning to the words in underlines.

91. Jerry, who is a good athlete, has been able to **keeps** place on the team.
    A) play   B) participate   C) maintain   D) recruit

92. Your **wages** will depend on how well you do the job.
    A) salary   B) skills   C) waves   D) employers

93. Raymond discovered several **errors** on his test.
    A) answers   B) corrections   C) mistakes   D) numbers

94. Chris became aware of his mistake **instantly**
    A) entirely   B) frequently   C) obviously   D) immediately

95. Mrs. Johnson said that the mayor was very **arrogant**.
    A) official   B) crude   C) haughty   D) attractive

96. The **complete** set of books will cost sixty dollars.
    A) entire   B) finish   C) common   D) interesting

97. After the football game, the field was a scene of total **chaos**.
    A) celebration   B) comprehension
    C) sports   D) confusion

98. Jean was unable to provide an **acceptable** explanation.
    A) simple   B) alternative   C) additional   D) satisfactory

99. If the mechanic had done the work **properly**, you wouldn't have had trouble with the car.
    A) on the engine   B) completely
    C) easily   D) correctly

100. Ted will **do well** in colleges
    A) have fun   B) be nice   C) work hard   D) be successful

TEST 3

1. _____ a pencil in my bag which you can borrow.
   A) That's   B) What's   C) It's   D) There's

2. It gets very hot there in the summer, _____ ?
   A) isn't it   B) is there   C) doesn't it   D) does there

3. Don't worry, I'll do the shopping for you today; I _____ the office early on Fridays.
   A) will leave   B) will be leaving
   C) leave   D) am leaving

4. Henry remembered Mary's birthday and _____ .
   A) her a gift sent   B) a gift to her sent
   C) to her a gift sent   D) sent her a gift

5. I see you are still doing your math home-work. How many problems _____ so far?
   A) will you finish   B) are you finished
   C) are you finishing   D) have you finished

6. My brother finished his dinner _____ than my sister.
   A) quickly   B) much quicker
   C) more quickly   D) the quickest

7. I _____ to get on the bus when the doors closed and I was left behind.
   A) was going   B) had gone   C) would go   D) was gone

8. He's already about _____ his father.
   A) so tall than   B) as tall as   C) as tall than   D) so tall as

9. Ali has been with us _____ three years.
   A) since   B) while   C) during   D) for

10. This morning you _____ me about your father's accident when we were interrupted. I'd like to hear the rest of the story.
    A) have told   B) were telling   C) told   D) are telling

11. A: Have you heard anything from Tom lately?
    B: Yes, let me be the first to tell you _____ good news about him.
    A) the   B) his   C) any   D) these

12. How _____ have you been to Germany?
    A) much time   B) long for   C) many times   D) long ago

13. Where have you been? I've been looking for you _____ .
    A) everywhere   B) all pieces   C) anywhere   D) some places

14. Jack is not only a good student _____ a fine athlete.
    A) rather than   B) as well as   C) but also   D) in addition

15. The police wanted _____ our car to a side street.
    A) us to move   B) well to move   C) we moved   D) is moved

16. This lesson is _____ than I expected.
    A) much harder   B) the hardest   C) most hard   D) more hard

17. A: He's the best person for the job.
    B: I _____ so, too; but now I'm not sure
    A) don't think   B) used to think   C) think   D) am thinking

18. You may find the end of the story quite _____ .
    A) surprised   B) surprised   C) surprising   D) surprise

19. A: Mary's very late. I hope nothing has happened to her.
    B: _____
    A) I don't either   B) Neither do I
    C) So do I   D) I hope to

20. The advisor has not yet returned the student lists, but when _____ they will be put on the bulletin board.
    A) he will   B) they do   C) he does   D) they are

21. A: Who cooks dinner at your house?
    B: It _____ by my elder sister.
    A) is cooked   B) is cooking   C) has cooked   D) can cook

22. Mary to Tom: I have something to show you.
    Mary told Tom that _____ had something to show _____ .
    A) I / you   B) she / him   C) you / him   D) she / you

23. A: What are you boiling that water for?
    B: _____ .
    A) To make tea   B) For make tea
    C) Making tea   D) Because of making tea

24. The students _____ . Don't interrupt them.
    A) are seeming busy   B) seem to be busy
    C) are seeming busily   D) seem busily

25. Father to son : Please, don't argue with me.
    The father _____ argue with him
    A) wanted that his son didn't   B) asked his son if he didn't
    C) asked his son not to   D) said that his son didn't

26. He is _____ that he has no time for regular meals.
    A) such a busy man   B) such busy man
    C) so busy man   D) a so busy man

27. He drove so fast _____ .
    A) when he was caught by the police
    B) as his car had broken down
    C) that the passengers became frightened
    D) than most men had done

28. Tourist to policeman: How far is it to the station?
    The tourist _____ to the station.
    A) inquired how far it was   B) asked me that was it far
    C) wanted to know if it was   D) said how far it was

29. Dear Mary, this is the first time _____ you a letter.
    A) of writing   B) for me write
    C) that I had written   D) I am writing

30. Who's that girl? I can't remember _____ her before.
    A) to see   B) if I see   C) seeing   D) did I see

31. I wish you _____ so much. It is bad for your health.
    A) won't be smoking   B) don't smoke
    C) aren't smoking   D) didn't smoke

32. A: Oh, your coat's wet!
    B: That's because _____ .
    A) the rainy weather   C) the rain is
    C) it's been raining   D) it might raining

33. A: Is the math problems very difficult?
    B: The problem _____ is not difficult, but it takes a long time to do.
    A) which   B) that   C) it   D) itself

34. The lab assistant made the students _____ the experiment all over again.
    A) did   B) doing   C) do   D) done

35. He has been very lonely since _____ .
    A) many years   B) a long time
    C) his dead wife   D) his wife died

36. I want to go to the station. Can you tell me which bus _____ ?
    A) to take   B) takes   C) I am taking   D) for me to take

37. Don't touch that hot stove. _____ .
    A) It'll get burned   B) It'll be burned
    C) You'll burn it   D) You'll get burned

38. The reason _____ I'm writing is to tell you about a party on Saturday.
    A) because   B) for   C) why   D) of

39. Let's stay at home tonight, _____ you want to watch TV.
    A) that   B) since   C) because of   D) whether

40. I wish I could find _____ .
    A) living quiet somewhere   B) a quit somewhere to live
    C) some quiet where to live   D) somewhere quiet to live

41. A: I wonder why my watch isn't working.
    B: You _____ it.
    A) must have dropped   B) could drop
    C) should have dropped   D) must be dropping

42. He is getting his latest novel _____ next month.
    A) to publish   B) publishing
    C) published   D) be published

43. Although Ali is quite short, _____ reach the apples on the tree.
    A) he can also   B) he just can't
    C) he's tall enough to   D) he's too short to

44. You can buy almost anything in this supermarket; _____ , it has a cafeteria serving good cheap meals.
    A) however   B) moreover   C) meanwhile   D) otherwise

45. If I had known that the book was so boring, _____
    A) I wouldn't buy it.   B) I wouldn't have bought it
    C) I would have bought it   D) I would buy it

46. A: How did the water feel?
    B: _____
    A) Warm   B) Warmth   C) Warmly   D) Warmest

47. A manager should have a good knowledge of labor _____ .
    A) organizer   B) organization   C) organized   D) organize

48. Petroleum _____ are getting more and more expensive everyday.
    A) produces   B) products   C) production   D) productivity

49. We had a very _____ time at the football match yesterday.
    A) excited   B) excitement   C) exciting   D) excitedly

50. He had to pay the library for the _____ book.
    A) lose   B) lost   C) loss   D) loser

51. Stop talking and _____ with your work.
    A) get on   B) get away   C) get after   D) get back

52. _____ the radio; I can't hear what you're saying.
    A) Turn up   B) Turn on   C) Turn away   D) Turn down

53. I am sorry I am so late. My car _____ .
    A) broke up   B) broke away   C) broke down   D) broke in

54. Will you _____ the baby this morning while I do my shopping.
    A) look over   B) look back   C) look up   D) look after

55. Did Alice _____ to live here?
    A) used   B) use   C) used to   D) ever

56. A: Are you still employed at the airport?
    B: Yes, I _____ there since 1978.
    A) had been working   B) worked
    C) have been working   D) am working

57. A: You mean there was no food left when you got to the reception?
    B: Exactly, they _____ everything up.
    A) will eat   B) had eaten   C) ate   D) have eaten

58. Wasn't he really doing any work at home? No, I found him _____ in an armchair
    A) sleep   B) to sleep   C) sleeping   D) slept

59. A: Which shoe of this pair did you say was too tight?
    B: _____ ; both of them fit me perfectly.
    A) None   B) Neither   C) Nor   D) No one

60. You look tired. What _____ ?
    A) did you do   B) were you doing
    C) have you been doing   D) you have done

61. A: Do you play snowball in Florida in the winter?
    B: No, it _____ for that.
    A) isn't so cold   B) is very cold
    C) isn't cold enough   D) isn't too cold

62. If I _____ your father, I would certainly punish you for this.
    A) am   B) were   C) had been   D) was

63. The journalist saw two brigands _____ an old man to death.
    A) beat   B) bit   C) bite   D) beaten

64. Thousands of traffic accidents _____ by careless drivers every day.
    A) are caused   B) will cause   C) caused   D) cause

65. I've just finished _____ my shopping.
    A) to make   B) doing   C) to do   D) making

66. She has no intention of _____ a poor man like you.
    A) marry   B) to marry   C) marrying   D) married

67. I wish _____ what to do in an emergency like this.
    A) I knew   B) I know   C) knowing   D) to know

68. You _____ watch what you are saying. The boss is very upset today.
    A) would rather   B) had better
    C) had rather   D) would sooner

69. The old woman knew about everything _____ was going on in the neighborhood.
    A) what   B) where   C) that   D) who

70. Very _____ people can learn how to read efficiently.
    A) less   B) few   C) little   D) a little

71. He sometimes wishes he _____ a computer.
    A) doesn't touch   B) will not touch
    C) had never touched   D) has never touched

72. Roy didn't go to school yesterday and _____ .
    A) nor didn't James   B) neither didn't James
    C) James didn't either   D) James didn't too

73. If you _____ your money carelessly, you wouldn't have been penniless in the middle of your holiday.
    A) hadn't spent   B) didn't spend
    C) haven't spent   D) wouldn't spent

74. The boss made him _____ the report all from the beginning.
    A) write   B) written   C) wrote   D) which

75. I was disappointed with my birthday present. It wasn't exactly _____ I expected.
    A) that   B) that what   C) what   D) which

76. We had a test yesterday. I wish _____ .
    A) we hadn't one   B) we hadn't had one
    C) we didn't have one   D) we don't have one

77. The baby is crying. I think she has been _____ by the noise.
    A) afraid   B) frightened   C) frighten   D) frightening

78. Your sister never saw me, _____?
    A) did she   B) does she   C) didn't you   D) doesn't she

79. Whether one will fail or succeed depends _____ himself.
    A) from   B) on   C) to   D) in

80. The moment she _____ her wounded husband, she burst into tears.
    A) will see   B) sees   C) has seen   D) saw

81. It's been rainy all afternoon, _____ it?
    A) wasn't   B) isn't   C) hasn't   D) doesn't

82. I am interested _____ English.
    A) at   B) to   C) for   D) in

83. After I _____ my dinner, I typed my report.
    A) had   B) have   C) had had   D) will have

84. If you're not feeling well, take a hot bath. It'll _____ you good.
    A) do   B) made   C) help   D) does

85. The twins look almost alike. None of us can _____ the difference between them.
    A) say   B) tell   C) make   D) prove

86. Now that I've bought a car, I _____ take the bus to work.
    A) needn't   B) must   C) mustn't   D) hadn't

87. It's time we _____ working.
    A) start   B) will start   C) started   D) had started

88. _____ strange car we saw near the post office belongs to the major.
    A) One of   B) The   C) An   D) Two

89. The river that runs _____ our town has now become a health hazard.
    A) in   B) through   C) over   D) from

90. I wonder if you could give me _____ advice about finding a job.
    A) an   B) a   C) any   D) many

91. How long ago did you _____?
    A) have painted your house   B) had your house painted
    C) have your house painted   D) have your house paint

92. I really think there is too _____ furniture in your office?
    A) much   B) more   C) many   D) most

93. My coffee is _____ hot that I can't drink it.
    A) very   B) much   C) so   D) too

94. I _____ him at 10:00 a.m. tomorrow.
    A) am supposed to see   B) am supposed to seeing
    C) supposed to see   D) am suppose to see

95. Paul studies his lessons the most carefully _____ all the students in class.
    A) than   B) from   C) as   D) of

96. Because it was raining, the children _____ out.
    A) wasn't going   B) hadn't gone
    C) didn't go   D) have gone

97. While they were mending the wall, the roof _____ in.
    A) falls   B) fell   C) is falling   D) had fallen

98. He found that the petrol tank _____ since he left the town.
    A) leaked   B) is leaking
    C) was leaking   D) had been leaking

99. It _____ me a long time to realize she had deceived me.
    A) take   B) took   C) takes   D) will be taken

100. The bus was crowded yesterday, so we _____ stand all the way.
    A) had   B) would have   C) had to   D) will have to

TEST 4

1. She traveled _____ the world.
   A) over   B) across   C) on   D) around

2. There's a park across the street _____ the hospital.
   A) of   B) to   C) from   D) for

3. I'm taking _____ some books.
   A) hers   B) her   C) to her   D) she

4. _____ bottle on the table.
   A) It has a   B) There's a   C) It's a   D) There are

5. A: Does your mother like Turkish coffee?
   B: Yes, she _____ .
   A) do   B) does   C) does like   D) likes

6. I have a very good radio. I don't need _____ .
   A) other one   B) any   C) some   D) another one

7. Helen is always reading books. She _____ like to read.
   A) will   B) would   C) must   D) can

8. I am not _____ to vote.
   A) very old   B) old enough   C) enough old   D) old for

9. Tom and Helen _____ the radio.
   A) are listening on   B) are listening to
   C) is listening on   D) is listening to

10. Where's the book?
    A) There's it   B) He's under the chair
    C) It's here   D) There's on a chair

11. What's her brother doing?
    A) They are playing   B) He is playing football
    C) They are playing golf   D) He is playing

12. I am not used to _____ strong coffee.
    A) drink   B) drinking   C) drank   D) drunk

13. A: Are you going to find a new job?
    B: I don't know. I _____ .
    A) should   B) might   C) must   D) will

14. Tom is tall, and _____ .
    A) Henry is, too   B) Henry is to
    C) George's too.   D) Henry is

15. A: Do Mr. and Mrs. Smith speak French?
    B: _____ .
    A) He does, but she doesn't
    B) He speaks, but she doesn't speak
    C) He speaks, but she isn't
    D) He is, but she doesn't

16. Do they live in England?
    A) Yes, they live   B) No, they don't have
    C) Yes, they do   D) No, they aren't

17. Helen is behind Mary. Mary is _____ Helen.
    A) beside   B) between   C) in front of   D) next

18. That's Helen. She _____ .
    A) is long hair   B) has long hair
    C) have long hair   D) have hair long

19. What's that man?
    A) He's Tom   B) He's a driver
    C) It's tom   D) Yes, he is

20. He _____ his own meals while his wife was at her mother's.
    A) often cooks   B) cooks quite often
    C) often cooked   D) has often cooked

21. Is that a dog?
    A) Yes, it is   B) Yes, that's
    C) Yes, it's that dog   D) Yes, a dog is that

22. There are _____ in the classroom but only one teacher.
    A) many student   B) much student
    C) a lot of students   D) a lot of student

23. Helen _____ .
    A) gave Tom the pen   B) gave the pen Tom
    C) gave to Tom the pen   D) gave to the pen Tom

24. The sun _____ in the east.
    A) is always rising   B) rises always
    C) always is rising   D) always rises

25. There isn't _____ at the bus-stop.
    A) anybody   B) any persons   C) people   D) somebody

26. He hasn't bought _____ oranges.
    A) a lot   B) any   C) much   D) some

27. _____ don't like red wine.
    A) Some people   B) Somebody
    C) Any people   D) Anybody

28. Tom didn't call the police. Helen didn't call _____ .
    A) them, either   B) him, either
    C) them, too   D) him, too

29. Sally is _____ George.
    A) as tall than   B) so tall as
    C) as tall as   D) so tall that

30. Who _____ on Sundays?
    A) do help you   B) you help
    C) do you help   D) you do help

31. A: What is Mary like?
    B: She _____ .
    A) is very well   B) likes ice-cream
    C) is like tall   D) is very pretty

32. _____ to California last month?
    A) Did he go   B) Was he
    C) Is like tall   D) Has he gone

33. A: Whose is that?
    B: It's _____ .
    A) my   B) of Tom
    C) my sister   D) ours

34. Helen never eats potatoes, and _____ .
    A) so doesn't Ken   B) neither doesn't Ken
    C) neither does Ken   D) neither Ken does

35. The party will start _____ Sunday.
    A) on 9 o'clock at   B) at 9 o'clock on
    C) at 9 o'clock in   D) 9 o'clock

36. This is _____ that.
    A) the same as   B) the same that
    C) different that   D) different

37. I don't know who _____ chocolate.
    A) like   B) likes   C) is liking   D) is like

38. Fred eats _____ bread.
    A) too many   B) fewer   C) too much   D) any

39. A: Who went to Bursa?
    B: Helen _____ .
    A) did   B) went   C) has   D) is

40. Ask him _____ .
    A) how old is he   B) how old he is
    C) Helen is   D) how old he has

41. This is _____ friend.
    A) of Helen   B) Helen's   C) Helen is   D) Helen

42. _____ the ball.
    A) Kicking   B) Kick   C) What if   D) What is

43. I can kick a ball, but I _____ play football.
    A) can   B) am   C) can't   D) will

44. _____ eat the ice-cream.
    A) Don't   B) Can't   C) Where   D) When

45. Please walk _____ the street.
    A) after   B) across   C) for   D) out

46. What _____ in her hand?
    A) she has   B) is she
    C) does she have   D) she is

47. Helen has _____ headache.
    A) a   B) the   C) some   D) an

48. Tom has _____ flu.
    A) a   B) the   C) some   D) an

49. Peter has a fever because he has _____ measles.
    A) a   B) the   C) some   D) of

50. The car is dirty. We ____ wash it.
    A) don't have to   B) have
    C) have to   D) do
51. How many ____ are there?
    A) shoe   B) pair of shoes
    C) pair   D) pairs of shoes
52. Whose slippers ____ ?
    A) this is   B) is this   C) are these   D) is this
53. We'll ____ swimming.
    A) go to   B) going   C) to   D) go
54. I'm ____ shopping.
    A) going   B) can't go   C) go   D) don't go
55. The ____ house is on Park Street.
    A) Bill's   B) friend   C) Browns'   D) boys
56. Peter wants ____ a pocket calculator now.
    A) uses   B) likes   C) to use   D) be
57. A: What ____ ?
    B: It's November 22, 1984.
    A) the date is   B) day   C) is the date   D) day is today
58. A: When is your birthday?
    B: It is ____ August.
    A) on   B) into   C) between   D) in
59. My birthday is ____ June 27.
    A) on   B) into   C) between   D) in
60. There isn't ____ at your house now.
    A) person   B) somebody   C) people   D) anybody
61. Is there ____ on the meat?
    A) anybody   B) thing   C) anything   D) somebody
62. Betty ____ come to the party.
    A) may not   B) is   C) maybe   D) does
63. The brown car is ____ than the white car.
    A) smaller   B) the smallest   C) smallest   D) small
64. The movie is ____ than the book.
    A) most interesting   B) interesting
    C) more interesting   D) interestingly
65. These apples aren't as ____ those.
    A) better than   B) good as
    C) good   D) better
66. That TV program is ____ than the other one.
    A) good   B) worst   C) worse   D) well
67. The man ____ you bought this car from cheated you.
    A) which   B) that   C) what   D) which that
68. ____ did Tom eat for breakfast?
    A) When   B) Where   C) What   D) How
69. A: ____ did you go there?
    B: To visit some friends.
    A) When   B) Why   C) How   D) What
70. I spent ____ time studying for the test.
    A) a lot of   B) hours of   C) a few   D) not much
71. They have been good friends ____ 1978.
    A) for   B) in   C) since   D) before
72. David has been ____ for three hours.
    A) working   B) to work   C) worked   D) not work
73. I can't find my book ____ .
    A) everywhere B) not here   C) where   D) anywhere
74. I want to go ____ this weekend.
    A) everywhere B) mountains C) somewhere   D) beach
75. Tom speaks English ____ .
    A) good   B) difficult C) easy   D) well
76. My friend drives ____ .
    A) fast   B) bad   C) good   D) careful
77. We work ____ every day.
    A) well   B) bad   C) good   D) much
78. Mrs. Brown feels ____ .
    A) beautifully B) nicely   C) terrible   D) easily
79. If he ____ really as happy as you say, why doesn't he smile occasionally?
    A) is   B) were   C) was   D) be
80. The movie ____ interesting at the end.
    A) stops   B) sees   C) goes   D) gets
81. A: My brothers speak English.
    B: So ____ .
    A) my brothers do   B) my brothers speak
    C) do my brothers   D) my brothers speak too
82. I went to New York. So ____ .
    A) I went   B) she goes
    C) did my friend   D) she also
83. I can't speak French, and my friend can't ____ .
    A) so   B) either   C) so too   D) neither
84. Tom's mother sent ____ a letter.
    A) him   B) for him   C) to him   D) by him
85. A: ____ can design computers?
    B: Engineers can.
    A) How   B) Who   C) Why   D) Whom
86. ____ do you write to about the job?
    A) What   B) Why   C) Whom   D) When
87. Kathy is wearing a hat ____ is red.
    A) it   B) so   C) that   D) such
88. Helen has a friend ____ plays football.
    A) who   B) always   C) he   D) his team
89. She showed me some pictures ____ were very interesting.
    A) that   B) all   C) their   D) they
90. Do you know where ____ a good dinner?
    A) a restaurant for   B) get
    C) we can get   D) can we get
91. It is difficult ____ English?
    A) to learn   B) having   C) have   D) speak
92. I don't understand how ____ the homework.
    A) write   B) doing   C) read   D) to do
93. This is my friend ____ house is near mine.
    A) who lives in   B) whose
    C) who is   D) in this
94. Do you know ____ car that is?
    A) if   B) with a   C) how fast   D) whose
95. It ____ this morning when I woke up.
    A) is raining B) will rain C) was raining D) would rain
96. I was sleeping ____ the alarm rang.
    A) when   B) how   C) why   D) which
97. If Frank had more time, he ____ to see more movies.
    A) would   B) would be able
    C) can   D) had
98. We will work on the problem ____ we solve it.
    A) why   B) how   C) until   D) by
99. I look forward ____ you soon.
    A) of visiting B) to visiting C) to visit   D) visiting
100. He is ____ to understand my instructions.
    A) very stupid   B) stupid enough
    C) too stupid   D) such a stupid

TEST 5

1. A: Did you read this book?
   B: No, I didn't. I wish I ____ it.
   A) read   B) can read   C) had read   D) will read

2. He will study ____ .
   A) until I will come back
   B) when I came back
   C) when I will come back
   D) until I come back

3. He has a headache so he ____ take an aspirin.
   A) must   B) ought   C) had to   D) must have

4. By the end of the year, I ____ this journey ten times.
   A) will do
   B) will have done
   C) will be doing
   D) will have been doing

5. He would have told me if he ____ it.
   A) knew
   B) would know
   C) has known
   D) had known

6. You will have a long holiday if you ____ your class.
   A) will pass
   B) are going to pass
   C) pass
   D) would pass

7. I didn't know that your book ____ into English until Charles told me.
   A) translating
   B) translated
   C) have been translated
   D) had been translated

8. The Browns will go on a picnic unless it ____ .
   A) doesn't rain   B) won't rain   C) rains   D) will rain

9. The teacher has Ali ____ the blackboard everyday.
   A) cleaned   B) clean   C) cleans   D) to clean

10. Don't mention it. It's the ____ I can do.
    A) little   B) least   C) less   D) likely

11. Don't you always feel very ____ when you are home?
    A) happy   B) hardly   C) happily   D) nicely

12. Helen has finished her school and ____ .
    A) so did her brother
    B) so has her brother
    C) so finished her brother
    D) so her brother has

13. Rose doesn't like horror films and ____ .
    A) James doesn't too
    B) James doesn't either
    C) James doesn't neither
    D) nor doesn't James

14. He must be the director. I remember ____ in school.
    A) to be him
    B) him to be
    C) seeing him
    D) saw him

15. Both boxers trained very ____ for several weeks before the fight.
    A) much   B) hardly   C) many   D) hard

16. A: Helen is leaving home to get a job in New York.
    B: I think ____ will make her father sad.
    A) her leaving
    B) she leaving
    C) she leaves
    D) her to leave

17. He ____ mistake in the examination.
    A) did a   B) was   C) made a   D) made

18. Do you know where ____ ?
    A) will they meet
    B) they will meet
    C) do they meet
    D) are they meeting

19. These grapes ____ in the sun.
    A) has been dried
    B) have been dry
    C) have been dried
    D) have being dried

20. He ____ for half an hour when he realized he was painting the wrong wall.
    A) worked
    B) had worked
    C) has worked
    D) has been working

21. I haven't eaten anything ____ .
    A) since five hours
    B) since yesterday morning
    C) for yesterday morning
    D) for five o'clock

22. The teacher told us ____ noise in class.
    A) don't make
    B) not to make
    C) not make
    D) not making

23. I can't remember the writer of the book ____ I have just read.
    A) who   B) whose   C) whom   D) that

24. Find the driver ____ car is blocking the entrance.
    A) which   B) whom   C) what   D) whose

25. We will have another test tomorrow. I wish ____ .
    A) we wouldn't have one
    B) we hadn't had one
    C) we don't have one
    D) we won't have one

26. I didn't take the test last week. I wish ____ .
    A) I took it
    B) I would have take it
    C) I had taken it
    D) I have taken it

27. I haven't had a peaceful day ____ six months.
    A) from   B) at   C) for   D) since

28. She likes Turkish coffee ____ .
    A) much   B) very much   C) very   D) as well as

29. Was the sound ____ you heard like a roar of lion?
    A) that   B) what   C) who   D) whose

30. Mary ____ the house early yesterday morning.
    A) left   B) leaves   C) has left   D) is leaving

31. She'd rather that ____ with her homework.
    A) you help   B) you to help   C) you helped   D) will help

32. Which book ____ ?
    A) Mary likes
    B) does Mary likes
    C) Mary like
    D) does Mary like

33. The United Kingdom and France made ____ its doors to European drug sellers in 1860.
    A) China to open
    B) China opened
    C) China open
    D) China opening

34. She swims ____ than I do.
    A) good   B) well   C) better   D) too good

35. ____ Germany nor England really cares for the rights of underdeveloped countries.
    A) Either   B) Nor   C) Not   D) Neither

36. You ____ the car carelessly because it is still very dirty.
    A) shouldn't clean
    B) could clean
    C) must have cleaned
    D) can't have cleaned

37. ____ help our friends, shall we?
    A) Let's   B) Shall we   C) To   D) Will we

38. I am interested ____ swimming.
    A) for   B) in   C) to   D) at

39. He's been with us ____ ten years.
    A) since   B) from   C) in   D) for

40. Children often cut ____ with a knife.
    A) himself   B) they   C) herself   D) themselves

41. The ____ names are Helen and Lucy.
    A) woman's   B) women   C) their   D) women's

42. I'm sure he ____ a job by the end of the year.
    A) will be finding
    B) will have found
    C) will be having
    D) will have been finding

43. It's been cloudy all morning, ____ it?
    A) hasn't   B) doesn't   C) isn't   D) wasn't

44. You never went there, ____ you?
    A) do   B) did   C) don't   D) didn't

45. Stress, ____ is a psychological problem, may lead to physical illness.
    A) which   B) what   C) that   D) whose

46. Helen must work hard, ____ she?
    A) mustn't   B) doesn't   C) must   D) does

47. A: How is your father's cold?
    B: ____ it get worse, we will call the doctor.
    A) Should   B) Might   C) If   D) Unless

48. Try to be a little more tactful, ____ you?
    A) don't   B) aren't   C) will   D) are

49. He said he ____ her.
    A) know   B) is knowing   C) known   D) knew

50. She told me where ____ .
    A) she lived   B) does she live
    C) has she lived   D) did she live

51. I was glad we ____ the candles when the lights went out.
    A) has had   B) have been having
    C) were having   D) had had

52. Jack asked me if ____ swimming.
    A) do I like   C) I was liked   B) I liked   D) did I like

53. He has written two books, and ____ is any good.
    A) both of them   B) neither
    C) one of them   D) all of which

54. I told him ____ close the door.
    A) do not   B) don't to   C) don't   D) not to

55. His teacher told them ____ hard.
    A) study   B) studied   C) to study   D) studying

56. When ____ to you?
    A) does that letter sent   B) was that book sent
    C) did that letter sent   D) can that book send

57. ____ waste any more time on this project.
    A) Do   B) Don't we   C) Let's   D) Let's not

58. He doesn't know anything about cars, so he ____ by a trained mechanic.
    A) repairs it   B) it repairs
    C) has it repaired   D) is repaired

59. Rarely ____ such terrible poverty as in this African city.
    A) she had seen   B) she was being seen
    C) had she seen   D) was she seen

60. ____ all that rubbish thrown away, will you?
    A) Please   B) Let   C) Do   D) Have

61. What do you want ____ ?
    A) to me to do   B) me to do   C) to me do   D) me do

62. We ____ shelter until it stops snowing, or we'll freeze.
    A) had better   B) had had   C) had rather to   D) would better

63. ____ that dress specially made for you?
    A) Have you   B) Hadn't you   C) Had you   D) Did you have

64. She finally admitted ____ the key.
    A) taking   B) took   C) to take   D) takes

65. I'd appreciate ____ from you.
    A) to hear   B) heard   C) hear   D) hearing

66. Does she deny ____ that?
    A) to say   B) says   C) saying   D) said

67. We're looking forward ____ the museum.
    A) visit   B) visiting   C) to visiting   D) to visit

68. It's no good ____ the door after the money has been stolen. It's too late.
    A) lock   B) locking   C) locks   D) to lock

69. Why don't you try ____ it with a hammer? It might work.
    A) hit   B) having hit   C) hitting   D) to be hitting

70. The police said he ____ arrested on several previous occasions.
    A) might be   B) would have been
    C) will be   D) had been

71. He never spends ____ money.
    A) many   B) some   C) much   D) a lot

72. We will work on the computer ____ .
    A) when he will come back   B) by the time he came back
    C) until he comes back   D) until he will come back

73. He has an exam tomorrow, so he ____ study.
    A) ought   B) must   C) had to   D) must have

74. You say you have gone to his office, but I think you ____ .
    A) ought to phone him   B) ought to have phoned him
    C) should has phoned him   D) should phone him

75. She would tell you so if she ____ it.
    A) had known   B) would know
    C) has known   D) knew

76. If you ____ your book, you will have a long holiday.
    A) finish   B) will finish
    C) are going to finish   D) finished

77. I would have called him right away if I ____ his telephone number.
    A) have known   B) will know
    C) had known   D) would know

78. We will not eat outside ____ it rains.
    A) until   B) since   C) unless   D) if

79. ____ have coffee after lunch?
    A) Did you   B) Were you   C) Are you   D) You were

80. When ____ born?
    A) did you   B) were you   C) are you   D) you were

81. This photograph, ____ I took five years ago, shows the harbor quite well.
    A) who   B) when   C) which   D) what

82. The patient ____ by the doctor.
    A) has being examined   B) has examined
    C) has been examined   D) has been exam

83. They haven't drunk anything ____ .
    A) since five hours   B) since yesterday morning
    C) for five o'clock   D) for yesterday morning

84. John has written a novel and ____ .
    A) so his sister, has   B) so got married his sister
    C) so has his sister   D) so did his sister

85. Rose didn't do anything yesterday, and ____ .
    A) nor James   B) neither James
    C) James didn't either   D) James hadn't either

86. He ____ less work than his wife.
    A) made   B) made a   C) was   D) did

87. Most of my students would rather ____ .
    A) play than study   B) play than studies
    C) plays than study   D) to play than to study

88. Does anybody know where ____ ?
    A) are they meeting   B) do they meet
    C) will they meet   D) they will meet

89. I think the roof needs ____ .
    A) mending   B) to mend
    C) be mended   D) to be mending

90. She had the servant ____ the windows.
    A) to clean   B) clean   C) cleans   D) cleaned

91. Aunt Elizabeth got the roof ____ .
    A) mends   B) mend   C) mended   D) to mend

92. I ____ the test when the bell rang.
    A) already have finished   B) have already finished
    C) had already finish   D) had already finished

93. She dances ____ than I do.
    A) badly   B) too badly   C) worst   D) worse

94. Mary ____ the house early yesterday morning.
    A) lived   B) left   C) has left   D) leaves

95. We had a test yesterday, I wish ____ .
    A) we hadn't one   B) we didn't have one
    C) we hadn't had one   D) we wouldn't have one

96. Has she ever ____ her leg?
    A) broken   B) breaking   C) broke   D) breaks

97. Will you ____ have lunch with us tomorrow?
    A) be able to   B) are able to   C) able to   D) be able

98. What kind of books ____ ?
    A) does Mary likes   B) Mary likes
    C) Mary like   D) does Mary like

99. I have to go to a dentist tomorrow. I wish ____ .
    A) I have gone there   B) I had gone there
    C) I wouldn't have to   D) I wouldn't have gone there

100. My son is seventeen years old. He is ____ to get married.
    A) too old   B) old enough
    C) too young   D) enough young

TEST 6

1. I ____ here for five years so far.
   A) worked B) have worked C) am working D) was working

2. George must go home now, but he wishes ____ .
   A) he hasn't had to B) hadn't had to C) he mustn't D) he didn't have to

3. The teacher told us ____ any mistakes.
   A) don't make B) not make C) not to make D) not made

4. I took a taxi so that I ____ miss the train.
   A) can't B) wouldn't C) won't D) don't

5. The ____ names are David and Samuel.
   A) man's B) men's C) men D) their

6. You never saw him, ____ you?
   A) did B) do C) didn't D) don't

7. They walked ____ the hospital.
   A) until to B) as far as C) until D) as much as

8. Who ____ ?
   A) for you waited B) did you wait for you C) did you wait for D) did wait for you

9. There's a boy over there, ____?
   A) doesn't there B) wasn't there C) isn't it D) isn't there

10. He'll take ____.
    A) them off B) of them C) them of D) bus on

11. We'll get ____ here.
    A) on bus B) the bus on C) on the bus D) bus on

12. She has been with us ____ ten years.
    A) since B) from C) for D) in

13. We must be very careful when we drive, ____ we?
    A) mustn't B) must C) oughtn't D) don't

14. It's been rainy all afternoon, ____ it?
    A) wasn't B) isn't C) hasn't D) doesn't

15. Children often hurt ____ while playing in the garden.
    A) themselves B) himself C) their D) they

16. New York is ____ important city in USA.
    A) the more B) the most C) more D) most

17. I am interested ____ flying kites.
    A) at B) to C) for D) in

18. The temperature is about 35C today, ____ it?
    A) isn't B) doesn't C) shall D) won't

19. His father told him ____ careful.
    A) being B) to be C) be D) been

20. She told him where ____.
    A) she lived B) does she live C) has she lived D) did she live

21. ____ their sister given a present last year?
    A) Are B) Is C) Was D) Does

22. She's ____ her lunch.
    A) already eaten B) still eaten C) eaten yet D) yet eaten

23. English ____ almost everywhere in the world.
    A) is speaking B) is spoke C) is spoken D) spoken

24. She asked me if ____ her.
    A) I had seen B) had I seen C) I have seen D) did I see

25. I asked him ____ close the door.
    A) do not B) don't to C) not to D) don't

26. Jack asked me if ____ swimming.
    A) did I like B) I liked C) do I like D) I was liked

27. When ____ to you?
    A) did that letter send B) does that letter send C) is that letter sending D) was that letter sent

28. Where do you want ____?
    A) me go B) to me go C) to me to go D) me to go

29. He said he ____ her before.
    A) meets B) has met C) had met D) was met

30. Mary wondered what ____ that I wanted.
    A) it was B) is it C) was it D) it is

31. I got the computer ____.
    A) repairing B) repaired C) repairs D) to repair

32. I ____ up early last year.
    A) use to get B) used to getting C) used get D) used to get

33. You are ____ I am.
    A) the same age as B) the same age with C) the same age like D) same age as

34. He's ____ dressed quickly.
    A) use getting B) use to getting C) used to get D) used to getting

35. I wish I ____ yesterday.
    A) met B) would meet C) had met D) meet

36. Do you mind ____ the window?
    A) closing B) to close C) close D) to closing

37. They came here ____ the second day of May.
    A) until B) in C) on D) at

38. She wrote her name on ____ book.
    A) most B) each C) all D) both

39. I'd ____ finish this book.
    A) not better to B) not better C) better not D) better not to

40. She ____ go there.
    A) would rather not B) wouldn't rather C) would rather not to D) would rather don't

41. ____ clever, he would not have passed.
    A) Was he not B) If he been C) If he will not be D) If he had not been

42. The policeman ____ that man if he doesn't stop disturbing neighbors.
    A) arrests B) will arrest C) would arrest D) had arrested

43. He would never have found such a good job ____ his uncle's help.
    A) if B) with C) unless D) but for

44. If only ____ , this wouldn't have happened.
    A) we have been careful B) had we been careful C) we were not careful D) we had been careful

45. John: I'm tired.
    Jerry: Yes, you look as if ____ a good night's sleep.
    A) you need B) you would be needed C) you would need D) you've needed

46. Would he have gone to Europe if ____ Europeans are racists?
    A) he had known B) he was knowing C) had he known D) was he knowing

47. No matter what he said to his girlfriend, she ____ listen to him.
    A) isn't B) wasn't C) wouldn't D) couldn't

48. Mary: Why didn't you call me?
    Jane: Well, ____ all this week.
    A) I was trying to call you B) Trying to call you C) I've been trying to call you D) I tried to call you

49. Tony: What a surprise to see you at the airport yesterday!
    Bill: Yes, ____ some friends.
    A) I've been seeing off B) I've seen off C) I was seeing off D) I would see off

50. We're delighted to see you back! ____ you so much!
    A) We've missed B) We were missing C) We had missed D) We are missing

51. Tom: I've been reading Turkish books.
    Ann: Oh, really? ____ you knew Turkish.
    A) I haven't known B) I didn't know C) I hadn't known D) I don't know

52. Dan: Have you ever seen her secret house?
    Bob: Yes, ____ last year
    A) I'd seen it B) I've seen it C) I saw it D) I did see it

53. I think you ____ this work yesterday evening.
    A) should have done B) had done C) should do D) would do

54. They discovered that the files ____ stolen while they were the other room.
    A) is B) will be C) had been D) was been

55. I asked you to get some white cheese! You ____ bought this!
    A) shouldn't have   B) hadn't to have
    C) mustn't have   D) wouldn't have
56. I always enjoyed ____ in that lake in summer.
    A) to have swum   B) been swimming
    C) to swimming   D) swimming
57. The boy told his teacher a lie to avoid ____.
    A) be punished   B) to be punished
    C) being punished   D) punishing
58. The two children ____ to look forward ____ to their grandparents house at Christmas
    A) use / to going   B) used / to going
    C) used to / to go   D) use to / to go
59. Having worked hard for three months, he succeeded ____ his exam.
    A) to pass   B) in to pass   C) in passing   D) passing
60. They accused him ____ a thief.
    A) for being   B) as being   C) of being   D) to be
61. We are very busy at the office. I must ____ my holiday for a while.
    A) put up   B) put through   C) put off   D) put in
62. We have an extra room in our house. We will gladly ____ you ____ for a week or two.
    A) put / up   B) put / off   C) put / through   D) put / in
63. How do you find your new neighbors? I've heard they are difficult to ____.
    A) get up   B) get on with   C) get down   D) get over
64. I tried to telephone my family several times last night, but I just couldn't ____.
    A) get up   B) get on with   C) get down   D) get through
65. Who do you think will ____ when he resigns?
    A) take over B) take in   C) take up   D) take off
66. With her blue eyes she seems to ____ her aunt.
    A) take after B) take off   C) take away   D) take for
67. There was so much noise I could hardly ____ what he was saying.
    A) make out   B) make for   C) make up   D) make off
68. Despite the snowstorm, we decided to ____ Chicago instead of sleeping in the car.
    A) make out   B) make for   C) make up   D) make off
69. After the operation one of the nurses stayed at his bedside, waiting for him to ____.
    A) come up   B) come around
    C) come off   D) come away
70. He's full of wonderful plans, but they very seldom ____.
    A) come in   B) come about   C) come off   D) come down
71. He got a low mark, but he ____ to have answered most of the questions correctly.
    A) contracts   B) claims   C) blames   D) conceives
72. She was fifteen minutes late because she was ____ by a traffic jam.
    A) bent on   B) fled   C) troubled   D) delayed
73. Teachers like _____ students.
    A) conscious   B) conscientious
    C) consenting   D) conscience
74. Her parents will never _____ such outrageous behavior.
    A) put up   B) endeavor   C) concentrate   D) tolerate
75. After trying for some time, he gave _____ working on it.
    A) way   B) up   C) in   D) on
76. Are you any good _____ making soup?
    A) by   B) for   C) at   D) from
77. _____ for his great courage, all lives would have been lost.
    A) It had not been   B) It wouldn't have seen
    C) Had it not been   D) Wouldn't it have been
78. Yes, I know you're tired this morning, but _____ to the party, you wouldn't have come home late.
    A) if you would have gone   B) if you hadn't gone
    C) if you have gone   D) if you wouldn't have gone
79. Unless he's offered more money elsewhere, _____ this job.
    A) he won't accept   B) he would accept
    C) he'll accept   D) he wouldn't accept
80. If I'd realized this before, I _____ in such a mess now.
    A) won't have been   B) wouldn't be
    C) wouldn't have been   D) won't be

81. If only _____ it, none of this would've happened.
    A) I wouldn't have mentioned   B) I hadn't mentioned
    C) I haven't mentioned   D) I would've mentioned
82. A: I've got a terrible headache.
    B: Yes, you look as if _____ an aspirin.
    A) you need   B) you would need
    C) you would've needed   D) you've needed
83. _____ to the market, when it started to the rain.
    A) I was just about to go   B) I would just go
    C) I'm just about to go   D) I've just about gone
84. _____ but I didn't have enough money.
    A) I would buy it   B) I will have bought it
    C) I was going to buy it D) I'll buy it
85. A: Why haven't you told me about your problems before?
    B: Well, _____ all this week.
    A) I was trying to tell you all about them
    B) I've been trying to tell you all about them
    C) I'm trying to tell you all about them
    D) I tried to tell you all about them
86. A: Did you see your boss at the airport yesterday!
    B: Yes, _____ his family.
    A) he's been seeing off B) he was seeing off
    C) he was seen off   D) he would see off
87. A: What is the most serious disadvantage of living in a city?
    B: The most serious one is _____ the city is too noisy.
    A) hich is   B) about which
    C) because of the fact that   D) that
88. How nice to be back home! _____ it so much!
    A) We've missed   B) We had missed
    C) We were missing   D) We are missing
89. A: I've been working a lot on my computer these days.
    B: Oh, really? _____ you had a computer.
    A) I haven't known   B) I hadn't known
    C) I didn't know   D) I don't know
90. A: Have you written to them?
    B: Yes, _____ twice last month.
    A) I'd written to them   B) I wrote to them
    C) I've written to them D) I would have written to them
91. A: How long has he been away?
    B: Oh, _____ three weeks on Friday.
    A) he'll be gone   B) he'll gone
    C) he will have been   D) he will have been gone
92. A: I do hope we can watch TV tonight.
    B: Oh, yes. I'm sure _____ the serial by now.
    A) they'll put up   B) they'll have put up
    C) they'd put up   D) they'll be put up
93. A: What excellent French you speak!
    B: So _____ ! I lived in Paris for twenty years.
    A) I must   B) I should   C) I am to   D) I have to
94. A: What was that noise?
    B: Oh, don't worry; it _____ the cat.
    A) should've been   B) can be
    C) must have been   D) ought to be
95. What a lovely carpet you've bought! It _____ expensive!
    A) should've been   B) has been
    C) must have been   D) ought to be
96. He is getting fatter and fatter. He _____ eating too much.
    A) must be   B) can be   C) may   D) might

Find the synonyms of the underlined words.

97. It's **incredible** to see him in such good health after the accident.
    A) creditable   B) increasing   C) unthinkable   D) unbelievable
98. She was angry because he **disregarded** her feelings in this matter.
    A) did not ignore   B) discharged
    C) paid no attention to D) considered
99. During the ten years he worked in Germany he **accumulated** a fortune.
    A) made   B) expanded   C) concentrated   D) increased
100. He did his work **reluctantly** because he did not like the director.
    A) slowly   B) unwillingly   C) inefficiently   D) unhesitatingly

TEST 7

1. A: I've eaten far too much!
   B: Oh _____ all that exercise.
   A) it has to be   B) it must be
   C) it ought to be   D) it should be

2. A: There was a lot of noise in this building last night.
   B: Well, _____ . I was out at a party all night.
   A) it might have been me   B) it mustn't have been me
   C) it couldn't have been me   D) it shouldn't have been me

3. A: I'm surprised your husband didn't stay longer.
   B: Well, _____ , had the weather been better.
   A) he should have done   B) he might've done
   C) he has done   D) he must have done

4. A: Must I always pay my rent by cheque?
   B: No, _____ . Pay it however you want to.
   A) you needn't   B) you mustn't
   C) you shouldn't   D) you oughtn't

5. A: I hate all this polite chat at cocktail parties.
   B: Oh, you _____ polite in my house. Say whatever you want!
   A) mustn't be   B) shouldn't be
   C) needn't be   D) oughtn't to be

6. I'm sorry but I can't _____ anybody at the moment because the bedrooms are being redecorated.
   A) put up   B) put up with   C) put off   D) put with

7. I must say I wouldn't buy it, but don't be _____ by me.
   A) put up   B) put up with   C) put off   D) put with

8. If he hadn't been so drunk, he would have _____ his ideas more convincingly.
   A) put across   B) put up with   C) put through   D) put with

9. The noise in the classroom is getting unbearable. I simply won't _____ it!
   A) put across   B) put up with   C) put through   D) put with

10. I'll never go to that grocer's again. He seems to _____ his prices every day.
    A) put up   B) put up with   C) put off   D) put with

11. A: How do you find your new colleague?
    B: I'm told he's difficult to _____ .
    A) get on with   B) get along with   C) get over   D) get off

12. They say he'll never _____ his dismissal.
    A) get on with   B) get along with   C) get over   D) get off

13. I tried to telephone Istanbul yesterday, but I just couldn't _____ .
    A) get on with   B) get along with
    C) get through   D) get off

14. Mr. Brown is so old now he just can't _____ as he used to.
    A) get about   B) get away   C) get around   D) off

15. There's no doubt that he's guilty and I'm sure he won't _____ .
    A) get about   B) get across   C) get off   D) get away

16. I'll have so much spare time, I'll probably _____ some kind of hobby.
    A) take up   B) take along   C) take down   D) take in

17. Have you any idea which son of his will _____ when he retires?
    A) take up   B) take along   C) take over   D) take in

18. He's very funny when he _____ his grandfather.
    A) takes off   B) takes to   C) takes after   D) takes for

19. She _____ her friends for advice on investing her money.
    A) looks after   B) looks away   C) looks to   D) looks into

20. It's very difficult to _____ a person who has so many prejudices.
    A) take to   B) take off   C) take in   D) take for

21. The line's very bad. It's difficult to _____ what he's saying.
    A) make off   B) make out   C) make for   D) make up

22. I don't really like his being absent so much, but he does _____ the most amusing excuses.
    A) make for   B) make up   C) make away   D) make out

23. They attacked the poor man and _____ every penny he had.
    A) stole him   B) stole of him   C) robbed him   D) robbed him of

24. To avoid paying death duties, he'll _____ his whole estate to his son this year.
    A) make over   B) make for   C) make off   D) make up

25. No, the burglar didn't take too much, but he did manage to _____ some of my best carpets.
    A) make for with   B) make out with
    C) make off with   D) make of with

26. Helen served tea _____ them.
    A) from   B) to   C) in   D) at

27. I want to pay _____ the book.
    A) at   B) for   C) of   D) to

28. She takes _____ her shoes when she enter the house.
    A) on   B) in   C) off   D) of

29. Put _____ your sweater before you get out.
    A) on   B) in   C) down   D) at

30. The tourist asked _____ some information.
    A) of   B) for   C) from   D) to

31. I don't like _____ hot drinks.
    A) serve   B) serving to   C) to serving   D) being served

32. They continued _____ songs.
    A) to singing   B) to sing   C) with singing   D) being singing

33. The costumer insists on _____ , so hurry up.
    A) serving   B) being served   C) serve   D) having served

34. She didn't finish _____ coffee.
    A) have   B) having   C) to have   D) have

35. The house is _____ for him to buy.
    A) made   B) did   C) had   D) making

36. The _____ we climbed, the thinner the air became.
    A) high   B) higher   C) highly   D) highest

37. They never _____ plans for the work.
    A) make   B) do   C) perform   D) ask

38. His brother was here _____ Saturday.
    A) in   B) by   C) on   D) at

39. Ali always goes to school _____ bus.
    A) with   B) by   C) on   D) in

40. She is still in school, _____ ?
    A) is she   B) isn't it   C) isn't she   D) is it

41. A: Don't you like this lesson?
    B: _____ .
    A) No, I'm not.   B) No, I don't   C) No, I don't like.   D) Yes, I don't.

42. The social problems of Spain are _____ those of Turkey.
    A) alike   B) similar   C) same as   D) the same as

43. Jim is not _____ a quick worker _____ you are.
    A) such / as   B) so / that   C) such / that   D) more / than

44. "You didn't understand what he was saying. I didn't, either." means:
    A) Either you or I understood what he was saying.
    B) Neither you nor I understood what he was saying.
    C) Both you and I understood what he was saying.
    D) Just as you understood what he was saying so did I.

45. The guest, _____ , apologized to the host for his attitude.
    A) his mistake is realized   B) he realized his mistake
    C) realizing his mistake   D) realized his mistake.

46. "He needn't have beaten the child." means:
    A) He didn't beat the child   B) The child needed to be beaten.
    C) He needed to beat the child.   D) He beat the child.

47. "I'd much rather have watched TV at home." means:
    A) I will watch TV at home.   B) I couldn't watch TV at home.
    C) I watched TV at home.   D) I won't watch TV at home.

48. "Jane didn't need to worry about Judy." means:
    A) Jane wanted Judy to worry.   B) Jane didn't need Judy to worry.
    C) Jane didn't worry about Judy.   D) Jane worried about Judy.

49. "You could have done more than you did to help her wash the car." means:
    A) You helped more than she wanted you to.
    B) You helped her but not much.
    C) You helped as much as you could.
    D) You didn't help her at all.

50. "If I hadn't been wearing my boots, I would have been sick." means:
    A) It's a pity I didn't wear my boots.
    B) It's pity I more my boots.
    C) It's a good thing I was wearing my boots.
    D) It's a good thing I didn't wear my boots.

51. The furniture _____ wonderful but _____ hard and uncomfortable.
    A) seems / sounds   B) looks / feels
    C) looks / sounds   D) feels / seems

52. "You can look after yourself and I can look after myself" means: "We can look after _____ "
    A) each other   B) yourself   C) ourselves   D) myself

53. _____ he does, his mother forgives him.
    A) Whenever   B) Wherever   C) Whatever   D) However

54. Witness: Two men and a woman stole the money.
    Detective: Did you actually see _____ the money?
    A) them to steal   B) him to steal
    C) them stealing   D) him stealing

55. I had lunch with my friends but I _____ dinner with my family now.
    A) have   B) have been having
    C) am not having   D) am having

56. The party _____ by my friend.
    A) being organized   B) is being organized
    C) organized   D) is organizing

57. He _____ the accident if he _____ drunk; but he was drunk and had the accident.
    A) wouldn't have / hadn't been   B) wouldn't have / weren't
    C) wouldn't have / weren't   D) wouldn't have had / hadn't been

58. A: What was he arrested _____ ?
    B: He smashed up a pub and left _____ paying.
    A) _ / on   B) for / on   C) for/ without   D) in/ without

59. You are talking to a foreigner in Turkish, but you don't think he understands you. So you say:
    "You _____ to understand me."
    A) aren't sure   B) can't   C) don't seem   D) shouldn't

60. _____ did it take her _____ all the dishes?
    A) How much / washing   B) How long / to wash
    C) How long / washing   D) How much / to wash

61. Who is that pretty girl _____ ?
    A) that everybody is looking   B) everybody is looking at her
    C) which everybody is looking   D) everybody is looking at

62. The bad smell in the kitchen was really _____ . We were all _____ .
    A) disgusting / disgusted   B) disgusting / disgust
    C) disgusted / disgusting   D) disgust / disgusting

63. Today many parents _____ their children go to bed late.
    A) get   B) let   C) do   D) force

64. Arthur: I must finish that work today.
    Arthur said he _____ finish the work that day.
    A) had to   B) must   C) would   D) might

65. I've been short of money _____ I bought a new house.
    A) although   B) when   C) because of   D) ever since

66. My friend broke one of the best vases, so she said: "I hope you'll excuse me _____ ."
    A) to break that vase   B) for breaking that vase
    C) for being broken   D) to be broken

67. Cindy: Is Manhattan near here?
    Cindy wanted to know _____ Manhattan was near here.
    A) what   B) which   C) where   D) if

68. Nobody wants to do anything about that problem _____ everybody knows it is serious.
    A) that's why   B) even though   C) thereby   D) because of

69. _____ , silent people or talkative ones?
    A) What you love is   B) Why do you love best
    C) Which you prefer is   D) Who do you hate most

70. The car is terribly dirty. I'm sure it _____ for weeks.
    A) isn't cleaned   B) hasn't been cleaned
    C) hadn't been cleaned   D) wasn't cleaned

71. A: Why do you save _____ money?
    B: To get married.
    A) up   B) for   C) with   D) to

72. I _____ to him because I thought I _____ him somewhere.
    A) had spoken / saw   B) spoke / saw
    C) spoke / had seen   D) had spoken / had seen

73. A: _____ the burglar before?
    B: No, I _____ him before I saw him in the bank.
    A) Did you ever see / hadn't met
    B) Had you ever seen / hadn't met
    C) Have you ever seen / didn't meet
    D) Had you ever seen / didn't meet

74. A: Why did you leave the concert early?
    B: Because I found _____ .
    A) it boring   B) it bored   C) bored   D) boring

75. I'd like you _____ spending all our money on that old car. In fact, you don't even have _____ that car.
    A) to stop / to drive   B) stopping / to drive
    C) to stop / driving   D) stop / to drive

76. No matter how hard they struggled with it, the window _____ open.
    A) isn't   B) wasn't   C) wouldn't   D) couldn't

77. "I think she might be on this bus." means: _____ on this bus.
    A) She is pure she is   B) She is possibly
    C) She won't be   D) She is definitely

78. A: I've got a terrible cold.
    B: You _____ .
    A) had better go to bed   B) had better not go to a doctor
    C) must go out   D) need to work harder

79. _____ have a cup of coffee if you don't mind.
    A) I decided to   B) I'm sure to   C) I'd rather   D) I prefer

80. The car _____ if you _____ to a mechanic.
    A) breaks down / will take it
    B) will break down / will take
    C) is going to break down / don't take it
    D) will break down / won't take it

81. Those policemen react _____ faster in emergencies.
    A) many   B) a lot of   C) some   D) much

82. That's the _____ car I've ever seen. It uses _____ petrol than any other car I know.
    A) cheapest / less   B) cheaper / less
    C) cheapest / the least   D) cheaper / more

83. Ali studies 3 hours a day. Emre studies 2 hours a day. Emre doesn't study _____ Ali does.
    A) so hard that   B) as hard as   C) as good as   D) less than

84. He always leaves _____ work at 5:30 and goes _____ home.
    A) from / to   B) _ / _   C) _ / to   D) from / _

85. How are we going to finish this work when we've got only _____ time and _____ people to do it?
    A) a few / a few   B) a little / a little
    C) a few / a little   D) a little / a few

86. There isn't _____ food left but there are _____ drinks.
    A) any / some   B) some / some   C) some / any   D) any / any

87. A: People have a duty to fight inflation.
    B: _____ .
    A) Neither does the Government   B) So does the Government
    C) So did the Government   D) The Government doesn't either

88. Don't disturb them. They _____ to an important lecture.
    A) listened   B) listen   C) are listening   D) have listened

89. What are those students in the line waiting _____ ?
    A) about   B) to   C) for   D) at

90. _____ you leave the letter on the table, my sister will post it for you.
    A) Unless   B) If   C) Wherever   D) Even though

91. A: Why didn't you answer me?
    B: I didn't hear _____ .
    A) why did you ask it   B) what did you ask
    C) what you asked   D) why you asked

92. "He isn't sure he can repair the damage but, he hopes to." Means "He _____ be able to repair it."
    A) will   B) should   C) may   D) would

93. "It's time salaries went up" means:
    A) This time salaries went up
    B) Salaries went up that time
    C) Salaries went up and it was the right time
    D) We think salaries ought to go up

94. A: When did they give the workers a rise?
    B: A rise _____ last month.
    A) was given to them   B) gave them
    C) was given for them   D) had been given to them

95. A: Did you manage to pass the exam?
    B: It was _____ , but I managed it all right.
    A) difficult enough   B) too difficult
    C) extremely difficult   D) such difficult

96. _____ his good work and manners he didn't get a promotion.
    A) Because of   B) In spite of   C) Even though   D) As a result of

97. It is clear that progress destroys beauty. That's why most people object to it _____ our surrounding this way.
    A) change   B) be changed   C) changed   D) changing

98. A: You ought to explain this matter to the union.
    B: It's already been explained _____ .
    A) them   B) to them   C) for them   D) to this matter

99. That scientist was one of the first _____ with bacteria.
    A) experimenting   B) to experiment
    C) experiment   D) experiments

100. She _____ found her photographs, because she is still looking for them.
    A) mustn't has   B) can't have   C) needn't have   D) oughtn't have

TEST 8

1. I'm not _____ that subject.
   A) interesting with   B) interested with
   C) interested in   D) interested by

2. Alice is unhappy today. She can't study _____ .
   A) something   B) anything
   C) nothing   D) everything

3. The student _____ something to write with.
   A) is need   B) needs   C) is needing   D) is needed

4. Who is going to answer _____ question?
   A) that   B) to that   C) for that   D) _

5. Can you tell me where _____ ?
   A) does John live   B) John is alive
   C) John lives   D) is John living

6. _____ you like some tea?
   A) Will   B) Would   C) Are   D) Can

7. Do you mind _____ the window?
   A) open   B) to open   C) opening   D) you open

8. My brother doesn't like coffee, _____ I do.
   A) neither   B) but   C) nor   D) so

9. She felt ill after _____ the food.
   A) being eaten   B) to eat   C) eating   D) eaten

10. Jane is the same age _____ Mary.
    A) like   B) with   C) as   D) so

11. He lives _____ 27 Gulf Street.
    A) at   B) on   C) in   D) of

12. Where is the new student from? _____ .
    A) He is coming from Bursa   B) He is from Bursa
    C) He can come from Bursa   D) He came from Bursa

13. When did your school begin? _____ .
    A) Since September   B) At September
    C) In September   D) For September

14. There are several kinds of mushrooms in Turkey _____ poisonous.
    A) they are   B) that are
    C) which they are   D) being

15. They would buy the car if they _____ enough money.
    A) would have   B) had   C) have had   D) had had

16. Did you like the house _____ yesterday?
    A) which I showed you   B) I showed you which
    C) which I showed you it   D) I showed it

17. George's father told him _____ .
    A) don't go out   B) not go out
    C) not to go out D) do not go out

18. How long have you lived here? _____ .
    A) Since ten years   B) For ten years
    C) From ten years   D) In ten years

19. Haven't you ever seen a tiger? _____ .
    A) No, never   B) Not, not never
    C) No, not ever D) Yes. Never

20. A: Which man is your teacher?
    B: _____ .
    A) The man is near the window is my teacher
    B) The man near the window is my teacher
    C) The man who is my teacher near the window
    D) The man is near the window who is my teacher

21. Turks _____ in Anatolia for a thousand years by 2099.
    A) will be living   B) have lived
    C) will have lived D) will live

22. A: What does Mary's mother do?
    B: _____ .
    A) She is a woman   B) She teaches English
    C) She is very well   D) She lives happily

23. What would you have done if you _____ a lot of money?
    A) had   B) have had
    C) had had D) should have had

24. Istanbul is _____ in Turkey.
    A) the most important city   B) most important a city
    C) the most important a city D) most important city

25. _____ four years in the country, he came back healthier than ever.
    A) Having spent   B) Spending
    C) After spent   D) After spend

26. Mary suggested that she _____ a pretty next week.
    A) will have   B) should have   C) will have to   D) has

27. A: What was happening at the TV studio when you visited it?
    B: Programs _____ and recordings _____ .
    A) were being produced / made
    B) produced / were being made
    C) were produced / made
    D) were being produced / were being made

28. The teacher wrote our names down _____ she should forget.
    A) because   B) in order to   C) lest   D) so as not to

29. The Government publish health warnings on cigarettes _____ people would become aware of the dangers of smoking.
    A) even though   B) so that   C) as soon as   D) in case

30. How can you leave him because of _____ ?
    A) his poverty   B) he is poor   C) his poor   D) he is poverty

31. If she ever decides to get married, I'm sure I will be the last person _____ .
    A) who has found about it   B) to find out about it
    C) will find out about it   D) who find out about it

32. Susan was introduced to Mr. Baker _____ had died in a car accident.
    A) whose younger son   B) the younger son of
    C) whom younger son   D) who younger son

33. The students didn't study for the exam. They _____ studied because most of them _____ passed.
    A) might / should have   B) should / might have
    C) should have / might have   D) might have / should have

34. Only when every possible treatment had been tried _____ decide for an operation.
    A) didn't they   B) did they   C) they did   D) they didn't

35. A: Did they type the letters in time?
    B: Yes, _____ in time.
    A) they were typed the letters   B) the letters were typed
    C) the letters typed   D) the letters have been typed

36. I don't mind your _____ it but I don't like you _____ it.
    A) think / say   B) think / saying
    C) thinking / saying D) thinking / say

37. My uncle is an engineer and _____ my aunt.
    A) so is   B) so does   C) so   D) does

38. It's difficult to make both ends meet these days the taxes _____ so high.
    A) with   B) are   C) being   D) to be

39. Our teacher is opposed _____ students read novels written 200 years ago.
    A) making   B) to make   C) make   D) to making

40. A: Have they taken the car to the garage?
    B: Yes, _____ to the garage.
    A) the car was taken   B) the car have been taken
    C) the car had been taken   D) the car has been taken

41. _____ the world's population is rising fast, food production is keeping pace with it.
    A) Because of   B) In spite of   C) Although   D) Unless

42. I don't know her well, but I've met her _____ times.
    A) plenty   B) another   C) several   D) more

43. Thousands of people have seen the exhibition _____ it opened last month.
    A) while   B) when   C) until   D) since

44. We should never forget how our ancestors have struggled _____ freedom.
    A) for   B) on   C) of   D) by

45. We know each other _____ we have never been officially introduced.
    A) even   B) if even   C) even though   D) however

46. I wouldn't ask for your help _____ I had no choice.
    A) since   B) despite   C) even if   D) although

47. He is sick of being mistaken _____ his brother.
    A) by   B) as   C) of   D) for

48. Since the coal mines closed, there _____ no jobs here.
    A) are   B) have been   C) is   D) were being

49. There must be some other reason for her failure _____ this.
    A) as well   B) too   C) also   D) besides

50. Their arguments are bound to result _____ a fight.
    A) to   B) on   C) with   D) in

51. A man who spends all the money he has is _____ .
    A) fool   B) a fool   C) foolishly   D) foolish man
52. Can you tell what model each of _____ ?
    A) them to be   B) them are   C) they are   D) them is
53. The diplomats haven't been able to arrive _____ an agreement yet.
    A) by   B) at   C) on   D) to
54. All athletes who have taken drugs will be disqualified _____ the race.
    A) out   B) to   C) against   D) from
55. _____ a drop of rain fell for months, and all the crops died.
    A) No   B) None   C) Not   D) Not any
56. He is _____ short-sighted to be pilot.
    A) so   B) too   C) not   D) enough
57. Most people _____ the dark.
    A) fear   B) are in fear   C) frightened   D) afraid of
58. He had difficulty _____ his wife to stay home.
    A) convince   B) to convince   C) convincing   D) for convincing
59. If you want to succeed, you must _____ .
    A) keep to try   B) keep in trying
    C) keep on trying   D) keep on to try
60. When he was a boy, he _____ to himself all day.
    A) will sing   B) would sing   C) has sung   D) is singing
61. _____ of the wine was spoilt.
    A) Few   B) Several   C) A good deal   D) A good many
62. The American Indians today are deprived _____ all the privileges the white man is enjoying.
    A) of   B) off   C) _   D) from
63. She was glad _____ the opportunity to discuss the matter.
    A) of   B) to   C) on   D) for
64. _____ he promises to quit gambling, we'll offer him the job.
    A) For   B) Although   C) Even   D) Provided
65. _____ hard I try, I can't seem to be of any help to anybody.
    A) Even though   B) However   C) When   D) So
66. No one _____ to enter the building until the police have checked the victim's identification.
    A) will allow   B) will be allowing
    C) has been allowed   D) is going to be allowed
67. I'm very satisfied _____ your last report.
    A) on   B) for   C) of   D) with
68. He is envious _____ his brother's success, and this makes him a sullen person.
    A) of   B) from   C) to   D) by
69. She isn't content _____ their present income and keeps nagging her husband.
    A) with   B) for   C) of   D) to
70. I was very tempted, but I refrained _____ the last glass.
    A) drink   B) to drink   C) drinking   D) from drinking
71. Everyone must pay a fee before _____ his certificate.
    A) to collect   B) collecting
    C) to have collected   D) collect
72. I wish I _____ of writing the report on the computer long ago.
    A) thought   B) think   C) had thought   D) have thought
73. The British contractors are said _____ half the government officials in the country.
    A) to have bribed   B) bribing   C) be bribed   D) has bribed
74. _____ of this land has been poisoned by chemicals.
    A) A good many   B) Several
    C) A good deal   D) Few
75. We have the pleasure _____ you that your book has been awarded the first prize.
    A) of informing   B) in informing
    C) on informing   D) informing
76. Spiders mainly feed _____ insects.
    A) by   B) at   C) from   D) on
77. Our company is three times _____ yours.
    A) bigger as   B) bigger   C) as bigger than   D) as big as
78. She did nothing but _____ excuses all the time.
    A) to making   B) to make   C) make   D) making
79. Tom _____ a computer, so he can't find a good job.
    A) uses   B) is using   C) cannot use   D) used

80. Tom, _____ no foreign languages, can't find a good job.
    A) speaking   B) spoke   C) speaks   D) is speaking
81. The detective asked the gangster where _____ .
    A) the gun was   B) was the gun
    C) did he hide the gun   D) the gun hidden
82. After Jack _____ his poem, he decided not to show it to anybody.
    A) finishing   B) had finished   C) was finishing   D) has finished
83. He thought he _____ able to find more information on British imperialism.
    A) will be   B) would be   C) is   D) was
84. If it _____ so expensive, Linda would often eat out.
    A) weren't   B) wasn't   C) isn't   D) won't be
85. Americans Indians _____ feel so unhappy if they were treated fairly.
    A) will   B) were   C) won't   D) would not
86. It is easy to develop bad study habits, but it is extremely difficult to rid _____ of them.
    A) ourselves   B) itself   C) themselves   D) yourselves
87. We will probably have to work _____ midnight today because the report should be ready tomorrow.
    A) for   B) until   C) under   D) by
88. _____ cause extensive damage to our city each year.
    A) Because of the winds during hurricanes
    B) The winds of hurricanes
    C) The winds which
    D) That the winds of hurricanes
89. Malaria _____ by the female mosquito.
    A) transmits   B) transmitted   C) is transmitted   D) to transmit
90. Water, _____ , is also one of the most abundant compounds on earth.
    A) is necessary for human survival
    B) one of the most critical elements for human survival
    C) it is necessary for human survival
    D) for human survival
91. The Social Security Act of 1935 was _____ .
    A) written to insure workers against unemployment
    B) it insured workers against unemployment
    C) written that it insured workers against unemployment
    D) workers against unemployment
92. Philosophers are not sure _____ .
    A) how can universal peace be secured
    B) universal peace can be
    C) precisely how universal peace can be secured
    D) can universal peace be secured
93. Overexposure to the sun _____ .
    A) more than damage to the skin
    B) damage to the skin
    C) can produce damage to the skin
    D) more damage to the skin
94. Antarctica is larger _____ , but it has no native human population.
    A) with some countries
    B) Europe and Australia put together
    C) from Europe or Australia
    D) than Europe or Australia
95. _____ paper was first used by the Chinese.
    A) That the belief   B) The belief that
    C) To believe that   D) It is believed that
96. Gold is the preferred choice of jewelry makers _____ indestructible.
    A) since it is   B) it is   C) because of   D) insofar as
97. _____ growing awareness of social ills, the philosophers wrote increasingly more to warn people.
    A) A   B) When a   C) Because her   D) Due to her
98. _____ categorized as lipids.
    A) Fats and also oils   B) While fats and oils
    C) Fats and oils are   D) Fats and oils
99. The overwhelming majority of people who _____ in the rescue operations were volunteers.
    A) they served   B) did they serve
    C) serving   D) served
100. _____ is found in many kinds of fruits and vegetables.
    A) Vitamin C   B) That vitamin C
    C) It is latex vitamin C   D) Because vitamin C

TEST 9

1. They asked a lot of questions _____ his job.
   A) about B) of C) for D) on

2. They need some gas. They're looking _____ a gas station.
   A) for B) to C) from D) at

3. She was _____ Paris last month.
   A) to B) at C) in D) from

4. There's park across the street _____ the hospital.
   A) of B) from C) to D) for

5. He has an apartment _____ Maple Street.
   A) at B) on C) into D) between

6. There aren't any pictures _____ the wall.
   A) to B) in C) at D) on

7. He never watches TV _____ Sunday.
   A) at B) in C) on D) with

8. I have only been here _____ 1983.
   A) for B) by C) since D) in

9. My uncle has not been here _____ the end of May.
   A) since B) during C) for D) while

10. I have not seen my best friend _____ nearly a fortnight.
    A) ago B) for C) since D) while

11. My brother was _____ all week.
    A) at the home B) at home C) in the home D) in home

12. You don't like hamburgers, _____ ?
    A) you don't B) don't you C) you do D) do you

13. She likes to exercise, _____ ?
    A) does she B) she doesn't C) doesn't she D) she does

14. There aren't any more books, _____ ?
    A) are they B) are there C) aren't there D) aren't they

15. She's found her money, _____ ?
    A) is she B) hasn't she C) isn't she D) has she

16. I'll be 29 next month, _____ ?
    A) am I B) aren't I C) will I D) won't I

17. Where are the glasses? _____ on the shelf.
    A) They're B) There C) Their D) There are

18. The boys are cleaning _____ shoes.
    A) there B) their C) theirs D) them

19. She _____ the bus every day.
    A) taking B) takes C) is taking D) take

20. I know it is here _____ .
    A) anywhere B) everywhere C) somewhere D) in

21. I can't find that book _____ .
    A) everywhere B) where C) not here D) anywhere

22. That book is not Helen's. It is _____ .
    A) her B) my C) his D) them

23. Is there _____ on the meat?
    A) anybody B) anything C) somebody D) thing

24. The _____ house is on Taylor Street.
    A) Bill's B) friend C) Brown's D) families

25. This is _____ friend.
    A) Helen B) Helen's C) one of Helen's D) of Helen's

26. My friend and _____ went for a walk.
    A) me B) my C) mine D) I

27. Maria _____ at home yesterday.
    A) is B) were C) was D) went

28. Did she _____ anything strange there?
    A) saw B) seeing C) see D) look

29. What has _____ ?
    A) he doing B) been done C) it does D) being done

30. They _____ football now.
    A) is playing B) plays C) play D) are playing

31. They _____ at the King's Restaurant last night.
    A) eat B) did eat C) eating D) ate

32. He _____ today.
    A) are working B) is working C) work D) working

33. Nancy _____ speak French.
    A) is B) wants C) want to D) can

34. Peter _____ the dinner although he was ordered to.
    A) didn't prepare B) wasn't prepared
    C) had to be prepared D) should have been prepared

35. A: Does Anne like music?
    B: Yes, she _____ .
    A) do B) likes C) does D) does like

36. He _____ at that office for a long time.
    A) works B) is working
    C) has been working D) working

37. Mary has been _____ English for three years.
    A) studied B) study C) studying D) to study

38. I _____ go shopping tomorrow.
    A) am B) may C) want D) think

39. A man who is very healthy _____ to see a doctor frequently.
    A) should go B) doesn't have C) ought D) has

40. Unfortunately, I _____ wash the dishes now.
    A) can B) like to C) have to D) try to

41. Do they always watch television? Yes, they _____ .
    A) watch B) do C) do watch D) does

42. _____ you like to go the movies tonight?
    A) How B) Had C) Would D) Why

43. We won't have _____ apples.
    A) much B) any C) some D) few

44. There's _____ milk in the refrigerator.
    A) a little B) a few C) much D) many

45. He doesn't drink _____ coffee.
    A) much B) a little C) some D) many

46. I spent _____ time studying for the test.
    A) a lot of B) a few C) not much D) hours

47. There aren't any glasses on the shelf. There aren't _____ on the table, either.
    A) some B) a few C) none D) any

48. There are _____ magazines in the living room.
    A) any B) a few C) much D) a little

49. She doesn't have any sugar. She needs _____ .
    A) any B) one C) some D) another

50. I'm only going to buy _____ stamps.
    A) many B) much C) a few D) a little

51. There wasn't _____ traffic on that street last night.
    A) many B) a lot of C) a little D) much

52. We bought _____ food today.
    A) much B) many C) a lot of D) plenty

53. If I _____ a chef, I would make a great meal.
    A) am B) was C) were D) had been

54. We _____ to go with him if we can't get permission.
    A) want to be B) won't be able
    C) don't D) can't

55. Leonard won't come here _____ it rains tomorrow.
    A) will   B) if   C) because   D) and

56. If Tom goes _____ movies, he won't be able to come to dinner.
    A) to   B) to the   C) the   D) inside

57. If Anita doesn't hurry, she _____ be able to finish her paper.
    A) won't   B) would   C) can   D) can't

58. A: _____ is responsible for all this confusion?
    B: It may be Jack.
    A) How   B) Why   C) Who   D) Whom

59. A: _____ do you go there?
    B: To visit some friends.
    A) When   B) Why   C) What   D) Where

60. _____ did Helen eat for breakfast?
    A) When   B) What   C) Where   D) Why

61. He hasn't bought _____ apples.
    A) a lot   B) any   C) much   D) some

62. Sarah, what _____ doing?
    A) she is   B) are   C) are you   D) is

63. Are there six books on the table?
    A) No, five are.   B) No, there is.
    C) No, there are three.   D) No, there are any.

64. A: _____ does she go to work?
    B: At nine o'clock.
    A) Why   B) Where   C) When   D) How

65. Wind power is both clean _____ .
    A) and expensive   B) but expensive
    C) but expensive also   D) cheap

66. Tom will mend the window when _____ home.
    A) he come   B) does he come
    C) he is coming   D) he comes

67. Are you making any more cakes?
    A) Yes, I do   B) Yes, I am
    C) Yes, I am doing   D) Yes, I am making

68. A: Were you singing when I came in?
    B: Yes, I _____ .
    A) sang   B) was   C) were   D) did

69. Lately, he has become interested in _____ antiques.
    A) collecting   B) to collect   C) collect   D) for collecting

70. I wonder when _____ home.
    A) is she coming   B) will she come
    C) she is coming   D) can she come

71. The singer _____ many compliments on her new album.
    A) paid   B) has been paid
    C) being paid   D) has been paying

72. He is _____ .
    A) artist   B) of artist   C) an artist   D) artistically

73. Gloria is a good dancer. She dances _____ .
    A) good   B) goodly   C) very good   D) well

74. We work _____ every day.
    A) hard   B) hardly   C) careful   D) good

75. _____ Helen reads in bed.
    A) Never   B) Seldom   C) Sometimes   D) Almost

76. You seem _____ a jazz fan.
    A) liking   B) to be   C) are   D) to himself

77. That man _____ terrible.
    A) cooks   B) feels   C) runs   D) works

78. The cookies taste _____ .
    A) well   B) much   C) good   D) beautifully

79. _____ bottle in the sink.
    A) It has a   B) It is   C) There's a   D) There are

80. _____ magazines in the closet.
    A) They're   B) Their   C) There   D) There are

81. _____ coffee in the pot.
    A) It's a   B) It has   C) There's a   D) There's some

82. A video set is _____ than a television set.
    A) more expensive   B) expensive
    C) most expensive   D) the most expensive

83. The yellow car is _____ car in the parking lot.
    A) dirtier   B) the dirtier   C) the dirtiest   D) the dirty

84. My hat is different _____ yours.
    A) to   B) as   C) like   D) from

85. Barbara doesn't have a car, _____ she takes the bus to work.
    A) as   B) because   C) then   D) so

86. _____ Tom nor his wife has a cold.
    A) Neither   B) Nor   C) Either   D) Or

87. We managed to reach our house _____ the road was flooded.
    A) whether   B) because   C) although   D) unless

88. He was late, _____ he took a taxi.
    A) as   B) so   C) then   D) since

89. Mrs. Simpson will visit _____ Spain or Greece.
    A) both   B) either   C) neither   D) between

90. The car is both fast _____ economical.
    A) if   B) and   C) or   D) but

91. Gold _____ in many countries.
    A) is found   B) finds   C) has found   D) finding

92. Many cameras _____ in Japan.
    A) made   B) are making   C) here   D) are made

93. There was a storm. Two trees _____ down.
    A) were blowing   B) were blown
    C) were to blow   D) blew

94. The electric light bulb _____ by Thomas Edison.
    A) is invented   B) was invented
    C) invented   D) invents

95. Even though construction costs are high, a new hospital _____ next year.
    A) will be built   B) would be built
    C) is built   D) builds

96. I don't know _____ book this is.
    A) interesting   B) who   C) whose   D) your

97. This is my friend _____ house is near mine.
    A) who lives is   B) who is   C) whose   D) in his

98. Helen is wearing a jacket _____ is red.
    A) it   B) as red   C) that   D) such

99. Do you know a good place _____ we can have lunch?
    A) somewhere   B) where   C) anywhere   D) there

100. This is the _____ suit I have ever bought.
    A) more expensive   B) most expensively
    C) most expensive   D) more expensively

TEST 10

1. _____ is going to the party.
   A) All   B) Everyone   C) Every   D) Some

2. Tom cut _____ while he was shaving this morning.
   A) him   B) his   C) himself   D) he

3. The food is on the table. Please help _____ to meat.
   A) you   B) your   C) it   D) yourself

4. We came out of the swimming pool and dried _____ carefully.
   A) us   B) our   C) ourselves   D) ours

5. Tom and Martha are learning judo so that they can protect _____ if necessary.
   A) them   B) their   C) theirs   D) themselves

6. My pen must be _____ but I can't find it.
   A) anywhere   B) somewhere   C) nowhere   D) anything

7. There isn't _____ at the door.
   A) anyone   B) someone   C) no one   D) nobody

8. The government _____ is in danger of falling.
   A) itself   B) its   C) it   D) they

9. Mary and Tom _____ the house.
   A) is looking   B) are looking at
   C) is looking at   D) are looking

10. Do they live in England?
    A) Yes, they live.   B) No, they don't.
    C) Yes, they are.   D) No, they don't live

11. What is his sister doing?
    A) Read.   B) He's reading.
    C) She's reading   D) It's reading

12. Where is the book?
    A) There is.   B) It's here.
    C) He's under the chair.   D) There's one chair.

13. Allan _____ his trip carefully.
    A) planning   B) had been planning
    C) he plans   D) has a plan for

14. Bruce _____ driving safely before the accident.
    A) hadn't been   B) always   C) he was   D) wasn't he

15. We often _____ dinner at six.
    A) having   B) has   C) are having   D) have

16. She _____ play tennis yesterday because it was raining.
    A) won't   B) always   C) couldn't   D) shouldn't

17. Carlos heard that you _____ in town.
    A) are   B) been   C) were   D) gone

18. He promised that they _____ the following Saturday.
    A) come   B) shall come   C) would come   D) are coming

19. The tree is _____ the door.
    A) between   B) in front   C) beside   D) next

20. Tom is in front of Helen. Helen is _____ Tom.
    A) beside   B) behind   C) before   D) between

21. She flew _____ high mountains.
    A) over   B) under   C) in   D) at

22. She looks _____ an actress.
    A) as   B) as if   C) like   D) as though

23. Paula hurried _____ station.
    A) into   B) as if   C) to the   D) as through

24. She's thinking _____ her house.
    A) to sell   B) of selling   C) on selling   D) she sell

25. I'm interested _____ getting a job at the airport.
    A) for   B) in   C) about   D) to

26. Peter received a letter _____ France yesterday.
    A) to   B) by   C) of   D) from

27. There are some good restaurants _____ our little town.
    A) at   B) for   C) in   D) from

28. She drives her husband _____ work.
    A) to   B) with   C) at   D) in

29. My friends _____ to play tennis.
    A) like   B) wants   C) can   D) likes

30. Do you know where _____ a passport?
    A) get me   B) can get me   C) to get   D) get

31. She's asking _____ some questions.
    A) them   B) to them   C) for them   D) of them

32. She will make dinner when she _____ home.
    A) gets   B) gets to   C) will get   D) is getting

33. They went _____ after school.
    A) to home   B) at home   C) home   D) to the home

34. You are the _____ person I've ever known.
    A) luckier   B) more lucky   C) too lucky   D) luckiest

35. She prefers playing cards _____ television.
    A) than watch   B) to watch   C) to watching   D) than watching

36. They work in the _____ building in Istanbul.
    A) modern   B) too modern
    C) more modern   D) most modern

37. He wasn't _____ to carry the case by himself.
    A) too strong   B) strong enough
    C) so strong   D) as strong

38. Is Helen _____ Kate?
    A) taller   B) so tall as   C) as tall as   D) tall than

39. Please tell me where _____ .
    A) does Peter live   B) Peter live
    C) Peter lives   D) Peter does live

40. Where _____ yesterday?
    A) was you   B) have you been
    C) did you   D) were you

41. How _____ to the station from here?
    A) to go   B) do you go   C) do one go   D) go we

42. Where _____ .
    A) Ali works?   B) works Ali?
    C) does Ali work?   D) Ali is working?

43. What's that man?
    A) He's Tom.   B) It's Tom   C) Yes, it's Tom   D) He's a pilot

44. Do you dance or draw?
    A) I'm dancing but drawing.   B) I'm dancing, but I not drawing.
    C) I dance, but I don't draw.   D) I dance, but I am not drawing.

45. If Mr. White _____ mayor, he will save the city park.
    A) will become   B) becomes   C) is becoming   D) became

46. They _____ raise animals if they lived on a farm.
    A) shall   B) should   C) can   D) could

47. If he had more time, he _____ take piano lessons.
    A) can   B) will   C) would   D) may

48. If I were you, I _____ take the bus.
    A) shall   B) can   C) will   D) would

49. They will work overtime if they _____ for it.
    A) get paid   B) will get paid
    C) would get paid   D) have gotten paid

50. We expect them _____ at nine o'clock.
    A) are coming   B) come   C) to come   D) will come

51. In cold countries people wear thick clothes _____ warm.
    A) for keeping   B) for to keep   C) to keep   D) keep

52. The movie _____ interesting at the end.
    A) goes   B) gets   C) sees   D) stops

53. The flowers smell _____ .
    A) much B) very much C) good D) well

54. The theater seems _____ small for all the people.
    A) to B) to be too C) it's to D) too much

55. Jean enjoys jogging and _____ .
    A) to swim B) a swim C) swimming D) swim

56. Edmond enjoys hiking and _____ .
    A) to camp B) to climb mountains
    C) fishing D) a fish

57. Tomorrow I'll go to the library _____ .
    A) and study B) for studying
    C) and studying D) reading

58. The cake is delicious, but I can't eat _____ more.
    A) some B) no C) any D) nothing

59. _____ people take the bus.
    A) Much B) A little C) A lot of D) Any

60. They don't have _____ clothes.
    A) much B) some C) few D) many

61. There wasn't _____ traffic on that street last night.
    A) many B) some C) a little D) much

62. He has spent a large _____ of money on his new house.
    A) deal B) amount C) number D) place

63. Helen has answered _____ questions.
    A) the more B) very much C) any D) a few

64. America _____ by Christopher Columbus in 1492.
    A) was here B) found
    C) was discovered D) had ships

65. The computer _____ guaranteed by the company.
    A) is B) are C) it's D) aren't

66. These houses _____ by settlers many yeas ago.
    A) are made B) were built C) built D) made

67. Where is the girl _____ saw the accident?
    A) whom B) _ C) she D) who

68. This is the watch _____ does not work properly.
    A) who B) that C) it D) _

69. You didn't lose your watch, _____ ?
    A) did you B) it's lost C) didn't you D) either

70. Linda was studying last night, _____ ?
    A) wasn't she B) she wasn't C) she was D) did she

71. You didn't mind waiting for us, _____ ?
    A) haven't you B) aren't you C) don't you D) did you

72. You didn't like our new computer, _____ ?
    A) didn't you B) you didn't C) you did D) did you

73. Helen and Tom were both excited about the project, _____ ?
    A) were they B) weren't they C) they were D) she was

74. Roberta wasn't in class today, _____ ?
    A) wasn't she B) was she C) weren't they D) very much

75. Jimmy isn't _____ to go out alone.
    A) very old B) enough old C) old enough D) old for

76. Last week Tom _____ his leg.
    A) falls and breaks B) fallen and broken
    C) fell and broke D) fell and has broken

77. _____ clever baby!
    A) What B) How C) What a D) How a

78. Tell _____ back tomorrow.
    A) Martha to come B) Martha come
    C) to Martha to come D) to Martha come

79. At the post office he asked _____ .
    A) stamps B) some stamps
    C) four stamps D) for stamps

80. I've just finished _____ my shopping.
    A) to make B) doing C) to do D) to

81. Do you know where _____ ?
    A) is the hotel B) can I find the hotel
    C) was the hotel D) the hotel is

82. The telephone rang _____ I was going out of the house.
    A) just B) just as C) even if D) even

83. Peter isn't very tall. _____ is John.
    A) So B) Neither C) Too D) Short

84. They don't have much free time. Neither _____ .
    A) do we have B) do we C) we do D) are we

85. She is hungry, and _____ am I.
    A) so B) nor C) neither D) too

86. This is the restaurant _____ we used to eat.
    A) which B) where C) that D) when

87. Many people _____ Mohammed Ali is the greatest boxer of all times.
    A) are believing B) believe
    C) do believe D) like

88. There _____ news tonight.
    A) are not many B) is not much
    C) are not much D) is not many

89. Albert is hungry. He _____ to have dinner now.
    A) can B) want C) wants D) likes

90. Please call Gloria when you _____ home.
    A) get B) will get C) get to D) are getting

91. May I ask a favor _____ you?
    A) of B) from C) for D) to

92. We are going _____ a party tomorrow.
    A) to have B) to go C) having D) to go

93. Betty couldn't help _____ when Oscar fell down.
    A) the laugh B) to laugh C) at laughing D) laughing

94. He took a shower before _____ dressed.
    A) he gets B) to get C) getting D) he has gotten

95. I enjoy _____ music.
    A) listen to B) listening C) listening to D) to listen to

96. Would you mind _____ the window?
    A) open B) to open C) opening D) opened

97. The doctor made me _____ in bed for a week.
    A) staying B) to stay C) stayed D) stay

98. I don't mind _____ for you.
    A) to wait B) waiting C) to waiting D) wait

99. I can't stand _____ the bus to work.
    A) riding B) ride C) the ride D) sitting

100. Sam likes to _____ on the weekends.
    A) go fish B) go to fish C) go fishing D) do fishing

TEST 11

1. _____ people don't know what the weather is like in other countries.
   A) The most   B) Most of   C) Most   D) A great

2. Our government spends _____ money on schools.
   A) much   B) many   C) a lot of   D) a great

3. We did _____ exercises yesterday without making _____ mistakes.
   A) some / any   B) some / some   C) some / no   D) any / some

4. The boys ate _____ sandwiches, but they didn't drink _____ milk at all.
   A) some / no   B) any / no   C) some / any   D) some / some

5. That man never does _____ work
   A) some   B) any   C) anything   D) something

6. They have _____ butter.
   A) some   B) any   C) a   D) one

7. They don't know _____ people in Florida.
   A) much   B) some   C) a few   D) many

8. _____ the volcanoes in Japan are active.
   A) However, of   B) Several of   C) Few   D) There are

9. The animal was hiding _____ a tree.
   A) in front of   B) behind   C) next to   D) with

10. _____ my friends live near me.
    A) Most   B) Most of   C) Of   D) Five

11. Helen works _____ a large office.
    A) on   B) in   C) at   D) for

12. My friends leads _____ a very easy life.
    A) with   B) in   C) _   D) to

13. A lot of students were standing _____ a queue.
    A) in   B) on   C) at   D) with

14. The women are not interested _____ the demonstration in the park.
    A) on   B) to   C) for   D) in

15. The party will start _____ Sunday.
    A) 8 o'clock at   B) 8 o'clock   C) on 8 o'clock   D) at 8 o'clock on

16. An old car was parked _____ the house.
    A) front of   B) at the front   C) in front of   D) in front

17. He takes good care _____ his motorcycle.
    A) for   B) of   C) to   D) with

18. A: Is this _____ book you were telling me about?
    B: Yes, it is about _____ life of Queen Victoria.
    A) _ / _   B) the / the   C) a / a   D) a / the

19. The whale is _____ of all living mammals.
    A) the largest   B) largest
    C) the largest which is   D) larger than

20. Tom plays tennis well, but he's not very good _____ basketball.
    A) in   B) at   C) on   D) for

21. I never _____ coffee.
    A) drink   B) am drinking
    C) from a cup of   D) drink like that coffee

22. Barbara and Tony _____ to the beach last Sunday.
    A) was   B) went   C) go   D) were

23. Don't forget to give him the message when you _____ him.
    A) see   B) will see   C) have seen   D) are seeing

24. Did Anne wash the dishes? Yes, she _____ .
    A) did   B) did wash   C) is washing   D) washed

25. Did they have dinner at home? No, they _____ .
    A) didn't have   B) have not   C) didn't   D) don't

26. We _____ a good movie last week.
    A) saw   B) have seen   C) were seeing   D) see

27. Have you been to the post office? Yes, I _____ .
    A) did   B) have   C) want   D) was

28. Nancy _____ to play tennis tomorrow.
    A) goes   B) is going   C) will like   D) likes

29. They _____ to the park yet.
    A) didn't go   B) have gone   C) haven't gone   D) don't go

30. They _____ the dishes when she left.
    A) was washing   B) were washing
    C) are washing   D) have washed

31. He's taking _____ some chocolates.
    A) her   B) to her   C) hers   D) she

32. She doesn't know _____ about sports.
    A) anything   B) something   C) nothing   D) none

33. Albert has a good radio. He doesn't need _____ .
    A) other one   B) any   C) some   D) another one

34. A: Whose is that?
    B: It's _____ .
    A) my   B) ours   C) of Tom   D) my sisters.

35. I didn't call the police. My son didn't call _____ .
    A) them, either   B) them, too
    C) him, either   D) him, too

36. Both of those men are tall. _____ of them is short.
    A) None   B) Neither   C) Any   D) Some

37. The girls are washing _____ clothes.
    A) there   B) theirs   C) their   D) them

38. Marie has two radios. _____ of them are good.
    A) Some   B) Any   C) Both   D) One

39. Albert likes Linda. He brought _____ a bar of chocolate yesterday.
    A) for her   B) hers   C) to her   D) her

40. I don't know _____ at the bank.
    A) anyone   B) any person   C) someone   D) nobody

41. You'd better take your umbrella. It _____ rain.
    A) might   B) must   C) can   D) would

42. He _____ play basketball in high school.
    A) use to   B) used to   C) like to   D) always

43. Linda _____ go to the market today.
    A) have to   B) has to   C) need to   D) likes to

44. Mr. Brown works very hard. He _____ relax more.
    A) likes to   B) would   C) shall   D) should

45. Last year Mr. Taylor _____ work 60 hours a week.
    A) must   B) had to   C) would   D) has to

46. I'm not used to _____ early.
    A) get up   B) getting up   C) I get up   D) be getting up

47. We would have to sign a lease, _____ ?
    A) do we   B) wouldn't we   C) haven't we   D) hadn't we

48. He'll have to stay home if he _____ to the bank.
    A) can't go   B) can't   C) been going   D) won't go

49. _____ children went on the flight.
    A) All of   B) Them   C) One of   D) Both

50. I _____ rather go shopping tomorrow. I have a lot of work today.
    A) would   B) can   C) much   D) will

51. If the projector _____ , we won't be able to see the movie.
    A) doesn't work   B) worked   C) didn't work   D) wasn't work

52. If people _____ , he will feel bad.
    A) will laugh   B) wouldn't laughed
    C) laugh   D) would laugh

53. If I had a car, I _____ to the theater.
    A) drive   B) would drive   C) would drove   D) drives

54. If they stand up, we _____ see the screen.
    A) doesn't   B) won't be able to
    C) haven't to   D) aren't

55. If my car _____ start, I will be late.
    A) didn't   B) doesn't   C) don't   D) did

56. I would come if I _____ enough time.
    A) had   B) have   C) will have   D) can have

57. He would feel better if he _____ more sleep.
    A) got   B) gets   C) will get   D) has gotten

58. You will succeed if you _____ .
    A) are trying   B) will try
    C) try   D) are going to try

59. _____ long books are interesting.
    A) Many   B) Many of   C) Many the   D) Of

60. _____ charming person she is!
    A) What   B) How   C) That   D) What a

61. _____ people came than I expected.
    A) Other   B) Fewer   C) Another   D) Few

62. I don't know where _____ .
    A) is the post-office   B) has the post-office
    C) the post-office   D) the post-office is

63. Tom sat near the fire _____ .
    A) to get warm   B) for to get warm
    C) for getting warm   D) get warm

64. She came _____ because her car had broken down.
    A) to walk   B) walk   C) by foot   D) on foot

65. She is very fond _____ modern art.
    A) in   B) of   C) with   D) at

66. I find English spelling _____ .
    A) it is difficult   B) is difficult   C) be difficult   D) difficult

67. It is not easy _____ me to tell you what happened.
    A) of   B) for   C) to   D) from

68. The film has finished, and the people _____ home.
    A) went   B) have gone   C) were going   D) going

69. She felt ill after _____ the food.
    A) eat   B) eating   C) to eat   D) eaten

70. I saw somebody _____ towards your house.
    A) going   B) went   C) gone   D) to go

71. _____ his experiments, Faraday made an important discovery.
    A) While   B) During   C) Since   D) For

72. Tom is _____ Helen.
    A) as tall as   B) as tall as   C) so tall as   D) so tall than

73. A dozen is _____ twenty.
    A) almost the same as   B) half as much as
    C) much more than   D) less than

74. I felt ill on Saturday, but I felt _____ on Sunday.
    A) worse   B) badly   C) worst   D) _

75. Are you interested in _____ a watch?
    A) by   B) for   C) buying   D) to buy

76. I hope everyone in your family is _____ good health.
    A) in   B) for   C) at   D) on

77. Our visitor will arrive _____ the airport soon after midnight.
    A) in   B) at   C) on   D) over

78. How long have you been working _____ hospital?
    A) this   B) that   C) at the   D) next door the

79. It is not always easy to pass thread _____ the eye of a needle.
    A) from   B) to   C) through   D) in

80. We stepped _____ the house _____ the garden.
    A) from / to   B) out of / into   C) out of / for   D) _ / into

81. I lost my keys _____ I was playing football.
    A) during   B) while   C) because of   D) for

82. _____ does she take the bus? Because she doesn't have a car.
    A) Why   B) Where   C) When   D) How

83. I don't need _____ money.
    A) no other   B) another   C) any   D) any other

84. How much money _____ in the bank?
    A) he has got   B) has he got   C) he had   D) he did

85. There isn't _____ water left, so we can't make tea.
    A) some   B) a little   C) any   D) more

86. How _____ men work for Mr. White?
    A) much   B) a lot of   C) hard   D) many

87. How _____ do you earn a month?
    A) many   B) hard   C) often   D) much

88. _____ some paper on the desk.
    A) It has   B) There are   C) They're   D) There's

89. A living room is usually _____ than the kitchen.
    A) bigger   B) the bigger   C) biggest   D) very big

90. This is an old photograph of me when I _____ .
    A) was having short hair   B) have short hair
    C) have had   D) had short hair

91. A: What is your new partner like?
    B: She _____ .
    A) likes football   B) is like any other partner
    C) likes almost nothing   D) is tall and slender

92. _____ is heavier, a kilo of gold or a kilo of feather?
    A) What   B) Which   C) How much   D) Who

93. _____ is the highest mountain in the world?
    A) What   B) Which   C) Who   D) How

94. _____ is the price of this blouse?
    A) What   B) Who   C) How   D) Which

95. _____ lives in that old house?
    A) What   B) Who   C) Which   D) How

96. _____ shall I give you, tea or lemonade?
    A) Where   B) How   C) What   D) Why

97. The rescue team _____ in the region hit by the recent earthquake last week.
    A) are   B) were   C) was   D) went

98. We _____ to London last Monday.
    A) can drive   B) will drive   C) drove   D) had driven

99. I will probably work _____ six.
    A) for   B) under   C) by   D) until

100. _____ the time Mr. Brown is sixty, he will have completed more than ten detective novels forty years.
    A) When   B) Until   C) Over   D) By

TEST 12

1. _____ is the climate like in your country?
   A) What B) Which C) Where D) How

2. _____ of these students studies hard?
   A) What B) How C) Which D) Who

3. She will come at 7 o'clock _____ evening.
   A) of this B) on this C) this D) at this

4. A: Are my shoes in the box?
   B: No, there _____ in the box.
   A) isn't anything B) isn't nothing
   C) aren't things D) isn't any

5. Alice is _____ as the boys.
   A) too strong B) so strong C) as strong D) also strong

6. I never eat potatoes, and _____.
   A) so doesn't Tom B) neither does Tom
   C) neither is Tom D) neither Tom does

7. What _____ on Sundays?
   A) Ali usually does B) does Ali usually do
   C) does Ali usually D) usually does Ali do

8. _____ lovely food!
   A) Which B) How C) What D) Where

9. I think there are _____ in the garden.
   A) nobody B) someone C) some people D) anybody

10. This is _____.
    A) the question thirty B) the question thirteenth
    C) question thirty D) thirteen question

11. The sun came _____ the windows.
    A) out of B) into C) with D) through

12. The old man came _____ the stairs.
    A) out of B) through C) down D) off

13. In Britain people drive _____ the left.
    A) on B) in C) at D) _

14. The distance _____ Ankara _____ Bursa is five hundred kilometers.
    A) from / to B) to / to C) _ / from D) from / _

15. You may write _____ a pencil or a pen.
    A) with B) for C) in D) from

16. Subtract two _____ ten.
    A) under B) out of C) than D) from

17. Mt. Everest is a little _____ 29,000 feet high.
    A) over B) than C) above D) for

18. Many women are afraid _____ mice.
    A) with B) of C) from D) than

19. There is a big difference _____ a cheap watch and an expensive one.
    A) with B) than C) from D) between

20. Tom was really delighted _____ your gift.
    A) with B) for C) about D) in

21. Wallace wasn't very careful when he drove the car, _____ ?
    A) wasn't he B) did he C) didn't he D) was he

22. She didn't tell Robert where her wife was, _____ ?
    A) wasn't she B) did she C) didn't she D) was she

23. Your friends aren't given any chance, _____ ?
    A) do they B) aren't they C) haven't they D) are they

24. Linda is thirsty. She wants _____ glass of milk.
    A) other B) some C) any D) another

25. I want to give my brother _____ for his birthday.
    A) a thing B) anything C) something D) any

26. Is that umbrella _____ ?
    A) you B) to you C) your D) yours

27. We bought a lamp for Mr. Pools. We gave it _____ last night.
    A) him B) to him C) his D) for him

28. Don't talk _____ .
    A) him B) he C) to him D) at him

29. A: Whose car is that?
    B: It's _____ .
    A) to her B) hers C) her D) Mrs. Jacobs

30. A: Whose is this?
    B: _____ .
    A) His B) He's C) It's D) It is

31. There isn't _____ in the restaurant.
    A) any people B) any persons C) anybody D) nobody

32. A: Have you got any apples?
    B: Yes, I've got _____ .
    A) a small B) one small
    C) two small ones D) two small

33. _____ don't like red wine.
    A) Some people B) Any people
    C) Somebody D) Anybody

34. I can hardly see _____ without my glasses.
    A) anything B) something C) nothing D) nowhere

35. The Nelsons enjoyed _____ on their vacation.
    A) themselves B) yourselves C) yourself D) ourselves

36. Mrs. Baker is fond of her students. She's giving _____ some candy.
    A) to them B) them C) they D) for them

37. My sister called last week. I haven't spoken _____ since.
    A) him B) she C) her D) to her

38. Is this typewriter _____ ?
    A) your B) yours C) to you D) you

39. He _____ in the heavy rain and came home dripping wet.
    A) was caught B) caught C) catch D) have caught

40. She has _____ strange in her handbag.
    A) something B) some things C) a thing D) anything

41. She's telling _____ an amusing story.
    A) they B) them C) to them D) their

42. All of the students did _____ homework.
    A) his B) her C) its D) their

43. I imagine _____ to have Italian ancestors.
    A) she B) his C) her D) their

44. When I returned home, my father asked me where I _____ .
    A) was B) had been C) have been D) went

45. Tom has just left for San Francisco. By six o'clock tomorrow he _____ New York.
    A) will have reached B) will reach
    C) reaches D) has reached

46. My brother told me that he _____ the letter.
    A) has posted B) will post C) had posted D) is posting

47. You can go home if you _____ your work.
    A) are finishing B) finished
    C) will finish D) have finished

48. When I arrived home at 7 o'clock, I was very surprised. Everybody _____ out.
    A) were B) has gone C) had gone D) is

49. He is sad because he _____ some money.
    A) lost B) had lost C) has lost D) was lost

50. Mohammed Ali _____ his first world title fight in 1960.
    A) has won B) is winning C) was winning D) won

51. Water _____ at a temperature of 100° C.
    A) is boiling B) boils C) boiled D) boil

52. In cold climates people _____ sitting in the sun.
    A) like   B) likes   C) are liking   D) do like

53. I was doing the shopping while you _____ tennis.
    A) played   B) were playing
    C) have played   D) have been playing

54. We _____ television when a bird flew into the room.
    A) was watching   B) were watching
    C) looked at   D) saw

55. Do they often go to the beach? Yes, they _____ .
    A) do   B) go   C) do go   D) are going

56. Does Albert have any new magazines? No, he _____ .
    A) does   B) doesn't   C) has   D) don't

57. He didn't understand me _____ I spoke to him slowly and clearly.
    A) although   B) however   C) since   D) because

58. _____ you open the window please?
    A) Could   B) Shall   C) Should   D) Must

59. She would rather read _____ listen to the radio.
    A) than   B) to   C) or   D) and

60. You look hungry. _____ you like a sandwich?
    A) Will   B) Would   C) Do   D) can

61. Professor Perkins _____ teach at your school.
    A) has   B) use to   C) is used to   D) used to

62. _____ to drive a bulldozer?
    A) Are you using   B) Did you use
    C) Do you use   D) Have you used

63. He _____ to go to college in his own hometown.
    A) uses   B) use   C) used   D) had used

64. Our suitcases _____ examined before anybody said anything.
    A) have been   B) is being   C) can't   D) had been

65. Let's drive _____ , shall we?
    A) to downtown   B) at downtown
    C) up downtown   D) downtown

66. The theater is located _____ .
    A) downtown   B) to downtown
    C) in downtown   D) into downtown

67. The guests are _____ .
    A) in upstairs   B) at door
    C) in the living-room D) downstairs

68. You can find many stores _____ of town.
    A) in center   B) the center   C) in the center   D) center

69. The fish moved _____ and silently through the water.
    A) swimming   B) rapid   C) to swim   D) quickly

70. _____ countries waged a war against poverty
    A) Both of   B) Both   C) None of   D) None

71. The whale _____ as a fish, but it is actually a mammal.
    A) regards   B) is regarded
    C) regarded   D) which has been regarded

72. The Empire State Building is different _____ the Parliament Building in Brasilia.
    A) between   B) from   C) to   D) for

73. The American pyramids are in some ways similar _____ the Egyptian pyramids.
    A) between   B) from   C) to   D) for

74. He was _____ than I was at playing chess.
    A) good   B) better   C) the best   D) best

75. Martha has been watching television, and _____ .
    A) Ralph has too   B) Ralph hasn't either
    C) so does Palph   D) neither has Ralph

76. Jack finished the assignment quickly and _____ .
    A) correctly   B) correct   C) rapid   D) hardly

77. Frank likes singing and _____ .
    A) to dance   B) a dance   C) dance   D) dancing

78. Harvey's new story is both short _____ interesting.
    A) but   B) nor   C) and   D) it's

79. A: Why don't you call Rita?
    B: I _____ call her a few minutes ago, but her phone was busy.
    A) am   B) do   C) will   D) did

80. Neither Jake _____ Diana can speak Japanese.
    A) and   B) or   C) nor   D) if

81. Many adult students of English wish they _____ their language studies earlier.
    A) would start   B) started
    C) would have started D) had started

82. Did they tell you whether or not they _____ there at 10 o'clock?
    A) would be   B) were gone   C) will go   D) can go

83. They'll work on the problem _____ they solve it.
    A) why   B) by   C) until   D) that

84. Have you ever thought _____ psychology?
    A) studied   B) to study   C) of studying   D) have studied

85. Tina was afraid of _____ home by herself.
    A) gone   B) going   C) go   D) goes

86. I look forward _____ you soon.
    A) of visiting   B) to visiting   C) to visit   D) will visit

87. Before _____ to the meeting, Harry was at his office.
    A) to come   B) comes   C) came   D) coming

88. Have you met the new secretary _____ last week?
    A) hired   B) she was hired
    C) was hired   D) when she was hired

89. _____ of the students gave their views on the subject.
    A) Each   B) Neither   C) All   D) One

90. Neither Nancy nor Lorna remembered to bring _____ camera.
    A) their   B) neither   C) them   D) her

91. I fell and hurt _____ .
    A) himself   B) myself   C) me   D) ourselves

92. You didn't damage car, _____ ?
    A) I hope   B) didn't it   C) you accident   D) did you

93. _____ of the students did well on their test.
    A) Each   B) Either   C) Neither   D) Most

94. Before I woke up, the burglars _____ most of my possessions.
    A) have taken   B) had taken   C) were taking   D) will take

95. Thomas _____ his vacation for several months.
    A) planning   B) had been planning
    C) is planning   D) been planning for

96. The dog _____ bit me wasn't mad, fortunately.
    A) that   B) who   C) whom   D) _

97. Tell me about the differences _____ this city and the one you come from.
    A) of   B) than   C) between   D) from

98. There are many differences _____ the styles of these two writers.
    A) between   B) from   C) to   D) for

99. It was nice _____ to remember my mother's birthday.
    A) don't forget   B) a present   C) for   D) of you

100. The child grew _____ when his father entered the room.
    A) silent   B) silently   C) happily   D) up

TEST 13

1. Her husband is ill in _____ hospital, so she has to stay at _____ home to look after _____ children instead of going to work.
   A) _ / _ / _   C) the / the / the
   B) _ / the / the   D) _ / _ / the

2. Because _____ sun was so strong, they decided to sleep during _____ day and travel by _____ night.
   A) the / the / _   C) the / the / the
   B) the / _ / _   D) _ / _ / _

3. Here is a picture of _____ village where I was born. It is about ten minutes by _____ car from Wellington, _____ big town.
   A) the / _ / a   B) the / the / _
   B) _ / the / _   D) the / _ / _

4. The two kinds of _____ dog that I detest most are _____ snow dogs and _____ lap dogs.
   A) the / _ / _   C) _ / _ / _
   B) _ / the / the_   D) _ / _ / _

5. Do you think that I could ever learn to speak _____ Japanese _____ way _____ Japanese speak it?
   A) _ / the / the_   C) _ / _ / _
   B) the / the / the_   D) _ / the / _

6. This is _____ toughest steak I have eaten. It is _____ last time I eat in this restaurant.
   A) _ / _   C) _ / the   B) the / _   D) the / the

7. I would like _____ there yesterday.
   A) being   C) to have been
   B) having to be   D) to be

8. I can't find my sister. Do you know _____ ?
   A) where is she   B) where she is
   C) somewhere she is   D) is she anywhere

9. Mr. Green has a _____ vacation.
   A) two weeks   B) two-week's
   C) two weeks'   D) two-week

10. Have you heard _____ weather forecast?
    A) yesterday   B) tomorrow's   C) for today's   D) next week

11. She ran in a _____ race.
    A) ten kilometer   B) ten-kilometer
    C) ten kilometer's   D) ten-kilometers

12. _____ weather will be great.
    A) Tomorrow   B) Yesterday's   C) Yesterday   D) Tomorrow's

13. I wish my car _____ make so much noise.
    A) won't   B) can't   C) didn't   D) doesn't

14. "Are you leaving, Sam?" asked Mabel. She asked Sam if he _____.
    A) is leaving   B) leaves   C) was leaving   D) would leave

15. Alice said that _____.
    A) I'm at my office   B) she was at her office
    C) I'm at her office   D) you have been at your office

16. Jack _____ to Tom.
    A) says that he had spoken   B) said that he had spoken
    C) say that he speaks   D) had spoken that he will say

17. "How have you been, Mona?" asked Fred. He asked Mona how _____.
    A) she was   B) she had been
    C) was she   D) had she been

18. He hoped that they _____ that question.
    A) don't ask   B) will ask   C) would ask   D) can't ask

19. The new system is more productive and _____.
    A) cheap   B) less dangerously
    C) less expensive   D) costing less

20. It was foolish _____ your advice.
    A) to be forgotten   B) for her forgetting
    C) of her to forget   D) to listen

21. She gave me a very nice book _____.
    A) reading   B) read   C) to read   D) will read

22. He can climb trees _____ a monkey.
    A) as though   B) like   C) as   D) as if

23. _____ poverty in the world.
    A) There are always   B) It has always
    C) It has always been   D) There has always been

24. _____ the children for me while I'm out.
    A) Look after   B) Take care   C) Look at   D) Care

25. Robert seems _____ ready.
    A) it is   B) to be   C) being   D) of being

26. He was working at the office when the telegram _____.
    A) was arriving   B) has arrived   C) arrived   D) arrives

27. This is the first time I _____ tennis this month.
    A) play   B) have played   C) was playing   D) played

28. Tom _____ carefully when he had the accident.
    A) hadn't been driving   B) hadn't been
    C) drives   D) driving very

29. The Browns family _____ about moving for several months.
    A) thinking   B) had been thinking
    C) been thinking   D) are thinking

30. We _____ for only a few minutes before you came.
    A) will wait   B) have to wait
    C) have been waiting   D) had been waiting

31. Julia _____ our visit.
    A) hadn't been expecting   B) was very surprised
    C) hadn't been to expect   D) had expected for

32. Tom: Have you seen that film?
    Bob: Yes, I have.
    Tom: When?
    Bob: I _____ it a week ago.
    A) would see   B) had seen   C) saw   D) have seen

33. He _____ the rent last Friday.
    A) pays   B) has paid   C) was paying   D) paid

34. Has Nick finished his work yet? Yes, he _____ half an hour ago.
    A) has finished   B) had finished   C) was finishing   D) finished

35. At eight o'clock last night I _____ a book.
    A) was reading   B) have read   C) read   D) am reading

36. They would have gone home if we _____ here.
    A) aren't   B) won't be   C) hadn't been   D) are

37. If Bruce had been careful, he _____ had an accident.
    A) has   B) have   C) wouldn't   D) wouldn't have

38. Wilma _____ called if she had forgotten her keys.
    A) had   B) was   C) would   D) would have

39. If they _____ harder, they would succeed.
    A) could try   B) try   C) tried   D) had tried

40. If Bruce _____ to a small country, his vacation would have been better.
    A) went   B) have gone   C) has gone   D) had gone

41. If I _____ a politician, I would never tell lies.
    A) was   B) were   C) am   D) cooked

42. _____ been made?
    A) Have the arrangements   B) When the invitations
    B) The urgent steps   D) A good salary was

43. "The letter _____ last week", Lola said.
    A) is sent   B) was sent   C) will be sent   D) sent

44. When the door _____ Frank was very surprised.
    A) opens   B) is opened   C) was opened   D) shuts

45. I'm teaching _____ to speak English.
    A) himself   B) yourself   C) us   D) myself

46. The work had _____ under extremely difficult conditions.
    A) for them   B) completed   C) to be done   D) slightly

47. Traffic was bad because the highway _____ repaired.
    A) will be   B) was being   C) is   D) being

48. _____ mountains that we climbed were high.
    A) All   B) All of   C) Of the   D) All of the

49. Do you know the man _____ lives across the street?
    A) which   B) there   C) who   D) what

50. I know a man _____ wife is a taxi driver.
    A) who's   B) his   C) the   D) whose

51. A special computer had _____ for use in space.
    A) to be   B) to be designed
    C) been used   D) developed

52. Jack's always reading books. He _____ like to read.
    A) will   B) must   C) would   D) can

53. He _____ buy a car so he could drive to work.
    A) has to   B) has had to   C) will have to   D) had to

54. The phone is ringing. _____ I answer it?
    A) Will   B) Would   C) Shall   D) Won't

55. They _____ rather see a larger apartment.
    A) had   B) have   C) would   D) will

56. When _____ the best time to call?
    A) it is   B) they would   C) have you   D) would be

57. Tom hasn't been working here since he came to Turkey, _____ ?
    A) did he   B) has he   C) didn't he   D) hasn't he

58. Coffee beans are picked by hand and then _____.
    A) drying   B) dried
    C) which are dried D) by drying

59. Ray and Ida were not at work today, _____ ?
    A) weren't they   B) they were   C) they weren't   D) were they

60. Ramon and Jorge weren't angry, _____ ?
    A) have they been   B) did they
    C) have they   D) were they

61. The European countries didn't stop the war, _____ ?
    A) could they   B) did they   C) would they   D) didn't they

62. Sandy likes the green dress. She's _____ now.
    A) trying for it.   B) trying it on
    C) trying them on   D) trying on it

63. We were at the train station _____ meet our father.
    A) to   B) for   C) in   D) on

64. Albert has gone to the market _____ some eggs.
    A) for buying   B) for buy   C) to buy   D) buy

65. It's no use _____. Nobody will take any notice of you.
    A) you complain   B) complaining
    C) to complain   D) complain

66. Isn't it about time _____ taking life seriously?
    A) you started   B) starting   C) you start   D) start

67. I'd rather _____ in tonight. There is too much pollution outside.
    A) stay   B) to stay   C) staying   D) stayed

68. There's no point _____ with him.
    A) to argue   B) you argue   C) in arguing   D) of arguing

69. _____ you stop that noise or I will.
    A) Either   B) If   C) Or   D) Rather

70. _____ Gordon or Sam will help you.
    A) Both   B) Because   C) Either   D) Neither

71. _____ you leave now, or you'll miss the bus.
    A) Neither   B) Nor   C) Either   D) Or

72. _____ the child nor her mother could play the violin.
    A) Either   B) Although   C) Both   D) Neither

73. Neither of the boys brought _____ lunch.
    A) his   B) its   C) their   D) he

74. Each of the countries sent _____ representative to the international conference.
    A) their   B) its   C) some   D) official

75. Please tell us about some of the dangers a detective _____ to face in his work.
    A) will   B) can   C) has   D) have

76. His choice of words _____ very good.
    A) is   B) are   C) will   D) being

77. _____ does Helen behave foolishly.
    A) Always   B) Sometimes   C) Usually   D) Never

78. _____ to become a film star.
    A) Every child want   B) Not every child wants
    C) Not every child want   D) Not children want

79. Next month you _____.
    A) will be as old as I am   B) will be so old as I am
    C) will be very old as me   D) will be so old as me

80. They need some envelopes. They don't have _____ left.
    A) some   B) any   C) a few   D) much

81. She runs _____ than her brother.
    A) faster   B) fastest   C) as fast   D) more fast

82. Ships are fun, but _____ to travel by plane.
    A) also faster   B) they were faster
    C) it is faster   D) they aren't as fast as

83. Peter's essay was different _____ Paul's.
    A) between   B) to   C) for   D) from

84. They live _____ than we do.
    A) comfortable   B) more comfortably
    C) comfortably   D) very comfortably

85. She isn't _____ to run a big business.
    A) so old   B) enough old   C) very old   D) old enough

86. Men _____ work is good receive high wages.
    A) whom   B) who   C) whose   D) of whom

87. Children _____ behavior is bad may be punished.
    A) who   B) of whom   C) whom   D) whose

88. Is that the man _____ sells newspapers?
    A) who is known   B) that is sometimes
    C) whose brother I know   D) who

89. Now that I've bought a car, I _____ walk to work.
    A) mustn't   B) must   C) needn't   D) hadn't

90. They are giving away _____ of their old furniture.
    A) any   B) many   C) few   D) some

91. The author still works hard, but not quite as _____ as he used to.
    A) hardly   B) –   C) hard   D) more

92. The film was _____ boring that we walked out in the middle.
    A) such   B) so   C) too   D) because

93. He drove so _____ that he lost his job.
    A) badly   B) quick   C) cowardly   D) worse

94. After _____ , I washed my face.
    A) got up   B) getting up   C) can get up   D) gotten up

95. How _____ from Leeds to Liverpool?
    A) far is there   B) far is it   C) long is there   D) long is it

96. Don't you think he's still _____ young to stay out so late?
    A) enough   B) very much   C) far too   D) extremely

97. Jimmy took a book from the shelf a few minutes ago. He's putting _____ now.
    A) it on   B) back it   C) it back   D) them back

98. Tom has never been to Turkey. _____ .
    A) Neither is Helen   B) Nor is Helen
    C) Neither has Helen   D) Helen isn't, either

99. It would be polite _____ to write and thank Martha for the gift.
    A) your letter   B) of you
    C) of you a letter D) a short letter

100. It was good _____ to return my tools.
    A) for you   B) about you   C) of you   D) you come

TEST 14

1. _____ English people are forever complaining about _____ weather, but in fact, _____ British Isles have a reasonable climate on the whole.
   A) the / the / the   B) __ / the / __
   C) __ / the / the   D) __ / __ / the

2. We always stay at the Palace Court Hotel because it is _____ only one with _____ facilities for _____ disabled.
   A) the / the / the   B) __ / the / the
   C) the / a / __   D) __ / __ / the

3. _____ Swiss Alps are a good place to go if you like _____ skiing. There is usually plenty of _____ snow during the winter months.
   A) The / __ / __   B) __ / __ / __
   C) __ / the / __   D) the / the / the

4. Most people in our country prefer tea _____ coffee.
   A) from   B) for   C) to   D) at

5. I never ask favors _____ anyone unless it is absolutely necessary.
   A) of   B) from   C) for   D) to

6. The large house was made _____ two flats.
   A) out of   B) into   C) from   D) than

7. I want to know what _____ .
   A) are those boys doing   B) were those boys doing
   C) will those boys do   D) those boys are doing

8. You're an intelligent person and you can take care of _____ .
   A) you   B) your   C) yourself   D) yourselves

9. Can't we eat _____ somewhere else?
   A) in   B) ___   C) on   D) at

10. She only has _____ free time on the weekends.
    A) much   B) a few   C) a little   D) any

11. Wind power is _____ and clean.
    A) either inexpensive   B) neither cheap
    C) both inexpensive   D) inexpensive also

12. _____ them went to the movies.
    A) All   B) Of both C) Both of   D) They all of

13. _____ paragraphs in Ben's essay are short.
    A) Few of them   B) All of them
    C) Most of the   D) They are all

14. A: Has Linda finished her homework yet?
    B: Yes, she _____ it a little while ago.
    A) had finished   B) has finished   C) is finishing   D) finished

15. She's doing her homework first. Then she _____ TV.
    A) watches B) would watch C) Shall watch D) will watch

16. The boys were playing football when we _____ the park.
    A) left   B) have left   C) were leaving   D) leave

17. She was making dinner when he _____ home.
    A) came   B) has come   C) was coming   D) comes

18. Felix _____ just spoken to the landlord when I called.
    A) was   B) had   C) will   D) were

19. She _____ breakfast when I called.
    A) had had B) did have C) have had D) has had

20. Ralph hadn't _____ carefully when he broke the machine.
    A) been very   B) working
    C) being worked   D) been working

21. Oscar _____ already left when you arrived.
    A) he   B) just   C) had   D) was

22. _____ they rented it before you called?
    A) How   B) Who   C) Did   D) Had

23. They promised that they _____ Mike next year.
    A) visit   B) will visit   C) would visit   D) won't visit

24. Mr. Brown was doing the shopping while his wife _____ .
    A) has been studying   B) was studied
    C) was studying   D) had been studying

25. Johnson would go to the beach if it _____ cold outside.
    A) weren't   B) isn't   C) wasn't   D) won't

26. Jim _____ study harder if he had more time.
    A) will   B) were   C) won't   D) would

27. If she _____ Peter her telephone number, he would call her.
    A) gave   B) will give   C) gives   D) has given

28. He would have met Mr. Taylor if he _____ to the meeting.
    A) goes   B) had gone   C) went   D) would go

29. If I were you, I _____ more exercise.
    A) would get   B) can get   C) will get   D) shall get

30. If Tom had been more careful, he _____ had an accident.
    A) has   B) have   C) wouldn't   D) wouldn't have

31. My son hopes _____ soon.
    A) for a job   B) to be hired
    C) about working   D) hired for a job

32. That computer _____ in another country.
    A) was assembled   B) repairs
    C) are guaranteed   D) makes

33. That information _____ over the telephone.
    A) were given   B) is giving
    C) isn't given   D) hadn't been giving

34. That product _____ sold in many countries.
    A) were   B) will   C) is   D) are being

35. _____ the answer given to you yesterday?
    A) Are   B) Could   C) Is   D) Was

36. These packages should _____ special care because they are fragile.
    A) have given   B) be given   C) be needed   D) be needing

37. We took the oranges _____ were in the refrigerator.
    A) that   B) who   C) there   D) those

38. The man with _____ she was arguing has a bad temper.
    A) who   B) that   C) whose   D) whom

39. A watch _____ is unreliable is not much use.
    A) ___   B) who   C) which   D) whose

40. The wrestler _____ leg was broken is better now.
    A) who is B) whom   C) whose   D) that

41. Jim and Andrew can't come tomorrow, and _____ .
    A) so can't I   B) we can't neither
    C) neither can we   D) so can't we

42. Rita wants to visit Nebraska, and _____ .
    A) Clive does too   B) also does Clive
    C) does Clive also   D) Clive wants too

43. John doesn't like cheese, and Mary _____ .
    A) so too   B) does either
    C) doesn't either   D) does neither

44. My friend has graduated from a college, and _____ .
    A) so do I   B) so have I   C) so did I   D) so had she

45. Your house is not comfortable, and _____ .
    A) so is mine   B) so mine is
    C) neither is mine   D) neither mine is

46. A: Do you think our team will win the big game on Sunday?
    B: I don't know. They _____ win.
    A) would   B) will   C) can   D) might

47. Before the invention of the automobile, people _____ use horses for transportation.
    A) to   B) to travel   C) always   D) used to

48. _____ it be possible to go next week if they were here?
    A) Can   B) How   C) Rather   D) Would

49. "Would you like _____ ?" he asked.
    A) dancing   B) a dance   C) to dance   D) dance

50. Mr. Jasper _____ to be a basketball player.
    A) was used   B) used   C) has been   D) is used

51. I shall not waste time _____ his letter.
    A) reply   B) replying   C) to reply   D) replied

52. It's nearly lunch time. Why don't we stop _____ a bite to eat?
    A) to have   B) have   C) having   D) had

53. We had to stand up _____ a better view of the game.
    A) to get   B) getting   C) get   D) ___

54. They earned a living by _____ old cars.
    A) sell   B) to sell   C) sold   D) selling

55. Mr. White is telling his wife _____ him tea.
    A) to make   B) make   C) making   D) made

56. Suzie's mother allowed her _____ to the party last night.
    A) go   B) to go   C) going   D) went

57. He kept on _____ the same mistakes.
    A) to make   B) to do   C) making   D) doing

58. Don't be nervous. I want you _____.
    A) not nervous   B) to relax   C) relax   D) relaxing

59. Excuse me, officer. I'd like you _____ me.
    A) helping   B) help   C) to help   D) for helping

60. There aren't enough men, _____ the work might take a long time.
    A) since   B) in order to   C) although   D) so

61. She took time to help me _____ she was very busy.
    A) since   B) because   C) although   D) so

62. Not only did he call on time, _____ he also left an important message.
    A) therefore   B) however   C) but   D) and

63. The mechanic can't fix the car, and _____.
    A) I can either   B) so do I   C) I can, too   D) neither can I

64. Alexander plays basketball very well, and _____.
    A) so I do   B) so do I   C) also do I   D) so what

65. We won't leave _____ we do all there is to do.
    A) that   B) until   C) by   D) don't

66. She dances as _____ as a professional dancer does.
    A) worse   B) good   C) better   D) fine

67. The Persian Empire is _____ empire history has ever seen.
    A) greedier
    C) the greediest
    B) too greedy
    D) greedy enough

68. I didn't _____ like Chinese food, but now I am fond of it.
    A) use to   B) used to   C) used   D) usually

69. It was _____ that we felt exhausted when we finally arrived at the camp.
    A) such a long journey   B) a long journey so
    C) a long journey   D) a journey so

70. Tom plays the piano _____ Arthur.
    A) well
    C) a lot better than
    B) more
    D) much more

71. Italian people usually speak _____ than Turkish people.
    A) somewhat quickly   B) more quickly
    C) too quickly   D) very quickly

72. All of those oranges are ripe. _____ of them are green.
    A) Some   B) Many   C) Neither   D) None

73. I think _____ took your umbrella.
    A) anyone   B) other   C) person   D) someone

74. Dr. Barnard has a lot of books. _____ of them were written in the Middle Ages.
    A) Some   B) Any   C) Neither   D) Both

75. None of those glasses are clean. _____ of them are as dirty as can be.
    A) Some   B) All   C) Both   D) Many

76. I don't think there's _____ home.
    A) any person   B) any people   C) someone   D) anyone

77. The _____ lamp is in the bedroom.
    A) other   B) another   C) any   D) other one

78. When would you like _____ you?
    A) that I call   B) I'm calling   C) me to call   D) I'd call

79. Be careful with that knife. You might cut _____.
    A) yourself   B) myself   C) itself   D) you

80. She taught _____ to play the piano.
    A) of herself   B) in herself   C) by herself   D) herself

81. You and Carl can help _____, can't you?
    A) myself   B) yourself   C) yourselves   D) we

82. Fortunately, the snake _____ bit the explorer wasn't poisonous.
    A) that   B) who   C) whose   D) whom

83. This poem is _____ long that I can't learn it by heart.
    A) very   B) too   C) so   D) enough

84. He's _____ to do any serious work.
    A) too lazy   B) lazy enough   C) very lazy   D) so lazy

85. _____ he was seriously wounded, he went on fighting.
    A) Even   B) Yet   C) Although   D) In spite

86. She isn't _____ to face all these misfortunes.
    A) strong for   B) strong enough
    C) enough strong   D) very strong

87. It was thoughtful _____ us your summer house.
    A) of you to offer   B) for your offer
    C) of your offering   D) of you offering

88. It was foolish _____ to Ronald's advice and buy this junk.
    A) of him listening   B) of him to listen
    C) he was listening   D) for him to listen to

89. Yesterday he had a terrible accident. He ran _____ a police car.
    A) with   B) on   C) for   D) into

90. Having lost their house in the disaster, they don't have _____ to go.
    A) nowhere   B) any where   C) somewhere   D) anywhere

91. Marry isn't going _____ this weekend.
    A) anywhere   B) somewhere   C) to anywhere   D) to somewhere

92. Joan was sick yesterday; _____ she didn't go to work.
    A) however   B) nevertheless   C) therefore   D) frequently

93. The new system is more wasteful than _____.
    A) economical   B) less efficiently
    C) less expensively   D) cost less

94. I saw a boy break your window with his ball. _____ it made me really mad.
    A) That he broke   B) What he broke
    C) He broke   D) He has broken

95. In back of the house _____ built almost a century ago.
    A) is a barn   B) there a barn
    C) a barn is   D) has a barn there

96. _____ kindly she talks to everybody!
    A) What   B) That   C) How   D) What a

97. _____ crowded city New York is!
    A) What a   B) How   C) That   D) What is

98. _____ the stamps in Dave's collection are rare ones.
    A) Many of   B) Some   C) Of all   D) Not any

99. Don't tell me about your problems. I've got enough problems of _____.
    A) my   B) me   C) my own   D) own

100. He has taken the exam six times so far and he _____ to pass it yet.
    A) isn't able   B) can't
    C) hasn't been able   D) wasn't able

TEST 15

1. A great many articles are made _____ nylon.
   A) from   B) than   C) of   D) out of

2. We have been working in terrible conditions _____ May.
   A) for   B) since   C) by   D) until

3. Please open your books _____ page 78.
   A) to   B) at   C) on   D) for

4. Why are those people _____ such a hurry?
   A) in   B) on   C) for   D) _____

5. My radio doesn't work very well, but I don't know what is wrong _____ it.
   A) for   B) to   C) on   D) with

6. Are there any objections _____ the committee's plan of action?
   A) to   B) for   C) at   D) _____

7. I am going to ask a few questions _____ that old gentleman.
   A) up   B) from   C) to   D) _____

8. There are a number of differences _____ the two theories.
   A) from   B) among   C) between   D) than

9. Susan will probably work _____ six.
   A) for   B) under   C) until   D) by

10. The package should be here _____ ten o'clock tomorrow.
    A) delivered   B) sent   C) by mail   D) by

11. There is only one way to win the battle _____ inflation.
    A) with   B) against   C) for   D) over

12. Sam has a lot friends in Ankara, but he doesn't know _____ in Bursa.
    A) someone   B) anyone   C) any friend   D) any person

13. Nancy traveled _____ the world.
    A) around   B) on   C) across   D) over

14. His friend lives _____ on the other side of town.
    A) near   B) here   C) somewhere   D) anywhere

15. Laura enjoys music, and _____ .
    A) either do I   B) neither can she
    C) I do too   D) she doesn't either

16. He hates liars, and so _____ .
    A) does he   B) she does   C) is she   D) works she

17. Tom has been very busy, and _____ .
    A) neither am I   B) I have too   C) so have I   D) so do I

18. James wants to buy a new car; _____ , he doesn't have enough money
    A) therefore   B) however   C) moreover   D) consequently

19. Mrs. Chunk doesn't enjoy driving, and _____ .
    A) either does she   B) she does too
    C) I do too   D) neither do I

20. Jack can play the piano, and _____ .
    A) so can Helen   B) either can Helen
    C) Helen plays either   D) neither does Helen

21. Last year at this time Tom Brown _____ Hollywood.
    A) lived at   B) was living at
    C) was living in   D) is living in

22. A: Has Barbara typed the letter yet?
    B: Yes, she _____ it a long time ago.
    A) typed   B) has typed
    C) was typing   D) has been typing

23. She was crossing the road when she _____ the package.
    A) drops   B) dropped   C) was dropping   D) has dropped

24. We _____ dinner when the guests arrived unexpectedly.
    A) was having   B) were having   C) have   D) has dropped

25. The telegram _____ at nine o'clock yesterday morning.
    A) has arrived   B) was arriving
    C) arrived   D) had arrived

26. I hope everyone _____ to the party tomorrow.
    A) will come   B) shall come   C) come   D) are coming

27. He said that he _____ me.
    A) have met   B) would meet   C) meet   D) are meeting

28. Did you think that they _____ their promise.
    A) would keep   B) won't keep   C) are keeping   D) have to keep

29. The painters _____ finished their work by tomorrow.
    A) have   B) will have   C) have been   D) had

30. By May 10, Tom _____ been in Turkey for two years.
    A) has   B) have   C) will   D) will have

31. Our family owns an antique piano. We _____ since 1915.
    A) have it   B) got it   C) have got it   D) have had it

32. A: Have you been to the United States?
    B: Yes, I _____ in 1989.
    A) went there   B) have gone there
    C) have been there   D) went

33. I will be glad when he _____ .
    A) went   B) had gone   C) has gone   D) will go

34. For years her only ambition _____ to become a film star.
    A) is   B) has been   C) have been   D) are

35. If you had got up earlier, you _____ not _____ the bus.
    A) will/miss   B) had/missed
    C) would/have missed   D) did/miss

36. If motorists were to drive more carefully, they _____ fewer accidents.
    A) will have   B) would have had
    C) would have   D) would be

37. He'll have to leave town soon if he _____ trouble.
    A) didn't want   B) hadn't   C) would rather   D) doesn't want

38. You can prolong your life, _____ , eat wisely, and avoid smoking.
    A) exercising   B) with exercising
    C) to exercise   D) if you exercise

39. They _____ if the movie weren't funny.
    A) not laugh   B) wouldn't laugh
    C) will laugh   D) aren't laughing

40. If Frank had more time, he _____ to see more movies.
    A) would like   B) will like   C) like   D) liked

41. The projector _____ if the shutter doesn't open.
    A) no work   B) don't work   C) work   D) won't work

42. People _____ like the movie better if the dialogues were shorter.
    A) would   B) can
    C) would be able   D) had

43. If he _____ from that window, he would be killed.
    A) fell   B) will fall   C) has fallen   D) would fall

44. If Mohammed Ali _____ his first fight with Sonny Liston, no one would have been surprised.
    A) lost   B) had lost
    C) has lost   D) would have lost

45. _____ you decide to go, call the station and reserve the tickets.
    A) Had   B) Do   C) Should   D) Would

46. Their passports _____ checked by the officer.
    A) already have   B) already been
    C) have already been   D) have already to be

47. The old patient _____ special care because his condition was critical.
    A) giving   B) is given   C) give   D) given

48. Many of the goods made in Japan _____ to other countries.
    A) export   B) exported   C) exporting   D) are exported

49. Two fishermen _____ in the open sea yesterday afternoon.
    A) have been rescued   B) rescued
    C) were rescued   D) are rescued

50. A: What are they doing to that old house?
    B: It _____ .
    A) pulled down   B) being pulled down
    C) is pull down   D) is being pulled down

51. She was seriously sick. _____ she didn't go to work last week.
    A) That's why   C) Owing to
    B) It is why   D) However

52. More people die in automobile accidents _____ in war.
    A) than   B) as   C) like   D) those

53. I feel sorry about the man _____ three sons were killed in a traffic accident.
    A) who had   B) of whose   C) that he had   D) whose

54. From _____ did you borrow that book?
    A) whom   B) who   C) that   D) which

55. This is the key _____ I lost yesterday.
    A) who   B) whom   C) ___   D) whose

56. We love to play tennis, but if they close the park we _____ play tennis any more.
    A) can't   B) won't be able to
    C) couldn't   D) won't have to

57. Sam has worked hard today. He _____ be tired now.
    A) shall   B) can   C) will   D) must

58. Barney has just found a job, and he is very happy. He _____ like his job.
    A) should   B) will   C) must   D) has to

59. The 100-year-old man _____ for the secret to his longevity.
    A) often asked   B) was often asked
    C) who was often asked   D) who often asked

60. I think that man is a burglar. _____ I call the police?
    A) Could   B) Will   C) Shall   D) Would

61. _____ he seems today, the old man was once a dangerous criminal.
    A) Peaceful   B) As peaceful as
    C) Although peaceful D) No matter peaceful

62. She _____ taken another course. She can use the computer well.
    A) was   B) isn't   C) has been   D) should have

63. When Jack was a child, he _____ to live on a farm with his family.
    A) likes   B) farmed   C) used   D) wishes

64. _____ speak to Felix?
    A) Would you like to   B) Had you
    C) Have you   D) When were you

65. You would like to see a good movie, _____ you?
    A) wouldn't   B) hadn't   C) haven't   D) weren't

66. The instructor wants us _____ for the test.
    A) student   B) study hard   C) to prepare   D) writing

67. _____ being useful, glass is also ornamental.
    A) Besides   B) Aside   C) Though   D) Because

68. Parents should always put medicine away after _____ it. Otherwise, children might take it and harm themselves.
    A) take   B) you took   C) took   D) taking

69. You should always check your tires before _____ your car.
    A) drive   B) driving   C) you drove   D) you're driving

70. She made him _____ the kitchen.
    A) to paint   B) painted   C) painting   D) paint

71. She has a very important report _____ .
    A) typing   B) to prepare
    C) which it was typed D) she prepared

72. Would you mind _____ home early?
    A) I came   B) coming   C) to come   D) you come

73. I can't stand _____ in a long line.
    A) wait   B) waiting   C) to wait   D) waited

74. We couldn't help _____ when she fell off the horse.
    A) the laugh   B) laughing   C) laugh   D) to laugh

75. Do you know the beautiful lady _____ ?
    A) sit in the car   B) she sat in the car
    C) sitting in the car   D) she is sitting in the car

76. If you don't _____ smoking, you'll never regain your health?
    A) give of   B) give away   C) give up   D) give off

77. The children _____ play with them.
    A) want that I   B) want me to   C) want me for   D) want my

78. Send him to the baker's _____ some bread.
    A) to buy   B) for buying
    C) in order that D) for I buy

79. I was very happy _____ him that he had won the prize.
    A) to tell   B) tell   C) telling   D) has told

80. It was a waste of time _____ him to keep quiet. He simply could not stop talking.
    A) ask   B) asking   C) asked   D) ____

81. Whoever _____ that picture was a fine artist.
    A) paints   B) was painted   C) has painted   D) had painted

82. What _____ here before you arrived?
    A) happens   B) had happened
    C) happening   D) happen

83. _____ ever painted an apartment before?
    A) Do you   B) Will you   C) Had you   D) Did you have

84. She had _____ late before.
    A) no   B) no ever   C) not been   D) not ever

85. The landlord _____ just rented the apartment before they called.
    A) is   B) has   C) was   D) had

86. _____ ever driven a car like this before?
    A) You had   B) Did you   C) Have you   D) Were you

87. Who _____ talking to before I came?
    A) you are   B) have they been
    C) are   D) had they been

88. I _____ rather not work in this office. It is terribly cold.
    A) would   B) had   C) have   D) will

89. When _____ possible to get some more information?
    A) Would it be   B) Had it   C) Has it   D) Would be it

90. The plan _____ will put a lot of people out of work.
    A) to mechanize the factory   B) has mechanized the factory
    C) is to mechanize the factory D) is to mechanize the factory.

91. The director _____ consulted about the plan.
    A) have been   B) should have been
    C) would   D) being

92. A: It's too bad you can't come tomorrow.
    B: I _____ come, but I'd rather stay home.
    A) can   B) did   C) have   D) do

93. Mace _____ a highly flavored spice used in foods.
    A) is   B) which is   C) as it is   D) to be like

94. Never _____ such a beautiful village before.
    A) I had seen   B) I saw
    C) have I seen   D) had I been seen

95. _____ difficult to work when you are tired.
    A) It is   B) It was   C) It   D) Its

96. _____ to read about the customs of other countries.
    A) That was extremely interesting
    B) It was interesting
    C) Is it very interesting
    D) That many students like

97. We have a lot of tasks this weekend, _____ .
    A) each one is demanding great attention
    B) each one has demanded great attention
    C) each one demanding great attention
    D) and each one has demanding great attention

98. Bethlehem, the city _____ Jesus was born, is regarded as a holy sanctum by Christians.
    A) which was   B) that where   C) where   D) whose city

99. Physical therapy _____ assuage his pain and speed his recovery.
    A) expects to   B) has expected
    C) expected   D) is expected to

100. _____ is that there is a risk of heart attack for the elderly.
    A) One important drawback of aerobics
    B) There is one important drawback of aerobics
    C) It is one important drawback of aerobics
    D) If there is one important drawback of aerobics.

TEST 16

1. I insisted that he _____ me the money.
   A) is paying   B) pays   C) was paying   D) pay

2. It is imperative that air pollution _____.
   A) eliminated   B) is eliminated
   B) be eliminated   D) was eliminated

3. It is essential that she _____ smoking.
   A) give up   B) is giving up
   C) gives up   D) gave up

4. I don't enjoy _____ at by other people.
   A) laughing   B) being laughed
   C) laughed   D) to laugh

5. It is easy _____ by his lies.
   A) to be fooled   B) fooling   C) to fool   D) fooled

6. It is _____ to study for a test and then to fail it.
   A) frustrating   B) frustrate   C) frustrated   D) frustration

7. She felt great _____ at not being able to ride a horse.
   A) frustration   B) frustrating   C) frustrate   D) frustrated

8. Usually a bird species gains public recognition _____ faces the danger of extinction.
   A) which only   B) only when it
   C) only when   D) which it

9. Why _____ at a given time is not known.
   A) does a drought occur   B) a drought should occur
   C) it is a drought that   D) a drought that occurs

10. It _____ the Titanic sank while crossing the Atlantic.
    A) is 1912 when   B) in 1912 that
    C) which was in 1912   D) was in 1912 that

11. _____ 1980 that Voyager transmitted photographs of Saturn to earth.
    A) When it was   B) During   C) It was   D) It was in

12. It was in 1901 _____ Roosevelt became President of the United States.
    A) when   B) which   C) that   D) who

13. He must run very fast _____ he wants to catch the bus.
    A) so that   B) because   C) unless   D) so

14. Father is not going to light the bonfire _____ we have gathered enough wood.
    A) because   B) although   C) if   D) so

15. "I will come to the meeting", Tom said to me.
    Tom promised me that _____.
    A) he will come to the meeting.
    B) I will come to the meeting.
    C) I would come to the meeting.
    D) he would come to the meeting.

16. "I will help you", Bob said to me.
    A) Bob told me he would help me.
    B) Bob told me that I will help you.
    C) Bob said that he would help you.
    D) Bob told me that he would help me.

17. _____ was more than mere nervousness: it was a real phobia.
    A) He was afraid of flying   B) His fear of flying
    C) Afraid of flying   D) If he was afraid of flying

18. It was Albert Einstein who developed the theory _____ relativity.
    A) of   B) that   C) was   D) in

19. The icy conditions made road travel dangerous, so _____ going by car we took the subway.
    A) therefore   B) instead of   C) as well as   D) in spite of

20. _____ the many hardships they had to face, the balloonists managed to reach their destination.
    A) Despite   B) In addition to
    C) Because of   D) In accordance with

21. _____ the extraordinarily good results, it was decided to try the same approach next year.
    A) In spite of   B) However   C) In view of   D) Despite

22. New oil deposits are being searched for; _____ they are very difficult to find.
    A) because   B) therefore   C) however   D) too

23. The rate of energy consumption has increased; _____ it continues to rise each year.
    A) because   B) moreover   C) consequently   D) therefore

24. Wilson works hard at school; _____, he does well on test.
    A) not only   B) correctly   C) consequently   D) studying

25. George, _____ speaks German, applied the job.
    A) whom   B) that   C) who   D) _ _ _ _

26. The beliefs _____ Moslems hold are based on the teachings of Prophet Mohammed.
    A) that   B) whom   C) who   D) whose

27. Although _____ named until 1782, aluminum was used as early as 5300 B.C.
    A) it was not   B) could not be
    C) there must not have been   D) which was never

28. In front of the house _____ looking at us threateningly.
    A) was a large dog   B) a large dog
    C) a large dog was   D) a dog was large

29. Never before _____ such ridiculous arguments.
    A) have we heard   B) we had heard
    C) we have heard   D) we could have heard

30. Not once _____ offer to help me.
    A) I have   B) did he   C) had his   D) for him to

31. Known reserves of petroleum are said to be sufficient only _____ the end of the century.
    A) by   B) since   C) until   D) unless

32. Not only _____ buildings, they also specify different kinds of materials for their buildings.
    A) architects to design   B) design architects do
    C) do design architects   D) do architects design

33. On top of the hill _____.
    A) standing a huge building   B) stood a huge building
    C) a huge building was   D) a huge building standing

34. Among the plays being presented _____ written by Eugene O.Neil.
    A) is as famous   B) is a famous one
    C) a famous play   D) one is famous

35. Never before _____ a war as bloody as the Vietnam War.
    A) history has seen   B) history has seen
    C) does history see   D) has history seen

36. Between the two trees _____.
    A) a flower garden was   B) garden was a flower
    C) a garden was flower   D) was a flower garden

37. Between the two mountains _____.
    A) a river is   B) is a river
    C) the river is there   D) along the river

38. In front of the station _____.
    A) some people are   B) stood several people
    C) did I wait   D) I am

39. Not once _____ the chance to talk to the project manager.
    A) did we get   B) we are   C) will be able   D) for us

40. _____ wants to come is welcome.
    A) Who   B) He   C) A person   D) Whoever

41. Never _____ a museum with as many paintings as this one.
    A) they had visited   B) they have visited
    C) had they visited   D) they must have visited

42. _____ but he must also avoid any evidence of partiality.
    A) If you are a judge, you must be unbiased
    B) A judge must be unbiased.
    C) Not only must a judge be unbiased
    D) Not just be punctual

43. _____ was obvious when she was caught with the stolen diamonds.
    A) If she was involved in the robbery
    B) She was involved in the robbery
    C) Because she was involved in the robbery
    D) That she was involved in the robbery

44. The world would be a better place _____ we could abolish wars.
    A) if   B) so that   C) unless   D) although

45. _____ sanitary conditions are so primitive, disease may be rampant all throughout the poverty-stricken country.
    A) Although   B) Due to   C) Because   D) With

46. They told their friends that they _____ a vacation in August and would visit them on their way to Ankara.
    A) would take   B) took   C) had taken   D) were taken

47. Some people think it's time we all _____ a single international language.
    A) learned   B) should learn   C) learn   D) will learn

48. It's no use _____ to learn a language just by studying a dictionary.
    A) to try   B) try   C) trying   D) in trying
49. _____ with a foreign family can be a good way to learn a language.
    A) Live   B) Living   C) Lived   D) Life
50. She turned off the tape recorder _____ pushing the stop button.
    A) by   B) with   C) in   D) be
51. Low-income families have a hard time _____.
    A) they buy enough meat   B) to buy enough meat
    C) buying enough meat   D) for buying meat.
52. He said that he _____ the film the day before.
    A) would see   B) has seen   C) had seen   D) saw
53. After Mohammed Ali _____ an Olympic gold medal, he became a professional boxer.
    A) has won   B) had won   C) won   D) was winning
54. A: It's too bad she's never worked in a real estate office.
    B: She _____ worked in one, but it was just a summer job.
    A) has   B) is   C) was   D) did
55. A: I'm sorry that Sam hasn't learned to drive yet.
    B: He _____ learned, but he doesn't like to drive.
    A) does   B) have   C) had   D) has
56. If we don't hurry, the wedding _____ before our arrival.
    A) took place   B) will have taken place
    C) takes place   D) should have taken place
57. In three years time, I _____ my studies.
    A) will have finished   B) finish
    C) will finish   D) am finishing
58. They never _____ the packages that they _____.
    A) had received / had ordered   B) received / ordered
    C) received / had ordered   D) received / has ordered
59. The secretary _____ the office after she _____ the letters.
    A) left / had typed   B) had left / had typed
    C) left / typed   D) had left / typed
60. For the past three days she _____ in a bad mood.
    A) were   B) have been   C) was   D) has been
61. One of the most effective ways of getting ahead in life _____.
    A) you work hard and regularly
    B) is to be a trustworthy person
    C) know how to solve problems quickly
    D) having invested in personal relationships
62. He _____ of Einstein before I gave him a book on relativity.
    A) did not hear   B) had not heard
    C) would not hear   D) would not have heard
63. Although he _____ the windows, they are still dirty.
    A) has cleaned   B) cleaned   C) will clean   D) had cleaned
64. Have you heard the _____ weather forecast?
    A) yesterday   B) three-week   C) today's   D) two weeks
65. Carl has a _____ vacation every year.
    A) two-week   B) two week   C) two weeks   D) of two weeks
66. Had they gone to the island a day earlier, they _____ the storm.
    A) will have avoided   B) would avoid
    C) would have avoided   D) had avoided
67. They _____ a better project if they had worked harder.
    A) might have   B) had had
    C) have   D) might have had
68. I would have come, _____ I been invited.
    A) should   B) when   C) if   D) had
69. _____ he studied more carefully, he could have improved his grade.
    A) However   B) Might   C) Had   D) Should have
70. _____ you need my help tomorrow, please call me.
    A) Should   B) Had   C) Might   D) Would
71. Have you been _____ today?
    A) to outside   B) from   C) outside   D) of outside
72. Many people with spinal cord injuries can, with the help of computer implants, _____.
    A) recovering some of their mobility
    B) they can recover some of their mobility
    C) recover some of their mobility
    D) who are recovering some of their mobility
73. She sang _____ and was admired by everybody.
    A) as beautiful as a bird   B) beautifying
    C) beautifully   D) beautiful like a bird
74. _____ require years of hard work to develop a successful software.
    A) It will   B) That will   C) Will it   D) The company

75. _____ possible that scientists will someday release the energy stored in water.
    A) That is   B) To be   C) It is   D) That it is
76. He ate a huge supper. He _____ very hungry.
    A) must be   B) can't be
    C) must have been   D) can't have been
77. I feel a draught. The windows _____ open.
    A) must be   B) were
    C) must have been   D) had to be
78. There wasn't any milk this morning. The milkman _____ to leave it.
    A) must forget   B) must have forgotten
    C) can't forget   D) can't have forgotten
79. According to some historians, if the United States had not used the atom bomb, the Japanese _____ half of the world.
    A) had conquered   B) would conquer
    C) would have conquered   D) had had conquered
80. Alice _____ have been told about the problem because she was on vacation and could not be reached.
    A) shouldn't   B) couldn't   C) needn't   D) must
81. Could the package _____ to the wrong address?
    A) being sent   B) to be sent   C) have been sent   D) will be sent
82. You are broke now because you spent all your money foolishly. You _____ your money foolishly.
    A) must spend   B) shouldn't have spent
    C) must have spent   D) mustn't have spent
83. Architects also design theaters, _____ is the Sydney Opera House.
    A) examples of which   B) example which
    C) an example of which   D) of which
84. English is quite difficult because of all the exceptions _____ have to be learned.
    A) which   B) what   C) they   D) those
85. We were impressed by the traditional architecture of Japan, _____ is in this picture.
    A) it   B) examples of which
    C) an example of which   D) that
86. Hydrogen peroxide _____ as a bleaching agent because it effectively whitens a variety of fibers and surfaces.
    A) which is used   B) housewives are using
    C) used   D) is used
87. The Bengal tiger, _____ can be seen in the local zoo, is an extremely interesting animal.
    A) of   B) examples of which
    C) where   D) of which
88. Niemeyer designed many buildings in Brazil, _____ are in Brasilia.
    A) an example of which   B) examples of which
    C) examples which   D) of which
89. Many of the items _____ were given to the employees.
    A) sell   B) sale   C) sold to   D) not sold
90. Even though Mohammed Ali has now lost his title, people _____ always remember him as a champion.
    A) would   B) did   C) will   D) shall
91. There is only one kind of species of snake _____ poisonous in Turkey.
    A) it is   B) that is   C) is   D) being
92. _____ I prefer Bangkok, my friend would rather live in Tokyo.
    A) Which   B) But   C) While   D) For example
93. Not only _____ come late, you also haven't brought my book.
    A) are you   B) you haven't   C) you did   D) have you
94. Neither my friend _____ I like playing soccer.
    A) or   B) and   C) but   D) nor
95. It is said that Chinese is perhaps the world's _____ language to master.
    A) harder   B) hardest   C) hard   D) too hard
96. Learning a second language is not the same _____ learning a first language.
    A) as   B) like   C) that   D) which
97. Fewer babies are born with birth defects _____ advances in prenatal care during this decade.
    A) because of   B) than   C) since   D) as to
98. The play was _____ one that I saw in London last year.
    A) it   B) similar from
    C) similar to   D) different between
99. Working provides people with personal satisfaction _____ wealth.
    A) apart from   B) as well as   C) beside   D) next to
100. A: Why don't you send your resume if you want the job?
     B: I _____ send it, but it got lost in the mail.
     A) did   B) do   C) can   D) will

TEST 17

1. Neither of the men gave _____ approval.
   A) their   B) his   C) its   D) they

2. Most of the women sent ____ applications to the director of the program.
   A) their   B) her   C) her own   D) them

3. Gold _____ to be the most alliable metal of all.
   A) know   B) has known   C) is known   D) knows

4. _____ enjoyed their meal.
   A) Every guest   B) Neither guest
   C) Each of the guests   D) Some guests

5. The cause of the series of disasters ____ not yet known, but an enquiry has been set up to find out what happened.
   A) are   B) is   C) has   D) were

6. Each team has received _____ new uniforms.
   A) their   B) them   C) his   D) its

7. It was ____ Dave to quit his job.
   A) fired because   B) stupid of
   C) foolish by   D) because of school

8. Robert didn't study for the test; _____ he did very well.
   A) consequently   B) nevertheless
   C) therefore   D) moreover

9. The sheep _____ to be brought down from the hills in bad weather, or some might die.
   A) has   B) would   C) must   D) have

10. I'll go to the station and _____ for you
    A) wait   B) to wait   C) waiting   D) have waited

11. Their ship was designed to make several trips and ____ equipment.
    A) carrying   B) to carry   C) for carrying   D) carries

12. _____ of measurement has ever equaled the metric system in simplicity.
    A) Another system   B) A new system
    C) No other system   D) Other systems

13. _____ to hear that Charles is doing well at his job.
    A) That is good   B) It is good   C) I am good   D) What is good

14. I don't care if we go to the beach or not. _____.
    A) It's up to you   B) Mind your own business
    C) We haven't got all day   D) It isn't worth it

15. She lost her job yesterday. _____.
    A) We are proud of her   B) I can't stand her
    C) I believe in her   D) I feel sorry for her

16. Susie said, "I'll wash the dishes." She said she _____ the dishes.
    A) would wash   B) will wash   C) shall wash   D) could wash

17. People respect Dr. Play. They _____ him because of his great knowledge.
    A) look up to   B) look at   C) look up   D) look for

18. It's high time _____ measures to protect our environment.
    A) we take   B) we took
    C) we have taken   D) we are taking

19. The Food and Drug Administration makes grocers and restaurant owners _____ all milk before selling it.
    A) pasteurized   B) had pasteurized
    C) pasteurize   D) should have pasteurized

20. She has always wanted other people _____ slowly.
    A) that they speak   B) to speak
    C) have spoken   D) had spoken

21. We would like _____ our radio.
    A) she's fixing   B) she'd fix   C) she had fixed   D) her to fix

22. The discovery was made after a _____ search.
    A) two years   B) twice a year
    C) two year   D) two year's

23. It's very important _____ before entering the contest.
    A) having practiced   B) to have practiced
    C) having to practice   D) practicing

24. ____ highway accidents may paralyze traffic for hours is known to all.
    A) These   B) That   C) As   D) Because

25. Mr. Nester can't swim, and _____.
    A) I can too   B) I can't either
    C) I swim neither   D) neither do I

26. It would be _____ to write George and thank him.
    A) a letter from you   B) kind of letter
    C) kind of you   D) of you

27. Every year, a _____ automobile race is held in Indianapolis.
    A) five hundred miles   B) five hundred-mile
    C) five hundred mile   D) of hundred miles

28. Rose ran in a _____ race.
    A) twenty-kilometer   B) twenty kilometer's
    C) of twenty kilometers   D) for twenty kilometers

29. A: Have you finished your book _____?
    B: No, I am _____ in the middle of it.
    A) yet/still   B) already/still   C) still/already   D) yet/yet

30. _____ lucky I am to see you this morning!
    A) What   B) What a   C) How   D) That

31. The delay was due _____ negligence, not to lack of funds.
    A) for   B) to   C) from   D) because

32. We insist _____ prompt attention.
    A) for   B) on   C) at   D) in

33. We shall agree _____ any reasonable proposal.
    A) for   B) with   C) to   D) for

34. I'm afraid we can't agree _____ each other _____ anything.
    A) with/on   B) with/with   C) on/on   D) on/with

35. The fluctuation in the money market is _____ worries the economists.
    A) what   B) which   C) that   D) whose

36. Is there a shop round here where they sell _____ clothes?
    A) children's   B) child's   C) children   D) childish

37. The building should be finished in about three _____.
    A) of months   B) month's   C) month   D) months

38. _____ motivate learning is well documented.
    A) That is computers   B) Computers that
    C) That computers   D) It is those computers

39. Raymond studies for several hours every evening; _____, he does very well on tests.
    A) however   B) not only   C) nevertheless   D) consequently

40. Dr. Osaka gives interesting lectures; _____, he is very popular with his students.
    A) however   B) consequently
    C) but also   D) not only

41. I wasn't in the office yesterday; _____, I didn't get the message you left for me.
    A) however   B) not only   C) therefore   D) nevertheless

42. Who was the first person _____ today?
    A) spoke to you   B) you spoke to
    C) you spoke   D) whom you spoke

43. _____ city life has its advantages, it also has its disadvantages.
    A) Like   B) While   C) But   D) For example

44. The argument soon developed _____ a quarrel.
    A) out   B) from   C) of   D) into

45. I am ashamed _____ my mistakes on that composition.
    A) of   B) from   C) for   D) with

46. _____ my opinion, English is a difficult language.
    A) For   B) To   C) In   D) With

47. The service in the restaurant is very poor; there aren't enough waiters to wait _____ people.
    A) to   B) on   C) for   D) at

48. Don't blame other people _____ your own mistakes.
    A) on   B) at   C) for   D) _____

49. This simple machine consists _____ three small wheels and a handle.
    A) of   B) for   C) from   D) at

50. Let's not have fish again tonight; I am tired _____ fish.
    A) from   B) with   C) of   D) _____

51. _____ I known you were coming, we would have stayed at home.
    A) Should   B) Had   C) Might   D) Would
52. _____ I not heard the warning, I would have had a serious accident.
    A) Had   B) If   C) Should   D) Would
53. _____ I listened to your advice, I wouldn't have had any trouble.
    A) When   B) Had   C) Although   D) Then
54. The car _____ with gas if the service station had been open.
    A) should have filled   B) would have been
    C) would have been filled   D) could be filled
55. _____ Bruce not driven so fast, he wouldn't have had an accident.
    A) Should   B) Had   C) Might   D) Would
56. Would Bruce _____ his car if he had driven slowly?
    A) damage   B) have damage
    C) have damaged   D) damaged
57. He wishes he _____ the exam.
    A) will pass   B) had passed   C) has passed   D) can pass
58. Intolerance between ethnic groups _____ on lack of information.
    A) usually based   B) which has been based
    C) which is usually based   D) is usually based
59. _____ bough gasoline if they had had more money?
    A) Would they have   B) Have they
    C) They had   D) Had they
60. If I had checked the gas, I wouldn't _____ to walk to the gas station.
    A) has had   B) have had   C) had had   D) had have
61. My mother, _____ you never met, works in a hospital.
    A) _____   B) that   C) who   D) whom
62. Helen's sister, for _____ we work, is really a good manager.
    A) _____   B) who   C) that   D) whom
63. Houses for _____ people pay high prices aren't always well built.
    A) _____   B) that   C) which   D) whom
64. Goods _____ we have paid for have not been delivered.
    A) that   B) of which   C) who   D) whose
65. The room in _____ Peter works is very small.
    A) that   B) which   C) _____   D) who
66. The girl to _____ I spoke comes from Italy.
    A) _____   B) who   C) whose   D) whom
67. The letter _____ I wrote to him was foolish.
    A) who   B) to which   C) _____   D) whose
68. Although he has money, with _____ he can do most things, he is rather unhappy.
    A) that   B) _____   C) which   D) who
69. Manuel asked _____ to the project.
    A) to work   B) to be assigned
    C) for a job   D) to be fired
70. The mechanic expects the car _____ by nylon.
    A) have fixed   B) have finished
    C) to have been repaired   D) repairing
71. What happened when the recipes _____ presented?
    A) were being   B) are past
    C) have been   D) will be
72. I expect all the arrangements _____ by tomorrow.
    A) to have been made   B) will be making
    C) have been made   D) were made
73. Irma wants _____ an opportunity to explain.
    A) being given   B) to be given   C) for   D) to giving
74. This book is said _____ in the fourteenth century.
    A) many times   B) to have been written
    C) when it was written   D) by being written
75. One of the primary causes of traffic accidents _____ .
    A) is reckless driving   B) people drive recklessly
    C) people who drive recklessly   D) driving recklessly
76. Land _____ in large cities that architects conserve space by designing skyscrapers.
    A) is more expensive   B) which is most expensive
    C) is so expensive   D) the most expensive thing

77. _____ is to visit Asia and Africa.
    A) It would be exciting   B) How interesting
    C) What I'd like to do   D) That's what I'd do
78. _____ I am talking about does not really concern you.
    A) What   B) That's what   C) Why   D) It's why
79. _____ requires a lot of patience to learn a second language.
    A) Teachers   B) Students   C) That   D) It
80. _____ to know is the address of Tim's house.
    A) What I will need   B) Had I needed
    C) That I will need   D) What directions are needed
81. Crocodiles are different from alligators _____ they have pointed snouts.
    A) in which   B) with which   C) in that   D) that
82. How long _____ here by the time she's sixty-five?
    A) will she work   B) she will work
    C) does she work   D) will she have worked
83. We _____ several possibilities before we made the decisions.
    A) had been   B) hadn't been
    C) been considering   D) had been considering
84. The lower the stock market falls, _____ .
    A) then the price of gold rises higher
    B) the higher the price of gold rises
    C) because the price of gold rises high
    D) the price of gold to rise higher
85. Rafts _____ the trunks of trees may have been the earliest vehicles.
    A) are made from   B) made from
    C) which they are made from   D) which made
86. For the past ten minutes I _____ for my friend to come. He hasn't arrived yet.
    A) wait   B) am waiting
    C) have been waiting   D) waiting
87. He _____ better as soon as he had eaten dinner.
    A) would feel   B) will feel   C) felt   D) could feel
88. They took a rest after they _____ the yard.
    A) had cleaned up   B) were cleaning up
    C) would clean up   D) have cleaned up
89. For three days we _____ the living room, and still haven't finished.
    A) paint   B) are painting
    C) have to paint   D) have been painting
90. When she left the building, she had the feeling she _____ .
    A) is watched   B) may be watched
    C) was being watched   D) has been watched
91. I expect him _____ the job by four o'clock.
    A) finishing   B) to be complete
    C) have been finished   D) to have completed
92. I would like _____ to the concert last night.
    A) to go   B) going
    C) to have gone   D) will have gone
93. A chameleon is a tree lizard _____ can change colors in order to conceal itself in the vegetation.
    A) with which it   B) that   C) whose life it   D) that it
94. He imagined the man _____ him.
    A) to be following   B) were following
    C) want to follow   D) follow
95. They were looking for a good _____ car.
    A) use   B) used   C) to use   D) using
96. They had their car _____ at Nick's Garage.
    A) repairing   B) to repair   C) repaired   D) repair
97. She was late to work. She _____ a taxi instead of waiting for the bus.
    A) would have taken   B) might have taken
    C) must have taken   D) should have taken
98. A new employee had _____ after Mr. Ferguson fired Oscar.
    A) to have been working   B) to be working
    C) to be hired   D) to be for the job
99. Hundreds of workers had _____ to build the pipeline.
    A) hired   B) to be hired   C) been hiring   D) hiring
100. No one realized that the document was important. It _____ thrown out.
    A) would have been   B) wouldn't have been
    C) should have been   D) might have been

TEST 18

1. _____ such as dogs and cats can teach children lessons in responsibility.
   A) Taking care of pets   B) If they take care of pets
   C) Take care of pets   D) Only when they take care of

2. Many of the health problems are found to result from _____ an unbalanced diet.
   A) people eat   B) eating   C) eaten   D) if people eat

3. Styles _____ in the 1940s have recently reappeared in high-fashion boutiques.
   A) have been popular
   B) were popular
   C) that were popular
   D) which they were universally popular

4. The idea of a set _____ the most fundamental concept in mathematics.
   A) which is   B) which it is   C) to be   D) is

5. It's easier to talk about a problem _____ to resolve it.
   A) that is difficult   B) than
   C) which is difficult   D) one finds it difficult

6. Nancy had imagined life on the campus _____ different.
   A) much   B) is   C) will be   D) to be

7. Wine _____ its flavor when it has not been properly sealed.
   A) which loses   B) loses   C) to lose   D) is lost

8. Don't forget _____ your lessons before you get to bed.
   A) study   B) to study   C) studying   D) studied

9. I promise _____ after movies, no matter how sleepy I feel.
   A) study   B) to study   C) studying   D) studied

10. Please go on _____ until you know all these words by heart.
    A) study   B) to study   C) studying   D) studied

11. Where is the body of the _____ man?
    A) murder   B) to murder   C) murdered   D) murdering

12. Mr. Tanner can't walk because he has a _____ leg.
    A) break   B) breaking   C) broke   D) broken

13. Have you ever seen a _____ fish?
    A) fly   B) to fly   C) flew   D) flying

14. I expected _____ last night, but I couldn't find my book.
    A) study   B) studying   C) to study   D) studied

15. Why did you decide _____ before breakfast instead of after dinner?
    A) studying   B) to study   C) study   D) studied

16. Can you finish _____ before the guests arrive?
    A) study   B) to study   C) studying   D) studied

17. I'd like to exchange this shirt _____ a large one?
    A) with   B) to   C) for   D) from

18. The prisoners were forced to work outside _____ the danger from wild animals and snakes.
    A) in spite of   B) for   C) because   D) of

19. The train arrived late _____ bad weather.
    A) due to   B) because   C) out of   D) from

20. His prices are too high; let's bargain _____ him.
    A) for   B) from   C) with   D) _____

21. Don't you ever feel bored _____ the same kind of music, day after day?
    A) from   B) with   C) on   D) at

22. The princess was dressed _____ green silk.
    A) in   B) on   C) from   D) _____

23. What is the use _____ to convince a foolish person?
    A) of trying   B) to try   C) from trying   D) for trying

24. _____ human being had ever traveled alone to the North Pole until 1984.
    A) No   B) If no   C) Although   D) There was no

25. If every country _____ more money on education the world would be a better place to live in.
    A) spends   B) spent   C) would spend   D) is spending

26. If nobody _____ taxes, governments would have no money.
    A) paid   B) would pay   C) pays   D) can pay

27. If every child _____ his teeth every day, dentists would not be very busy.
    A) brushes   B) would brush   C) brushed   D) had brushed

28. If I _____ English perfectly, I wouldn't be studying English now.
    A) spoke   B) speak   C) am speaking   D) would speak

29. Mr. Bell's car _____ a taxi last night if he hadn't been driving too fast.
    A) would not hit   B) didn't hit
    C) had not hit   D) wouldn't have hit

30. If they _____ to me, they wouldn't have made that mistakes.
    A) listened   B) could listen   C) would listen   D) had listened

31. An old lady, _____ looks younger than her years, takes care of the library.
    A) that   B) _____   C) who   D) whom

32. Chocolate, for _____ I have a great liking, is going up in price.
    A) _____   B) that   C) which   D) whom

33. My doctor, from _____ I have few secrets, is a close friend of mine.
    A) _____   B) who   C) that   D) whom

34. Mr. Black, _____ opinion I value, told me to look for a new job.
    A) _____   B) which   C) that   D) whose

35. Two tables, _____ were beautifully polished, stood in the middle of the room.
    A) _____   B) that   C) which   D) who

36. Mrs. Brown is almost _____ tall _____ her husband.
    A) so/so   B) so/as   C) as/as   D) like/as

37. I saw the paintings _____ were in the living room.
    A) that   B) who   C) there   D) those

38. We've looked _____ for the keys we lost.
    A) in all places   B) at all places   C) over all   D) everywhere

39. Jean has _____ paid a good salary.
    A) been   B) being   C) had   D) _____

40. Al repairs are _____ without charge.
    A) did   B) doing   C) made   D) making

41. Why _____ sent late?
    A) the order was   B) it was
    C) they were   D) was the order

42. _____ the stamps put on the package or in it?
    A) Do   B) Does   C) Are   D) Will

43. Kevin's suitcase _____ examined already by the customs officer?
    A) carefully   B) is   C) has   D) has been

44. Much of the work _____ done yesterday.
    A) being   B) was   C) will be   D) won't be

45. Was the package _____ carefully?
    A) opens   B) opening   C) opened   D) open

46. Traffic was bad because the highway _____ repaired.
    A) will be   B) was being   C) is   D) being

47. They were in danger of _____ .
    A) injured   B) injure   C) been injured   D) being injured

48. The English test was _____ yesterday.
    A) being   B) being here   C) giving   D) given

49. _____ her never-ending energy, the project turned out to be a failure.
    A) Nevertheless   B) Although
    C) Despite   D) On condition that

50. _____ happened after she left the house is difficult to explain.
    A) That   B) Which   C) Before   D) What

51. _____ was to have dinner after the movie.
    A) What   B) What I want
    C) What we are to do   D) What I wanted to do

52. _____ best is riding horses.
    A) She likes   B) What she likes
    C) That she likes   D) What she is like

53. We heard that _____ called the mayor.
    A) you would   B) they will   C) we are   D) she had

54. Did Smith tell the reporter that the small boats ____.
    A) were crowding   B) crowded
    C) were the crowd   D) were crowded

55. ____ next year, the highway will have been started.
    A) At   B) Until   C) By   D) On

56. ____ its fragile appearance, a newborn infant is extremely sturdy.
    A) In spite of   B) Although   C) For   D) Unlike

57. They will ____ to build the highway by next year.
    A) starting   B) have started   C) had started   D) started

58. The smoke ____ from the oil refinery distorts the view.
    A) is rising   B) that is rising   C) has risen   D) must rise

59. The landlord ____ just rented the apartment when I got there.
    A) was   B) had been   C) have   D) had

60. Nucleoproteins are the essential chemicals ____ living matter duplicates itself.
    A) which all   B) what   C) whose   D) with which

61. ____ and a strict sleeping schedule are necessary to sound health.
    A) If you exercise daily   B) With daily exercise
    C) You exercise   D) Daily exercise

62. ____ are brightly colored beetles that help farmers by eating harmful insects.
    A) Because ladybugs   B) Ladybugs
    C) Due to ladybugs   D) If ladybugs

63. I got a letter from an old friend. It was a ____ surprise for me.
    A) pleasantly   B) pleased   C) pleasant   D) to please

64. She ____ take a taxi because she was in a hurry.
    A) has to   B) had to   C) must   D) should

65. It was very cold today. You ____ your sweater.
    A) could wear   B) should wear
    C) should have worn   D) couldn't worn

66. After strict safety regulations have been introduced, only rarely ____.
    A) does an accident occur   B) accidents occur
    C) occurring accidents   D) an accident has occurred

67. I thought that he ____ something for me.
    A) was supposed to do   B) was supposed to
    C) is supposed to do   D) is supposed to

68. Tom ____ more for the test yesterday.
    A) can always study   B) could have studied
    C) will be able to study   D) always studied

69. Did Alice really ____ to live in this small town?
    A) used   B) use   C) used to   D) ever

70. The alarm clock is ringing. It ____ be time to get up.
    A) must   B) can't   C) will   D) should

71. The higher a mountaineer climbs, ____.
    A) the thinner the air will become.
    B) there will be thinner air
    C) the air will become thinner
    D) thinner the air will become

72. A: That desk is exactly what I need.
    B: Would you consider ____ it then?
    A) to buy   B) buy   C) buying   D) about buying

73. Today isn't ____ cold ____ yesterday.
    A) __/as   B) so/like   C) so/as   D) so/so

74. There are apricots on our tree ____ large ____ a fist.
    A) like/as   B) so/as   C) as/like   D) as/as

75. Tokyo isn't quite ____ far from Beijing ____ Istanbul is.
    A) so/so   B) so/like   C) __/as   D) so/as

76. I have ____ experience than you do.
    A) as much   B) less   C) little   D) fewer

77. ____ a person earns, the more the family spends.
    A) The most   B) When   C) The more   D) How much

78. Sue is ____ Lucy.
    A) a lot pretty than   B) a lot prettier than
    C) pretty than   D) prettier as

79. Why is there ____ traffic on the streets in August than in September?
    A) fewer   B) less   C) little   D) few

80. Helen hardly ever goes to ____ the theatre.
    A) the cinema nor   B) neither the cinema nor
    C) either the cinema or   D) the cinema or

81. ____ depends on good preparation and strong delivery.
    A) If you want to win a debate   B) People winning a debate
    C) Winning a debate   D) Some people win a debate

82. Of the four girls, Mary is the ____.
    A) prettier   B) prettiest   C) pretty   D) far prettier

83. We've missed the bus. There's nothing we can do now ____ wait for the next one.
    A) although   B) unless   C) except   D) if

84. Some women are wearing jeans ____ skirts.
    A) to wearing   B) until were
    C) for wearing   D) instead of wearing

85. ____ did Ellen enter the contest, but she also won the first prize.
    A) How   B) Both   C) Neither   D) Not only

86. To judge a person, ____ what he says but observe what he does.
    A) do not listen to   B) when you do not listen to
    C) your not listening to   D) listening not to

87. Not only were the students late, but they ____ their books.
    A) forgot them   B) also forgot
    C) forget   D) were forgetting

88. She plays tennis ____ that everyone thinks she is a professional player.
    A) so good   B) very well   C) too well   D) so well

89. Since it ____ for more than a week, everything in the house felt damp.
    A) has rained   B) had been raining
    C) it rained   D) will have rained

90. A: Where is Tom working these days?
    B: He's still at Gima ____ I know.
    A) as   B) because   C) that   D) as far as

91. Only when every possible treatment had been tried ____ decide for an operation.
    A) didn't they   B) they did   C) they didn't   D) did they

92. She doesn't ____ English.
    A) either speaks or writes   B) neither speak nor write
    C) speak or write   D) speak nor write

93. I'm bad ____ remembering face.
    A) at   B) in   C) with   D) on

94. These are nice apples. How ____ a kilo.
    A) many are there   B) much are there
    C) much are they   D) many are they

95. Very small hotels ____ this serve good food.
    A) as   B) with   C) in   D) like

96. A sports car is expensive ____.
    A) to run   B) running   C) run   D) ran

97. Because early balloons were at the mercy of shifting winds, ____ not considered a practical means of transportation.
    A) they were   B) which were   C) so they were   D) were

98. Tom is waiting ____ the doctor.
    A) to see   B) for to see   C) for seeing   D) see

99. I haven't a chair ____.
    A) to sit   B) for to sit on   C) to sit on   D) for sitting

100. In any line of business, it is ____ customers.
    A) important pleasing   B) important to please
    C) important for pleasing   D) important pleased

TEST 19

1. Several ____ friends attended last night's concert.
   A) them   B) my   C) of my   D) of them

2. The actor ____ house we visited was Robert Redford.
   A) which   B) whose   C) who   D) of whom

3. A person who talks to ____ is not necessarily mad.
   A) himself   B) oneself   C) him   D) itself

4. My sister taught ____ to cook Chinese dishes.
   A) myself   B) themselves   C) himself   D) herself

5. Sometimes it's a good idea to study ____.
   A) by yourself   B) itself   C) by itself   D) in yourself

6. ____ of the men brought his tools.
   A) Both   B) Neither   C) Some   D) Not all

7. ____ you decide to take violin classes let me know.
   A) While   B) Should   C) Do   D) Because

8. I wish I ____ what to do now.
   A) know   B) knew   C) have known   D) had known

9. The whole house ____ if he hadn't called the fireman.
   A) would be destroyed   B) would have been destroyed
   C) will have been destroyed   D) would destroy

10. ____ been late if he hadn't forgotten his keys?
    A) Would he have   B) He had
    C) Had he   D) Have he

11. ____, which is essential in learning a language, can be difficult for beginners.
    A) Students ask questions   B) If students ask questions
    C) Students who ask questions   D) Asking questions

12. If Bruce ____ the top up, his car wouldn't have gotten wet.
    A) put   B) has put   C) had put   D) puts

13. If she ____ somewhat taller, she would join the team.
    A) were   B) be   C) am   D) will be

14. They would refuse to read the book if they ____ it.
    A) like   B) doesn't like   C) didn't like   D) don't like

15. Nancy would have ____ a vacation if she had had enough money.
    A) take   B) taken   C) takes   D) took

16. They ____ to the cinema if they had known it was the last night of the film.
    A) will go   B) would go
    C) would have gone   D) had gone

17. ____ said under oath was disputed by several other witnesses.
    A) It is the man   B) What the man
    C) That the man   D) The man

18. ____ is prevalent in both primitive societies and advanced cultures.
    A) They believe in life after death
    B) Life after death
    C) Their life after death
    D) The belief in life after death

19. Holman's Department Store ____ business in the same location for fifty years before it moved.
    A) doing   B) had been
    C) had been doing   D) is doing

20. She will be late unless she ____ now.
    A) leaves   B) is leaving   C) is going to leave   D) will leave

21. She ____ the bus before the accident took place.
    A) had gotten off   B) was getting off
    C) has gotten off   D) would get off

22. ____, measles can now be prevented by a vaccine.
    A) Although a serious health hazard
    B) It was once a serious health hazard
    C) That once a serious health hazard
    D) Once a serious health hazard

23. Jimmy and Linda were walking home when they ____ a loud noise.
    A) saw   B) were hearing   C) heard   D) met

24. The library ____ since last Wednesday.
    A) has been closed   B) was closed
    C) closed   D) is closed

25. She ____ television since she got home a couple of hours ago.
    A) watched   B) is watching
    C) has been watching   D) watched

26. The last time ____ to the library was last week.
    A) I have gone   B) I have been to
    C) I was   D) I went

27. The old man died not of injuries ____ in the accident but of a heart attack.
    A) were sustained   B) sustained
    C) to sustain   D) what sustained

28. It was recently reported that a young research scientist ____ a blood test to diagnose cancer.
    A) found   B) finding   C) who found   D) to have found

29. There are over 12000 people ____ in New York.
    A) they don't have any fixed address
    B) don't have any fixed address
    C) whose fixed address
    D) with no fixed address

30. In the desert ____ for water is of primary importance.
    A) all living things need   B) if there is no need
    C) the need   D) all living things that need

31. ____, generally found in the desert, is useful as a water softener in the laundry industry.
    A) When Borax   B) Borax   C) It is Borax   D) Borax is

32. Pete ____ by the time the meeting starts.
    A) arrived   B) had arrived   C) will have arrived   D) has arrived

33. No sooner ____ the door than the thief fled.
    A) had I opened   B) have I opened
    C) did I open   D) I had opened

34. Linda hoped ____ to Ralph's party.
    A) to be invited   B) to have invitation
    C) for being invited   D) she will be invited

35. After working on the same project for several months, Mr. Williams asked ____ a different assignment.
    A) for a more interesting   B) to be interested for
    C) to be given   D) for giving him

36. Before the computer could be repaired, a special part had ____ from Japan.
    A) to import   B) to be imported
    C) a very long delivery   D) to have been important

37. If it keeps on raining the game may ____.
    A) delay   B) be delayed   C) have delayed   D) have to delay

38. ____ the president given a warm welcome?
    A) Did   B) Have   C) Should   D) Was

39. ____ your company's products guaranteed?
    A) Do   B) Are   C) Would   D) Will

40. The packages ____ at the post office.
    A) weighs   B) was weigh   C) weigh   D) are weighed

41. The Sea of Marmara ____ so much that it can now support only little life.
    A) is polluted   B) with dangerous pollution
    C) has been polluted   D) has polluted

42. The answers ____ into Spanish.
    A) were translated   B) are translate
    C) is translated   D) are translating

43. The order ____ sent last month.
    A) is   B) will   C) was   D) will be

44. All developed countries are running out of space ____ their garbage.
    A) it discards   B) in which to discard
    C) which discards   D) which they discard

45. If Charles Lindbergh ____ across the Atlantic, another person would have done that sooner or later.
    A) hasn't been   B) would not fly   C) did not fly   D) hadn't flown

46. Gilberto ____ more precise instructions; he couldn't do the job.
    A) must be given   B) should be given
    C) should have been given   D) must have been given

47. ____ the legendary land of the lost continent of Atlantis may some day be found.
    A) The belief   B) It is believed that
    C) Believing   D) That belief

48. Do you intend ____ English while you are visiting England?
    A) to study   B) study   C) studying   D) studied

49. I'd appreciate ____ an answer as soon as possible.
    A) receive   B) to receive   C) receiving   D) received

50. Do you want me ____ that doctor's address for you.
    A) to copy   B) copy   C) copying   D) copied

51. Won't you let the children ____ a little longer?
    A) stay   B) to stay   C) staying   D) stayed

52. Most teachers don't permit their students ____ dictionaries during an examination.
    A) use   B) to use   C) using   D) used

53. She doesn't allow her daughter ____ high heels.
    A) wear   B) wearing   C) to wear   D) _ _ _

54. Her mother makes her ____ to bed before ten every evening.
    A) to go   B) going   C) go   D) went

55. Please have the doctor ____ that report.
    A) sign   B) to sign   C) signing   D) _ _ _

56. Shall we request the committee ____ our suggestion again?
    A) consider   B) considering   C) to consider D) _ _ _

57. Oscar is expected to pick up the products and ____ them to customers.
    A) he delivers   B) to deliver   C) then delivers   D) delivering

58. ____, Horace returned to the house.
    A) Tired of waiting   B) Tiring of wait
    C) Of waiting tiring   D) After tired from waiting

59. Recycling ____ the process of collecting used materials and manufacturing them into new products.
    A) which is   B) which is done by
    C) which has   D) is

60. A person ____ eventually deceives only himself.
    A) tells lies   B) who tells lies
    C) can tell lies well   D) has told lies

61. Learning to live with a chronic illness such as diabetes ____ an ongoing process.
    A) that has to be   B) it has to be
    C) has to be   D) and has to be

62. The package ____ been sent to the wrong person; we've never seen it.
    A) must have   B) would have   C) should have   D) can't have

63. The ____ the thief is caught, the happier everyone will be.
    A) quickly   B) quickest   C) fast   D) sooner

64. He may have got delayed. This sentence means:
    A) He will arrive shortly.
    B) He has permission to arrive late.
    C) It is probable that he has been delayed.
    D) He was delayed.

65. He is very tired. He ____ hard today.
    A) might have worked   B) must have worked
    C) should have worked   D) would have worked

66. You ____ drive carefully. The roads are wet.
    A) would rather   B) had better   C) had rather   D) are better

67. Mary ____ be in Paris because I saw her here in Ankara only two hours ago.
    A) can't   B) mustn't be   C) isn't able to   D) may not

68. He's ____ to know the answer.
    A) likely   B) probably   C) maybe   D) obviously

69. She ____ a lot by cutting down on the luxuries, but she didn't.
    A) could save   B) could have saved
    C) should save   D) would save

70. As we drove on, the countryside became ____ and more beautiful.
    A) beautiful   B) very beautiful   C) more   D) so beautiful

71. Jack's ability to wrong things at the wrong time ____.
    A) it amazes us   B) is amazed
    C) which is amazing   D) is amazing

72. She ____ terribly disappointed in her low grade because she ____ very hard the night before.
    A) ___ / has studied   B) was / had studied
    C) would be / has studied   D) was /can't have studied

73. I should ____ my assignment last night, but there was no electricity.
    A) have done   B) do   C) had done   D) did

74. ____ has enough natural resources so as to be practically self-sufficient in the event of war.
    A) Our country which   B) Only when our country
    C) Our country   D) If our country

75. ____ is to study Chinese.
    A) What I plan to do   B) A very difficult language
    C) The language that   D) What language

76. Were you ____ when the car started skidding?
    A) frightening   B) frightened
    C) being frightening   D) frighten

77. ____ is to finish this test.
    A) That's what I want   B) What I want to do
    C) This is what I want   D) It was easy of me

78. ____ I'm calling about is the job advertised in Sunday's newspaper.
    A) Where   B) What   C) Why   D) How

79. Mr. Smart, ____, walks five miles every day.
    A) whose is sixty   B) he is sixty five
    C) who is seventy   D) almost eighty old

80. Mary has three children, ____.
    A) who likes toys   B) all of which like toys
    C) one of whom likes toys   D) both of them enjoy toys

81. The students, ____, did extremely well on today's English test.
    A) most of them had studied hard
    B) most of whom to study hard
    C) most of whom had studied hard
    D) they all studied very hard

82. The Wilson's had three children, ____.
    A) and both of them are musicians
    B) all who became musicians
    C) all of whom became musicians
    D) two musicians and one is salesman

83. The children, ____, were not injured in the crash.
    A) frightened and seriously hurt in the crash
    B) all of whom were frightened
    C) all of them were frightened
    D) both of them were frightened

84. There are two trails up the mountain, ____.
    A) both of which are difficult   B) either of them is difficult
    C) that are difficult trails   D) they are difficult

85. I ate two sandwiches, ____ were delicious.
    A) one of them   B) both of which
    C) either of which   D) none of whom

86. ____ I go, I seem to bump into people I was at school with.
    A) Wherever   B) Where   C) When   D) How

87. ____ you lost your job, what would you do then?
    A) When   B) After   C) So   D) Supposing

88. Take an umbrella ____ you won't get wet.
    A) so that   B) in case   C) so   D) _ _ _

89. Take an umbrella ____ it rains.
    A) so that   B) in case   C) so   D) _ _ _

90. Have something to eat ____ you can't get anything to eat later.
    A) in case   B) so that   C) so   D) _ _ _

91. This picnic site ____ quite tidy is now a disgrace.
    A) used to be   B) could be
    C) which used to be   D) would be

92. He failed his driving test ____ he practiced a lot.
    A) so   B) because   C) even though D) so that

93. She is fit and healthy ____ she doesn't get much exercise.
    A) so   B) because   C) even though D) so that

94. ____ my friend works at home, I have to drive to work.
    A) While   B) Like   C) For example D) But

95. Neither the housing shortage ____ the problem of pollution can be solved easily.
    A) and   B) or   C) neither   D) nor

96. If our friend had not warned us of the danger, we ____ now.
    A) must have been dead   B) would have been all dead
    C) would all be dead   D) had all died

97. ____ did Oswald damage his skis, but he also broke his leg.
    A) Neither   B) How   C) Not only   D) Why

98. Not only did Oscar lose his job, but he ____ his car.
    A) also damaged   B) and an accident
    C) lost also   D) and

99. I shall say no more ____ I be misunderstood.
    A) so   B) in order that   C) lest   D) even though

100. Children are forbidden to play with matches ____ they may get burned.
    A) so that   B) for fear that   C) if   D) when

TEST 20

1. He won't be able to finish studying those reports at the office. He wants to ____ at home.
   A) look for them   B) look after them
   C) look them over   D) look them up

2. Some of the tenants are upset because the landlord won't ____ the building.
   A) keep off   B) keep on   C) keep up with   D) keep up

3. Many of the items ____ were given to the poor.
   A) sell   B) sale   C) sold to   D) not sold

4. Mr. Green received all the complaints ____ to our office.
   A) sent   B) were sent   C) sending   D) be sent

5. Anyone ____ in hunting can come with me.
   A) interesting   B) interested
   C) was interested   D) was interesting

6. War and Peace is a long novel ____ by Leo Tolstoy.
   A) written   B) it was written
   C) was written   D) wrote

7. Have you met the new secretary ____ last week?
   A) hired   B) was hired
   C) she was hired   D) when she was hired

8. ____ entering the hall, he found everyone waiting for him.
   A) At   B) While   C) On   D) In

9. His parents died when he was young, so he was ____ by his aunt.
   A) brought out   B) grown up
   C) brought up   D) grown

10. You can't rely ____ him to do the job properly.
    A) on   B) with   C) to   D) in

11. Don't make him ____ it if he doesn't want to.
    A) do   B) doing   C) to do   D) done

12. He rushed out of the room, ____ the door as he went.
    A) slam   B) slamming   C) slams   D) slammed

13. He arrived without ____ us that he was coming.
    A) warn   B) having warned
    C) have warned   D) to warned

14. The man ____ for a bus were knocked down when a lorry skidded and ran off the road.
    A) wait   B) waiting   C) waited   D) were waiting

15. After ____ all the doors and windows thoroughly, I went to bed.
    A) check   B) have checked
    C) having checked   D) have been checked

16. The man is going to drown ____ nobody jumps into the river to save him.
    A) in case   B) unless   C) so   D) that

17. Martin hasn't got a library ticket, ____ he can't borrow books from the library.
    A) so   B) unless   C) if   D) that

18. ____ you have driven a car like this, you will never want to drive any other car.
    A) Once   B) In case   C) Although   D) Therefore

19. He looked ____ he had seen a ghost.
    A) as   B) as if   C) like   D) because

20. Don't use the car ____ it is absolutely necessary.
    A) if   B) so   C) because   D) unless

21. You can take books out of the library ____ you bring them back.
    A) provided   B) unless   C) because   D) so

22. It is ____ an expensive hotel that only the rich can afford it.
    A) ___   B) very   C) so   D) such

23. The restaurant was ____ crowded that we couldn't get a table.
    A) ___   B) such   C) so   D) very

24. He has ____ large feet that he can't get shoes to fit him.
    A) so   B) ___   C) very   D) such

25. He gave me ____ good advice that I was able to save thousands of pounds.
    A) ___   B) very   C) so   D) such

26. ____ it is getting late; I suggest we break off now.
    A) As though   B) So   C) As   D) Where

27. ____ I can see, he has no intention of paying the bill.
    A) As far as   B) So   C) Because   D) When

28. We will have a picnic on Saturday ____ it rains.
    A) if   B) as if   C) however   D) unless

29. He meets ____ people that he can't remember all their names.
    A) so many   B) so much   C) very many   D) too many

30. ____ he does his work, I don't mind what time he arrives at the office.
    A) As long as   B) As   C) Unless   D) So

31. ____ a good thing you didn't get caught.
    A) That's   B) It's   C) What is   D) There is

32. We'll go to Paris for our holiday ____ it isn't too expensive.
    A) unless   B) provided   C) so   D) except

33. It looks ____ it is going rain.
    A) that   B) as   C) as if   D) like

34. ____ the weather was fine, I opened all the windows.
    A) As   B) Because of   C) Due to   D) Since that

35. I'll leave him a note ____ he'll know where we are.
    A) so that   B) that   C) in order that   D) for

36. ____ he worked all day, he couldn't finish the job.
    A) Even   B) In case   C) So   D) Although

37. ____, the music company cancelled the record contract.
    A) The band having broken up
    B) The band has broken up
    C) They have broken up the band
    D) The band broke up

38. It's difficult to make both ends meet these days, the taxes ____ so high.
    A) with   B) being   C) are   D) be

39. Customers ____ with the product can return it to the store.
    A) who buy   B) bought   C) purchased   D) not satisfied

40. He ate all the meat ____.
    A) giving him   B) given to him
    C) gave to him   D) had given to him

41. Most tarantulas, ____ occur in the temperate zone, live in the tropics.
    A) which they   B) some of them
    C) several species of which   D) several species also

42. ____ two years ago, Rita's car costs five thousand dollars.
    A) Purchased less than   B) To buy a car
    C) Expensive cars   D) Buying automobile

43. Mrs. Smith answers all the letters ____ to her husband.
    A) sent   B) send for   C) are sent   D) sending

44. I have two cars, ____.
    A) and so do I   B) both of which are old
    C) all of them stolen   D) and I do too

45. Ronald Eliot, ____, is in my English class.
    A) his brother is a pilot   B) whose brother is a pilot
    C) who's his brother a pilot   D) whose not a pilot

46. Anyone ____ in taking the course can enroll next week.
    A) wants   B) is interested   C) interested   D) wanting

47. "Sunflowers" is one of many beautiful pictures ____ by Vincent van Gogh.
    A) painted   B) was painted
    C) it was painted   D) when it was painted

48. Raymond has two brothers, ____.
    A) both of whom live in Turkey   B) whom they live in Turkey
    C) both of them live in Turkey   D) one of them lives in Turkey

49. ____ only two elderly people who were enjoying the beautiful weather.
    A) ___   B) As many as   C) There were   D) It was

50. There were twenty people near the scene, ____ saw the accident.
    A) all of whom   B) most   C) whom   D) both of them

51. Two men ____ on the bridge were injured yesterday afternoon.
    A) working   B) work   C) worked   D) were working

52. She bought many beautiful objects in Japan, ____ is this painting.
    A) an example of which   B) example of which
    C) examples of which   D) of which

53. According to black leaders, ____ the most malignant cancer in the body of America.
    A) it is racism   B) racism which is
    C) racism is   D) nothing but racism

54. The interest on savings accounts at HSBC Bank are ____ Bank of Rome.
    A) higher than   B) higher than that of
    C) higher of   D) as high as

55. Fresh fruit costs twice ____ canned fruit.
    A) more expensive than   B) higher than
    C) much as   D) as much as

56. She was ____ I met at the party.
    A) the one   B) whom   C) who   D) that

57. ____ she needs is a good rest.
    A) That   B) What
    C) The thing what   D) Which

58. Is this ____ looking for?
    A) you were   B) that you were
    C) what you were   D) which you were

59. The UN has destroyed an Iraqi factory which ____ to produce biological weapons.
    A) it is claimed   B) claimed   C) claiming   D) is claimed

60. My father, ____ knows two languages, works for a publisher.
    A) whom   B) that   C) who   D) whose

61. The man ____ were all actors.
    A) to those I talked   B) I talked to
    C) whom I talked   D) talked

62. He didn't thank me for the present. That is ____ annoyed me.
    A) ---   B) the thing   C) what   D) the thing what

63. The reason ____ I'm writing is to tell you about a party next week.
    A) because   B) why   C) for   D) as

64. ____ in my first visit to Turkey that I went to Bodrum.
    A) It is   B) It was   C) It has been   D) Its

65. ____ to see that you are feeling better.
    A) It is nice   B) Therefore   C) That's fine   D) I went

66. It is less expensive for me to take the bus to work, but ____ to take my car.
    A) I will   B) for I will   C) it is less than   D) it is faster

67. ____ requires years of practice to play the guitar as well as Carlos.
    A) Music of high quality   B) That music of high quality
    C) It   D) Playing music

68. ____ to spend that much money for a shirt.
    A) Consequently, foolish   B) Not only
    C) Foolish of him   D) It is foolish

69. ____ to hear from Lillian after so many years.
    A) Consequently, nice   B) It was nice
    C) That was nice   D) She was nice

70. ____ to watch the dancers perform.
    A) Interesting nevertheless   B) That was interesting
    C) Not only was it interesting   D) It was interesting

71. ____ an enjoyable way to spend an evening.
    A) Therefore   B) It was
    C) Was it   D) Going to a movie

72. Prime Minister ____ by members of his own party of using undemocratic methods.
    A) who was accused   B) whom they have accused
    C) has been accused   D) had accused

73. ____ the bus yesterday morning, Mr. Gomez saw a terrible automobile accident.
    A) On his way to work   B) Because it was crowded
    C) Waiting for   D) Missed

74. ____ down the street, Lionel lost his watch.
    A) Running   B) Fall   C) Ran fast   D) Run

75. ____ the problem, Susan was able to correct it.
    A) Having recognized   B) Recognize
    C) Having been recognized   D) Recognized

76. Not having ____ instructions, George could not do the job properly.
    A) been given   B) given   C) giving   D) given the

77. ____ in the city for several years, he was able to help the tourists.
    A) They have lived   B) Have lived
    C) Having lived   D) Having live

78. ____ by the noise, the bird flew away.
    A) Fearing   B) Afraid   C) Frightened   D) Building

79. ____ in 1795, the house has many interesting features.
    A) Later   B) Built
    C) When it was built   D) Building

80. ____ her problem, Tom wrote Susan a letter.
    A) Because   B) Hearing about
    C) Write about   D) What about

81. This ____ the fourth time you've asked me the same difficult question.
    A) had to be   B) must be   C) to be   D) have been

82. He told the police that he ____ there since March.
    A) not be   B) hasn't been   C) wasn't   D) hadn't been

83. I'm not going to miss the chance of seeing this performance ____ it is.
    A) however expensive   B) although expensive
    C) nevertheless expensive   D) how expensive

84. She demanded that she ____ given the exact figures.
    A) be   B) are   C) were   D) have

85. No sooner ____ the match than flames shot across the floor.
    A) did he drop   B) he dropped
    C) he had dropped   D) plans

86. Not until now ____ popularly recognized that man is destroying his environment.
    A) it has become   B) it becomes
    C) does it become   D) has it become

87. Not for one moment ____ my friend's innocence.
    A) I doubted   B) I did doubt   C) did I doubt   D) I doubt

88. Hardly ____ the harbor when a storm broke out.
    A) had we left   B) we had left   C) we left   D) we did leave

89. You will pass the exam ____ you get over 50% in each section.
    A) provided   B) unless   C) so   D) otherwise

90. There will be even greater unemployment ____ the government radically alters its policies.
    A) provided   B) unless   C) as if   D) in case

91. I have taken out a life insurance to protect my wife and children ____ something should happen to me.
    A) unless   B) otherwise   C) in case   D) provided

92. We'll have a good crop of beans this summer ____ an unexpected frost damages the plants.
    A) unless   B) if   C) provided   D) so

93. The east of Argentina is agricultural, ____ the west is industrialized.
    A) whereas   B) because   C) so   D) since

94. They would rather cut down on a few luxuries now ____ not be able to go away on holiday in the summer.
    A) than   B) on   C) to   D) for

95. The government aims ____ inflation by at least 20% this year.
    A) reducing   B) to reduce   C) reduce   D) reduced

96. "Don't go out alone after dark in that city, Tom," said Martha. Martha ____ Tom not to go out after dark in that city.
    A) said   B) promised   C) threatened   D) warned

97. They prohibited him ____ going in.
    A) from   B) to   C) for   D) in

98. I have dissuaded Mary ____ involving the police.
    A) from   B) to   C) in   D) for

99. The guard prevented the prisoner ____ escaping.
    A) for   B) to   C) from   D) than

100. Life is full of secrets, many ____ will never be explained.
    A) of where   B) of whose   C) of whom   D) of that

ELEMENTARY TEST - 1

Choose the correct answer. Only one answer is correct.

1. A) The sun is in a sky.   B) The sun is in the sky.
   C) Sun is in a sky.   D) A sun is in a sky.

2. What _____ John doing?
   A) are   B) do   C) does   D) is

3. John and Mary _____ the radio.
   A) are listening on   B) are listening to
   C) is listening on   D) is listening to

4. Bill and I _____ here.
   A) we're   B) we   C) we are   D) are

5. Sarah, what _____ doing?
   A) she is   B) are you   C) are   D) is

6. Mary's _____ the garden.
   A) in   B) at   C) on   D) into

7. Are there six books on the table?
   A) No, are five?   B) No, there are three.
   C) No, there's the one.   D) No, there are any.

8. Tom often sings, but _____ .
   A) sings Sarah?   B) Sarah sings?
   C) Sarah does?   D) does Sarah?

9. Tony is looking at _____ .
   A) she   B) he   C) her   D) here

10. Who's that boy?
    A) Is Bill.   B) It's Tom.   C) It's a boy.   D) Peter's that.

11. Where's the book?
    A) There's it.   B) He's under the chair.
    C) It's here.   D) There's on a chair.

12. Are you happy?
    A) Yes, I'm.   B) No, I aren't.   C) Yes, I am.   D) No, I not.

13. What's his name?
    A) It's name Jack.   B) It's Jack.
    C) It's Jack's name.   D) It's a Jack.

14. Do you dance or draw?
    A) I'm dance but I'm not draw.
    B) I dance but I don't draw.
    C) I'm dancing but I not drawing.
    D) I dance but I'm not drawing.

15. Is that a book?
    A) Yes, there is.   B) Yes, it is.
    C) Yes, that's.   D) Yes, is a book.

16. Is that horse big?
    A) No, that's a little.   B) No, that's little horse.
    C) No, it's little horse.   D) No, it isn't.

17. What's her brother doing?
    A) Playing football.   B) Is playing football.
    C) He playing football.   D) She's playing football.

18. How many chairs are there in the room?
    A) Are four.   B) Are five chairs there.
    C) There's one.   D) There's a chair.

19. A) Is that table big brown?   B) Is that big brown table?
    C) Is that big table brown?   D) Is brown that big table?

20. A) Mary can dance tomorrow.
    B) Mary cans dance tomorrow.
    C) Mary she can dance tomorrow.
    D) Mary can tomorrow dance.

21. The lamp is _____ the television.
    A) at   B) next to   C) near of   D) between

22. The tree is _____ the door.
    A) between   B) in front   C) beside   D) next

23. What's that girl?
    A) It's a student.   B) She's student.
    C) She's a student.   D) She's a student girl.

24. Do the girls know Tom?
    A) Yes, they knows her.   B) No, they isn't.
    C) Yes, they know.   D) No, they don't.

25. A) John's looking at I and you.   B) Your looking at John and I.
    C) I'm looking at you and John.   D) John and I am looking at you.

26. A) That girl is some of my friends.
    B) This girl is one of my friends.
    C) That girl is me friend.
    D) This girl's are friends.

27. A) This is Mr. Smith there.   B) That is the Mr. Smith there.
    C) This is the Mr. Smith here.   D) That is Mr. Smith there.

28. Our house is _____ Washington Street.
    A) in   B) from   C) at   D) on

29. A) Who now in London lives?   B) Who in London live?
    C) Who lives in London now?   D) Who live now in London?

30. Monday is the first day.
    A) Tuesday is the second.   B) The second is Thursday.
    C) Tuesday is the fourth.   D) The fourth is Thursday.

31. Jane is in front of Tom. Tom is _____ Jane.
    A) beside   B) behind   C) before   D) between

32. Tom is Mrs. Smith's son.
    A) She is his son.   B) She is her son.
    C) He is her son.   D) He is his son

33. A) Come here to us!   B) Go here to we!
    C) Go there to us!   D) Come here to my!

34. A) Don't look at us!   B) Don't looking at us!
    C) No looking at we!   D) Not look at us!

35. A) Some girl are listening to the old men.
    B) An old man is listening to the girl.
    C) An old men are listening the girl.
    D) The old man are listening to a girl.

36. A) Listen to he and he's brother!
    B) Listen to he and his brother!
    C) Listen to him and his brother!
    D) Listen to him and he's brother!

37. Whose hats are those? They are _____ hats.
    A) he's   B) Mr. Black's   C) Mrs.' Black's   D) She's

38. A) Where are you going to put the cups?
    B) Where are you going put the cups?
    C) Where you're going put the cups?
    D) Where you are going to put the cups?

39. Jane's tall and _____ .
    A) John's, too.   B) Tom is, too.
    C) Tom is to.   D) Tom are two.

40. Does Brian play football?
    A) Yes, and Sam doesn't, too.   B) No, but Sam doesn't.
    C) Yes, but Sam doesn't.   D) No, and Sam does, too.

41. James is talking to _____ .
    A) they   B) them   C) she   D) your

42. These pens are _____ .
    A) Pats   B) of Pat   C) Pat's   D) to Pat

43. Sarah _____ cat.
    A) haves a   B) haves some   C) has some   D) has a

44. This is _____ .
    A) second lesson   B) the lesson two
    C) lesson the second   D) lesson two

45. A) Lena cans have Mikes' radio.   B) Lena can has Mike's radio.
    C) Lena can have Mike's radio.   D) Lena can has Mikes' radio.

46. It's 21.00.
    A) Yes, it's nine in the evening.   B) Yes, it's nine clocks.
    C) Yes, it's nine in the afternoon.   D) Yes, it's nine hours.

47. 164 is _____ .
    A) hundred sixty four.   B) a hundred sixty four.
    C) hundred sixty and four.   D) a hundred and sixty four.

48. A) The girls don't do the homework.
    B) The girls don't the homework.
    C) The girls doesn't do the homework.
    D) The girls don't does the homework.

49. Do Mr. and Mrs. Smith speak English?
    A) He does but she doesn't.   B) He speak but she doesn't.
    C) He do but she don't.   D) He speak but she don't.

50. Who are those boys? One is my brother and _____ .
    A) the big boy is Peter.   B) a big boy is Peter.
    C) the big boy is a Peter.   D) a big boy is a Peter.
51. A) Some sun is in a sky.   B) Sun is in some sky.
    C) A sun is in a sky.   D) The sun is in the sky.
52. Where _____ Mary standing?
    A) do   B) does   C) is   D) are
53. Tom and Anne _____ the table.
    A) are sitting in   B) are sitting on
    C) is sitting in   D) is sitting on
54. Sarah and I _____ here.
    A) we   B) are we   C) we're   D) are
55. John, what _____ doing?
    A) are you   B) is   C) your   D) he's
56. Anne's _____ the bedroom.
    A) at   B) on   C) in   D) into
57. Are there many trees near the house?
    A) There's one. B) Are four. C) There five. D) Three of trees.
58. Mary speaks English, but _____ .
    A) speaks Bill. B) Bill speaks? C) Bills does? D) does Bill?
59. Barbara is looking at _____ .
    A) there   B) them   C) we   D) my
60. Who's that woman?
    A) Anne is it.   B) Is Sarah.   C) He's Barbara. D) It's Jane.
61. Where's the cat?
    A) There's on the table.   B) It's on the table.
    C) There's under a table.   D) It's under table.
62. Is Mary pretty?
    A) Yes, she is.   B) No, she's n't.
    C) No, isn't.   D) Yes, she's.
63. What's her name?
    A) The name Anne.   B) Anne is she name.
    C) It's Anne.   D) It's Anne's name.
64. Do you draw or sing?
    A) I draw and I sing.   B) I'm drawing and singing.
    C) I do draw and singing.   D) I drawing and singing.
65. Is that a table?
    A) Yes, there is.   B) Yes, it is.
    C) Yes, that's.   D) Yes, it's that table.
66. Is that house small?
    A) No, it isn't.   B) No, there's a big house.
    C) No, a big house is that.   D) No, that's big house.
67. What's his sister doing?
    A) Reading.   B) She reading.
    C) He's reading.   D) It's reading.
68. How many trees are there?
    A) There's a tree.   B) There are any.
    C) There are three.   D) There are trees.
69. A) Is this little book red?   B) Is this little red book?
    C) Is this little book a red? D) Is red this little book?
70. A) Fred cans tomorrow work.   B) Fred can working tomorrow.
    C) Fred he can work tomorrow. D) Fred can work tomorrow.
71. The cup is _____ the radio.
    A) at   B) near   C) between   D) next
72. The window is _____ the door.
    A) next   B) between   C) with   D) beside
73. What's that man?
    A) He's my brother.   B) It's an old man.
    C) Yes, it's that man.   D) He's a teacher.
74. Do they live in England?
    A) Yes, they live.   B) Yes, they live in it.
    C) No, they don't.   D) No, they don't live.
75. A) Mary is sitting near you and me.
    B) You and me is sitting near Mary.
    C) Mary and you sitting near me.
    D) You and Mary's sitting near me.

76. A) These boy is a good friend.
    B) My friends are these goods boys.
    C) This boy is some good friend.
    D) My friend is that good boy.
77. A) This is my shoes there.   B) Those are my shoes there.
    C) These are my shoes there.   D) Those are my shoes here.
78. My brother is looking _____ his cat. It may be in the garden.
    A) in   B) out   C) at   D) for
79. A) Does Milly now living in Scotland?
    B) Is Milly now in Scotland living?
    C) Does Milly in Scotland now live?
    D) Does Milly live in Scotland now?
80. Monday is the first day.
    A) Tuesday is the fourth.   B) Thursday is the fourth.
    C) The second is Tuesday.   D) The second is Thursday.
81. Ken is behind Mary. Mary is _____ Ken.
    A) beside   B) in front of C) between   D) next
82. Carrie is Mr. Smith's daughter.
    A) He is of her the father.   B) He is of she the father.
    C) He is her father.   D) He is she's father.
83. A) Come here to my!   B) Come here to us!
    C) Come there to me!   D) Come here at me!
84. A) Not listen to me radio!   B) No listen at my radio!
    C) Don't listen on my radio!   D) Don't listen to my radio!
85. A) A old woman lives near me.
    B) A young woman live near my house.
    C) The old woman lives near me.
    D) An old women lives near my house.
86. Listen to _____ sister!
    A) she and she's   B) she and her
    C) her and she   D) her and her
87. Whose cats are they? They are _____ cats.
    A) Miss Smith's   B) Miss's Smith's
    C) the Miss Smith's   D) Miss's Smith
88. Where _____ bottles?
    A) you are going to take this B) are you going take the
    C) you are going take those   D) are you going to take these
89. A) Tom's clever and they are, too
    B) Tom's brother clever and they are, too
    C) Tom clever but they're two
    D) Tom's clever but they are two
90. Can Bill sing?
    A) Yes, and Peter can't, too   B) No, and Peter can, too
    C) No, but Peter can't   D) Yes, but Peter can't
91. Tony is talking to _____ .
    A) my   B) we   C) them   D) your
92. This ball is _____ Chris.
    A) of   B) to   C) at   D) for
93. A) Mark's some pen   B) Mark's some pens
    C) Mark has some pens   D) Mark has some pen
94. A) This is two lessons   B) This is lesson two.
    C) This is second lesson.   D) This is lesson the second.
95. A) Pat can have Jim's hat.   B) Pat can to have Jim's hat.
    C) Pat can have Jims' hat.   D) Pat can to have Jims' hat.
96. It's 11.45.
    A) Yes, it's fifteen to eleven.   B) Yes, it's fifteen from twelve.
    C) Yes, it's a quarter to twelve. D) Yes, it's a quarter past twelve.
97. 140 is _____ .
    A) one hundred forty.   B) one hundred fourteen.
    C) one hundred and forty.   D) one hundred and fourteen.
98. A) Tom don't plays football.   B) Tom doesn't play football.
    C) Tom don't plays the football.   D) Tom don't play the football.
99. Does father read the newspaper?
    A) Yes, he reads.   B) No, he doesn't.
    C) No, he not read.   D) No, he reads not.
100. That's Jane. She _____ .
    A) have hair long.   B) have long hair.
    C) has hair long.   D) has long hair.

ELEMENTARY TEST - 2

Choose the correct answer. Only one answer is correct.

1. A) The bird are in the sky.　　B) A bird's in a sky.
   C) The birds in a sky.　　　　 D) The bird's in the sky.

2. What _____ doing?
   A) are they　B) do they　C) does they　D) is they

3. Jane and Tom _____ the door.
   A) are walking at　　B) walks to
   C) walks to　　　　　D) are walking to

4. Charles and I _____ .
   A) am here　B) we are here　C) are here　D) we here

5. Anne, what _____ ?
   A) is doing　B) she's doing　C) are doing　D) are you doing

6. Tom's _____ street.
   A) in the　B) at the　C) into the　D) under

7. How many girls are there in the room?
   A) There are any.　　B) There's one.
   C) A girl.　　　　　　D) There two.

8. Mary works, but _____ .
   A) works Tom?　B) does Tom?　C) Tom does?　D) Tom works?

9. Liz is looking at _____ .
   A) them　B) they　C) there　D) their

10. Who's that girl?
    A) He's Elizabeth.　　B) Her name Sarah.
    C) She's a good girl.　D) It's Anne.

11. Where's the dog?
    A) He's under chair.　　B) There's on a table.
    C) It's near the window.　D) Its here.

12. Is John tall?
    A) Yes, he's.　B) No, he'sn't.　C) No, his not.　D) Yes, he is.

13. What's his name?
    A) It John.　　　　　　B) It's John.
    C) John it's the name.　D) Its John.

14. Do you draw or write?
    A) I'm draw and write.　　　　B) I drawing and writing.
    C) I'm not draw but I'm write.　D) I draw and I write.

15. Is that a chair?
    A) Yes, that's.　　B) Yes, there is.
    C) Yes, it is.　　 D) Yes, it's that chair.

16. Is this chair brown?
    A) No, isn't brown chair.　B) No, this is green chair.
    C) Yes, it's brown.　　　　D) Yes, it is a brown.

17. What's her father doing?
    A) Her working in the garden.　B) Working in the garden.
    C) Is working in the garden.　　D) She is working in the garden.

18. How many books are there?
    A) They're many.　　B) There are any.
    C) There are eight.　D) Are two books there.

19. A) Is that red book a big?　B) Is that book a big red?
    C) Is red that big book?　　 D) Is that red book big?

20. Anne _____ tomorrow.
    A) can sing　　　　B) can to sing
    C) is going sing　　D) going to sing

21. The pen is _____ his pocket.
    A) in　B) into　C) at　D) to

22. The car is _____ the tree.
    A) near of　B) with　C) beside　D) next

23. What's that man?
    A) He's John.　　B) Yes, it's a man.
    C) It's John.　　 D) He's a teacher.

24. Do you like the boat?
    A) No, I don't like it.　B) Yes, I like him.
    C) No, I like not.　　　D) Yes, I like.

25. A) Ken is talking to Jane and we.
    B) We and Jane is talking to Ken.
    C) Jane and we talking to Ken.
    D) We are talking to Ken and Jane.

26. A) Is you friend that pretty girl?
    B) Is that friend you're pretty girl?
    C) Is that girl pretty your friend?
    D) Is that pretty girl your friend?

27. A) Is this your hat there?　B) Are those your hats there?
    C) Are those your hats here?　D) Is this your hats here?

28. There are _____ people on the street.
    A) any　B) a little　C) a lot of　D) much

29. A) Do Gary live in Bristol now?　B) Does Gary live in Bristol now?
    C) Is living in Bristol, now?　　　D) Does now Gary live in Bristol?

30. Monday is the first day.
    A) Tuesday is the second.　B) The second is Thursday.
    C) Tuesday is the fourth.　 D) The fourth is Thursday.

31. Mike is beside Pat. Pat is _____ Mike.
    A) behind　B) between　C) beside　D) in front of

32. Tom is Mrs. Black's son.
    A) She is his daughter.　B) He is his son.
    C) She is her son.　　　D) He is her son.

33. A) Go over there to they!　B) Go over there to them!
    C) Come over there to me!　D) Come to them over here!

34. A) Look my garden, Susan!　　B) Susan looks my garden.
    C) Susan is look at my garden.　D) Look at my garden, Susan!

35. A) You know not the old man.　B) You know a old man.
    C) An old man knows you.　　　D) An old man don't knows you.

36. Watch _____ .
    A) him and his dog!　B) he and he's dog!
    C) he and his dog!　 D) him and its dog!

37. Whose house is this? It's _____ house.
    A) the Mr. Smith's　B) our
    C) Mrs.' Smith　　　D) she's

38. A) Where are they going put the books?
    B) Where there are going to put the books?
    C) Where are they going to put the books?
    D) Where are there going put the books?

39. A) Jack's English and Anne are two.
    B) Jack's English and Anne is too English.
    C) Jack's English and Anne's, too.
    D) Jack's English and Anne is, too.

40. Do pigs fly?
    A) No, and dogs don't.　B) No, and not dogs, too.
    C) No, and dogs not.　　D) No, and dog doesn't fly.

41. Jack is standing beside _____ .
    A) us　B) its　C) they　D) your

42. This car is _____ .
    A) of John　B) to John　C) John's　D) Johns'

43. A) Betty has some flower.　B) Betty's has any flowers.
    C) Betty's any flowers.　　 D) Betty has some flowers.

44. A) These are the third lesson.　B) This is the lesson two.
    C) This is a lesson, too.　　　　D) This is third lesson.

45. A) Tom cans have Joan's bicycle.
    B) Tom can have Joan's bicycle.
    C) Tom can to have Joan's bicycle.
    D) Tom can has Joan's bicycle.

46. It's 11.30.
    A) Yes, it's thirty past eleven.　B) Yes, it's half past eleven.
    C) Yes, its' thirty to twelve.　　 D) Yes, its half to twelve.

47. 439 is _____ .
    A) four hundred and thirty nine.　B) four hundreds and thirty nine.
    C) four hundred thirty nine.　　　D) four hundreds thirty and nine.

48. A) The teacher don't like some book.
    B) The teacher doesn't likes some book.
    C) The teacher don't like his book.
    D) The teacher doesn't like her book.

49. Mother washes the girls' hair. Look, she _____ .
    A) is washing it now.　　B) washes it now.
    C) is washing them now.　D) washes them now.

50. The cat has _____ .
    A) the long legs.   B) long legs.
    C) the legs long.   D) legs long.

51. I'm not looking _____ .
    A) at sun   B) at a sky   C) at the sun   D) at some sky

52. Where _____ standing?
    A) is they   B) are they   C) do they   D) does they

53. Mary and John _____ the house.
    A) is looking   B) are looking at
    C) is looking at   D) are looking

54. Anne and I _____ here.
    A) are   B) we're   C) is   D) am

55. Fred, what _____ doing?
    A) is   B) are   C) he's   D) are you

56. A) Charles in the street.   B) Charles at the street.
    C) Charles is in the street.   D) Charles is at the street.

57. How many books are there on the table?
    A) There is one on.   B) There are three.
    C) There are three of books. D) There are any books.

58. Anne works, but _____ .
    A) does Peter? B) Peter does? C) works Peter? D) Peter works?

59. Mike is looking at _____ .
    A) they   B) she   C) my   D) us

60. Who's that man?
    A) He's teacher.   B) It's John.
    C) Is Peter.   D) That's a man.

61. Where's the chair?
    A) The chair near the table.   B) Its there.
    C) It's in the room.   D) There's near the door.

62. Are you writing?
    A) No, I aren't.   B) Yes, I am.
    C) Yes, I'm.   D) No, I not.

63. What's her name?
    A) There's Mary.   B) She name Mary.
    C) Her name's Mary.   D) She's name is Mary.

64. Do you sing or dance?
    A) I'm sing but not dance.   B) I singing and dancing.
    C) I do sing and dance.   D) I sing and I dance.

65. Is that a dog?
    A) Yes, it is.   B) Yes, that's.
    C) Yes, it's that dog. D) Yes, there is.

66. Is this book red?
    A) No, is this book green.   B) No, this is green book.
    C) No, it's a green.   D) No, it's green.

67. What's his mother doing?
    A) He's shopping.   B) His shopping.
    C) Her shopping.   D) Shopping.

68. How many books are there?
    A) Five.   B) They're five.
    C) There are five.   D) There's a book.

69. A) Is this big red chair?   B) Is this a big chair red?
    C) Is red this big chair?   D) Is this big chair red?

70. Bill _____ play tomorrow.
    A) going to   B) can   C) is going   D) can to

71. The knife is _____ the bottle.
    A) at   B) next   C) near   D) between

72. The bicycle is _____ the house.
    A) near of   B) front of   C) next   D) behind

73. What's that woman?
    A) She's a doctor.   B) She calls Jane.
    C) Her name Jane.   D) It's Jane.

74. Do you know Peter?
    A) Yes, I know.   B) No, I'm not.
    C) Yes, I do.   D) No, I don't know.

75. A) They're live near you and I.   B) You live near them and me.
    C) They and I'm live near you.   D) They lives near you and me.

76. Are _____ brothers?
    A) those big boys some   B) some those big boys
    C) those big boys   D) big boys those

77. A) Is that her dog there?   B) Is this her dogs here?
    C) Are these her dogs there?   D) Are those her dogs here?

78. Brenda is writing _____ .
    A) with a book   B) on a paper   C) by a pencil   D) in paper

79. A) Where now lives Alan?   B) Where is now Alan living?
    C) Where does now Alan live?   D) Where is Alan living now?

80. Monday is the first day.
    A) Tuesday is the fourth.   B) Thursday is the fourth.
    C) The second is Tuesday.   D) The second is Thursday.

81. Bill is in front of Carrie. Carrie is _____ Bill.
    A) behind   B) between   C) next   D) beside

82. Elizabeth is Mr. Brown's daughter. Mr. Brown is _____ father.
    A) her   B) his   C) its   D) their

83. A) Come here to my!   B) Come here to we!
    C) Come here to us!   D) Go here to us!

84. A) Jack listen my radio.   B) Listen on my radio, Jack!
    C) Jack is listen to my radio.   D) Listen to my radio, Jack!

85. A) An old men is sitting on the park.
    B) The old men is sitting in the park.
    C) An old man is sitting in the park.
    D) The old man are sitting on the park.

86. Look at _____ cat!
    A) her and she's   B) her and her
    C) she and her   D) she and she's

87. Whose car is that? It's _____ car.
    A) our   B) hour   C) there   D) theirs

88. Where _____ put the cups?
    A) are you going to   B) you going to
    C) you are going   D) are you going

89. A) Sally's sister pretty and they are, too.
    B) Sally's pretty and they're, too.
    C) Sally's pretty and they are, too.
    D) Sally's pretty but they are.

90. Is Jane in the bedroom?
    A) No, but Pat isn't.   B) No, but Pat is.
    C) Yes, and Pat isn't too. D) Yes, but Pat isn't too.

91. Barry is sitting near _____ .
    A) my   B) your   C) me   D) we

92. Whose flowers are they?
    They're _____ .
    A) to Mary   B) of Mary   C) Maries   D) Mary's

93. A) Ken have any books.   B) Ken has some books.
    C) Ken has any books.   D) Ken have some books.

94. A) This is a lesson, too.   B) These are lessons two.
    C) This is the lesson fourth. D) This is the lesson two.

95. A) Mary can has John's bicycle.
    B) Mary can have the bicycle of John.
    C) Mary can to have John's bicycle.
    D) Mary can have John's bicycle.

96. It's 7.30.
    A) Yes, it's half past seven.   B) Yes, the clock is half past seven.
    C) Yes, it's half past eight.   D) Yes, the clock is half past eight.

97. 316 is _____ .
    A) three hundred and sixteen.   B) three hundred sixteen.
    C) three hundred and sixty.   D) three hundred sixty.

98. A) Mary plays not the tennis.   B) Mary does not play the tennis.
    C) Mary plays not tennis.   D) Mary does not play tennis.

99. Do Mr. and Mrs. Brown live in England?
    A) Yes, they do live.   B) Yes, they lives.
    C) Yes, they do.   D) Yes, they live.

100. Mrs. Johnson is washing the girls' hair.
    A) He is washing her hair.   B) She is washing her hair.
    C) He is washing their hair.   D) She is washing their hair.

ELEMENTARY TEST - 3

Choose the correct answer. Only one answer is correct.

1. There are _____ in the classroom but only one teacher.
   A) many people   B) much pupils
   C) a lot people   D) a lot of pupils

2. Kate _____ .
   A) gave to Peter the pen   B) gave the pen to Peter
   C) give to Peter the pen   D) give the pen to Peter

3. The sun _____ in the East.
   A) is always rising   B) always is rising
   C) rises always   D) always rises

4. Which girls _____ ?
   A) John likes   B) likes John
   C) does John like   D) do John like

5. There isn't _____ at the bus stop.
   A) anybody   B) people   C) any persons   D) somebody

6. Kim and Fred _____ home.
   A) are at   B) are in   C) they are in   D) they are at

7. What color are your new shoes?
   A) They are brown color.   B) Their brown.
   C) They're brown.   D) They are colour brown.

8. A) Are the big nice apples?   B) Are nice the big apples?
   C) Are big and nice the apples?   D) Are the big apples nice?

9. He hasn't bought _____ oranges.
   A) a lot   B) much   C) any   D) some

10. A) Go there to they.   B) Go there to them!
    C) Go here to we.   D) Go here to us!

11. How _____ from London to Gatwick?
    A) it is going   B) to go   C) we can go   D) can we go

12. _____ Mary reads in bed.
    A) Always   B) Seldom   C) Sometimes   D) Never

13. Millie _____ at the flowers in the garden.
    A) is seeing   B) is looking   C) is washing   D) is watching

14. _____ don't like red wine.
    A) Some people   B) Any people
    C) Somebody   D) Anybody

15. Did you visit Canada last year?
    A) No, I went never there.   B) No, I never was there.
    C) No, I've never been there.   D) No, I never have been there.

16. Tom didn't call the police. Brenda didn't call _____ .
    A) them, either.   B) them, too.   C) him, either.   D) him, too.

17. Sally is _____ Paul.
    A) as tall than   B) as tall as   C) so tall as   D) so tall that

18. Do you like that shop? Yes, I _____ every week.
    A) come there   B) come here   C) go there   D) go here

19. Brian is the man _____ .
    A) of a hat   B) of no hat   C) with hat   D) without a hat

20. Pauline's _____ as the boys.
    A) too strong   B) of no hat   C) as strong   D) also strong

21. Are my shoes in the box? No, there _____ in the box.
    A) isn't anything   B) aren't no things
    C) isn't nothing   D) isn't any things

22. Have you got any apples? Yes, I've got _____ .
    A) a small   B) one small
    C) two small ones   D) two small

23. Whose are those dogs? They're _____ .
    A) of them   B) to them   C) their   D) theirs

24. A) How is your age?   B) How old are you?
    C) What age have you got?   D) How many years have you?

25. Who _____ on Saturdays?
    A) do help you   B) you help   C) do you help   D) you do help

26. 572 is _____ .
    A) five hundred and seventy two
    B) five hundred seventy two
    C) five hundreds seventy two
    D) five hundreds and seventy two

27. Molly is the girl _____ brown hair?
    A) of many   B) with many   C) of a lot of   D) with a lot of

28. What time _____ breakfast?
    A) does Mary have the   B) does Mary have
    C) has Mary   D) has Mary the

29. His mother will come at 8 o'clock _____ evening.
    A) of this   B) on this   C) this   D) at this

30. I feel very well because I went to bed very early _____ .
    A) last night   B) tonight   C) this night   D) in the night

31. What is Mary like? She _____ .
    A) is very well   B) likes ice-cream
    C) is like tall men   D) is very pretty

32. Have the people got the money now? Yes, the police gave _____ .
    A) them to them   B) it to it
    C) it to them   D) them to it

33. Terry is behind Belinda. Yes, Belinda is _____ Terry.
    A) in front of   B) behind   C) between   D) next

34. Pauline is _____ radio.
    A) listening to   B) listening to the
    C) listening in   D) listening in the

35. Are those books in the car? Yes, Alice _____ yesterday.
    A) put them   B) put them into
    C) puts them in   D) put them in

36. _____ to Scotland last month?
    A) Did Andrew go   B) Was Andrew
    C) Has Andrew been   D) Has Andrew gone

37. This is an old photograph of me when I _____ .
    A) have short hairs   B) had short hairs
    C) have short hair   D) had short hair

38. Whose is that? It's _____ .
    A) my   B) my sisters   C) of Tom   D) ours

39. My brother was _____ all week.
    A) at the home   B) at home   C) in the home   D) in home

40. Barry never eats potatoes and _____ .
    A) so doesn't Molly   B) neither doesn't Molly
    C) neither does Molly   D) neither Molly does

41. James _____ to play tomorrow.
    A) is going   B) can   C) shall   D) will

42. How is your brother?
    A) That's he.   B) That's him.
    C) He's very well.   D) He's very good.

43. Is there _____ the bottle?
    A) much water into   B) much water in
    C) many water into   D) many water in

44. The party will start _____ Saturday.
    A) on 8 o'clock at   B) on 8 o'clock
    C) 8 o'clock at   D) at 8 o'clock on

45. Are you going to shops? No, _____ .
    A) I cycle there   B) usually on the bus
    C) to the work   D) I've already been

46. Here are three girls. _____ .
    A) Which girl is the bigger?   B) What girl is the bigger?
    C) Which girl is the biggest?   D) What girl is the biggest?

47. Jack is writing _____ .
    A) with pen   B) on the wall   C) by a pen   D) out of a pen

48. What _____ on Saturdays?
    A) Ken usually does   B) does Ken usually do
    C) does Ken usually   D) usually does Ken do

49. "Have you been to America?" " _____ "
    A) Ever   B) Already   C) Yet   D) Never

50. Tony _____ make some cakes tomorrow.
    A) is going to   B) he'll   C) want to   D) can to

51. Fred _____ to the shops.
    A) went just   B) just was going
    C) has just gone   D) just has gone

52. Ann gave _____ .
    A) my the flowers   B) the flowers mine
    C) the flowers me   D) me the flowers
53. Mary _____ to school.
    A) never walks   B) is never walking
    C) walks never   D) never is walking
54. Where _____ .
    A) Mary works?   B) works Mary?
    C) does Mary works?   D) does Mary work?
55. Who _____ .
    A) Tom usually helps?   B) Tom does usually help?
    C) does Tom usually help?   D) usually Tom does help?
56. What color is your dog?
    A) It's grey.   B) It's a grey.
    C) It's color grey.   D) It's the grey color.
57. A) Is the little clever boy?   B) Is clever the little boy?
    C) Is the little boy a clever?   D) Is the little boy clever?
58. Mary hasn't got _____ .
    A) no friend   B) many friends
    C) some friend   D) much friend
59. A) Not to do that!   B) No do that!
    C) Don't do that!   D) Don't that!
60. A) Come here to me!   B) Come there to me!
    C) Go here to they!   D) Go there to he!
61. How _____ to the station from here?
    A) to go   B) do you go   C) do one go   D) go we
62. Brian is _____ Pamela.
    A) as old as   B) not old as   C) as old that   D) not old that
63. Mother _____ the children through the window.
    A) is seeing   B) is looking   C) is watching   D) is washing
64. _____ going to the party.
    A) Everyone are   B) Everyone is
    C) Every people are   D) Every people is
65. Did your brother go to America last year?
    A) No, he did never go there.   B) No, he has never gone there.
    C) No, he never was there.   D) No, he's never been there.
66. Jenny hasn't got a dog. Mike hasn't _____ .
    A) got, either.   B) got, too.
    C) got one, either.   D) got one, too.
67. 215 is _____ .
    A) two hundred fifty   B) two hundred and fifty
    C) two hundred fifteen   D) two hundred and fifteen
68. Have you been to the United States? Yes, I _____ in 1965.
    A) went there   B) went here   C) came there   D) came here
69. Janet is the girl _____ in her hand.
    A) with anything   B) with nothing
    C) of anything   D) of nothing
70. Anne's older _____ .
    A) that Mary   B) than Mary's   C) than us   D) that I'm
71. Are the bicycles in the garage? No, there _____ in the garage.
    A) is nothing   B) isn't nothing
    C) isn't something   D) is anything
72. Have you got any brown socks? No, but I've got _____ .
    A) some blue ones   B) some blues
    C) some blue one   D) a blue ones
73. Whose is this house? It's _____ .
    A) our   B) ours   C) our one   D) ours one
74. A) How old he is?   B) How many years has he?
    C) What age he has?   D) How old is he?
75. There isn't _____ in the restaurant.
    A) any people   B) any persons   C) anybody   D) nobody
76. Laura's _____ her sister.
    A) very taller than   B) much taller than
    C) very taller that   D) much taller that
77. Pat's a girl _____ long arms.
    A) with some   B) with her   C) with   D) with the

78. What time _____ dinner?
    A) Peter has   B) do Peter has
    C) does Peter has   D) does Peter have
79. Her father will come 8 o'clock _____ .
    A) this evening   B) this afternoon
    C) in this evening   D) in this afternoon
80. I feel fine today because I _____ .
    A) have gone to bed early tonight.
    B) have gone to bed early last night.
    C) went to bed early tonight.
    D) went to bed early last night.
81. What is Tom like? He _____ .
    A) likes a cup of tea.   B) is liking football.
    C) isn't very nice.   D) isn't very well.
82. Has Susan got the money? Yes, John gave _____ yesterday.
    A) to her them   B) to her it   C) her them   D) it to her
83. Debbie is beside Jane. Yes, Jane is _____ Debbie.
    A) behind   B) beside   C) next   D) between
84. Sam is _____ the radio.
    A) listening to   B) listening in   C) hearing to   D) hearing in
85. The shoes are in the box. I know, because my brother _____ yesterday.
    A) has put them in   B) put them in
    C) has put them   D) put them
86. Last month _____ to Scotland.
    A) was Ian   B) Ian was   C) went Ian   D) Ian went
87. Which student is near the teacher? Malcolm is _____ .
    A) much near   B) very nearer   C) the nearest   D) the next
88. Whose is this? It's _____ .
    A) my   B) his   C) her   D) our
89. Tomorrow my sister will come _____ late.
    A) home   B) at home   C) to home   D) to the home
90. Nancy works in a shop and _____ .
    A) so does Alan too   B) so Alan does
    C) that does Alan too   D) that Alan too does
91. Rose _____ to sing on Saturday,
    A) can   B) will   C) is going   D) shall
92. What is your cousin?
    A) That's she.   B) This is her.
    C) I haven't got any.   D) She's a doctor.
93. Can you see _____ the bottles?
    A) many beer into   B) much beer into
    C) many beer in   D) much beer in
94. We'll do it _____ .
    A) 11 o'clock in this morning   B) on 11 o'clock this morning
    C) this morning at 11 o'clock   D) in this morning at 11 o'clock
95. Are you going to work? No, _____ .
    A) I'm take a bus.   B) to the doctor's.
    C) by train.   D) I'm riding by bicycle.
96. Here are three books. _____ like best?
    A) Which book do you   B) Which book you
    C) What book do you   D) What book you
97. The old man came _____ the stairs.
    A) out of   B) through   C) off   D) down
98. What _____ on Saturday?
    A) does Jim usually   B) John usually does
    C) usually does Jim   D) does John usually do
99. "Have you been to Scotland?" "_____ "
    A) Not ever.   B) Not yet.   C) Not already.   D) Not never.
100. Beryl _____ sing tomorrow.
    A) going to   B) is going   C) can   D) can to

ELEMENTARY TEST - 4

Choose the correct answer. Only one answer is correct.

1. Jack gave _____.
   A) to her the flowers.   B) the flowers to hers.
   C) her the flowers.   D) hers the flowers.

2. The sun _____ early in summer.
   A) always rises   B) rises always
   C) is always rising   D) is rising always

3. What _____ at the weekend?
   A) Jane does do   B) does Jane do
   C) do Jane   D) Jane does

4. Who _____.
   A) do Mary likes?   B) Mary likes?
   C) do Mary like?   D) does Mary like?

5. Bill and Carrie _____ the street.
   A) they are at   B) they are in   C) are in   D) are at

6. What color's your bicycle?
   A) It's the red.   B) It's red.
   C) It's a red color.   D) It's color's red.

7. A) Is the black cat your?   B) Is the black cat yours?
   C) Is your the black cat?   D) Is the your black cat?

8. Bill hasn't seen _____.
   A) much boats   B) any boat   C) many boats   D) some boats

9. _____ the room!
   A) Don't go in   B) Don't going to
   C) Not to go in   D) Not go into

10. A) Go here to me!   B) Go to my here!
    C) Come to my here!   D) Come here to me!

11. Where _____ some stamps for this letter?
    A) can I buy   B) I can buy   C) I buy   D) to buy

12. Ken is as good _____.
    A) is Brian.   B) Brian is.   C) as Brian.   D) than Brian.

13. Lynn _____ television every evening.
    A) looks at   B) locks at   C) washes at   D) watches at

14. _____ good weather.
    A) Every person likes   B) Every person like
    C) Everybody like   D) Everybody likes

15. Did you go to Scotland last year?
    A) No, I did never go there.   B) No, I've never been there.
    C) No, I've never gone here.   D) No, I never went here.

16. I didn't see the people there. I didn't see _____.
    A) him, too.   B) him either.   C) them, too.   D) them either.

17. Pat and Jane are _____ her.
    A) clever than   B) clever that   C) as clever as   D) so clever as

18. Do you _____?
    A) come often here   B) come here often
    C) go often here   D) go here often

19. Mary is the girl _____.
    A) about the television.   B) of the red hair.
    C) at the kitchen.   D) by the window.

20. Do you go to school?
    A) No, I work.   B) Yes, I am.
    C) No, I go home.   D) No, I cycle.

21. Are my pencils on your desk? No, there _____ on my desk.
    A) aren't something   B) isn't something
    C) aren't anything   D) isn't anything

22. Have you got some red shoes? No, but I've got _____.
    A) some yellow pair.   B) some yellows.
    C) some yellow.   D) some yellow ones.

23. Whose is that car? It's _____.
    A) theirs   B) there's   C) their   D) there

24. A) What age has she?   B) How many years has she?
    C) How old is she?   D) How old she is?

25. There wasn't _____ in the garden.
    A) some people   B) anybody
    C) any people   D) no persons

26. 333 is _____.
    A) three hundreds and thirty three.
    B) three hundred and thirty three.
    C) three hundreds thirty and three.
    D) three hundred thirty and three.

27. Carol is the girl _____ in her hand.
    A) without anything   B) without nothing
    C) of anything   D) of something

28. What time _____ dinner?
    A) has John   B) John has he
    C) does John have   D) has John got

29. Bill will come _____.
    A) at 9 o'clock this afternoon.   B) at 9 o'clock this evening.
    C) in this afternoon at 9 o'clock.   D) in this evening at 9 o'clock.

30. I feel fine because I _____ night.
    A) have gone to bed early last   B) have gone to bed early this
    C) went to bed early last   D) went to bed early this

31. What is Shirley like? She _____.
    A) is like my sister.   B) likes us.
    C) like my brother.   D) is liking ice-cream.

32. Has Colin got a pen? Yes, the teacher has _____.
    A) lent one him.   B) lent him one.
    C) borrowed one him.   D) borrowed him one.

33. Carrie is in front of David. Yes, David is _____ Carrie.
    A) beside   B) between   C) before   D) behind

34. Eva is _____ my radio.
    A) hearing to   B) hearing on   C) listening to   D) listening on

35. Are the papers in your room? Yes, my mother _____ yesterday.
    A) put them there   B) puts them there
    C) put it there   D) puts it there

36. Last year _____ to Canada.
    A) went Mary   B) did Mary go   C) Mary went   D) Mary was

37. Mary was going to a wedding so she brushed _____ well.
    A) her hair   B) her hairs   C) the hair   D) the hairs

38. Whose are those?
    A) It's of the teacher.   B) It's theirs.
    C) They're Jill's brother's. D) They're our.

39. This evening I'll come _____ early.
    A) to home   B) at home   C) in home   D) home

40. Mary likes ice-cream and _____.
    A) so John too does.   B) so does John too.
    C) John likes too.   D) John too likes.

41. Boris usually _____ breakfast at eight o'clock.
    A) has got the   B) has   C) take   D) eats the

42. How is your sister?
    A) She's fine.   B) She's good.   C) She s there.   D) That's her.

43. There's _____ those bottles there.
    A) much beer on   B) much beers in
    C) a lot of beer in   D) a lot of beer on

44. Paula's singing _____ afternoon.
    A) at this   B) in this   C) on this   D) this

45. Are you going to the doctor's? No, _____.
    A) to the police station.   B) I'm coming there.
    C) usually by bus.   D) he's going to me.

46. There are the two boys.
    A) What boy is the clever?   B) What boy is the clever one?
    C) Which is the clever?   D) Which boy is the clever one?

47. The sun came _____ the windows.
    A) out of   B) into   C) with   D) through

48. When _____ her homework?
    A) does Wendy usually   B) does Wendy usually
    C) Wendy usually does   D) usually does Wendy

49. Have you been to the mountains?
    A) does Wendy usually do   B) does Wendy usually
    C) Wendy usually does   D) usually does Wendy

50. Joan _____ play on Saturday.
    A) going to   B) can   C) is going   D) can t
51. The bicycle is _____ the car.
    A) front of   B) near of   C) next   D) behind
52. Tom gave _____ .
    A) Pat the book   B) the book Pat
    C) to Pat the book   D) the book a Pat
53. Sarah _____ tennis on Sundays.
    A) plays never   B) never plays
    C) is never playing   D) never is playing
54. When _____ football?
    A) do Jim plays   B) plays Jim   C) Jim plays   D) does Jim play
55. Who _____ .
    A) do Tom love?   B) do love Tom?
    C) does Tom love?   D) Tom loves?
56. John and I _____ school.
    A) are at   B) are to   C) we are at   D) we are to
57. What color are your gloves?
    A) They are some brown.   B) Some brown gloves.
    C) They are color brown.   D) They are brown.
58. A) Are the big cars blue?   B) Are the cars big blue?
    C) Are big the blue cars?   D) Are the big blue cars?
59. Did you see _____ people?
    A) much   B) a   C) any   D) a lot
60. _____ your homework?
    A) Don't   B) Don't do   C) Not do   D) Not to do
61. A) Go here to us!   B) Go there to they!
    C) Come there to we!   D) Come here to us!
62. How _____ telephone to England?
    A) do I   B) can   C) I do   D) to
63. This is _____ .
    A) the question thirty.   B) the question thirteen.
    C) the question thirty.   D) question thirteen.
64. Jack _____ football on Saturday afternoon.
    A) looks   B) locks   C) washes   D) watches
65. _____ live in the town.
    A) Somebody   B) Anybody   C) Some people   D) Any people
66. Did you go to Ireland last year?
    A) No, I've never been to Ireland.
    B) No, here I have never gone.
    C) No, I haven't gone to Ireland.
    D) No, I did never go there.
67. Molly hasn't got your money. Jack hasn't got _____ .
    A) it, too.   B) them, too.   C) it, either.   D) them, either.
68. Bill and I _____ good as you.
    A) are as   B) am as   C) as   D) we're as
69. Mary's here. She's just _____ .
    A) gone   B) been   C) got   D) come
70. Jeremy is the man _____ .
    A) of the long legs   B) of the tall legs
    C) with the long legs   D) with the tall legs
71. Fred's _____ Charles.
    A) much better that   B) much better than
    C) very better that   D) very better than
72. Are my books on the table? No, there _____ on the table.
    A) aren't anything   B) isn't anything
    C) aren't something   D) isn't something
73. Have you got some brown eggs? No, but I've got _____ .
    A) any white ones   B) some white ones
    C) some white one   D) any white one
74. Whose is the table? It's _____ .
    A) of us   B) to us   C) ours   D) our
75. A) How old are you?   B) How many years are you?
    C) How old you are?   D) What age do you have?

76. There wasn't _____ on the bus.
    A) no person   B) nobody   C) any person   D) anyone
77. Jim is _____ boy in the class.
    A) the smaller   B) smaller   C) the smallest   D) smallest
78. Margaret is the girl _____ .
    A) between my brother   B) at the back
    C) on the tree   D) at the street
79. What time _____ dinner?
    A) does Jane have   B) does Jane have the
    C) has Jane   D) has Jane the
80. Sally will come at 8 o'clock _____ .
    A) this day   B) this afternoon
    C) this night   D) this evening
81. I feel fine because I went _____ .
    A) to the bed early last night   B) to bed early last night
    C) to the bed early tonight   D) to bed early tonight
82. What is Peter like? He _____ .
    A) is very well   B) is very nice   C) like football   D) is liking tennis
83. Has Jimmy got his books now? Yes, my brother _____ yesterday.
    A) gave them to him   B) gave to him them
    C) has given them to him   D) has given to him them
84. Arthur is beside Penny. Yes, Penny is _____ Arthur.
    A) behind   B) before   C) beside   D) between
85. Are the pencils in the box? Yes, Norma _____ on Saturday.
    A) put them   B) puts them
    C) put them there   D) puts them there
86. _____ to Ireland last year?
    A) Mary went   B) Did Mary go   C) Mary was   D) Was Mary
87. It was a bad day so Mike _____ his raincoat.
    A) puts on   B) put on   C) takes on   D) took on
88. Whose are these? _____ .
    A) Theirs.   B) Are my sister's.
    C) It's mine.   D) They're her.
89. My brother _____ early.
    A) often goes to home   B) goes often to home
    C) often goes home   D) goes often home
90. John doesn't like beer and _____ .
    A) so I do   B) so do I   C) neither I do   D) neither do I
91. Kathie always _____ lunch in a restaurant.
    A) is eating   B) take   C) has   D) has got
92. What's that man?
    A) He's Eric.   B) It's Bill.
    C) He's student.   D) He's a teacher.
93. I've put _____ water in the bottles.
    A) a lot of   B) much   C) many   D) any
94. You can't see the sun _____ .
    A) at the night   B) at night   C) at the nights   D) at nights
95. Are you going to school? No, _____ .
    A) I take the bus.   B) I'm cycling.
    C) to the shops.   D) I'm coming to school.
96. Here are three pens. _____ you like best?
    A) What one do   B) What one
    C) Which one do   D) Which one
97. Mary is writing _____ .
    A) in paper   B) with a pen   C) by a pen   D) with pen
98. Where _____ in the summer?
    A) usually Lena goes   B) goes usually Lena
    C) does Lena usually go   D) usually does Lena go
99. Have you visited Edinburgh?
    A) Not yet   B) Not ever   C) Already   D) Ever
100. Donald _____ sixteen tomorrow.
    A) is being   B) going to be   C) shall be   D) will be

ELEMENTARY TEST - 5

Choose the correct answer. Only one answer is correct.

John: Mr. Jackson __1__ the children to the zoo yesterday. When they got there they __2__ a bell, and when they were inside they saw a man in the lion house.
Mary: Why __3__ ?
John: He __4__ the lions their food.
Mary: How much __5__ ?
John: The children didn't __6__. Did you know that __7__ two restaurants in the zoo? So people __8__ go out if __9__ eat something.
Mary: What time __10__ the restaurants?
John: Oh, the children __11__ remember times. They __12__ times aren't important.

1. A) was taking B) did take C) took D) has taken
2. A) heard B) were hearing C) listened D) were listening
3. A) was he here B) has he been there C) has he been here D) was he there
4. A) was just giving B) has just given C) gave just D) had given just
5. A) he gave to them B) did he give them C) gave he to them D) did he to them give
6. A) tell it me B) say me C) tell me D) say it to me
7. A) are there B) are they C) they are D) there are
8. A) mustn't to B) mustn't C) don't need to D) don't need
9. A) they want to B) they want C) he wants to D) he wants
10. A) do open B) do they open C) are open D) are opening
11. A) can't B) may not C) aren't able D) couldn't to
12. A) say to me what B) say me which C) tell me what D) tell me that
13. A) How is your age? B) How old are you? C) What age have you got? D) How many years you are?
14. Mary had _____ money.
    A) enough B) many C) fewer D) any
15. A) What shoes are they made? B) What shoes are made of? C) What are shoes made of? D) What are made of shoes?
16. _____ are very clever.
    A) Both them B) Both of them C) The both boys D) Both of boys
17. What _____ on Sundays?
    A) does John usually do B) do John usually does C) John usually does D) does John usually
18. There wasn't _____ in the park.
    A) some people B) anybody C) any people D) no people
19. This is _____ that.
    A) the same as B) the same that C) different that D) the different from
20. Michael always wants _____ money.
    A) a few B) too many C) so much D) another
21. When _____ give her this book.
    A) Alison will arrive B) is Alison arriving C) Alison arrive D) Alison arrives
22. I think there are _____ in the garden.
    A) nobody B) someone C) some people D) anybody
23. Michael stayed with us _____ three weeks.
    A) since B) in C) for D) through
24. Carrie is _____ Hilary.
    A) pretty than B) prettier than C) so pretty as D) more pretty that
25. Did you buy _____ cheese?
    A) so many B) too C) these D) a lot of
26. _____ the men's a doctor?
    A) What B) Both C) Which of D) Who of
27. John was _____ the bus for ten minutes.
    A) waiting for B) expecting C) attending D) hoping for
28. Have you been to the USA? _____ .
    A) Ever B) Never C) Already D) Yet
29. Shall I buy some apples? Yes, _____ .
    A) get a kilo of big B) bring a kilo C) take few big ones D) buy a lot of
30. Ken doesn't come from London. _____ .
    A) Neither Tom does B) Tom isn't coming, too C) Tom also D) Nor does Tom
31. Do you need any water? No, _____ .
    A) I needn't any B) I've got some C) I don't need D) I haven't got any
32. _____ lovely food!
    A) Which B) Which a C) What D) What a
33. I'm going to give _____ .
    A) to him a record B) him a record C) a record him D) some record to him
34. I don't know who _____ chocolate.
    A) is liking B) like C) are liking D) likes
35. _____ we don't get home before midnight.
    A) Sometimes B) Always C) Never D) Every time
36. _____ to become a film star.
    A) No every child wants B) No every children want C) Not every child wants D) Not every children want
37. Whose is this?
    A) His B) He's C) Its D) It's
38. Were you singing when I came in? Yes, I _____
    A) sang B) sung C) was D) were
39. Where's the record?
    A) There's it. B) He's under the chair. C) There's on a chair. D) It's here.
40. Are you making cakes?
    A) Yes, I do. B) Yes, I am. C) Yes, I'm doing. D) Yes, I'm making.
41. Next month _____ seventeen.
    A) I'll be B) shall I be C) I'm being D) I have
42. How's the baby?
    A) He's Alison's. B) She's very well. C) That's the baby. D) She's a girl.
43. When did you last _____ Mr. Brown?
    A) meat B) met C) meeting D) meet
44. Have you ever _____ the Atlantic?
    A) flown along B) flowed along C) flown across D) flowed across
45. Yesterday Mary _____ to me with a problem.
    A) came B) goes C) went D) come
46. _____ lots of trees round the house?
    A) Were always there B) Have there always been C) Had there always D) Were they always
47. What date is it?
    A) The third of march. B) The third march. C) Of march the third. D) March the third.
48. His daughter is _____ .
    A) as old as yours B) as old as your one C) so old as yours D) so old as your one
49. He _____ his hat and went out.
    A) takes on B) took on C) puts on D) put on
50. A) Was the English women old?
    B) Was the English woman an old?
    C) Were the English women some old?
    D) Were the English women old?

"Peter __51__ back from the shop," said Mr. James. "He __52__ some new football boots, but he __53__ find any that were right for him." "__54__ the same?" I asked. "He said they showed __55__ but he __56__ any of them." "What __57__ do about his boots, then?" I asked. "Well, the shop told __58__ next week. It's not a big problem because he __59__ to have them before the new school term. But he __60__ to arrange his things early. For example, he __61__ late for school." "My daughter is different," I said. "I __62__ throw her out when it's time for school."

51. A) has just come B) came just
    C) just went D) was just arriving
52. A) wanted buying B) like to buy
    C) had liked to buy D) wanted to buy
53. A) didn't able B) wasn't able to
    C) couldn't to D) mustn't
54. A) Have all of them been B) Were all they
    C) Were they all D) Have they all been
55. A) to him different pairs B) different pairs for him
    C) him different pairs D) for him different pairs
56. A) wasn't liking B) didn't like
    C) hasn't liked D) hadn't liked
57. A) Peter will B) will Peter to
    C) is Peter going D) is Peter going to
58. A) him to come back B) to him come back
    C) him coming back D) he could come back
59. A) needs not B) doesn't need
    C) mustn't D) may not
60. A) is beginning always B) is always beginning
    C) begins always D) always begins
61. A) is never coming B) never is
    C) has never been D) comes never
62. A) need B) may C) have to D) can
63. A) What age has she? B) How many years she has?
    C) How old is she? D) How old she is?
64. Fred eats _____ bread.
    A) too many B) so much C) fewer D) any
65. A) Of what cups are made? B) Of what are cups?
    C) What cups are made of? D) What are cups made of?
66. _____ are very good.
    A) Both those boys B) The both boys
    C) Both of they D) Both they
67. Where _____ at the weekend?
    A) usually Mary goes B) does Mary usually go
    C) goes usually Mary D) do Mary usually goes
68. There isn't _____ at the station.
    A) people B) some persons
    C) anyone D) somebody
69. Cars are _____ lorries.
    A) as different to B) not same as
    C) not as same as D) different from
70. Mary has answered _____ questions.
    A) the more B) any C) very much D) a few
71. John will mend the window when _____ .
    A) he comes B) does he can C) is he coming D) he will come
72. I haven't seen _____ this week.
    A) much people B) no people
    C) someone D) anybody
73. Next year we are going to stay in Scotland _____ two weeks.
    A) on B) for C) through D) in
74. Pat isn't _____ Val.
    A) so heavy as B) heavy than C) heavier than D) so heavy than
75. They have visited _____ countries.
    A) a lot of B) so much C) the both D) every

76. _____ those books do you want?
    A) What are B) Which of C) Which are D) What
77. Mary was waiting _____ bus stop.
    A) for a B) at the C) by D) the
78. Have you ever been to Ireland?
    A) Not yet. B) Not already. C) Not ever. D) Not still.
79. Shall I get some apples? Yes, _____ red ones.
    A) bring some B) take a few C) take any D) bring a little
80. John never eats meat.
    A) That does Tom. B) Tom doesn't too.
    C) Neither does Tom. D) Tom does neither.
81. Do you want a drink?
    A) Yes, I want. B) Yes, I do want.
    C) No, I don't. D) No, I don't want.
82. _____ clever idea!
    A) What a B) What C) So D) How
83. Mary got _____ .
    A) for her birthday a pen. B) at her birthday a pen.
    C) a pen for her birthday. D) a pen at her birthday.
84. Ask him _____ .
    A) how old he is. B) how old is he.
    C) how old has he D) how old he has
85. _____ we didn't visit John in hospital.
    A) Already B) Sometimes C) Never D) Always
86. _____ to get rich.
    A) Not every young man try B) Not every young man tries
    C) No every young men try D) No every young man tries
87. Whose is this?
    A) There's. B) There. C) Their. D) Theirs.
88. Who went to Paris? John _____ .
    A) has B) did C) does D) was
89. Where's the dog?
    A) It's on the table. B) There's on the table.
    C) There's under a table. D) It's under a table.
90. Are you going to school?
    A) No, I don't. B) No, I'm cycling.
    C) No, to the shops. D) No, to shops.
91. Next month Jane _____ twenty three.
    A) is having B) has C) shall be D) will be
92. How's John's sister?
    A) She's fine. B) That's she. C) This is her. D) She's good.
93. Have you _____ the cups with tea?
    A) felt B) feel C) filled D) full
94. Did John _____ to drive a car?
    A) teach you B) taught you C) learn you D) learnt you
95. Why have you _____ to me?
    A) gone B) come C) came D) went
96. Last Sunday _____ thousands of people at the beach.
    A) it was B) they were C) there was D) there were
97. What's today's date?
    A) Of January the second. B) Of January second.
    C) The January second. D) January the second.
98. My daughter is older _____ .
    A) that his one B) than his C) than his one D) that his
99. She _____ her hat and left the room.
    A) takes on B) took on C) puts on D) put on
100. A) Was the big car expensive? B) Was the expensive car a big?
     C) Was expensive the big car? D) Was the expensive a big car?

ELEMENTARY TEST - 6

Choose the correct answer. Only one answer is correct.

Tom: Hello, Ann. How are you?
Ann: Well, I __1__ the doctor's yesterday.
Tom: What __2__ you?
Ann: He said that I have a weak stomach, but I __3__ take any medicine.
Tom: How __4__ that you were ill?
Ann: I was teaching __5__ a bicycle, and I couldn't run as fast as I __6__
Tom: Well, what __7__ tomorrow evening?
Ann: I __8__ __9__ invite me for dinner?
Tom: __10__ __11__ in town this week, and I want __12__ with me.

1. A) was to B) went to C) have been to D) have gone to
2. A) did he tell to B) he has told C) did he tell D) has he told to
3. A) mustn't B) don't need to C) couldn't D) may not
4. A) did you notice B) have you noticed it C) were you noticing it D) you noticed
5. A) to my cousin ride B) my cousin riding C) my cousin to ride D) my cousin ride
6. A) did need B) needed to C) must D) had to
7. A) are you doing B) are you going do C) will you to do D) do you
8. A) didn't plan anything B) haven't planned something C) didn't plan something D) haven't planned anything
9. A) Do you like to B) Are you wanting C) Are you going to D) You will
10. A) Not this B) No that C) No this D) Not that
11. A) There are some good films B) It's some good film C) There's some good film D) They are some good films
12. A) you going B) that you go C) you to go D) that you'll go
13. A) How old he is? B) How many years has he? C) What age he has? D) What is his age?
14. Sheila put in _____ water.
    A) any B) so much C) few D) enough of
15. A) What are cars made of? B) What cars are made of? C) What off are made cars? D) What are made of cars?
16. _____ sing beautifully.
    A) These both girls. B) Both of they. C) Both of them. D) These two girls.
17. When _____ his homework?
    A) Tom usually does B) does Tom usually C) does Tom usually do D) usually does Tom
18. There was _____ on the train.
    A) no persons B) anyone C) any person D) nobody
19. Newspapers _____ magazines.
    A) aren't same that B) are different of C) aren't the same as D) are the different from
20. I spoke to _____ people at the bus stop.
    A) a few B) a pair of C) much D) another
21. I'll talk to Mary when _____ time.
    A) has she B) she has C) she have D) she'll have
22. There wasn't _____ in the box.
    A) any things B) anything C) something D) nothing
23. Last year Joan stayed in London _____ weeks.
    A) through six B) on six C) six D) in six
24. Jack is _____ Joe.
    A) as quite than B) so quiet as C) more quite than D) quieter than
25. They bought _____ bread.
    A) any B) a lot of C) many D) much

26. _____ these girls do you know?
    A) Which of B) Who are C) What of D) How many
27. Yesterday John _____ the bus.
    A) waited for ten minutes B) was expecting ten minutes C) waited ten minutes for D) expected for ten minutes
28. Have you ever visited Rome?
    A) Ever. B) Still. C) Already. D) Never.
29. What sort of car shall I get?
    A) Get no English! B) Get none English! C) Don't get any one English! D) Don't get an English one!
30. Mary doesn't like cats. _____ .
    A) So does John B) John doesn't either C) John doesn't too. D) John also.
31. Do you want some milk? No, _____ .
    A) I've got any B) I don't want C) I haven't got any D) I've got some
32. _____ clever women!
    A) Which B) What a C) What D) How
33. Mary bought _____ .
    A) to Peter a pen B) a pen to Peter C) for Peter a pen D) a pen for Peter
34. Tell me who _____ blue eyes.
    A) is having B) are having C) has D) have
35. _____ work on Saturdays.
    A) Sometimes didn't I B) Sometimes I didn't C) Never didn't I D) Never I didn't
36. _____ to get married.
    A) Not every girl wants B) Not every girl want C) No every girl wants D) No every girl want
37. Whose is that? It's _____ .
    A) he's B) there's C) theirs D) she's
38. Were you working when I came in? Yes, _____ .
    A) I was. B) was I. C) I did. D) did I.
39. Where's my cup?
    A) It here B) It's near window. C) He's under chair. D) There's on a table.
40. Is Mary doing her homework?
    A) No, she doesn't. B) No, she isn't doing. C) No, she doesn't do. D) No, she isn't.
41. Next month you _____ .
    A) shall be as old as I B) will be so old as I C) will be as old as me D) shall be so old as me
42. How many times have you been?
    A) One times. B) Quite much. C) Two months. D) Twice.
43. Has Mary _____ the ring?
    A) fond B) found C) find D) fined
44. Mary _____ that expensive show.
    A) walked and see B) gone and saw C) got and seen D) went and saw
45. Did you _____ here by bus this morning?
    A) go B) went C) come D) came
46. At 10 o'clock yesterday _____ hundreds of people outside.
    A) there were B) there was C) there were being D) there was being
47. What date is it? It's _____ .
    A) July twentieth first. B) of July twenty first. C) the twenty first of July. D) the twentieth first of July.
48. My car was _____ .
    A) between his one B) between his C) beside his one D) beside his
49. Mary _____ her boots because it was raining.
    A) put on B) puts on C) takes on D) took on
50. A) Was black the little dog? B) Was the little dog black? C) Was the little black dog? D) Was the little dog a black?

Ann: Look! Tom __51__ a dress for my birthday.
Pat: It's lovely __52__ it at Bromley's?
Ann: No, he __53__ one there, but they didn't show __54__ that he __55__.
Pat: That's odd. They __56__ dresses that are all right for me. My birthday was two months ago.
Ann: What __57__ for you?
Pat: He __58__ tell him something that he __59__ buy. I said, "I __60__ anything at all. I __61__ a lot of clothes." "That's true," he said. "__62__ out for dinner instead."

51. A) gave to me B) has given to me
    C) have given me D) has given me
52. A) Was he buying B) Did he buy
    C) He bought D) Had he bought
53. A) tried get B) wanted have
    C) wanted to get D) tried to have
54. A) to him something B) anything him
    C) something to him D) him anything
55. A) was happy B) interested C) liked D) pleased
56. A) are always having B) always have
    C) have often D) do have often
57. A) did Peter buy B) Peter bought
    C) has Peter bought D) Peter has bought
58. A) asked me B) said me to C) asked me to D) said to me
59. A) could B) was able to C) may D) can
60. A) needn't B) mustn't need
    C) haven't to need D) don't need
61. A) still have got B) already have got
    C) have already got D) have got still
62. A) We'll be going B) Let us to go
    C) Will we go D) Let's go
63. A) What is your age? B) How many years you have?
    C) How old you are? D) What age do you have?
64. John bought _____ cheese.
    A) enough of B) too many C) fewer D) more
65. A) What pencils made of?
    B) What are pencils made of?
    C) What pencils are they made of?
    D) What are made of pencils?
66. _____ like music.
    A) The both girls B) Both this girls
    C) Both of them D) Both they
67. What _____ on Saturday.
    A) Ken usually does B) does Ken usually
    C) usually does Ken do D) does Ken usually do
68. There isn't _____ in the garden.
    A) anyone B) no person C) persons D) any people
69. He thinks John _____.
    A) the same as I B) is the same as me
    C) is same as me D) is the same I am
70. Cathie has read _____ French books.
    A) so much B) a few C) the more D) every
71. When _____, I'll talk to him.
    A) does Peter come B) Peter will come
    C) Peter comes D) can Peter come
72. I don't know _____ geography.
    A) something about B) anything about
    C) something of D) anything of
73. Next year we're going to stay there _____ a week.
    A) in B) through C) during D) for
74. Is Chris _____ Kate?
    A) taller that B) so tall as C) as tall as D) taller as
75. Tom gave us _____ apples.
    A) a lot of B) so much C) same D) this

76. _____ those newspapers have you read?
    A) What are B) Which C) What of D) Which of
77. It was raining when Mary _____ the bus.
    A) waited B) expected
    C) was expecting D) was waiting for
78. Have you been to the museum?
    A) Not yet. B) Not already. C) Not ever. D) Not still.
79. What kind of watch shall I buy? Get _____.
    A) one Swiss B) a French
    C) a Japanese one D) some American one
80. Mary doesn't speak Russian.
    A) Laura doesn't either. B) Neither Laura does.
    C) Laura doesn't neither. D) Laura doesn't too.
81. Do you want another cake? No, thank you. I've still got _____.
    A) some B) someone's C) some ones D) ones
82. _____ clever people!
    A) What a B) What C) How D) So
83. They gave _____.
    A) the girls some books B) to the girls some books
    C) to them some books D) some books the girls
84. I can't say who _____ the answer.
    A) is knowing B) knows C) are knowing D) know
85. _____ I don't work on Saturday.
    A) Always B) Never C) Sometimes D) Seldom
86. _____ the homework.
    A) No every students do B) No every student does
    C) Not every students do D) Not every student does
87. Whose is this? It's _____.
    A) yours B) to Mary C) of him D) a mine
88. Have you ever been to Scotland? Yes, I _____ last year.
    A) was B) was being C) have gone D) went
89. Where's the lamp?
    A) The chair near the table. B) Its there
    C) It's in the room. D) There's near the door.
90. Are you going to work?
    A) No, to the shops. B) No, to shopping.
    C) No, I don't. D) No, I take the bus.
91. Next month _____ twenty-one.
    A) has my sister B) my sister will be
    C) my sister shall have D) my sister going to be
92. How's the old man?
    A) He's sixty-five. B) That's him.
    C) He's much better. D) Mr Smith is the old man.
93. Did John _____ with the band yesterday?
    A) sing B) sung C) song D) sang
94. Last week John _____ his leg.
    A) felt and broken B) fell and broke
    C) feels and breaks D) fallen and broken
95. When did you _____ to see me last?
    A) go B) went C) came D) come
96. What _____ behind the house when you were a child?
    A) was there B) there were C) were there D) there was
97. What date is it? It's _____.
    A) the July fourth. B) the fourth of July.
    C) of July the fourth. D) fourth July.
98. My car was _____.
    A) in front of the his B) in front of his
    C) in front the his D) in front of he's
99. Jack _____ his thick coat because it was snowing.
    A) puts on B) put on C) takes on D) took on
100. A) Was the big brown book? B) Was the brown book a big?
     C) Was the big book brown? D) Was the brown a big book?

INTERMEDIATE TEST - 1

Choose the correct answer. Only one answer is correct.

Last June my brother __1__ a car. He had had an old scooter before, but it __2__ several times during the spring. "What you want is a second-hand Mini," I suggested. "If you give me the money," he said, "__3__ one tomorrow." "I can't give you the money," I replied, "but what about Aunt Myra. She must have enough. We __4__ her since Christmas but she always hints that we __5__ go and see her more often."

We told our parents where we were going. They weren't very happy about it and asked us not to go. So __6__ But later that same day something strange __7__. A doctor __8__ us that Aunt Myra __9__ into hospital for an operation. "__10__ go and see her at the same time," said my mother. "You two go today, but don't mention the money."

When we __11__ Aunt Myra __12__ "I'm not seriously ill," she said, "but the doctor insist that __13__ to drive my car. You can have it if you promise __14__ me to the seaside now and again." We agreed, and now we quite enjoy our monthly trips to the coast with Aunt Myra.

1. A) wanted to buy B) wanted buying C) liked to buy D) liked buying
2. A) was breaking down B) was breaking up C) had broken down D) had broken up
3. A) I get B) I'm going C) I'm going to get D) I'll get
4. A) are not seeing B) haven't seen C) didn't see D) don't see
5. A) should B) shall C) would D) will
6. A) that we haven't B) that we didn't C) we haven't D) we didn't
7. A) occurred B) took the place C) passed D) was there
8. A) rang for telling B) rang to tell C) rung for telling D) rung to tell
9. A) had gone B) had been C) has gone D) has been
10. A) We may not all B) We can't all C) All we can't D) All we may not
11. A) have come there B) were arriving C) got there D) came to there
12. A) was seeming quite happily B) was seeming quite happy C) seemed quite happily D) seemed quite happy
13. A) I'm getting so old B) I'm getting too old C) I get so old D) I get too old
14. A) taking B) bringing C) to take D) to bring
15. Can this camera _____ good photos?
    A) make B) to make C) take D) to take
16. Who was the first person _____ today?
    A) spoke to you B) you spoke to C) you spoke D) whom you spoke
17. I can't find the book _____ .
    A) nowhere B) everywhere C) anywhere D) somewhere
18. There was a house at _____ .
    A) the mountain foot B) the foot of the mountain C) the feet of the mountain D) the mountain's foot
19. A person who talks to _____ is not necessarily mad.
    A) himself B) oneself C) yourself D) itself
20. I'll be 13 tomorrow, _____ ?
    A) am I B) aren't I C) won't I D) will I
21. Did you hear _____ Julie said?
    A) what B) that C) that what D) which
22. Spanish people usually speak _____ than English people.
    A) quicklier B) more quicklier C) more quickly D) more quicker
23. That old lady can't stop me _____ the tennis match on my radio.
    A) to listen B) listening C) listen to D) listening to
24. I haven't got a chair _____ .
    A) to sit B) for to sit on C) to sit on D) for sitting

25. _____ at the moment, I'll go to the shops.
    A) For it doesn't rain B) As it doesn't rain C) For it isn't raining D) As it isn't raining
26. Bill drinks _____ whisky.
    A) any B) none C) too many D) so much
27. _____ are very intelligent.
    A) Both of them B) Both them C) Both they D) The both
28. In a shop _____ customers.
    A) it is important pleasing B) it is important to please C) there is important pleasing D) there is important to please
29. Don't leave your shoes on the table.
    A) Put off them! B) Take them off! C) Pick them off! D) Pick up them!
30. _____ in my class likes the teacher.
    A) All persons B) All pupils C) Everyone D) All people
31. We expected about 20 girls but there were _____ people there.
    A) another B) others C) some D) more
32. Your bicycle shouldn't be in the house!
    A) Take it out! B) Get out it! C) Put it off! D) Take away it!
33. What time does the bus _____ Bradford?
    A) go away to B) go away for C) leave to D) leave for
34. She _____ be Canadian because she's got a British passport.
    A) can't B) isn't able to C) mustn't D) doesn't need
35. "Our daughter _____", they said.
    A) was born since three years B) is born for three years C) was born three years ago D) has been born since three years ago
36. When _____ English?
    A) has he begun to study B) has he begun study C) did he begin to study D) did he begin study
37. Do you want some cheese? No, _____ .
    A) I've some still B) I still haven't much C) I don't want D) I've still got much
38. Brenda likes going to the theatre and _____ .
    A) so do I B) so go I C) so I like D) so I am
39. _____ from London to Edinburgh!
    A) How long there is B) What a long way it is C) What distance is there D) How long is
40. He's a good guitarist, but he plays the piano _____ .
    A) quite well B) too hardly C) very good D) much better
41. When you go to the shops, bring me _____ .
    A) a fruit tin B) a fruits tin C) a tin of fruit D) a tin of fruits
42. Molly doesn't eat fish.
    A) So doesn't John. B) Neither does John. C) John doesn't too. D) John doesn't that either.
43. The airport is five miles _____ .
    A) away from here B) from here away C) far from here D) far away from here
44. Please ask _____ and see me.
    A) to Bill come B) Bill to come C) to Bill come D) Bill come
45. She always buys _____ my birthday.
    A) anything nice to B) anything nice for C) something awful to D) something awful for
46. Aren't they friends _____ ?
    A) of yours B) of you C) to yours D) to you
47. She hardly ever eats _____ potatoes.
    A) or bread or B) bread or C) neither bread or D) neither bread nor
48. This is the record we _____ .
    A) like so much B) are liking so much C) like it much D) are liking it much
49. She's going to buy _____ new trousers.
    A) some pair of B) some C) a couple of D) this
50. Is she going to school? No, _____
    A) she doesn't B) she's cycling C) she gets by bus D) to the shops

Nowadays __51__ quite early what kind of work they would __52__. When I was at school, we had to choose what to study when we were fifteen. I chose scientific subjects. "In the future, scientists __53__ a lot of money," my parents said. __54__ to learn physics and chemistry, but in the end I decided that I would never be a scientist. It was a long time __55__ my parents that I wasn't happy at school. "I didn't think you were," said my mother. "__56__," said my father. "Well, the best __57__ now is to look for a job."

I talked about it with my friends Frank and Lesley. Neither of them __58__ suggest anything, but they promised that they __59__ their friends. A few days later while I __60__ bed, someone telephoned. "Is that Miss Jenkins?" a man's voice asked. "I understand your hobby is photography and I've got a job that might interest you in my clothes factory. My name is Mr. Thomson." He seemed pleasant on the phone so I went __61__. I was __62__ I almost forgot to say goodbye. "Good luck!" my mother __63__ me.

I arrived a bit early and when Mr. Thomson came he asked me if __64__ for a long time. "No, not long," I replied. After talking to me for about twenty minutes he offered me a job —not as a photographer though, as a model!

51. A) the most people decide B) the most people decides
    C) most people decide D) most people decides
52. A) like to do B) like to make C) do D) make
53. A) shall I earn B) will earn C) going to earn D) are earning
54. A) During three years I've tried B) During three years I tried
    C) For three years I've tried D) For three years I tried
55. A) that I didn't tell B) before I told
    C) when I wasn't telling D) before telling
56. A) Nor I did B) I didn't neither
    C) I didn't either D) I didn't too
57. A) to do B) you should do
    C) thing to do D) thing that you do
58. A) may B) might C) can D) could
59. A) should ask B) would ask C) were asking D) have asked
60. A) was still in B) still was in C) was still in the D) still was in the
61. A) that I should see him B) for seeing him
    C) to see him D) for to see him
62. A) so excited than B) so excited as
    C) so much excited D) so excited that
63. A) told B) said C) told to D) said to
64. A) I had been waiting B) I had been expecting him
    C) I have been waiting D) I have been expecting him
65. Is her _____ than mine?
    A) shorter hair B) hair shorter
    C) hair more short D) more short hair
66. Phone me when you get _____.
    A) to home B) at home C) in home D) home
67. When _____ a game of football?
    A) had you last B) did you last have
    C) last had you D) did you have last
68. I can't find the book _____.
    A) nowhere B) everywhere C) anywhere D) somewhere
69. There's not much news in today's paper, _____?
    A) isn't it B) are there C) is there D) aren't there
70. Fred doesn't like babies _____ Jill.
    A) Nor does B) So doesn't C) So does D) Nor doesn't
71. He often tells stories _____.
    A) what people laugh at B) which people laugh
    C) that people laugh at D) at what people laugh
72. Let's not _____ tonight. There's a good film on television.
    A) to go somewhere B) go to somewhere
    C) go nowhere D) go anywhere
73. The baby is crying! Will you _____ while I prepare his milk?
    A) tear him up B) look after him
    C) care him D) make him up
74. A secretary's job isn't always easy _____.
    A) of to do B) for doing C) of doing D) to do

75. _____ was fine, I sat out in the garden.
    A) For it B) As it C) For there D) As there
76. While we were traveling _____, it started to rain.
    A) towards London in my car B) towards London by my car
    C) against London in my car D) against London by my car
77. Jack brought us _____ cheese.
    A) enough of B) too many C) some more D) a lot
78. _____ draw very well.
    A) These both children B) Both of they
    C) Both them D) Both these girls
79. To travel from England to Scotland you _____ a passport.
    A) mustn't have B) haven't got C) don't need D) needn't
80. Your pen's on the floor.
    A) Pick it up! B) Pick up it! C) Take it up! D) Take up it!
81. I like bacon and eggs _____.
    A) for breakfast B) for the breakfast
    C) with breakfast D) with the breakfast
82. Do you like the cakes? I don't like _____.
    A) all them B) them all C) every D) everyone
83. Children shouldn't leave their toys on the floor. They should _____.
    A) put out them B) put off them
    C) put them away D) put them off
84. Where can we get a ball? Let's _____.
    A) lend one from John B) lend John's one
    C) borrow one of John D) borrow one from John
85. I _____ home at half past six.
    A) was at B) come at C) arrive in D) go to
86. I _____ early, but on Sundays I stay in bed late.
    A) usually go up B) usually get up
    C) used to go up D) used to get up
87. When _____ Mr. Jones?
    A) you have met B) you did meet
    C) you met D) did you meet
88. The girls _____ talked to were quite happy.
    A) we B) which we C) those we D) what we
89. Tony likes walking in the country and _____.
    A) also does Mary B) so does Mary
    C) Mary likes also D) so Mary likes
90. _____ it is from Bristol to Glasgow!
    A) What long a way B) What distance
    C) How long way D) How far
91. I _____ meet her every day.
    A) used to B) wanted C) liked D) am not able
92. You said the books were on the desk, but _____ there.
    A) there was no one B) there were none
    C) there were no ones D) was none
93. Have you got a _____, please?
    A) fishes tin B) fish tin C) tin of fishes D) tin of fish
94. John's not been to New York.
    A) Neither has Ben. B) Ben hasn't also.
    C) Nor is Ben. D) Ben isn't too.
95. How _____ have you been to America?
    A) much time B) many times C) long for D) long ago
96. Tell _____ back tomorrow.
    A) Pam to come B) Pam come
    C) to Pam to come D) to Pam come
97. There was a lot of post today but _____ you.
    A) it's nothing for either of B) it's nothing for either
    C) there's nothing for either of D) there's nothing for either
98. He doesn't _____ English.
    A) neither speak or write B) neither speak nor write
    C) speak or write D) speak nor write
99. Is that the man _____ yesterday?
    A) you've met B) has met you
    C) you met D) met you
100. The restaurant had plenty of tables but _____.
    A) one only empty B) only one empty
    C) no one empty D) no ones empty

INTERMEDIATE TEST - 2

Choose the correct answer. Only one answer is correct.

"Hello, Jill. How nice to see you here," said Jack. "__1__ here often?" "Not as much as I'd like. I often used to meet my friends here, but now I live a long way away," Jill explained. "In fact, it's exactly three years __2__." "Well," said Jack, "tell me what __3__ here today, then." "Last week my mother had an accident in her car. She __4__ when it happened. Suddenly a motorcycle came out of another street and she __5__ stop very quickly, and she __6__ another car from behind. She banged her head on the car roof." "__7__ her safety belt on at the time?" Jack asked. "No, she never wears one. I don't think __8__ in that car," Jill explained. "I hope your mother __9__" said Jack. "No, thank goodness, but the doctor said she __10__ stay in hospital __11__ completely better," explained Jill. "And so you __12__ see her now?" Jack wanted to know. "Yes," said Jill, "every day someone goes to the hospital __13__. She's a lot better now." "I'm glad to hear that," said Jack. "Anyway __14__ coffee."

1. A) Are you coming   B) Are you going
   C) Do you come   D) Do you go
2. A) since then we moved   B) since we moved
   C) that we moved us   D) that we move
3. A) you're doing   B) you do
   C) do you do   D) takes you
4. A) went the Oxford Street along
   B) was going Oxford Street along
   C) was going along Oxford Street
   D) went along the Oxford Street
5. A) must   B) had to   C) ought to   D) had better
6. A) was beaten with   B) was hit with
   C) was beaten by   D) was hit by
7. A) Was she having   B) Did she have
   C) Has she put   D) She was wearing
8. A) they were any   B) there were any
   C) they were any ones D) there were any ones
9. A) wasn't badly hurt   B) wasn't hurt bad
   C) wasn't so much hurt   D) wasn't too much hurt
10. A) need   B) ought   C) should   D) would rather
11. A) until she is   B) until when she will be
    C) until she will be D) until she's going to be
12. A) just were at   B) just were in
    C) have just gone to   D) have just been to
13. A) for seeing her   B) for to see her
    C) that we see her   D) to see her
14. A) let me pay you your   B) let me to pay your
    C) let me pay for your   D) let me to pay for your
15. Where _____ yesterday?
    A) went you   B) was you
    C) have you been D) were you
16. I've just finished _____ my shopping.
    A) to make   B) doing   C) to do   D) making
17. The girl _____ the bicycle is Jane.
    A) riding on   B) driving in   C) driving on   D) riding in
18. He's lived in London _____ .
    A) for some time   B) since he is born
    C) since a long time D) since some time
19. At the post office he asked _____ .
    A) stamps   B) some stamps
    C) four stamps   D) for four stamps
20. The girl _____ house he visited was Elizabeth.
    A) of which   B) of whom   C) which   D) whose
21. I have a _____ paper in my desk.
    A) lot   B) little   C) loss   D) little of
22. "Can't you read?" Mary said _____ to the notice.
    A) and pointed angry   B) angrily pointed
    C) pointing angrily   D) and angrily pointing
23. Tom is waiting _____ the doctor.
    A) to see   B) for to see   C) for seeing   D) for see
24. I'm not sure which restaurant _____ .
    A) to eat on   B) eating at   C) to eat at   D) for eating

25. _____ the weather was fine, I opened all the windows.
    A) As   B) For   C) Because of   D) Since that
26. I've just seen Mary _____ the village.
    A) to walk towards   B) to walk against
    C) walking towards   D) walking against
27. Sally didn't put in _____ water.
    A) no   B) so much   C) enough of   D) few
28. _____ like ice-cream.
    A) Every children   B) Every child
    C) All of children   D) All children
29. When you go abroad, do you _____ take your passport?
    A) have to   B) ought to   C) need   D) must
30. You don't need your hat.
    A) Put off it!   B) Put it off!   C) Take off it!   D) Take it off!
31. How many elephants did you see? _____ .
    A) None   B) No one   C) Not many ones   D) No many
32. We're going to go _____ car.
    A) in France in John's   B) in France by John's
    C) to France in John's   D) to France by John's
33. It's dark without the lights. Let's _____ .
    A) switch on them   B) turn them on
    C) to turn on them   D) to switch them on
34. What time does the train _____ Bristol?
    A) arrive into   B) come at   C) go into   D) get to
35. How _____ here?
    A) long you stay   B) often you stay
    C) long are you staying D) often are you staying
36. Everybody _____ in bed.
    A) has to spend some time   B) have to spend some time
    C) has to spend sometimes   D) have to spend sometimes
37. These are nice apples. How _____ in a kilo?
    A) much are there   B) many are there
    C) much are they   D) many are they
38. Paul's ill, so he _____ a doctor tomorrow.
    A) is going to be visit   B) goes to meet
    C) is going to see   D) goes to tell
39. How _____ from Leeds to Liverpool?
    A) far is there   B) long is there   C) far is it   D) long way is
40. She's _____ singer in England.
    A) most known   B) the most known
    C) most famous D) the most famous
41. _____ to finish quickly.
    A) No every student wants   B) No every student want
    C) Not every student wants   D) Not every student want
42. My mother usually has _____ bed.
    A) the breakfast in   B) breakfast in
    C) the breakfast in the   D) breakfast in the
43. Beryl isn't going to the dance.
    A) Neither Pat is.   B) Pat isn't too.
    C) Pat also.   D) Nor is Pat.
44. Who taught you _____ a car?
    A) driving   B) to drive   C) riding   D) to ride
45. A lot of letters and cards came today, but _____ you.
    A) there wasn't anything for   B) there wasn't something for
    C) it wasn't anything for   D) it wasn't something for
46. Sarah hardly ever goes to _____ the theatre.
    A) neither the cinema or   B) neither the cinema nor
    C) either the cinema nor   D) the cinema or
47. _____ the girls came on the trip.
    A) Neither   B) Nobody of   C) None of   D) No one of
48. I've thrown away my old trousers. I'll have to buy _____ .
    A) a new pair   B) a new one
    C) some new   D) some new pair
49. Kim and Tony weren't the only people in the garden. There _____ .
    A) were some other ones   B) were some others
    C) was another   D) was someone more
50. I want to leave my car. Can you tell me _____ near here?
    A) if there's a car park   B) is there a car park
    C) if there's a parking   D) is there a parking

I work at Poleson Ltd. __51__ there since 1967. Last month the manager asked __52__ one morning __53__ time. He was new so I wondered __54__. When I went to see him, he said "I'd like __55__ me with a special project. I've heard that you speak German." He said that a factory in Germany wanted a specialist for six months. "Tell me __56__ go." I __57__ a few days to think about it. "All right," he said, "and if you want all the details, my secretary __58__ them to you." So I asked his secretary __59__ give me the papers. "I don't know where they are," she said. "When I __60__ them, I'll phone you. Oh! Here they are. Let me __61__ them back after you've read them."

When I told my friends about it they all said, "__62__!" "__63__," I said. But next day I told the manager I wanted to go and he said, "I hoped __64__."

51. A) I'm working B) I've been working
    C) I am worker D) I have been worker
52. A) I should see him B) me see him
    C) that I saw him D) me to see him
53. A) when I should have B) then I should have
    C) when I had D) the I had
54. A) how he would be B) how he should be
    C) what he would be like D) how he should like me
55. A) that you will help B) that you should help
    C) you to help D) you helping
56. A) if you may B) if you can C) may you D) can you
57. A) explained him I liked B) explained him I'd like
    C) told him I liked D) told him I'd like
58. A) will give B) is going to give
    C) gives D) is giving
59. A) please B) to C) please to D) that she
60. A) am going to find B) will find
    C) find D) am finding
61. A) to have B) have C) to get D) get
62. A) It looks to be marvelous B) It looks marvelously
    C) It seems marvelous D) It seems marvelously
63. A) didn't yet say that yes B) haven't said yes yet
    C) haven't yet said that yes D) didn't yet say yes
64. A) that you'd agree B) that you agreed
    C) for you to agree D) you to agree
65. Must we _____ this homework tonight?
    A) to do B) to make C) do D) make
66. My piano is magnificent _____ since I was 18.
    A) I got it B) I've got it C) I have it D) I've had it
67. The last time _____ to the library was last week.
    A) I have gone B) I have been C) I was D) I went
68. My parents _____ in this evening.
    A) are both B) all are C) both are D) are all
69. I don't want _____ .
    A) that anybody saw me B) anybody to see me
    C) that anybody sees me D) anybody see me
70. Can I _____ this book back to you?
    A) to take B) to bring C) take D) bring
71. Why is there _____ traffic on the streets in February than in May?
    A) less B) fewer C) few D) little
72. _____ it's raining, we'll stay at home.
    A) As B) Like C) How D) Because of
73. Tim sat near the fire _____ warm.
    A) for to get B) for get C) to get D) for getting
74. I don't know where _____ .
    A) the lavatory to be B) is the lavatory
    C) be the lavatory D) the lavatory is
75. We watched carefully _____ the houses.
    A) during she walked against B) during she walked towards
    C) while she walked against D) while she walked towards

76. Jane had _____ furniture for her room.
    A) enough B) many C) all D) any
77. I like _____ two records.
    A) these both B) both these C) all these D) these all
78. To drive a car safely it is _____ good brakes.
    A) essential with B) essential having
    C) essential to have D) essential have
79. If you've read my book, please _____ to me.
    A) give it again B) give again it C) give it back D) give back it
80. _____ people came than I expected.
    A) Other B) Fewer C) Another D) Few
81. In some countries children normally go _____ bikes.
    A) to school on B) to the school on
    C) to school by D) to the school by
82. You'll get cold without your coat.
    A) Take on it! B) Take it on! C) Put on it! D) Put it on!
83. We haven't got a record player. Let's _____ .
    A) to borrow the Mary's B) borrow Mary's
    C) to lend one of Mary D) lend Mary's one
84. Mary _____ be in Paris because I saw her in town only an hour ago.
    A) mustn't B) isn't able to C) can't D) may not
85. The station? Take the second turning _____ .
    A) to left, then go straight on B) to the left, then go straight on
    C) to left, then go right forward D) to the left, then go right forward
86. Simon _____ the club.
    A) often plays tennis at B) often plays tennis on
    C) plays often tennis at D) plays often tennis on
87. Do you want another cake? No, thank you, _____ .
    A) I still have got some left B) I've still got some left
    C) I still have some ones D) I have still some ones
88. The men _____ were all office workers.
    A) which I talked B) to those I talked
    C) those I talked to D) I talked to
89. _____ is Oxford from Cambridge?
    A) How far B) How long
    C) How long away D) What distance
90. She _____ the cinema, but her husband doesn't go with her.
    A) used to go B) usually sees
    C) often goes to D) visits sometimes
91. We've looked _____ for the keys we lost.
    A) in all places B) at all places C) over all D) everywhere
92. There's something wrong with the table. Yes, I can _____ .
    A) feel it that it's moving B) touch its moves
    C) touch it moving D) feel it moving
93. Sally never goes to pubs.
    A) Tom doesn't that either. B) Tom doesn't too.
    C) Neither does Tom. D) Tom does neither.
94. Agnes was the first girl _____ when you got here.
    A) you talked to whom B) you talked to
    C) whom you talked D) who talked you
95. Many parents allow their children _____ own decisions.
    A) making their B) making the C) to make their D) to make the
96. The teacher says that Mary _____ work hard next year.
    A) will have to B) has better
    C) would rather to D) had rather
97. The American film I saw was _____ .
    A) not very funny B) not much funny
    C) not very fun D) not too much fun
98. Try to find me _____ scissors.
    A) a pair B) two C) some D) one
99. Teresa wasn't the only one in the car
    A) It was some other. B) It was someone else.
    C) There was some other. D) There was someone else.
100. I'd like to leave my car near here. Where's the _____ please?
    A) nearest parking B) next parking
    C) nearest car park D) next car park

INTERMEDIATE TEST - 3

Choose the correct answer. Only one answer is correct.

I __1__ to your letter, which __2__ before __3__ for Rome. __4__ yesterday that the company __5__ me there next week for a business conference. If I __6__ about it earlier I would have told you. Anyway, I'll ring you as soon as I __7__ there.

John Marshall came into my office while I __8__ the arrangements for my flight to Rome. You __9__ him last year when you were in England. If you __10__ him, you would remember him because he is over two meters tall. He told me that he __11__ for the previous two months on the plans for the new factory in Naples. He __12__ very hard because he looked very tired. By the time I come to Rome he __13__ them so I'll bring them with me.

1. A) like to reply   B) would like replying
   C) would like to reply   D) am wanting to reply

2. A) arrived two days ago   B) has arrived two days ago
   C) arrived since two days   D) has arrived since two days

3. A) to go out   B) to leave   C) leave   D) leaving

4. A) I was said   B) It was said me
   C) I was told   D) It was told me

5. A) shall have sent   B) is going to send
   C) shall be sending   D) shall send

6. A) knew   B) had known
   C) would have known   D) would know

7. A) get   B) will get   C) shall get   D) will have got

8. A) made   B) did make   C) had made   D) was making

9. A) can have met   B) may have met
   C) can meet   D) may meet

10. A) meet   B) met   C) were meeting   D) would meet

11. A) has worked   B) has been worked
    C) had been worked   D) had been working

12. A) must have worked   B) had to work
    C) need have worked   D) needed to work

13. A) will finish   B) will be finished
    C) will have finished D) has finished

14. Take an umbrella _____ it rains.
    A) in any case   B) in case   C) because   D) for

15. I _____ have coffee than tea.
    A) like more to   B) prefer   C) would rather   D) had better

16. He didn't thank me for the present. That is _____ annoyed me.
    A) the which   B) that which
    C) the thing what D) what

17. I'll have to buy _____ trousers.
    A) a   B) two   C) a pair of   D) a couple of

18. She looks _____ .
    A) pleasant   B) to be pleasant
    C) that she's pleasant D) pleasantly

19. When you _____ the furniture, please tell me.
    A) will finish to move   B) finish to move
    C) will finish moving   D) have finished moving

20. The reason _____ I'm writing is to tell you about a party on Saturday.
    A) because   B) why   C) for   D) as

21. Don't make him _____ it if he doesn't want to.
    A) do   B) to do   C) doing   D) that he do

22. He's _____ to know the answer.
    A) likely   B) probable   C) maybe   D) probably

23. She came _____ because her car has broken down.
    A) walking   B) by foot   C) with foot   D) on foot

24. That's the man _____ yesterday.
    A) which I was talking to   B) what I was talking to
    C) I was talking to   D) with who I was talking

25. I've been looking for you _____ .
    A) everywhere   B) anywhere   C) for all places   D) in all places

26. _____ he was tired he went on working.
    A) Even   B) Yet   C) Although   D) In spite

27. Send him to the baker's _____ the bread.
    A) to buy   B) in order he buys
    C) for to buy   D) for buying

28. Wanda is _____ Jane.
    A) a lot pretty than   B) a lot prettier that
    C) much more pretty that D) much prettier than

29. He didn't know _____ or go home.
    A) to wait   B) if that he should wait
    C) if to wait   D) whether to wait

30. _____ me _____ .
    A) Tell / what is this   B) Tell / what this is
    C) Say / what is this   D) Say / what this is

31. If you _____ help you, you only have to ask me.
    A) want me to   B) want that I
    C) want I should   D) are wanting me to

32. "I'm going to the theatre tonight." "So _____ "
    A) will I   B) I will   C) am I   D) do I

33. How _____ is it from here to New York?
    A) long way   B) long   C) far   D) much far

34. I wish I _____ what to do.
    A) knew   B) have known   C) know   D) would know

35. He likes playing _____
    A) the football   B) football   C) at football   D) at the football

36. My brother, _____ lives in Iceland, is coming to visit us.
    A) which   B) that   C) whom   D) who

37. He's already about _____ his father.
    A) so tall than   B) as tall than   C) as tall as   D) so tall as

38. _____ him go out if he wants to.
    A) Allow   B) Leave   C) Let   D) Permit

39. I didn't hear what he was _____
    A) telling   B) saying   C) talking   D) speaking

40. I _____ watching this program because it is very interesting.
    A) amuse   B) please   C) delight   D) enjoy

41. That student _____ his hand every time I ask a question.
    A) gets out   B) gets up   C) rises   D) puts up

42. I _____ hands with him when he came in.
    A) gave   B) greeted   C) shook   D) offered

43. He wants to get a better _____ and earn more money.
    A) job   B) work   C) employ   D) employment

44. _____ the children for me while I'm out.
    A) Look after   B) Look to   C) Take care   D) Care

In this series of questions, three words have the same sound but one does not. Choose the one that does not.

45. A) ball   B) call   C) fall   D) shall

46. A) freeze   B) piece   C) please   D) trees

47. A) lose   B) chose   C) rose   D) nose

48. A) what   B) cat   C) sat   D) fat

49. A) fair   B) wear   C) hear   D) their

50. A) days   B) says   C) ways   D) plays

I __51__ asleep while I was working because it took me a long time to realize that the telephone __52__. When I answered it, my girl friend __53__ "__54__ that we __55__ to the cinema tonight? __56__. If you __57__ soon, we'll miss the film."

I suddenly remembered that __58__ for the first performance of a new film. If I __59__ so much work to do, I would have taken her out to dinner before __60__ to the cinema. I said: "by the time I get there, the film __61__. __62__ out to dinner instead." "You are a nuisance," she said. "I __63__ the tickets. Anyway, I've already had dinner."

51. A) should fall   B) ought to fall
    C) had to fall   D) must have fallen

52. A) rang   B) was ringing
    C) has rung   D) has been ringing

53. A) said   B) told   C) was saying   D) was telling

54. A) Aren't you remembering   B) Aren't you remembered
    C) Doesn't you remember   D) Don't you remember

55. A) would go   B) go   C) are going   D) will be going

56. A) It's half an hour I am waiting here.
    B) I'm waiting here since half an hour.
    C) I've been waiting here for half an hour.
    D) I've been waiting here since half an hour.

57. A) aren't coming   B) don't come
    C) won't come   D) wouldn't come

58. A) Sarah had been given some tickets
    B) some tickets to Sarah had been given
    C) to Sarah some tickets had been given
    D) they had been given some tickets to Sarah

59. A) should not have   B) would not have
    C) had not have   D) would not have

60. A) to go   B) go   C) going   D) I was going

61. A) will have started   B) shall have started
    C) has started   D) has to start

62. A) Let's going   B) Let's go   C) Will we go   D) Would we go

63. A) hadn't accept   B) mustn't have accept
    C) didn't need to accept D) needn't have accepted

64. Take hold of it firmly _____ in falls.
    A) because   B) for   C) in case   D) in any case

65. He looks _____ .
    A) to be sad   B) sad   C) sadly   D) that he's sad

66. Would you like some more coffee? There's still _____ left.
    A) a little   B) little   C) a few   D) few

67. I gave her _____ stocking for her birthday.
    A) a pair of   B) a couple of   C) a   D) any

68. Frank plays _____ Alex.
    A) a lot more better that   B) much more better that
    C) a lot better than   D) much more well than

69. How _____ is your house from here?
    A) long   B) far   C) much far   D) long way

70. You can't rely _____ him to do the job properly.
    A) to   B) with   C) in   D) on

71. I'd never allow my children _____ like that.
    A) that they behaved   B) behave
    C) to behave   D) behaving

72. I can't stop. I _____ .
    A) am going running   B) am at a run
    C) am in a hurry   D) have a hurry

73. He asked me _____ stay.
    A) how long I was going to
    B) how long was I going to
    C) how long time I was going to
    D) how long time was I going to

74. _____ he worked all day, he couldn't finish the job.
    A) Although   B) Even   C) In case   D) In spite

75. That's the hotel _____ last year.
    A) which we stayed   B) at which we stayed at
    C) where we stayed at   D) where we stayed

76. I'll leave him a note _____ he'll know where we are.
    A) so that   B) that   C) in order   D) for

77. You _____ drive carefully. The roads are wet.
    A) had rather   B) would rather   C) had better   D) would better

78. She broke a _____ while she was washing up.
    A) glass wine   B) wine glass   C) glass for wine   D) glass of wine

79. I'm going to the hairdresser's to _____ .
    A) cut my hair   B) have my hair cut
    C) have cut my hair   D) cut me my hair

80. He couldn't help _____ that his wife was worried.
    A) except notice   B) notice
    C) to notice   D) noticing

81. He wanted to know the reason _____ I was late.
    A) as   B) for   C) why   D) because

82. I'm bad _____ remembering faces.
    A) at   B) in   C) with   D) on

83. She _____ read her a story.
    A) wants that I   B) wants me for
    C) is wanting that I D) wants me to

84. He hasn't been here _____ .
    A) three weeks ago   B) since three weeks
    C) during three weeks   D) for three weeks

85. He is _____ a horse.
    A) as strong like   B) as strong as
    C) so strong as   D) so strong than

86. "Which is your sister?" "She's the girl _____ is wearing the green dress."
    A) who   B) who's   C) which   D) what

87. There's no one to _____ .
    A) look the children after   B) look after the children
    C) take care the children   D) care the children

88. I wanted to go there by plane but I hadn't enough money to pay for the _____ .
    A) journey   B) travel   C) voyage   D) fly

89. He failed the examination three times but _____ he passed.
    A) at the end   B) at finish   C) at last   D) at least

90. She _____ the cups and some of them broke.
    A) dropped   B) fell   C) let   D) let fall

91. Tennis is a _____ invented by an Englishman a hundred years ago.
    A) game   B) play   C) toy   D) match

92. He got a job in a furniture _____ .
    A) society   B) industry   C) fabric   D) factory

93. He has spent a large _____ of money on his new house.
    A) deal   B) amount   C) number   D) piece

94. His parents died when he was young so he was _____ by his aunt.
    A) brought out   B) grown up   C) brought up   D) grown

In this series of qestions, three words have the same sound but one does not. Choose the one that does not.

95. A) word   B) lord   C) heard   D) bird

96. A) run   B) done   C) none   D) won

97. A) great   B) beat   C) treat   D) seat

98. A) tries   B) wise   C) twice   D) buys

99. A) town   B) grown   C) shown   D) known

100. A) head   B) bed   C) said   D) paid

INTERMEDIATE TEST - 4

Choose the correct answer. Only one answer is correct.

When I went to bed last night, I __1__ asleep immediately. I __2__ tired because I __3__ so hard for several hours. So I forgot to close the windows before __4__ into bed. If I had remembered, the thief __5__. But __6__ a perfect opportunity to enter the house. The next time I __7__ late I will lock the house carefully.

A policeman came to see me about the theft. "__8__ investigate," he said. "So I __9__ ask you some questions. First, how __10__?" I told him that I __11__ the window open. "You __12__ more careful," he said. "If people __13__ their houses properly, we wouldn't have so much work to do."

1. A) fell   B) did fell   C) was falling   D) have fallen
2. A) had to be   B) ought to be
   C) must have been   D) needed to be
3. A) have been working   B) had been working
   C) have being working   D) had being working
4. A) getting   B) to get   C) going   D) to go
5. A) has not got in   B) had not got in
   C) would not get in   D) would not have got in
6. A) it was given to him   B) there was given to him
   C) he has been given   D) he was given
7. A) shall work   B) will work
   C) work   D) will be working
8. A) I've been said to   B) I've been told to
   C) It has been said to me   D) It has been told me
9. A) would   B) would to
   C) am wanting to   D) want to
10. A) the thief got in   B) was the thief getting in
    C) has the thief got in   D) did the thief get in
11. A) had let   B) had left   C) was letting   D) was leaving
12. A) would be   B) ought be   C) should be   D) had to be
13. A) looked after   B) looks after
    C) have looked after   D) should look after
14. There are so many cars _____ nowadays.
    A) for all places   B) in all the place
    C) anywhere   D) everywhere
15. Ask him to go to the post office _____ some stamps.
    A) to get   B) for getting
    C) in order he gets   D) that he gets
16. The reason _____ I can't come is that I have to work late.
    A) because   B) for   C) as   D) why
17. She cut the cloth with _____ scissors.
    A) a couple of   B) a pair of   C) two   D) a
18. _____ me _____ .
    A) Tell / where are you going   B) Tell / where you are going
    C) Say / where are you going   D) Say / where you are going
19. The children _____ play with them.
    A) want that I   B) want me for
    C) want me to   D) are wanting that
20. He may be able to come to the party. _____ the other hand, he may be too busy.
    A) On   B) In   C) By   D) For
21. I haven't seen him _____ .
    A) last week   B) during last week
    C) for last week   D) since last week
22. I'm fond _____ good music.
    A) to the   B) to   C) of the   D) of
23. John is _____ .
    A) a friend of me   B) a friend mine
    C) a friend of mine   D) one friend of mine
24. She's the girl _____ .
    A) whose money was stolen   B) the which money was stolen
    C) whose money was robbed   D) the which money was robbed
25. It's the _____ film I've ever seen.
    A) more interesting   B) most interesting
    C) more interested   D) most interested
26. He doesn't know the answer _____ I've told him several times.
    A) in spite   B) even   C) while   D) although
27. _____ English?
    A) How long time are you studying
    B) How long do you study
    C) How long have you been studying
    D) How long time have you studied
28. The little boy keeps the insect in a _____ .
    A) match box   B) box of matches
    C) box of the matches   D) box match
29. She's going to the photographer's _____ .
    A) to take her photograph   B) to have taken her photograph
    C) to have her photograph   D) that he takes her photograph
30. He looks _____ .
    A) to be unhappy   B) unhappily
    C) unhappy   D) that he's unhappy
31. Where have you been? I've been playing _____ .
    A) the tennis   B) at tennis   C) at the tennis   D) tennis
32. It's very kind _____ invite me.
    A) from you to   B) of you to   C) by you to   D) that you
33. I can't break. It's _____ iron.
    A) as hard as   B) so hard as   C) as hard than   D) so hard than
34. I didn't know _____ him or not.
    A) whether to help   B) if to help
    C) to help   D) if that I should help
35. _____ of them knew about the plan because it was secret.
    A) Some   B) Any   C) No one   D) None
36. Mont Blanc, _____ we visited last summer, is the highest mountain in Europe.
    A) where   B) which   C) that   D) what
37. This question is _____ difficult for me.
    A) so much   B) too much   C) too   D) enough
38. It _____ the village where we spent our holidays last summer.
    A) reminds me of   B) remembers me of
    C) reminds me to   D) remembers me to
39. Living here at the top of the mountain with no one else near you must be very _____ .
    A) sole   B) alone   C) only   D) lonely
40. The tailor made him a new _____ .
    A) clothes   B) suit   C) dress   D) wear
41. The clock _____ and we realized it was two o'clock.
    A) hit   B) struck   C) turned   D) rang
42. Good _____ ! I hope you win the race.
    A) sort   B) wish   C) luck   D) chance
43. My car _____ so I had to come by bus.
    A) fell down   B) fell over   C) broke down   D) broke up
44. Look what Father _____ me when he came home from work.
    A) brought   B) took   C) carried   D) fetched

In this series of questions, three words have the same sound but one does not. Choose the one that does not.

45. A) force   B) sauce   C) horse   D) worse
46. A) good   B) wood   C) blood   D) stood
47. A) but   B) put   C) cut   D) shut
48. A) lost   B) most   C) post   D) ghost
49. A) talk   B) pork   C) fork   D) work
50. A) mass   B) pass   C) grass   D) class

I went to the doctor's yesterday. I __51__ for half an hour before he __52__ see me. "I __53__ abroad next week," I said. "I __54__ to Africa on business. But __55__ two days. __56__ I'll be well enough to go?" "When I __57__ you, I'll be able to tell you," the doctor said.

"I __58__ in the garden when I suddenly felt the pain," I told the doctor. "If I __59__ immediately, it would have been all right, I suppose. But I __60__ any exercise in my job so I went on working." After __61__ me carefully, the doctor said: "You __62__ a bone in your back. I __63__ you to hospital for an X-ray."

51. A) must wait B) had to wait C) should wait D) ought to wait
52. A) can B) may C) might D) could
53. A) shall be go B) will be go C) am going D) go
54. A) am sent B) am being sent
    C) am send D) be sent
55. A) I've had a pain for B) I've had a pain since
    C) I'm having a pain for D) I'm having a pain since
56. A) Do you think B) Are you thinking
    C) Does you think D) You are thinking
57. A) am examining B) will examine
    C) will have examined D) have examined
58. A) worked B) have worked
    C) was working D) have been working
59. A) had stopped B) would have stopped
    C) stopped D) would stop
60. A) never get B) don't get ever
    C) am never getting D) am not ever getting
61. A) examine B) to examine
    C) examining D) that he had examined
62. A) can be hurt B) may be hurt
    C) can have hurt D) may have hurt
63. A) would send B) would like to send
    C) am wanting to send D) will like to send
64. It's _____ I expected.
    A) much bigger than B) much bigger that
    C) a lot more big than D) a lot more big that
65. They'll hurt _____ if we don't stop them fighting.
    A) one to another B) one the other
    C) each the other D) each other
66. I've brought you _____ flowers for your birthday.
    A) few B) a few C) little D) a little
67. He didn't know _____ or stay at home.
    A) to go B) if that he should go
    C) if to go D) whether to go
68. Would you mind _____ the window?
    A) that I open B) open C) to open D) opening
69. Are you interested _____ tennis tomorrow?
    A) in playing B) for playing C) on playing D) to play
70. I wouldn't rely _____ him if I were you.
    A) to B) for C) on D) in
71. Her father didn't let her _____ out with him.
    A) to go B) go C) going D) that she went
72. Don't wait for me if you _____ .
    A) have a hurry B) are in a hurry
    C) have speed D) are in a speed
73. _____ beautiful flowers!
    A) What a B) What C) How D) So
74. I'm going to the passport office _____ .
    A) to stamp my passport
    B) for stamping my passport
    C) to have stamped my passport
    D) to have my passport stamped

75. Who is responsible _____ the arrangements?
    A) for make B) to make C) to making D) for making
76. Speak to him slowly _____ he will understand you better.
    A) in order B) so that C) for D) that
77. He wanted to know _____ there.
    A) how long time I had been B) how long had I been
    C) how long time had I been D) how long I had been
78. He works too hard. That is _____ is wrong with him.
    A) that which B) the what
    C) what D) the thing what
79. I know it's not important but I can't help _____ about it.
    A) except to think B) thinking
    C) think D) to think
80. He finally _____ the driving test after failing three times.
    A) succeeded in passing B) succeeded to pass
    C) could pass D) managed passing
81. She's very fond _____ modern art.
    A) of the B) of C) to the D) to
82. "I went to the cinema last night." "So _____ "
    A) I have B) have I C) I did D) did I
83. I won't allow you _____ for the meal.
    A) pay B) paying
    C) to pay D) that you should pay
84. She hasn't written to me _____ .
    A) for last month B) during last month
    C) since last month D) a month ago
85. It was _____ that we felt tired when we arrived.
    A) a so long travel B) such a long travel
    C) such a long journey D) a so long journey
86. Is this _____ looking for?
    A) you were B) that you were
    C) what were you D) what you were
87. That's the man _____ killed my cat.
    A) whose dog B) the dog of whom
    C) which dog D) the which dog
88. I learnt how to _____ a bicycle when I was six years old.
    A) drive B) ride C) conduct D) lead
89. I don't think I could _____ another night without sleep.
    A) stand B) support C) put up D) carry
90. They _____ on holiday in Switzerland and became good friends.
    A) found B) knew C) met D) encountered
91. They were very happy when they _____ the end of their journey.
    A) arrived B) arrived to C) arrived at D) reached at
92. He _____ .
    A) robbed me my coat B) stole me my coat
    C) robbed my coat from me D) stole my coat from me
93. _____ at the door before you come into the room.
    A) Hit B) Knock C) Touch D) Strike
94. If you don't _____ smoking you'll never get better.
    A) give off B) give out C) give from D) give up

In this series of questions, three words have the same sound but one does not. Choose the one that does not.

95. A) love B) move C) above D) glove
96. A) gone B) bone C) stone D) own
97. A) want B) plant C) aunt D) can't
98. A) weak B) peak C) break D) speak
99. A) low B) cow C) grow D) slow
100. A) eyes B) rise C) price D) dies

INTERMEDIATE TEST - 5

Choose the correct Answer. Only one answer is correct.

My wife and I went to the Airport to meet some friends. Their plane landed but they weren't on it.

"__1__ if there is a massage for us," my wife said.

"They __2__ the plane. Or perhaps they __3__ from coming for some reason."

After __4__ information At the information desk without success, I had an idea" __5__ their letter?" I asked my wife. She found it in her handbag.

"Here you Are," she said. "We __6__ at 10 o'clock on the 7th and __7__ us."

"But today's the 6th," I said. "We should have looked at the date before. If we had, we wouldn't have had this journey for nothing."

"How silly!" my wife said. " I __8__ this letter around for days without looking at it."

1. A) Let's see B) Let's to see C) Will we see D) We are seeing
2. A) can have missed B) may have missed C) can have lost D) may have lost
3. A) would be prevented B) would be avoided C) have been prevented D) have been avoided
4. A) asking for B) to ask for C) asking D) to ask
5. A) Do you yet have B) Do you already have C) Have you yet got D) Have you still got
6. A) Are arriving B) would arrive C) will be arrive D) will be arrived
7. A) want you to wait B) want that you look for C) would like you to meet D) would like that find
8. A) am carrying B) have been carrying C) carry D) must carry
9. I've often _____ at hotel.
   A) remained B) rested C) stayed D) passed
10. I didn't know what do but then an idea suddenly _____ to me.
    A) happened B) entered C) occurred D) hit
11. When they arrived at the crossroads, he went the wrong _____.
    A) way B) direction C) route D) street
12. Your work has been _____ so we're going to give you a rise in salary.
    A) regular B) well C) satisfactory D) available
13. That's the best horse in the _____ .
    A) career B) run C) rate D) race
14. The weather _____ says it will rain tomorrow.
    A) provision B) forecast C) advertisement D) advise
15. There are a lot of mistakes in this exercise. I'll have to _____ it again with you.
    A) come though B) go over C) repass C) instruct
16. If there are no buses, we'll have to take a taxi. We must get there _____.
    A) somehow or other B) somewhere or other C) on one way or another D) anyway or other
17. _____ I read, the more I understand.
    A) The more B) So much C) How much D) For how much
18. _____ he does his work, I don't mind what time he arrives at the office.
    A) So far as B) So long as C) In case D) Meanwhile
19. _____ entering the hall, he found everyone waiting for him.
    A) At B) While C) On D) In
20. It's years _____ a picture.
    A) that I don't paint B) that I didn't paint C) since I painted D) ago I painted
21. I found the first question _____ .
    A) to be easy B) the easy C) that it was easy D) easy
22. _____ an empty seat at the back of the bus.
    A) She happened to find
    B) She happened to meet
    C) It happened her that she found
    D) It happened her that she met
23. It was raining, _____ was a pity.
    A) what B) that C) the which D) which
24. Your car is _____ mine.
    A) the same that B) as C) similar to D) alike
25. I'm going away for a _____ .
    A) holiday of a week B) week holiday C) holiday week D) week's holiday
26. Why _____ ? It's not very important.
    A) to worry B) worry C) you are worried D) you worry
27. I don't like _____ at me.
    A) them shouting B) them shout C) their shout D) that they shout
28. It often snows _____ January.
    A) on B) in C) for D) at
29. I'll meet you again _____ the weekend.
    A) by B) on C) at D) for
30. It's the first turning _____ the left after the traffic lights.
    A) on B) in C) by D) for
31. He wasn't _____ to lift the case.
    A) too strong B) enough strong C) strong enough D) so strong
32. He can climb trees _____ a monkey.
    A) as B) like C) the same that D) similarly than
33. He _____ lives in the house where he was born.
    A) already B) yet C) still D) every
34. It's ten o'clock in the morning so he's still _____.
    A) at the bed B) at bed C) in bed D) in the bed
35. He was a good swimmer so he _____ swim to the river bank when the boat sank.
    A) could B) might C) succeeded to D) was able to
36. She's been very kind, _____ ?
    A) isn't she B) hasn't she C) wasn't she D) doesn't she
37. He was left alone, with _____ to look after him.
    A) someone B) anyone C) not one D) no one
38. I pulled the handle _____ I could.
    A) so hardly as B) as hardly as C) so hard as D) as hard as
39. Have you got match? I've left my _____ at home.
    A) cigarette lighter B) cigarettes lighter C) cigarette's lighter C) lighter for cigarettes
40. That's the dog _____ .
    A) we've been looking after
    B) after which we've been looking
    C) what we've been looking after
    D) we've been taking care for
41. I made him _____ what I had told him.
    A) repeating B) that he repeated C) repeat D) to repeat
42. I was _____ tired that I had to rest.
    A) so much B) so C) enough D) too
43. He _____ live in the country than in the city.
    A) prefers B) likes better to C) had better D) would rather
44. He _____ his sister.
    A) remembers me of B) remembers me C) reminds me of D) reminds me
45. Put on your raincoat _____ it rains.
    A) because B) for C) in any case D) in case

In this series of questions, three words have the same sound but one does not. Choose one that does not.

46. A) raise B) trays C) says D) stays
47. A) crown B) thrown C) brown D) town
48. A) prove B) move C) groove D) love

49. A) were   B) spare   C) chair   D) pair
50. A) water   B) porter   C) daughter   D) laughter

My wife's mother was taken ill two days ago so my wife had to go and look after her. Before __51__ my wife said, "I had better tell you where everything is or you __52__ know what to do. But my train is leaving in half an hour's time and I must get to mother's house as soon as I __53__"

"__54__," I said. "I can look after myself."

Now I realize that I __55__ for a map of the house. If I __56__, I would have found all the food I needed.

But when my wife __57__ back tomorrow, she won't have any dirty dishes to wash up because I __58__ in restaurants since she went away.

51. A) she was leaving   B) that she left
    C) leaving   D) to leave
52. A) shan't   B) shouldn't   C) wouldn't   D) won't
53. A) can   B) may   C) could   D) might
54. A) Not to mind   B) Don't worry
    C) Not to import   D) Don't mater
55. A) had to ask   B) ought to ask
    C) must have asked   D) should have asked
56. A) had   B) have   C) did   D) would
57. A) comes   B) come   C) shall come   D) will come
58. A) am eating   B) eat
    C) have been eating   D) ate
59. He's _____ his sister.
    A) much taller than   B) much taller that
    C) much more tall than   D) much more tall that
60. She had three sons, all _____ became doctors.
    A) of which   B) which   C) of whom   D) who
61. You _____ go now. It's getting late.
    A) had rather   B) would rather   C) would batter   D) had better
62. I'm going to spend a few days with some _____ of mine, who live in the north of Scotland.
    A) relatives   B) familiars   C) neighbors   D) companies
63. The _____ outside the house said "No Parking".
    A) advice   B) single   C) label   D) notice
64. He has no _____ of winning.
    A) occasion   B) luck   C) opportunity   D) chance
65. Those people over there are speaking a language I don't understand. They must be _____.
    A) foreign   B) strange   C) rare   D) outlandish
66. I didn't write it. That is not my _____ on the cheque.
    A) mark   B) letter   C) firm   D) signature
67. The actors have to _____ before they appear in front of the strong lights on television.
    A) cover up   B) paint up   C) make up   D) do up
68. It is a difficult problem but we must find the answer _____.
    A) by one way or other   B) somehow or other
    C) anyhow or other   D) anyway or other
69. I want _____ immediately.
    A) That this work is made   B) this work made
    C) That this work is done   D) this work done
70. He's used to _____ in public.
    A) be speaking   B) the speaking
    C) speaking   D) speak
71. You can fly to London this evening _____ you don't mind changing planes in Paris.
    A) provided   B) except   C) unless   D) so far as
72. It's ages _____ him.
    A) that I don't see   B) that didn't see
    C) ago I saw   D) since I saw
73. He made me _____.
    A) angry   B) be angry
    C) to be angry   D) that I got angry

74. Do what you think is right, _____ they say.
    A) however   B) whatever   C) whichever   D) for all
75. He arrived late, _____ was annoying.
    A) what   B) that   C) which   D) the which
76. His job is _____ yours.
    A) the same that   B) as
    C) alike   D) similar to
77. He needs a _____.
    A) few days' rest   B) few days rest
    C) little days' rest   D) little days rest
78. Do you know _____ the repairs?
    A) to do   B) how to do   C) to make   D) how to make
79. We usually have fine weather _____ summer.
    A) at   B) on   C) in   D) while
80. My flat is _____ the third floor of the building.
    A) by   B) at   C) in   D) on
81. They live _____ the other side of the road.
    A) in   B) on   C) for   D) by
82. He isn't _____ to reach the ceiling.
    A) so tall   B) as tall   C) enough tall   D) tall enough
83. They treated him _____ a king when he won all that money.
    A) as   B) as being   C) like   D) like he was
84. I've told him several times but he _____ doesn't understand.
    A) yet   B) already   C) no longer   D) still
85. _____ did you go in the car this morning?
    A) How far   B) How much far
    C) How long   D) How much
86. He'd done that before, _____ ?
    A) wouldn't he   B) shouldn't he   C) hadn't he   D) didn't he
87. _____ of them understood him.
    A) None   B) No one   C) anyone   D) someone
88. It's _____ mountain in the world.
    A) the more high   B) the higher
    C) the highest   D) the most high
89. I'm going to a concert tomorrow evening. So _____.
    A) I am   B) am I   C) I will   D) will I
90. That's the firm _____.
    A) what we've been dealing with
    B) we've been dealing with
    C) We've been treating with
    D) what we've been treating with
91. She let the children _____ to play.
    A) going out   B) that they went out
    C) to go out   D) go out
92. It was _____ that he couldn't finish it alone.
    A) a so difficult work   B) a so difficult job
    C) such a difficult job   D) such a difficult work
93. I _____ photographs.
    A) enjoy taking   B) enjoy to take
    C) amuse taking   D) amuse to take
94. I _____ me what happened.
    A) would like you tell   B) would like you to tell
    C) would like you telling   D) would like that tell
95. _____ he wasn't hungry, he ate a big meal.
    A) Although   B) In spite   C) Unless   D) Even

In this series of questions, three words have the same sound but one does not. Choose one that does not.

96. A) cleared   B) feared   C) beard   D) heard
97. A) shoes   B) goes   C) blows   D) knows
98. A) wait   B) state   C) great   D) heat
99. A) among   B) wrong   C) rung   D) sung
100. A) broad   B) load   C) showed   D) road

ADVANCED TEST - 1

Choose the correct answer. Only one answer is correct.

I had been sitting __1__ in my usual compartment __2__ at least ten minutes, waiting __3__. The trains from Littlebury never seemed to start __4__ and I often thought that I could have __5__ in bed a little longer or had __6__ cup of tea before __7__ Suddenly I heart someone shouting __8__ the platform outside. A young girl was running towards the train. The man __9__ put out his hand to stop her but she run past him and opened the door of my compartment. Then the whistle blew and the train started.

"I nearly missed it, __10__?" the girl said. "How long does it take to __11__ London?"

"It depends on the __12__" I said. "Some days it's __13__ others."
"I'll have to __14__, __15__ late again tomorrow," she said. "It's my first day __16__ with a new firm today and they told me that the man __17__ is very strict. I __18__ him yet so I don't know __19__ but he sounds a bit frightening.

She talked about her new job __20__ the way to London and before long, I realized that she was going to work for my firm. My __21__ secretary had just left so I must be her new boss __22__ only fair to tell her.

"Oh, dear," she said." __23__ mistake! I wish I __24__"

"Never mind," I said. "At least you'll know when your train's late that __25__"

1. A) for myself   B) only myself   C) by myself   D) in my own
2. A) for   B) during   C) since   D) meanwhile
3. A) the train to start   B) for the train start
   C) the train's start   D) for the train to start
4. A) on their hour   B) on time
   C) at their hour   D) at time
5. A) lain   B) laid   C) lied   D) lay
6. A) other   B) some other   C) another   D) one other
7. A) I had left the home   B) leave from home
   C) leaving home   D) to leave home
8. A) at   B) by   C) in   D) on
9. A) at place   B) on duty   C) for control   D) in post
10. A) haven't I   B) don't I   C) wasn't I   D) didn't I
11. A) get to   B) arrive to   C) reach to   D) make to
12. A) driver to the engine   B) driver engine
    C) engine's driver   D) engine driver
13. A) far slower that   B) much slower than
    C) a lot more slow than   D) a great deal more slow than
14. A) mend me the watch   B) mend me my watch
    C) have my watch mended   D) have mended my watch
15. A) in order not are   B) so as not to be
    C) for not being   D) so that it's not
16. A) at job   B) in job   C) in work   D) at work
17. A) I'm going to work for   B) what I'm going to work for
    C) for which I'm going to work   D) which I'm going to work
18. A) didn't meet   B) haven't met
    C) didn't know   D) haven't known
19. A) what he is like   B) what is he like
    C) how he is   D) how is he
20. A) through   B) by   C) on   D) in
21. A) proper   B) own   C) same   D) self
22. A) There was   B) That was   C) It was   D) Was
23. A) What a terrible   B) What terrible
    C) How terrible   D) So terrible a
24. A) had known   B) have known
    C) knew   D) would have known
25. A) so will the mine be   B) the mine will be, too
    C) So will mine   D) mine will be, too

Hello, Mary! I __26__ you before now but I __27__ so hard at the office that I didn't have time. My boss __28__ to holiday tomorrow and he __29__ arrange everything before he __30__ If he had given me sensible instruction I could have done the work next week. But you __31__ the same problems with your boss. Anyway, __32__ two tickets for the new play at the Grand Theatre on Saturday __33__ and see it together?

26. A) should have rung   B) must have rung
    C) had to ring   D) ought to ring
27. A) must work   B) must have worked
    C) have had to work   D) ought to work
28. A) will go   B) is going
    C) shall go   D) shall be going
29. A) wants that I   B) would that I
    C) would like that I   D) wants me to
30. A) leaves   B) shall leave   C) will leave   D) is leaving
31. A) have to have   B) can have
    C) ought to have   D) must have
32. A) they have been given to me   B) I have been given
    C) I am given   D) they are given to me
33. A) May we go   B) Do you like to go
    C) Shall we go   D) Will we go
34. The lift is out of _____ so we'll have to walk.
    A) function   B) order   C) running   D) work
35. Dinner will be ready _____ but we have time for a drink before than.
    A) currently   B) lately   C) presently   D) suddenly
36. What do you _____ to do about the problem now that this solution has failed.
    A) attempt   B) think   C) pretend   D) intend
37. We have _____ for a new secretary but we haven't had any replies yet.
    A) advertised   B) advised   C) announced   D) noticed
38. I've _____ for the job and I hope I get it.
    A) appointed   B) applied   C) presented   D) succeeded
39. He threw the box out of the window and it fell to the _____ outside.
    A) flat   B) floor   C) plain   D) ground
40. 100 competitors had _____ the race.
    A) put their names for   B) entered for
    C) put themselves for   D) taken part
41. I'm very _____ to you for your help.
    A) grateful   B) agreeable   C) pleased   D) thanks
42. He's so mean that he wouldn't give a beggar a _____ of bread.
    A) peel   B) shell   C) crust   D) skin
43. Will you be able to come to the party? I _____ .
    A) believe yes   B) am afraid not
    C) don't hope so   D) don't expect
44. I never expected you to turn _____ at the meeting. I thought you were abroad.
    A) A round   B) on   C) in   D) up
45. The plane is just going to take _____.
    A) away   B) out   C) off   D) up

In this series of questions, three words have the same sound but one does not. Choose one that does not.

46. A) knees   B) peace   C) freeze   D) keys
47. A) home   B) sum   C) crumb   D) come
48. A) straighter   B) greater   C) water   D) later
49. A) ache   B) shake   C) steak   D) weak
50. A) another   B) bother   C) brother   D) mother

I __51__ don't believe in ghosts __52__ my experience at the Rose Inn. __53__ I have never seen one. But ghost stories have made me __54__ uncomfortable since then I __55__ the inn late at night and asked __56__.

"There's nothing left," he said, "__57__ to sleep in Number 7."

"Why not?" I said. "What's wrong with it?", I was so tired that I would have slept __58__.

"Nothing," he said slowly. " but something happened there a few months ago."

Every old inn has __59__ strange stories, so I thought that __60__ he told me about it, the better. I was willing to listen to anything for __61__ a bed to sleep in.

"A man came here late at night, __62__ you," the landlord said. "I thought there was something odd __63__ him because he kept looking __64__ his shoulder while he was signing his name in the book. He asked me __65__ have and I offered __66__." "__67__ a man who has said he'll kill me," he said suddenly. "With a knife." He looked __68__ that I thought I had better __69__ him to his room. I locked the door and left him __70__. The next day we __71__ him dead, with a knife beside him. He had __72__," the landlord said. "or someone else had done it. Do you mind sleeping there now you know the story?". "Well," I said. "__73__ is following me. But I wish you __74__ the story in morning __75__ I'll sleep here on the bar if you've got a couple of blankets."

51. A) Already   B) Yet   C) no longer   D) still
52. A) Even though   B) even after   C) although   D) in spite
53. A) At least   B) At last   C) At first   D) At once
54. A) To feel   B) feel myself   C) feel   D) that I feel
55. A) arrived to   B) arrived at   C) reached to   D) reached at
56. A) room of the landlord   B) room from the landlod
    C) the landlord a room   D) the landlord for a room
57. A) If you didn't like   B) If you don't like
    C) Unless you are liking   D) Unless you'd like
58. A) anywhere   B) somewhere
    C) nowhere   D) in whatever place
59. A) his   B) its   C) their   D) the
60. A) so soon as   B) as soon as   C) the soonest   D) the sooner
61. A) the sake of   B) the lack of   C) the need of   D) the wish of
62. A) as   B) like   C) the same that   D) similar with
63. A) with   B) of   C) about   D) around
64. A) through   B) back   C) over   D) after
65. A) what room could he   B) what room he may
    C) which room could he   D) which room he could
66. A) to him the number 7   B) to him number 7
    C) him number 7   D) him the number 7
67. A) It's   B) There's   C) That's   D) He's
68. A) to be so frightened   B) so frightened
    C) with such fright   D) with such fright
69. A) to bring   B) to take   C) bring   D) take
70. A) by himself   B) by his self   C) only himself   D) in his own
71. A) met   B) knew   C) found   D) uncovered
72. A) cut himself the throat   B) himself cut the throat
    C) his throat cut   D) cut his throat
73. A) None   B) No one   C) Anyone   D) Any one
74. A) told me   B) had told me
    C) would tell me   D) would have told me
75. A) As it is   B) Like it is
    C) Being like that   D) Being as that

"Darling! There's hardly any petrol left in the tank. I __76__ it up before we left home. __77__ a garage quite near but I __78__ drive carefully until we __79__ there. If only I __80__ the petrol before we started out! Damn! I __81__ this to happen for the last ten minutes. I'll have to push the car to the side of the road because we __82__ if we leave it here. But I can't imagine what __83__ to let this happen.

76. A) must have filled   B) should have filled
    C) would have filled   D) had to fill
77. A) There may be   B) It may be
    C) There can be   D) It can be
78. A) like better   B) would better
    C) had better   D) prefer
79. A) shall get   B) will get
    C) are getting   D) get
80. A) checked   B) would have checking
    C) had checked   D) have checked
81. A) am expecting   B) expect
    C) have been expecting   D) was expecting
82. A) will be fined   B) will fine
    C) will be being fined   D) will be fining
83. A) was I thinking about   B) I was thinking about
    C) did I think about   D) I thought about
84. He _____ me by two games to one
    A) beat   B) conquered   C) gained   D) won
85. His office is on the third _____ of the building.
    A) floor   B) flat   C) ground   D) level
86. How long are you thinking of _____ in this country?
    A) reminding   B) staying   C) resting   D) inhabiting
87. I don't want to go into the sea. I'd rather lie on the _____.
    A) coast   B) beach   C) bank   D) seaside
88. I'm _____. I didn't pass the examination but I'll do better next time.
    A) deceived   B) despaired   C) disillusioned   D) disappointed
89. The lecture was so _____ that everyone went to sleep.
    A) boring   B) bored   C) tiring   D) tired
90. I _____ an answer to my letter within a few days.
    A) hope   B) wait   C) look forward   D) expect
91. When he _____ he wants to be an architect.
    A) ages   B) grows   C) grows up   D) increases
92. It's on the top shelf, out of _____.
    A) distance   B) reach   C) touch   D) attempt
93. He's worked so _____ that he deserves a rest.
    A) roughly   B) intensive   C) hardly   D) hard
94. They're staying with us _____ the time being until they find a place of their own.
    A) during   B) in   C) since   D) for
95. Ill call _____ you at 8.30 and give you a lift to work.
    A) in   B) for   C) at   D) up

h this series of qestions, three words have the same sound but one does not. Choose one that does not.

96. A) blood   B) stood   C) flood   D) mud
97. A) word   B) third   C) stirred   D) lord
98. A) war   B) bar   C) far   D) star
99. A) eyes   B) prize   C) lies   D) buys
100. A) build   B) mild   C) wild   D) child

ADVANCED TEST - 2

Choose the correct answer. Only one answer is correct.

I can clearly remember the first time I __1__ Mr. Andrews, my old headmaster, __2__ __3__. During the war, I had been __4__ school in the north of England but my family had just returned to London. __5__ for children to go to and my father had to go from __6__ asking them __7__ __8__ pupil. I used to go with him but he had __9__ hard time trying to persuade people __10__ him that I seldom had to do __11__. We had been to all the schools __12__ we lived, but __13__ my father argued, the more impossible it became. In the end, we went to a school __14__ from home. The headmaster __15__ for at least an hour. While we were waiting, I looked round that the __16__, __17__ was one of those old Victorian structures, completely __18__ but still standing. I could hear the boys playing in the playground outside. When the headmaster's secretary finally let us __19__ his office, Mr. Andrews spoke to me first. "Why do you want to come here?" he said. I had been thinking __20__ something about studying but I couldn't help __21__ the boys outside. "I don't know __22__ in London," I said." I'd like __23__ with the other boys. I read a lot of books, too" I added. "All right," Mr. Andrews said. "We have one place free, __24__"

My two years at that school were among the __25__ of my life.

1. A) met   B) knew   C) found   D) discovered
2. A) even   B) nevertheless C) although   D) in spite
3. A) it's now since over 20 years
   B) it's over 20 years ago now
   C) it's since more than 20 years now
   D) it makes more than 20 years now
4. A) in the   B) in   C) at   D) at the
5. A) There were not enough schools left
   B) There were not still enough schools
   C) There didn't stay enough schools
   D) Not enough schools rested
6. A) one to another   B) each to other
   C) one to other   D) the ones to the others
7. A) that they took me   B) for taking me
   C) for to take me   D) to take me
8. A) as   B) as a   C) like   D) like a
9. A) such   B) such a   C) so   D) a so
10. A) just for seeing   B) just for to see
    C) even seeing   D) even to see
11. A) no test   C) any test   B) one test   D) some test
12. A) near where   B) near
    C) near to   D) near the place there
13. A) the most   B) the more
    C) how much   D) for how much
14. A) at five miles   B) five miles long
    C) about five miles away D) about five miles far
15. A) kept us to wait   B) kept us waiting
    C) made us to waiting   D) made us waiting
16. A) building of the school B) building school
    C) school's building   D) school building
17. A) which   B) that   C) what   D) it
18. A) of the old time   B) outside its time
    C) past its date   D) out of date
19. A) to enter B) to pass in C) to come into D) into
20. A) of saying B) to say   C) of telling   D) to tell
21. A) to remember   B) remembering
    C) to remind   D) reminding
22. A) no one   B) none   C) someone   D) anyone
23. A) that I played B) the play C) to play   D) playing
24. A) in truth B) it's the truth C) in fact D) it's fact
25. A) happier   B) happiest   C) more happy   D) most happy

"Excuse me, Mrs. Jones. Would you mind __26__ me a favor? I __27__ shopping. But as soon as I shut my front door I realized I had left my key in the house. So when I __28__ back I __29__ get in. It was very silly of me. I __30__ at all because all the groceries __31__ I only wanted some mustard. __32__ come in and climb over the fence into my back garden? That is very kind of you. I wish I __33__ give you so much trouble."

26. A) making   B) doing   C) to make   D) to do
27. A) have just been   B) have just gone
    C) would just go   D) was just going
28. A) get   B) am getting
    C) shall get   D) will get
29. A) can't   B) won't be able to
    C) haven't been able to   D) couldn't
30. A) needn't have come out B) didn't need to come out
    C) mustn't have come out D) hadn't to come out
31. A) have already been delivered B) already have delivered
    C) are being delivered already D) already are being delivered
32. A) Shall I   B) Will I
    C) May I   D) Do you want me to
33. A) don't have to   B) haven't to
    C) hadn't to   D) didn't have to

Choose the correct answer. Only one answer is correct.

34. Would you _____ holding this box for me while I open the door?
    A) like   B) matter   C) mind   D) object
35. He is _____ dark glasses to protect his eyes from the sun.
    A) carrying B) fitting   C) bearing   D) wearing
36. He has told to get off the bus because he couldn't pay the _____.
    A) bill   B) journey   C) travel   D) fare
37. They have put the bird in a cage to _____ it from flying away.
    A) avoid   B) prevent   C) hinder   D) resist
38. He has some very _____ habits. He always has a bath with his clothes on.
    A) strange   B) rare   C) uneven   D) foreign
39. The _____ outside the house said "Private".
    A) advice   B) label   C) notice   D) signal
40. If the boss sees you doing that, you'll get into _____.
    A) trouble   B) nuisance   C) mess   D) problem
41. I was so _____ by the news that I don't know what to say.
    A) admired   B) marveled   C) amazed   D) wondered
42. He's _____ because he has won the prize.
    A) nervous   B) satisfying C) excited   D) exciting
43. He likes lying in bed. He still wasn't _____ when I rang him at 10 o'clock.
    A) out   B) away   C) up   D) in
44. If you don't know how to spell a word, look it _____ in the dictionary.
    A) up   B) after   C) out   D) for
45. He carries _____ as if he were the boss.
    A) through   B) off   C) out   D) on

In this series of questions, three words have the same sound but one does not. Choose one that does not.

46. A) dull   B) bull   C) wool   D) pull
47. A) earth   B) birth   C) worth   D) north
48. A) done   B) none   C) won   D) son
49. A) warn   B) dawn   C) scorn   D) barn
50. A) wise   B) cries   C) rice   D) sighs

We arrived __51__ Spain for the first time __52__. And I decided to buy a car because we had sold __53__ we had in England before leaving. Yesterday the office rang us __54__ the car was ready. I had tried out a model __55__ it before but as I was __56__ in this city, my wife didn't __57__ it on my own so we went together to __58__. We paid __59__ and signed the papers. They told us that __60__ us to a garage, __61__ we could fill up. The __62__ the office was __63__ and we got there safely. But when I turned into the main road I suddenly saw a lot of cars racing towards me. I got __64__ __65__ by backing into the garage __66__ and the man behind me shouted at me. "__67__ problem to __68__ on the right, isn't it?" my wife said. "Yes, if only I __69__ a few lessons for practice" I replied. "You __70__ go carefully __71__ home," my wife said. "You'd be sorry if you had an accident __72__ the first day, __73__ "Would you __74__ me when you are thinking of leaving? Or are you going to sit in your car __75__ day?"

51. A) to B) in C) at D) on
52. A) few weeks since B) since a few weeks
    C) few weeks ago D) a few weeks ago
53. A) that B) which C) the one D) the one what
54. A) for saying B) to say C) for telling D) to tell
55. A) as B) like C) the same that D) similar
56. A) no longer used to driving B) still not used to drive
    C) not yet used to driving D) already not used to drive
57. A) want me to collect B) like me to collect
    C) want that I collected D) like that I collected
58. A) bring it B) take it C) fetch it D) carry it away
59. A) the car B) the car for
    C) for the car D) how much the car
60. A) there was enough petrol to take
    B) there was enough petrol for taking
    C) it was enough petrol to take
    D) it was enough petrol for taking
61. A) where at B) there C) there where D) where
62. A) nearest garage at B) nearest garage to
    C) garage most near D) most near garage to
63. A) at 100 yards away B) at 100 yards far
    C) about 100 yards away D) about 100 yards far
64. A) away from their way B) away from their road
    C) out of their way D) out their road
65. A) as far as I could B) so fast as I could
    C) as fast s I may D) so fast as I may
66. A) once more B) one more time
    C) one other time D) another time
67. A) It's so much B) It's such a
    C) That's such a D) That's so much a
68. A) remind to drive B) remind driving
    C) remember to drive D) remember driving
69. A) would have B) would have had
    C) was having D) had had
70. A) had better B) would better
    C) had rather D) would better
71. A) in the way to B) on the way to
    C) in the way D) on the way
72. A) in B) on C) at D) by
73. A) hadn't you? B) shouldn't you
    C) wouldn't you? D) won't you?
74. A) mind to tell B) object telling
    C) mind telling D) upset to tell
75. A) every B) each C) all the D) all

" I wonder why __76__ yet. I told Jim how to get here but perhaps I __77__ a map. The traffic __78__ them, of course. But I'm sure they would have telephoned us if they __79__ lost."
"Yes, but by the time they __80__ here , the dinner __81__. What a nuisance! I __82__ to all this trouble. __83__ getting everything ready."

76. A) they didn't arrive B) didn't they arrive
    C) they haven't arrived D) haven't they arrived
77. A) should have given him B) had to give him
    C) ought to give him D) must have given him
78. A) can delay B) may delay
    C) can have delayed D) may have delayed
79. A) would get B) had got
    C) would have got D) would be got
80. A) will get B) would get C) get D) are getting
81. A) has been spoilt B) will be spoilt
    C) shall be spoilt D) is spilt
82. A) needn't have gone B) didn't need to go
    C) mustn't have gone D) hadn't to go
83. A) I am working for hours B) I have been working for hours
    C) It's hours I'm working D) It's hours I've been working

Choose the correct Aswer. Oly one answer is correct.

84. He was killed in a car _____.
    A) blow B) crash C) shock D) hit
85. All the hotel in the town was full up so we stayed in a _____ village.
    A) close B) neighbor C) near D) nearby
86. He won the first _____ in the competition.
    A) prize B) price C) reward D) premium
87. Sixty per cent of television viewers chose him as their _____ actor.
    A) popular B) preferred C) favorite D) favored
88. We've been _____ with that firm for many years.
    A) treating B) making business
    C) dealing D) supplying
89. I cant give you an answer yet. I'd like _____ more time to consider my decision.
    A) quite B) fairly C) hardly D) rather
90. I learnt to _____ a bicycle when I was six years old.
    A) drive B) ride C) guide D) conduct
91. The lady who had invited us heard me telling my wife that the dinner was terrible so I was _____.
    A) confused B) nervous C) shameful D) embarrassed
92. Sometimes a bus _____ gets on the bus and checks the tickets.
    A) inspector B) agent C) conductor D) officer
93. Where do you _____ the writing paper? In this desk.
    A) keep B) hold C) maintain D) guard
94. PTO stands _____ "Please turn over"– the page, of course.
    A) as B) like C) for D) by
95. He'll soon get _____ his disappointment and be quite cheerful again by the morning.
    A) over B) out of C) away D) through

h this series of qestions,three words have the same sound but one does not. Choose one that does not.

96. A) case B) phrase C) base D) lace
97. A) eight B) height C) weight D) freight
98. A) wrong B) young C) sung D) tongue
99. A) lower B) shower C) tower D) power
100. A) sound B) ground C) drowned D) owned

ADVANCED TEST - 3

Choose correct answer. Only one answer is correct.

One crossing of the Atlantic is very much like __1__; and people who cross it frequently do not __2__ for the __3__ of its interest. Most of us are quite happy when we feel __4__ to go to bed and pleased when the journey __5__. On the first night this time I felt especially lazy and went to bed __6__ earlier than usual. When I __7__ my cabin, I was surprised __8__ that I __9__ a companion during my trip. I had expected __10__ but there was a suitcase __11__ mine in the opposite corner. I wondered who __12__. Soon afterward he came in. He was the sort of man you might meet __13__, except that he was wearing __14__ good clothes that I made up my mind that we would not __15__, __16__, and did not say __17__.

I suppose I slept for several hours because when I woke up it was the middle of the night. I felt cold but covered __18__ __19__ and tried to __20__. Then I realized that a draught was coming from somewhere. I got up __21__ the door but found it already locked from the inside. The cold air was coming from the window opposite. I crossed the room and __22__ the moon shone through it on to the other bed. __23__ there. It took me a minute or two to __24__ the door myself. I realized that my companion __25__ through the window into the sea.

1. A) other B) the other C) another D) one other
2. A) make the travel B) make the voyage C) do the travel D) do the voyage
3. A) reason B) motive C) cause D) sake
4. A) tired enough B) enough tired C) ourselves tired enough D) our selves enough tired
5. A) is achieved B) finish C) is over D) is in the end
6. A) quite B) rather C) fairly D) somehow
7. A) arrived in B) reached to C) arrived to D) reached at
8. A) for seeing B) that I saw C) at seeing D) to see
9. A) am to have B) should have had C) would have D) ought to have
10. A) being lonely B) to be lonely C) being alone D) to be alone
11. A) like B) as C) similar than D) the same that
12. A) could he be and how he would be
    B) he could be and what he would be like
    C) could he be and what would he be like
    D) he could be and he would be
13. A) in each place B) for all parts C) somewhere D) anywhere
14. A) a so B) so C) such a D) such
15. A) treat together well B) pass together well C) get on well together D) go by well together
16. A) whoever he was B) whoever was he C) however he was D) however was he
17. A) him a single word B) him not one word C) a single word to him D) not one word to
18. A) up me B) up myself C) up to myself D) myself up
19. A) so well as I could B) as well as I could C) so well that I might D) as well that I might
20. A) go back to sleep B) go back to sleeping C) put myself to sleep again D) put myself for sleeping again
21. A) to shut B) for shutting C) in order that I shut D) so as for shutting
22. A) while doing like that B) as I did like that C) as I did so D) at doing so
23. A) It was no one B) There was no one C) It any one D) There was any one
24. A) remind to lock B) remember to lock C) remind locking D) remember locking
25. A) had to jump B) was to have jumped C) must have jumped D) could be jumped

"__26__ I ask the waiter for the bill, darling, when you __27__ your coffee?"
"Yes I think you __28__. I __29__ this film for such a long time that I __30__ any of it."
"Waiter! The bill, please. Oh dear, I haven't got my wallet. I __31__ it in my other jacket. I wish I __32__ it before we came out."
"Good heaven! Now I suppose they'll make us __33__"

26. A) Shall B) Will C) Am I going D) Ought
27. A) will finish B) shall finish C) will have finish D) have finished
28. A) had rather B) would rather C) had better D) would better
29. A) am looking forward to seeing
    B) am looking forward to see
    C) have been looking forward to seeing
    D) have been looking forward to see
30. A) wouldn't like that we miss
    B) wouldn't like to miss
    C) wouldn't miss
    D) wouldn't like that we missed
31. A) must have left B) had to leave C) should have left D) ought have left
32. A) would check B) have checked C) would have checked D) had checked
33. A) to wash up B) wash up C) washing up D) the washing up
34. He _____ out of the window for a moment and then went on working.
    A) glanced B) viewed C) glimpsed D) regarded
35. It's the _____ in this country to go out and pick flower on the first day of spring.
    A) use B) custom C) habit D) normal
36. He made a swift _____ from his illness.
    A) repair B) survival C) relief D) recovery
37. It gave me a strange feeling of excitement to see my name in _____.
    A) news B) print C) publication D) press
38. You'd better add it up. I am no good at _____.
    A) counters B) characters C) summaries D) figures
39. Our main concern is to raise the voters' _____ of living.
    A) standard B) capacity C) degree D) condition
40. I'd like to take _____ of this opportunity to thank you all for your cooperation.
    A) profit B) benefit C) advantage D) occasion
41. He _____ to hit me if I didn't do as he said.
    A) pretended B) thought C) threatened D) warned
42. He does not feel like playing tennis because he's _____.
    A) out of condition B) off condition C) off fitness D) out of fitness
43. He's been working too hard and he's _____. He needs a rest.
    A) broken apart B) broken up C) run down D) run over
44. We went to the station to _____.
    A) see them out B) see them off C) goodbye them D) say them goodbye
45. New problems are always _____ in the factory.
    A) raising B) going up C) waking up D) coming up

In this series of questions, three words have the same sound but one does not. Choose the one that does not.

46. A) spear B) wear C) dare D) prayer
47. A) spread B) tread C) bread D) bead
48. A) blow B) allow C) owe D) sew
49. A) goose B) prose C) flows D) knows
50. A) crime B) limb C) climb D) rhyme

The news did not come directly to Ella herself __51__ her indirectly in hints that she had won the prize. But as she was a calm, quiet girl, she __52__ without __53__, __54__ the whole school was full of rumors and statements from students who had no right to be __55__ at all because __56__ really knew __57__ what result of this year's art competition was.

But Ella was __58__ good artist, her lines so sure that __59__ student in the art class was expected to win. But you never __60__. Last year nobody had expected Frank Peters to win with the funny modern painting he had __61__ the city bridge. __62__, it was hard to __63__ the bridge until you looked at the picture for a long time. Still, Frank had got the prize and the President of the Board of Governors had presented __64__ at a big dinner in the Ritz Hotel.

Ella was a rather shy girl but her classmates seldom thought of her __65__ shy. She was pretty and intelligent and __66__ very well with everyone. She played games well, had taken part in the school play, and never seemed to __67__, except in pleasant ways. She liked her school. She was very fond of her art teacher, Miss Drake, __68__ was natural. __69__ wonderful about Miss Drake was that she brought out the best in her students-not __70__ but theirs. __71__ best, __72__, was not good enough to please Miss Drake. So Ella was __73__ the prize, not just for herself and her parents but because she had heard Miss Drake __74__ that it was the __75__ seen from one of her students.

51. A) It reached B) They reached
    C) It arrived at D) They arrived wt
52. A) went on to work B) went on working
    C) went back for working D) went back working
53. A) telling nothing B) telling anything
    C) saying nothing D) saying anything
54. A) in spite B) nevertheless
    C) although D) however
55. A) doing advertisements B) making advertisement
    C) doing announcements D) making announcements
56. A) no one B) some one C) anyone D) not anyone
57. A) still B) already C) yet D) any lounger
58. A) such a B) such C) a so D) so
59. A) not another B) no one other
    C) no other D) none other
60. A) might know B) could be sure
    C) can learn D) may be secure
61. A) done for B) made about C) done of D) made on
62. A) In the reality B) To say truth C) Surely D) In fact
63. A) pick up B) see through C) take hold of D) make out
64. A) him it B) it to him C) it him D) him for it
65. A) as B) like C) to be D) for
66. A) got on B) got by C) passed D) carried
67. A) distinguish B) stand off C) stand out D) stand up
68. A) which B) what C) where D) whose
69. A) The thing what was B) What was
    C) The D) The which was
70. A) her best herself B) her best self
    C) her own best D) her proper best
71. A) Other person's B) Other peoples'
    C) Anybody's else D) Anybody else's
72. A) for how good it might be B) for how good might it be
    C) however good it was D) however good was it
73. A) looking forward to win B) looking forward to winning
    C) wishing to win D) waiting for winning
74. A) say B) tell C) to say D) to tell
75. A) better painting she ever had B) best painting she ever had
    C) better painting she had ever D) best painting she had ever

"I have been looking for this office since I arrived at the station. It __76__ be in the main street. I __77__ me a hotel, please."

"Certainly, sir. But you __78__ so far. If you'd turned left at the station, you __79__ it straightaway. Now, __80__ see if we can find you something suitable?"

"I only want a room for one night but I can not stand sleeping in noisy rooms."

"All the hotels here are near the main road. You __81__ come home with me, sir. You'll be more comfortable. In fact, when you __82__ my wife's cooking, you'll realize you __83__ have come to a better place."

76. A) should B) has to C) ought D) must have
77. A) would like finding B) would like you to find
    C) would like that you find D) am wanting you to find
78. A) did not need to walk B) needn't have walked
    C) must not have walked D) were not to walk
79. A) would have found B) had found
    C) should have found D) would find
80. A) let's to B) are we going to
    C) will we D) shall we
81. A) had better B) would better
    C) had rather D) would rather
82. A) will be tasting B) shall taste
    C) taste D) will taste
83. A) can not B) might C) may not D) couldn't
84. She chose some very pretty _____ paper for the present.
    A) covering B) involving C) packing D) wrapping
85. Everyone else was killed in the accident. I was the only one to _____.
    A) relive B) survive C) alive D) outlive
86. That's a nice dress. It _____ you perfectly.
    A) suits B) costumes C) matches D) goes
87. The _____ stuck on the outside of the envelope said "By Air".
    A) label B) ticked
    C) signal D) advertisement
88. She died after a long _____.
    A) disease B) sickness C) illness D) failing
89. I _____ to inform you that there's nothing we can do to help you.
    A) sorry B) respect C) resent D) regret
90. I'll put the flowers in this _____ They'll look nice there.
    A) mug B) vase C) crystal D) bucked
91. _____ I didn't understand the job but now I'm making progress.
    A) On the beginning B) At first
    C) For a start D) In principle
92. Would you mind paying for the tickets _____?
    A) in advance B) forward C) primarily D) now and then
93. How long did it take you to realize he was dishonest? I _____ from the start.
    A) looked him through B) saw through him
    C) looked forward to him D) saw him through
94. We're going to have our house _____. The decorators are coming next week.
    A) done up B) done in
    C) made over D) made away with
95. He asked me what was _____ in the street outside.
    A) succeeding B) making out
    C) doing up D) going on

h this series of qestions, three words have the same sound but one does not. Choose the one that does not.

96. A) freeze B) ease C) seize D) lease
97. A) weight B) great C) wheat D) freight
98. A) palm B) calm C) warm D) harm
99. A) hint B) mint C) print D) pint
100. A) stuff B) cough C) rough D) enough

ANSWER KEY

BOOK 1 - PART A

ELEMENTARY Test: 1 (Page 2)

1-A	2-B	3-C	4-C	5-A	6-C	7-D	8-A
9-A	10-C	11-D	12-C	13-A	14-C	15-A	16-C
17-D	18-C	19-C	20-B	21-C	22-C	23-C	24-C
25-C	26-C	27-C	28-C	29-C	30-C	31-A	32-B
33-C	34-D	35-B	36-A	37-B	38-A	39-B	40-B
41-A	42-B	43-A	44-A				

ELEMENTARY Test: 2 (Page 3)

1-D	2-B	3-B	4-A	5-C	6-B	7-A	8-C
9-C	10-A	11-B	12-D	13-B	14-B	15-C	16-C
17-A	18-C	19-A	20-C	21-C	22-A	23-C	24-C
25-B	26-C	27-B	28-C	29-D	30-C	31-A	32-C
33-A	34-B	35-A	36-B	37-D	38-C	39-B	40-C
41-C	42-D	43-A	44-C	45-B	46-A	47-A	48-D
49-D	50-B	51-A	52-C	53-B	54-D	55-D	56-A
57-A							

ELEMENTARY Test: 3 (Page 4)

1-D	2-B	3-A	4-C	5-C	6-A	7-C	8-C
9-A	10-C	11-B	12-C	13-D	14-B	15-D	16-A
17-D	18-D	19-A	20-B	21-C	22-B	23-C	24-A
25-C	26-D	27-B	28-B	29-B	30-B	31-C	32-B
33-A	34-C	35-C	36-A	37-A	38-C	39-B	40-C
41-A	42-A	43-D	44-D	45-B	46-B	47-D	48-B
49-C	50-B	51-A	52-C	53-B	54-C	55-A	56-A
57-D	58-C	59-C	60-D				

ELEMENTARY Test: 4 (Page 6)

1-D	2-A	3-B	4-D	5-C	6-B	7-C	8-A
9-B	10-C	11-D	12-C	13-C	14-A	15-A	16-D
17-A	18-B	19-C	20-C	21-C	22-A	23-C	24-C
25-D	26-B	27-B	28-D	29-B	30-C	31-A	32-C
33-A	34-B	35-B	36-B	37-B	38-A	39-C	40-B
41-B	42-B	43-B	44-C	45-A	46-C	47-D	48-B
49-A	50-B	51-C	52-B	53-A	54-D	55-B	56-B
57-C	58-A	59-A	60-C	61-A	62-B	63-B	64-C
65-A	66-D	67-B	68-C	69-B	70-A	71-A	72-A
73-A	74-C	75-B	76-C	77-A	78-D	79-A	80-A
81-A	82-B	83-B	84-C				

ELEMENTARY Test: 5 (Page 8)

1-C	2-A	3-B	4-D	5-A	6-C	7-A	8-C
9-D	10-A	11-C	12-D	13-A	14-C	15-B	16-D
17-A	18-C	19-C	20-B	21-C	22-A	23-C	24-B
25-C	26-C	27-A	28-A	29-B	30-C	31-B	32-A
33-C	34-B	35-D	36-B	37-B	38-A	39-B	40-B
41-C	42-B	43-A	44-C	45-A	46-D	47-B	48-A
49-C	50-A	51-B	52-C	53-A	54-B	55-A	56-A
57-C							

ELEMENTARY Test: 6 (Page 9)

1-B	2-D	3-A	4-C	5-A	6-D	7-C	8-B
9-A	10-B	11-D	12-A	13-C	14-B	15-D	16-A
17-B	18-C	19-D	20-B	21-B	22-A	23-B	24-B
25-C	26-D	27-B	28-B	29-A	30-B	31-A	32-B
33-B	34-D	35-C	36-A	37-C	38-B	39-C	40-A
41-B	42-B	43-B	44-B	45-C	46-B	47-A	48-C
49-A	50-D	51-B	52-B	53-C	54-C	55-C	56-A
57-B	58-B	59-A	60-C	61-B	62-A	63-A	64-A
65-C	66-B	67-C	68-B	69-B	70-C	71-B	72-B
73-C	74-A	75-C	76-A	77-B			

ELEMENTARY Test: 7 (Page 11)

1-A	2-C	3-B	4-D	5-A	6-C	7-B	8-C
9-A	10-B	11-A	12-D	13-B	14-C	15-A	16-D
17-A	18-C	19-B	20-A	21-B	22-A	23-C	24-B
25-B	26-C	27-A	28-C	29-A	30-C	31-C	32-A
33-C	34-B	35-C	36-C	37-C	38-C	39-A	40-C
41-C	42-D	43-A	44-C	45-A	46-C	47-C	48-C
49-D	50-D	51-A	52-C	53-D	54-C	55-D	56-A
57-A	58-B						

ELEMENTARY Test: 8 (Page 13)

1-A	2-A	3-B	4-D	5-A	6-C	7-B	8-D
9-B	10-D	11-A	12-B	13-B	14-B	15-B	16-D
17-A	18-B	19-C	20-B	21-A	22-B	23-C	24-A
25-B	26-C	27-A	28-C	29-A	30-C	31-B	32-A
33-A	34-B	35-C	36-D	37-D	38-D	39-C	40-A
41-C	42-A	43-B	44-B	45-C	46-B	47-A	48-B
49-D	50-A	51-B	52-D	53-C	54-A	55-B	56-C
57-A	58-B	59-B	60-A	61-C	62-D	63-A	64-C
65-D	66-A	67-D	68-A	69-C	70-B	71-D	72-A
73-B	74-C	75-A	76-D	77-A	78-C	79-A	80-D
81-A	82-C	83-C	84-B	85-D	86-B	87-C	88-B
89-A	90-A	91-B	92-A	93-D	94-D	95-A	96-C
97-C	98-B	99-A	100-A				

ELEMENTARY Test: 9 (Page 15)

1-B	2-C	3-A	4-C	5-A	6-B	7-C	8-B
9-B	10-B	11-C	12-A	13-B	14-B	15-D	16-B
17-A	18-D	19-D	20-B	21-C	22-D	23-B	24-B
25-C	26-C	27-B	28-A	29-A	30-B	31-D	32-A
33-B	34-D	35-D	36-C	37-D	38-B	39-A	40-D
41-A	42-C	43-A	44-D	45-A	46-C	47-B	48-D
49-D	50-D	51-A	52-A	53-B	54-D	55-D	56-C
57-B	58-D	59-A	60-A	61-B	62-B	63-C	64-A
65-D	66-B	67-B	68-C	69-A	70-A	71-B	72-C
73-D	74-B	75-A	76-C	77-B	78-B	79-C	80-A

ELEMENTARY Test: 10 (Page 16)

1-C	2-B	3-A	4-A	5-C	6-D	7-D	8-C
9-A	10-D	11-B	12-C	13-C	14-C	15-C	16-C
17-B	18-A	19-A	20-A	21-D	22-C	23-C	24-C
25-B	26-B	27-B	28-C	29-C	30-D	31-C	32-C
33-A	34-A	35-C	36-B	37-A	38-C	39-A	40-B
41-A	42-C	43-B	44-D	45-B	46-B	47-C	48-D
49-A	50-B	51-B	52-A	53-C	54-D	55-A	56-B
57-A	58-D	59-B	60-C	61-B	62-C	63-C	64-A
65-B	66-C						

ELEMENTARY Test: 11 (Page 18)

1-C	2-A	3-C	4-D	5-A	6-A	7-C	8-D
9-A	10-C	11-D	12-C	13-B	14-A	15-C	16-A
17-C	18-B	19-D	20-A	21-C	22-C	23-A	24-B
25-C	26-B	27-A	28-A	29-C	30-B	31-C	32-D
33-B	34-C	35-B	36-B	37-B	38-D	39-B	40-C
41-B	42-B	43-B	44-D	45-B	46-B	47-D	48-C
49-C	50-C	51-C	52-B	53-C	54-D	55-C	56-D
57-C	58-A	59-C	60-B	61-D			

ELEMENTARY Test: 12 (Page 19)

1-D	2-B	3-A	4-C	5-B	6-C	7-D	8-B
9-A	10-C	11-B	12-B	13-D	14-A	15-C	16-D
17-C	18-D	19-C	20-A	21-D	22-C	23-A	24-C
25-C	26-B	27-C	28-B	29-C	30-A	31-A	32-B
33-C	34-D	35-C	36-D	37-B	38-A	39-B	40-C
41-B	42-A	43-B	44-A	45-B	46-D	47-A	48-B
49-D	50-B	51-C	52-B	53-B	54-C	55-D	

ELEMENTARY Test: 13 (Page 21)

1-A	2-B	3-B	4-B	5-C	6-B	7-D	8-C
9-C	10-B	11-C	12-D	13-D	14-C	15-B	16-C
17-D	18-B	19-A	20-D	21-C	22-B	23-C	24-D
25-C	26-D	27-A	28-B	29-D	30-C	31-D	32-A
33-C	34-A	35-B	36-A	37-B	38-A	39-C	40-D
41-A	42-B	43-C	44-D	45-A	46-A	47-A	48-B
49-A	50-D	51-B	52-B	53-A	54-C		

ELEMENTARY Test: 14 (Page 22)

1-C	2-B	3-B	4-D	5-D	6-D	7-C	8-A
9-C	10-C	11-B	12-C	13-B	14-A	15-B	16-D
17-D	18-D	19-D	20-B	21-A	22-D	23-D	24-C
25-A	26-D	27-C	28-A	29-C	30-B	31-D	32-B
33-A	34-D	35-D	36-B	37-B	38-A	39-D	40-B
41-B	42-D	43-D	44-B	45-C	46-D	47-A	48-C
49-B	50-C	51-D	52-A	53-B	54-C	55-A	

PRE-INTERMEDIATE Test: 1 (Page 24)

1-D	2-B	3-C	4-C	5-A	6-D	7-D	8-B
9-C	10-D	11-B	12-C	13-D	14-C	15-B	16-C
17-B	18-C	19-A	20-B	21-A	22-D	23-C	24-D
25-B	26-C	27-D	28-A	29-B	30-C	31-A	32-D
33-C	34-B	35-A	36-B	37-B	38-B	39-C	40-C
41-A	42-B	43-C	44-C	45-A	46-B	47-C	48-A
49-D	50-A	51-A	52-C	53-B	54-C	55-D	56-C
57-A	58-C	59-B	60-D	61-A	62-B	63-B	64-D
65-A							

PRE-INTERMEDIATE Test: 2 (Page 26)

1-B	2-C	3-A	4-C	5-D	6-C	7-C	8-D
9-A	10-B	11-D	12-A	13-B	14-C	15-D	16-C
17-A	18-C	19-D	20-C	21-B	22-A	23-B	24-B
25-C	26-B	27-C	28-D	29-A	30-D	31-C	32-C
33-B	34-D	35-C	36-C	37-C	38-B	39-A	40-C
41-C							

PRE-INTERMEDIATE Test: 3 (Page 27)

1-C	2-A	3-B	4-B	5-C	6-C	7-B	8-A
9-D	10-D	11-C	12-C	13-D	14-B	15-D	16-C
17-B	18-B	19-D	20-A	21-B	22-A	23-D	24-D
25-B	26-B	27-A	28-C	29-D	30-B	31-B	32-C
33-D	34-B	35-C	36-D	37-B	38-C	39-C	40-C
41-B	42-A	43-D	44-D	45-C	46-C	47-B	48-C
49-D	50-D						

PRE-INTERMEDIATE Test: 4 (Page 28)

1-C	2-A	3-B	4-A	5-B	6-A	7-D	8-C
9-B	10-B	11-D	12-C	13-A	14-C	15-B	16-C
17-D	18-D	19-D	20-C	21-D	22-C	23-A	24-C
25-D	26-C	27-B	28-B	29-C	30-D	31-A	32-B
33-A	34-A	35-D	36-C	37-C	38-A	39-C	40-B
41-A	42-C	43-A	44-B	45-D	46-C	47-B	48-C
49-C	50-A						

PRE-INTERMEDIATE Test: 5 (Page 29)

1-C	2-B	3-D	4-C	5-D	6-C	7-B	8-A
9-C	10-B	11-B	12-C	13-B	14-C	15-D	16-A
17-C	18-B	19-D	20-C	21-C	22-A	23-B	24-A
25-D	26-B	27-A	28-B	29-B	30-A	31-B	32-C
33-A	34-A	35-D	36-B	37-D	38-B	39-A	40-D
41-B	42-C	43-B	44-B	45-D	46-A	47-C	48-B
49-B	50-B						

PRE-INTERMEDIATE Test: 6 (Page 30)

1-A	2-D	3-B	4-C	5-A	6-B	7-D	8-C
9-B	10-A	11-C	12-D	13-C	14-A	15-B	16-C
17-D	18-B	19-C	20-B	21-D	22-C	23-B	24-A
25-C	26-B	27-C	28-A	29-C	30-C	31-B	32-A
33-C	34-B	35-C	36-D	37-A	38-D	39-C	

PRE-INTERMEDIATE Test: 7 (Page 31)

1-B	2-A	3-D	4-A	5-D	6-B	7-B	8-C
9-D	10-B	11-A	12-C	13-B	14-C	15-A	16-D
17-C	18-A	19-A	20-A	21-D	22-B	23-B	24-C
25-A	26-B	27-D	28-B	29-C	30-B	31-C	32-A
33-B	34-D	35-C	36-B	37-C	38-A	39-D	40-A
41-A	42-C	43-B	44-D	45-C	46-C	47-B	48-A
49-D	50-C						

PRE-INTERMEDIATE Test: 8 (Page 32)

1-B	2-D	3-A	4-B	5-C	6-C	7-A	8-C
9-D	10-B	11-C	12-D	13-A	14-C	15-A	16-C
17-A	18-B	19-D	20-C	21-B	22-D	23-C	24-A
25-B	26-D	27-B	28-D	29-C	30-B	31-A	32-D
33-A	34-B	35-C	36-D	37-A	38-B	39-C	40-D
41-D	42-A	43-A	44-D	45-C	46-A	47-D	48-D
49-C	50-D						

PRE-INTERMEDIATE Test: 9 (Page 34)

1-C	2-B	3-A	4-A	5-A	6-B	7-D	8-B
9-D	10-D	11-C	12-A	13-C	14-D	15-B	16-D
17-A	18-B	19-D	20-B	21-C	22-A	23-D	24-C
25-C	26-C	27-B	28-D	29-C	30-D	31-B	32-C
33-D	34-D	35-A	36-A	37-B	38-D	39-A	40-B
41-C	42-B	43-B	44-A	45-B	46-C	47-D	48-C
49-D	50-C						

PRE-INTERMEDIATE Test: 10 (Page 35)

1-C	2-D	3-D	4-A	5-C	6-C	7-A	8-B
9-C	10-B	11-D	12-B	13-C	14-D	15-C	16-A
17-D	18-A	19-C	20-D	21-A	22-C	23-D	24-B
25-A	26-B	27-A	28-C	29-B	30-A	31-C	32-A
33-B	34-D	35-D	36-A	37-B	38-B	39-B	40-C
41-C	42-B	43-C	44-A	45-D	46-B	47-A	48-D
49-C	50-C						

PRE-INTERMEDIATE Test: 11 (Page 36)

1-C	2-A	3-C	4-D	5-D	6-B	7-A	8-D
9-C	10-B	11-B	12-D	13-C	14-A	15-D	16-B
17-A	18-B	19-C	20-C	21-B	22-D	23-A	24-D
25-B	26-C	27-B	28-C	29-C	30-D	31-C	32-B
33-D	34-B	35-A	36-B	37-C	38-D	39-B	40-B
41-B	42-D	43-D	44-A	45-C	46-B	47-C	48-B
49-D	50-B						

PRE-INTERMEDIATE Test: 12 (Page 37)

1-C	2-B	3-C	4-D	5-B	6-C	7-D	8-C
9-B	10-C	11-D	12-C	13-D	14-B	15-C	16-D
17-D	18-D	19-C	20-D	21-C	22-B	23-C	24-A
25-C	26-B	27-D	28-B	29-B	30-B	31-C	32-B
33-B	34-D	35-D	36-B	37-D	38-B	39-D	40-B
41-D	42-A	43-C	44-D	45-D	46-D	47-B	48-C
49-D	50-B						

PRE-INTERMEDIATE Test: 13 (Page 39)

1-C	2-B	3-D	4-A	5-A	6-D	7-D	8-C
9-B	10-B	11-C	12-D	13-C	14-B	15-C	16-C
17-A	18-C	19-A	20-D	21-D	22-D	23-B	24-D
25-A	26-D	27-B	28-D	29-A	30-C	31-B	32-C
33-D	34-B	35-D	36-C	37-C	38-C	39-B	40-A
41-D	42-B	43-D	44-A	45-D	46-B	47-A	48-A
49-B	50-C						

PRE-INTERMEDIATE Test: 14 (Page 40)

1-C	2-B	3-B	4-A	5-C	6-D	7-B	8-B
9-A	10-D	11-C	12-D	13-C	14-B	15-A	16-C
17-B	18-D	19-D	20-A	21-A	22-C	23-B	24-A
25-B	26-A	27-C	28-B	29-A	30-A	31-D	32-B
33-B	34-C	35-B	36-D	37-B	38-C	39-D	40-D
41-C	42-A	43-C	44-B	45-B	46-C	47-C	48-B
49-C	50-C						

INTERMEDIATE Test 1 (Page 42)

1-B	2-D	3-A	4-C	5-B	6-D	7-A	8-D
9-A	10-B	11-B	12-D	13-B	14-D	15-B	16-D
17-D	18-C	19-B	20-B	21-A	22-B	23-C	24-C
25-A	26-D	27-C	28-C	29-A	30-B	31-C	32-D
33-B	34-A	35-A	36-D	37-D	38-D	39-B	40-D

INTERMEDIATE Test 2 (Page 43)

1-C	2-A	3-C	4-C	5-B	6-D	7-C	8-B
9-A	10-C	11-D	12-A	13-D	14-B	15-A	16-C
17-A	18-A	19-D	20-C	21-A	22-D	23-C	24-D
25-A	26-B	27-A	28-C	29-C	30-A	31-D	32-B
33-A	34-C	35-B	36-D	37-D	38-C	39-A	40-D
41-D	42-D	43-C					

INTERMEDIATE Test 3 (Page 44)

1-D	2-A	3-C	4-A	5-C	6-B	7-C	8-A
9-D	10-B	11-C	12-A	13-B	14-D	15-C	16-D
17-A	18-D	19-A	20-A	21-C	22-C	23-B	24-A
25-C	26-B	27-D	28-B	29-B	30-A	31-D	32-A
33-C	34-A	35-D	36-B	37-A	38-D	39-B	40-C
41-B	42-A						

INTERMEDIATE Test 4 (Page 45)

1-D	2-B	3-C	4-A	5-A	6-B	7-A	8-C
9-A	10-B	11-C	12-A	13-B	14-C	15-D	16-B
17-B	18-D	19-C	20-C	21-B	22-B	23-A	24-C
25-B	26-D	27-D	28-D	29-D	30-C	31-B	32-D
33-A	34-D	35-C	36-D	37-B	38-A	39-C	40-C

INTERMEDIATE Test 5 (Page 46)

1-B	2-B	3-A	4-B	5-A	6-B	7-B	8-B
9-D	10-B	11-A	12-B	13-B	14-A	15-B	16-D
17-C	18-A	19-A	20-B	21-C	22-A	23-A	24-A
25-A	26-A	27-B	28-B	29-B	30-B	31-B	32-A
33-A	34-A	35-B	36-A	37-C	38-B	39-A	40-B
41-C	42-D	43-B					

INTERMEDIATE Test 6 (Page 47)

1-B	2-A	3-B	4-A	5-A	6-D	7-D	8-C
9-D	10-C	11-C	12-A	13-C	14-D	15-C	16-C
17-D	18-C	19-C	20-D	21-C	22-B	23-C	24-A
25-B	26-B	27-A	28-C	29-A	30-C	31-A	32-A
33-C	34-A	35-A	36-B	37-A	38-A	39-A	40-C
41-C	42-B	43-A	44-B	45-D	46-C	47-A	48-A
49-B	50-A	51-D	52-B	53-D	54-D	55-C	56-C
57-D	58-A	59-A	60-B	61-A	62-B	63-B	64-A
65-C	66-C	67-B	68-A	69-C	70-B	71-A	72-D
73-A	74-D	75-D	76-B				

INTERMEDIATE Test 7 (Page 48)

1-C	2-A	3-A	4-D	5-B	6-D	7-B	8-B
9-D	10-B	11-C	12-D	13-C	14-A	15-B	16-A
17-A	18-B	19-A	20-B	21-B	22-C	23-B	24-C
25-B	26-D	27-A	28-D	29-C	30-B	31-D	32-D
33-B	34-A	35-B	36-A	37-B	38-A	39-A	40-C
41-B	42-C	43-B	44-C	45-D	46-B	47-A	48-D
49-A	50-C	51-B	52-A	53-D	54-D	55-B	56-A
57-C	58-B	59-C	60-C	61-B	62-D	63-B	64-D
65-C	66-D	67-C	68-C	69-A			

INTERMEDIATE Test 8 (Page 50)

1-A	2-A	3-D	4-C	5-D	6-A	7-B	8-A
9-D	10-D	11-A	12-A	13-C	14-B	15-A	16-C
17-B	18-D	19-B	20-A				

BOOK 1 - PART B

Pronouns - adverbs - adjectives - determines
(Elementary / Pre-Intermediate) 1 *(Page 51)*

1-B	2-A	3-D	4-C	5-C	6-B	7-C	8-B
9-B	10-A	11-C	12-D	13-D	14-D	15-B	16-A
17-D	18-B	19-C	20-D	21-D	22-B	23-A	24-A
25-B	26-C	27-D	28-B	29-A	30-A	31-B	32-D
33-C	34-D	35-A	36-B	37-A	38-B	39-D	40-D
41-A	42-D	43-C	44-B	45-C	46-A	47-C	48-A
49-C	50-B	51-D	52-B	53-D	54-A	55-B	56-D
57-B	58-D	59-A	60-C	61-D	62-C	63-C	64-A
65-D	66-D	67-A	68-A	69-D	70-B	71-C	72-A
73-B	74-C	75-A	76-D	77-A	78-C	79-B	80-C
81-D	82-A	83-A	84-B	85-C	86-A	87-C	88-A
89-C	90-D	91-B	92-A	93-B	94-A	95-B	96-A
97-D	98-B	99-D	100-A	101-A	102-C	103-C	104-B
105-A	106-C	107-B	108-D	109-D	110-A	111-A	112-B
113-B	114-D	115-D	116-D	117-A	118-C	119-B	120-D
121-C	122-B	123-A	124-C	125-D	126-A	127-D	128-C
129-A	130-B	131-D	132-C	133-B	134-A	135-B	136-D
137-A	138-A	139-C	140-A	141-A	142-A	143-D	144-C
145-D	146-B	147-D	148-A	149-C	150-B	151-C	152-A
153-D	154-B	155-C	156-A	157-D	158-A	159-C	160-C
161-D	162-B	163-D	164-C	165-D	166-A	167-C	168-B
169-A	170-B	171-B	172-C	173-B	174-A	175-B	176-B
177-C	178-D	179-A	180-A	181-C	182-B	183-B	184-C
185-D	186-C	187-C	188-A	189-B	190-A	191-A	192-B
193-C	194-A	195-D	196-A	197-B	198-C	199-A	200-C
201-B	202-C	203-D	204-A	205-B	206-B	207-C	208-B
209-B	210-D	211-C	212-A	213-B	214-D	215-D	216-B
217-B	218-D	219-A	220-A	221-C	222-B	223-B	224-B
225-A	226-B	227-B	228-C	229-C	230-B	231-B	232-A
233-C							

Pronouns - adverbs - adjectives - determines
(Intermediate / Upper-Intermediate) 2 *(Page 55)*

1-C	2-A	3-C	4-A	5-C	6-C	7-B	8-A
9-A	10-A	11-C	12-B	13-C	14-A	15-A	16-B
17-C	18-B	19-A	20-C	21-B	22-A	23-C	24-A
25-C	26-C	27-D	28-C	29-A	30-D	31-D	32-A
33-B	34-B	35-A	36-A	37-A	38-B	39-C	40-D
41-A	42-B	43-A	44-C	45-D	46-B	47-A	48-B
49-D	50-A	51-D	52-B	53-B	54-C	55-A	56-B
57-B	58-A	59-C	60-B	61-C	62-D	63-A	64-C
65-B	66-C	67-D	68-B	69-A	70-C	71-B	72-D
73-C	74-B	75-D	76-C	77-D	78-A	79-D	80-A
81-C	82-A	83-D	84-B	85-D	86-B	87-C	88-C
89-A	90-A	91-A	92-D	93-B	94-A	95-C	96-D
97-B	98-A	99-A	100-C	101-A	102-B	103-D	104-A
105-A	106-A	107-B	108-C	109-D	110-C	111-A	112-D
113-A	114-C	115-A	116-C	117-B	118-A	119-B	120-C
121-C	122-D	123-D	124-B	125-A	126-A	127-C	128-D
129-B	130-D	131-C	132-D	133-D	134-B	135-C	136-B
137-A	138-D	139-C	140-B	141-D	142-C	143-D	144-A
145-B	146-B	147-C	148-C	149-D	150-B	151-A	152-D
153-C	154-D	155-A	156-C	157-D	158-A	159-C	160-C
161-B	162-C	163-A	164-A	165-D	166-C	167-A	168-C
169-C	170-D	171-C	172-B	173-A	174-D	175-B	176-D
177-C	178-B	179-B	180-A	181-D	182-A	183-C	184-D
185-A	186-D	187-B	188-A	189-D	190-A	191-B	192-A
193-C	194-A	195-B					

Tenses - Passives (Elementary / Pre-Intermediate) 3
(Page 59)

1-B	2-D	3-A	4-B	5-C	6-D	7-D	8-C
9-B	10-A	11-B	12-D	13-C	14-A	15-C	16-B
17-A	18-D	19-A	20-D	21-D	22-B	23-A	24-D
25-D	26-C	27-B	28-D	29-A	30-D	31-A	32-B
33-C	34-B	35-C	36-D	37-B	38-B	39-C	40-A
41-D	42-A	43-C	44-A	45-D	46-A	47-B	48-B
49-C	50-D	51-A	52-B	53-D	54-B	55-D	56-C
57-A	58-B	59-D	60-A	61-C	62-A	63-C	64-B
65-D	66-C	67-A	68-B	69-D	70-D	71-C	72-A
73-C	74-D	75-A	76-B	77-B	78-D	79-C	80-C
81-A	82-D	83-B	84-D	85-D	86-C	87-A	88-D
89-D	90-D	91-D	92-D	93-B	94-D	95-B	96-C
97-A	98-A	99-B	100-C	101-D	102-B	103-C	104-A
105-B	106-D	107-D	108-D	109-D	110-D	111-D	112-C
113-A	114-C	115-A	116-C	117-B	118-B	119-C	120-A
121-C	122-C	123-B	124-B	125-B	126-B	127-C	128-A
129-D	130-B	131-A	132-A	133-A	134-C	135-C	136-D
137-B	138-B	139-A	140-C	141-C	142-D	143-B	144-D
145-D	146-B	147-A	148-C	149-A	150-B	151-B	152-A
153-C	154-A	155-A	156-D	157-C	158-A	159-B	160-A
161-B	162-C	163-D	164-B	165-A	166-C	167-D	168-A
169-A	170-B	171-A	172-A	173-C	174-C	175-D	176-C
177-B	178-B	179-A	180-A	181-B	182-C	183-D	184-C
185-B	186-B	187-C	188-C	189-A	190-C	191-A	192-A
193-D	194-C	195-B	196-D	197-B	198-C	199-A	200-D
201-A	202-C	203-A	204-A	205-D	206-C	207-B	208-D
209-C	210-B	211-C	212-C	213-B	214-D	215-A	216-C
217-D	218-B	219-A	220-A	221-C	222-D	223-B	224-C
225-D	226-A	227-A	228-A	229-D	230-B	231-D	232-D
233-B	234-A	235-C	236-B	237-D	238-D	239-B	240-A
241-A	242-D	243-B	244-D	245-B	246-B	247-B	248-A
249-D	250-D	251-A	252-D	253-C	254-A	255-C	256-D
257-C	258-B	259-C	260-C	261-C	262-D	263-A	264-A
265-D	266-B	267-C	268-A	269-A	270-B	271-A	272-A
273-C	274-D	275-C	276-B	277-D	278-A	279-B	280-C
281-B	282-A	283-B	284-B	285-D	286-C	287-C	288-B
289-B	290-C	291-A	292-D	293-B	294-D	295-A	

Tenses - Passives (Intermediate / Upper-Intermediate) 4
(Page 65)

1-C	2-A	3-C	4-C	5-C	6-D	7-C	8-B
9-C	10-A	11-B	12-B	13-A	14-B	15-A	16-A
17-C	18-B	19-B	20-A	21-C	22-C	23-A	24-B
25-D	26-D	27-C	28-B	29-C	30-D	31-A	32-B
33-B	34-C	35-B	36-A	37-C	38-D	39-A	40-B
41-A	42-D	43-B	44-B	45-D	46-A	47-A	48-C
49-D	50-D	51-C	52-C	53-C	54-C	55-D	56-B
57-A	58-B	59-C	60-A	61-B	62-A	63-C	64-C
65-D	66-A	67-C	68-C	69-C	70-A	71-D	72-C
73-D	74-A	75-A	76-D	77-D	78-B	79-B	80-B
81-B	82-B	83-A	84-A	85-A	86-C	87-C	88-B
89-C	90-B	91-C	92-C	93-B	94-D	95-B	96-C
97-B	98-D	99-B	100-C	101-D	102-D	103-A	104-D
105-B	106-D	107-C	108-D	109-B	110-B	111-D	112-D
113-C	114-A	115-D	116-C	117-B	118-C	119-A	120-C
121-A	122-D	123-C	124-A	125-D	126-A	127-C	128-B
129-C	130-A	131-A	132-C	133-A	134-C	135-B	136-B
137-D	138-B	139-A	140-A	141-D	142-B	143-A	144-C
145-C	146-B	147-C	148-B	149-C	150-B	151-D	152-B

Clauses (Elementary / Pre-Intermediate) 5 (Page 69)

1-B	2-A	3-C	4-C	5-D	6-C	7-A	8-B
9-C	10-A	11-B	12-A	13-D	14-B	15-D	16-B
17-B	18-C	19-A	20-B	21-A	22-A	23-C	24-D
25-C	26-C	27-D	28-D	29-B	30-D	31-A	32-C
33-D	34-B	35-A	36-A	37-B	38-A	39-C	40-D
41-D	42-A	43-C	44-C	45-C	46-C	47-A	48-D
49-D	50-D	51-C	52-B	53-B	54-A	55-B	56-D
57-D	58-C	59-C	60-B	61-A	62-D	63-C	64-A
65-B	66-C	67-A	68-A	69-B	70-D	71-C	72-A
73-C	74-D	75-B	76-B	77-A	78-B	79-A	80-C
81-C	82-A	83-A	84-D	85-B	86-D	87-C	88-A
89-D	90-D	91-A	92-C	93-D	94-C	95-B	96-A
97-D	98-C	99-B	100-A	101-B	102-A	103-C	104-C
105-A	106-A	107-B	108-C	109-B	110-A	111-A	112-D
113-D	114-C	115-B	116-B	117-B	118-C	119-B	120-D
121-A	122-B	123-A	124-A	125-C	126-D	127-A	128-B
129-D	130-B	131-B	132-D	133-A	134-C	135-C	136-A
137-D	138-A	139-C	140-A	141-D	142-B	143-C	144-C
145-A	146-B	147-A	148-C	149-C	150-B	151-A	152-D
153-B	154-D	155-B	156-C	157-C	158-B	159-C	160-C
161-B	162-A	163-D	164-A	165-A	166-A	167-A	168-C
169-C	170-A	171-D	172-C	173-A	174-C	175-B	176-C
177-A	178-A	179-B	180-A				

Clauses (Intermediate / Upper-Intermediate) 6 (Page 73)

1-D	2-C	3-B	4-B	5-D	6-A	7-D	8-B
9-A	10-D	11-A	12-B	13-A	14-C	15-A	16-B
17-C	18-C	19-B	20-A	21-B	22-A	23-B	24-C
25-A	26-C	27-B	28-B	29-A	30-D	31-A	32-C
33-B	34-B	35-D	36-B	37-A	38-C	39-C	40-A
41-C	42-C	43-D	44-C	45-B	46-D	47-D	48-C
49-B	50-A	51-B	52-B	53-B	54-A	55-A	56-B
57-D	58-A	59-C	60-C	61-D	62-D	63-C	64-B
65-D	66-C	67-D	68-B	69-D	70-D	71-B	72-D
73-B	74-A	75-D	76-D	77-C	78-D	79-B	80-A
81-B	82-A	83-C	84-A	85-B	86-B	87-C	88-C
89-D	90-B	91-B	92-B	93-A	94-B	95-A	96-A
97-D	98-B	99-C	100-B	101-A	102-B	103-B	104-B
105-B	106-A	107-C	108-B	109-D	110-C	111-B	112-D
113-A	114-D	115-A	116-B	117-B	118-C	119-C	120-B
121-A	122-C	123-B	124-A	125-C	126-B	127-C	128-D
129-A	130-D	131-A	132-C	133-D	134-C	135-B	136-C
137-B	138-A	139-B	140-A	141-C	142-A	143-B	144-B
145-B	146-C	147-B	148-D	149-C	150-A	151-D	152-B
153-C	154-C	155-A	156-C	157-B	158-C	159-D	160-A
161-B	162-A	163-B	164-D	165-D	166-C	167-A	168-D
169-B	170-A	171-D	172-C	173-A	174-D	175-D	176-C
177-B	178-A	179-C	180-B	181-B	182-A	183-B	184-D
185-A	186-B	187-A	188-B	189-C	190-A	191-B	192-C
193-B	194-C	195-D	196-A	197-A	198-D	199-C	200-B
201-B	202-D	203-D	204-C	205-A	206-B	207-A	208-C
209-D	210-B	211-A	212-C	213-D	214-A	215-C	216-A
217-B	218-D	219-D	220-B	221-C	222-B	223-A	224-C
225-A	226-B	227-A	228-C	229-C	230-A	231-C	232-A
233-B	234-D	235-D	236-A	237-A	238-A	239-D	240-D
241-A	242-C	243-B	244-B	245-D	246-C	247-C	248-B
249-C	250-A	251-B	252-D	253-C	254-A	255-C	256-A
257-B	258-A	259-B	260-D	261-C	262-A	263-C	264-B
265-B	266-B	267-A	268-A	269-D	270-D	271-A	272-C
273-A	274-C	275-B	276-C	277-A	278-C	279-B	280-C

Modals (Elementary / Pre-Intermediate) 7 (Page 80)

1-C	2-A	3-C	4-B	5-C	6-A	7-B	8-B
9-A	10-B	11-A	12-C	13-A	14-C	15-B	16-D
17-B	18-B	19-C	20-A	21-A	22-C	23-B	24-D
25-B	26-B	27-A	28-A	29-D	30-B	31-C	32-B
33-C	34-B	35-C	36-A	37-D	38-B	39-C	40-A
41-B	42-A	43-C	44-B	45-B	46-B	47-C	48-A
49-A	50-C	51-C	52-A	53-B	54-B	55-B	56-A
57-A	58-C	59-A	60-B	61-A	62-C	63-B	64-C
65-A	66-D	67-B	68-A	69-C	70-A	71-C	72-A
73-C	74-C	75-B	76-B	77-A	78-D	79-C	80-B
81-D	82-B	83-B	84-D	85-B	86-B	87-A	88-D
89-C	90-B	91-B	92-C	93-A	94-C	95-A	96-C
97-A	98-B	99-A	100-C				

Modals (Intermediate / Upper-Intermediate) 8 (Page 82)

1-C	2-A	3-C	4-D	5-A	6-D	7-D	8-C
9-A	10-A	11-D	12-C	13-B	14-A	15-C	16-D
17-C	18-A	19-B	20-B	21-A	22-D	23-A	24-C
25-D	26-B	27-A	28-B	29-B	30-C	31-B	32-D
33-B	34-A	35-B	36-D	37-C	38-B	39-B	40-D
41-C	42-C	43-A	44-C	45-A	46-C	47-D	48-A
49-B	50-C	51-B	52-D	53-D	54-C	55-C	56-D
57-D	58-B	59-B	60-A	61-C	62-C	63-C	64-C
65-D	66-B	67-D	68-A	69-A	70-A	71-B	72-D
73-A	74-B	75-D	76-A	77-D	78-D	79-A	80-B
81-B	82-C	83-A	84-D	85-B	86-D	87-C	88-B
89-C	90-D	91-A	92-B	93-B	94-C	95-B	96-D
97-D	98-D	99-A	100-C	101-D	102-C	103-D	104-C
105-B	106-B	107-B	108-D	109-B	110-A	111-C	112-B
113-B	114-C	115-B	116-A	117-C	118-B	119-C	120-C

Prepositions (Elementary / Pre-Intermediate) 9 (Page 85)

1-D	2-B	3-A	4-D	5-A	6-B	7-C	8-B
9-D	10-D	11-A	12-B	13-C	14-A	15-B	16-D
17-C	18-A	19-C	20-A	21-B	22-C	23-D	24-A
25-D	26-C	27-B	28-D	29-A	30-B	31-C	32-A
33-D	34-A	35-C	36-A	37-D	38-B	39-A	40-C
41-C	42-B	43-D	44-B	45-C	46-B	47-A	48-A
49-B	50-A	51-D	52-D	53-A	54-C	55-C	56-B
57-A	58-D	59-C	60-C	61-B	62-C	63-A	64-C
65-A	66-D	67-A	68-C	69-B	70-B	71-D	72-C
73-D	74-A	75-A	76-B	77-C	78-C	79-D	80-A
81-A	82-B	83-B	84-C	85-A	86-D	87-D	88-B
89-C	90-B	91-B	92-D	93-A	94-D	95-C	96-C
97-A	98-A	99-C	100-A	101-B	102-A	103-D	104-A
105-C	106-B	107-C	108-A	109-C	110-B	111-A	112-C
113-C	114-A	115-B	116-C	117-A	118-C	119-A	120-B
121-D	122-C	123-C	124-C	125-C	126-B	127-D	128-C
129-D	130-A	131-C	132-D	133-A	134-C	135-B	136-B
137-A	138-B	139-C	140-D	141-C	142-A	143-B	144-B
145-C	146-A	147-D	148-D	149-C	150-B		

Prepositions (Intermediate / Upper-Intermediate) 10
(Page 88)

1-A	2-A	3-C	4-B	5-A	6-A	7-B	8-A
9-D	10-A	11-C	12-C	13-B	14-A	15-D	16-A
17-C	18-D	19-D	20-A	21-D	22-A	23-B	24-A
25-D	26-C	27-B	28-D	29-C	30-B	31-A	32-D
33-A	34-D	35-A	36-D	37-B	38-D	39-C	40-D
41-A	42-B	43-B	44-B	45-A	46-D	47-B	48-C
49-A	50-D	51-D	52-B	53-C	54-D	55-D	56-B
57-B	58-C	59-D	60-A	61-B	62-C	63-D	64-A
65-A	66-C	67-B	68-C	69-B	70-D	71-A	72-B
73-D	74-C	75-D	76-A	77-C	78-B	79-A	80-C
81-B	82-D	83-C	84-A	85-B	86-B	87-D	88-C
89-A	90-C	91-A	92-C	93-D	94-A	95-B	96-B
97-A	98-C	99-A	100-D	101-B	102-B	103-B	104-D
105-A	106-C	107-D	108-C	109-A	110-B	111-A	112-C
113-C	114-A	115-C	116-B	117-D	118-B	119-C	120-C
121-B	122-A	123-B	124-D	125-D	126-D	127-B	128-A
129-C	130-B	131-C	132-B	133-C	134-A	135-B	136-A
137-A	138-A	139-A	140-C	141-A	142-A	143-B	144-D
145-D	146-A	147-D	148-D	149-A	150-D	151-B	152-B
153-B	154-A	155-A	156-B	157-A	158-B	159-D	160-B
161-A	162-B	163-D	164-B	165-D	166-D	167-B	168-C
169-C	170-B	171-D	172-B				

Prepositions after adjectives (Intermediate / Upper-Intermediate) 11
(Page 91)

1-B	2-D	3-B	4-D	5-A	6-A	7-B	8-C
9-C	10-B	11-D	12-A	13-D	14-D	15-C	16-A
17-B	18-A	19-C	20-A	21-B	22-D	23-A	24-D
25-A	26-A	27-C	28-C	29-A	30-D	31-D	32-A
33-D	34-A	35-C	36-C	37-A	38-B	39-D	40-B
41-D	42-B	43-C	44-B	45-A	46-D	47-A	48-C
49-B	50-C	51-B	52-B	53-A	54-C	55-A	56-D
57-D	58-A	59-C	60-A	61-A	62-B	63-D	64-D
65-A	66-C	67-D	68-B	69-D	70-C	71-D	72-B
73-A	74-B	75-A	76-C	77-C	78-A	79-C	80-D
81-D	82-A	83-C	84-A	85-B	86-B	87-A	88-D
89-A	90-B	91-C	92-A	93-C	94-D	95-D	96-B
97-B	98-C	99-A	100-D	101-D	102-B	103-B	104-A
105-D	106-C	107-C	108-B	109-B	110-A	111-B	112-A
113-B	114-A						

Prepositions after verbs (Intermediate / Upper-Intermediate) 12
(Page 93)

1-B	2-A	3-D	4-C	5-D	6-C	7-B	8-B
9-A	10-C	11-D	12-B	13-A	14-B	15-D	16-C
17-A	18-B	19-D	20-A	21-C	22-C	23-D	24-B
25-A	26-D	27-A	28-C	29-B	30-D	31-B	32-D
33-B	34-A	35-C	36-B	37-D	38-A	39-B	40-C
41-D	42-C	43-D	44-A	45-C	46-C	47-C	48-D
49-B	50-B	51-A	52-D	53-C	54-A	55-D	56-B
57-A	58-D	59-B	60-B	61-A	62-D	63-C	64-A
65-B	66-D	67-D	68-D	69-C	70-A	71-C	72-A
73-D	74-B	75-C	76-A	77-D	78-D	79-C	80-A
81-B	82-B	83-A	84-B	85-B	86-A	87-D	88-A
89-B	90-B	91-D	92-A	93-D	94-B	95-C	96-B
97-D	98-C	99-A	100-A	101-C	102-C	103-A	104-C
105-A	106-B	107-A	108-C	109-C	110-D	111-A	112-C
113-B	114-A	115-C					

Gerund - infinitive (Elementary / Pre-Intermediate) 13
(Page 95)

1-B	2-A	3-D	4-C	5-D	6-B	7-A	8-C
9-A	10-D	11-D	12-B	13-A	14-C	15-C	16-A
17-C	18-D	19-A	20-C	21-A	22-D	23-A	24-C
25-A	26-B	27-B	28-D	29-B	30-A	31-D	32-B
33-A	34-B	35-A	36-B	37-A	38-A	39-A	40-C
41-B	42-B	43-A	44-B	45-A	46-D	47-C	48-C
49-A	50-A	51-C	52-A	53-B	54-B	55-A	56-C
57-C	58-B	59-D	60-B	61-C	62-A	63-C	64-A
65-D	66-A	67-C	68-A	69-A	70-C	71-A	72-C
73-B	74-B	75-A	76-C	77-A	78-C	79-C	80-B
81-A	82-C	83-D	84-D	85-B	86-A	87-B	88-C
89-A	90-C	91-D	92-C	93-D	94-B	95-A	96-C
97-B	98-A	99-C					

Gerund - infinitive (Intermediate / Upper-Intermediate) 14
(Page 97)

1-A	2-A	3-A	4-C	5-C	6-B	7-B	8-D
9-B	10-A	11-B	12-C	13-C	14-B	15-A	16-D
17-C	18-B	19-B	20-A	21-C	22-D	23-A	24-C
25-B	26-A	27-D	28-C	29-C	30-C	31-B	32-B
33-D	34-D	35-B	36-C	37-D	38-B	39-D	40-A
41-A	42-C	43-B	44-D	45-B	46-A	47-B	48-C
49-C	50-B	51-D	52-B	53-A	54-B	55-B	56-D
57-A	58-D	59-C	60-A	61-D	62-C	63-A	64-C
65-A	66-C	67-A	68-D	69-B	70-D	71-B	72-A
73-C	74-B	75-D	76-A	77-A	78-A	79-D	80-B
81-C	82-D	83-C	84-A	85-B	86-A	87-C	88-C
89-A	90-A	91-A	92-B	93-B	94-C	95-B	96-B
97-C	98-A	99-A	100-C	101-A	102-A	103-C	104-A
105-B	106-D	107-C	108-B	109-A	110-C	111-B	112-C
113-A	114-D	115-B	116-A	117-A	118-C	119-C	120-A
121-C	122-D	123-D	124-C	125-A	126-D	127-B	128-A
129-C	130-B	131-C	132-D	133-C	134-C	135-B	136-D
137-A	138-C	139-B	140-B	141-D	142-A	143-A	144-C
145-B	146-D	147-B	148-C	149-A	150-D	151-C	152-A
153-D	154-B	155-A	156-C	157-D	158-B	159-A	160-C
161-C	162-B	163-A	164-D	165-D	166-B	167-A	168-C
169-A	170-A	171-A	172-D	173-C	174-A	175-B	176-D
177-C	178-C	179-C	180-A	181-C	182-D	183-D	184-C
185-D	186-A	187-A	188-B	189-D	190-C	191-C	192-D
193-B	194-A	195-C	196-D	197-A	198-A	199-B	200-C
201-C	202-A	203-A	204-C	205-A	206-C	207-C	208-B
209-D	210-A	211-B	212-D	213-C	214-B	215-C	216-C
217-A	218-B	219-A	220-C	221-D	222-B	223-D	224-C
225-A	226-B	227-D	228-C	229-A	230-C	231-D	232-C
233-A	234-C	235-C	236-B	237-C	238-D	239-D	240-B
241-D	242-D	243-A	244-A	245-C	246-C	247-C	

BOOK 1 - PART C

Test 1: Articles (Page 103)

1-B	2-A	3-B	4-A	5-A	6-A	7-A	8-B
9-B	10-A	11-A	12-C	13-B	14-D	15-B	16-B
17-C	18-B	19-A	20-E	21-A	22-C	23-B	24-E
25-A	26-D	27-E	28-A	29-A	30-A	31-C	32-E
33-B	34-A	35-A	36-A	37-A	38-A	39-A	40-A
41-D	42-C	43-B	44-D	45-E	46-D	47-C	48-D
49-A	50-C	51-B	52-A	53-E	54-A	55-A	56-B
57-C	58-D	59-C	60-C	61-C	62-D	63-A	64-B
65-D	66-A	67-A	68-B	69-B	70-D	71-D	72-C
73-A	74-C	75-D	76-C	77-A	78-C	79-D	80-B
81-A	82-A	83-E	84-C	85-E	86-D	87-B	88-C
89-C	90-B	91-C	92-B	93-B	94-D	95-A	96-B
97-C	98-A	99-D	100-C				

Test 2: Prepositions (Page 106)

1-D	2-D	3-A	4-B	5-B	6-C	7-C	8-D
9-B	10-C	11-C	12-B	13-C	14-E	15-C	16-E
17-E	18-E	19-C	20-B	21-C	22-A	23-D	24-C
25-C	26-A	27-A	28-C	29-A	30-E	31-B	32-D
33-C	34-A	35-E	36-A	37-B	38-A	39-C	40-A
41-B	42-B	43-E	44-A	45-C	46-B	47-B	48-B
49-C	50-D	51-E	52-D	53-A	54-B	55-A	56-D
57-E	58-D	59-B	60-A	61-E	62-B	63-C	64-A
65-A	66-E	67-C	68-B	69-B	70-B	71-D	72-B
73-A	74-E	75-D	76-D	77-E	78-B	79-B	80-C
81-C	82-C	83-B	84-E	85-A	86-B	87-D	88-E
89-C	90-A	91-E	92-C	93-B	94-B	95-A	96-B
97-D	98-C	99-B	100-D				

Test 3: Pronouns (Page 109)

1-B	2-B	3-B	4-C	5-C	6-E	7-D	8-B
9-B	10-E	11-C	12-C	13-C	14-A	15-A	16-C
17-B	18-B	19-D	20-D	21-C	22-E	23-C	24-D
25-B	26-E	27-E	28-C	29-A	30-A	31-C	32-D
33-D	34-E	35-B	36-C	37-C	38-C	39-B	40-C
41-C	42-D	43-B	44-B	45-C	46-A	47-D	48-C
49-D	50-C	51-E	52-D	53-A	54-C	55-D	56-D
57-C	58-B	59-A	60-B	61-B	62-D	63-D	64-C
65-C	66-D	67-A	68-C	69-D	70-C	71-C	72-B
73-B	74-B	75-D	76-A	77-D	78-C	79-B	80-C
81-B	82-B	83-C	84-A	85-D	86-D	87-C	88-D
89-C	90-C	91-D	92-E	93-D	94-E	95-B	96-B
97-D	98-C	99-B	100-D	101-A	102-A	103-A	104-B
105-B	106-B	107-C	108-E	109-D	110-C	111-D	112-B
113-B	114-C	115-C	116-C	117-D	118-D	119-B	120-A
121-B	122-D	123-A	124-B	125-E	126-C	127-E	128-B
129-A	130-B	131-C	132-D	133-E	134-C	135-A	136-B
137-C	138-B	139-B	140-D	141-E	142-D	143-C	144-B
145-E	146-E	147-B	148-A	149-A	150-D	151-A	152-A
153-D	154-B	155-A	156-A	157-A	158-A	159-C	160-C
161-B	162-C	163-C	164-B	165-C	166-D	167-A	168-E
169-E	170-B	171-B	172-C	173-E	174-E	175-A	176-B
177-E	178-C	179-D	180-C	181-C	182-C	183-E	184-B
185-E	186-A	187-A	188-C	189-B	190-D		

Test 4: Present Tenses (Page 114)

1-A	2-B	3-A	4-A	5-B	6-A	7-A	8-C
9-B	10-C	11-A	12-D	13-C	14-E	15-D	16-C
17-E	18-C	19-B	20-C	21-E	22-C	23-C	24-A
25-C	26-B	27-B	28-B	29-B	30-D	31-B	32-B
33-C	34-B	35-C	36-C	37-A	38-C	39-D	40-B
41-D	42-A	43-C	44-A	45-D	46-D	47-D	48-A
49-A	50-C	51-C	52-B	53-D	54-D	55-B	56-C
57-D	58-C	59-D	60-E	61-B	62-C	63-D	64-A
65-E	66-B	67-D	68-C	69-B	70-C	71-E	72-B
73-A	74-C	75-A	76-B	77-D	78-D	79-C	80-C
81-D	82-C	83-E	84-E	85-C	86-D	87-A	88-E
89-E	90-A	91-B	92-E	93-E	94-C	95-A	96-B
97-C	98-C	99-D	100-E	101-B	102-D	103-B	104-C

Test 5: Future Tenses (Page 117)

1-B	2-C	3-E	4-E	5-A	6-D	7-C	8-C
9-A	10-E	11-B	12-B	13-B	14-A	15-B	16-D
17-C	18-A	19-C	20-C	21-C	22-B	23-C	

Test 6: Past Tenses (Page 118)

1-E	2-A	3-C	4-B	5-E	6-B	7-E	8-C
9-C	10-C	11-D	12-C	13-B	14-E	15-D	16-C
17-D	18-B	19-D	20-B	21-A	22-E	23-C	24-B
25-A	26-A	27-B	28-B	29-D	30-A	31-C	32-C
33-C	34-A	35-C	36-B	37-C	38-D	39-D	40-D
41-C	42-A	43-C	44-D	45-A	46-E	47-B	48-C
49-D	50-D	51-C	52-C	53-E	54-B	55-B	56-C
57-D							

Test 7: Mixed Tenses (Page 120)

1-D	2-D	3-B	4-C	5-B	6-C	7-B	8-B
9-A	10-D	11-D	12-C	13-E	14-A	15-D	16-C
17-B	18-B	19-C	20-C	21-B	22-B	23-B	24-B
25-D	26-E	27-B	28-A	29-A	30-B	31-E	32-B
33-E	34-E	35-B	36-E	37-E	38-D	39-C	40-A
41-A	42-A	43-C	44-B	45-C	46-B	47-A	48-D
49-B	50-C	51-E	52-B	53-A	54-A	55-B	56-B
57-A	58-B	59-A	60-A	61-B	62-D	63-B	64-E
65-A	66-C	67-C	68-B	69-C	70-C	71-D	72-A
73-A	74-C	75-D	76-C	77-C	78-B	79-A	80-D
81-A	82-B	83-D	84-C	85-D	86-E	87-D	88-A
89-D	90-B	91-C	92-B	93-C	94-C	95-A	96-B
97-D	98-A	99-E	100-D	101-A	102-B	103-B	104-A
105-B	106-B	107-A	108-C	109-B	110-C	111-B	112-B
113-B	114-C	115-E	116-A	117-A			

Test 8: Modals (Page 124)

1-C	2-A	3-A	4-A	5-A	6-A	7-A	8-A
9-D	10-A	11-A	12-E	13-A	14-E	15-C	16-D
17-D	18-E	19-D	20-E	21-A	22-E	23-A	24-C
25-B	26-E	27-B	28-D	29-C	30-B	31-A	32-A
33-A	34-C	35-B	36-D	37-C	38-D	39-B	40-A
41-D	42-E	43-B	44-C	45-E	46-C	47-A	48-B
49-D	50-C	51-B	52-D	53-D	54-A	55-B	56-E
57-C	58-D	59-B	60-B	61-B	62-C	63-A	64-C
65-D	66-E	67-E	68-A	69-B	70-A	71-A	72-E
73-A	74-C	75-E	76-C	77-C	78-E	79-D	80-E
81-D	82-B	83-E	84-E	85-E	86-C	87-A	88-D
89-C	90-C	91-D	92-E	93-C	94-D	95-D	96-B
97-B	98-B	99-B	100-C	101-C	102-C	103-E	104-C
105-A	106-B	107-E	108-B	109-C	110-C	111-E	112-B
113-A	114-C	115-C	116-B	117-A	118-C	119-B	120-C
121-A	122-B	123-D	124-E	125-E	126-B	127-C	128-E
129-D	130-B	131-C	132-D	133-B	134-D	135-D	136-D
137-C	138-B	139-A	140-D	141-D	142-B	143-B	144-C
145-B	146-C	147-D	148-C	149-D	150-A	151-C	152-C
153-D	154-D	155-E	156-E	157-B	158-D	159-D	160-C
161-D	162-D						

Test 9: Conditionals (Page 129)

Type 1

1-E	2-D	3-E	4-D	5-E	6-A	7-C	8-A
9-B	10-C	11-E	12-D	13-B	14-C	15-C	16-A
17-A	18-B	19-C	20-E	21-C	22-B	23-D	24-E
25-A	26-B	27-A	28-B	29-E	30-D	31-C	32-B
33-C	34-D	35-D	36-B	37-A			

Type 2

1-B	2-C	3-A	4-B	5-D	6-E	7-C	8-D
9-B	10-D	11-A	12-E	13-D	14-B	15-B	16-B
17-D	18-D	19-A	20-C	21-A	22-C	23-C	24-E
25-D	26-C	27-D	28-C				

Type 3

1-E	2-E	3-D	4-D	5-C	6-A	7-D	8-B
9-C	10-A	11-C	12-D	13-B	14-C	15-D	16-B
17-A	18-D						

Mixed

1-A	2-C	3-A	4-C	5-D	6-A	7-C	8-B
9-E							

Test 10: Comparatives - Superlatives (Page 133)

1-C	2-C	3-E	4-C	5-B	6-D	7-C	8-E
9-C	10-C	11-E	12-B	13-A	14-B	15-C	16-B
17-D	18-C	19-B	20-D	21-B	22-C	23-D	24-C
25-B	26-A	27-B	28-B	29-D	30-D	31-C	32-B
33-B	34-D	35-D	36-E	37-B	38-D	39-D	40-D
41-D	42-C	43-E	44-C	45-E	46-D	47-B	48-D
49-E	50-D	51-C	52-B	53-C	54-B	55-C	56-A
57-E	58-B	59-E	60-C	61-C	62-C	63-B	64-B
65-B	66-A	67-E	68-C	69-C	70-D	71-B	72-E
73-D	74-C	75-D	76-B	77-D	78-D	79-D	80-E
81-D	82-E	83-C	84-B	85-D	86-D	87-A	88-A
89-D	90-B	91-C	92-B	93-C	94-B	95-B	96-E
97-B	98-D	99-A	100-C	101-B	102-D	103-B	104-E
105-A	106-B						

Test 11: Infinitive - Gerund (Page 136)

1-A	2-B	3-B	4-C	5-E	6-A	7-D	8-D
9-A	10-B	11-C	12-B	13-B	14-A	15-D	16-A
17-C	18-A	19-C	20-A	21-D	22-C	23-A	24-A
25-C	26-B	27-C	28-A	29-C	30-A	31-A	32-C
33-D	34-D	35-C	36-E	37-B	38-D	39-B	40-A
41-E	42-B	43-E	44-C	45-C	46-A	47-C	48-B
49-B	50-A	51-E	52-D	53-A	54-A	55-B	56-A
57-B	58-C	59-C	60-D	61-C	62-C	63-E	64-D
65-B	66-A	67-C	68-B	69-C	70-D	71-B	72-B
73-A	74-E	75-A	76-B	77-C	78-C	79-B	80-A
81-D	82-C	83-D	84-D	85-D	86-A	87-D	88-B
89-B	90-C	91-B	92-D	93-E	94-A	95-D	96-C
97-E							

Test 12: Passive voice (Page 139)

1-B	2-D	3-D	4-D	5-E	6-E	7-A	8-D
9-B	10-B	11-D	12-C	13-E	14-C	15-D	16-C
17-B	18-D	19-C	20-D	21-A	22-C	23-C	24-B
25-C	26-B	27-C	28-B	29-C	30-D	31-B	32-C
33-C	34-E	35-E	36-C	37-C	38-B	39-D	40-D
41-C	42-B	43-B	44-B	45-A	46-D	47-C	48-D
49-A	50-C	51-D	52-C	53-A	54-B	55-E	56-D
57-E	58-D	59-C	60-A	61-C	62-D	63-C	64-E
65-C	66-B	67-E					

Test 13: Indirect speech (Page 142)

1-C	2-D	3-A	4-A	5-B	6-C	7-A	8-B
9-C	10-D	11-B	12-C	13-A	14-E	15-B	16-B
17-B	18-C	19-D	20-B	21-B	22-B	23-A	24-D
25-C	26-A	27-B	28-C	29-B	30-D	31-C	32-D
33-A	34-B	35-D	36-A	37-B	38-C	39-E	40-C
41-E	42-D	43-E	44-A	45-E	46-B	47-C	48-D
49-B	50-B	51-B	52-C	53-C	54-D	55-E	56-A
57-D	58-C	59-C	60-B	61-B	62-C	63-C	64-B
65-C	66-A	67-A	68-D	69-C	70-B	71-C	72-B
73-D	74-C	75-B	76-B	77-B	78-E	79-A	80-B

Test 14: When - While - Where - As soon as (Page 146)

1-C	2-C	3-A	4-D	5-A	6-A	7-C	8-B
9-B	10-C	11-C	12-C	13-C	14-E	15-B	16-C
17-C	18-C	19-B	20-B	21-E	22-B	23-A	24-B
25-D	26-A	27-A	28-C	29-B	30-E	31-A	32-C
33-D	34-A	35-A	36-A	37-D	38-D	39-A	40-E
41-B	42-C	43-B	44-D	45-A	46-A	47-D	48-C
49-D	50-D	51-B	52-C	53-A	54-A	55-D	56-B
57-B	58-B						

Test 15: Questions tags (Page 148)

1-B	2-C	3-B	4-D	5-D	6-B	7-A	8-D
9-B	10-B	11-E	12-C	13-C	14-D	15-D	16-D
17-C	18-E	19-C	20-A	21-D	22-A		

Test 16: Additions to remarks (Page 149)

1-C	2-A	3-C	4-D	5-A	6-D	7-B	8-A
9-A	10-C	11-A	12-C	13-A	14-D	15-C	16-A
17-C	18-D	19-D	20-B	21-B	22-C	23-E	24-D
25-E	26-D	27-B	28-E	29-D	30-C	31-A	32-D
33-C	34-A	35-D	36-D	37-E	38-B	39-D	40-C
41-A	42-D	43-C					

BOOK 1 - PART D

Test 1 (Page 151)

1-D	2-A	3-D	4-C	5-D	6-A	7-B	8-C
9-B	10-D	11-A	12-B	13-B	14-C	15-B	16-D
17-D	18-B	19-A	20-B	21-D	22-C	23-B	24-D
25-C	26-C	27-A	28-B	29-A	30-D	31-C	32-C
33-B	34-C	35-A	36-D	37-D	38-C	39-C	40-B
41-D	42-A	43-A	44-D	45-C	46-C	47-C	48-B
49-A	50-B	51-B	52-D	53-B	54-B	55-D	56-A
57-D	58-C	59-B	60-A	61-C	62-A	63-A	64-B
65-A	66-B	67-C	68-B	69-A	70-C	71-A	72-B
73-D	74-B	75-C	76-A	77-C	78-B	79-D	80-B
81-C	82-A	83-B	84-C	85-D	86-D	87-A	88-A
89-C	90-B	91-C	92-B	93-A	94-A	95-D	96-C
97-A	98-B	99-B	100-B				

Test 2 (Page 153)

1-C	2-C	3-D	4-D	5-C	6-A	7-A	8-C
9-B	10-A	11-B	12-B	13-A	14-D	15-D	16-B
17-A	18-C	19-C	20-B	21-B	22-B	23-D	24-C
25-D	26-C	27-B	28-A	29-D	30-B	31-C	32-D
33-D	34-C	35-B	36-C	37-C	38-D	39-A	40-B
41-C	42-C	43-C	44-C	45-A	46-C	47-C	48-B
49-D	50-A	51-B	52-B	53-C	54-C	55-C	56-C
57-B	58-C	59-D	60-B	61-A	62-D	63-B	64-C
65-B	66-B	67-D	68-C	69-B	70-D	71-B	72-D
73-A	74-C	75-C	76-D	77-A	78-C	79-B	80-B
81-C	82-D	83-B	84-B	85-C	86-B	87-B	88-A
89-B	90-C	91-C	92-A	93-C	94-A	95-C	96-A
97-D	98-D	99-D	100-D				

Test 3 (Page 155)

1-D	2-C	3-C	4-D	5-D	6-C	7-A	8-B
9-D	10-B	11-A	12-C	13-A	14-C	15-A	16-A
17-B	18-C	19-C	20-C	21-A	22-B	23-A	24-B
25-C	26-A	27-C	28-A	29-D	30-C	31-D	32-C
33-D	34-C	35-D	36-A	37-D	38-C	39-B	40-D
41-A	42-C	43-C	44-B	45-B	46-A	47-B	48-B
49-C	50-B	51-A	52-D	53-C	54-D	55-C	56-C
57-B	58-C	59-B	60-C	61-C	62-B	63-A	64-A
65-B	66-C	67-A	68-B	69-C	70-B	71-C	72-C
73-A	74-A	75-C	76-B	77-B	78-A	79-B	80-D
81-C	82-D	83-C	84-A	85-B	86-A	87-C	88-B
89-B	90-C	91-C	92-A	93-C	94-A	95-D	96-C
97-B	98-D	99-B	100-C				

Test 4 (Page 157)

1-D	2-C	3-B	4-B	5-B	6-D	7-C	8-B
9-B	10-C	11-B	12-B	13-B	14-A	15-A	16-C
17-C	18-B	19-B	20-C	21-A	22-C	23-A	24-D
25-A	26-B	27-A	28-A	29-D	30-C	31-D	32-A
33-D	34-C	35-B	36-A	37-D	38-C	39-A	40-B
41-B	42-B	43-C	44-A	45-B	46-C	47-A	48-B
49-B	50-C	51-D	52-C	53-D	54-A	55-C	56-C
57-C	58-D	59-A	60-D	61-C	62-A	63-A	64-C
65-B	66-C	67-B	68-C	69-B	70-A	71-C	72-A
73-D	74-C	75-D	76-A	77-A	78-C	79-A	80-D
81-C	82-C	83-B	84-A	85-B	86-C	87-B	88-A
89-A	90-C	91-A	92-D	93-B	94-C	95-A	96-A
97-B	98-C	99-B	100-C				

Test 5 (Page 159)

1-C	2-D	3-A	4-B	5-D	6-C	7-D	8-C
9-B	10-B	11-A	12-B	13-B	14-C	15-D	16-B
17-C	18-B	19-C	20-B	21-B	22-A	23-D	24-D
25-A	26-C	27-B	28-B	29-A	30-A	31-D	32-D
33-C	34-C	35-D	36-C	37-A	38-C	39-D	40-D
41-D	42-B	43-A	44-B	45-A	46-A	47-A	48-C
49-D	50-A	51-D	52-C	53-B	54-D	55-C	56-B
57-D	58-C	59-C	60-D	61-B	62-A	63-D	64-A
65-D	66-C	67-C	68-B	69-C	70-D	71-C	72-C
73-B	74-B	75-D	76-A	77-C	78-D	79-A	80-B
81-C	82-C	83-B	84-C	85-C	86-D	87-A	88-D
89-A	90-C	91-C	92-D	93-D	94-B	95-C	96-A
97-A	98-D	99-C	100-C				

Test 6 (Page 161)

1-B	2-D	3-C	4-B	5-B	6-A	7-B	8-C
9-D	10-A	11-C	12-C	13-A	14-C	15-A	16-B
17-D	18-A	19-B	20-A	21-C	22-A	23-C	24-A
25-C	26-B	27-C	28-D	29-C	30-A	31-B	32-D
33-A	34-C	35-C	36-A	37-C	38-B	39-C	40-A
41-D	42-B	43-C	44-D	45-C	46-A	47-C	48-C
49-C	50-A	51-B	52-C	53-A	54-C	55-A	56-D
57-C	58-C	59-C	60-C	61-C	62-A	63-B	64-D
65-A	66-A	67-A	68-B	69-B	70-B	71-B	72-D
73-B	74-D	75-B	76-C	77-C	78-B	79-C	80-C
81-B	82-A	83-A	84-C	85-B	86-B	87-D	88-B
89-B	90-B	91-D	92-B	93-A	94-C	95-C	96-A
97-D	98-C	99-A	100-B				

Test 7 (Page 163)

1-B	2-C	3-B	4-A	5-C	6-A	7-C	8-A
9-B	10-A	11-B	12-C	13-C	14-A	15-C	16-A
17-C	18-A	19-C	20-A	21-B	22-B	23-D	24-A
25-C	26-B	27-B	28-C	29-A	30-B	31-D	32-B
33-B	34-B	35-A	36-B	37-A	38-C	39-B	40-C
41-B	42-D	43-A	44-B	45-C	46-D	47-B	48-C
49-B	50-C	51-B	52-C	53-C	54-C	55-D	56-B
57-D	58-C	59-C	60-B	61-D	62-A	63-B	64-A
65-D	66-B	67-D	68-B	69-D	70-B	71-A	72-C
73-B	74-A	75-A	76-C	77-B	78-A	79-C	80-C
81-D	82-A	83-B	84-B	85-D	86-A	87-B	88-C
89-C	90-B	91-C	92-C	93-D	94-A	95-C	96-B
97-D	98-B	99-B	100-B				

Test 8 (Page 165)

1-C	2-B	3-B	4-A	5-C	6-B	7-C	8-B
9-C	10-C	11-A	12-B	13-C	14-B	15-B	16-B
17-C	18-B	19-A	20-B	21-C	22-B	23-C	24-A
25-A	26-B	27-D	28-C	29-B	30-A	31-B	32-A
33-C	34-B	35-B	36-C	37-A	38-C	39-D	40-A
41-C	42-C	43-D	44-A	45-C	46-C	47-D	48-B
49-D	50-D	51-B	52-D	53-B	54-D	55-C	56-B
57-A	58-C	59-C	60-B	61-C	62-A	63-D	64-D
65-B	66-C	67-D	68-A	69-A	70-D	71-B	72-C
73-A	74-C	75-A	76-D	77-D	78-D	79-C	80-A
81-A	82-B	83-B	84-A	85-D	86-C	87-B	88-B
89-D	90-B	91-A	92-C	93-C	94-D	95-D	96-A
97-D	98-C	99-D	100-A				

Test 9 (Page 167)

1-A	2-A	3-C	4-B	5-B	6-D	7-C	8-C
9-A	10-B	11-B	12-D	13-C	14-B	15-B	16-D
17-A	18-B	19-B	20-C	21-D	22-C	23-B	24-C
25-B	26-D	27-C	28-C	29-B	30-D	31-D	32-B
33-D	34-A	35-C	36-C	37-C	38-B	39-B	40-C
41-B	42-C	43-B	44-A	45-A	46-A	47-D	48-B
49-C	50-C	51-D	52-C	53-C	54-B	55-B	56-B
57-A	58-C	59-B	60-B	61-B	62-C	63-C	64-C
65-A	66-D	67-B	68-B	69-A	70-C	71-B	72-C
73-D	74-A	75-C	76-B	77-B	78-C	79-C	80-D
81-D	82-A	83-C	84-D	85-D	86-A	87-C	88-B
89-B	90-B	91-A	92-D	93-B	94-B	95-A	96-C
97-C	98-C	99-B	100-C				

Test 10 (Page 169)

1-B	2-C	3-D	4-C	5-D	6-B	7-A	8-A
9-B	10-B	11-C	12-B	13-B	14-A	15-D	16-C
17-C	18-C	19-C	20-B	21-A	22-C	23-A	24-B
25-B	26-D	27-C	28-A	29-A	30-C	31-A	32-A
33-C	34-D	35-C	36-D	37-B	38-C	39-C	40-D
41-B	42-C	43-D	44-C	45-B	46-D	47-C	48-D
49-A	50-C	51-C	52-B	53-C	54-B	55-C	56-C
57-A	58-C	59-C	60-D	61-D	62-B	63-D	64-C
65-A	66-B	67-D	68-B	69-A	70-A	71-D	72-D
73-B	74-B	75-C	76-C	77-C	78-A	79-D	80-B
81-D	82-B	83-B	84-B	85-A	86-B	87-B	88-B
89-C	90-A	91-A	92-A	93-D	94-C	95-C	96-C
97-D	98-B	99-A	100-C				

Test 11 (Page 171)

1-C	2-C	3-A	4-C	5-B	6-A	7-D	8-B
9-B	10-B	11-B	12-C	13-A	14-D	15-D	16-C
17-B	18-B	19-A	20-B	21-A	22-B	23-A	24-A
25-C	26-A	27-B	28-B	29-C	30-B	31-A	32-A
33-D	34-B	35-A	36-B	37-C	38-C	39-D	40-A
41-A	42-B	43-B	44-D	45-B	46-B	47-B	48-A
49-D	50-A	51-A	52-C	53-B	54-B	55-B	56-A
57-A	58-C	59-A	60-D	61-B	62-D	63-A	64-D
65-B	66-D	67-B	68-B	69-B	70-A	71-B	72-B
73-D	74-A	75-C	76-A	77-B	78-C	79-C	80-B
81-B	82-A	83-C	84-B	85-C	86-D	87-D	88-D
89-A	90-D	91-D	92-B	93-B	94-A	95-B	96-C
97-C	98-C	99-D	100-D				

Test 12 (Page 173)

1-A	2-C	3-C	4-A	5-C	6-B	7-B	8-C
9-C	10-C	11-D	12-C	13-A	14-A	15-A	16-D
17-A	18-B	19-D	20-A	21-D	22-B	23-D	24-D
25-C	26-D	27-B	28-D	29-D	30-A	31-C	32-C
33-A	34-A	35-A	36-B	37-D	38-B	39-A	40-A
41-B	42-D	43-C	44-B	45-A	46-C	47-D	48-C
49-C	50-D	51-B	52-A	53-B	54-B	55-A	56-B
57-A	58-A	59-A	60-B	61-D	62-B	63-C	64-D
65-D	66-A	67-D	68-C	69-D	70-B	71-B	72-B
73-C	74-B	75-A	76-A	77-D	78-C	79-D	80-C
81-D	82-A	83-C	84-C	85-B	86-B	87-D	88-A
89-C	90-A	91-B	92-D	93-D	94-B	95-B	96-A
97-C	98-A	99-D	100-A				

Test 13 (Page 175)

1-D	2-A	3-A	4-C	5-D	6-D	7-C	8-B
9-D	10-B	11-B	12-D	13-C	14-C	15-B	16-B
17-B	18-C	19-C	20-C	21-C	22-B	23-D	24-A
25-B	26-C	27-B	28-A	29-B	30-C	31-A	32-C
33-D	34-D	35-A	36-C	37-D	38-C	39-C	40-D
41-B	42-A	43-B	44-C	45-D	46-C	47-B	48-D
49-C	50-D	51-B	52-B	53-D	54-C	55-C	56-D
57-B	58-B	59-D	60-D	61-B	62-B	63-A	64-C
65-B	66-A	67-C	68-C	69-A	70-C	71-C	72-D
73-A	74-B	75-C	76-A	77-D	78-B	79-A	80-B
81-A	82-C	83-D	84-B	85-D	86-C	87-D	88-D
89-C	90-D	91-C	92-B	93-A	94-B	95-B	96-C
97-C	98-C	99-B	100-C				

Test 14 (Page 177)

1-A	2-A	3-A	4-C	5-A	6-B	7-D	8-C
9-B	10-C	11-C	12-C	13-C	14-D	15-D	16-A
17-A	18-C	19-A	20-D	21-C	22-D	23-C	24-C
25-A	26-D	27-C	28-B	29-A	30-D	31-B	32-A
33-C	34-C	35-C	36-B	37-A	38-D	39-B	40-C
41-C	42-A	43-C	44-B	45-C	46-D	47-D	48-D
49-C	50-B	51-B	52-A	53-A	54-D	55-A	56-B
57-C	58-B	59-C	60-D	61-C	62-C	63-D	64-B
65-B	66-B	67-C	68-A	69-A	70-C	71-B	72-D
73-D	74-A	75-B	76-D	77-A	78-C	79-A	80-D
81-C	82-A	83-C	84-A	85-C	86-B	87-A	88-B
89-D	90-D	91-A	92-C	93-A	94-A	95-A	96-C
97-A	98-A	99-C	100-C				

Test 15 (Page 179)

1-C	2-B	3-A	4-A	5-D	6-A	7-C	8-C
9-C	10-D	11-B	12-B	13-A	14-C	15-C	16-A
17-C	18-B	19-D	20-A	21-C	22-A	23-B	24-B
25-C	26-A	27-B	28-A	29-B	30-D	31-D	32-A
33-C	34-B	35-C	36-C	37-D	38-C	39-B	40-A
41-D	42-A	43-A	44-B	45-C	46-C	47-B	48-D
49-C	50-D	51-A	52-A	53-D	54-A	55-C	56-B
57-D	58-C	59-B	60-C	61-B	62-D	63-C	64-A
65-A	66-C	67-A	68-D	69-B	70-D	71-B	72-B
73-B	74-B	75-C	76-C	77-B	78-A	79-A	80-B
81-D	82-B	83-C	84-C	85-D	86-C	87-D	88-A
89-A	90-A	91-A	92-A	93-A	94-C	95-A	96-B
97-C	98-C	99-D	100-A				

Test 16 (Page 181)

1-D	2-B	3-A	4-B	5-A	6-A	7-A	8-B
9-B	10-D	11-D	12-C	13-B	14-B	15-D	16-A
17-B	18-A	19-B	20-A	21-C	22-C	23-B	24-C
25-C	26-A	27-A	28-A	29-A	30-B	31-C	32-D
33-B	34-B	35-D	36-D	37-B	38-B	39-A	40-D
41-C	42-C	43-D	44-A	45-C	46-A	47-A	48-C
49-B	50-A	51-C	52-C	53-B	54-A	55-D	56-B
57-A	58-C	59-A	60-D	61-B	62-B	63-A	64-B
65-A	66-C	67-D	68-D	69-C	70-A	71-C	72-C
73-C	74-A	75-C	76-C	77-A	78-B	79-C	80-B
81-C	82-B	83-D	84-A	85-C	86-D	87-B	88-B
89-D	90-C	91-B	92-C	93-D	94-D	95-B	96-A
97-A	98-C	99-B	100-A				

Test 17 (Page 183)

1-B	2-A	3-C	4-D	5-B	6-D	7-B	8-B
9-D	10-A	11-B	12-C	13-B	14-A	15-D	16-A
17-A	18-B	19-C	20-B	21-D	22-C	23-B	24-B
25-B	26-C	27-B	28-A	29-A	30-C	31-B	32-B
33-C	34-A	35-A	36-A	37-D	38-C	39-D	40-B
41-C	42-B	43-B	44-D	45-A	46-A	47-B	48-C
49-A	50-C	51-B	52-A	53-B	54-C	55-B	56-C
57-B	58-D	59-A	60-B	61-C	62-D	63-C	64-A
65-B	66-D	67-C	68-C	69-B	70-C	71-A	72-A
73-B	74-B	75-A	76-C	77-C	78-A	79-D	80-A
81-C	82-D	83-D	84-B	85-B	86-C	87-C	88-A
89-D	90-C	91-D	92-C	93-B	94-A	95-B	96-C
97-D	98-C	99-B	100-D				

Test 18 (Page 185)

1-A	2-B	3-C	4-D	5-B	6-D	7-B	8-B
9-B	10-C	11-C	12-D	13-D	14-C	15-B	16-C
17-C	18-A	19-A	20-C	21-B	22-A	23-A	24-A
25-B	26-A	27-C	28-A	29-D	30-D	31-C	32-C
33-D	34-D	35-C	36-C	37-A	38-A	39-A	40-C
41-D	42-C	43-D	44-B	45-C	46-B	47-D	48-D
49-C	50-D	51-D	52-B	53-D	54-D	55-C	56-A
57-B	58-B	59-D	60-D	61-D	62-B	63-C	64-B
65-C	66-A	67-A	68-B	69-B	70-A	71-A	72-C
73-C	74-D	75-D	76-B	77-C	78-B	79-B	80-C
81-C	82-B	83-C	84-D	85-D	86-A	87-B	88-D
89-B	90-D	91-D	92-C	93-A	94-C	95-D	96-A
97-A	98-A	99-C	100-B				

Test 19 (Page 187)

1-C	2-B	3-A	4-D	5-A	6-B	7-B	8-B
9-B	10-A	11-D	12-C	13-A	14-C	15-B	16-C
17-B	18-D	19-C	20-A	21-A	22-D	23-C	24-A
25-C	26-D	27-B	28-A	29-D	30-C	31-B	32-C
33-A	34-A	35-C	36-B	37-B	38-D	39-B	40-D
41-C	42-A	43-C	44-B	45-D	46-C	47-B	48-A
49-C	50-A	51-A	52-B	53-C	54-C	55-A	56-C
57-B	58-A	59-D	60-B	61-C	62-A	63-D	64-C
65-B	66-B	67-A	68-A	69-B	70-C	71-D	72-B
73-A	74-C	75-A	76-B	77-B	78-B	79-C	80-C
81-C	82-C	83-B	84-A	85-B	86-A	87-D	88-A
89-B	90-A	91-C	92-C	93-C	94-A	95-D	96-B
97-C	98-A	99-C	100-B				

Test 20 (Page 189)

1-C	2-D	3-D	4-A	5-B	6-A	7-A	8-C
9-C	10-A	11-A	12-B	13-B	14-B	15-C	16-B
17-A	18-A	19-B	20-D	21-A	22-D	23-C	24-D
25-D	26-C	27-A	28-D	29-A	30-A	31-B	32-B
33-C	34-A	35-A	36-D	37-A	38-B	39-D	40-B
41-C	42-A	43-A	44-B	45-B	46-C	47-A	48-A
49-C	50-A	51-A	52-A	53-C	54-B	55-D	56-A
57-B	58-C	59-D	60-C	61-B	62-C	63-B	64-B
65-A	66-D	67-C	68-D	69-B	70-D	71-B	72-C
73-C	74-A	75-A	76-A	77-C	78-C	79-B	80-B
81-B	82-D	83-A	84-A	85-A	86-D	87-C	88-A
89-A	90-B	91-C	92-A	93-A	94-A	95-B	96-D
97-A	98-A	99-C	100-D				

BOOK 1 - PART E

Elementary test 1 (Page 191)

1-B	2-D	3-B	4-D	5-B	6-A	7-B	8-D
9-C	10-B	11-C	12-C	13-B	14-B	15-B	16-D
17-A	18-C	19-C	20-A	21-B	22-C	23-C	24-D
25-C	26-B	27-D	28-D	29-C	30-A	31-B	32-C
33-A	34-A	35-B	36-C	37-B	38-A	39-B	40-C
41-B	42-C	43-D	44-D	45-C	46-A	47-D	48-A
49-A	50-A	51-D	52-C	53-B	54-D	55-A	56-C
57-A	58-D	59-B	60-D	61-B	62-A	63-C	64-A
65-B	66-A	67-A	68-C	69-A	70-D	71-B	72-D
73-D	74-C	75-A	76-D	77-B	78-B	79-D	80-B
81-B	82-C	83-B	84-D	85-C	86-D	87-A	88-D
89-A	90-D	91-C	92-D	93-C	94-B	95-A	96-C
97-C	98-B	99-B	100-D				

Elementary test 2 (Page 193)

1-D	2-A	3-D	4-C	5-D	6-A	7-B	8-B
9-A	10-D	11-C	12-D	13-B	14-D	15-C	16-C
17-B	18-C	19-D	20-A	21-A	22-C	23-D	24-A
25-D	26-D	27-B	28-C	29-D	30-A	31-C	32-D
33-B	34-D	35-C	36-A	37-B	38-C	39-D	40-A
41-A	42-C	43-D	44-C	45-B	46-B	47-A	48-D
49-A	50-B	51-C	52-B	53-B	54-A	55-D	56-C
57-B	58-A	59-D	60-B	61-C	62-B	63-C	64-D
65-A	66-D	67-D	68-A	69-D	70-B	71-C	72-D
73-A	74-C	75-B	76-C	77-A	78-B	79-D	80-B
81-A	82-A	83-C	84-D	85-C	86-B	87-A	88-A
89-C	90-B	91-C	92-D	93-B	94-A	95-D	96-A
97-A	98-D	99-C	100-D				

Elementary test 3 (Page 195)

1-D	2-B	3-D	4-C	5-A	6-A	7-C	8-D
9-C	10-B	11-D	12-C	13-B	14-A	15-C	16-A
17-B	18-C	19-D	20-C	21-A	22-C	23-D	24-B
25-C	26-A	27-D	28-B	29-C	30-A	31-D	32-C
33-A	34-B	35-D	36-A	37-D	38-D	39-B	40-C
41-A	42-C	43-C	44-D	45-D	46-C	47-B	48-B
49-D	50-A	51-C	52-D	53-A	54-D	55-C	56-A
57-D	58-B	59-C	60-A	61-B	62-A	63-C	64-B
65-D	66-C	67-D	68-A	69-B	70-C	71-A	72-A
73-B	74-D	75-C	76-B	77-C	78-D	79-A	80-D
81-C	82-D	83-B	84-A	85-B	86-A	87-C	88-B
89-A	90-A	91-C	92-D	93-D	94-C	95-B	96-A
97-D	98-D	99-B	100-C				

Elementary test 4 (Page 197)

1-C	2-A	3-B	4-D	5-C	6-B	7-B	8-C
9-A	10-D	11-A	12-C	13-A	14-D	15-B	16-D
17-C	18-B	19-D	20-A	21-D	22-D	23-A	24-C
25-B	26-B	27-A	28-C	29-B	30-C	31-A	32-B
33-D	34-C	35-A	36-C	37-A	38-C	39-D	40-B
41-B	42-A	43-C	44-D	45-A	46-D	47-B	48-A
49-C	50-B	51-D	52-A	53-C	54-D	55-C	56-A
57-D	58-A	59-C	60-B	61-D	62-A	63-D	64-D
65-C	66-A	67-C	68-A	69-D	70-C	71-B	72-B
73-B	74-C	75-A	76-D	77-C	78-B	79-A	80-D
81-B	82-B	83-A	84-C	85-C	86-B	87-B	88-A
89-C	90-D	91-C	92-D	93-A	94-B	95-C	96-C
97-B	98-C	99-A	100-D				

Elementary test 5 (Page 199)

1-C	2-A	3-D	4-A	5-B	6-C	7-D	8-C
9-A	10-B	11-A	12-D	13-B	14-A	15-C	16-B
17-A	18-C	19-A	20-C	21-D	22-C	23-C	24-B
25-D	26-C	27-A	28-B	29-B	30-D	31-B	32-C
33-B	34-D	35-C	36-C	37-A	38-C	39-D	40-B
41-A	42-C	43-C	44-C	45-A	46-B	47-D	48-A
49-D	50-C	51-A	52-D	53-B	54-C	55-C	56-B
57-B	58-A	59-B	60-D	61-C	62-C	63-C	64-B
65-D	66-A	67-B	68-C	69-D	70-D	71-A	72-D
73-B	74-C	75-A	76-B	77-B	78-A	79-A	80-C
81-C	82-A	83-C	84-A	85-B	86-B	87-D	88-B
89-A	90-C	91-D	92-A	93-C	94-A	95-B	96-D
97-D	98-B	99-D	100-A				

Elementary test 6 (Page 201)

1-B	2-C	3-B	4-A	5-C	6-B	7-A	8-D
9-C	10-A	11-A	12-C	13-D	14-B	15-A	16-D
17-C	18-D	19-C	20-A	21-B	22-B	23-C	24-D
25-B	26-A	27-C	28-C	29-D	30-B	31-D	32-C
33-D	34-C	35-B	36-A	37-C	38-A	39-B	40-D
41-C	42-D	43-B	44-D	45-C	46-A	47-C	48-D
49-A	50-B	51-D	52-B	53-C	54-D	55-C	56-B
57-A	58-C	59-A	60-D	61-C	62-D	63-A	64-D
65-B	66-C	67-D	68-A	69-B	70-B	71-C	72-B
73-D	74-C	75-A	76-D	77-D	78-A	79-C	80-A
81-A	82-B	83-A	84-B	85-C	86-D	87-A	88-D
89-C	90-A	91-B	92-C	93-A	94-B	95-D	96-A
97-B	98-B	99-B	100-C				

Intermediate test 1 (Page 203)

1-A	2-C	3-D	4-B	5-A	6-D	7-A	8-B
9-A	10-B	11-C	12-D	13-B	14-C	15-C	16-B
17-C	18-B	19-A	20-C	21-A	22-C	23-D	24-C
25-D	26-D	27-A	28-B	29-B	30-C	31-D	32-A
33-D	34-A	35-C	36-C	37-D	38-A	39-B	40-D
41-C	42-B	43-D	44-B	45-D	46-A	47-B	48-A
49-B	50-D	51-C	52-A	53-B	54-D	55-B	56-C
57-C	58-D	59-B	60-A	61-C	62-D	63-D	64-A
65-D	66-B	67-B	68-C	69-C	70-A	71-C	72-D
73-B	74-D	75-B	76-A	77-C	78-D	79-C	80-A
81-A	82-B	83-C	84-D	85-A	86-B	87-D	88-A
89-B	90-D	91-A	92-B	93-D	94-A	95-B	96-A
97-C	98-C	99-C	100-B				

Intermediate test 2 (Page 205)

1-C	2-B	3-A	4-C	5-B	6-D	7-B	8-B
9-A	10-C	11-D	12-D	13-D	14-C	15-D	16-B
17-A	18-A	19-D	20-C	21-B	22-D	23-A	24-C
25-A	26-C	27-B	28-D	29-A	30-D	31-A	32-C
33-B	34-D	35-C	36-A	37-B	38-C	39-C	40-D
41-C	42-B	43-D	44-B	45-A	46-D	47-C	48-A
49-B	50-A	51-B	52-D	53-C	54-C	55-C	56-B
57-D	58-A	59-B	60-C	61-B	62-C	63-B	64-A
65-C	66-D	67-B	68-A	69-B	70-D	71-A	72-A
73-C	74-D	75-D	76-A	77-B	78-C	79-C	80-B
81-A	82-D	83-B	84-C	85-B	86-A	87-B	88-D
89-C	90-C	91-D	92-D	93-C	94-B	95-C	96-A
97-A	98-C	99-D	100-C				

Intermediate test 3 (Page 207)

1-C	2-A	3-D	4-C	5-B	6-B	7-A	8-D
9-B	10-B	11-D	12-A	13-C	14-B	15-C	16-D
17-C	18-A	19-D	20-B	21-A	22-A	23-D	24-C
25-A	26-C	27-A	28-D	29-D	30-B	31-A	32-C
33-C	34-A	35-B	36-D	37-C	38-C	39-B	40-D
41-D	42-C	43-A	44-A	45-D	46-B	47-A	48-A
49-C	50-B	51-D	52-B	53-A	54-D	55-C	56-C
57-B	58-A	59-C	60-C	61-A	62-B	63-D	64-C
65-B	66-A	67-A	68-C	69-B	70-D	71-C	72-C
73-A	74-A	75-D	76-A	77-C	78-B	79-B	80-D
81-C	82-A	83-D	84-D	85-B	86-A	87-B	88-A
89-C	90-A	91-A	92-D	93-B	94-C	95-B	96-D
97-A	98-C	99-A	100-D				

Intermediate test 4 (Page 209)

1-A	2-C	3-B	4-A	5-D	6-D	7-C	8-B
9-D	10-D	11-B	12-C	13-A	14-D	15-A	16-D
17-B	18-B	19-C	20-A	21-D	22-D	23-C	24-A
25-B	26-D	27-C	28-A	29-C	30-C	31-D	32-B
33-A	34-A	35-D	36-B	37-C	38-A	39-D	40-B
41-B	42-C	43-C	44-A	45-D	46-C	47-B	48-A
49-D	50-A	51-B	52-D	53-C	54-B	55-A	56-A
57-D	58-C	59-A	60-A	61-C	62-D	63-B	64-A
65-D	66-B	67-D	68-D	69-A	70-C	71-B	72-B
73-B	74-D	75-D	76-B	77-D	78-C	79-B	80-A
81-B	82-D	83-C	84-C	85-C	86-D	87-A	88-B
89-A	90-C	91-C	92-D	93-B	94-D	95-B	96-A
97-A	98-C	99-B	100-C				

Intermediate test 5 (Page 211)

1-A	2-B	3-C	4-A	5-D	6-A	7-C	8-B
9-C	10-C	11-A	12-C	13-D	14-B	15-B	16-A
17-A	18-B	19-C	20-C	21-D	22-A	23-D	24-C
25-D	26-B	27-A	28-B	29-C	30-A	31-C	32-B
33-C	34-C	35-D	36-B	37-D	38-D	39-A	40-A
41-C	42-B	43-D	44-C	45-D	46-C	47-B	48-D
49-A	50-D	51-C	52-D	53-A	54-B	55-D	56-A
57-A	58-C	59-A	60-C	61-D	62-A	63-D	64-D
65-A	66-D	67-C	68-B	69-D	70-C	71-A	72-D
73-A	74-B	75-C	76-D	77-A	78-B	79-C	80-D
81-B	82-D	83-C	84-D	85-A	86-C	87-A	88-C
89-B	90-B	91-D	92-C	93-A	94-B	95-A	96-D
97-A	98-D	99-B	100-A				

Advanced test 1 (Page 213)

1-C	2-A	3-D	4-B	5-A	6-C	7-C	8-D
9-B	10-D	11-A	12-D	13-B	14-C	15-B	16-D
17-A	18-B	19-A	20-C	21-B	22-C	23-A	24-A
25-D	26-A	27-C	28-B	29-D	30-A	31-D	32-B
33-C	34-B	35-C	36-D	37-A	38-B	39-D	40-B
41-A	42-C	43-B	44-D	45-C	46-B	47-A	48-C
49-D	50-B	51-D	52-B	53-A	54-C	55-B	56-D
57-D	58-A	59-B	60-D	61-A	62-B	63-C	64-C
65-D	66-C	67-B	68-B	69-D	70-A	71-C	72-D
73-B	74-B	75-A	76-B	77-A	78-C	79-D	80-C
81-C	82-A	83-B	84-A	85-A	86-B	87-B	88-D
89-A	90-D	91-C	92-B	93-D	94-D	95-B	96-B
97-D	98-A	99-B	100-A				

Advanced test 2 (Page 215)

1-A	2-C	3-B	4-C	5-A	6-A	7-D	8-B
9-B	10-D	11-C	12-A	13-B	14-C	15-B	16-D
17-A	18-D	19-D	20-D	21-B	22-D	23-C	24-C
25-B	26-B	27-D	28-A	29-B	30-A	31-A	32-C
33-D	34-C	35-D	36-D	37-B	38-A	39-C	40-A
41-C	42-D	43-D	44-C	45-D	46-A	47-D	48-C
49-D	50-C	51-B	52-D	53-C	54-B	55-B	56-C
57-A	58-C	59-C	60-A	61-D	62-B	63-C	64-C
65-A	66-A	67-B	68-C	69-D	70-A	71-D	72-B
73-C	74-C	75-D	76-C	77-A	78-D	79-B	80-C
81-B	82-A	83-B	84-B	85-D	86-A	87-C	88-C
89-D	90-B	91-D	92-C	93-A	94-C	95-A	96-B
97-B	98-A	99-A	100-D				

Advanced test 3 (Page 217)

1-C	2-B	3-D	4-A	5-C	6-B	7-A	8-D
9-C	10-D	11-A	12-B	13-D	14-D	15-C	16-A
17-C	18-D	19-B	20-A	21-A	22-D	23-B	24-D
25-C	26-A	27-D	28-C	29-C	30-B	31-A	32-D
33-B	34-A	35-B	36-D	37-B	38-D	39-A	40-C
41-C	42-A	43-C	44-B	45-D	46-A	47-D	48-B
49-A	50-B	51-A	52-B	53-D	54-C	55-D	56-A
57-C	58-A	59-C	60-B	61-C	62-D	63-D	64-B
65-A	66-A	67-C	68-A	69-B	70-C	71-D	72-C
73-B	74-A	75-D	76-A	77-B	78-B	79-A	80-D
81-A	82-C	83-D	84-D	85-B	86-A	87-A	88-C
89-D	90-B	91-B	92-A	93-B	94-A	95-D	96-D
97-C	98-C	99-D	100-B				

www.ingramcontent.com/pod-product-compliance
Lightning Source LLC
Chambersburg PA
CBHW081107080526
44587CB00021B/3481